Social Media Data Extraction and Content Analysis

Shalin Hai-Jew
Kansas State University, USA

A volume in the Advances in Data Mining and
Database Management (ADMDM) Book Series

www.igi-global.com

Published in the United States of America by
IGI Global
Information Science Reference (an imprint of IGI Global)
701 E. Chocolate Avenue
Hershey PA, USA 17033
Tel: 717-533-8845
Fax: 717-533-8661
E-mail: cust@igi-global.com
Web site: http://www.igi-global.com

Library of Congress Cataloging-in-Publication Data

Names: Hai-Jew, Shalin, editor.
Title: Social media data extraction and content analysis / Shalin Hai-Jew,
  editor.
Description: Hershey : Information Science Reference, 2016. | Includes
  bibliographical references and index.
Identifiers: LCCN 2016017814| ISBN 9781522506485 (hardcover) | ISBN
  9781522506492 (ebook)
Subjects: LCSH: Social media. | Data mining. | Qualitative research.
Classification: LCC HM742 .S628196 2016 | DDC 302.23/1--dc23 LC record available at https://lccn.loc.gov/2016017814

This book is published in the IGI Global book series Advances in Data Mining and Database Management (ADMDM) (ISSN: 2327-1981; eISSN: 2327-199X)

British Cataloguing in Publication Data
A Cataloguing in Publication record for this book is available from the British Library.

For electronic access to this publication, please contact: eresources@igi-global.com.

Advances in Data Mining and Database Management (ADMDM) Book Series

David Taniar
Monash University, Australia

ISSN: 2327-1981
EISSN: 2327-199X

MISSION

With the large amounts of information available to organizations in today's digital world, there is a need for continual research surrounding emerging methods and tools for collecting, analyzing, and storing data.

The **Advances in Data Mining & Database Management (ADMDM)** series aims to bring together research in information retrieval, data analysis, data warehousing, and related areas in order to become an ideal resource for those working and studying in these fields. IT professionals, software engineers, academicians and upper-level students will find titles within the ADMDM book series particularly useful for staying up-to-date on emerging research, theories, and applications in the fields of data mining and database management.

COVERAGE

- Cluster Analysis
- Quantitative Structure–Activity Relationship
- Data quality
- Heterogeneous and Distributed Databases
- Association Rule Learning
- Database Security
- Decision Support Systems
- Data Mining
- Sequence Analysis
- Data Analysis

IGI Global is currently accepting manuscripts for publication within this series. To submit a proposal for a volume in this series, please contact our Acquisition Editors at Acquisitions@igi-global.com or visit: http://www.igi-global.com/publish/.

Titles in this Series

For a list of additional titles in this series, please visit: www.igi-global.com

Collaborative Filtering Using Data Mining and Analysis
Vishal Bhatnagar (Ambedkar Institute of Advanced Communication Technologies and Research, India)
Information Science Reference • copyright 2017 • 309pp • H/C (ISBN: 9781522504894) • US $195.00 (our price)

Effective Big Data Management and Opportunities for Implementation
Manoj Kumar Singh (Adama Science and Technology University, Ethiopia) and Dileep Kumar G. (Adama Science and Technology University, Ethiopia)
Information Science Reference • copyright 2016 • 324pp • H/C (ISBN: 9781522501824) • US $195.00 (our price)

Data Mining Trends and Applications in Criminal Science and Investigations
Omowunmi E. Isafiade (University of Cape Town, South Africa) and Antoine B. Bagula (University of the Western Cape, South Africa)
Information Science Reference • copyright 2016 • 386pp • H/C (ISBN: 9781522504634) • US $210.00 (our price)

Intelligent Techniques for Data Analysis in Diverse Settings
Numan Celebi (Sakarya University, Turkey)
Information Science Reference • copyright 2016 • 353pp • H/C (ISBN: 9781522500759) • US $195.00 (our price)

Managing and Processing Big Data in Cloud Computing
Rajkumar Kannan (King Faisal University, Saudi Arabia) Raihan Ur Rasool (King Faisal University, Saudi Arabia) Hai Jin (Huazhong University of Science and Technology, China) and S.R. Balasundaram (National Institute of Technology, Tiruchirappalli, India)
Information Science Reference • copyright 2016 • 307pp • H/C (ISBN: 9781466697676) • US $200.00 (our price)

Handbook of Research on Innovative Database Query Processing Techniques
Li Yan (Nanjing University of Aeronautics and Astronautics, China)
Information Science Reference • copyright 2016 • 625pp • H/C (ISBN: 9781466687677) • US $335.00 (our price)

Handbook of Research on Trends and Future Directions in Big Data and Web Intelligence
Noor Zaman (King Faisal University, Saudi Arabia) Mohamed Elhassan Seliaman (King Faisal University, Saudi Arabia) Mohd Fadzil Hassan (Universiti Teknologi PETRONAS, Malaysia) and Fausto Pedro Garcia Marquez (Campus Universitario s/n ETSII of Ciudad Real, Spain)
Information Science Reference • copyright 2015 • 500pp • H/C (ISBN: 9781466685055) • US $285.00 (our price)

www.igi-global.com

701 E. Chocolate Ave., Hershey, PA 17033
Order online at www.igi-global.com or call 717-533-8845 x100
To place a standing order for titles released in this series, contact: cust@igi-global.com
Mon-Fri 8:00 am - 5:00 pm (est) or fax 24 hours a day 717-533-8661

For R. Max

Editorial Advisory Board

Table of Contents

Section 1
Modeling with Social Data

Chapter 1

    Jonathan Bishop, Centre for Research into Online Communities and E-Learning Systems,
        UK

Chapter 2

    Eric Poitras, University of Utah, USA
    Negar Fazeli, University of Utah, USA

Chapter 3

    Davide Di Fatta, University of Messina, Italy
    Roberto Musotto, University of Messina, Italy
    Vittorio D'Aleo, University of Messina, Italy
    Walter Vesperi, University of Messina, Italy
    Giacomo Morabito, University of Messina, Italy
    Salvatore Lo Bue, University of Messina, Italy

Chapter 4

    Duygu Mutlu-Bayraktar, Istanbul University, Turkey

Section 2
Analytics from the Online Crowd

Section 3
Tapping Specific Social Media Platforms

Detailed Table of Contents

Section 1
Modeling with Social Data

Chapter 1

> *Jonathan Bishop, Centre for Research into Online Communities and E-Learning Systems,*
> *UK*

Academia is often plagued with those who define themselves by whether they are "quantitative" or "qualitative." This chapter contests that when it comes to researching social media the two are inseparable in datafying user generated content. Posts on Twitter for instance have a textual element to the narratives that could be considered qualitative, but also quantitative criteria can be applied. Interviewing approaches can allow for the exploration of discourses to produce new theories, which may then rely of those approaches commonly thought of as quantitative. This chapter tests out a variety of different approaches to show how it is only through using all approaches available can social media be triangulated to produce accurate modelling of user behaviour.

Chapter 2

> *Eric Poitras, University of Utah, USA*
> *Negar Fazeli, University of Utah, USA*

The rapid proliferation of Web 2.0 technologies during the last decade has led to online communities of learners, where members share prerequisite knowledge and skills to further professional growth. The educational affordances of blogs offer a wealth of online resources that can be mined in order to gain better understanding of community members and their contributions. In this chapter, we outline a web content mining technique to extract and analyze information from educational blogs, resulting in networks of online resources where content is linked in terms of the underlying semantic relationships. This type of representation is referred to as a network-based model, and has implications for e-learning personalization systems that seek to suggest similar content to those preferred by other learners. The applications of this method are discussed in terms of enhancing teacher professional development in the context of nBrowser, an intelligent web browser designed to support pre-service teachers in building lesson plans that integrate technologies in the classroom.

Chapter 3

The rapid rise in internet economy is reflected in increased scholarly attention on the topic, with researchers increasingly exploring the marketing approaches and strategies now available through social media. The network provides a value for companies, thus becomes essential acquire greater awareness to evaluate and quantify its value. What are practical implications for managers? Social network analysis is nowadays an essential tool for researchers: the aim of this chapter is to extend the internet economy research to network theories. Today, there are emerging observations on the global internet economy, but there is a big gap in literature indeed. At first, literature focused on people. Now, on digitalized information. Firms are connected in a virtual network and there are undefined distances in terms of space and time. Traditional methods of analysis are no more efficient: to analyze the relationship in the network society, we need a different paradigm to approach network issue.

This chapter describes usability studies of website-based and mobile application-based social media sites. In the study including 10 university students, the completion time of assigned tasks were measured along with click numbers and completion situations. These measures were analyzed. Data obtained from eye tracking movements was analyzed, and the results were evaluated. According to the results, the users can complete most of the tasks, but completion time varied. The participants had difficulties completing settings menu tasks except menus previously used in social media. When eye tracking results were examined, it was revealed that they mostly focused on the left side of websites and mobile applications. The participants stated that mobile applications were more useful than websites. According to eye-tracking data obtained in the study and the users' opinions, mobile social media applications were more functional than their websites.

Section 2
Analytics from the Online Crowd

Marlene Goncalves, Universidad Simón Bolívar, Venezuela
Patrick Rengifo, Universidad Simón Bolívar, Venezuela
Daniela Andreina Rodríguez, Universidad Simón Bolívar, Venezuela
Ivette C. Martínez, Universidad Simón Bolívar, Venezuela

Due to the rise of the social networks it's possible to use techniques based on crowdsourcing to easily gather real-time information directly from citizens in order to create recommendation systems capable to employ knowledge that is shared from the crowd. Particularly, in Twitter, the users publish a big amount of short messages; however, to automatically extract useful information from Twitter is a complex task. In order to provide an informed recommendation of the current best route between two city points, this chapter introduces a workflow that integrates natural language techniques to build an vector of features for training two linear classifiers which obtain current information from Twitter, and integrates that information with historical information about possible routes using exponential smoothing; current and historical data to feed a route selection algorithm based on Dijkstra. The effectiveness of the proposed workflow is shown with routes between two interest points in Caracas (Venezuela).

Antonia Estrella-Ramón, University of Almeria, Spain
Alba Utrera-Serrano, University of Almeria, Spain

Nowadays social networks have a high potential to disseminate information, positive and negative, of any person, organization or product generating electronic word of mouth through customers' comments and complaints. Consequently, this paper proposes a novel research on the content related to the users' online complaints and seeks to understand the power of social networks as creating electronic word of mouth. For this task, the user-generated social network Critizen is used, especially critiques related to one of the most criticised sectors in Spain, that is, the telecommunication industry. The main results of this paper reveal that content analysis is an effective technique to extract business value from the vast amount of data available on the Internet, and especially in social networks.

Shalin Hai-Jew, Kansas State University, USA

NVivo 11 Plus, a qualitative data analysis software tool, enables some types of "distant reading" albeit within the text data processing limits of the desktop machine. Some "distant reading" applications include the following: (1) word frequency counts (visualized as word clouds, tree maps, cluster analyses graphs, dendrograms, and ring graphs/circle graphs), (2) text searches (as word trees), (3) theme and sub-theme extractions (as bar charts), (4) matrix queries (as various types of data visualizations), (5) sentiment analyses (as bar charts, hierarchical treemaps, hierarchical sunburst diagrams, and text sets), (6) autocoding by existing pattern, and (7) geolocational mapping. While "distant reading" is still evolving, these unsupervised and semi-supervised machine reading approaches broaden the capabilities of researchers and may serve as a bridge to even more complex distant reading methods.

Chapter 8

Shalin Hai-Jew, Kansas State University, USA

One new feature in NVivo 11 Plus, a qualitative and mixed methods research suite, is its sentiment analysis tool; this enables the autocoding of unlabeled and unstructured text corpora against a built-in sentiment dictionary. The software labels selected texts into four categories: (1) very negative, (2) moderately negative, (3) moderately positive, and (4) very positive. After the initial coding for sentiment, there are many ways to augment that initial coding, including theme and subtheme extraction, word frequency counts, text searches, sociogram mapping, geolocational mapping, data visualizations, and others. This chapter provides a light overview of how the sentiment analysis feature in NVivo 11 Plus works, proposes some insights about the proper unit of analysis for sentiment analyses (sentence, paragraph, or cell) based on text dataset features, and identifies ways to further explore the textual data post-sentiment analysis—to create coherence and insight.

Section 3
Tapping Specific Social Media Platforms

Chapter 9

Shalin Hai-Jew, Kansas State University, USA

Network Overview, Discovery and Exploration for Excel (NodeXL Basic) enables the extraction of "user" (entity), "video" (content), and pseudo multi-modal networks from YouTube. This open-source add-on to NodeXL captures a wide range of data, enables data processing for analysis, and then visualization in a variety of graphs (based on different layout algorithms). This chapter summarizes some of the "askable" questions using this approach. Various types of data extractions are shared to give a sense of the breadth of some approaches, including the following: (1) entities, (2) in-world phenomena, (3) imaginary phenomena, (4) themes, (5) reputations by name, (6) genres, (7) language-specific phenomena, and (8) location-specific phenomena.

Chapter 10

Shalin Hai-Jew, Kansas State University, USA

Using the emotion words of Robert Plutchik's "Wheel of Emotions" (based on his multidimensional emotion model) as seeding terms to extract related tags networks (and related thumbnail imagery) from Flickr (at 1 deg., 1.5 deg., and 2 deg.), it is possible to formulate (1) insights about emotions and their interrelationships (through the lens of collective folksonomic tagging), (2) understandings about what the related tags in the networks may suggest about the image item holdings on Flickr, and (3) awareness of the collective mental models of the Flickr users regarding particular emotions, and (4) fresh methods of research to folk tagging through the extraction and analysis of related tags networks and related thumbnail imagery. This chapter introduces this case of analyzing related tags networks to more deeply understand public conceptualizations of emotions through data labels.

Chapter 11

Shalin Hai-Jew, Kansas State University, USA

If human-created objects of art are historically contingent, then the emergence of (social) network art may be seen as a product of several trends: the broad self-expression and social sharing on Web 2.0; the application of network analysis and data visualization to understand big data, and an appreciation for online machine art. Social network art is a form of cyborg art: it melds data from both humans and machines; the sensibilities of humans and machines; and the pleasures and interests of people. This chapter will highlight some of the types of (social) network art that may be created with Network Overview, Discovery and Exploration for Excel (NodeXL Basic) and provide an overview of the process. The network graph artwork presented here were all built from datasets extracted from popular social media platforms (Twitter, Flickr, YouTube, Wikipedia, and others). This chapter proposes some early aesthetics for this type of electronic artwork.

Section 4
Applied Uses of Social Media Data for Awareness and Problem-Solving

Chapter 12

E. Pınar Uça-Güneş, Anadolu University, Turkey
Gülsün Eby, Anadolu University, Turkey

Distance Education is more preferable by both learners and institutions in the 21st century. The technology, teaching-learning and communication processes are in a change that each stakeholder should comply with. One up-to-date form of these processes is social networking. Social networks have the potential of providing access to more resources and improving the quality of communication and interaction. Social Network Analysis and Network Weaving approaches are useful to determine the social network structure and improve it. Further to that, in this chapter, "Social Network Synthesis" approach is introduced, obtained by applying synthesis process on Social Network Theory. The approach is thought to allow for the establishment of optimum relationships between the concerned actors in a newly configured goal-directed social network. An illustrative framework that can be used for building Distance Education programs is also presented.

Chapter 13

Vindaya Senadheera, Deakin University, Australia
Matthew Warren, Deakin University, Australia
Shona Leitch, RMIT University, Australia
Graeme Pye, Deakin University, Australia

Understanding the motives that encourage users to adopt social media to communicate with businesses is very important. This research study was conducted with Australian banks and adds to the development of empirically tested social media adoption model consisting of technological and social communication aspects. This chapter presents the findings of the research study based on analysis of wall posts gathered from Australian banks' Facebook presence in the year 2013. The research study involves a thematic analysis of frequently used words by Australian banks in their respective Facebook wall posts following an outcome of a word frequency test conducted using NVivo. This analysis was conducted with the proposed adoption model as the basis to determine whether banks' Facebook content addresses the basic user requirements driving them to adopt social media to communicate with Australian banks. The results strengthens the robustness and the applicability of the social media adoption model.

The reuse of code can be used to add or update functionalities with little or no modifications to new or existing software applications. Developers have reused sections of code when the code is available but have been hindered by finding the code that is needed for an application. By creating a code repository, code would be available to developers in a systemic method. The code would be available for functional and nonfunctional uses in applications. Since the code has already be written, during the discovery phase of projects the developers involved should be able to search the repository for the code that is needed for strategies and problems that have already been successfully been implemented. Quality, cost, and time should be the focus of code reuse. To maximize code reuse, a code repository that is properly categorized and indexed would add to the software development lifecycle by making code available to developers that they can use with confidence. The code repository will improve the application process.

Foreword

Why Datafy Social Media?

With data about each of us having value to so many others (mostly to better sell us things—or refuse to sell us things if we look too "risky"), it seems inevitable that as social media matured, the various players already interested in our personal data would want to mine this type of information to add to the data they have already gathered. Noncommercial research into our connections, opinions, and personal situations as embedded in social media has only recently begun, however, as data mining and other analytical techniques weren't originally designed for the messiness of social media and the malleable, episodic nature of much of its content. Commercial entities investigating social media in an attempt to "datafy" it usually keep their results proprietary, which doesn't advance wider research and prevents outside oversight of data ownership and privacy issues. Not helpful.

Why try to abstract data and content from the World Wide Web, multiple social media platforms, microblogging sites, e-mail platforms, geolocation devices, and text and multimedia collections? Why analyze it, visualize it, and apply it to other situations? What do the researchers hope to learn?

The possibilities range widely, with almost as many options as motives for digging into the data. Commercial motives for evaluating data we already know fairly well:

- Selling more effectively by identifying the specific audience for a product
- Modifying a product to better fit consumer needs and wants
- Reducing risk by *not* selling (insurance, for example) or lending (mortgages) to people who fit an industry's risk profile
- Developing long-term loyalty relationships with customers
- Fine-tuning tools to search and evaluate data in real time

What about noncommercial motives for this type of research?

- Tracking health emergencies and outbreaks
- Making sense of citizen science for migrations, population counts, temperature variations by time and location, etc.
- Identifying and correcting bottlenecks and flaws in networks or other technology services
- Evaluating the completeness of content collections
- Spotting cultural, political, and other trends as they develop
- Learning breaking news from the people observing it

- Sharing key concepts and lessons teased out through analysis and presented using advanced visualization techniques
- Developing tools to search all types of data and metadata in real time and quickly analyze the likely meaning as it becomes visible

Both types of research have many more drivers—these short lists barely touch on the reasons researchers and their backers want to collect, analyze, and visualize data from social media networks and platforms. This book takes a closer look at the authors' specific interests, providing their insights into a still new type of research that has many benefits—and risks—for all of us. Whether you agree with their conclusions, the datafication of social media continues. It behooves the worldwide community to keep up with what's happening behind the scenes and speak up with ethical concerns, ideas for further research, and proposals for openness and privacy rules to get a handle on this exploding area of research that peers so closely into our personal and professional lives. Our social media interconnections mean that what researchers, governments, and industries do with *our* data has vital importance now and in the future.

Nancy Hays
EDUCAUSE, USA

Foreword

Using Social Media to Track People

In addition to the intensive information flow in our age, daily technological developments make possible the tracking of individuals. This intensive information should be presented to desired places with the final version to be delivered very quickly after checking for accuracy with advanced tools and adapting according to our interests.

Social Media platforms enable people to follow and to be followed; in short, appropriate social media platforms bring together people and their respective audiences. Social media are media channels that everyone (individuals, companies, brands, institutions) can use to communicate with each other, and they can share information without any limit. Social media have rapidly become an integral part of our community life. The use of social media differs according to individuals. Social media platforms respond to many desires such as socialization, escape, enlightenment, communication, and time spending. While responding to these desires, it became the fastest and most encompassing tool for people today.

To summarize social media in a sentence, it is all of the media whose content is created and distributed by the user, who interacts with the community in which user-generated content is shared and co-produced. Namely, the platforms that anyone or any corporation can share desired content in any platform and can take feedback shortly after sharing are called social media.

Social media are different from traditional media channels in terms of putting users at the center of the content production process by providing the opportunity to contribute to the content. Traditional media no longer determine the form and content of mass communications. Traditional media address mainline populations and take no account of individual features; they make interface design, settings and new arrangements by taking common features of specific target group into consideration.

Traditional media production mostly requires specialized skills and training. This is not the case for most of social media; namely, everyone can produce digital contents for sharing.

The fact that those from all walks of life and various cultures use social media means that there are new dimensions to socialization. People at are once local citizens but also global ones. To understand this new socialization, it is important to understand for what purpose the contents were developed in social media and how these are used. It has become important to know how online contents are developed and how the usability of tools can be investigated for improvement.

The analysis of all shares people have published on via social media is called social media content analysis. Social media tools present numerous collectible and ethnographically searchable data in different formats. With the formation of this vast content pool published by people, it is important to identify what is important for research and knowledge.

The existence of social networks in many areas in Turkey is important for both the individual end-users and companies. Social networks are used for making friends. The most important factor shaping the sort of social network density in Turkey is the Internet usage habits of the Turkish people.

Social network sites can be easily used by being flexible and user-friendly when compared to other education management systems. Forming a group via following easier steps by students and researchers and sharing among themselves provide facilities in terms of communication and feedback. In addition to facilities provided in terms of general use, use limitations of some settings can cause lost during navigating. To form a more useful network via defining these limitations, eye tracking studies are also considered to be important.

Duygu Mutlu-Bayraktar
Istanbul University, Turkey

Preface

If social media started in the late 1990s and early 2000s, we are now some 18 years into the Web 2.0 phenomenon. In this time, there have been a lot of takers, and a global electronic culture has emerged. Users, globally, have been posting status updates through microblogging messages, short messaging services, and social networking wall posts. They have been labeling their messages and online resources with tags. They have been #hashtagging their microblogged messages and liberally using keywords, and many of these are new words created on-the-fly (word mash-ups and new creations, if you will). Virtually everyone has learned how to strike a pose towards the business end of selfie sticks and to create attention-worthy spectacles. There are a rich variety of "go fund me" efforts online. Social media platforms are up-tempo spaces where people go to see and be seen, where people perform socially to audiences—both real and imagined. (People are sensitive to the realization that they are observed and will changed their behaviors.) There is profligate oversharing on food, friends, travel, and dating, in competitions for social approval and fame. Online is a space leavened by the human imagination and games of pretense. Online is a virtual social playground and collaboration space for the world's youth and adults. For most, it is "TMI" (too much information).

The overflow of amateur-created work has sometimes put the pros out-of-business or dropped the bottoms out of pro work, whether in journalism or entertainment or porn. Online, there are groups and individuals advocating for social and political changes for, if not some conceptualized utopias, at least some betterment. Messages are shaped to activate people to action, and the respondents are the savvy and the gullible. Many are working to create online norms against trolling, fraud, and advantage-taking, and to make the online spaces safer. It's a mix of signals and mixed signals. Collectively and individually, people form understandings of each other through electronically mediated ways. Social media platforms are a little like "stone soup" concoctions: people need to bring their own ingredients, and the resulting mix is sometimes a savory one.

Users have been going short—short texts, short videos (think Vines), and quick image captures—and moving on. The messages and contents are narrow-casted to friends and others with like-minded interests but also often simultaneously broadcast to anyone who cares to follow, observe, and engage. The argument is that with digital contents, the sharing will be non-rivalrous. There is no actual limit to the sharing as long as a commercial site is willing to host the contents and enable others to access it. Human largesse and goodwill do not have a cost except in the initial investment to build the particular digital good; thereafter, it can be consumed any number of ways and exist part of a digital record into digital eternity. Maintaining communications with a small group of friends will be the same as maintaining that of a large followership with the electronic affordances.

SOME EMPIRICAL RESEARCH-BASED INSIGHTS

At first blush, sharing on a planetary or global scale still inspires awe. Over time, even as one's eyes adjust, this is all still astounding, but other observations also come to the fore. While the "world" is participating online, there are actual and real limits. For those engaged in various research topics, there can be limited sources for certain types of information or only a few trustworthy sources. On many topics, there is silence—no sharing. For many crowd-sourced projects, the general dynamic still is in the rabid support of a few and mass free-riding from others. In a global possible pool of contributors, few select in to volunteer—especially as real-world costs for skills, hard (or boring) work, and investments mount. Enthusiasms and skills carry contributors a way, and then interests wane, or relationships break, and there is a fast drop-off of contributions. Those who work in open-source do burn out because users of their resources have needs for support and for updates of the tools and resources. It gets harder for those who provision resources for free to continue in goodwill. In the few anomalous crowd-sourcing projects that have been accepted as broad successes, like Wikipedia, the developer base of those who maintain the core of this are fairly well funded (albeit as a non-profit organization), the contributors well supported with an annual conference, and the endeavor underpinned by a powerful open-source technology and also friendly robots that help present a potent information space. In this space, Wikipedia stands out…in part because of the rarity of effective continuing crowd-sourced resources. For massive open online courses, at least in the early generations, they would attract many potential learners, but a majority would not make it past the first log-in, and in terms of those that actually finished, these would be in the low single digits as a percentage of the mass that first enrolled. Follow-through or stick-to-it-iveness is often wanting.

So much social information is now available in the Internet wilds, and the sharing continues at a rollicking pace. At global scale, in the vernacular, the Internet responds; it thinks; it emotes; it sparks and runs; it breaks. There are mass-scale emotive reactions. There are debates over "the dress" and its colors, and other trivialities. It's all spectacle. And then there's the near-constant *sousveillance,* with mobile phone videos and stills of observed events, often as they unfold.

In the meantime, researchers have surfaced some insights into online human sociality. Online, everything is the "court of public opinion," and for years now, researchers have been tapping those spaces for sentiment. For all the affordances of mediated connectivity, there are real limits to human sociality, a kind of Dunbar number limit. It does take real effort to build and maintain relationships in every context. To usurp Charles de Gaulle's famous quote about nation-states, in one sense, people really have no friends online, only interests. When those interests wane, the weak links break.

Online, the follower-following dynamic does apply, with the masses engaged in following a few and the few not reciprocating followership but having an outsized influence on the many (who often engage in one-sided parasocial relationships). While unreciprocated one-way relationships may be unsustainable, oftentimes, in dyadic contexts, they seem to maintain well over time in various types of fandom; it may be that people want to live in certain imaginary or pretend connections with others. The Pareto principle seems to apply to social media platforms, with a minority few creating a majority of the contents and the others consuming the goods mostly passively as lurkers.

In the 1990s, online spaces were conceptualized as those for people experimenting and exploring, coming into their own identities, no matter what those might look like; it was a space for the imagination. Back then, it was thought that people could explore in full anonymity; it was thought that pseudonymity could be maintained over time. For many social sharers, there was not the conceptualization of an electronic record that would remain in the practical forever. There was not the sense that a deletion was not a real hard deletion, with complete erasure of records. Now, with the revelations of Edward Snowden and others, it is clear that most of what happens online—whether on the Surface Web or Deep Web, it is all quite knowable and explorable. The access is not only for those with high-end access and super technology skills but mainline academic researchers. There is plenty to interpret online already even if it were only on the level of explicit messaging. Researchers have evolved a number of ways to study and access pattern data that is less obvious or hidden. For example, they have created sophisticated stylometric analyses techniques to identify authorship based on hidden metrics (such as parts-of-speech counts). Online forensic investigations turn on when accounts were made, the account handles used, what information was shared, and how; all it would take for a person wanting to remain anonymous or pseudonymous over time would be one small slip-up. Network analysis enabled the capture of trace data to look at human relating. There are machine learning approaches to tap mass data and to extract hidden patterns (often not otherwise findable).

In the attention economy, there is huge competition for "shares," "likes," "favorites," "upvotes," and hotness measures; followers, and "friends." In that light, people have gone online to game socially, sharing their gaming talents with varied guilds and engaging with other players globally. On professional social networks, they share their professional and educational data and work-based slideshows, publications, and presentation videos. On social networking sites, they socialize. On dating sites, they spark, burn out, and more often than not, dim out. In 3D immersive virtual worlds, they create avatars and engage with virtual environments and each other and automated robots. They collaborate around fund-raising, tagging online contents, co-creating encyclopedias and publications, building and sharing digital learning objects, and co-teaching and co-learning through free online courses. On content sharing sites, they engage in special interest groups. Through electronic connectivity, something like global culture has spawned. It is said that everyone can find their own community, no matter how small it is on the long tail. If people prefer the company of others like themselves (homophily), then it may be said that people self-select into certain groups based on self-interests and objectives.

With so much socializing, it seems inevitable that marketplaces of conveniences also form. Many have gone online to create hand-made goods for broad sale and online reputations built up over time based on the various interactions they've had with others on the site. In a sense, electronic social affordances have changed up the calculus of human expectations, with many subscribing to swift trust enabled by third-party sites that hold reputations in escrow. Here, people are engaging in sharing economies, inviting rent-paying strangers into their cars and homes. The boundaries of the electronic marketplace have moved well into people's homes and what might have been thought of as private spaces.

Throughout, there have been small voices emphasizing security. With data, you are always giving away more than you intend—through data leakage and slippage. Those who are practiced in inference attacks can read-back data and read information—like age, gender, culture, personality, intellect, education level, and then some. Even if people cannot see your content data, they can capture your trace and metadata: who you are engaging with, when you are sharing, and often where you are sharing from (geolocation data). Unless pseudonyms are created in a randomized way, they can be interpreted and read-back as well, with varying levels of inferential accuracy.

DATAFICATION OF SOCIAL MEDIA DATA

All this interacting and broad sharing through web-accessible platforms means that there is a lot of available (albeit noisy) data for research and analysis: content data (messaging, articles, images, videos, and others); trace data (log and interaction data); and metadata (data describing data). On a surface level, this data seems highly unstructured. After all, it includes string or text data, imagery, multimedia, and URLs. However, with various types of data scraping and data extraction methods, the data may be categorized into data tables and treated as semi-structured and structured data. Different types of information may be extracted in different ways based on the social media platform and its technological affordances.

In a typical dataset from Twitter, for example, there are columns for user account names, the microblogging message (Tweet), date information, time information, geolocational data, scraped imagery, and so on. Data may be extracted based on certain keywords, hashtags, physical locations, profile Tweetstreams, and other methods. On Wikipedia, which is built on the open-source MediaWiki understructure, its contents may be captured in various ways: articles, article networks, author page networks, edit networks, and other data. And so forth.

On a very superficial level, information shared on social media platforms is lightweight. The information is about people in their respective contexts sharing information with friends and colleagues and maybe the larger publics. Intentions are pretty easy to discern, and it is possible to maybe read some personality into what is shared. The informational value for outsiders may be minimal.

From an applied research perspective, the informational value of social media data tends to be in the aggregate insights: the trends, the public conversations being held, the shared events, the geographically-based occurrences, cultural features, and so forth. If learning from social media is a narrative, the data scientist is striving to enable writing with millions of voices from the perspective of an omniscient narrator. Social media data are at once both subjective and objective. The first draft of history is not achieved through journalism but is in the hands of people who share their moment-by-moment insights and who collectively have described their world at any slice-in-time. The dynamic reading of #hashtagged conversations, Tweetstreams, posting walls, may be achieved with computerized "distant reading," which enables the capture of summary data and trends. To be clear, the same technologies enable viewing not only at the 30,000 foot level but zooming in to the level of an individual node (ego) and the level of a single voice, a single dyadic pair and their electronic interchanges, a three-some in a three-way short messaging interchange, or a cluster of actors engaging around an obscure topic.

The data are already in electronic format. With various tools, accessing the data results in minimal effort, with application programming interfaces (APIs), web browser add-ons, and command-line capabilities in programming languages (many with packages that enable various text-based analytics). There is a pursuit of hidden patterning in the data—what is latent or non-obvious—beyond intended revelations. What may be understood from social media data depends on the questions asked (or the discovery approach), the data extraction tools and methods used, the application of analytical processes (and tools), and the sophistication of the researchers. Some common analytical approaches include natural language processing, geolocational data processing, geoprocessing, network analysis, sentiment analysis, time-based analyses, content mapping, and others. Various types of machine learning applications may be applied to social media data in order to extract patterns and create models; these models come with validation methods.

Instead of speculating on what others are thinking, it is actually possible to tap empirical data to see what is being expressed (by at least part of the population). It is possible to explore breaking events and issues to see what is trending and who is participating in various conversations. It is possible to see into people's profiles and their ego neighborhoods and networks. It is possible to explore geographically-based phenomena as well as those of certain tribes and people groups. For those more used to traditional research methods, the datasets from social media tend to be a lot bigger than typical, and often, it is much easier to acquire the data. There is often a strong discovery element to such data—because there are revelatory insights, even for aspects that were not necessarily considered.

And yet, for all the data bounty, there is also the sense that access to data is constantly changing. Those who run social media platforms do not constantly enable access through their application programming interfaces (APIs); rather, the terms of access and use do change. There is the sense that those who control the data have better things to do with it than to give it away for free (back to those who actually contributed the original data). Also, the intermediary tools used to access data can be quite limited and limiting based on pre-set data extraction parameters and other tool features. To scrape an N of all from planet-scale social media, researchers would generally have to go with a commercial entity that enables full access to social media data and have a way to engage big data (with the necessary training, the proper data handling software, and access to cloud-based data). They also have to be comfortable with abstracted data in different data formats.

Computer science researchers have made impressive headway in areas of machine vision, and there are companies offering services to machine-sort imagery (with machine learning tools trained on the Web corpus of imagery). These technologies are still quite cutting edge and have not been fully integrated into the toolkits of contemporary researchers.

OPEN CHALLENGES

So what are "open challenges" in social media data extractions and content analysis? If I were to speculate, the list would include the following:

First, there is constant surveillance over what the next big popular social application may be and what its features are and how people might engage that application in their daily lives. Next-generation social media platforms may well be built into the Internet of Things (IoT) and hidden in the physical environment and encapsulated in apparent simplicity. The social ecosystem is in constant motion, and changes are the norm. The next game changers are likely already being conceptualized and built.

Second, there is constant work on advancing computational analytics. As-is, there are technologies for "distant reading" of small-to-large text corpora. There are ways to extract sentiment, emotion, and valence from texts. There are ways to read and interpret the personality of writers using computational means. There are ways to map "http networks" to understand web page ties and relationships. There are ways to map social networks within and across platforms. Geolocational data may be plumbed to understand the physical locational aspects of social media interactions. There are ways to anticipate people's physical locations in the future (with a high degree of confidence), based on a sufficient amount of underlying locational data. There are ways to plumb the Dark Web for virtually all the same insights as the Surface Web. Of late, there have been rich advancements in data visualization to communicate complex and large-scale data and data changes over time. All the prior may be done dynamically on newly created data in real-time. On the cutting edge is machine vision (such as object recognition, facial recognition, context recognition, and others) and image analytics on-the-fly. There is work also on video analytics on-the-fly. There is a need for easier ways to conduct analyses cross-lingually. In the years since social media has popularized, there have many methods developed to fuse data from disparate sources and to plumb that data for otherwise-latent insights. Indeed, there is nascent progress to expand knowability on a variety of technological fronts based on commercial and security needs. On the long tail is work on applications to particular domains and unique research cases.

Third, there will be continuing efforts to bring research and analytical methods to researchers. There is not only the push for new ways of datafying and analyzing social media data but also endeavors to make it easier and lower-cost for researchers to analyze social media data. Using "big data" to understand consumers and the broad public has been *de rigueur* in industry, but big data analyses are still not that common in academia. Machine learning has been enabled for years, but that also has been slow to be accepted by academic researchers (even though these capabilities have been integrated into software analytics packages for years). Acceptance of computational methods in academic fields will require leadership, funding, advocacy, validated research and analytics methods, and potent research cases and exemplars. There will have to be work training up researchers in new methods and technologies. Concomitant with this methods work will be advancements in theory and modeling, which enable academic research work to advance.

Fourth, there are people groups joining social media and others leaving—in a constant churn. Still, even today, according to one application of the diffusion of innovations model, there are still many of the "late majority" and "laggards" coming online and joining social media, especially as technological infrastructures are put into place and mobile devices become more capable in various regions of the world. As others come online and engage socially, many research insights may be attainable. (Of course, at the same time, there are others who are exiting social media and going through temporary or even permanent "digital detox". Still others have never gotten on board to begin with because of the common truism that when social media services are free, what they are selling is their users' data and access to the users—for advertisers. People who do not want their private selves to be bought and sold and used for commercial ends choose to remain socially inert or non-present on social media platforms. A social media platform is only as good as its current verified users, in a sense.)

Certainly, there are other open challenges in social media data extractions and content analysis. The above four are general areas as I see it: the next-gen social media applications, advancing computational analytics, the expansion of research and analytical methods to researchers in a range of fields, and the changing populations using social media (and what they each bring).

GETTING TO "YES" WITH BOOK CONTRIBUTORS

Some of my colleagues speak dreamily of research, writing, editing, and publishing. The script that they are running often has something to do with fame and fortune, which are life aspects which are rarely factually associated with this work. For some of them, there is still a mystique to the process. Take it from me: if there is fear when facing a blank page, facing an unfilled text without any pages as-yet defined is multiply "frightening".

After coming up with the initial inspiration for an edited text, what is actually required is just plain doggedness. Initially, an editor works to recruit talent through as many channels as possible. Not all gatekeepers are necessarily willing to offer access to their electronic mailing lists or email networks or other electronic venues. The call for chapter proposals is scattershot. Online word-of-mouth can be pretty iffy. The targeting itself is fairly imprecise because the book topic on social media research draws those from a range of educational and professional backgrounds.

A call for chapter proposals temporarily focuses time for those few working in a particular area of a field to achieve the works that ultimately make it into the book. I think of this as a kind of extended "moment" when particular interests align and commitments to the work are made. The book development cycle proceeds during a year. A year is rarely sufficient for researchers to fully acquire new skill sets and technologies, much less the insights required to know what is somewhat novel in the field. This is especially so in the exploration of social media for research purposes because while researchers are expert in their respective areas, engaging social media with their complexities, applying new technologies and research methods, and re-conceptualizing statistical applications, are hard endeavors. There are substantial real-world challenges to understanding how to use software tools to "read" texts (think stopwords lists, regular expressions, matrix queries, and data visualizations) and "interpret" imagery. The harnessing of computational methods to understanding social media is seen as potentially up-ending long-practiced analytical processes and so is not without controversy.

Not only do they have to be pre-positioned for the work, the researchers and writers first have to be willing to invest that much of their own efforts and "head space" into the research. Ultimately, contributors have to self-select into a book project; they cannot be charmed or talked into one because the work itself is simply too demanding.

Research and writing are hard work that draw a few. The work cycle for a chapter, roughly, goes something like this: inspiration, a thorough review of the literature, research design, conduct of the research, data analytics, data visualizations, writing, revision, re-review of the literature, submittal, peer review, revision, and finalization. If the work is being achieved by a team, there is the additional layer of work involving coordination—a complex social dance of high expectations, cross-field expertise, and mutual accommodation. Regardless, there are many sacrifices to make the space to actually execute on the work.

Then, too, besides investing in the hard work, all sides have to work on the shared trust. It does not take more than one misstep or wrong messaging to break that trust. Even if all sides start out with good will and a respect for each other's public reputations, it's in the interactions that collaborations are made or broken. In this text, two chapters did not make because of broken trust. Trust is a two-way relational phenomenon, and in some cases, it is ephemeron. Publishing is about convergence of shared interests around a particular project, and in the fragile year leading up to the finalization of a work, that trust has to be built and cultivated; it has to be maintained into a practical foreseeable future as well (professional worlds are small).

Some publications use their posted rejection rate as a metric for the value of a publication. The harder it is to have a work accepted for publication, the more elite and selective a publication may be. That is not my intention here. Ideally, in every context, every potential author and authoring team would have a fair hearing and fair judgment through double-blind peer review. Not all works get to that stage of an actual submitted draft chapter. For this work, a half-dozen would-be contributors had works that did not make it through the process. For two teams, their chapter drafts were mere summaries of the research literature with no original primary research, and neither was able to recover when they received that feedback. One of the more counterintuitive messages to authors is that their local knowledge is critical to the value and uniqueness of their work. It is interesting to identify wide gulfs in thinking across different spaces. So often, researchers do not see the value in what they know intimately because such details are normal and mundane to them. If outside research is to be summarized, as these two teams chose, then there still has to be something else in the work that is original—such as the creation of a new model or the application of the research to a local setting.

One potential author self-selected out and retracted his approved chapter when he did not like the anonymized draft chapter he was to peer-critique. He erroneously suggested that the author of that work had plagiarized based on running the text through an anti-plagiarism tool and not actually apparently reading the work. He also seemed frustrated that he would only be receiving one complimentary copy of the published text, and he wanted more recognition and reward for his work. (All first-author contributors receive one complimentary copy of the published text, nothing more. This is why, as an editor, I am hoping that the contributors acquire other benefits from their work, such as professional advancement and professional recognition.) While it can be annoying when potential authors self-select out of a project, it is a healthy sign of the field where researchers and authors advocate for themselves and their own interests and that they have a wide range of potential publishers they may access to help polish and present their work to the world.

Another work was declined when the contributor made it clear that she would not abide by the strictures of the publishing contract. She did not like the terms of the contract, and she wanted to create derivative (read: self-plagiarised) works from her research. That chapter did not make it into the peer review process. Several others did not complete their work in time. Ultimately, people self-select in or out; they follow through, or they do not; they choose one project or another. And after a number of book projects, I think there should be no offense taken if a work does not make for a particular project. Sometimes, the "fit" is simply not there, and no one should feel the worse for it. Maybe next time. Still, it is helpful to conduct a "traceback" and review how things may be done better next time to be still more inclusive while upholding tough standards.

Interestingly, in one of the email exchanges with a potential author, he asked if I reviewed the chapters directly. *Of course.* I read the contributors' chapters multiple times, even before I send it out in anonymized format for double-blind peer review. I do provide feedback to the authors and authoring teams. I also read all reviews and make sure that those are shared appropriately with the authors. I see my role as shepherding a work through the peer editing and publishing process. While I have my own standards, I am conscious of the importance of protecting and respecting author freedom and voice. I understand that feedback has to be constructive and not harmful to the authors' confidence. The idea is to support the authors' highest and best, and what that looks like differs.

While much research is occurring on social media, much of it is proprietary and protected by corporations (as it should be in those contexts). A lot of work is on-going without documentation for public consumption. Most publications in this area seem to be coming from academia, with a few from corporate research labs.

INITIAL AMBITIONS FOR THE TEXT

In the original conceptualization, it was hoped that *Social Media Data Extraction and Content Analysis* would include works that encompassed research not only on the Surface Web but also the Deep (Hidden) Web and maybe even the Dark Web. Also, there were expectations that there could be broad inclusion of a wide range of social media platforms and the introduction of a wide range of technologies and research methods for data extractions and analytics. The general concept is to not artificially limit the possibilities by thinking in too small, but to conceptualize broadly and to let the real world limitations determine the ultimate Table of Contents (TOC).

When I say that editing is an emergent process, I mean that it involves a lot of ambiguity. One has to make a certain amount of progress before the next considered decisions are made and the proper steps taken. This is especially so for determining the ultimate contents of a text. As such, the TOC is set up in four sections.

Section 1: Modeling with Social Data
Section 2: Analytics from the Online Crowd
Section 3: Tapping Specific Social Media Platforms
Section 4: Applied Uses of Social Media Data for Awareness and Problem-Solving

SECTION 1: MODELING WITH SOCIAL DATA

Jonathan Bishop's "Devising Parametric User Models for Processing and Analysing Social Media Data to Influence User Behaviour: Using Quantitative and Qualitative Analysis of Social Media Data" (Ch. 1) thoughtfully argues for using a range of theoretically informed and practical methods for studying social media data. Drs. Eric Gilbert Poitras and Negar Fazeli Dehkordi describe the application of the intelligent nBrowser to enhancing the work of teacher professional development, in "Mining the Edublogosphere: Towards Modeling Networks of Online Resources to Enhance Teacher Professional Development" (Ch. 2). This work stands to advance education through the harnessing of relevant socially mediated educational contents across a range of online platforms. In a theoretically important work, Drs. Davide Di Fatta, Roberto Musotto, Vittorio D'Aleo, Walter Vesperi, Giacomo Morabito, and Salvatore Lo Bue argue that network analysis is especially relevant in terms of the global Internet economy, in "Weak Ties and Value of a Network in the New Internet Economy" (Ch. 3). Dr. Duygu Mutlu-Bayraktar, in "Usability Evaluation of Social Media Web Sites and Applications via Eye-Tracking Method" (Ch. 4), takes a human usability approach in evaluating social media sites based on eye-tracking.

SECTION 2: ANALYTICS FROM THE ONLINE CROWD

The second section, "Analytics from the Online Crowd," focuses on the phenomenon of "crowd-sourcing," or reaching out to the people connecting online to collaboratively address interests and issues. Drs. Marlene Goncalves, Patrick Rengifo, Daniela Andreina Rodriguez, and Ivette C. Martinez, in "A Route Recommender System Based on Current and Historical Crowdsourcing" (Ch. 5) describes a clever approach to use Twitter information for traffic awareness between any two geographical points in Caracas, Venezuela. In Chapter 6, Drs. Antonia Estrella-Ramón and Alba Utrera-Serrano describe a content analysis approach to exploring and understanding "Customer Complaints in Social Networks in the Spanish Telecommunication Industry: An Analysis using the 'Critizen'"; this is a work about enhancing business-based decision-making. With the outpouring of so much digital data shared through social media platforms and the Social Web, software developers have been extending capabilities for "distant reading," or using machines to extract meaning from text. Dr. Shalin Hai-Jew's "Applied Analytical 'Distant Reading' using NVivo 11 Plus" (Ch. 7) explores some of the distant reading capabilities of a widely used qualitative data analytics tool. The last chapter of this section describes a sentiment analysis feature and its applications for research. "Sentiment Analysis and Post-Sentiment Data Exploration through Automated Means" (Ch. 8), by Hai-Jew, describes the ways that "sentiment" in textual corpora may be understood computationally and applied to research.

SECTION 3: TAPPING SPECIFIC SOCIAL MEDIA PLATFORMS

In Section 3, "Tapping Specific Social Media Platforms," the chapters highlight some of the types of information that may be extracted from various social platforms and how such data may be used for various purposes. The platforms include social networking platforms, content-sharing sites, microblogging platforms, and others. Chapter 9, "Exploring 'User,' 'Video,' and (Pseudo) Multi-Mode Networks on YouTube with NodeXL," describes the drawing of various social and content networks from Google's YouTube using a freeware tool (NodeXL Basic). The fact that the same graphs can no longer be extracted with the same tool highlights the constantly changing levels of access to social media platform data and the sense that researchers must seize the moments which are ephemeral and fast-moving. "Flickering Emotions: Feeling-based Associations from Related Tags Networks based on Flickr Contents" (Ch. 10) is a multi-layered work. Based on Robert Plutchik's "Wheel of Emotions" model, the author captures related tags networks and related thumbnail imagery from Flickr in order to explore a more diffracted sense of what those emotions mean as described in tagging (based on socially shared imagery). In "Creating "(Social) Network Art" with NodeXL' (Ch. 11), Shalin Hai-Jew displays a sense of experimentation and whimsy in using social media platform data to draw various graphs in artistic ways with aesthetic appeal.

SECTION 4: APPLIED USES OF SOCIAL MEDIA DATA FOR AWARENESS AND PROBLEM-SOLVING

This final section, "Applied Uses of Social Media Data for Awareness and Problem-Solving," captures some of the applied uses of social media data for awareness and problem solving. Taking a page from the hyper-social online environment, Drs. E Pinar Uca-Günes and Gülsün Eby, both of Anadolu University, explore the potential benefits of tactically created social networks to build distance education programs, in "Social Network Synthesis: A Dynamic Approach for Building Distance Education Programs" (Ch. 12). In the final chapter, an authoring team explores how Australian banks engage the online community through Facebook. Drs. Vindaya Senadheera, Matthew Warren, Shona Leitch, and Graeme Pye explore themes in Facebook wall posts using NVivo in "Facebook Content Analysis: A Study into Australian Banks' Online Community Engagement" (Ch. 13). Donna Bridgham, in "Code Reuse," proposes a solidly conceptualized and developed repository for the sharing of code to benefit the work of developers; here is an idea for work-purposive social sharing (Ch. 14).

How a book ultimately shapes out is serendipitous in one sense and a result of a lot of hard and purposeful work on the other. The only appeal of a print (and electronic) book—which is somewhat anachronistic—is that it will be packaged and indexed in a way that may be referenced in the near-present and the far future. Sometimes, it may seem that a more strategic way to achieve a large audience is to create a video for a social media site, but chapters capture irreducibly complex information that would be difficult to present in other ways. I hope that this text may be a building block for others' insights and professional endeavors and achievements. Writing, classically, enables shared understandings with others. It is hard to bridge different understandings among people about a particular topic. There are discordant mental models between people about particular topics. Even an author will find past writings somewhat unrecognizable and maybe even jarring; one way to understand why this may be is because the person who wrote the earlier work was in a different place in life than the more recent individual reading that work. In shared synchronous time, differing individuals may have different cultural, historical, educational, linguistic, and geographical backgrounds, and these may influence how they approach a particular topic.

By itself, a book will not draw future human attention per se; rather, the quality of the work will determine whether any chapter has any value beyond that of a few readers in the near-present. What future readers may find valuable is not predictable given so many factors. What may be highly popular at a point in time may easily become part of the so-called forgotten literature. The foremost work of editors and peer reviewers then is to ensure quality, so authors and authoring teams achieve their highest and best possible at the time of the work's creation.

Steve Simon, the photographer, talks about how single images placed in a set creates a kind of interplay and a momentum, and that analogy applies here to this collection as well. The respective works are powerful on their own, but their interplay in this set of writing really brings potency to the conceptualization of social media platforms as sources of usable data for exploration and study.

Acknowledgment

I am deeply grateful to all the authors who contributed in person because we are mostly collaborating from a distance. Their talent and goodwill are hugely apparent and much appreciated.

I am grateful for their act of trust in me and also in IGI-Global, which has been a strong partner on a number of texts. Thanks to Janine Haughton for her work in supporting this project and all the others on this team who work so diligently to bring a text to reality. So much hard work is required behind-the-scenes. Creating a textually and visually coherent text, particularly with so many moving parts, is a complex challenge. The typographers especially rise to the task.

I hope to be worthy of the trust of all who are part of *Social Media Data Extraction and Content Analysis*, whether as authors-contributors, publisher, and/or readers.

I am deeply appreciative of the editorial board (listed in alphabetical order) who served on this project. They include:

Nancy Hays, *EDUCAUSE, USA*

Duygu Mutlu-Bayraktar, *Istanbul University, Turkey*

Marc A. Smith, *Social Media Research Foundation, USA*

Section 1
Modeling with Social Data

Chapter 1

Devising Parametric User Models for Processing and Analysing Social Media Data to Influence User Behaviour:
Using Quantitative and Qualitative Analysis of Social Media Data

Jonathan Bishop
Centre for Research into Online Communities and E-Learning Systems, UK

ABSTRACT

Academia is often plagued with those who define themselves by whether they are "quantitative" or "qualitative." This chapter contests that when it comes to researching social media the two are inseparable in datafying user generated content. Posts on Twitter for instance have a textual element to the narratives that could be considered qualitative, but also quantitative criteria can be applied. Interviewing approaches can allow for the exploration of discourses to produce new theories, which may then rely of those approaches commonly thought of as quantitative. This chapter tests out a variety of different approaches to show how it is only through using all approaches available can social media be triangulated to produce accurate modelling of user behaviour.

INTRODUCTION

Researching social media is challenging and publishing such research may be even more challenging. Even after a generation of expanded use of the world wide web, the methods and approaches to researching cyberspace are highly disputed. A positivist might say that only quantifiable facts can be studied, such as web metrics. A phenomenologist on the other hand might say that it is only through understanding the meaning behind internet postings and those who post them is it possible to understand Internet cul-

DOI: 10.4018/978-1-5225-0648-5.ch001

ture. Even worse, the positivist might want to position themselves as a 'quantitative' researcher and the phenomenologist as a 'qualitative' researcher. Both points of view leave a lot to be desired. In order to properly understand life in cyberspace, one needs to triangulate various different methods to achieve a comprehensive account. This chapter explored in depth various forms of data collection and data analysis and how these, whether based around words or numbers, can contribute to the creation of models that allow for those who use the Internet and social media to be understood and influenced.

BACKGROUND

Scientists of all kinds are trying to understand the ways in which people communicate with respect of social media. Social media as a term can be seen to refer to all the forms of under-generated content that have existence since the second wave of social networking services, which include Twitter and Facebook. This period could be referred to as post-modem history. The reason being that social media platforms offer little above earlier social networking services like Friendster and MySpace, but as a result of affordable broadband connections more people are using the Internet, whereas previously they might have been technophobic. At present, many scientists seeking to understand social media have turned to Big Data. In other words they are using number-crunching algorithms to systematically understand why people might make certain postings at certain times.

As time goes on, there will be increasing pressure for education institutions to integrate social media functionalities into their managed learning environments. This will need to be done in such a way that the integration is seamless and invisible and not a central focus for the user. Such acts would allow for the creation of networked learning communities, where student-centred learning can be enabled. So far, approaches to this has followed an e-tivities model reliant on the use of message boards and other web-based communities. Whilst these are inevitably essential to online learning, they will no doubt attract the same sorts of problems found in social media platforms. Problems such as lurking, flaming and defriending can result in a loss of sense of community and result in disengagement with the learning process. It is therefore important to develop methods in which these behaviours can be identified and those behaviours influenced before they are able to occur.

This chapter seeks to set out a rationale and methodology of why this is inappropriate and why instead an approach based on making use of the senses of the researcher – to systematically draw out meanings from social media postings – is a better alternative. To demonstrate this it is first essential to understand the persuasive and seductive properties of hypermedia that give rise to varying behaviours in social media services and how these can be systematically detected and influenced. It will then be shown how drawing out meanings from social media can assist with enhancing sense of community in networked learning communities.

DEVISING A DATA THEORY: CONSIDERING METHODOLOGICAL APPROACHES TO SOCIAL MEDIA RESEARCH

This section sets out the methodological approaches for the overall study.

Approaches to Data Collection

This section sets out the data collection methods that can be used to triangulate the various forms of and approaches to social media. In particular this section looks at questionnaires, interview-based critical event recall, subjective and systematic data capture, and website metrics.

Questionnaires

Questionnaires are one of the most used methods for data collection. They are easy to administer and can produce consistent data. However, questionnaires do not always allow for the expression of accurate statements because those taking the survey might want to answer in a way that is not possible. There are means to overcome this, such as by asking users open-ended questions with written answers and then encoding those into more measurable numerical data (Bishop, 2015).

Interview-Based Critical Event Recall

Interviews are one of the most established methods of inquiry in various research disciplines. An interview allows for the collection of data based on the spontaneous reactions of others to questions. Whilst a questionnaire uses predefined questions that can result in researcher bias, interviews can be better at correcting this, providing questions are open ended and seek to elicit the interviewees opinions as opposed to confirm the researcher's point of view. Because of the speed that activities take online – in many cases due to being in a state of flow – much of the detail is forgotten (De Laat & Lally, 2003; De Laat & Lally, 2005). On this basis, an interviewer can more effectively elicit information from a participant, which they might not have though possible. This could be done with open-ended questions. The problem with open-ended interviews, however, is that it can sometimes be difficult to code the transcripts with a framework that is universally applicable, again without relying on preconceived ideas. Even those based on the 'framework' approach, which seems to pull the codes from the minds of the researcher, who is making a judgement, may confirm a preconceived mental model, whether the researcher wants to admit it or not.

The author therefore proposes a new approach to interviewing and critical event recall, using predefined modal verbs, which are supported in the interview with pronouns. For instance, an interviewee might be asked as a follow up question; "Would you say that you don't like that type of navigational structure?" Or they might be asked: "How much would you say this represents *your* view on a scale of 1 to 7 – 'I don't like navigational structures that get in the way of interaction.'" As can be seen from Table 1 there are a number of pronoun supported modal verbs that can be used to elicit responses and provide a coding framework at the same time. It might be that the pronoun supported modal verbs could be a coding into a different a priori model, or even the associations derived after the coding. It might seem clear however that the words allow for a more objective interview seeking the interviewees opinions and not the interviewers.

Table 1 presents an approach for conducting interviews. As can be seen a number of pronouns and verbs are placed together, which will enable the research more easily entice the participant into expressing statements that can be clearly coded with the M-MARS ethnographical approach (Bishop, 2011) or a similar approach.

Table 1. Possible interview approaches

Factor	Communication Orientated	Experience Orientated	Achievement Orientated
Recurrent Needs	Relationships (I want/don't want)	Recognition (I can/can't)	Responsibility (I think/I don't think)
Situational Constraints	Group Dynamics (I offer/don't accept)	Antecedent State (I need/don't need)	Prospects (I am/I am not)
Compound Identity	Social Self (I shall / shall not)	Situational Self (I must/must not)	Symbolic Self (I'll always/I'll never)
Situated Actions	Cooperative (I will / I won't)	Impulsive (I should/shouldn't)	Cautious (I like/don't like)

Subjective and Systematic Data Capture

Monitoring activities and gathering of data from virtual communities is challenging task, with it being argued that even in simple NLCs and wikis, these do not properly store all available data about behaviour of users and/or changes of content (Štogr, 2011). It has been argued that in most cases analysing these datasets can provide enough information for completion assessment, but cannot be used for modelling simulated experiences (Štogr, 2011). The most promising NLCs are those where one has full access to both datasets and tools that can be used for "replaying" past activities it has been concluded (Štogr, 2011).

Website Metrics

Website audiences are broad and come to them freely, often with no registration or prior identification, most data gathered comes from web metrics (which reveal behaviour but not attitudes or intent) or from surveys and interviews of a self-selecting group of users (Carson, Kanchanaraksa, Gooding, Mulder, & Schuwer, 2012). In the source selection, methods such as web metrics can be used to evaluate the information source, and inputs from industry experts are essential to providing a complete picture (Xie, Wang, & Chen, 2012).

As can be seen from Table 2 there are a number of factors that can influence involvement. Reactionary influences result in low involvement – because not much effort is needed to achieve the behaviour. Ulterior motives means in the situation that a person will do things for their own ends or the websites they use, such as clicking on adverts to increase income for this site. This may be seen as a form of trolling, as the person is causing harm to another – the advertiser – for their own or that site's benefit. Angular influences are those where the person will not change, such as where an elder won't change to accommodate new members of the group or point out 'flaws' in others arguments, if they don't match their own. In terms of Flow this has a direct impact on involvement. Flow is high when a person has little involvement in a task though increased effort. Flow is low when involvement is high as the person's actions are not fluid because of the extra effort being put into the task at hand.

It is known that whether a test is parametric or non-parametric that having a good theory on which to base one's assumptions can avoid pitfalls of data collection and analysis. The Consumer Resource Exchange Model (CREM) is based upon the theory that consumers seek to manage resources in order to engage in exchange activities directed at achieving goals (Bristow & Mowen, 1998). The resources

Table 2. Elements to build into website metrics

Involvement	Considerations	Examples
Reactionary	1 aspect: Needs and constraints	Rapid clicking of a mouse, facial expressions, heart rate.
Ulterior	2 aspects: Needs and constraints	Clicking on adverts that financially support a website one uses.
Angular	3 aspects: Needs, constraints and identity	Not willing to change one's attitudes, believe or practices for others regardless of the impact it has on them.
Flow	1 aspect: High level involvement	Speed of transition from one page to the next and one contribution to another.

in the model have been operationalised as available, accumulative assets that are readily transmittable or exchangeable between individuals (ibid). This might be one model for testing a subjective approach that looks at individual difference.

Another framework – The SARM Model – includes the elements of Situational Constraint Theory (SCT) as a basis for explaining the factors that restrict a social actors ability to achieve their goals (Peters, O'Connor, & Eulberg, 1985; Pritchett, 2009). Situational constraints are "a set of circumstances that is likely to influence the behaviour of at least some individuals, and that is likely to reoccur repeatedly in essentially the same form" (Peters et al., 1985). This definition helped researchers build an approach to gather applicable research about situational constraints of a job or task that has or will interfere with past or present work performance (Pritchett, 2009). Hybrid versions of these models can perhaps be found in (Zikmund & Scott, 1973), which was in existence thirty to forty years before these models. The factors making up all these models are presented in Table 3.

Parametric modelling has most frequently been spoken about in human-computer interaction in relation to programming concepts such as objects and classes (Aggarwal, 2003; Szewczyk, 2003). Equally parametric testing of users to derive statistical models are usually developed using so-called objective techniques like questionnaires and other so-called quantitative approaches. The authors however argue that subjectivity is inherent in research studies both from the participant and the researcher. However, many people claim they are being objective in looking at a dataset, when it is necessary for models to be

Table 3. Possible models for constructing a subjectively devised parametric user mode.

SARM (Situational Constraints)	CREM (Motivations)	William Zikmund (Perceived Risk)	Coding Factors
Environmental	Physical	Physical	Motifs
Capital	Financial	Financial	Cognitions
Group Dynamics	Social	Social	Bleasure/Pleasure intention, Befriending strategy
Antecedent State		Psychological	Metrics
Prospects	Informational	Opportunity	Sentiment; Prospect choice biases; Befriending strategy; Means to avoid defriending; Mediator/Dismediator
Time		Time	Seduction time; knol

Table 4. Elements to elicit from websites matrices

SARM (Angular Responses)	Karen Horney (Orientation)	Mantovani (Situated Actions)
Cooperative	Compliant	Cooperation
Impulsive	Aggressive	Conflict
Cautious	Detached	Negotiation

constructed – by the researcher – materialist paradigms go out of the window as the researchers need to rely on their mind to construct a model or influence a dataset (e.g. through rotation), meaning research bias is inevitable. Table 4 presents possible factors that could be drawn from parametric modelling of neurological behaviour.

These models evolved from the study of human personality and motivation in the social sciences.

Document Inspection

Document inspection is a broad term. Documents can be used to refer to not just printed publications, but also to physical records, such as sculptures representing historical persons or events. In the context of this chapter, documents refer to social media postings and indeed the befriending services on which they are held. Document inspection involves looking at these and finding those postings which are most relevant. The advantage most social media postings have over traditional records is that they are already indexed, meaning so long as one selects the correct keyterms, one can find records that document the most relevant information one is seeking to explore.

APPROACHES TO DATA ANALYSIS

The overall approach used in the data analysis involve coding data in one form or another. All coding techniques assume that the internal signifiers and processes of actors are represented through the external signifiers that they express (De Laat & Lally, 2003; De Laat & Lally, 2005). Specifically, this section looks at narrative analysis and concept mapping.

Narrative Analysis

Narrative analysis is a tool that researchers can use to explore the intersection between the individual and society (Kil, 2010). Narrative analysis in Internet studies essentially uses both text and online "talk" to construct a holistic view of the online interactions, looking at cognition as well as affect (Yukawa, 2005). Narrative analysis is the most prevalent approach that has emphasized alternatives to categorising analysis, but much of narrative research, broadly defined, involves categorising as well as connecting analysis, and the distinction has not been clearly defined (Maxwell & Miller, 2008). Narrative analysis requires the encoding of the content being interrogated, which can be seen as an approach for extracting, generalising, and abstracting original messages to look for evidence of systematic processes in human behaviour (De Laat & Lally, 2003; De Laat & Lally, 2005).

Figure 1. An adaption of Kommers's hybrid entry road for resources

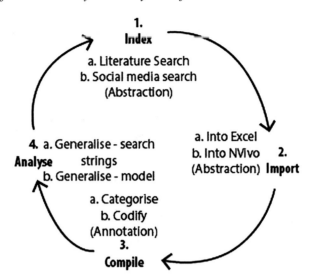

A number of ways in which hypertext can be created and stored, namely compiling, importing and indexing (Kommers, Ferreira, & Kwak, 1998). Indexing allows for the storing of information in the format in which it exists. Importing brings the data into a database. Compiling transforms the data into an internal format suitable for further use. Figure 1 presents an adaption of this model, introducing a further process of Analysing, which is the process of making use of the hypertext database generated. It is argued that this allows for the effective extraction and analysis of social and other data in networked learning communities.

Figure 4 shows a table of data that has gone through the compile stage (3), which was sourced from research into devising a praxis (De Laat & Lally, 2003). This is the approach that will be taken in the main studies, with the changes being that a significant number of threads will be used and so instead of using use names, the actors (HBs) taking part will be assigned a role or category. Namely, the actor who starts the thread will be identified as the protagonist (PUA) who may target various people (HBs/Various). The non-targeted actor who criticises them or disrupts the thread shall be the antagonist (AMOG/Hater), and the one who is joking around will be the fool (CB/Lolcow). This will be followed by the regular participating actors, namely the deuterogamists (AFOG/Bzzzter) and finally the bit players are the ones who like/share/favourite, etc., but are not really too involved with or noticed by others (JAW/Eyeball). All of these are presented in Figure 5.

Personas are descriptions of particular types of users that engage with a system in a particular way (Cunliffe & Elliott, 2005, p.71). Personas can be described through avatars and character traits (Bishop, 2008). Their avatar allows for them to be related to, even if they are not a real person, and their character traits and background allow for their persona to be fleshed out (Cunliffe & Elliott, 2005, p.71). An example of such a persona is in Figure 2 (Cunliffe & Elliott, 2005, p.71).

Building scenarios of users and their profiles involves determining their background, their knowledge, skill level, motivation and indeed, any other relevant background information (Brinck, Gergle, & Wood, 2002, p.208). An example of a scenario is in Figure 3.

Figure 2. Example of a Persona

Jonathan
30 years old
Male
Single

Laboratory assistant earning £24K
Educated to degree level in chemistry

Typically reads a book a week, likes to follow particular authors, but is always looking for new authors who write similar types of book. Also interested in series and masterwork collections. Likes to read books which are recommended by friends with similar tastes. He has a large collection of books and sometimes finds it difficult to remember which ones he has.

Uses the internet most evenings, generally for checking email. Doesn't use it for long periods as modem is slow and access costs are high. Reluctant to use online shopping as he is concerned about security.

Wants to see new titles from favourite authors
Wants easy access to favourite authors
Wants to see titles from similar authors
Wants recommendations from people with similar interests
May wish to make recommendations
May wish to be able to record which books he already has
May wish to create 'wish-list'
Wants ordered books to arrive quickly
May wish to use offline payment methods
May be interested in opening an account
May like to have notification of new titles sent by email

Does not want to spend long browsing site
Speed of site will be important
Needs to be reassured about security and confidentiality

Site needs to provide convenience beyond that provided by a bookshop

Table 5. Acronyms for identifying user behaviour and goals

Acronym	Meaning	Description
PUA	Player, User or Actor	The person who initiates a thread or topic.
HB	Human Being	The person the PUA is seeking to befriend, persuade, etc.
AMOG	Antagonistic Malcontent of the Group	The person who seeks to cause problems for the PUA so they can't covey their arguments or objectives easily.
CB	Chat-blocker	The person who disrupts the flow of the thread for their own purposes with disregard for others, including the PUA.
AFOG	Attention-Focuser of the Group	The person who adds anecdotes to the thread in a constructive, if not overbearing manner, taking attention of the HB from the PUA.
JAW	Just Another Watcher	The person who watches what others are doing until the opportune moment, in their eyes, to build kudos. This could be either helpful or damaging for the PUA, but might not help their own case either.

Figure 3. Example of scenario

1. Janet is a regular user of the site and has the URL stored in her bookmarks.
2. On arrival at the site Janet is presented with a list of new releases since her last visit, in her favourite categories of music.
3. She browses the list, marking some to be added to her 'wish-list'.
4. Janet spots a new release from her brother's favourite band and emails the details to him.
5. Janet has just had a pay rise, and decides to treat herself to a couple of new CDs so she reviews her 'wish-list' which now includes the latest releases which she has just added.
6. Browsing down she notices that some of the CDs are marked 'bought as gift for you' – she guesses that her brother has bought these for her birthday next week. Knowing that her brother likes the same music as she does, Janet leaves these CDs on her 'wish-list' in case her brother decides to keep them for himself. She can always remove the 'bought as gift for you' mark later.
7. She notices a CD on her 'wish-list' that she has been meaning to buy for a while, so she adds it to her shopping basket.
8. Another CD on the list catches her eye, she opens up the track list and plays a sample track. Deciding that she likes the sound of it, she adds it to her shopping basket.
9. Janet does this for several other CDs, then notices that the shopping basket total, which is continuously displayed on the screen, has reached £75. This is more than she wanted to spend because she also wants to treat herself and her fiancé to a meal to celebrate her pay rise.
10. She decides to review her shopping basket and reluctantly removes some of the CDs back to her 'wish-list', watching as the basket total is reduced to £50. She knows that the price displayed includes VAT and postage, so this is the actual amount that she will pay.
11. Janet's credit card details are already stored, so all she has to do is enter her password to verify the transaction. A confirmation message is displayed confirming her purchases. Janet prints this for her records, then leaves the site.

Figure 4. An approach by De Laat's to coding text in order to create a praxis

Units of meaning coded for learning processes during the beginning phase (note: pseudonyms are used here and in the rest of this paper)

Type of learning process	Learning processes of individual community members								
	Bill	Katie	Brian*	Pauline	Andrea	Felicity	Charles	Margaret	Total
Cognitive	0	2	4	1	17	5	11	6	46
Affective	0	2	1	0	4	1	3	0	11
Metacognitive	0	1	1	1	4	3	4	1	15
Miscellaneous	1	0	1	0	2	0	1	0	5
Total	1	5	7	2	27	9	19	7	77

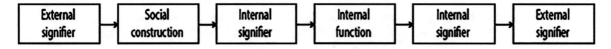

Scenarios can be used to determine what functionality is required in a given system, especially if they are based on the profiles of actual users (Brinck et al., 2002, p.208). Such scenario building by considering users as 'people in motion,' can allow for systems to be regularly adapted to help users move to parts of the system that make them happier (Wodtke, 2003, p.51).

In terms of bringing these various narratives, an appropriate way of presenting such data can be seen in Figure 4. This shows a table from a study into online behaviour (De Laat & Lally, 2003), which itself shows the observable narrative forms (i.e. cognitive, affective, etc.) and the different personas to which these relate (i.e. Bill, Kate, etc.). Through analysing the narratives in such a way, the resulting personas and scenarios can be used to better understand and influence participation.

Discourse Analysis

Discourse analysis is a form of content analysis like narrative analysis, but with key differences. Narrative analysis focuses primarily on secondary sources of spoken information, such as social media postings. Discourse analysis on the other hand has some intentions behind it, namely the researcher has directed the discourse, such as through interviewing. Whilst narrative analysis might focus on shared meaning, discourse analysis focuses specifically on the person being investigated.

Statistical Analyses

Statistical analysis is one of the most efficient ways of analysing questionnaires where the data gathered is either numerical or categorical. In most statistical tests there is an assumption that data is parametric, such as that there is normal distribution and a significant number of variables. However, increasingly non-parametric tests are being used which assume quite the opposite. In the case of this study it is expected that in order to derive parametric user models it is first important to test data using non-parametric approaches, such as those that do not assume homogeneity of The parametric user model that is devised would then be subject to confirmation through confirmatory tests, such as structural equation modelling.

APPROACHES TO DATA VERIFICATION

The section sets out the methods that will be used for verifying the data. In the case of card sorting it is unlikely there will be the time for this one to be conducted. It is well known that producers of a technology may have in mind a group of individuals as potential users while designing, producing and marketing it (Wang, Tucker, & Rihll, 2011). It is known that targeting of specific niches as a viable marketing strategy to overcome the disadvantage of smaller network size (Morsillo, 2011). A review of practices of marketing towards diverse ethnics by (Cui, 1997) revealed several perspectives: traditional marketing, separated marketing, integrated marketing and multicultural marketing. This shows the importance of data verification.

Card-Sorting

Card-sorting studies can provide insights into the mental modes of actors and the way in which they categorise and use information (Rosenfield & Morville, 2002, p.235). An appropriate way to conduct this is Q-methodology. In order to design the statements for a Q-Methodology based card sorting exercise, doing a paper prototype exercise to familiarize participants with a new technological application does not prevent participants from forming their own mental models can be effective (Slegers & Donoso, 2012). This is confirmed by the fact that paper prototyping exercises that are done before doing card sorting exercises may result in deeper insights into the participants' mental models which is useful for (re)designing application interface structures (Slegers & Donoso, 2012). The various dimensions of card-sorting are presented in Table 6 (Rosenfield & Morville, 2002, pp.235-236).

Observational Recordings

Observational recordings can provide a useful insight into how users make use of a system and interact with all the elements of it. Face-to-face sessions involving one user at a time is known to be a central part of effective research (Rosenfield & Morville, 2002, p.233). To devise and test a parametric user model one might first determine the factors that influence the decision-making processes of social actors in a particular user group by testing several dependent variables that may affect the way a social actor uses a

Table 6. Dimensions of card-sorting

Dimension	Description
Open/Closed	It totally open card sorts, users write their own card and category labels. Totally closed sorts allow only pre-labelled cards and categories. Open sorts are used for discovery. Closed sorts are used for validation. There's lots of room in the middle.
Phrasing	The levels on cards might be a word, a phrase, a sentence, or a category with sample sub-categories. You can even affix a picture. One might phrase the card levels as a question or an answer, or one may use topic-or task-orientated words.
Granularity	Cards can be high-level or detailed. One's labels might be main page categories or the names of subsites, or one may focus on specific documents or even content elements within documents.
Heterogeneity	Early on, one may want to cover a lot of ground by mixing apples and oranges (e.g. name of subsite, document title, subject heading) to elicit rich qualitative data. This will really get users talking as they puzzle over the heterogeneous mix of cards. Later, one may want high consistency (e.g. subject headings only) to produce quantitative data (e.g. 80% of users grouped these three items together).
Cross-listing	One might be fleshing out the primary hierarchy of an application or exploring alternative navigation paths. If the latter, one might allow users to make copies of cards, cross-listing them in multiple categories. One may also ask them to write descriptive terms (i.e. metadata) on the cards or category labels.
Randomness	One can strategically select card labels to prove a hypothesis, or one can randomly select labels from a pool of possible labels. As always, your power to influence outcomes can be used for good or evil.
Quantitative / Qualitative	Card sorting can be used as an interview instrument or as a data collection tool and can be effectively used for assessing qualitative data.

Table 7. The effect of dopamine, serotonin, flow and involvement on prefrontal cortex functioning

Factor	Self-Control	Conscience	Working Memory	Empathy	Deception
Dopa-mine	Increasing dopamine can improve focus	Increasing dopamine can produce thoughts of guilt due to greater awareness	Increased dopamine can overload working memory or enable more creative thinking.	Increasing dopamine can impair empathy because a person may be focussed more on their own thoughts. Reducing dopamine can lead to disinterest in others.	Increased dopamine makes deception difficult because of over focus. Reducing dopamine can make deception easier due to being more relaxed.
Sero-tonin	Reducing serotonin can reduce task-focussed anxiety	Increasing serotonin can exacerbate feelings of guilt due to anxiety around unwanted thoughts.	Increased serotonin can impair working memory by making it difficult to focus because of resultant anxiety.	Increased serotonin can improve empathy where another person is also experiencing it.	Increased serotonin can make deception more difficult due to task focussed anxiety.
Flow	Increased flow can reduce self-control	Increased low can reduce awareness of guilt or consequences of actions.	Increased flow can improve effectiveness of working memory	Increased flow can make conversations more fluid and empathy easier.	Increased flow can make it easier to deceive others because of an ability to avoid distractions.
Involve-ment	Increased involvement can improve task-focus	Increased involvement can make it difficult to avoid conscience	Increased involvement depends on working memory	Increased involvement can make empathy difficult due to lack of fluidity of thinking.	Increased involvement can make masking deceptive behaviour more difficult.

virtual environment (e.g. VR-based, iTV, Web). One approach that might to be used to object the effectiveness of a parametric user model in a live setting would be a study that follows a quasi-experimental research design in which the experimenter controls the independent variables within the virtual environment the participant is using. The participants in such a study may not need to be randomly allocated, as they will either be a member of one user group or another. Using a video prototyping technique, certain elements of the virtual environment are changed (e.g. navigation, graphics, etc) and the effect of this on the participant recorded.

Concept Mapping

On its own, narrative analysis, and indeed content analysis more generally, is cumbersome and time consuming, as often choosing coding categories for a given context is complex and subjective (De Laat & Lally, 2003; De Laat & Lally, 2005). To provide some form of objectivity to the study, in validating the conceptual framework based on the narratives being coded as cognitions, these are given numerical values to allow the design of a parametric user model which in addition to the conceptual framework will form an overall praxis. An important part of this numerical coding is to associate the behaviours with neurological processes such as those identified in Table 7. This allows for the systematic modelling of behaviour

Testing Out: Quantitative Studies

The pilot studies play and important role in verifying the existence of key cognitions and to provide a basis to show that lurking, flaming and defriending are problems that manifest online. All the studies are quantitative.

In order to understand the background to the concepts being researched, namely lurking, flaming and defriending, three pilot studies were conducted into how these concepts are reflected online. These took the form of investigating consumer attitudes, personalities and behaviour (CAPB) is a challenging task and completely parametric models seem to throw up the same answers to the wrong questions. Whilst quantitative survey designs can be used to define the operational aspects involved in the decision-making processes of consumers, on its own these studies lack the reality of subjectivity in human interactions. The design of CAPB surveys need to take into account that traditional designs for assessing consumer attitudes do not always take into account technological changes in commerce, which may be approached differently by a consumer because of different opinions towards it. Whilst parametric methods for determining the attitudes, personality and behaviour make claim to generalisability due to the randomly allocated participants that take part in them, all this can offer is a rough and ready insight into the user group they represent. One could argue to the contrary that a clear picture of the factors that form part of the Parametric User Model will develop following subjective analyses and not as a result of parametrically derived ones which rely too heavily on researcher bias.

Quantitative Study 1: Lurking Study

The premise of this study is that those persons whom predominantly lurk share common personality traits with people who suffer from social phobia, which is also called social anxiety disorder. This study is important because it establishes key differences in the personalities of those who lurk compared to those who do not.

The study was designed to compare those who take part in virtual communities with those that take part in organic communities. A questionnaire was developed based on the Social Thoughts and Beliefs Scale (Turner, Johnson, Beidel, Heiser, & Lydiard, 2003). The questionnaire was administered to support the principle of ecological validity through the questions being asked through a website to the respondents in the virtual communities, and the questions being asked through an interviewer to those in the organic communities. A control question was used to determine whether the respondent was a drone and the same question was asked in both the online and organic communities.

Quantitative Study 2: Flaming Study

The premise of this study is that there will be measurable differences in the brain activity when someone is flaming compared to when they are not. To verify this data is used to assess in theory the thresholds of when someone is most likely to be harmed by being flamed and when they are not. This study made use of secondary data from an ICM Research study (Couldry, Markham, & Livingstone, 2005) and freedom of information requests into the number of incidents of trolling recorded by the police in the UK between 2009 and 2011. Phase One of the ICM research project comprised of detailed qualitative work across six regions of England. The diaries of 37 participants' media consumption were analysed, initial and subsequent interviews were conducted with those respondents, and focus group interviews

Table 8. Scenarios used in the Wizard of Oz pilot study

Scenario No.	Scenario Text
Scenario 1	Edward is interested in astronomy, as a teenager he was a member of an astronomy group and has been intrigued by astronomy ever since. He wants to find out more about astronomy so visits his local library. He looks up astronomy and finds its classification number. He uses this number to find the shelves and whilst browsing them comes across a video on Black Holes. He puts the video in the player, decides it looks interesting and keeps it with him. Edward continues to browse the shelves, finds a book for beginners on astronomy so opens it up and looks up 'black holes' in the index. He finds a good introduction to black holes, takes a photocopy of the page, returns the book and borrows the video for watching at home later.
Scenario 2	Edward is interested in astronomy, as a teenager he was a member of an astronomy group and has been intrigued by astronomy ever since. He wants to find out more about astronomy so he uses an e-learning system. He enters 'black holes' into a search box and presses the search button. He comes across and entry with a video icon next to it so clicks the link. He presses the 'play' button to watch the video and then stops it by pressing the 'stop' button. He reads the text on the page and clicks the 'add to favourites' button to store it for later use.

were conducted with diarists. Phase Two involved a telephone survey of 1,017 people, conducted by ICM Research across the United Kingdom that aimed to produce conclusions on the detailed issues about consumption and citizenship raised in Phase One.

Quantitative Study 3: Wizard of Oz Evaluation Study

Current methods have been able to establish the overall persuasiveness of a system, but there are few techniques for evaluating the persuasiveness of mediating artefacts. This pilot study made use of the Wizard of Oz approach to do just that. Actors were asked to act out Scenario 2 (Table 8) by searching for a video clip on black holes, and were interviewed about their experience afterwards. The e-learning system that was developed allowed the experimenter to monitor the actions of the user whilst they used the system, as well as allow them to modify the system using the Wizard of Oz approach by adding mediating artefacts to specific locations. The users were presented with a page with links to a news article and an article on the solar system that led to the article on black holes containing the video clip, accessible through clicking on textual mediating artefacts – the graphical and button-based mediating artefacts were not immediately visible to the users but were added during their interaction with the system by the experimenter.

Testing Out: Quantitative Study

The Preliminary Studies prepare the data for the main studies by taking into account the pilot studies. The point of the preliminary studies is to establish whether there is a prima facie case to explore the concepts of lurking, flaming and defriending. Pilot studies will explore each of these concepts.

Qualitative Study 1: Defriending Study

This study investigates the nature of defriending. By quantifying the postings to weblogs that refer to acts of defriending the study draws out characteristics, such as gender, that impact on defriending. The study was designed to use a narrative analysis to analyse defriending activity and extend the under-standing the ECF brings to virtual community research. Narratives were selected from Google's Blog

Search by searching for the terms, "I deleted him as a friend", "he deleted me as a friend". "I deleted her as a friend" and "She deleted me as a friends". The ethnomethodological narrative analysis approach of (Bishop, 2011) was then used to code the text in the blog posts to identify the different 'Methods', 'Memes', 'Amities', 'Rules' and 'Strategies' that impact on the decision to defriend someone or why someone was defriended.

Qualitative Study 2: Interview (Do the Pilot Studies Provide a Way Forward for Solving the Problems of a Real Person?)

Selecting from different web-based communities can be a challenging process for individuals in their search for potential friends and partners. There is a plethora of social networking services available on the Web that individuals have to navigate their way through in order to achieve their goals. A number of questions can be asked, including what do people look to get out of social networking services, what makes a good social networking service and can current psychological frameworks be used to understand these applications. Some of the most widely used methods for researching online are interviewing, observation and document analysis (Mann & Stewart, 2000). Interviewing is the most widely applied technique for conducting systematic social inquiry in academic, clinical, business, political and media life with qualitative research being well established in this area (*ibid.*). Interviewing participants is one way of accessing information beyond what has been observed, and that is related to the meaning of the experience (Thyer, 2009). There is no correct or incorrect way of interviewing participants (Barton, 2006), though it has been recommended to use follow-up interviews when conducting a study, as interviewing can form a core part of a case study (Goodwyn & Stables, 2004). The basic case study entails the detailed and intensive analysis of a single case with some of the best known studies in business and management research being based on this method, which can be an investigation of a single organization, a single location, a person, or an event (Bryman & Bell, 2003). Some case studies investigating an organization have provided insights into the types of problems usability studies are likely to encounter, as well as some valuable lessons learned along the way in the organization (Rowley, 1994).

The case in question was of a young male in his early 20s who was educated to university level who took part in university social activities such as debating, book club and political activities, suggesting he had reasonable social skills and capabilities. The case over a period of a year used various online communities that could be used as online dating services and engaged with them to develop relationships with others. The interviewing model in Table 1 was used to ask questions that would allow him to discover how the case used social networking services and how they interacted with others in them. The model allowed the researcher to investigate the process by which the interviewee perceived and responded to a stimulus, and investigate the cognitions they hold and develop and how this relates to the way they perceive the worlds around them.

Qualitative Study 3: Abstraction (Language and Narrative Structure of Artefacts: What is the Quality of the Discourse?)

The language and narrative structure in communications within NLCs gives significant insight into how certain behaviours are likely to trigger other behaviours. In order for such actions to occur an external signifier needs to be made available (Norman, 2013), that signifier then needs to be socially constructed by the receiver (Berger & Luckmann, 1991; De Laat, 2002), which then activates an internal signifier

(Vygotsky, 1930), through which a higher order function is then accessed (Vygotsky, 1930). The outcome of that internal higher order function will then be the development of further internal signifiers which the person may then express in such a way they become external signifiers. This process is known as 'referentiality' and is presented in Figure 5, of which the stages of referentiality are based on the functions associated with 'particularity,' as discussed below.

Referentiality is the process by which a person makes reference to their internal processes in order to understand an external event (Leyton Escobar, Kommers, & Beldad, 2014). It involves the comparison of the *mise en scene* of a current situation with pre-existing knowledge from an earlier situation (Escobar, Kommers, & Beldad, 2014). Table 9 presents the first four phases of the referentiality model in Figure 5, with the fifth stage being the same as the third, and the sixth stage being the same as the first. The external signifiers are based on an extended version of the M-MARS model (Bishop, 2011); the social construction is based on established research on who social constructions occur online (De Laat, 2002), internal signifiers are based on those in the ecological cognition framework and the internal functions are those associated with the prefrontal cortex and inferior parietal lobule.

Another consideration are 'particularities.' Particularities are those aspects of narratives that are present in current situations that are different to those experienced in previous situations that are otherwise the same as the current ones (Escobar et al., 2014). Particularities are closely linked with referentiality, which can be seen as a way to understand the common elements among previous and current narratives. Table 10 uses the findings of the study on defriending above in terms of the process of constructing a narrative to show how this is associated with the particularity factors that make up a referentiality, and to further associate these with the seduction stages of ecological cognition seduction theory as embodied in the adapted transitional flow of persuasion model in Figure 6.

Table 10, by extending the original transitional flow of persuasion model (Solo & Bishop, 2015), introduces two new transitions, namely social context and situation action. These are introduced to reflect the fact that during seduction there are an exchange of indications of interest (IOIs) where the participants to the process test the other to see if they reciprocate. These terms are drawn from works into situated action theory, which consider the role of social context (Mantovani, 1996a; Mantovani, 1996b). As can be seen from Figure 6, which is an amended version of the transitional flow of persuasion model (TFP), the transition of social context (soc) is associated with compression, and the transition of situated action (sac) is associated with decompression.

The first stage (a) starts with a systematic literature search. A number of key texts in online communities are identified and the discussion text from them, such as from message boards, chatrooms and emails are then abstracted. These are then entered into Microsoft Excel and categorised as part of the

Table 9. Understanding language and 'referentiality'

External Signifier	Social Construction	Internal Signifier	Internal Function
Strategy	Discover / Explore	Goal	Problem-solving
Method		Plan	Self-control
Rule	Sharing / Comparing	Value	Conscience
Meme		Belief	Working memory
Amity	Negotiation / Co-construction	Interest	Empathy
Enmity		Detachment	Deception

Table 10. Understanding narrative structure of posts to online communities through 'particularities'

Particularity	Narrative Stage	Seduction Stage	Description
External signifier	Provocation	Disruption (A+)	There is a spark that makes someone want to post a message. This provokes someone into seizing the opportunity to make a contribution.
Social construction	Awareness	Severance (A+)	Someone who has been incentivised to post will attempt to gain an awareness of what happened to understand it better
Internal signifier	Realisation	Social Context (C+)	Someone with an awareness of how a situation affects them will realise its wider impacts on them, such as its relevance
Internal function	Reaction	Contrience (C+)	There are some people who will react straight away to a situation, often not appreciating the consequences of their actions.
Internal signifier	Organisation	Situated Action (C+)	It is often the case that after planning what one wants to say or do, one doubts the benefits. Weighing up pros and cons of a situation can be helpful in deciding what to communicate.
External signifier	Testimony	Equilibrium (S+)	Someone with a full awareness of a situation from both their point of view and others can explain a considered opinion, often taking into account not only their own views, but others' also.

compiling process – according to whether the text is a flame or kudos, and which online community character it most represents. The text is then generalised at the analysing process, including by using wildcards, into a search string that can be used to identify further posts.

In terms of the second stage (b), the indexing is done through using the search strings identified from the first stage (a) to identify threads on social media. This is then imported into NVivo before being codified, including using auto-code, as part of the compiling process. Finally, the analysing process is conducted so that the data can produce parametric models that are generalised beyond the research

Figure 6. The amended transitional flow of persuasion model

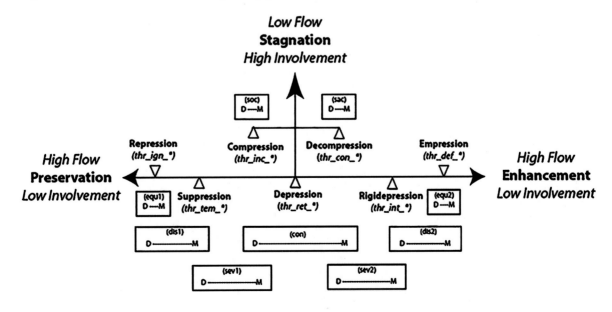

Figure 7. An annotation framework for explaining causes of lurking, flaming, and defriending

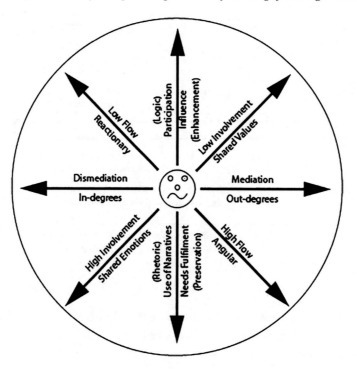

study. Using Figure 1 as a reference, processes 1 to 4 of the first stage (a) and processes 1 to 2 of the second stage (b) are pretty menial. Stages 3 and 4 of the second stage, however, are quite complex, and this section sets out in detail how they are conducted.

TOWARDS A NEW APPROACH FOR SOCIAL MEDIA ANALYSIS

The main studies will generate much of the data used in the rest of the study. The conceptual framework in Figure 7 is based on a fundamental premise that cognitive dissonance is an on-going issue for all social actors. The emoji in the centre is one of a confused actor, feeling overwhelmed. The arrows shooting out from the actor represent all the things they have to consider at the same time. The constraints of this may often lead to Reactionary behaviours of flight (i.e. lurking), fight (i.e. flaming), or fall-out (i.e. defriending). Ulterior motives may lead to follow (i.e. lurking), foray (i.e. flaming) or flout (i.e. defriending). Angular motives may lead to feast (i.e. lurking), firebomb (i.e. flaming), or feign (defriending). Angular behaviours can include being cooperative, impulsive, and cautious.

Figure 7 shows how aspects of the annotation framework can be used to explain the problems of lurking, flaming and defriending that result from a sub-optimal social orientation. To identify narratives that fit within these in order to query social networking services a systematic abstraction of chat phrases taken out of established books on virtual communities that cover these issues was conducted.

Social actors that are communication-orientated want to use virtual marketplaces that allow them to share their views with other consumers and seek their opinion on potential purchases. Social actors that are experience-orientated require shopping environments that allow them to 'touch' and 'feel' products.

Table 11. Aspects of the self and possible models for measuring value system

Self-Type (Value System)	Source	Codes
Substantial Self (Opportunity)	(Harris & Goode, 2010)	Aesthetic Appeal [Originality of Design *[Acceptance, Openness]*, Visual Appeal *[Validity, Certainty]*, Entertainment Value *[Ingratiation, Information]*
Synthetic Self (Understanding)	(Harris & Goode, 2010)	Financial Security [Perceived Security [Claim, Community, Security], Ease of Payment [Impermanence, Imitation, Focus]]
Social Self (Relevance)	(Harris & Goode, 2010)	Layout & Functionality [Usability *[Consistency]*, Relevance of Information *[Backing, Ambivalence]*, Customisation *[Applicability]*, Interactivity *[Inspiration, Encouragement]*]
Situational Self (Aspiration)	(Harris & Goode, 2004)	Trust [Service Quality [Unsatisfactoriness], Personal Value [Warrant, Fairness], Satisfaction [Instigation], Loyalty [Challenge, Recognition]]
Symbolic Self (Choice)	(Goode & Moutinho, 1996)	Overall Satisfaction [Overall Expectations *[Conclusion]*, Perceived Risk *[Introspection]*, Recommend to Others *[Confirmation]*, Confidence *[Efficacy]*, Frequency of Use *[Self-Direction]*, Full Use of Services *[Approval]*
Saturated Self (Expression)	(Jamal & Goode, 2001)	Brand Preference [Education *[Evidence]*, Occupation *[Interaction]*, Gender *[Cooperation]*, Income *[Reciprocity]*, Age *[Tolerance]*, Marital Status *[Complacence]*]

These are less likely to enjoy shopping in static virtual marketplace and are more suited to highly interactive Web sites. Experience-orientated social actors are more likely to adapt to virtual environments that employ direct manipulation techniques and 3D graphics. Social actors that are achievement-orientated want to use virtual marketplaces in which they can be seen to be an important.

Stage 1: Considering the Central Participants in the Discourse (Identity and Dominance)

The abstraction process will encode a dataset of chat expressions according to the character type the person appears to be and whether or not that posting is a flame or kudos. When being annotated the identity of all in the discussion will be identified. It will also be recorded whether the identity of the poster identified using the chat string matches their actual perceived identity, based on both their avatar and narrative.

It has been argued that devising a grounded theory of annotation categories can provide an authentic summary of the data being interrogated (De Laat & Lally, 2003; De Laat & Lally, 2005). In the case of this research the ecological cognition framework has been used to derive the annotation categories in the form of character types (see Table 14), posting types (see Table 13) and the cognition-based Signifiers.

Table 11 presents an amalgamation of various models from the authors that could be used to populate the fields in a parametric user model.

Stage 2: Considering How Active the Members in the Discourse Are (Intention and Nature of Artefacts)

Understanding the intention and nature of artefacts is an important part understanding participation in networked learning communities. This study, by making use of the character theory, will show the links between these and group identity, fun, love, punishments, rewards, meaning, autonomy.

Table 12. Codes used to understand dominance, intensity, collaboration, and nature of posts (hypothesis 2)

Metric Code	Relevance	Measurements
Total number of posts	The total number of posts an actor has made, such as their tweet-count. Measures intensity and dominance.	A higher number of posts equates to the more phantasies in existence
Numbers of buddies	The total number of buddies an actor has, such as their followers. Measures collaboration.	The more buddies a person has the more likely a person has a high interest (friends) and/or detachment (foes) in them.
Number of buddies in thread	The number of people in a thread that an actor has in their buddy list. Measures collaboration and dominance.	The more friends in a thread the more likely the phantasies include the interest cognition
Number of posts in thread	Measures intensity.	The more posts in a thread by an actor the more likely the phantasies will include the belief cognition
Number of replies to posts	Measures collaboration and dominance.	The more posts an actor replies to, the more likely the value cognition will be reflected across all of them in a phantasy.
Number of posts replied to	Measures collaboration.	The more posts other actors reply to, the more likely the value cognition will be reflected across all of them in a phantasy and the more likely there will be higher detachment or interest in the actor being replied to.
Number of posts referred to within	Measures dominance.	The more posts an actor is referred to in the more likely the other actor's phantasies include an interest or detachment relating to them.

Table 13. Types of posting and interface cues that explain breach of canonicity and intentional state entailment

Stimulus Code	Interface Cue Codes	Descriptions and Manifestations
Social (Snacking)	Group identity, fun, love	Snacking is where users post short bursts or information and consume a lot of others' as well. On Twitter this is common as users are fed various comments to which they may respond to one or more of. Not all snacking is positive, but it is usually always in response to something.
Emotional (Mobiling)	Punishments, rewards	Mobiling derives from the fact that mobile devices can result in highly emotive reactions due to lack of access to complete information. This is also a problem on Twitter because 140 character tweets make miscommunications common.
Relaxational (Lurking)	Meaning, autonomy	Lurking might be seen to apply to posts where they are not a reply to another post, but appear to come from nowhere, or in other words directly from a thoughts of a user who read or experienced something others reading did not. Such commenting is common on Twitter.

In the context of this section, in-degrees will be measured according to how many postings occur prior to the observed actor posting in pursuit of a goal and out-degree will be measured how many posts are made in succession by an actor while achieving that goal. Understanding members is an important part of narrative analysis (De Laat, Lally, Lipponen, & Simons, 2005; De Laat, 2002). Members will be measured according to how many people are in the conversion, whether they are friends or followers of the participation, and/or whether they have been blocked or threated with being blocked or otherwise defriending. In addition to membership, needs fulfilment, influence and participation are important for understanding intention and nature of artefact (Escobar et al., 2014) and form part of measuring flow.

Table 14. The four categories of troll associated emotions

Identity Type	Example Emotions Expressed in Signifiers
Lolcows	Chatroom Bob: Intoxicated, devoted, erotic, hopeful, merry, obscene, romantic, sexy Ripper: Sadness, failure, depressed, despairing, distressed, embarrassed, gloom, guilty, helpless, horror, misery, regretful, sad, stress, suicide, unhappy, upset, pity. Big Man: Critical, thoughtful, moral, rigid, rude, selfish, serious, sceptical, thought, snob
Haters	Snert: Disgust, annoyed, irritated, bothered, unfriendly, disdainful, disgusted, hostile, jealous, menacing, insecure, nasty, obnoxious, rejected, resentful. Iconoclast: Aggressive, hateful, alarmed, antagonistic, suspicious, disbelieving, freethinker, disgusted, ridicule. E-Venger: Angry, contemptuous, hurt, enraged, displeased, hate, hatred, hurt, outrage, rage, scornful, scorn, violent.
Bzzzters	Flirt: Neutral, glad, pleased, calm, serene, delighted, liked, child, friendly, impressed, natural, nice, pleasure, relaxed, satisfied. Wizard: Cheerful, excited, cheerful, elated, excitement, lively, optimism, triumphant. MHBFY Jenny: Surprised, astonished, content, acceptance, trusting, kind., grateful, repentant, reverent, startled, subdued, thoughtful, timid, warmth, sissy.
Eyeballs	Lurker: Nervous, afraid, lonely, fear, discouraged, fear, fearful, loneliness, nervous, reserved, scared terrified Elder: Boredom, sleepy, tired, fatigued, rusty, sleep, wise, detached) Troll: Happiness, joy, amused, enjoyment, happy, joy, joyful, mischief, silly, tease, wit

The study into lurking above showed a number of factors that are core to understanding intensity and collaboration. These included the number of people in a thread, the number of post types in a thread and the number of friends, contacts or followers a user has. These observation in addition to the other evident cues within the mise en scene of a virtual community can help understand the narrative structures that exist. Social networking services like Twitter and Facebook pose challenges for understand mise en scene because each person has a different timeline and thus every sees a thread in a different context. Some might argue this is what happens in any case, as each person is likely to perceive the same content on a computer screen differently from others.

The breach of canonicity and state entailment are also important factors in understanding the intensity to which an actor participates in an NLC, how they collaborate with other actors and how they social construct the *mise en scene*. Breach of canonicity refers to the fact that an interaction must seek to deviate from some form of norm or status quo, such as in the way a canonical script can be breached, violated or deviated from (Escobar et al., 2014). State of entailment refers to that fact that some actors will strong goals can appear as protagonists in a discussion, where regardless of how others might try to take a discussion off track – in their view – they can still keep that discussion directing towards their goals and not those of others. Such an actor will therefore have low out-degrees as they are not really interested in others, yet may have high in-degrees because they need to read others' posts in order to bring the discussion back on track – to meet their goals.

In such a set-up the cognitions that come into play are easy to see. An actor seeking to dominate will have a goal at the maximum amount of 9, their interest in themselves will be at the maximum of 10 and their detachment from others will be at the maximum of 6. One might therefore measure in-degrees according to whether the selected actor appears to be responding to others posts through collaboration, and in-degrees according to the intensity of the posts made by the selected actor is greater than that of the others, or where others are directly responding to that actor instead of others. As can be seen from Table 13, the study will focus on plans/Methods which appear to be based on snacking, mobiling and lurking and goals that appear to be based around specific interface cues. It is therefore assumed when computing the phantasies that the selected user (see Table 14 for identities that will be selected) will have an interest in themselves of 10 and a detachment from all the others of 6.

Stage 3: Intensity, Collaboration, and Mise en Scene Constructions: How Dense Is the Participation within the Network?

This study will seek to associate the following factors with the emotions associated with each persona (i.e. Hater, Lolcow, Bzzzter, Eyeball): Total number of posts, Numbers of buddies, Number of buddies in thread, Number of posts in thread, Number of replies to posts, Number of posts replied to, Number of posts referred to within.

By understanding actors within an NLC according to a fixed number of character types will make understanding how they will act in specific circumstances easier. As can be seen from Table 14 there are a number of emotions observable in external signifiers that might give an indication as to the character/identity type of the actor. The character type of the main poster, and the others in the conversation will then feed into the dataset constructed for analysis. One method of understanding the data collected on specific actors, categorised by character type, that will be used is the sociogram (De Laat, 2002). Table 14 shows the emotions associate with the four categories of troller.

Stage 4: Analysis (Define a Conceptual Framework)

Based on all the research in the study, the ecological cognitive framework will be updated to be a suitable reference point for the subsequent parametric user model and praxis. This confirmatory study will take all the results from the pilot studies and main studies to change the ecological cognition framework into one suitable for the post-modem time in which we exist. The ecological cognition framework produced at the start of this study was designed for a time when not all generation to part in Internet use, and in particular when older generations were not using the Internet for surveillance and escapism (Leung, 2003). It therefore needs to be updated to take account of the added complexity of social networking services.

Stage 5: Analysis (Create and Describe a Parametric User Model)

This first part will confirm whether the proposed parametric user model can be used to compute the knol of the user to determine how susceptible they are to being flamed, defriending, or at risk of lurking or defriending themselves. One might like to think of this confirmatory study as a logical experiment. In the same way that Einstein used his mind to compute the speed of light, so this study will show how analysis of linguistic components and metrics such as number of posts, number of buddies, etc. can be used to predict knol. A user's knol is the speed at which they are processing information. To calculate someone's knol one first needs to identify one or more phantasies, then calculate a Pression, and from this a knol can be calculated. Phantasies are compute my paring together cognitions, namely goals, plans, values, beliefs, interests and detachments. A Pression is the amount of pressure being put on the brain, namely though computing the number of phantasies burdening an actor's working memory. Finally, the knol is calculated by calculating the amount of time an actor is able to dedicate to a specific task according to a baseline of 48 hours, which is drawn of the European Union's Working Time Directive.

Stage 6: Create a Praxis and Test It in a System: Is It Possible for the Praxis Embodied into an NLC to Have the Intended Effect of Reducing Lurking, Flaming, and Defriending?

To help resolve flame trolling abuses in e-learning systems online, the author proposes a plug-in for platforms like Moodle called "Paix" – The Persuasive and Adaptive Interaction Extension. Paix is based around a general interface add-on that can be extended through plug-in-able strategy modules that use the Open Social Platform, which can create additional strategies, or 'games' to analyses and influence behavior of those using the system.

A PROPOSAL AND PILOT STUDY FOR VALIDATING THE PRAXIS

In order to evaluate whether the praxis is workable or not is necessary to first explore through a pilot study the various elements that will make it up. This section therefore shows how this will be achieved.

Defining the Hypothetical Study: Lurking, Flaming, and Defriending

This study will focus on using the terms "lurking," "flaming" and "defriending." Whilst it is now common to use "Internet trolling" to refer to what was once called flaming (Bishop, 2014), this study will preserve the original terms rather than be forced to use "flame trolling" to refer to flaming. Regardless of what names they are given, the practices of larking, flaming and defriending are significant problems for maintaining virtual communities, especially in educational environments through which networked learning communities are enabled.

At a time when social mobility is at its lowest and the need end social exclusion and encourage greater social equality, this study is desperately needed. Whether an actor continues to use a system is based on the extent to which it is acceptable to them (Nielsen, 1993, p.25). As can be seen from Figure 8, there are many factors that affect system acceptability, with the most relevant to this study being to make a system "subjectively pleasing." It is quite obvious that if a virtual community's design encourages lurking, defriending or flaming then it is quite possible it is not subjectively pleasing to those who experience these. Lurking can be seen to be a sign that people do not feel comfortable posting to a virtual community (Bishop, 2013). For example, people may feel the group is not for them (Preece, Nonnecke, & Andrews, 2004). Flaming, whereby someone posts an offensive message to others, will be a problem regardless of which form of public electronic communications network is used (Alzouma, 2014; Best, 2014; Bishop, 2013), and regardless of what jargon the mass media choose to use (Bishop, 2014; Bishop, 2015). Flaming, or perceived flaming, can result in defriending and/or lurking. It is therefore essential to identify the subjective nuances that give rise to flaming and to understand how such interactions can be intervened in so both lurking and defriending, and indeed further flaming can be avoided in order that flamewars do not develop. Whilst it has been argued that a system needs to be subjectively pleasing to be acceptable, this is not the case with those who use a system as part of their work or study space are less likely to be concerned with a system's acceptability (Nielsen, 1993, p.33). However, as distance learning is becoming the norm, so a system needs to maintain its appeal as users will lose motivation otherwise (Bishop, 2004; Bishop, 2012; Mbakwe & Cunliffe, 2002; Mbakwe & Cunliffe, 2003).

Figure 8. Nielsen's model of the attributes of system acceptability

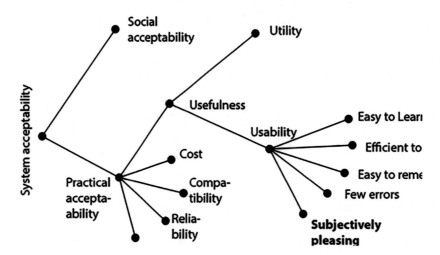

This study will achieve that by devising a conceptual framework that can be used to devise parametric user model that through a praxis allows a system to analyse a user's behaviour in and to influence it. This study will therefore advance scientific knowledge through providing new ways to systematically understand users' subjectivities and the impact their behaviours will have on others and others' behaviour will have on them.

It has been argued that there are a number of important considerations in understanding narratives that are produced in virtual environments, such as networked learning communities. These include understanding the quality of discourse, understanding the central participants in the discourse, understanding how active the members are in the discourse, and understanding the density of participation in the discourse (De Laat, 2002). Whilst one might argue such questions have been answered in the past, answering them against in relation to a new data set is essential in achieving the objective of designing a solid conceptual framework from which parametric user models of users can be devised. Table 15 sets out the questions that will be asked for each of the factors that will be controlled by a system based on the praxis.

Table 16 sets out the overall research hypotheses for the study. In particular these relate to activity, narrative, and evaluation.

Table 15. Overview of research questions

Topic	Research Question
Lurking	Is there a difference between lurkers and posters in terms of the extent to which they show symptoms of social phobia?
Befriending	Are there distinctions to be drawn between the number of buddies someone has and the posts they have made and replies they have received?
Flaming	Is there a difference in the mental effort required to take part in flaming as compared to other forms of participation?
Defriending	Is there a difference in social orientation between those who defriend and those who do not?

Table 16. Overview of research hypotheses

Factor	Hypothesis
Activity	There will be will be differences between those who take part in flaming, lurking and defriending and those who do not
Narrative	There will be linguistically identifiable differences in the narratives of those who participate in a constructive matter and those who do not.
Evaluation	By designing a system that varies based on metric and linguistic parameters a conceptual framework and parametric user model can form a praxis to aid the reduction of problematic behaviours and participation inequality in NLC.

Table 17. Three approaches to generating data

Approach	Question
Wizard of Oz	Can the Wizard of Oz approach to systems evaluation be used to assess networked learning communities?
Interview	Do the pilot studies provide a way forward for solving the problems of real persons who have experienced lurking, flaming and defriending?
Abstraction	Language and narrative structure of artefacts: What is the quality of the discourse and which codes are most prominent?

Not only would there be research questions relating to the factors that make up the praxis, but also those relating to the methods that will be used to explore the factors relating to the praxis. These are set out in Table 17.

As with all models for understanding online communities, the behavioural aspects of those explained are also important. Table 18 sets out the questions that need to be answered relating to such behavioural activities and concepts.

In addition, it is important to consider how the model will affect the process of systems analysis, design, development and evaluation. Table 19 sets out these questions.

Table 18. Factors related to behavioural activities and concepts in online communities

Factor	Question
Identity and dominance	Who are central participants in the discourse and how does this affect linguistic properties?
Intention and nature of artefacts	How active are the members in the discourse and how does this affect linguistic properties?
Intensity, collaboration and mise en scene constructions	How dense is the participation within the network and how does this affect linguistic properties?

Table 19. Research questions related to design stages

Design Stage	Research Question
Systems analysis	What are the common conceptual themes in the data that could form a revised conceptual framework?
Systems design	What are the evident quantifiable elements that can be used to form a parametric user model to analyse behaviour in networked learning communities?
Systems development and evaluation	What generalizable findings can be made from applying the conceptual framework and parametric user model as a praxis in a mock networked learning community?

Piloting the Hypothetical Study through Generation of Data for Analysis

This section sets out the results for the pilot studies conducted. These involved using website metrics, observational recordings, document inspection, narrative analysis, discourse analysis, interview-based critical-event recall, questionnaires and statistical analyses.

Website Metrics and Observational Recordings Using the Wizard of Oz Approach

An e-learning system was constructed using the above model and example and was evaluated by users of Internet applications with varying levels of computer literacy. Those who had high digital literacy are referred to as experts ($N=2$), those with low digital literacy are referred to as novices ($N=3$). The users were asked to act out Scenario 2 by searching for a video clip on black holes, and were interviewed about their experience afterwards. The e-learning system that was developed allowed the experimenter to monitor the actions of the user whilst they used the system, as well as allow them to modify the system using the Wizard of Oz approach by adding mediating artefacts to specific locations. The users were presented with a page with links to a news article and an article on the solar system that led to the article on black holes containing the video clip, accessible through clicking on textual mediating artefacts – the graphical and button-based mediating artefacts were not immediately visible to the users but were added during their interaction with the system by the experimenter.

None of the users managed to find the black holes article within 2 minutes of starting so the first hidden mediating artefact was displayed - a graphic of a site map, which when clicked displayed 6 textual mediating artefacts leading to articles on black holes - and was clicked on by users within an Mean time of 33.7 seconds of it being displayed, suggesting it was very persuasive. After clicking on the first article on black holes, the experts clicked on the accompanying graphic within a Mean time of 11.5 seconds of viewing the page, whereas none of the novice users did, suggesting that graphics offer the perceived affordance of clicking to those with greater experience of Internet applications. One of the experts (E1) continued to click on graphics until they found the one that linked to the video clip, but the other expert (E2) did not, suggesting that expert E2 developed a belief that clicking on a graphic did not do anything. When interviewed expert E1 indicated that they often click on graphics that they believed to be movies, suggesting that the history a user has with a particular type of mediating artefact determines whether it offers the perceived affordance of clicking. When the graphic was changed to include a film-reel icon

Figure 9. A mediating artefact that offers the perceived affordance of clicking

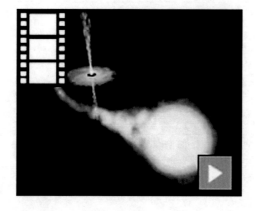

Figure 10. Twitter reporting a post does not breach their community rules

Hello.

Thanks for letting us know about your issue. Here are some tips to help you with your situation:

- **Do not respond to the user. We have found that responding to someone who is intentionally attempting to aggravate you or others encourages them to continue their behavior.**
- **Block the user. You can block the user using the blocking feature described here:** https://support.twitter.com/articles/117063
- **Learn more about how to deal with abusive users:** https://support.twitter.com/articles/15794
- **Learn how to flag inappropriate media here:** https://support.twitter.com/articles/20069937

We've investigated the account and reported Tweets for abusive behavior, and have found that it's currently not violating the Twitter Rules (https://twitter.com/rules**).**

and 'play' button, it took novices a Mean time of 7 seconds to click the mediating artefact after viewing the page and expert E2 took 3 seconds. This suggests that by using symbols or signs that have a historical meaning to the user (such as a 'play' button) a mediating artefact can offer the perceived affordance of clicking and persuade the user to click on it.

Document Inspection and Narrative Analysis

The process of abstraction, and the subsequent annotation and analysis is an important part of understanding the nature of posts made to online befriending services, which is especially important in environments where e-moderating is the norm. For this pilot studies the de facto Wild West of online befriending communities, namely Twitter, was investigated. Even if a message is illegal, Twitter tries to exercise "sysop prerogative" where it has none. For instance, even where a court has ruled particular content is illegal, Twitter will not remove it if it thinks it does not breach its own "community rules" (Figure 10).

The particular type of postings chosen were those that implied threats, such as threats to kill and rape-threats. As can be seen from Table 20, a number of terms were drawn from news articles of what people convicted of trolling are claimed to have said online. These includes Peter Nunn and Isabella Sorley, who were convicted of sending rape threats.

Table 20. Expressions used to guide querying of Twitter

Rape Threat	General Threat
I'll rape you	I will find you
You'll be raped	I'd do a lot worse than
You will be raped	Go kill yourself
You're pathetic	Happy to see you buried
	I will find you

The study results show that many of the rape threats on Twitter are not supposed to be real threats, as they lack menace. They are used in the same comfortable way as saying "I'll kill you" to a friend who was playing a trick on one, where what they said is not intended to be offensive, but pleasant for both sides.

I'll Rape You

This would appear to be a direct rape threat, but whether it is menacing depends on the context. Tweets collected when this and similar terms were queried using the platform. The data shows that on the one hand the first posts could be that seeing suggest that you could suffer a serious sexual assault if you were to visit the San Francisco area. It is in fact, it's satire, suggesting that if you vote a certain way, you agree to unfair forms of policing. The suggestion is that the police in the Golden Gate Bridge area of San Francesco are as exploitative as a sex offender, yet does not suggest the police actually commit sexual offenses. The statement collected, "I will rape you, my friend," appeared to be based on the Middle East meme where an insult is followed with "my friend" to soften the blow. For example, in the Japanese Manga Cartoon, Street Fighter II, a fighter who by another goes away without saying a word, is referred to as "my friend" by the person that he does not say goodbye to. On this basis, the rape threat should not be taken as such.

One of the messages was clearly intended to be jovial and not a threat. It read: "@GDKJordie This has gone way to far you will be caught and you will be raped in prison:D" One might want to interpret this as being harassment and stalking, or a threat of battery, but the smiley signifies laughter, which suggests strongly it is a joke. It is quite easy to see how someone untrained in forensic linguistics in the context of social media could interpret this the wrong way.

I Will Find You

"I will find you" was another string that was queried on Twitter in relation to identifying the extent of rape-threats and threats more generally. The first message explored, "@TheRetailGay Nu. Pls nu. Don't do it:(I will find you and slap that knife or whatever the fuck out of your hand if I have to," was in fact a supportive message, where the person was suggesting they would do all they could to support the person at their tough time. The use of the emoticon, ":(" implies that the person was not happy about the situation in which the other person was in.

Many of the messages related to a quotation from the Liam Neason film, Taken, which like those posted directly relating to "I'll rape you" were intended as jokes and for parody, not offense. The remainder were persons expressing personal gripes, but were not targeted at the people to whom they referred directly. For instance, one read: "If you ever invite me again to any #game..farm..saga..cruch..I will find you and I will kill you!" This was a person expressing annoyance with those in their buddy list inviting them to take part in online games, which they clearly do not want to take part in. Many people who use Facebook can relate to this, as Farmville for instance is popular with some and despised as a waste of time by others. It could be quite easy for a person not trained in forensic linguistics in relation to social media to not understand this, meaning someone could be wrongly found to have committed a wrong under statute, tort or contract law, when anyone trained in social media could easily see such messages are men to express exasperation and are not intended to be menacing or threatening.

I'd Do a Lot Worse Than

One phrase investigated was "I'd do a lot worse than." One message could be translated as "If I eat the pussy and you don't let me fuck I'm going to do more than rape you I'm going to kill you." The message appears to be more of a social complaint about sexual inequality, namely that the person believes that if he is asked to perform oral sex on someone that he should expect the sexual intercourse in return. On this basis, whilst it might appear to the uninformed as a rape threat, it is actually a statement about scruples in a relationship. It could be presented as a form of duress, that the poster is saying that if he is not given sexual intercourse in return for oral sex that he will rape the person. This is, however, not the case, making it easy to see how those untrained in forensic linguistics might misinterpret the meaning leading to an unethical use of the law.

Most of the other statements involving "I'd do a lot worse things than" are used to indicate that if the poster didn't take the course of action they are doing, there would be a lot worse things they could do, which are less moderate. The statement, "I'd do a lot worse things than eat a Tesco burger than Orthodox with the tampon girl" is simply saying that the person is confident in their choices and not those of someone else. The statement, "I'd do a lot worse things than I already do if I didn't have friends & family that cared so much" is simply saying that because of the social support afforded to the poster, there are much worse circumstances they could be in. One of the statements that came up was one of those that instigated this study, namely "rape?! I'd do a lot worse things than rape you!!"

Go Kill Yourself

In terms of "go kill yourself" two statements investigated were the creation of a meme by the media relating to "fuck off and die you worthless piece of crap" where they in effect repost the content someone has been prosecuted for, which may cause the same offense in those who see it. Most of the remaining posts are discussion of the media reporting the original tweets. Most of the other threats were sent in relation to celebrities, whom use such language themselves, so would likely have been taken in an endearing way, as it would be the reaction they would want. Some might be offended by the way one of the posters used the word "nigga," by wrongly thinking this was the same as the racist word, "nigger." In fact, "nigga" is a term of endearment towards someone who is Black, and even more so to someone who is White, who would interpret it as being an equal to those who are Black and mostly associated with the term, such as through hip-hop music where the term is extensively used.

Happy to See You Buried

The term, "happy to see your buried" might not seem endearing to some, but in fact that was not on the whole the case. Two examples made use of an exclamation mark, which has the imputation it is intended as a joke. In the first of these it is quite clearly a provocative response, and is to be seen as no more menacing than saying "I would be glad to see the back of you" in other discourses. The second example is a person saying they were inconvenienced by being contacted in the early hours and were glad when the person decided to go to sleep, by being "buried" under the duvet.

You're Pathetic

Considering "you're pathetic," the outcomes were very similar to the use given to "go kill yourself." As can be seen, it is a way of dismissing what a person has to say. Considering the statement: "Just because you can't see someone everyday isn't a reason to cry and throw a fit." This captures many of the posts where calling someone pathetic is comparing them to an ideal state, which on the whole is what the person posting the message believes to be the case. One could therefore argue that saying "you're pathetic" is not something that someone should be going to court over, whether the civil courts or criminal courts.

Document Inspection and Statistical Analysis

A study was designed to use a narrative analysis to analyse defriending activity and extend the understanding the ECF brings to virtual community research. Narrative analysis is a tool researchers can use to explore the intersection between the individual and society (Kil, 2010). Narrative analysis in Internet studies essentially uses both text and online "talk" to construct a holistic view of the online interactions, looking at cognition as well as affect (Yukawa, 2005). Narrative analysis is the most prevalent approach that has emphasized alternatives to categorising analysis, but much of narrative research, broadly defined, involves categorising as well as connecting analysis, and the distinction has not been clearly defined (Maxwell & Miller, 2008). Narratives were selected from Google's Blog Search by searching for the terms, "I deleted him as a friend", "he deleted me as a friend". "I deleted her as a friend" and "She deleted me as a friends". The ethnomethodological narrative analysis approach of (Bishop, 2011a) was then used to code the text in the blog posts to identify the different 'Methods', 'Memes', 'Amities', 'Rules' and 'Strategies' that impact on the decision to defriend someone or why someone was defriended.

The difficulties of a romantic relationship accounted for just over 2,700 (13.4%) of the cases where a female was defriended compared to less than 50 (0.47%) for men, suggesting that when a romantic relationship doesn't work out women are more likely to be defriended than men, or at least, people are more likely to disclose on a blog that they defriended a female because of relationship problems than they would males. Less than 20 males were defriended for a sex related issue compared to over 9,500 females. This may be because as (Thelwall, 2008) suggests, men use online social networking more for dating and women more for other forms of friendship. It became clear in the discourses there were often other people involved in the event leading to a person being defriended. In around 65 percent of cases where males were defriended and 90 percent where females were defriended there was another person involved. Over 3,000 females (16.4%) were defriended because someone was offended compared to only 4 males (0.08%) for the same reason.

Analysing the data resulted in four key findings. Firstly, actors are provoked into responding to a state of disequilibrium, such as being defriended. Second, actors need to develop an awareness of the change in the environment before they are able to realise its impact on them. Thirdly, actors will first have a reaction to a state of disequilibrium before organising a response that causes them least dissonance. Fourthly and finally, actors will testify their experiences to others as a way of expressing their understanding in order to restore a state of equilibrium.

Finding 1: Actors are provoked into responding to a state of disequilibrium.

Understanding what drives actors to act is crucial to developing human-computer systems that adapt to and influence them. There has been extensive research into discovering what drives people, which has led to a number of theories, including psychoanalytic theory (Freud, 1933), hierarchical needs theory (Maslow, 1943), belief-desire-intention theory (Rao & Georgeff, 1998), which see desires as goals, and other desire-based theories, which see desires as instincts that have to be satisfied (Reiss, 2004). All of these theories suggest that actors are trying to satisfy some internal entity. This assumption ignores the role of the environment in shaping the behaviour of an actor and suggests that actors are selfish beings that only do things for shallow reasons.

There seemed from most of the narratives that there was something in the environment that provoked the actor to write about their defriending action. For instance, Era talking about a male she had known since the age of 12 who "made lots of sexual innuendos and jokes i.e. wolf whistles/comments about my make up, perfume etc." ended her narrative saying, "I told him goodbye and removed him as a friend on FB. I wished him all the best in his life. Then he replies and says he only likes me as a friend. He denied that he ever flirted with me and said I was crazy and that I over-analyse things," suggesting that recognition of her experience was important and writing in the blogosphere might be a way she saw to achieve it.

Finding 2: Actors need to develop an awareness of the change in the environment before they are able to realise its impact on them.

It was apparent in the data that those writing their narratives needed to gain an awareness of how the stimulus that provoked them affects them, so that they can understand its impact more appropriately. In one of the weblog narratives, a blogger, Julie, said; "I deleted her as a friend on Facebook because after waiting six months for her to have time to tell me why she was upset with me I got sick of seeing her constant updates (chronic posting I call it)". This supports the view accepted among many psychologists that perception and action are linked and that what is in the environment has an impact on an actor's behaviour. Some have thought that an actor's actions are reflexes to stimuli (Watson, 1913) and these can be conditioned (Watson & Rayner, 1920) so that when an actor perceives a stimulus, such as an artefact, they respond with an action without reference to any cognitions. This concept will be referred to as stimuli-response theory. The idea that all animal behaviour could be explained by stimulus–response connections formed by reinforcements, such as rewards was a highly influential idea during the first half of the 20th century, but has been abandoned by many because experimental evidence did not support it (Cahill, McGaugh, & Weinberger, 2001). The core principle of traditional stimuli-response theory is that all behaviour is a reflex to stimuli. Whilst this appears to acknowledge the role of the environment in influencing behaviour it fails to acknowledge that aspects of the environment can create an impetus that leads to action. Perceptual psychologists have introduced a new dimension to the understanding of perception and action, which is that artefacts suggest action through offering affordances, which are visual properties of an artefact that determines or indicates how that artefact can be used and are independent of the perceiver (Gibson, 1986). This suggests that when an actor responds to a visual stimulus that they are doing so not as the result of an internal reflex, but because of what the artefact offers.

Finding 3: Actors will first have a reaction to a state of disequilibrium before organising a response that causes them least dissonance.

Cognitive dissonance is what an actor experiences when their cognitions are not consonant with each other (Festinger, 1957). For example if an actor had a plan to be social, but a belief that it would be inappropriate they would experience dissonance as a result of their plan not being consonant with their belief. Resolving this dissonance would achieve a state of consonance that would result in either temperance or intemperance. If this actor held a value that stated that they must never be social if it is inappropriate they could achieve consonance by abandoning the plan to be social which results in

Table 17. Role of different factors in defriending narratives

Defriending Discourse Type	Males Defriended	Females Defriended
Effect of male on female friend	3,315	19,226
Effect of female on male friend	3,249	18,359
Employment mentioned	2,167	12,951
Sex	11	9,665
Break-ups and Dating	24	2,759
Offence	4	3,372
Little in common	3	1,835
Email related	25	1,386
Text message related	7	0
Application related	1	0
Total	5,084	20,572

temperance. If the same actor had an interest in being social and a belief that it was more important to be social than not be social they might resolve to disregard their belief resulting in intemperance. If an actor experiences a desire without experiencing any dissonance they experience deference, as they will act out the desire immediately.

It became quite apparent early on in the analysis that those writing narratives would do to in such a way to cause least dissonance. For instance, one female blogger when writing about a relationship breakdown with her friend, said, "I'm not sure if anything I write tonight will make any sense, but it's not as if anyone else reads these anyway so I guess it doesn't really matter how organized I keep it."

Finding 4: Actors will testify their experiences to others as a way of expressing their understanding in order to restore a state of equilibrium.

It became apparent from looking at the weblog entries that bloggers got some sort of closure from writing the narratives. For instance, closing one of her blogs, a user said, "As you can see, my brain is a ridiculously tangled ball of yarn at the moment and my thoughts are all over the place. Maybe some good old REM's sleep will massage the knots out. Until next time." Psychological closure, it is argued, is influenced by the internal world of cognition as well as the external world of (finished or unfinished) actions and (challenging or unchallenging) life events. Weblogs, according to some, serve similar roles to that of papers on someone's office desk, for example allowing them to deal with emerging insights and difficult to categorise ideas, while at the same time creating opportunities for accidental feedback and impressing those who drop by (Efimova, 2009).

Interview-Based Critical Event Recall and Discourse Analysis

The case in question was of a young male in his early 20s who was educated to university level who took part in university social activities such as debating, book club and political activities, suggesting he had reasonable social skills and capabilities. The case over a period of a year used various online communities that could be used as online dating services and engaged with them to develop relationships with others. The interview explored the cognitions held by the case, including his goals for using social networking sites. While initially he didn't claim to have any goals, it soon became clear that they select people they would interact with based on whether they were looking for a relationship. The case indicated that they wouldn't interact with another person without first finding out about them on their profile, suggesting that the ecological cognition framework is equally relevant to relationship building in that there needs to be some encoding of beliefs, values and interests before an actor will develop goals and plans to interact with someone, suggesting that there needs to be a degree of intimacy and liking before a relationship can progress. Also clear from the interview was that this particular case was concerned whether the people on the sites masked some malicious intention, such as to send them SPAM messages. The case claimed that along with photographs he assessed how much the individual used the service as an indication of whether they were genuine, suggesting that online dating communities could be more effective if the profile pages show that the individual has participated in community life, such as through taking or setting up quizzes, posting messages or leaving comments on others' pages. A feature that seemed important to the case was that the dating services should offer recommendation systems that suggest specific individuals that they might be interested in, and he suggested that he is more likely to be encouraged to interact with someone if the site recommends it, suggesting that online dating services need to be persuasive in their approach to helping people find their match.

Questionnaires, Statistical Analysis, and Concept Mapping

This study made use of secondary data from an ICM Research study (Couldry, Markham, & Livingstone, 2005) and freedom of information requests into the number of incidents of trolling recorded by the police in the UK between 2009 and 2011. Phase One of the ICM research project comprised of detailed qualitative work across six regions of England. The diaries of 37 participants' media consumption were analysed, initial and subsequent interviews were conducted with those respondents, and focus group interviews were conducted with diarists. Phase Two involved a telephone survey of 1,017 people, conducted by ICM Research across the United Kingdom that aimed to produce conclusions on the detailed issues about consumption and citizenship raised in Phase One.

Preliminary Data Coding and Analysis

The variables in the secondary dataset needed to be re-computed to match those in the equations. One of these was the trolling magnitude scale. The computation made the TM values relative to the number of hours spent on the Internet. This was because it was assumed that the longer one is on the Internet the more likely one would be abusive towards others, even if unintentionally (Cassidy, Jackson, & Brown, 2009). On that basis, a trolling magnitude (TM) of 1, which is Playtime, where people are more likely to act in the heat of the moment, was assigned to all the participants who used the Internet 0 to 1 hours. A TM of 2 (i.e. Tactical) was assigned to people who used the Internet for 1 to 3 hours. A TM of 3 (i.e. Strategic) was assigned to people who used the Internet for 3 to 5 hours, and finally, a TM of 4 was assigned to people who used the Internet for between 5 and 7 hours, or greater than 7 hours. This study is important because it will allow for not only the automated pre-screening of Internet content but by linking knol to trolling magnitude will make it easier to prove injury towards someone by someone else in relation to the offences linked with trolling magnitude scale. In this case it would be when engaging with media in general or art in particular. In Equation 1 the variable F reflects the normal force a human can handle in an average week, measured in hours, which is taken to be 48, based on the European Union's Working Time Directive [2003/88/EC]. In the case of this investigation, phantasies were computed through the use of a type of cognition called a detachment (rated from 0 to 6) and a plan (rated from -2 to +2). A detachment is an attitude towards a person that makes one anxious and which the mind tries to suppress. A plan is a willingness, or lack of, to perform a particular action.

The detachments were calculated through linking six regions in the UK where data on reports of electronic message faults between 2009 and 2011 were known. This was done by the region with the lowest number of EMF incidents being 0 and the highest number of incidents of flame trolling being 6. This resulted in Yorkshire and the Humber being ranked 0, with 42 incidents and the East of England being ranked 1, with 114 incidents. Wales was ranked 2 with 135 incidents, Scotland 3 with 174 incidents, and South West England 4 with 578 incidents. Northern Ireland was ranked 5 with 1485 incidents and South East England 6 with 1903 incidents.

The three plans used in the study were, 'People like me don't get involved in the arts and culture,' 'There are other things besides arts and culture that I prefer to do in my leisure time,' and 'It's expensive to get involved in arts and culture.' Using the lookup table in (Bishop, 2011b) for the $x1$ and $y1$ variables, Equation 1 was used to produce three phantasies from combining the detachment with the associated plan for each participant.

Participants were asked to state whether they worked full-time, part-time, were a homemaker, registered unemployed, a full-time student, or not working at all. The number of hours worked were harmonized based on official government figures to reflect the 'potential' as opposed to 'actual'. Those working full-time were assigned to 30 hours and those working part-time were assigned to 24 hours. These are the hours required for the respective rates on the UK's Tax Credits system. A homeworker was assigned 35 hours, which is the number of hours required to claim Carers Allowance and a person who was not working or seeking work was assigned 0 hours. Someone registered unemployed and seeking work was as-signed 15 hours, which is the maximum one can work and still receive out-of-work benefits, and a full-time student was assigned 21 hours, which is the number of hours one needs to be studying to qualify as a full-time student to receive a reduction in council tax.

The baseline figure, which is a person's individual production possibility in terms of workable hours is then added to the maximum a person can work in an healthy environment, which is 48 hours as signified by F. Adding the baseline and the force together and dividing them by the Pression calculated by Equation 2 then produces a persons speed and performing in a particular setting. In terms of phantasies containing detachments, 0.81 is an ideal figure for someone achieve as they are likely to be able to withstand most abusive content due to media content of a GOIOM nature being suppressed. A knol based on a detachment phantasy score of 0.98 or over is not ideal as this could put a lot of pressure on the prefrontal cortex of the brain, which is quite vulnerable. And a knol of below 0.5 is below also not ideal as the phantasy in question is likely to be affecting the person's mental wellbeing and participation in society. Where this reaches around 0.6 then there is an increasing chance the person would not be as productive as they would be at either 0.81 or 0.50.

Table 16. Relationship between trolling magnitude (TM) and knol (k)

TM	N	Mean k	L Bound k	U Bound k	Description
1	90	0.7265	0.6926	0.7604	The prefrontal cortex is operating nearing its most optimal (0.81) means a person is likely to act in the heat of the moment when their knol is at is greatest.
2	285	0.7061	0.6884	0.7239	The prefrontal cortex has decreased from its optimal state by 0.2 points, meaning a decrease in the value of knol increases self-sanctioned trolling activity.
3	519	0.7094	0.6960	0.7228	The prefrontal cortex becomes further sub-optimal as the magnitude of a trolling offence increases, which might explain why the most determined of trolls have social orientation impairments.
4	81	0.6843	0.6527	0.7160	The prefrontal cortex is at its most sub-optimal when the person has to put a lot of effort into their trolling.

Analysis of Results

Using a One-Way ANOVA, the data was then analysed to see whether there was a significant difference between the knol of those assigned to the 4 groups, to make it worthwhile proceeding with further analysis of difference between the groups. The ANOVA was successful. The degree of freedom numerator for the dataset of 975 participants was 3 and the degrees of freedom denominator was 971. This gave a CV of 2.08380. As the F for the dataset was 1.145 (0.9388) this was not an ideal outcome, but further inspection of the dataset showed it was the best outcome possible. An eight-factor model gave an F of 0.568 and CV of 1.71672 (a difference of 1.14872) and a five- factor model, as currently used by the police gave an F of 0.891 and CV of 1.94486 (a difference of 1.05386). This shows the four-factor model to be most appropriate for determining media ratings based on knol and number of hours spent on the Internet.

Table 16 shows the number of persons assigned to each trolling magnitude, the Mean knol (k) for each group and the upper and lower knol for those groups using the means from the ANOVA. As can be seen, there is a negative relationship between trolling magnitude and knol. That is, as trolling magnitude increases then knol decreases. This can be interpreted as meaning that in order to troll at a higher magnitude that more effort is needed in the brain to do so. It could also mean that those who have been traumatized to the extent their knol is very low, may be at more risk of trolling at a higher magnitude. The upper and lower bounds of knol in Table 16 could be used to develop models, such as based on neural networks, to understand the breaking points for different people in terms of stimulus and response to develop effective automated content screening.

LIMITATIONS AND FUTURE RESEARCH DIRECTIONS

This study has explored a variety of research approaches to exploring social media use in order to develop models, such as a praxis based on a parametric user model. The major weakness in this chapter is that they have not been explored in great depth or in most case with huge sample sizes. This should not be unexpected. The aim of the chapter was to explore what might be possible. The next step is to test the approaches in this chapter on a wider scale to see whether it is possible to develop a praxis that can explain social media user beyond those models that are currently in use.

DISCUSSION

Scientists of all kinds are trying to understand the ways in which people communicate with respect of social media. Social media as a term can be seen to refer to all the forms of under-generated content that have existence since the second wave of social networking services, which include Twitter and Facebook. This period could be referred to as post-modem history. The reason being that social media platforms offer little above earlier social networking services like Friendster and MySpace, but as a result of affordable broadband connections more people are using the Internet, whereas previously they might have been technophobic. At present, many scientists seeking to understand social media have turned to Big Data. In other words they are using number-crunching algorithms to systematically understand why people might make certain postings at certain times.

As time goes on, there will be increasing pressure for education institutions to integrate social media functionalities into their managed learning environments. This will need to be done in such a way that the integration is seamless and invisible and not a central focus for the user. Such acts would allow for the creation of networked learning communities, where student-centred learning can be enabled. So far, approaches to this has followed an e-tivities model reliant on the use of message boards and other web-based communities. Whilst these are inevitably essential to online learning, they will no doubt attract the same sorts of problems found in social media platforms. Problems such as lurking, flaming and defriending can result in a loss of sense of community and result in disengagement with the learning process. It is therefore important to develop methods in which these behaviours can be identified and those behaviours influenced before they are able to occur.

Academia is often plagued with those who define themselves by whether they are "quantitative" or "qualitative." This chapter contested that when it comes to researching social media the two are inseparable in datafying user generated content. Posts on Twitter for instance have a textual element to the narratives that could be considered qualitative, but also quantitative criteria can be applied. Interviewing approaches can allow for the exploration of discourses to produce new theories, which may then rely of those approaches commonly thought of as quantitative. This chapter tested out a variety of different approaches to show how it is only through using all approaches available can social media be triangulated to produce accurate modelling of user behaviour. This chapter, by setting out a rationale and methodology of why this is inappropriate and why instead an approach based on making use of the senses of the researcher, has shown how it is possible to systematically draw out meanings from social media postings to produce conceptual frameworks and praxes. This chapter has shown that it is first essential to understand the persuasive and seductive properties of hypermedia that give rise to varying behaviours in social media services and how these can be systematically detected and influenced. Through doing so the chapter has proved that it is possible to drawout meanings from social media can assist with enhancing sense of community.

REFERENCES

Aggarwal, C. C. (2003). Towards systematic design of distance functions for data mining applications. In *Proceedings of the Ninth ACM SIGKDD International Conference on Knowledge Discovery and Data Mining*. doi:10.1145/956750.956756

Alzouma, G. (2014). Between flaming and laudation: Political websites, social media, and democratic participation in niger. *The International Journal of Internet Trolling and Online Participation, 1*(1), 29–61.

Barton, B. (2006). *Stripped: Inside the lives of exotic dancers.* New York, NY: New York University Press.

Berger, P. L., & Luckmann, T. (1991). *The social construction of reality: A treatise in the sociology of knowledge.* Penguin.

Best, R. S. (2014). *Social media and criminal offences* (First Report). London: House of Lords.

Bishop, J. (2004). *The potential of persuasive technology for educating heterogeneous user groups. (Unpublished MSc).* Pontypridd, UK: University of Glamorgan.

Bishop, J. (2008). Increasing capital revenue in social networking communities: Building social and economic relationships through avatars and characters. In C. Romm-Livermore & K. Setzekorn (Eds.), *Social networking communities and eDating services: Concepts and implications* (pp. 60–77). Hershey, PA: IGI Global.

Bishop, J. (2011a). *The equatrics of intergenerational knowledge transformation in techno-cultures: Towards a model for enhancing information management in virtual worlds. (Unpublished MScEcon).* Aberystwyth University, Aberystwyth, UK.

Bishop, J. (2011b). *The role of the prefrontal cortex in social orientation construction: A pilot study.* Poster Presented to the BPS Welsh Conference on Wellbeing, Wrexham, UK.

Bishop, J. (2012). Cooperative e-learning in the multilingual and multicultural school: The role of 'Classroom 2.0' for increasing participation in education. In P. M. Pumilia-Gnarini, E. Favaron, E. Pacetti, J. Bishop, & L. Guerra (Eds.), *Didactic strategies and technologies for education: Incorporating advancements* (pp. 137–150). Hershey, PA: IGI Global. doi:10.4018/978-1-4666-2122-0.ch013

Bishop, J. (2013). The art of trolling law enforcement: A review and model for implementing 'flame trolling' legislation enacted in great britain (1981–2012). *International Review of Law Computers & Technology, 27*(3), 301–318. doi:10.1080/13600869.2013.796706

Bishop, J. (2014). Representations of 'trolls' in mass media communication: A review of media-texts and moral panics relating to 'internet trolling'. *International Journal of Web Based Communities, 10*(1), 7–24. doi:10.1504/IJWBC.2014.058384

Bishop, J. (2015). Using 'on-the-fly corpus linguistics' to systematically derive word definitions using inductive abstraction and reductionist correlation analysis: Considering seductive and gratifying properties of computer jargon. In J. Bishop (Ed.), *Psychological and social implications surrounding internet and gaming addiction* (pp. 153–170). Hershey, PA: IGI Global. doi:10.4018/978-1-4666-8595-6.ch009

Brinck, T., Gergle, D., & Wood, S. D. (2002). *Usability for the web: Designing web sites that work.* London: Morgan Kaufmann Publishers.

Bristow, D. N., & Mowen, J. C. (1998). The consumer resource exchange model: An empirical investigation of construct and predictive validity. *Marketing Intelligence & Planning, 16*(6), 375–386. doi:10.1108/02634509810237587

Bryman, A., & Bell, E. (2003). *Business research methods*. Oxford, UK: Oxford University Press.

Cahill, L., McGaugh, J. L., & Weinberger, N. M. (2001). The neurobiology of learning and memory: Some reminders to remember. *Trends in Neurosciences, 24*(10), 578–581. doi:10.1016/S0166-2236(00)01885-3 PMID:11576671

Carson, S., Kanchanaraksa, S., Gooding, I., Mulder, F., & Schuwer, R. (2012). Impact of OpenCourse-Ware publication on higher education participation and student recruitment. *International Review of Research in Open and Distance Learning, 13*(4), 19–32.

Cassidy, W., Jackson, M., & Brown, K. N. (2009). Sticks and stones can break my bones, but how can pixels hurt me? students' experiences with cyber-bullying. *School Psychology International, 30*(4), 383–402. doi:10.1177/0143034309106948

Couldry, N., Markham, T., & Livingstone, S. (2005). *Media consumption and the future of public connection*. London: London School of Economics and Political Science.

Cui, G. (1997). Marketing strategies in a multi-ethnic environment. *Journal of Marketing Theory and Practice, 5*(1), 122–134. doi:10.1080/10696679.1997.11501756

Cunliffe, D., & Elliott, G. (2005). *Multimedia computing. Newcastle under Lyme*. Lexden Publishing Ltd.

De Laat, M. (2002). *Network and content analysis in online community discourse.Third International Conference on Networked Learning*.

De Laat, M., & Lally, V. (2003). Complexity, theory and praxis: Researching collaborative learning and tutoring processes in a networked learning community. *Instructional Science, 31*(1-2), 7–39. doi:10.1023/A:1022596100142

De Laat, M., & Lally, V. (2005). Investigating group structure in CSCL: Some new approaches. *Information Systems Frontiers, 7*(1), 13–25. doi:10.1007/s10796-005-5335-x

De Laat, M., Lally, V., Lipponen, L., & Simons, P. (2005). *Patterns of interaction in a networked learning community: Squaring the circle*. Manuscript Submitted for Publication.

Efimova, L. (2009). Weblog as a personal thinking space. In *Proceedings of the 20th ACM Conference on Hypertext and Hypermedia*. doi:10.1145/1557914.1557963

Escobar, M. L., Kommers, P., & Beldad, A. (2014). Using narratives as tools for channeling participation in online communities. *Computers in Human Behavior, 37*, 64–72. doi:10.1016/j.chb.2014.04.013

Festinger, L. (1957). *A theory of cognitive dissonance*. Evanston, IL: Row, Peterson.

Freud, S. (1933). *New introductory lectures on psycho-analysis*. New York: W.W. Norton & Company, Inc.

Gibson, J. J. (1986). *The ecological approach to visual perception*. Lawrence Erlbaum Associates.

Goode, M. M. H., Moutinho, L. A. C., & Chien, C. (1996). Structural equation modelling of overall satisfaction and full use of services for ATMs. *International Journal of Bank Marketing, 14*(7), 4–11. doi:10.1108/02652329610151331

Goodwyn, A., & Stables, A. W. (2004). Learning to read critically in language and literacy. *Sage (Atlanta, Ga.).*

Harris, L. C., & Goode, M. M. (2004). The four levels of loyalty and the pivotal role of trust: A study of online service dynamics. *Journal of Retailing, 80*(2), 139–158. doi:10.1016/j.jretai.2004.04.002

Harris, L. C., & Goode, M. M. H. (2010). Online servicescapes, trust, and purchase intentions. *Journal of Services Marketing, 24*(3), 230–243. doi:10.1108/08876041011040631

Jamal, A., & Goode, M. M. (2001). Consumers and brands: A study of the impact of self-image congruence on brand preference and satisfaction. *Marketing Intelligence & Planning, 19*(7), 482–492. doi:10.1108/02634500110408286

Kil, S. H. (2010). Telling stories: The use of personal narratives in the social sciences and history. *Journal of Ethnic and Migration Studies, 36*(3), 539–540. doi:10.1080/13691831003651754

Kommers, P. A. M., Ferreira, A., & Kwak, A. (1998). *Document management for hypermedia design.* Berlin: Springer-Verlag. doi:10.1007/978-3-642-95728-4

Leung, L. (2003). Impacts of net-generation attributes, seductive properties of the internet, and gratifications-obtained on internet use. *Telematics and Informatics, 20*(2), 107–129. doi:10.1016/S0736-5853(02)00019-9

Leyton Escobar, M., Kommers, P. A. M., & Beldad, A. (2014). The key is not to forget to be awesome: Identifying narratives in an online community. *International Journal of Web Based Communities, 10*(4), 490–505. doi:10.1504/IJWBC.2014.065396

Mann, C., & Stewart, F. (2000). *Internet communication and qualitative research: A handbook for research online.* London: Sage Publications.

Mantovani, G. (1996a). *New communication environments: From everyday to virtual.* London: Taylor & Francis.

Mantovani, G. (1996b). Social context in HCI: A new framework for mental models, cooperation, and communication. *Cognitive Science, 20*(2), 237–269. doi:10.1207/s15516709cog2002_3

Maslow, A. H. (1943). A theory of motivation. *Psychological Review, 50*(4), 370–396. doi:10.1037/h0054346

Maxwell, J. A., & Miller, B. A. (2008). Categorizing and connecting strategies in qualitative data analysis. Handbook of Emergent Methods, 461-477.

Mbakwe, C., & Cunliffe, D. (2002). *Towards systematically engineered seductive hypermedia.* Unpublished manuscript.

Mbakwe, C., & Cunliffe, D. (2003). *Conceptualising the process of hypermedia seduction.* The 1st International Meeting of Science and Technology Design: Senses and Sensibility – Linking Tradition to Innovation through Design, Lisbon, Portugal.

Morsillo, R. (2011). One down, two to go: Public policy in service of an available, affordable and accessible national broadband network for people with disability. *Telecommunications Journal of Australia, 61*(2)

Nielsen, J. (1993). *Usability engineering*. London: Academic Press.

Norman, D. A. (2013). *The design of everyday things: Revised and expanded edition*. Basic books.

Peters, L. H., O'Connor, E. J., & Eulberg, J. R. (1985). Situational constraints: Sources, consequences, and future considerations. *Research in Personnel and Human Resources Management, 3*, 79–114.

Preece, J., Nonnecke, B., & Andrews, D. (2004). The top 5 reasons for lurking: Improving community experiences for everyone. *Computers in Human Behavior, 2*(1), 42.

Pritchett, J. E. (2009). *Identification of situational constraints in middle school business information technology programs*. (Doctor of Education Dissertation). The University of Georgia in Partial.

Rao, A. S., & Georgeff, M. P. (1998). Decision procedures for BDI logics. *Journal of Logic and Computation, 8*(3), 293–342. doi:10.1093/logcom/8.3.293

Reiss, S. (2004). Multifaceted nature of intrinsic motivation: The theory of 16 basic desires. *Review of General Psychology, 8*(3), 179–193. doi:10.1037/1089-2680.8.3.179

Rosenfield, L., & Morville, P. (2002). *Information architecture for the world wide web*. Sebastopol, CA: O'Reilly & Associates, Inc.

Rowley, D. E. (1994). Usability testing in the field: Bridging the laboratory to the user. Boston, MA: Academic Press.

Slegers, K., & Donoso, V. (2012). The impact of paper prototyping on card sorting: A case study. *Interacting with Computers, 24*(5), 351–357.

Solo, A. M. G., & Bishop, J. (2015). Avoiding adverse consequences from digital addiction and retaliatory feedback: The role of the participation continuum. In J. Bishop (Ed.), *Psychological and social implications surrounding internet and gaming addiction* (pp. 62–77). Hershey, PA: IGI Global. doi:10.4018/978-1-4666-8595-6.ch005

Štogr, J. (2011). Surveillancebased mechanisms in MUVEs (MultiUser virtual environments) used for monitoring, data gathering and evaluation of knowledge transfer in VirtuReality. *Journal of Systemics, Cybernetics & Informatics, 9*(2), 24-27. Retrieved from http://libezproxy.open.ac.uk/login?url=http:// search.ebscohost.com/login.aspx?direct=true&db=a9h&AN=83259035&site=eds-live&scope=site

Szewczyk, J. (2003). Difficulties with the novices' comprehension of the computer-aided design (CAD) interface: Understanding visual representations of CAD tools. *Journal of Engineering Design, 14*(2), 169–185. doi:10.1080/0954482031000091491

Thelwall, M. (2008). Social networks, gender, and friending: An analysis of MySpace member profiles. *Journal of the American Society for Information Science and Technology, 59*(8), 1321–1330. doi:10.1002/ asi.20835

Thyer, B. (2009). *The handbook of social work research methods*. Sage.

Turner, S. M., Johnson, M. R., Beidel, D. C., Heiser, N. A., & Lydiard, R. B. (2003). The social thoughts and beliefs scale: A new inventory for assessing cognitions in social phobia. *Psychological Assessment, 15*(3), 384–391. doi:10.1037/1040-3590.15.3.384 PMID:14593839

Vygotsky, L. S. (1930). *Mind in society*. Cambridge, MA: Harvard University Press.

Wang, V., Tucker, J. V., & Rihll, T. E. (2011). On phatic technologies for creating and maintaining human relationships. *Technology in Society.*

Watson, J. B. (1913). Psychology as the behaviorist views it. *Psychological Review*, *20*(2), 158.

Watson, J. B., & Rayner, R. (1920). Conditioned emotional reactions. *Journal of Experimental Psychology*, *3*(1), 1–14. doi:10.1037/h0069608

Wodtke, C. (2003). *Information architecture: Blueprints for the web*. Indianapolis, IN: New Riders.

Xie, X., Wang, Q., & Chen, A. (2012). Analysis of competition in chinese automobile industry based on an opinion and sentiment mining system. *Journal of Intelligence Studies in Business*, *2*(1).

Yukawa, J. (2005). Story-lines: A case study of online learning using narrative analysis. In *Proceedings of the 2005 Conference on Computer Support for Collaborative Learning: Learning 2005: The Next 10 Years!*. doi:10.3115/1149293.1149389

Zikmund, W. G., & Scott, J. E. (1973). A multivariate analysis of perceived risk, self-confidence and information sources. *Advances in Consumer Research. Association for Consumer Research (U. S.)*, *1*(1), 406–416.

KEY TERMS AND DEFINITIONS

Discourse Analysis.: Discourse analysis is the form of content analysis that is applied to documents that are created by a researcher through engaging with participants, such as through interviews.

Interviews: Interviews are an approach to research that involve the researcher interrogating a participant through questions, either spoken or via a messaging service.

Narrative Analysis: Narrative analysis is used to understand the themes that exist in documents that have been discovered by a researcher but not created by them.

Questionnaires: Questionnaires are an approach to data collecting that involved the participants recording on a form their responses to questions.

Social Media: Social media is the form of user generated content that came about following the introduction of buddy-lists into platforms hosting user generated content.

Website Metrics: Website metrics are those pieces of meta data that are collected through a website being used, such as the hyperlinks clicked on and the pages referred from.

Chapter 2
Mining the Edublogosphere to Enhance Teacher Professional Development

Eric Poitras
University of Utah, USA

Negar Fazeli
University of Utah, USA

ABSTRACT

The rapid proliferation of Web 2.0 technologies during the last decade has led to online communities of learners, where members share prerequisite knowledge and skills to further professional growth. The educational affordances of blogs offer a wealth of online resources that can be mined in order to gain better understanding of community members and their contributions. In this chapter, we outline a web content mining technique to extract and analyze information from educational blogs, resulting in networks of online resources where content is linked in terms of the underlying semantic relationships. This type of representation is referred to as a network-based model, and has implications for e-learning personalization systems that seek to suggest similar content to those preferred by other learners. The applications of this method are discussed in terms of enhancing teacher professional development in the context of nBrowser, an intelligent web browser designed to support pre-service teachers in building lesson plans that integrate technologies in the classroom.

INTRODUCTION

Web 2.0 technologies refer to any type of technology or service that serves as a tool, allowing individuals and groups to actively transform and share information (Alexander, 2006; Siemens, 2008). These tools include, but are not limited to blogs, wikis, social networking, and social bookmarking platforms (Aijan & Hartshorne, 2008; Grosseck, 2009). Weblogs, commonly known as blogs, are time-stamped entries that are archived in a site, allowing visitors to leave comments. The subject material of blog posts vary considerably according to the intended audience, and in the case of educators, may address technologies

DOI: 10.4018/978-1-5225-0648-5.ch002

that are available to teachers and students. The comments written by site visitors are often organized as a threaded discussion, allowing visitors to rate answers, share posts, and write replies (Martindale & Wiley, 2005). As an example, the blog site Edutech for Teachers (i.e., edutech4teachers.edublogs.org/), which is hosted by Edublogs, shares information about latest technologies and trends for teachers that engage students in meaningful learning experiences. Site visitors are able to comment on these posts and share their views about the online resources and their usefulness in the classroom. In this case, the blog serves as a professional learning network, however, blogging may also serve as an instructional tool in the classroom. Teachers often rely on blogging platforms to create a realistic writing assignment, enabling students to help each other by commenting on the post to share feedback or ask questions. Educational researchers have relied on metaphors to characterize the instructional affordances of such tools, referring to them as cognitive and metacognitive tools, to describe how their design supports mental processes that are conducive to better learning (Azevedo, 2005; Lajoie & Azevedo, 2006).

Educational blogs also hold great promise as an informal learning environment for teacher professional development (Hou, Chang, & Sung, 2009; Ranieri, Manca, & Fini, 2012; Rutherford, 2010). Blogs allow pre-service teachers to connect with more experienced peers to gain useful tips and resources about best practices in the classroom. These resources may include videos, pictures, e-books, links to external websites, and so on. A community of teachers may share greetings, quotes, humorous comments, as well as discuss about their frustrations and provide emotional support (Bissessar, 2014; Sumuer, Esfer, & Yildirim, 2014). External links to resources are particularly prevalent in Twitter feeds that are indexed through popular education-related hashtags such as #edchat and #edtech, allowing for the dissemination of websites, blogs, and newspaper articles pertaining to education (Holmes, 2013). Furthermore, the use of blogging services embedded in social networking providers such as Facebook and Twitter is already widespread amongst college students. In a survey conducted by Ellison, Steinfield, and Lampe (2007), a total of 94% of responders were registered to Facebook, while users of the social networking site spent from 15 to 45 minutes viewing their accounts, sometimes multiple times during the day. A comparable finding was obtained with users of Twitter, a microblogging service that enable registered users to share brief posts. College students tweeted an average of 7.5 tweets on a daily basis for the purposes of replying to on-going discussions related to class or share private messages (Ebner, Lienhardt, Rohs, and Meyer, 2010), but less often while contributing to a live Twitter feed from inside the classroom (Elavsky, Mislan, & Elavsky, 2011).

Despite the pervasive use of this medium, instructors are often reticent to use blogs for educational purposes, preferring instead to use them for personal reasons, and to stay in touch with friends (Roblyer, McDaniel, Webb, Herman, & Witty, 2010). A similar finding is reported in studies that examined the use of social networking in college students, claiming that its use is limited to staying in touch with friends from high school and classmates, and to maintain these old relationships (Ellison et al., 2007; Roblyer et al., 2010). The barriers to the educational affordances of blogs include the instructors' perception of their own competence in using technology, its perceived usefulness, ease of use, and the compatibility of the tool with the curricular content (Aijan & Hartshorne, 2008). These findings suggest a pressing need to change common beliefs regarding the educational affordances of this tool and to implement blogs as part of the training of pre-service teachers, using them as a platform to develop knowledge about classroom practices.

In this chapter, we outline an analytical method that captures the content of educational blogs and leverages their benefits for teachers to attain the knowledge and abilities of integrating technology into classroom. Educational web mining is an emerging field of research in education that aims to discover knowledge about students, and how they learn in educational settings, such as traditional classroom settings, online courses, learning content management systems, and adaptive instructional systems (Baker & Yacef, 2009; Romero & Ventura, 2007, 2010). Mining the web involves the application of data mining techniques to discover and extract information, and is further distinguished in terms of focusing on either web content (e.g., information within web pages and search results), structure (i.e., hyperlink interconnections between pages), or usage (i.e., page access patterns and trends) (Johnson & Gupta, 2012). To study online communities of teachers in the blogosphere, it is important to understand the content of the blogs, and how their meaning is similar to or different from one another. Due to the large amount of blog posts, it is often difficult for humans to manually code the data, which warrants the use of automated web and text mining techniques to identify patterns and facilitate further analysis.

The proposed analytical approach to extract information from the content of educational blogs relies on similarity metrics in order to represent individual posts as networks of linked resources. Based on this semi-automated approach, we address the following questions:

1. Does semi-automated techniques, namely, the representation of blogs as vectors of terms by documents and the calculation of the cosine distance between these vectors, allow to identify groups of online resources on similar topics?;
2. What are the properties of networks of online resources?;
3. What are the implications of these properties for enhancing pre-service teacher professional development?

In the first section, we outline the theoretical framework that informs our research. This is followed by a description of the proposed network-based approach to web content mining and learner modeling. We then turn our attention to the implications of the proposed approach for personalizing instruction, drawing on preliminary findings obtained in the context of our research on nBrowser, an intelligent web browser designed to support pre-service teachers to build lesson plans that implement technologies in the classroom.

BACKGROUND

Technological pedagogical and content knowledge (TPACK) is a theoretical construct that characterizes the knowledge base that is necessary to successfully integrate technologies into the classroom (Mishra & Koehler, 2006, 2009). The model of technology extends Shulman's (1986) theory of pedagogical content knowledge, which describes the knowledge that enables teachers to adapt the teaching process of a particular topic to learners' needs, interests, and proficiency, resulting in better comprehension and retention. This process necessitates teachers' understanding of how to represent concepts in a domain using technology as well as use pedagogical strategies that leverage technology to teach these concepts. An important aspect of this process is teachers' performance of design tasks, and how their design leverages the affordances of technology that map onto content representations and the pedagogical/learning processes (Angeli & Valanides, 2009; Graham, 2011). For instance, the affordances of technology to record sound, allowing for an auditory representation that can be repeatedly accessed by learners to strengthen word recognition. A library of symbols and pictures may be used by students to visualize complex narratives, animating them to demonstrate key aspects of a story and how the plot unfolds.

The use of technology is justifiable by the difficulty of achieving such representations or pedagogical approaches through traditional means, and the selection of appropriate technologies that enable student-centered instruction.

The design of technology-enhanced instructional lessons requires prerequisite skills and knowledge. However, pre-service teachers generally experience significant challenges in planning the integration of technology in a manner that adds value to teaching practices in the classroom and support students in attaining deeper understanding (Angeli & Valanides, 2009; Kramarski & Michalsky, 2010, 2015). Educational blogs are a promising approach to teacher professional development, serving as an informal learning environment where pre-service teachers co-construct knowledge, share relevant resources, materials, experiences, advice, and so on (Bissessar, 2014). In particular, pre-service teachers may learn from more experienced in-service teachers about useful technologies to implement in the classroom as well as receive support and guidance in doing so.

An important factor in learning with open-ended hypermedia-based environments such as educational blogs is the ability to engage in self-regulated learning processes (Azevedo & Cromley, 2004; Greene & Azevedo, 2007). Self-regulated learners make active efforts to gain better understanding of the requirements of a task. They plan and control how they spend their time, find relevant resources, and seek assistance when necessary. Learners' knowledge and relevant experiences inform goal-setting activities prior to task performance. Information is gathered and processed strategically in an effort to achieve these objectives. Learners regulate their own learning by coordinating different sources of information, looking for specific content, and evaluating it on the basis of their prior experiences, interests, as well as their objectives. In doing so, the outcomes of their efforts are monitored as a means to make any necessary re-adjustments (Greene & Azevedo, 2007; Winne & Hadwin, 2008). Likewise, pre-service teachers should regulate their own learning while designing lesson plans by monitoring, controlling, and adjusting their efforts. This requires an awareness of a plan for using technology in the classroom, and the motivation to progressively improve this plan based on learners' growing understanding of the situation and the anticipation of issues that may arise during the activity. In doing so, pre-service teachers should know "what to learn, how to learn, whether they understand the material, when to change plans and strategies, and when to increase effort, based on their own needs and interests" (Kramarski & Michalsky, 2009; 2010).

However, recent empirical research provides ample evidence that learners have difficulties to regulate certain aspects of their own learning (Azevedo & Cromley, 2004; Azevedo, 2008). Learners' inability to regulate several aspects of their learning may be attributable to lack of prior knowledge in effective study skills, the cognitive demands of the task, and the amount of relevant resources (Azevedo & Feyzi-Behnagh, 2011). This becomes a more important issue while navigating through open-ended learning environments such as educational blogs and hypermedia. Learners often fail to monitor and judge their performance appropriately, as well as use effective strategies to learn about a particular topic (Azevedo, 2008; Azevedo & Cromley, 2004; Biswas, Kinnebrew, & Mack, 2013). The inability of pre-service teachers to appropriately engage in self-regulated learning processes has detrimental impacts on learning and task performance, resulting in poor lesson plan design (Kramarski, 2008; Kramarski & Michalsky, 2009, 2010). This suggests a need to train pre-service teachers in regulating their own learning with the aim of improving their ability to design lesson plans that implement technologies in the classroom. For instance, Kramarski and Michalsky (2009) outlined the IMPROVE method, which relies on professional development workshops and the use of self-questioning prompts to externally regulate preservice teachers' learning. A total of 194 pre-service teachers were randomly assigned to each experimental condition, where the prompts were either made available or were unavailable in the context of learning in a face-to-face or online setting. In both settings, learners who had the benefit of these prompts outperformed their unsupported peers in their performance on design tasks. In addition, learners also benefit from metacognitive support while collaborating with peers in a web-based learning environment (Kramarski & Gutman, 2006; Kramarski & Mizrachi, 2006).

To realize the potential of educational blogs as a promising platform to connect pre- and in-service teachers, and build a common knowledge base for implementing technologies in the classroom, we aim to design an intelligent web browser that is tailored to the needs of pre-service teachers. In doing so, the web browser serves as a metacognitive tool (Lajoie & Azevedo, 2006) as a means to train pre-service teachers' ability to engage in self-regulated learning processes. Research results suggest that pre-service teachers often fail to engage in appropriate goals, monitor their progress, and use strategies while designing lesson plans that implement technologies in the classroom. The underlying assumption for the proposed network-based approach to learner modeling is to improve the adaptive capabilities of web-based learning environments, enabling the intelligent web browser to assess and respond to learners' self-regulated learning processes and tailor the delivery of instruction to their specific needs and interests.

NETWORK-BASED APPROACH TO LEARNER MODELING

In this section, we outline a semi-automated approach to the analysis and representation of educational blogs as networks of online resources as a means to foster technological pedagogical content knowledge. Figure 1 depicts the series of steps involved in this approach, which are performed both off-line, prior to student learning, and on-line, as students learn with a web-based learning environment. Before a learning session, the proposed approach involves (1) crawling educational blogs; (2) extracting and processing linguistic features from the content; (3) clustering blogs on the basis of the linguistic features; and (4) visualizing the clusters of blogs in the form of a network of nodes and their interconnections. In doing so, we purposely sample educational blog sites in order to crawl and extract specific content from the web. The content is then processed using a series of text pre-processing algorithms, resulting in a vector of term occurrences by blog posts or post elements. The term co-occurrence across each pair of blog post is then computed, using cosine similarity as a similarity measure. The cosine similarity values determine the link weights that interrelate each blog post within the network of online resources. In doing so, we rely on popular open source tools for data mining (i.e., RapidMiner) and visualization (i.e., Gephi) to facilitate the dissemination of the proposed analytical approach to a broad range of web-based learning environments. During learning, an activation spread and path overlay algorithm enable systems to dynamically update the network of online resources on the basis of learner interactions. In the following, we describe each step of the proposed method in more detail.

Crawling Educational Blogs

The web mining extension of RapidMiner (RapidMiner, 2015) was used to crawl educational blog sites of interest and store the retrieved pages in a database. The web crawler connected to blog hosting providers using standard HTTP protocol (i.e., GET request method), starting at a pre-determined URL to download pages. From this top-level domain, the web crawler followed links that are descendants of the root URL address. We set a number of parameters for the crawler to send a GET request to the servers

Figure 1. Semi-automated approach to mining the web and building network-based models of online resources

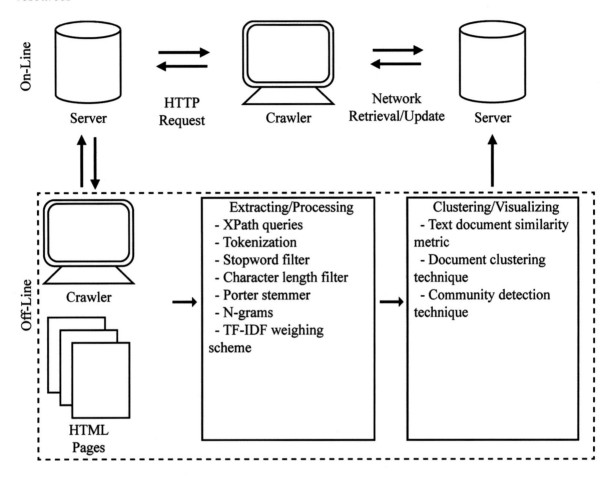

and acquire a page. The crawler operated as a single thread to reduce server load. The crawler engine extracted URL links from blog sites by waiting for a maximum of 10 seconds for a server to respond and limiting queries to 1 second between pages within each website. A maximum file size of 10 MB was set, otherwise a page was skipped. Although the sites varied in their amount of pages, the maximum sitemap generated by the web crawler was limited to 50,000 pages for each site and the maximum depth of the crawling process to 20. In crawling a blog site, the crawler was set to obey the robot exclusion rule specified by the blog hosting provider.

The crawling process was performed in two steps. First, a sample of educational blog sites was purposefully chosen on the basis of their intended audience and subject matter, dealing with the implementation of instructional technologies in the classroom. The URL links of each web page was retrieved from these sites following the crawling parameters mentioned earlier. Second, the URL links were filtered using several inclusion and exclusion criteria prior to extracting information for further analysis. A URL link was included for analysis if the web address matches the following sequence of characters: "htm", which is short for ".html" file extensions. However, it was excluded from further analysis if it was found to match any of these regular expressions: "pdf", "jpeg", "png", "share", "tag", "comment", "Comment", "feed", "category", "label", and "archive". To manage memory constraints, we randomly selected amongst the URL links that were included for further analysis while specifying a desired sample size. The resulting list of URL links was then submitted to the crawler to retrieve each page and download the content for further analysis.

Extracting and Processing Linguistic Features

After a page was downloaded, a series of text pre-processing algorithms were applied in order to extract linguistic features that characterized the page content. The linguistic features were extracted and represented as a vector of words by documents. A term frequency-inverse document frequency (i.e., tf-idf) weighing scheme was used to reflect the relative importance of a word within each document. The weight value increases to the amount of term mentions within the document, while taking into account the frequency of mentions within the entire corpus of documents. In doing so, the weighing scheme allows to control for terms that occur commonly in sentences (e.g., "the", "and", "is", and so on), which may bias the analysis by lessening the importance of less common terms that convey the unique meaning of each document. In creating the vector of words by documents, a series of XPath queries using the *"text()"* function was performed to segment the constituent elements of an HTML page. These elements include paragraph <p> and article <article> HTML tags (i.e., //h:p/text(); //h:article/text(), respectively), which convey the textual content of the page, the later following the latest HTML5 semantic element standards, which may include multiple embedded paragraphs. A similar approach was used to identify title tags and headers ranging from the first to the sixth level in the HTML page. The resulting content was further processed while storing the type of HTML element as an attribute of each document.

A series of steps were followed to segment each document into a list of tokens or terms mentioned in the document. First, the text characters of each document were converted to lower case. Tokenization of the document was performed at the level of individual words using non-letter characters as the splitting point. The text of a document was thus split into a sequence of tokens, and was then filtered for the occurrence of English stop words. The built-in stop word list includes common function words (e.g., the, is, at, which, on, and so on) that have little or ambiguous meaning and serve only grammatical purposes in a sentence. The list of tokens is then again filtered on the basis of the length of text characters, ranging from 2 to 25 characters for inclusion in the resulting vector. In some cases, it is also desirable to filter tokens using a part-of-speech algorithm, which recognizes tokens classified as nouns and removes adjectives, adverbs, and so on. The Porter stemmer for English words (Porter, 1980) is then applied to reduce word variations to their common stem by removing common morphological and inflexional endings from words (e.g., "weakness" and "weak" is both reduced to "weak"). Finally, contiguous sequence of tokens are represented as bi-grams to capture the context in which words are mentioned in a sentence (e.g., "weak" followed by "usabl" is represented as the following bi-gram: "weak_usabl"). This last step is also optional given the choice of similarity measure used in the following stage of the analysis, but it may facilitate interpretation of the tokens by reflecting the context in which terms occur in the document.

Detecting Clusters of Educational Blogs

In order to detect groups of educational blogs with similar topics, the analysis was conducted at the level of the document, which corresponds to either a whole blog post, the content of an article HTML tag within the page (i.e., <article> tags), or a paragraph tag (i.e., <p> tags) featured in the HTML markup of the page. In the case of paragraphs, a minimum amount of 100 characters was set in order to ensure the interpretability of the content, and any duplicate paragraph featured in a single page was removed from further analysis. To compare each pair of pages or page elements, cosine similarity was used as a similarity measure to capture the amount of word co-occurrence between each document (Huang, 2008). Cosine similarity is a popular approach to represent content overlap amongst documents, alongside other alternative similarity metrics such as Euclidean distance, Jaccard coefficient, and the Pearson correlation coefficient. The measure consists of the angle between the word frequency vectors of both documents. A null value indicates that there is no overlap between words mentioned in the pair of documents, while a maximum value of 1 suggests that their content is identical. The formula for cosine similarity is shown below, where W represents the tf-idf weight attributed to each term i mentioned in a pair of documents denoted by d.

$$sim_{(d=1,d=2)} = \frac{\sum_{i=1}^{n} W_{(1,i)} \times W_{(2,i)}}{\sqrt{\sum_{i=1}^{n} W_{(1,i)}^2} \times \sqrt{\sum_{i=1}^{n} W_{(2,i)}^2}} \tag{1}$$

Using this similarity measure, a broad variety of text document clustering techniques may be applied to form clusters of similar documents, such as agglomerative and hierarchical clustering, distance-based partitioning, and hybrid algorithms (see Aggarwal & Zhai, 2012). Community structure detection algorithms are also a popular method in analyzing the properties of text documents represented as networks of nodes that are interconnected through edges. These algorithms aim to uncover the underlying structure of nodes within networks, where the groups have dense interconnections or links between their constituent nodes, and sparse connections with other nodes from other groups. These methods may include traditional approaches mentioned previously as well as vertex similarity techniques, greedy optimization algorithms, spectral clustering methods, as well as alternative approaches to find overlapping communities (see Fortunato, 2010).

Visualizing Clusters of Educational Blogs

Network visualizations enable researchers to gain better understanding of the clusters of nodes identified during the previous stage of the analysis. In order to build network visualizations, we relied on Gephi, an open-source and interactive visualization platform (Bastian, Heymann, & Jacomy, 2009). As an example, we review the case of a small network that featured 39 educational blog posts about the use of technologies in teaching K-12 mathematics. The Gephi implementation of the Louvain method for community detection (Bastian, Heymann, & Jacomy, 2009) was applied to extract the underlying structure of the network. The Louvain method enables the decomposition of a larger network into sub-units or communities by optimizing modularity (Blondel, Guillaume, Lambiotte, & Lefebvre, 2008). A community with high modularity has dense connections between the nodes within sub-units but sparse connections between nodes in different units. In order to discover communities with high modularity within the larger network, the Louvain method computes the modularity density of different community arrangements by removing and placing nodes together. This process is repeated multiple times to evaluate different network arrangements, while retaining the solution that resulted in the highest modularity value. The modularity density measure ranges from -1 to 1, where a value above 0.4 indicates the discovery of one or more well-defined communities. The Louvain method was applied to this network while filtering for the amount of links, including a subset of links that corresponded to a 100%, 75%, 50%, and 25% of links with the highest weight. In doing so, a total of 7 different clusters of educational blogs was discovered within the larger network. However, the highest modularity density value obtained was 0.063, which fails to reach the 0.4 threshold for the quality of the division of a larger network into sub-units. Figure 2 depicts a visualization of this network with the node colors assigned to the different communities detected by the Louvain algorithm.

The use of text document clustering and network analysis techniques allow researchers to validate the arrangements of networks into a particular configuration. For instance, the dimension of nodes featured in the network with 25% of links with the highest weights, shown in Figure 2, is scaled according to the link weights spanning through the node, resulting in larger nodes being more highly interconnected to other nodes within the network. A force vector algorithm was applied to the network to determine the position of nodes. This algorithm relies on the connection weights to attract and converge nodes to each other, ensuring that nodes that are close to each other have greater amounts of words that overlap across the contents of the blog posts. A closer inspection of this visualization suggests that 7 nodes grouped into 4 distinct communities are outliers as the words mentioned in the blog posts do not substantially overlap with others within the network. However, the 32 nodes that belong to the 3 other communities are clustered at the center of the network and all share strong interconnections. This arrangement is further

Figure 2. An example network-based model pertaining to educational blogs on the use of technologies for mathematics K-12 classrooms

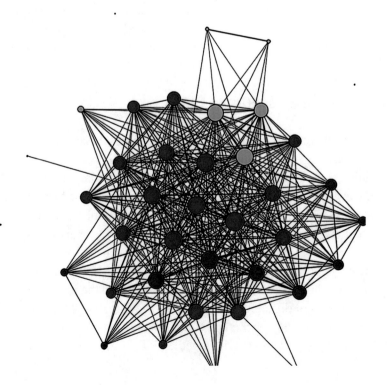

confirmed by the examination of the average betweenness centrality of nodes featured in each community, an indicator of how often connections spanning through a particular node serve as the shortest path between two other nodes in the network. A node with high betweenness centrality means that there is a greater amount of shortest paths that pass through that node to interconnect other nodes within the network. The average betweenness centrality of nodes in the outlier communities range from 0 to 0.9, while the 3 communities that include more nodes central to the network range from 4.5 to 8.8. As such, the central communities are more highly interconnected than the outlier communities of blog posts.

In this case, the nodes or blog posts featured within the 7 distinct communities were not significantly different in the topics or words mentioned to warrant the division of the network into sub-units. This suggests that the network of blogs on mathematics education may be considered as a cohesive representation of a well-defined body of knowledge. However, the detection of outlier nodes with substantially different content, or groups of nodes that appear to address a distinct topic, serves as an initial basis for either pruning an existing network or building an entirely new one. In a similar manner, learners may rate a blog post or node within the network more favorably, which suggests that other nodes that belong in the same community may also be of interest to the learners. In crawling additional blogs, these nodes may provide a benchmark for researchers to determine which ones to include or exclude from the network. In the following section, we elaborate further on the applications of network-based models in the context of web-based learning environments, drawing on examples from our own research on intelligent tutoring systems.

IMPLICATIONS OF NETWORK-BASED LEARNER MODELS

Adaptive learning environments analyze learner behaviors in order to infer the learners' progress towards achieving instructional objectives (Desmarais & Baker, 2012; Shute & Zapata-Rivera, 2012; Sottilare, Graesser, Hu, & Holden, 2013). These processes occur during learning and typically involve a model or representation of the domain, the learner, and pre-determined instructional strategies. The domain model reflects a set of skills, misconceptions, ideal answers, or emotional states that are targeted by the system for the purposes of assessment. The learner model is continually updated by the system using the domain model as a reference, and allowing the system to intervene when necessary by selecting and delivering content from the instructional model. Another key feature is the timing of these interventions. VanLehn (2006) distinguishes between micro- and macro-level system processes. Micro-level processes occur during the course of task performance, and involve the delivery of content such as hints, prompts, and feedback. Macro-level processes are responsible for determining the sequence of task performance or the next material to learn, and typically occur at the end of a learning session or activity.

In this chapter, we claim that networks of online resources can serve as the basis for learner modeling in adaptive web-based learning environments. In support of this claim, we describe the nBrowser learning environment, an intelligent web browser designed to support pre-service teachers in developing knowledge on the integration of technologies in the classroom. An activation spread and path overlay algorithm is described in the following section, allowing the system to update the network-based model on the basis of learner interactions with nBrowser. We also report on preliminary findings obtained from simulated learner experiments conducted in the laboratory. The network-based model embedded in nBrowser is shown to enable the system to adapt the delivery of content at both the micro- and macro-level, as the online resources and example lesson plans delivered by the system are tailored towards the specific interests of different learners.

Web-Based Learning Environment

The nBrowser environment is an intelligent web browser designed to support pre-service teachers in building lesson plans that integrate technologies in the classroom. The teachers navigate the web to find online resources and are supported by the system in setting the objectives of the lesson, monitoring their progress, and using strategies to process and produce information incorporated in the lesson plan. In doing so, the design guidelines of the system are based on the metaphor of using software as cognitive and metacognitive tools to support learners in engaging in self-regulated learning processes that are critical to task performance (Azevedo, 2005; Azevedo & Aleven, 2013; Azevedo & Lajoie, 2006). Theoretical models of self-regulated learning (Winne & Hadwin, 2008; Azevedo, 2008) and technological pedagogical content knowledge (Koehler & Mishra, 2009) inform how the system appraises learner interactions and responds to pre-service teacher needs and interests. The assumption is that pre-service teachers' professional growth requires the acquisition of lifelong learning skills, allowing them to be autonomous in the use of technologies in their future practice. The system also shares similar characteristics to open-ended learning environments, where learners are actively involved in setting goals for their own learning, and are autonomous in making choices with respect to the learning activities (Hannafin, Hall, Land, & Hill, 1994; Land, 2000; Segedy, Biswas, & Sulcer, 2014).

As mentioned previously, the proposed network-based approach to learner modeling leverages web mining techniques to represent online resources as networks of nodes interconnected through links that capture their semantic relationship. The nBrowser system tracks learners' navigational profiles in order to dynamically update the network during learning and personalize instruction. The two modes to using nBrowser aim to train pre-service teachers on the use of self-regulated learning processes. In the *Create* mode, pre-service teachers are free to choose their own topic of interest to build a lesson plan with the benefit of all the networks made available in a particular version of the nBrowser system. The *Solve* mode begins with a case description, wherein an in-service teacher is facing a challenge in the classroom, which the learner is expected to solve by designing a lesson plan that implements technologies in the classroom. As an example, the case of Linda the math teacher, shown in Figure 3, describes her students' reticence to be in front of the class and solve math problems on the board. The nBrowser system relies on a network that is tailored towards a subject matter, in particular, the network that featured educational blogs about teaching with technology in mathematics K-12 classrooms. To support pre-service teachers in building their lesson plans while engaging in self-regulated learning processes, the nBrowser interface features a set of tools that are available in the Lesson Plan sidebar, which is organized into the Details, Assets, and Builder panels.

Pre-service teachers begin a learning session by engaging in goal-setting activities, which are supported through the Lesson Plan Details panel. A textbox enables them to write the objective of their lesson plan. A list of dropdown menus allow them to further specify the subject matter, grade level, type of technology, as well as the timing of the planned activity. A checked list box is available to indicate the relevant Common Core State Standards and the International Society for Technology in Education standards that are targeted by the lesson plan. Learners monitor their own progress using the progress indicator numeric up-down control. A complete list of relevant resources rated by the learners is shown in a list box.

Figure 3. The nBrowser learning environment that implements network-based models to inform recommendations of online resources and example lesson plans

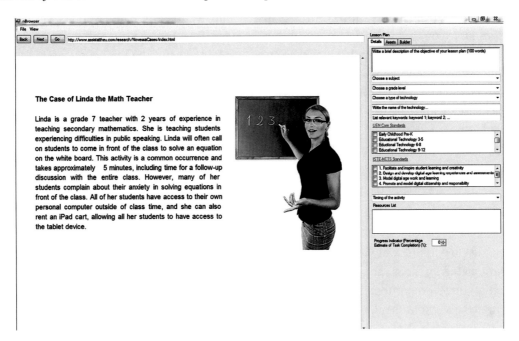

In order to continually monitor their progress and evaluate the content of online resources, learners rely on the Lesson Plan Assets panel while navigating the web. Pre-service teachers may request online resources from nBrowser by clicking on a search button shown in the panel. A brief description of the recommended resource (i.e., the web page title) is displayed on request in a textbox, and learners may visit the site by clicking on the navigation button. The relevant resource is then shown in the browser window, and the learner can also evaluate its content by rating its usefulness, using a 5-point Likert type scale displayed as a slider bar that ranges from useful to not useful. The ranked page then appears in the list of resources visited by the learner, allowing the learner to revisit the page at a later time. Alternatively, the learner may also rely on the navigation sidebar to search for online resources without relying on system recommendations. The web browser search bar enable learners to type in any URL address and navigate to popular search engines such as Google or Bing.

In order to write their lesson plan, learners engage in a broad range of strategic activities to process and produce information, which are supported through the Lesson Plan Builder panel. Learners have access to a split screen option to coordinate multiple sources of information. A list of online resources enable learners to re-visit specific pages of interest and the case description may also be viewed upon request. Finally, a learner may request lesson plans written by other members of the nBrowser user community to assist them in their own writing. A tree view control displays a hierarchical list of key elements to consider in writing a lesson plan, and each one is associated with an example. In the following sections, we outline the activation spread and path overlay algorithms that enable the system to dynamically update the network-based model embedded in nBrowser on the basis of learner interactions with the aim of personalizing instruction.

Activation Spread Algorithm

The activation spread algorithm allows nBrowser to dynamically update the link weights within networks of online resources on the basis of learner usefulness ratings. Learners consult online resources and rate their usefulness using a slider bar that ranges from not useful to useful shown in the Lesson Plan Assets panel. This 5-point Likert type scale is used to assign a constant value to each rating option, ranging from -4, -2, 0, 2, and 4, and denoted as *u*. For each ranking of an online resource, a sigmoid function is applied to the network to update the incoming link weights spanning towards the node under examination in the browser window. The link weight value, referred to as *LS*, where *d* refers to a pair of nodes or documents *d*, is calculated through this function:

$$LS_{(d=1,d=2)} = \frac{1}{1 + e^{-(U \cdot sim_{(1,2)})}}$$

(2)

Where the current link weight value, $sim_{(d=1,d=2)}$, is multiplied with the constant value *u* that was assigned through the learners' rating of the usefulness of the online resource. In doing so, the link weight is updated at a rate proportional to the original network configuration, which reflects the amount of overlapping terms across the document. The connections spanning across groups of similar resources becomes progressively denser as learners rank online resources as useful. In contrast, the link weights are progressively decreased as learners' rate online resources as not useful in building lesson plans. The nBrowser system follows links with the highest weights in order to generate recommendation of online resources and support learner navigation. In doing so, the current version of the system arbitrarily chooses an initial location for the learner to traverse the network of online resources. This approach enables the learners to learn from content that is sequenced in a coherent manner, while also guiding them towards resources that are often rated as being most useful to building lesson plans.

Path Overlay Algorithm

The path overlay algorithm enables nBrowser to search amongst different learner trajectories across the network of online resources, which are associated to lesson plans stored by the system. Learners are able to request example lesson plans in the builder panel of the nBrowser sidebar. In doing so, the path taken by the learner through the network of online resources is compared to all other trajectories of past learners. For each ranking of an online resource, the rating option *c*, ranging from 1 to 5, is assigned to a specific node in the trajectory. The current path taken by a learner is used to multiply and add these ratings across all possible trajectories stored in the system.

$$TW_{(t=1,t=2)} = \sum_{d=1}^{n} c_{(1,d)} \times c_{(2,d)}$$

(3)

where *TW* refers to the weight assigned to a pair of trajectories *t* taken by a learner using nBrowser. The system filters the learner trajectories stored in the database in order to find the one that overlaps the most with the path taken by the current learner. In doing so, the relevant trajectory is retrieved by the system and the lesson plan displayed as an example in the Lesson Plan Builder panel. The nBrowser system thus supports pre-service teachers to engage in strategic activities while emulating each other's writing of lesson plans.

PRELIMINARY FINDINGS

In order to test the activation spread algorithm, a series of simulation experiments were conducted under controlled conditions. A total of 100 simulated learners re-enacted probable learning trajectories under different network configurations. In doing so, the amount of nodes featured in the network was manipulated (i.e., 10, 20, 30, 40, 50, 60, 70, 80, 90, and 100) to determine how the links are weighed by the system as a function of the size of the network. The link weights consist of random values ranging from 0 to 1, where a null value signifies that a pair of online resources do not include any overlapping terms, while a value of 1 indicates that their content is identical. A single node within each of these networks, referred to as the target node, was rated by simulated learners as the most useful in building a lesson plan. The remaining nodes within the network were arbitrarily rated by the simulated learners, with appraisals ranging from 1 (i.e., Not useful) to 5 (i.e., Most useful). The amount of steps taken in the simulated trajectories was also arbitrarily determined at the onset of a learning session, with values ranging from a single step to the maximum amount, where simulated learners visited all the nodes featured in the network. The initial placement of the simulated learner within the network, corresponding to the initial resource recommended by the system, was also randomly chosen amongst all the nodes available in the network.

Under these conditions, we tested the spreading activation algorithm, which dynamically updates link weights within the network in accordance with simulated learner ratings of resource usefulness. Our first experiment examined the distribution of link weight values spanning across the target node as a function of the size of the network and the amount of simulated learners. In doing so, we tested the convergence hypothesis, which states that link weight values spanning through the target node increases accordingly to the amount of simulated learners that navigate across the network. Furthermore, the size of the network mediates this relationship, as the rate of convergence is expected to decrease for larger networks, where more learners are required in order to visit all the nodes. Figure 4 shows the rate of convergence of the links spanning through the target node while simulating a 100 learners' ratings for online resources. This finding suggests that the network of online resources converge efficiently to an optimal solution within a minimum of ten simulated learners using the system, thus increasing the probability that nBrowser will recommend the most useful resource within the network. Contrary to expectations, the convergence rate did not seem to differ on the basis of the size of the network. A proper verification of this claim may require running the experiment repeatedly to reduce the impact of anomalous data while varying the initial configuration of link weights for networks of different sizes. This effect may also be more evident by adjusting the number of steps for the simulated learner trajectories on the basis of data collected from human learners, as opposed to relying solely on an arbitrary value.

Our second simulation focused on the step in the simulated learner trajectory when the online resource associated to the target node is recommended by the system. The underlying assumption of the convergence hypothesis is that networks that have stabilized to an optimal arrangement enable a system

Figure 4. The link weight values spanning trough the target node as a function of the different network sizes and simulated learners

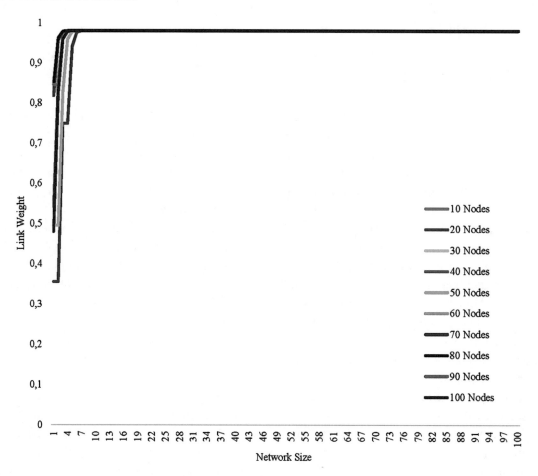

to recommend online resources rated by learners as the most useful towards task performance. This means that the targeted online resource should be recommended most often by the system during the initial steps of the simulated trajectories as opposed to later during the learning session. Figure 5 shows at which step the targeted resource was recommended by the system, arranged into bins of 10 steps performed by the 100 simulated learners across networks of varying sizes (i.e., 1st to 9th step, 10th to 19th step, and so on). The results suggest that 79.9% of recommendations made in relation to the target node occurred between the initial and 9th step in the simulated learner trajectories; furthermore, the system failed to recommend the target node to the simulated learners on only 3.3% of occasions. This finding suggests that network-based models recommend useful resources earlier rather than later during simulated learning sessions with nBrowser, allowing pre-service teachers to quickly access these online resources to build their lesson plans while navigating the web. In the following section, we situate the network-based approach to learner modeling in the context of the broader literature pertaining to web mining and personalized e-learning systems.

Figure 5. The count of recommendations of the target node made by the system as a function of the amount of steps in the simulated learner trajectories

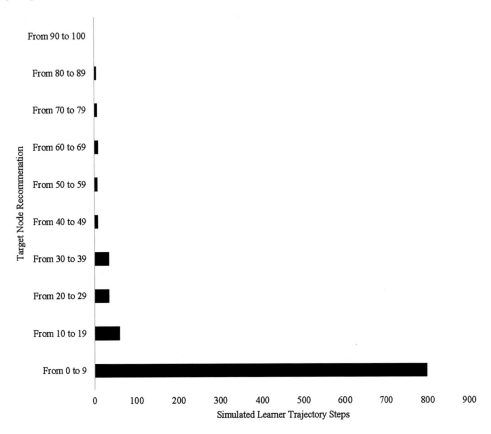

Relevance to Mining the Web and Personalized E-Learning Systems

Personalized e-learning systems aim to adapt the delivery of online educational materials to the specific needs and interests of different learners. In designing such web-based learning environments, it is common practice to individualize instruction on the basis of learner behaviors or the characteristics of the online materials. As an example, structural analysis techniques such as community organization algorithms and filtering algorithms based on vector space models have been used to analyze learner interactions in server log profiles or software interface ratings of learning resources, scores on tests, document access frequency, and so on. Based on the self-organized communities of learners with similar interests, the system is able to recommend a list of online resources (Li, Luo, & Yuan, 2007), and may allow members of the community to recommend resources to one another (Yang, Han, Shen, & Hu, 2005). Hierarchical Bisecting Medoids algorithms have also been used to cluster time-framed learner navigation sessions in order to recommend web pages that are usually visited together in a single session (Wang & Shao, 2004). In contrast, alternative approaches to web mining, such as document clustering techniques, focus exclusively on the document characteristics in order to inform system recommendations. Online resources are represented as a vector of words by documents, and are clustered using maximal frequent itemsets as a similarity measure to increase computational efficiency (Su, Song, Lin, & Li, 2008).

Learner interactions from user sessions have also been analyzed in real-time in combination with off-line analysis of learning resources by domain experts to establish their difficulty (Lu, Li, Liu, Yang, Tan, & He, 2007) or by machines to map keywords to a set of HTML pages (Khribi, Jemni, & Nasraoui, 2008). In the latter case, the top relevant terms from the last pages viewed by learners are used for information retrieval purposes in order to recommend URL links of interest. The learners' usage and ratings of online resources may also serve as the basis for updating the collection of relevant online resources that are crawled from the web, with pages being deleted on the basis of learner ratings. At the same time, learner browsing behaviors are clustered and their ratings are filtered for the purposes of recommending links of relevance (Tang & McCalla, 2005). In the case of educational blogs, the keywords taken from blogs written by learners have been automatically extracted and submitted to Google's blog search engine to search for similar articles. The results are filtered through an extended Serial Blog Article Composition Particle Swarm Optimization (SBACPSO) algorithm, and asynchronously pushed into the user interface (Huang, Cheng, & Huang, 2009). Interestingly, this approach captured blog writing activities by weighing terms while taking into account their relative importance in a document as well as the different type of learner behaviors (i.e., term appears while reading a post, writing a post, or commenting on a post).

The proposed network-based approach to delivering recommendations in web-based learning environments such as nBrowser relies on both learner behaviors and online material characteristics as a means to individualize instruction. The learning materials are analyzed off-line to build and validate the network of online resources, which is continually updated in real-time by the personalized e-learning system on the basis of learner behaviors. The recent advances in personalized e-learning systems provides several directions for furthering the design of nBrowser and the embedded network-based model. For instance, an alternative implication of network-based models is to recommend bloggers rather than blog posts, allowing members of these online communities to interact with learners through written comments (Yang, Han, Shen, & Hu, 2005). Furthermore, the possibility to update the network-based model on the basis of terms weighed depending on the nature of the learners' activity may stand to converge networks in a more efficient manner, rather than solely relying on learner ratings of resource usefulness (Huang, Cheng, & Huang, 2009).

One of the most important limitation to using networks as learner models is the need to diversify the indicators of usefulness for online resources used to update the network. Alternative approaches to designing personalized e-learning systems that analyze real-time learner interactions leverage user interactions such as the number of access or the time spent on a document, its use during the writing task, and so on. The efficiency in which a network converges to an optimal arrangement may be improved drastically by considering several latent behaviors rather than overt choices made by the learners regarding the usefulness of online resources. The later approach assumes that the learners will engage in the behavior, or that they are relying on valid criteria to guide their choices, which may both prove to be incorrect. The behaviors of novice pre-service teachers may also be compared to those of experienced in-service teachers as a means to extend the proposed path-overlay algorithm using methods traditionally employed in novice-expert overlay models. Further research is necessary to determine the relative merits of these different directions.

CONCLUSION

Educational blogs support teacher professional development by serving as platforms for communities of learners to share online resources. The widespread use of social networking services holds great promise to connect pre- and in-service teachers, fostering lifelong learning opportunities for professional growth. However, the affordances of blogs are often limited to personal rather than professional use, such as staying in touch with friends. The study of online communities of teachers, and how they learn in these settings, enable researchers to discover and extract knowledge from the blog content. This knowledge may in turn be useful for professional development solutions, such as personalized e-learning systems, adaptive hypermedia, and intelligent web-based learning environments.

Network-based models represent educational blogs as networks of online resources, relying on similarity metrics to relate elements of web pages to one another. The networks of nodes are interconnected through the use of web mining techniques to capture the amount of overlapping content. In particular, the calculation of the cosine distance between vectors of terms by documents, where the later consists of blog pages or elements within each page. This requires a series of steps, beginning with the extraction of features that characterize the blog content as well as the identification of groups of similar resources. A visualization eases interpretation of the network properties, and the clusters of topics that were identified during the later stages of the analysis.

The implications of a network-based approach to learner modeling is to improve the recommendation of online resources in the context of adaptive instructional technologies. The spreading activation and path overlay algorithms enable instructional systems to update the properties of the network on the basis of the learner usefulness ratings of online resources. In doing so, the network converges to an optimal arrangement, allowing the system to recommend the most useful resources. Furthermore, the navigational path of learners across the network of online resources can be stored by the system to facilitate retrieval of the most relevant lesson plan examples, which enable learners to emulate each other's writing.

This chapter has outlined the methodological foundations of building network-based models by mining the edublogosphere, which offers a wealth of online resources for teachers to implement technologies in the classroom. In clustering the nodes within the network, the method allows to establish the cohesiveness of topics addressed in the collection of resources. We have reviewed recent findings from simulated learners conducted to test the spread of activation algorithm, and demonstrated how networks converge to an optimal arrangement, enabling adaptive systems to recommend the most useful online resources.

FUTURE RESEARCH DIRECTIONS

In order to foster additional research on network-based models, we have outlined several assumptions regarding the personalization of instruction in the context of web-based learning environments. These assumptions are listed below:

- **Cohesion Effect:** A network-based model facilitates learning under the condition that (1) the nodes form a cohesive semantic relationship of a well-defined body of knowledge; (2) new nodes are added to the network as novel resources are mined from the web; and (3) old nodes are pruned on the basis of the usefulness and quality of the content.

- **Convergence Effect:** A network-based model facilitates learning by converging to an optimal arrangement as activation spreads through links at a rate proportional to the amount of learners rating the usefulness of online resources and the dimension of the network.
- **Emulation Effect:** A network-based model facilitates learning by enabling learners to emulate each other in their writing of lesson plans at a rate proportional to the amount of learners that navigated across the network.
- **Disengagement Effect:** If a network fails to meet the conditions for cohesion, convergence, and emulation, then learners are more likely to engage in disengaged behaviors and fail to regulate their own learning.

In testing these assumptions, our preliminary findings from simulations conducted in the laboratory and mining the edublogosphere for online resources provides methodological and empirical foundations for the investigation of the cohesion and convergence effects. There is a need for further investigation and improvement of these methods however, in particular with respect to the range of learner behaviors that are indicative of interest towards a resource as well as to the instructional benefits of emulating each other's writing of lesson plans. Although the spreading activation algorithm enables networks of online resources to converge to an optimal solution, researchers should further substantiate this claim by validating the simulation parameters with data obtained from actual learners. The web mining technique outlined in this chapter serves as a means to appraise the cohesiveness of networks, but the steps involved do not address the need to dynamically update nodes featured in a particular network on the basis of input obtained from other learner behaviors and the ratings of resource usefulness made by domain experts.

The proposed modeling framework is used as a platform for an intelligent web browser to adapt the delivery of instructional content, acting as a metacognitive tool for pre-service teachers to navigate the web and find educational blogs that are most relevant to their own interests. The assumption is that pre-service teachers should engage in settings goals, monitoring their own progress, and adjusting their efforts while navigating online resources in search of helpful resources. In doing so, we expect that pre-service teachers will gain better understanding of how to implement technologies in the classroom.

REFERENCES

Aggarwal, C. C., & Zhai, C. X. (2012). A survey of text clustering algorithms. In C. C. Aggarwal & C. X. Zhai (Eds.), *Mining Text Data* (pp. 77–128). Springer. doi:10.1007/978-1-4614-3223-4_4

Ajjan, H., & Hartshorne, R. (2008). Investigating faculty decisions to adopt Web 2.0 technologies: Theory and empirical tests. *The Internet and Higher Education, 11*(2), 71–80. doi:10.1016/j.iheduc.2008.05.002

Alexander, B. (2006). Web 2.0. A New Wave of Innovation for Teaching and learning. *EDUCAUSE Review*, (March/April), 33–44. Retrieved from http://www.educause.edu/ir/library/pdf/erm0621.pdf

Angeli, C., & Valanides, N. (2009). Epistemological and methodological issues for the conceptualization, development, and assessment of ICT–TPCK: Advances in technological pedagogical content knowledge (TPCK). *Computers & Education, 52*(1), 154–168. doi:10.1016/j.compedu.2008.07.006

Azevedo, R. (2005). Computer environments as metacognitive tools for enhancing learning. *Educational Psychologist, 40*(4), 193–197. doi:10.1207/s15326985ep4004_1

Azevedo, R. (2008). The role of self-regulation in learning about science with hypermedia. In D. Robinson & G. Schraw (Eds.), *Recent innovations in educational technology that facilitate student learning* (pp. 127–156). Charlotte, NC: Information Age Publishing.

Azevedo, R., & Aleven, V. (2013). Metacognition and learning technologies: An overview of the current interdisciplinary research. In R. Azevedo & V. Aleven (Eds.), *International handbook of metacognition and learning technologies* (pp. 1–16). Amsterdam: Springer. doi:10.1007/978-1-4419-5546-3_1

Azevedo, R., & Cromley, J. G. (2004). Does training on self-regulated learning facilitate students' learning with hypermedia? *Journal of Educational Psychology, 96*(3), 523–535. doi:10.1037/0022-0663.96.3.523

Azevedo, R., & Feyzi-Behnagh, R. (2011). Dysregulated learning with advanced learning technologies. *Journal of e-Learning and Knowledge Society-English Version, 7*(2).

Baker, R. S. J. D., & Yacef, K. (2009). The state of educational data mining in 2009: A review and future visions. *Journal of Educational Data Mining, 1*(1), 3–16.

Bastian, M., Heymann, S., & Jacomy, M. (2009). Gephi: An open source software for exploring and manipulating networks. *Proceedings of the 3rd International AAAI Conference on Weblogs and Social Media*.

Bissessar, C. S. (2014). Facebook as an informal teacher professional development tool. *Australian Journal of Teacher Education, 39*(2), 121–135. doi:10.14221/ajte.2014v39n2.9

Biswas, G., Kinnebrew, J. S., & Mack, D. L. C. (2013). How do students' learning behaviors evolve in scaffolded open-ended learning environments? *Proceedings of the 21st International Conference on Computers in Education*.

Blondel, V. D., Guillaume, J. L., Lambiotte, R., & Lefebvre, E. (2008). Fast unfolding of communities in large networks. *Journal of Statistical Mechanics, 2008*(10), P10008. doi:10.1088/1742-5468/2008/10/P10008

Desmarais, M. C., & Baker, R. S. (2012). A review of recent advances in learner and skill modeling in intelligent learning environments. *User Modeling and User-Adapted Interaction, 22*(1-2), 9–38. doi:10.1007/s11257-011-9106-8

Ebner, M., Lienhardt, C., Rohs, M., & Meyer, I. (2010). Microblogs in higher education – A chance to facilitate informal and process-oriented learning? *Computers & Education, 55*(1), 92–100. doi:10.1016/j.compedu.2009.12.006

Elavsky, C. M., Mislan, C., & Elavsky, S. (2011). When talking less is more: Exploring outcomes of Twitter usage in the large-lecture hall. *Learning, Media and Technology, 36*(3), 215–233. doi:10.1080/17439884.2010.549828

Ellison, N. B., Steinfield, C., & Lampe, C. (2007). The benefits of Facebook "friends:" Social capital and college students' use of online social network sites. *Journal of Computer-Mediated Communication, 12*(4), 1143–1168. doi:10.1111/j.1083-6101.2007.00367.x

Fortunato, S. (2010). Community detection in graphs. *Physics Reports, 486*(3-5), 75–174. doi:10.1016/j.physrep.2009.11.002

Graham, C. R. (2011). Theoretical considerations for understanding technological pedagogical content knowledge (TPACK). *Computers & Education, 57*(3), 1953–1960. doi:10.1016/j.compedu.2011.04.010

Greene, J. A., & Azevedo, R. (2007). A theoretical review of Winne and Hadwin's model of self-regulated learning: New perspectives and directions. *Review of Educational Research, 77*(3), 334–372. doi:10.3102/003465430303953

Grosseck, G. (2009). To use or not to use web 2.0 in higher education? *Procedia: Social and Behavioral Sciences, 1*(1), 478–482. doi:10.1016/j.sbspro.2009.01.087

Hannafin, M. J., Hall, C., Land, S., & Hill, J. (1994). Learning in open-ended environments: Assumptions, methods, and implications. *Educational Technology, 34*(8), 48–55.

Holmes, B. (2013). School teachers' continuous professional development in an online learning community: Lessons from a case study of an eTwinning learning event. *European Journal of Education, 48*(1), 97–112. doi:10.1111/ejed.12015

Hou, H.-T., Chang, K.-E., & Sung, Y.-T. (2009). Using blogs as a professional development tool for teachers: Analysis of interaction behavioral patterns. *Interactive Learning Environments, 17*(4), 325–340. doi:10.1080/10494820903195215

Huang, A. (2008). Similarity measures for text document clustering. *Proceedings of the Sixth New Zealand Computer Science Research Student Conference* (pp. 49-56).

Huang, T.-C., Cheng, S.-C., & Huang, Y.-M. (2009). A blog article recommendation generating mechanism using an SBACPSO algorithm. *Expert Systems with Applications, 36*(7), 10388–10396. doi:10.1016/j.eswa.2009.01.039

Johnson, F., & Gupta, S. K. (2012). Web content mining techniques: A survey. *International Journal of Computers and Applications, 47*(11), 44–50. doi:10.5120/7236-0266

Khribi, M. K., Jemni, M., & Nasraoui, O. (2008). Automatic recommendations for e-learning personalization based on web usage mining techniques and information retrieval. *Proc. IEEE Int. Conf. Adv. Learning Technol.* (pp. 241-245). doi:10.1109/ICALT.2008.198

Koehler, M. J., & Mishra, P. (2009). What is technological pedagogical content knowledge? *Contemporary Issues in Technology & Teacher Education, 9*(1).

Kramarski, B. (2008). Promoting teachers' algebraic reasoning and self-regulation with metacognitive guidance. *Metacognition and Learning, 3*(2), 83–99. doi:10.1007/s11409-008-9020-6

Kramarski, B., & Gutman, M. (2006). How can self-regulated learning be supported in mathematical E-learning environments? *Journal of Computer Assisted Learning, 22*(1), 24–33. doi:10.1111/j.1365-2729.2006.00157.x

Kramarski, B., & Michalsky, T. (2009). Three metacognitive approaches to training pre-service teachers in different learning phases of technological pedagogical content knowledge. *Educational Research and Evaluation, 15*(5), 465–485. doi:10.1080/13803610903444550

Kramarski, B., & Michalsky, T. (2010). Preparing preservice teachers for self-regulated learning in the context of technological pedagogical content knowledge. *Learning and Instruction*, *20*(5), 434–447. doi:10.1016/j.learninstruc.2009.05.003

Kramarski, B., & Michalsky, T. (2015). Effect of a TPCK-SRL Model on Teachers' Pedagogical Beliefs, Self-Efficacy, and Technology-Based Lesson Design. In Technological Pedagogical Content Knowledge (pp. 89-112). Springer US.

Kramarski, B., & Mizrachi, N. (2006). Online discussion and self-regulated learning: Effects of instructional methods on mathematical literacy. *The Journal of Educational Research*, *99*(4), 218–231. doi:10.3200/JOER.99.4.218-231

Lajoie, S. P., & Azevedo, R. (2006). Teaching and learning in technology-rich environments. In P. Alexander & P. Winne (Eds.), *Handbook of educational psychology*. Mahwah, NJ: Erlbaum.

Land, S. M. (2000). Cognitive requirements for learning with open-ended learning environments. *Educational Technology Research and Development*, *48*(3), 61–78. doi:10.1007/BF02319858

Li, X., Luo, Q., & Yuan, J. (2007). Personalized recommendation service system in e-learning using web intelligence.*Proceedings 7th Int. Conf. Comput. Sci.* (pp. 531-538). doi:10.1007/978-3-540-72588-6_86

Lu, F., Li, X., Liu, Q., Yang, Z., Tan, G., & He, T. (2007). Research on personalized e-learning system using fuzzy set based clustering algorithm.*Proc. Int. Conf. Comput. Sci.* (pp. 587-590). doi:10.1063/1.2747485

Martindale, T., & Wiley, D. A. (2005). An introduction to teaching with weblogs. *TechTrends*, *49*(2), 55–61. doi:10.1007/BF02773972

Mishra, P., & Koehler, M. (2006). Technological pedagogical content knowledge: A framework for teacher knowledge. *Teachers College Record*, *108*(6), 1017–1054. doi:10.1111/j.1467-9620.2006.00684.x

Porter, M. F. (1980). An algorithm for suffix stripping. *Program*, *14*(3), 130–137. doi:10.1108/eb046814

Ranieri, M., Manca, S., & Fini, A. (2012). Why (and how) do teachers engage in social networks? An exploratory study of professional use of Facebook and its implications for lifelong learning. *British Journal of Educational Technology*, *43*(5), 754–769. doi:10.1111/j.1467-8535.2012.01356.x

RapidMiner. (2015). *RapidMiner 6 Operator Reference Manual*. RapidMiner GmbH.

Roblyer, M. D., McDaniel, M., Webb, M., Herman, J., & Witty, J. V. (2010). Findings on Facebook in higher education: A comparison of college faculty and student uses and perceptions of social networking sites. *The Internet and Higher Education*, *13*(3), 134–140. doi:10.1016/j.iheduc.2010.03.002

Romero, C., & Ventura, S. (2007). Educational data mining: A survey from 1995 to 2005. *Expert Systems with Applications*, *33*(1), 125–146. doi:10.1016/j.eswa.2006.04.005

Romero, C., & Ventura, S. (2010). Educational data mining: A review of the state-of-the-art. *IEEE Transactions on Systems, Man and Cybernetics. Part C, Applications and Reviews*, *40*(6), 601–618. doi:10.1109/TSMCC.2010.2053532

Rutherford, C. (2010). Facebook as a source of informal teacher professional development. *Education*, *16*(1), 60–74.

Segedy, J. R., Biswas, G., & Sulcer, B. (2014). A model-based behavior analysis approach for open-ended environments. *Journal of Educational Technology & Society, 17*(1), 272–282.

Shulman, L. S. (1986). Those who understand: Knowledge growth in teaching. *Educational Researcher, 15*(2), 4–14. doi:10.3102/0013189X015002004

Shute, V. J., & Zapata-Rivera, D. (2012). Adaptive educational systems. In P. Durlach (Ed.), *Adaptive technologies for training and education* (pp. 7–27). New York, NY: Cambridge University Press. doi:10.1017/CBO9781139049580.004

Siemens, G. (2008). *A World without courses*. Retrieved from http://www.elearnspace.org/media/world-withoutcourses/player.html

Sottilare, R., Graesser, A., Hu, X., & Holden, H. (Eds.). (2013). *Design recommendations for intelligent tutoring systems: Learner modeling* (Vol. 1). Orlando, FL: Army Research Laboratory.

Su, Z., Song, W., Lin, M., & Li, J. (2008). Web text clustering for personalized e-learning based on maximal frequent item sets.*Proc. Int. Conf. Comput. Sci. Softw. Eng.* (pp. 452-455).

Sumuer, E., Esfer, S., & Yildirim, S. (2014). Teachers' Facebook use: Their use habits, intensity, self-disclosure, privacy settings, and activities on Facebook. *Educational Studies, 40*(5), 537–553. doi:10.1080/03055698.2014.952713

Tang, T., & McCalla, G. (2005). Smart recommendation for an evolving elearning system. *International Journal on E-Learning, 4*(1), 105–129.

VanLehn, K. (2006). The behavior of tutoring systems. *International Journal of Artificial Intelligence in Education, 16*(3), 227–265.

Wang, F. H., & Shao, H. M. (2004). Effective personalized recommendation based on time-framed navigation clustering and association mining. *Expert Syst. Appl. J., 27*(3), 265–377. doi:10.1016/j.eswa.2004.05.005

Winne, P., & Hadwin, A. (2008). The weave of motivation and self-regulated learning. In D. Schunk & B. Zimmerman (Eds.), *Motivation and self-regulated learning: Theory, research, and applications* (pp. 297–314). Mahwah, NJ: Erlbaum.

Yang, F., Han, P., Shen, R., & Hu, Z. (2005). A novel resource recommendation system based on connecting to similar e-learners.*Proc. Int. Conf. Web-Based Learning* (pp. 122-130). doi:10.1007/11528043_12

KEY TERMS AND DEFINITIONS

Adaptive Web-Based Learning Environment: Any type of learning environment where web technologies are used for the purposes of personalizing the delivery of instructional content.

Edublogosphere: A collection of blogs where the intended audience is learners, and the content is meant to disseminate information on relevant knowledge and skills in implementing technologies in the classroom.

Network-Based Model: A representation of online resources mined from the web as nodes that are interconnected through links with weights reflecting their semantic relationships, such as the amount of words that overlap or any other relevant characteristics.

Self-Regulated Learning: The learning processes that mediate how learners process and produce information while building lesson plans, including setting-goals, monitoring one's own progress, and using strategies.

Technological Pedagogical Content Knowledge: The knowledge base that allows teachers to implement technologies in the classroom.

Chapter 3
Weak Ties and Value of a Network in the New Internet Economy

Davide Di Fatta
University of Messina, Italy

Walter Vesperi
University of Messina, Italy

Roberto Musotto
University of Messina, Italy

Giacomo Morabito
University of Messina, Italy

Vittorio D'Aleo
University of Messina, Italy

Salvatore Lo Bue
University of Messina, Italy

ABSTRACT

The rapid rise in internet economy is reflected in increased scholarly attention on the topic, with researchers increasingly exploring the marketing approaches and strategies now available through social media. The network provides a value for companies, thus becomes essential acquire greater awareness to evaluate and quantify its value. What are practical implications for managers? Social network analysis is nowadays an essential tool for researchers: the aim of this chapter is to extend the internet economy research to network theories. Today, there are emerging observations on the global internet economy, but there is a big gap in literature indeed. At first, literature focused on people. Now, on digitalized information. Firms are connected in a virtual network and there are undefined distances in terms of space and time. Traditional methods of analysis are no more efficient: to analyze the relationship in the network society, we need a different paradigm to approach network issue.

INTRODUCTION

Sociologists and anthropologists who initially studied networks didn't pay attention to their economic relevance (Barnes,1979). Some industrial sociologists (Roy, 1954; Dalton, 1959) had long stressed the role of informal networks as an antidote to formal organization practices and structures (Doerr and Powell, 2005). However, there is not much previous literature that applied internet economy research to network theories: this chapter aims to fill this gap.

DOI: 10.4018/978-1-5225-0648-5.ch003

Noting this gap, the research question, around which this work is build, is: built the present work: is there a contact point between network theories and the internet economy? Assuming an affirmative answer, as we will discuss later, what are the advantages of applying the network theory in the Internet economy?

The aim of this chapter is to highlight the importance of network theories for the internet economy (among all, Rosenbaum et al., 1990). This manuscript contributes to the understanding of a mutable economic environment: the environment is worth studying because it is characterized by an increasing dynamism of the network. In order to get this objective, network theories will be discussed. Such a review seeks to add new foundations to the internet economy paradigm into economic literature.

This study is consistent with the Milgram experiment (Milgram, 1967), which is probably one of the most well-known experiments in social science: Milgram and his staff randomly distributed preaddressed and stamped letters to 296 people in Nebraska who were asked to pass the letters on to the correct recipient in Massachusetts. Milgram's team tabulated the rate at which the letters were picked up and sent to the correct recipient: the mean number of intermediaries between starters and targets was 5,2 people. This is a cornerstone for the degrees of separation theory which will be explained in the next paragraphs.

However, in the Milgram experiment, there is something else interesting to note: during the delivery process of the letters there was an apparent crucial point in the network, because 48 per cent of the chains passed through the same three people before reaching the target. In other words, there was some hub in the network. Therefore, a network is not egalitarian: it is a small world structure (Travers and Milgram, 1969). Small world networks show how a social world is interconnected, having only six degrees a social world such that it has only six degrees of separation among its elements (Buchanan, 2003), as it will be explained in subsequent sections.

The present chapter is structured as follows: the next paragraph shows the state of the art and the theoretical background through a literature review; in the main body, it is possible to identify three conceptual areas: Internet Economy, Network Value, Strong and Weak Ties. These themes correspond to the sections in which this chapter is ideally divided. Nevertheless, these aspects are mutually interconnected and they form a unified framework; then, a solution and recommendation will be proposed, with further research directions and a conclusion given to highlight the practical implications of the theoretical arguments discussed above.

BACKGROUND

The necessary starting point is to introduce some insight about network theories. The issue has its origins in the studies of Granovetter who argued that, although the strong social ties could appear necessary to hold together a social system, in truth weak ties are crucial, specifically the so-called strength of weak ties (Granovetter 1973, 1983).

We assume a network of individuals (nodes) and friends (connections) that bind individuals: individuals within a group have, in fact, many elements connected to each other by generating a redundancy of strong ties. The disappearance of one of these links does not affect the interconnection between the network elements.

However, considering the system as social network (i.e. friendship), we realize that there are weak links between different groups of friends that hold it together: they work as a sort of bridge between social groups. The disappearance of one of these weak bonds would result in serious harm to the degree of connection of the system: indeed, these specific weak ties are known as social bridges. On social network websites, such as Facebook, most ties are weak and they are bridges between social group (De Meo et al., 2014).

From a theoretical point of view, in order to study these connections it is useful to consider graph theory: this is a branch of mathematics that studies the various ways in which certain points are connected, regardless of the specific nature of the objects. In more detail, a graph consists of two sets (called vertices and edges) and an incidence relation between them (Gross and Yellen, 2005). Graph theory tends to explain the configuration of these nodes and connection occurring in a great diversity of applications such as social networks, the internet etc.

We start from the analysis of an ordered theoretical network: each node is connected to the next; to move from point 1 to point 3, you must necessarily pass through point 2. We realize that there are many degrees of separation that combine elements are spatially distant: if you have to move from point 1 to point 4, you must necessarily pass through point 2 and then through point 3.

Let's introduce some random connections: inputting a minimum number of random connections, elements previously furthest approach exponentially, reducing more than proportionally the distances (or degrees of separation).

For instance, if we have to build the roads that link 50 urban centres with each other, using the fewest possible resources, theoretically from a strictly mathematical point of view, 1225 different combinations of possible roads exist. It's possible to show that building only 98 roads (8% of the possible total combinations) ensures the connection of the vast majority of points: this is the trick of the so-called random connections (Erdos, 1961).

The studies developed on the basis of the Milgram's experiment are still relevant today, but there is a big gap in literature. At first, literature focused on people. Now, it focuses on digitalised information (Fuchs, 2009). The advent of the digital economy has radically changed our society at all levels: relational, social, economic, political (just to name a few).

These are the basic concepts that define the network theory. To understand its intersections with the internet economy is necessary to define what it is and what its boundaries are. Therefore, the main body of this chapter is divided into three conceptual areas: first of all, we have to deal with the Internet Economy.

The next section will follow an approach based on "differences": it will analyse peculiarities of the internet economy, highlighting the conceptual differences with e-business. The intent is to clarify a distinction that often is not clear in literature.

INTERNET ECONOMY AND E-BUSINESS

There are multiple definitions of internet economy and e-business (Norris et al., 2000). Some of them are even conflicting: internet economy is not a synonym of e-business. In fact, the internet economy is a broader concept. It includes e-business, but it covers a wider sphere of economic activities. Such activities aim at multiple purposes (Dominici, 2012): exploitation of the network, construction with the purchase and implementation of the infrastructure of the network.

What is meant by the term internet economy? In this regard, it is important to mention the first studies of the C.R.E.C. (acronym of the Centre for Research and Electronic Commerce of the University of Texas)[1].

The C.R.E.C. outlines a conceptual framework of the operation of the Internet Economy by breaking it down into 4 segments (Barua et al., 1999): Physical infrastructure also defined Information and Communication Technology; it includes companies that provide the hardware and equipment to connect to the network. Business infrastructure; it refers to companies that produce software to facilitate online transactions and web consulting companies. Intermediaries; they are businesses that connect buyers and sellers in the network by providing virtual markets online. Traders; these are firms that sell goods or services directly to consumers (B2C) or other businesses (B2B).

In other words, the internet economy is based on electronic goods and services traded in the electronic commerce. It refers to conducting business through markets whose infrastructure is based on the World-Wide Web (Dominici, 2012). The WWW is a complex system. It is based on the exchange of information through links between a plurality of nodes (websites and servers).

At this point, it is possible to define the concept of e-business. It refers to the integrated management processes and tools for the creation and transfer of value (Kolakota and Robinson, 1999). Handling this definition, it might be easy to get wrong. E-business might be confused with the e-commerce. The first is that set of strategies, policies and tactics that enable the company to effectively and efficiently exploit digital technologies. Instead, e-commerce can be defined as the set of levers for managing the digital distribution channel.

What is more, e-business can be seen as a system that includes three sub-systems: e-commerce, digital information and electronic cooperation (Bartelt and Lamersdorf, 2001).

With regard to the concept of e-business, some basic elements that weave the main features of an e-business model have been identified in the literature, also known as an internet based business model (Mahadevan, 2000): technology aspect, software domain, management aspect, statutory and legal dimension.

The starting point is the technology aspects dealing with infrastructural issues; then software domain including technicalities such as programming languages, page design etc; management aspects are related with the business strategy in order to create value for stakeholders and satisfaction for customers; last, but not least the statutory and legal dimensions should be considered to take into account cyber laws.

Other authors (Sanders, 2007; Prajogo and Olhager, 2012) have focused their attention on the study of the impact of e-business on organizational collaboration and performance. Sanders (2007), using a structural equation model, shows that use of e-business technologies impacts performance both from a

Figure 1. Internet economy vs. e-business
Bartelt & Lamersdorf, 2001.

direct and indirect point of view: in other words, intra-firm collaboration is found to have a (positive) direct impact on organizational performance; on the other hand, the impact of inter-organisational collaboration on performance is found to be only indirect, through the impact of intra-organizational collaboration.

Other authors (Koellinger, 2008; Oliveira and Martins, 2009; Yuan et al., 2010) instead analysed the issue of impact of e-business innovation. As was expected, empirical results by Koellinger show that internet based technologies and an e-business model were important enablers of innovation. Even if innovative activity is not necessarily associated with higher profitability, businesses that operate online have shown a greater capacity for innovation.

Although existing literature has shown a relationship between knowledge management processes and technology adoption (Fink, 2006), Chong (2014) empirically verifies an adoption model based on knowledge management processes. The results show that knowledge management processes such as knowledge acquisition and knowledge application are significant in affecting Malaysian SMEs' decision to adopt e-business in their supply chain. Knowledge dissemination was found not to be significant in affecting the adoption of e-business. Without wanting to digress from the objectives of the present work, what matters here it is the concentric relationship between internet economy, e-business and e-commerce.

As the Internet Economy has now been defined, the next section will deal with a very important question for our research in order to understand the intersections with network theory: how to estimate the value of a network? Considering the internet as a network, how to define its value?

NETWORK VALUE

In literature, there is not unanimous thought about the definition of the value of a network (Domingos and Richardson, 2001; Peppard and Rylander, 2006). The objective of this paragraph is not, therefore, a simple historical survey, but an examination of the problems that may arrive at the formulation of an evaluation criterion valid for the analysis of network. In other words, how it is practically possible to calculate the value of a network?

The solution of this question is of particular interest for online business and for those that want to know the value of their networks, but in a broad sense can be extended to the consideration of all other types of networks (relational, social, work, etc.)

The first informal definition of the value of the network dates back to the early decades of the twentieth century: according to Kovarik (2015), Sarnoff states that the value of a broadcast network is directly proportional to the number of viewers. In its simplicity, the Sarnoff's law has the merit of opening the way to a line of studies on the value of a network. A more interesting is that proposed by Bob Metcalfe, the inventor of Ethernet[2].

Metcalfe's Law

Metcalfe's law states that the value of a telecommunications network is proportional to the square of the number of connected users of the system. Metcalfe's law was originally presented in 1980, not in terms of users, but rather of compatible communicating devices (for example, fax machines, telephones, etc.).

Recently, with the diffusion of the internet, this law exploits its power because it is also very much related to the internet economics (Hendler and Golbeck, 2008): in fact, network externalities are what lie behind Metcalfe's law (Shapiro et al., 1999). If there are n people in a network, and the value of the network to each of them is proportional to the number of other $(n-1)$ users, then the total value of the network is proportional to:

$$n(n-1) = n^2 - n$$

For instance, if the value of a network to a single user is \$1 for each other user on the network, then a network made by 10 users has a total value of \$90. In opposition, a network of size 100 has a total value of 9.801 \$, roughly \$10.000. Therefore, according to Metcalfe's law, a tenfold increase in the size of the network leads roughly to a hundredfold increase in its value. A review on the subject is proposed by a formulation from the same author in order to express the law through a triangular number which converges asymptotically to n^2 :

$$\frac{n(n-1)}{2}$$

If Metcalfe's Law works perfectly for the communication device, but from a strictly economic point of view it is necessary to provide some clarifications: all companies would theoretically combine with another partner in order to increase the value of the network. Does it really work in this way?

A Refutation of Metcalfe's Law

Often, only equal firms are willing to interconnect with one another. In the case of a larger firm and a smaller one, the larger feels that the smaller one is benefiting on a much larger scale. The larger firm gains little in comparison to the small one. The fundamental fallacy underlying Metcalfe's law is in the assumption that all connections are equally valuable (Odlyzko and Tilly, 2005; Arakji and Lang, 2007).

Another problem is that Metcalfe's law provides irresistible incentives for all networks relying on the same technology to merge or at least interconnect. For example, consider two networks composed by n members. By Metcalfe's law, each one is worth n^2 so the total value of both (by summing) is $2n^2$. But suppose these two networks decide to interconnect (by merger or acquisition), then the result will be a single network with $2n$ members. By Metcalfe's law, the value of the new network will be $4n^2$; twice as much as the two separate networks. Since Metcalfe's law tends to overestimate the value of a network, the Odlyzko's proposal is to use an alternative rule-of-thumb:

$$n \log(n)$$

This growth rate is faster than the linearity of Sarnoff's law, but only slightly: this helps explain why interconnection often requires time, effort and in many case regulatory pressure to achieve. As before, consider a new interconnected network made by a merger: its value by the suggested formula will be only about 5% gain over the total valuation of the separate networks.[3]

While steps are being made towards solving the problem, some issues still remain unresolved: the value of a network lies in its connections, but some connections are more valuable than others. Which matter most?

Reed's Law

Reed's law is based on the assumption that, given a set of n people, it has at most 2^n possible subsets. However, this includes the empty set, and n subset composed by a single element, which are not properly subsets. Therefore, the known formulation of Reed's law subtracts from the maximum number of all possible subgroups (2^n), the n subsets composed by a single element and the empty set:

$$2^n - n - 1$$

Like Metcalfe's law and also Reed's law, as n increases, it tends asymptotically to 2^n. However, from a theoretical point of view, Reed introduces a fundamental difference: for the first time, he considers the possibility that not all the ties in networks have the same value. In the specific case Reed simply does not recognize the value to the empty set and the single subset that in fact do not generate any network effect.

A recent study (Fuentelsaz et al., 2015) extends previous research on network industries (Carter and Wright, 1999) by analyzing the role that firm strategy plays in markets where network effects are important. The result is that firms can benefit from the existence of network effects through their strategic choices.

With the advent of the new Web 2.0, it becomes also interesting to consider the contribution of so-called user-generated content. This expression is usually referred to content precisely generated by users on the web to create new information: in this sense, the reference point is definitively Wikipedia (Ransbotham et al. 2012; Jullien, 2012), but other scholars (Smith, et al., 2012) have studied how brand-related user-generated content differs across social network as YouTube, Facebook, and Twitter.

The two-mode social network analysis by Ransbotham (2012) demonstrates that embedding content in the content–contributor network (i.e. Wikipedia) positively affects viewership.

Why so much attention specifically on Wikipedia? In this regard it is interesting to note that in the past Welser et al. (2011) dealt with the theme and starting from the species "Wikipedia", we got to the genus "wiki" by which is meant to be a (generally) free access website on which users can insert, add, modify, or delete content, the above mentioned user-generated content, using a simplified mark-up language or a rich-text editor.

In other words, Wikipedia is not just a website, but has in effect created an e-business model based on the free movement of information created and shared by users (user generated content) and subject to revision and moderation by the same users who are therefore the main judges as well as users. This mechanism involves, therefore, a process of continuous improvement aimed at refining and purifying the information from any possible distortions.

The aforementioned research (Welser et al. 2011) also suggests the presence of social roles within Wikipedia that, therefore, act as a social network. More deeply, the comparison is between two samples of Wikipedia users: long term dedicated editors and editors from a one-month window of new arrivals. Welser team found that, in the two groups, the proportions of editor types are similar; it's interesting to note that the number of new editors (from a one-month window) playing helpful roles is nearly equal the number found in the long term dedicated sample.

What are the practical implications of this reasoning? Informal socialisation has the potential provide decisive role-related labour despite growth and continuous change inside Wikipedia.

In this regard, the contribution of Mayer et al. (2015) is particularly suitable for investigating the activity of passive content consumers: typically, the impact on social media sites is difficult to measure, but Mayer's team explore the influence on Wikipedia page views, based on evidence derived from Reddit. Reddit is a web community which frequently links to Wikipedia articles. In brief, the week in which a post published on Reddit references a specific Wikipedia article is associated with a substantial increase in page views, taking as a reference prior and successive weeks (Mayer et al. 2015).

This analysis leads to a further critical point: in order to make a comprehensive study of a network's value, the quality of the links (bonds or ties) must be considered. Given the above, it is useful and appropriate to say a few words about the classical bipartition of network ties. As probably many readers already know, there are two kinds of ties: strong and weak.

STRONG AND WEAK TIES

In our lives, we categorize relationships in two types: strong ties, the strongest links, correspond to family and best friends; and weak ties, the weaker dealings, such as acquaintances. The set of our links constitutes our (social) network.

One of the most striking findings is that the more the network enlarges, the lower the percentage of minimum connections to tie the network together is (Erdos, 1961). In a network of 300 nodes, there were almost 50,000 possible connections, but it only takes 2% to ensure complete connection. In the case of 1000 points, the percentage drops to 1%. For a network of 6 billion people, the percentage produced by the calculations of Erdos is about 0,000000004%.

More analytically, in a network with n nodes, the percentage of connections needed to hold together the entire network is given by the formula:

$$\frac{\log\left(n\right)}{n}$$

Barabási and Albert (1999) proposed an upgrade with respect to the version of the Erdos theory of random networks to account for the scaling properties of a number of systems, including the link structure of the World Wide Web: clustering coefficient distribution. It decreases as the node degree increases. This distribution also follows a power law (Adamic and Huberman, 2000). This implies that the low-degree nodes belong to very dense sub-graphs. But Whereas the Barabási and Albert model predicts that older sites have more time to acquire links and gather links at a faster rate than newer sites, other scholars (Adamic et at., 2001) found no significant correlation between the age of a site and its number of links: an exciting site that appeared last year will have more links than a bland site created five years ago. Therefore, Adamic concluded that the rate of acquisition of new links is related not only to the website age, but also to the number of links the site already has: in other words, the more links a site has, the more visible it becomes and the more new links it will get.

These findings are based on the structure of the world wide web. A computer robot started from the site of the University of Notre Dame explores the web. The power law was found by 325.729 documents connected by 1.469.680 hypertext links. All these connections were characterised by the well-known long-tail. This example allows us to state that a limited number of nodes has a high number of connections. A very large number of nodes has a limited number of connections (Albert et al., 2000).

Albert and Barabási's team (2000) has also calculated the so-called the diameter of the web: the distance between internet pages is conceptually similar to the degrees of separation computed by Milgram. Ideally, it is possible to choose two pages at random and count the number of clicks needed to switch between them.

In the 2000's the diameter was found to be about 19. Even in a first approximation the discovered result appears divergent from the six degrees of separation (traditional small world network). This result is surprisingly good considering that on the internet there are several billion pages: This experiment on the diameter of the web, with regard to the subject of this work, it is important to provide further evidence of the strength of weak ties. Even in a network of enormous dimensions as is the case with the internet, the degree of separation is only 19.

In order to calculate this result, the internet applies a logarithmic dependence between the diameter of the web and the total number of documents in the network. This implication means that, even assuming a 1000% increase of the size of the web, the diameter would only increase from 19 to 21. In other words, this implication confers a great robustness to Barabási's research.

Once again Granovetter's social studies (1973) are of great relevance by focusing on the intensity of the links within the network: the introduction of weak ties randomly does not alter the aggregation coefficient within the network, but drastically reduces the degrees of separation between the points.

The relevance of weak ties found empirical evidence also on social media. The increasing ease of access to information through social media to communicate with a wide audience at a cost close to zero, initiates a process of democratisation of information (Farrel, 2012). Social networks marked a turning point in our era: the best in class is Facebook (Catenese, 2001; Ferrara, 2012).

According to De Meo et al. (2014), on Facebook most ties are weak. Indeed strong ties connect individuals in the same community; weak ties connect individuals in different communities. Managers have to take into consideration the importance of weak ties as a "bridge" between social groups. These figures serve as opinion leaders (Li and Du, 2001) through the word-of-mouth marketing in online blogs and social networks to become real trend setter (Phan et al., 2011).

SOLUTIONS AND RECOMMENDATIONS

Nowadays, economic literature has in realizing the importance of the internet in many sectors, from financial issues (Khan and Omar, 2013) to healthcare industry (Minor-Cooley et al., 2015), but also communication and connectivity (Gilinsky Jr et al. 2015).

However, the practical implications for companies and managers are not always very clear. Especially with respect to networks and social network websites there is not a unanimous way of thinking. The final section (conclusion) will be dedicated to the development of practical managerial implications, but with regard to this paragraph it must be emphasized that this study represents a bridge between the internet economy and the social network sciences.

To this end, in the course of this work three latent recommendations emerged and, here, they will be formalized in detail: first, this chapter shows that internet economy is not simply a synonym of e-business. Internet economy is a broader concept, with multiple features: inside the internet economy there is the e-business concept. Therefore, companies that carry out e-business must realise the importance of internet economy as strategic factor.

Secondly, this chapter presents the value of a network under a different light, which needs future research. Indeed, the next section will show research paths on which literature has not focused yet. Network analysis is not a distant concept from internet theories: most of the theories presented here were theorised years before internet diffusion. Therefore, our recommendation is that internet economy and network theories work together to create synergies.

Thirdly, the issue of weak ties is shown through the new light of possible applications to the internet economy. A larger network requires less effort (in percentage) in order to connect each node through weak ties: this is the power of social network websites, like Facebook, Twitter, LinkedIn, YouTube, falling into the classic definition of social networks, not to mention the phenomenon Wikipedia. Wikipedia, as mentioned in the previous chapter, has created a model of e-business that is often imitated and replicated. Therefore, social networks are no longer just a means of communication between people, but a business opportunity: through social media, managers can reach so many users (potential buyers) with minimal effort.

At this point, a final recommendation is useful in order to systematise the extensive literature analyzed: the aim of the following table is to offer to the reader concise and easy to read summary

Table 1 highlights the most relevant literature in order to simplify any future research, while the complete references are listed in the bibliography. All these works are listed not by relevance, but following a chronological criterion.

Table 1. Classification

Internet Economy and E-Business	Network Value	Strong and Weak Ties
Kolakota and Robinson, 1999	Shapiro and Varian, 1999	Erdos and Renyi, 1961
Barua et al., 1999	Carter and Wright, 1999	Granovetter, 1973
Norris et al., 2000	Domingos and Richardson, 2001	Granovetter, 1983
Mahadevan, 2000	Odlyzko and Tilly, 2005	Watts and Strogatz, 1998
Bartelt and Lamersdorf, 2001	Peppard and Rylander, 2006	Barabasi and Albert, 1999
Kogut, 2003	Arakji and Lang, 2007	Albert et al, 2000
Fink, 2006	Hendler and Goldbeck, 2008	Adamic and Huberman, 2000
Sanders, 2007	Welser et al. 2011	Adamic et al., 2001
Koellinger, 2008	Ransbotham et al., 2012	Li and Du, 2001
Oliveira and Martins, 2009	Jullien, 2012	Phan et al., 2011
Yuan et al., 2010	Fuentelsaz, 2015	Catanese, 2011
Prajogo and Olhager, 2012	Mayer et al, 2015	Farrel, 2012
Dominici, 2012	Kovarik, 2015	Ferrara, 2012
Chong 2014		De Meo et al., 2014

Having established a theoretical framework for the topic, this background will be the base from which to deduce the practical implications (in the concluding section) and, at the same time, a springboard for further researches.

FUTURE RESEARCH DIRECTIONS

This study aims to open a research path that leads on a specific theme that has not received enough attention in the previous literature. Considering the internet and websites as social networks, it would be possible to envisage an extension of the studies in the field of social capital (Ellison and Lampe, 2008), knowledge quality and inertia on the evolution of networks (Demirkan et al., 2012).

From a more closely organizational point of view, another interesting field of research could deepen the studies related to the so-called network orchestration (Paquin and Howard-Grenville, 2013) defined as the process of assembling and developing an inter-organizational network (Schiller et al. 2014).

The common denominator in all these new fields of research is the premise of considering the internet, websites and SNSs as social networks with the aim of studying their mechanisms in order to derive the economic implications helpful to the full understanding of the internet economy.

Finally, the works mentioned above have provided a support for the contribution of positive network effects, but they have not focused on the study of the internet as a competition network. Future research could also investigate the competitive relations within the internet.

CONCLUSION

According to Hollesen (2015), internet marketing management is the future not only for e-commerce, but also for traditional retailing. As previously stated, network analysis and social media marketing (SMM) are the new frontier (Stelzner, 2011)[4].

Indeed, other studies (Hoffman and Fedor, 2010), have confirmed the importance of frequent updates and incentives for participation in social media content. In addition, several creative strategies have been associated with customer engagement, image, and exclusivity messages (Ashley and Tuten, 2015).

In the light of what has been said, what is SMM? It is a set of strategies, on one hand to dominate the flow of communication on the web and, on the other hand, to exploit the network to obtain some benefits from social media. In other words, it is precisely what we were searching for: the contact point between network theories and the internet economy.

Following a broad interpretation of the internet economy as a broader concept than mere e-business (Bartelt and Lamersdorf, 2001), the SMM allows not only the management of social media, but the exploitation of the full potential of the Internet network.

What are the practical advantages? Social networks are no longer just a means of communication between people, nor an opportunity to be exploited for mere advertising investments. Social networks are, in effect, a new strategic business unit (SBU) and, as such, they require special attention and targeted resources both in financial terms and in terms of intellectual capital. In other words, social media marketing is emerging as a strong success factor for companies that believe in its power.

According to Stelzner (2011) benefits of social media marketing are: generating exposure for the business, increased traffic on website and, consequently, more subscribers, improved search ratings using SEO techniques, new business partnerships, generating qualified leads, reduced overall marketing expense (online advertising is cheap and more efficient that traditional communication) and improved sales.

These theoretical suggestions must be translated in practical implication: A substantial change of perspective is requested of the companies because managers should consider the need for the incorporation of new human resources specially dedicated to activities on the web: social media managers, web strategists, SEO (search engine optimization) consultants.

In more detail, the SEO techniques allow users who use search engines to be directed to a particular web page. Similarly, the techniques of SMM allow viral spread of promotional content and advertising.

The SMM requires the use of specific resources within the organization. As suggested by some authors recognizing the importance of the SMM (Smith et al, 2012; Andzulis et al., 2012). Another practical implication could be the creation of specific performance indicators. The reference point is the so-called SMM-ROI, Social Media Marketing Return on Investment (Hofman and Fodor, 2010): it is a simple and useful tool to measure the impact of the SMM on profitability.

Subsequently, other authors extended this concept and proposed a methodology to integrate SMM-ROI and WOM value, a customer's word-of-mouth (Kumar et al., 2013). They created a unique metric to measure the net influence wielded by a user in a social network, which they named customer influence effect (CIE), and then predicted the user's ability to generate the spread of viral information.

Therefore, the main advantage of the techniques of SMM is that, with a very low access cost, businesses are able to reach an extremely vast public. Moreover, through social media websites businesses can select a specific target: for instance, Facebook offers demographic (age, gender), social (education, occupation) and cultural filters (interests, religion, sport) in order for advertising campaigns to be directed to the selected target.

Further expanding the perspective of this investigation, it is necessary to involve not only enterprises, but also the institutions (schools, universities, educational centres) for the development of new professional figures who will become part of a new labour market which is a fertile territory to discover: web marketing strategy and social media management.

REFERENCES

Adamic, L. A., Huberman, B. A., Barabási, A.-L., Albert, R., Jeong, H., & Bianconi, G. (2000). Power-law distribution of the world wide web. *Science, 287*(5461), 2115–2115. doi:10.1126/science.287.5461.2115a

Adamic, L. A., Lukose, R. M., Puniyani, A. R., & Huberman, B. A. (2001). Search in power-law networks. *Physical Review E: Statistical, Nonlinear, and Soft Matter Physics, 64*(4), 046135. doi:10.1103/PhysRevE.64.046135 PMID:11690118

Albert, R., Jeong, H., & Barabási, A. L. (2000). Diameter of the World Wide Web. *Nature,* (401): 130–131.

Andzulis, J. M., Panagopoulos, N. G., & Rapp, A. (2012). A review of social media and implications for the sales process. *Journal of Personal Selling & Sales Management, 32*(3), 305–316. doi:10.2753/PSS0885-3134320302

Arakji, R. Y., & Lang, K. R. (2007). Digital consumer networks and producer-consumer collaboration: Innovation and product development in the digital entertainment industry. In *System Sciences, 2007. HICSS 2007. 40th Annual Hawaii International Conference on* (pp. 211c-211c). IEEE.

Ashley, C., & Tuten, T. (2015). Creative strategies in social media marketing: An exploratory study of branded social content and consumer engagement. *Psychology and Marketing, 32*(1), 15–27. doi:10.1002/mar.20761

Barabási, A. L., & Albert, R. (1999). Emergence of scaling in random networks. *Science, 286*(5439), 509–512. doi:10.1126/science.286.5439.509 PMID:10521342

Barnes, J. A. (1979). Network analysis: orienting notion, rigorous technique or substantive field of study? In P. W. Holland & S. Leinhardt (Eds.), *Perspectives on Social Network Analysis* (pp. 403–423). New York: Academic. doi:10.1016/B978-0-12-352550-5.50024-9

Bartelt, A., & Lamersdorf, W. (2001). A multi-criteria taxonomy of business models in electronic commerce. *International Conference on Distributed Systems Platform*, Heidelberg, Germany. doi:10.1007/3-540-45598-1_18

Barua, A., Pinnel, J., Shutter, J., & Whinston, A. B. (1999). Measuring the internet economy. Center for Research in Electronic Commerce, University of Texas.

Buchanan, M. (2003). *Nexus: small worlds and the groundbreaking theory of networks*. WW Norton & Company.

Carter, M., & Wright, J. (1999). Interconnection in network industries. *Review of Industrial Organization, 14*(1), 1–25. doi:10.1023/A:1007715215394

Castells, M. (2000). The information age: economy, society and culture.: Vol. 1. *The rise of the network society*. Oxford, UK: Blackwell.

Castells, M. (2003). The power of identity: The information Age: Economy, society and culture: Vol. 2. *The information age*. Oxford, UK: Blackwell.

Castells, M. (2007). Communication, power and counter power in the network society. *International Journal of Communication*, 238–266.

Catanese, S. A., De Meo, P., Ferrara, E., Fiumara, G., & Provetti, A. (2011). Crawling Facebook for social network analysis purposes. In *Proceedings of the international conference on web intelligence, mining and semantics* (p. 52). ACM. doi:10.1145/1988688.1988749

Chesbrough, H., & Rosembloom, R. (2002). The role of the business model in capturing value from innovation: Evidence from Xerox Corporation's technology spin-off companies. *Industrial and Corporate Change, 11*(3), 529–555. doi:10.1093/icc/11.3.529

Chong, S. (2014). Business process management for SMEs: An exploratory study of implementation factors for the Australian wine industry. *Journal of Information Systems and Small Business, 1*(1-2), 41–58.

Dalton, M. (1959). *Men who manage New York*. John Wiley and Sons.

De Meo, P., Ferrara, E., Fiumara, G., & Provetti, A. (2014). On Facebook, most ties are weak. *Communications of the ACM, 57*(11), 78–84. doi:10.1145/2629438

Demirkan, I., Leeds, D. L., & Demirkan, S. (2012). Exploring the role of network characteristics, knowledge quality and inertia on the evolution of scientific networks. *Journal of Management, 39*(6), 1462–1489. doi:10.1177/0149206312453739

Doerr, L. S., & Powell, W. W. (2005). Networks and economic life. In The Handbook of economic sociology. Russell Sage foundation and Princeton University Press.

Domingos, P., & Richardson, M. (2001). Mining the network value of customers. In *Proceedings of the seventh ACM SIGKDD international conference on Knowledge discovery and data mining* (pp. 57-66). ACM. doi:10.1145/502512.502525

Dominici, G. (2012). E-business Model: a content based taxonomy of literature. *International Journal of Management and Administrative Sciences, 1*, 10-20.

Duff, A. S., Craig, D., & McNeill, D. A. (1996). A note on the origins of the information society. *Journal of Information Science, 22*(2), 39–45. doi:10.1177/016555159602200204

Ellison, N. B., & Lampe, C. (2008). Social, capital, self-esteem and use of online social network sites: A longitudinal analysis. *Journal of Applied Developmental Psychology, 29*(6), 434–445. doi:10.1016/j.appdev.2008.07.002

Erdos, P., & Renyi, A. (1961). On the strength of connectedness of a random graph. *Acta Mathematica Hungarica*, 152–163.

Farrell, H. (2012). The consequences of the internet for politics. *Annual Review of Political Science, 15*(1), 35–52. doi:10.1146/annurev-polisci-030810-110815

Fink, D. (2006). The professional doctorate: Its relativity to the PhD and relevance for the knowledge economy. *International Journal of Doctoral Studies, 1*(1), 35–44.

Fuchs, C. (2009). Information and communication technologies and society a contribution to the critique of the political economy of the internet. *European Journal of Communication, 24*(1), 69–87. doi:10.1177/0267323108098947

Fuentelsaz, L., Garrido, E., & Maicas, J. P. (2015). A strategic approach to network value in network industries. *Journal of Management, 41*(3), 864–892. doi:10.1177/0149206312448399

Gilinsky, A. Jr, Thach, E. C., & Thompson, K. J. (2015). Connectivity & Communication: A Study of How Small Wine Businesses Use the Internet. *Journal of Small Business Strategy, 14*(2), 37–57.

Granovetter, M. (1973). The strength of weak ties. *American Journal of Sociology, 78*(6), 1360–1380. doi:10.1086/225469

Granovetter, M. (1983). The strength of weak ties: A network theory revisited. *Sociological Theory, 1*, 201–233. doi:10.2307/202051

Gross, J. L., & Yellen, J. (2005). *Graph theory and its applications*. CRC Press.

Hendler, J., & Golbeck, J. (2008). Metcalfe's law, Web 2.0, and the Semantic Web. *Web Semantics: Science, Services, and Agents on the World Wide Web, 6*(1), 14–20. doi:10.1016/j.websem.2007.11.008

Hoffman, D. L., & Fodor, M. (2010). Can you measure the ROI of your social media marketing. *MIT Sloan Management Review, 52*(1), 41–49.

Hollensen, S. (2015). *Marketing management: A relationship approach.* Pearson Education.

Jullien, N. (2012). *What we know about Wikipedia: A review of the literature analyzing the project (s).* Available at SSRN, 2053597.

Kalakota, R., & Robinson, M. (2001). *E-business 2.0: Roadmap for Success.* Addison-Wesley Professional.

Khan, M. N. A. A., & Omar, N. A. (2013). A Study of Importance Items of Internet Financial Reporting: A Case of Malaysian Auditors. *Middle-East Journal of Scientific Research, 17*(3), 395–406.

Koellinger, P. (2008). The relationship between technology, innovation, and firm performance—Empirical evidence from e-business in Europe. *Research Policy, 37*(8), 1317–1328. doi:10.1016/j.respol.2008.04.024

Kogut, B. (2003). Is there global convergence in regulation and electronic markets? The global internet economy. MIT Press.

Kovarik, B. (2015). *Revolutions in communication: Media history from Gutenberg to the digital age.* Bloomsbury Publishing.

Kumar, V., Bhaskaran, V., Mirchandani, R., & Shah, M. (2013). Practice prize winner-creating a measurable social media marketing strategy: Increasing the value and ROI of intangibles and tangibles for hokey pokey. *Marketing Science, 32*(2), 194–212. doi:10.1287/mksc.1120.0768

Li, F., & Du, T. C. (2011). Who is talking? An ontology-based opinion leader identification framework for word-of-mouth marketing in online social blogs. *Decision Support Systems, 51*(1), 190–197. doi:10.1016/j.dss.2010.12.007

Mahadevan, B. (2000). Business models for Internet-based e-commerce. *California Management Review, 42*(4), 55–69. doi:10.2307/41166053

Metcalfe, B. (1995). Metcalfe's law: A network becomes more valuable as it reaches more users. *InfoWorld,* (October), 2.

Milgram, S. (1967). The small-world problem Psychology Today. Sussex Publishers LLC.

Minor-Cooley, D. O., Bush, A., & Madupu, V. (2015). How Consumers are Searching: The Importance of the Internet to the Healthcare Industry. In *Proceedings of the 2008 Academy of Marketing Science (AMS)Annual Conference* (pp. 176-176). Springer International Publishing.

Norris, G., Balls, J. D., & Hartley, K. M. (2000). *E-business and ERP: Transforming the Enterprise.* John Wiley and Sons, Inc.

Odlyzko, A., & Tilly, B. (2005). *A refutation of Metcalfe's Law and a better estimate for the value of networks and network interconnections.* Manuscript.

Oliveira, T., & Martins, M. F. (2009). Firms' Patterns of e-Business Adoption: Evidence for the European Union-27. In *Proceedings of the 3rd European Conference on Information Management and Evaluation*. Academic Conferences Limited.

Peppard, J., & Rylander, A. (2006). From value chain to value network: Insights for mobile operators. *European Management Journal, 24*(2), 128–141. doi:10.1016/j.emj.2006.03.003

Phan, M., Thomas, R., & Heine, K. (2011). Social media and luxury brand management: The case of Burberry. *Journal of Global Fashion Marketing, 2*(4), 213–222. doi:10.1080/20932685.2011.10593099

Prajogo, D., & Olhager, J. (2012). Supply chain integration and performance: The effects of long-term relationships, information technology and sharing, and logistics integration. *International Journal of Production Economics, 135*(1), 514–522. doi:10.1016/j.ijpe.2011.09.001

Ransbotham, S., Kane, G. C., & Lurie, N. H. (2012). Network characteristics and the value of collaborative user-generated content. *Marketing Science, 31*(3), 387–405. doi:10.1287/mksc.1110.0684

Reed, E. P. (1999). *The sneaky exponential- beyond Metcalfe's law to the power of community building*. Context Magazine.

Reed, E. P. (2001). The law of the pack. *Harvard Business Review*, (March), 63–78. PMID:11213694

Rosenbaum, J. E., Kariya, T., Settersten, R., & Maier, T. (1990). Market and network theories of the transition from high school to work: Their application to industrialized societies. *Annual Review of Sociology, 16*(1), 263–299. doi:10.1146/annurev.so.16.080190.001403

Roy, D. (1954). Efficiency and 'the fix': Informal intergroup relations in a piecework machine shop. *American Journal of Sociology, 60*(3), 255–267. doi:10.1086/221535

Sanders, N. R. (2007). An empirical study of the impact of e-business technologies on organizational collaboration and performance. *Journal of Operations Management, 25*(6), 1332–1347. doi:10.1016/j.jom.2007.01.008

Schiller, F., Penn, A. S., & Basson, L. (2014). Analyzing networks in industrial ecology–a review of Social-Material Network Analyses. *Journal of Cleaner Production, 76*, 1–11. doi:10.1016/j.jclepro.2014.03.029

Shapiro, C., Varian, H. R., & Becker, W. E. (1999). Information rules: A strategic guide to the network economy. *The Journal of Economic Education, 30*(2), 189–190. doi:10.2307/1183273

Smith, A. N., Fischer, E., & Yongjian, C. (2012). How does brand-related user-generated content differ across YouTube, Facebook, and Twitter? *Journal of Interactive Marketing, 26*(2), 102–113. doi:10.1016/j.intmar.2012.01.002

Stelzner, M. A. (2011). Social media marketing industry report. *Social Media Examiner*, 41.

Travers, J., & Milgram, S. (1969). An experimental study of the small world problem. *Sociometry*, 425–443.

Watts, D. J., & Strogatz, S. H. (1998). Collective dynamics of small world networks. *Nature, 393*(6684), 440–442. doi:10.1038/30918 PMID:9623998

Welser, H. T., Cosley, D., Kossinets, G., Lin, A., Dokshin, F., Gay, G., & Smith, M. (2011, February). Finding social roles in Wikipedia. In *Proceedings of the 2011 iConference* (pp. 122-129). ACM. doi:10.1145/1940761.1940778

Yuan, L., Zhongfeng, S., & Yi, L. (2010). Can strategic flexibility help firms profit from product innovation? *Technovation, 30*(5), 300–309. doi:10.1016/j.technovation.2009.07.007

KEY TERMS AND DEFINITIONS

E-Business: Integrated management processes and tools for the creation and transfer of value (Strategic relevance).

E-Commerce: Set of levers for managing the digital distribution channel (Operational relevance).

Internet Economy: Set of factors which form an online market. It is composed of: physical infrastructure (ICT), business infrastructure, intermediaries and traders.

Power Law: Functional relationship between two quantities. When a quantity changes (independent variable) the other quantity (dependent variable) changes more than proportionally.

SEO (Search Engine Optimization): Method to improve search engine rating through organic positioning.

SMM (Social Media Marketing): Set of strategies to dominate the flow of communication on the web and to exploit the network to obtain some benefits from social media.

Strong Ties: The strongest links; correspond to family and best friends.

Weak Ties: The weaker dealings, such as acquaintances. A weak tie becomes a "bridge" when it connects social groups (not only in a spatial sense) that would otherwise be disconnected.

ENDNOTES

[1] Already in 1999, The internet economy was in full swing in France. There was already an active research program affiliated with the institute of International Business at the Stockholm school of Economics and with the Science Centre in Berlin.

[2] Probably the first formulatio is dated by George Gilder, but the spread of the law is uniquely traced back to Metcalfe that made it famous through the application to Ethernet (Shapiro et al., 1999).

[3] In the projection proposed by Odlyzko and Tilly (2005), if we have two networks each with $n = 2^{20} = 1.048.576$ embers, then (assuming the logarithm is to base 2, and the constant of proportionality is 1) each is valued at $20n$. If these two networks interconnect, the resulting new single network will have size $n = 2^{21} = 2.097.152$ that is only about 5% gain over the total variation of the two separate networks.

[4] In this regard, to further deepen the importance of social networks, the Appendix shows the results of the Social Media Marketing Industry Report: How Marketers Are Using Social Media to Grow Their Businesses (Stelzner, 2011).

APPENDIX: SOCIAL MEDIA MARKETING INDUSTRY REPORT

How Marketers Are Using Social Media to Grow Their Businesses

Data Source: Stelzner, M. A. (2011). Social media marketing industry report. *Social Media Examiner*, 41

Commonly Used Social Media Marketing Tools

Facebook = 92%
Twitter = 84%
LinkedIn = 71%
Blogs = 68%
YouTube = 56%
Social Bookmarking =26%
Forums = 24%
Foursquare =17%
MySpace: = 6%

Social Media Tools People Want to Learn

Facebook = 70%
Blogs = 69%
Social Bookmarking/news site = 59%
Twitter = 59%
LinkedIn = 55%
YouTube or other video = 55%
Geolocation (Foursquare) = 46%
Forums = 40%
Groupon = 30%
MySpace = 10%

Survey Participant Demographics

3342 participants
Market segment:
50% business-to-business marketers;
50% business-to-consumer marketers
Sex: 60% female - 40% male

Table 7. Survey participants

Age	0 - 19	20 - 29	30 - 39	40 - 49	50 - 59	> 60
Perc.	0%	19%	26%	29%	19%	7%

Country of origin:

64% from the United States
7% from Canada
6% from United Kingdom
4% Australia
2% Netherlands
16% Other countries combined

Chapter 4
Usability Evaluation of Social Media Web Sites and Applications via Eye-Tracking Method

Duygu Mutlu-Bayraktar
Istanbul University, Turkey

ABSTRACT

This chapter describes usability studies of website-based and mobile application-based social media sites. In the study including 10 university students, the completion time of assigned tasks were measured along with click numbers and completion situations. These measures were analyzed. Data obtained from eye tracking movements was analyzed, and the results were evaluated. According to the results, the users can complete most of the tasks, but completion time varied. The participants had difficulties completing settings menu tasks except menus previously used in social media. When eye tracking results were examined, it was revealed that they mostly focused on the left side of websites and mobile applications. The participants stated that mobile applications were more useful than websites. According to eye-tracking data obtained in the study and the users' opinions, mobile social media applications were more functional than their websites.

1. INTRODUCTION

Communication, stating an opinion, looking for a job, and sharing via social media have been among the most common uses of the Internet. There are globally about 1.96 billion social network users in the year of 2015, and it is suggested that the number of the social network audience will be total 2.44 billion as of 2018 (Statista, 2015). Social media is used to share and discuss experiences and knowledge of Internet tools and other people in electronic media (Bryer and Zavattaro, 2011; Gursakal, 2009; Ito, et al., 2008; Boyd, 2007).

DOI: 10.4018/978-1-5225-0648-5.ch004

Social media provides us ways to communicate with other individuals over the Internet, and those people can be our target market, customers, colleagues, or anyone corresponding with us through conversations (Stratten, 2012).

The Internet statistics of Turkey laid out in the report "We Are Social" are as follows: There are 37.7 million active internet users in Turkey. According to this, it seems that active Internet user penetration is 49% in Turkey, which has 76.7 million citizens. In Turkey, in which there are 40 million active social media accounts, the penetration rate of social media accounts is 52%.

In terms of mobile application usage, there are 32 million active social media accounts. According to this, it seems that 80% of 40 million active social media accounts are accessed from mobile.

When the statistics of Internet and social media users were compared with the report of 2014, it was revealed that the numbers of active Internet users, active social media users and mobile users in Turkey increased 5%, 11%, and 2%, respectively.

During the day, the Internet users in Turkey spend about their four hours 37 minutes on the Internet, two hours 51 minutes in mobile internet, and two hours 56 minutes in social media. The time users spending to watch television was determined as average two hours 17 minutes per day. When the most widely used social networks in Turkey were examined, Facebook, WhatsApp, and Facebook Messenger were in the first three places, and they were followed by Twitter, Google+ and Skype (Kemp, 2014).

Social media are different from traditional media channels in terms of putting users at the center of the content production process and providing the opportunity to share that content. Traditional media production mostly requires specialized skills and training. This is not the case for most of social media; in some cases, required skills are completely different in some cases. Namely, everyone can provide self-produced contributions to social media.

The use of social media became such a habit of virtual environment users and the communication environment that broad masses from all cultures and every walk of life have shown interest, and this massness has added a new dimension to the concept of socialization.

As smartphone use increases along with faster connectivity speeds (Mobile Marketer, 2009). The Mobile Web will be used more than the desktop-based Web in future days (MobileBeyond, 2010). The accessibility and practicality of social media increased with the uses of mobile devices and mobile apps to access social media platforms and tools (Cooke & Buckley, 2008). Moreover, it has been statistically revealed that individuals started to spend more online time (Facebook, 2011). One of the important aspects of the fast growth of the mobile Web is the use of increasing numbers of smartphone Web browsers for access to social media, mainly social networking sites (Gonsalves, 2010; MobileBeyond, 2010).

Individuals should feel safe during surfing social media, and they should be able to find solutions in the interface of the website as soon as possible during any adverse situation. The authors report that Facebook is mostly used to have fun and to share information about activities occurring in one's social network, and instant messaging (IM-ing) serves to meet the need to maintain and develop relations (Quan-Haase & Young, 2010; Pentina, et al., 2013; Lee & Moonhee, 2011).

When people interact with social media platforms, the issue of usability comes to the fore. Human-computer interaction (HCI) focuses on usable design and development of technologies used in different environments. Usability can be assessed in terms of effectiveness, productivity, and satisfaction. Usability can be measured with the data obtained from the use of system by target users. In this method called the usability test, required data is gathered following each step during test application, and the data is then evaluated.

While various interface evaluation tasks are performed in traditional usability tests, participants sometimes get lost, and researchers work to determine which interface features cause distractions (Akcapinar, et al., 2012; Mutlu-Bayraktar & Bayram, 2015). In addition to obtaining data about their experiences, researchers also want to know how much time participants spent and where they focused on the site (Nielsen & Pernice, 2009; Mutlu-Bayraktar & Bayram, 2013).

It was stated that the data obtained from eye movement tracking method was more useful than the data collected from a normal survey. On the contrary to the thinking aloud method, recording eye movements of participants may allow us to answer many questions about usability during fulfilling any task that requires human-computer interaction (Karn, Ellis & Julliano, 1999).

In the usability studies, Goldberg and Kotval (1999) suggest that tracking eye movements provides important information about detecting the strategies of users. In the design of a website interface, eye tracking data can provide information about where people pay attention, which information they ignore, and what they are mostly disturbed by (Russel, 2005). According to the result of the study carried out by Josephson and Holmes (2002), when the participants were asked to visit three different websites constantly, it was found that some participants followed a particular visual way in line with their habits.

Acartürk and Cagiltay (2006) stated that usability degree was obtained from assessment of effectiveness, productivity, and satisfaction together. Efficiency represents how much of the tasks given to people using site or software are fulfilled (Tonbuloglu & Bayram, 2012). Productivity is evaluated by determining how long the user does the assigned work in website, which path the user follows, and how many step it takes. For users, achieving to the right place with the right steps and the shortest route can be explained by productivity. Usability concept can be explained by the sum of the efficiency and productivity concepts. According to Bayram and Yeni (2011), usability is a measure related about how easily the process can be completed by individuals according to the specific roles within the scope of a product or system. User satisfaction represents whether the user appreciates the application and their experiences with it. Although satisfaction does not have the same significance with efficiency and productivity, it is affected by them. Satisfaction is determined by satisfaction surveys designed for this purpose (Cagiltay, 2006).

Paying attention to the design of websites and their usability has become an important issue today. In this concept, many variables such as people's interest and characteristics and intended use of product have priority during defining the necessary features of websites because these variables are accepted as important (Lee & Koubek, 2010).

The usability of social media (Twitter, Facebook, and LinkedIn) has been not previously evaluated via the eye tracking method (according to the best knowledge of this author). However, Schiessl, et al. (2003) performed eye tracking, application usability and media search in Humboldt University, Berlin. According to the research, eye tracking, visual attention and conventional boundaries of usability methods were used, and more realistic results were obtained than traditional methods. According to the results, individuals focused on pictures and the left side of websites.

In usability studies, perceptions of the users were generally measured via surveys and the time needed for tasks and the success rate was recorded. However, these methods cannot give information about what the users do and when they do those actions, or the methods provide subjective results (Fukuda & Bub, 2003).

According to Goldberg and Kotval (1999), following eye movement in usability studies gives important information to define strategies of users. Nowadays, traditional usability tests are still widely used in determining the quality of designs. Traditional testing generally includes participants having to perform several tasks while the researcher performs observations. The following aspects are measured (Namahn, 2000): time to complete a task, success percentage of participants, number and types of errors, and subjective perceived levels of user friendliness of the system.

Usability evaluation techniques can be listed in two main topics: expert analysis and yser participation (Dix, et al., 2004).

1. **Expert Analysis:** Here, an expert examines design in this method and searches for the effect on a typical user. The main goal is to determine the sections causing difficulties. Expert Analysis methods include the following (Schneiderman & Plaisant, 2005):
    a. Scenario-based (Heuristic) Evaluation,
    b. Directive criticism,
    c. Consistency control,
    d. Mental/Logical Instructions,
    e. Formal Usability Control.
2. User participation methods include the following (Dix, et al., 2004):
    a. Experimental Studies,
    b. Interrogation Techniques,
    c. **Observational Techniques:**
        i. **Think Aloud:** It is a kind of observation format including to tell what participants perform and observe momentarily or retroactively.
        ii. **Cooperative Evaluation:** Change in saying what they think is known as cooperative evaluation. At the beginning of the session, evaluators want users to tell what they think or they ask questions to users.
        iii. **Protocol Analysis:** It is the method that user actions and verbal situations are recorded. Paper and pencil method is limited by the writing speed of analyst. Audio recording is useful during thinking aloud. Video recording has advantage due to showing what participants do and special equipment is needed.
        iv. **Automated Analysis:** Video, audio and system recordings are performed and analyzed with a multimedia work station. Post-task Walkthroughs: After the case, it reflects the actions of participants not speaking during the actual observation.
        v. **Psychological Measurement:** Heart activity, activity of sweat glands, provocative situation or mental effort, activities of muscles and brain are observed to determine factors that cause stress and relieve user.
        vi. **Eye-Tracking:** Eye tracking method provides eye movement data about focused areas while people following content on screen, objects that they ignore and they are disturbed (Underwood & Radach, 1998; Russell, 2005). Eye tracking measurements are quite valuable in terms of supporting and verifying the results previously produced in multimedia studies. Moreover, eye movements deeply provide qualitative and quantitative data about processing information by users. This method helps to find individual differences via tracking eye movements and to interact with source provided (Liu, Lai, & Chuang, 2011).

Eye movements are related to cognitive operations in the brain, so that it provides to obtain information about these operations and processes via observing and interpreting eye movements (Biedert, Buscher, & Dengel, 2009). It is quite important that experimental environments prepared with this method measuring cognitive processes should be natural and they should be in a way that participants will not feel like they are in experimental environment. Simple-to-use eye-tracking device located away from should be preferred to the device mounted on head (Namahn, 2000). Within the scope of this study, it was integrated under the monitor in Human-Computer Interaction laboratory and unnoticed eye tracking device was used.

Definitions of some terms used for eye tracking data were listed below (Jacob and Karn, 2003):

- **Fixation:** Fixing eye, looking at object or areas generally with 2-degree distribution threshold and minimum 100-200 ms duration.
- **Gaze Duration:** The duration that eye looks at a certain point via keeping on.
- **Scan Path:** Roaming pattern of fixed gaze on screen (See Figure 1).
- **Area of Interest:** Attractive picture or visual environmental area that researcher specifies (See Figure 2).
- **Heat Map:** The screens are rated with colors on heat maps according to gaze duration and number (See Figure 3).

In addition to these data, images are obtained from video records saved by cameras found in HCI laboratory. It provides important information via enabling to observe individuals' reactions and behaviors in video and via being an information store including visual and audio sides.

The eye tracking method provides eye movement data about areas where users paid attention, the areas which subjects ignored, and the perceived irritating things when people follow content on screen (Underwood & Radach, 1998; Russell, 2005). Eye tracking measurements are quite valuable in terms of support and confirmation of the results produced in previous multimedia environment studies. More-

Figure 1. Scan path data

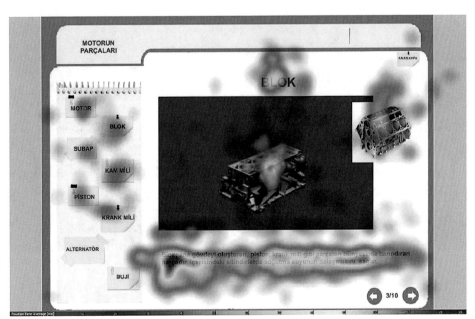

Figure 2. Area of interest data

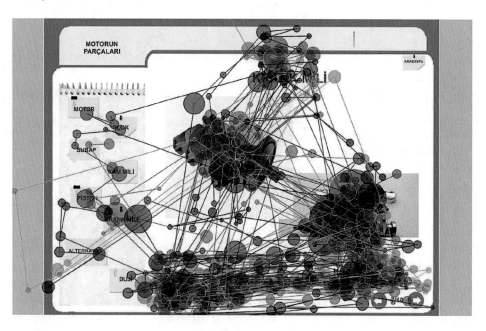

Figure 3. Heat map data

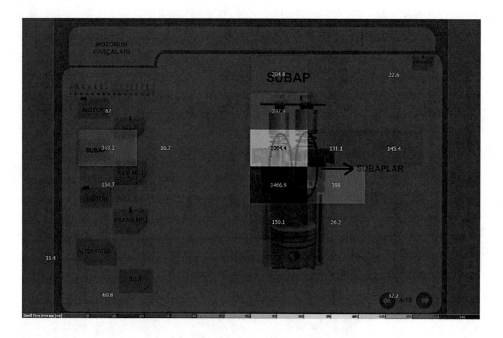

over, eye movements deeply provide qualitative and quantitative data about processing of information by users. This method helps about finding individual differences and interacting with presented source via tracking eye movements (Liu, Lai, & Chuang, 2011).

Eye movement is related with cognitive processes in the brain. This means that observing and interpreting eye movements may be suggestive of cognitive processes and steps in the brain (Biedert, Buscher & Dengel, 2009). It is really important that experimental environments should be as natural as possible, so that participants do not feel that they are in an artificial experimental environment. Simple-to-use eye-tracking devices located away from a person's face should be preferred over head-mounted device (Namahn, 2000). Within the scope of this study, an unobtrusive eye tracking device integrated under screen was used in Human-Computer Interaction laboratory.

This study was designed to study the usability of social media platforms as websites and as mobile applications. This study included 10 university students, and it measured the completion time of tasks given to the users, the numbers of clicks, and task completion situations. Meanwhile data obtained from eye tracking movements was analyzed, and the results were evaluated.

1.1. The Intended Use of Social Media

The use of Facebook by users varies from culture to culture. For example, while students in France use Facebook to keep in touch with their friends and to refresh their old friendships, they do not prefer memberships to applications containing entertainments and groups (Facebook.com). While Japanese adolescents do not prefer Facebook too much due to "safety" issues, the social networks in Mexico are used to keep in touch with friends, to make new friends, and to find girl/boyfriends (Kennedy, 2009).

When we look at Facebook which is preferred in Turkey as in the world, Turkey with 12,382,000 users, is the fourth largest country of Facebook users after the USA, England, and Indonesia.

In a study performed to reveal the use status of Facebook in Turkey by Sener (2010), a total of 254 users answered the survey performed on a group. While 98% of the users participating in Facebook Research added people they have already known, 42.5% added newly met people, and 15.7% added friends of friends. Only 6.6% of the users added people they didn't know. According to this result, unlike other social networks, it seems that Facebook is a place that users communicate with people they have already known rather than making new friends. Moreover, the high adding rate of newly met people face-to-face gives an impression about that users use Facebook to know these people better and to keep in touch with them. In this sense, Facebook helps to protect and maintain daily-life friendships on virtual platforms. The most important feature of Facebook distinguishing it from other social network is that communication is among known people, and the environment of confidence is present. Therefore, Facebook has created an Internet-based social environment where people chosen from different social environments can be found together.

In the Sener (2010)'s study, the users indicate that the most important reasons to use Facebook are to communicate with friends (66.2%), to find friends they lost track of (37.7%) and to share videos/photos they like (20.6%). Using other applications of Facebook, forming group, solving tests, and playing a game are among the least preferred activities. In a similar study, the first reason among the use purposes of social network site is to communicate with people they are familiar with ("to communicate with people I know 96.5%"). The second reason is to get information about events related to the agenda. In accordance with this result, it can be said that the participants see social networks as a source of information (to get information about events related to the agenda 93.1%).

The relationship between loneliness levels and the use of social networks of students in Turkey was investigated, and it was revealed that loneliness points increased according to the frequency of use of social networks. Moreover, 48.3% of the users feeling asocial agree with the opinion "I don't feel alone thanks to Facebook". So, this shows that Facebook can be a loneliness troubleshooting tool for this group.

The aim of the study performed by Dal and Dal (2014) was to investigate social website usage habits of individuals and to reveal the relationship between personality characteristics and the use of social websites and to lay out personality differences between individuals as members of social websites. In this context, a quantitative research was performed with 350 university students who are in 15-24 age range and who use social websites actively. The results of the study showed that there was a significant and linear relationship between the average time spent daily on social websites and the average scores of personality dimension of Compatible and Openness to Experiences. It was revealed that the daily average time male users spent on social networks was higher than the time female users spent.

In the research performed to measure social media addiction of young people by Kırık et al., (2015), the study group included 271 students in 13-19 age range. According to the results, although there was no significant difference between genders in terms of social media addiction, a significant difference was present in terms of age, daily time spent on the Internet and the frequency of daily visit of profiles on social networks. The results revealed that while social media addiction which is lowest at age of 14 increased with the age until 17 and then decreased at age of 18. In addition, it showed that social media addiction significantly increased when daily time spent on the Internet and the frequency of profile visit on social networks increased. In the study, the recommendations on what needs to be done were also presented to prevent the addiction.

Social media usage status and the intended usage of students studying in vocational schools and their opinions on the use of social media in the educational context were investigated. The study has been carried out in the screening model. The sampling of the study included 344 individuals containing 12 female and 332 male. As a result of the study, it was revealed that social websites had a positive effect on high school education and educational use of social networks could be useful in terms of communication, cooperation and sharing sources according to the students' opinions. It was found that the intended uses of social websites by the students were mostly to communicate with old friends, to join groups containing common interests and needs and to share more information in a short time.

According to the students participating in the study, while social websites have positive effects in terms of communication, socialization, sharing, self-expression and psychological relief, they also have negative effects such as spending too much time, decreasing course productivity, distraction and prevention of socialization. Therefore, although social websites can have positive effects on increasing learning performance in education, it is needed to be careful during usage process and to be prepared against students who can be negative examples (Uysal, 2013).

In the thesis study of Bostanci (2010), the development of social media and the usage habits of communication faculty students were investigated.

Social media taking a place in our daily life with the Internet is felt to be important day by day. Therefore, social media dealt with mass media plays an important role in socialization. Our aim was to introduce social media adding a new dimension to the Internet which influences our lives in recent years and to reveal which social media tools are used by communication faculty students for which purposes and what their priorities are. In the study, literature search and survey methods were used. The basic assumptions before the study are that social networks, important parts of social media, are frequently used among young people and these people tend to communicate with their friends and make new friends via social networks. At the end of the study, it is revealed that these assumptions are true and Facebook is the most frequently used social network among the participants. In addition, it is found that the primary purpose of using social networks is to communicate with friends, in other words to be aware of social environment.

2. METHODOLOGY

2.1. The Aim of Study

In this study, how the users implement the activities that they want to perform in social media such as Facebook, Twitter, and LinkedIn are evaluated. The study aims to evaluate usability by analyzing information about how, how long and which results the participants perform the assigned tasks. With the data obtained from the study results, it is aimed to reveal incomplete and non-functional aspects of Facebook, Twitter and LinkedIn websites and their mobile applications.

2.2. Method

The study model was designated as a case study. The case study method is used to longitudinally investigate a case or an event in detail rather than to investigate a limited number of variables and to follow certain rules. Case studies are the studies to look at what happens in real environment, to collect data systematically, to analyze and to reveal results (Davey, 1991). In the study, 5 tasks were given to the participants for each Facebook, Twitter, LinkedIn websites and mobile applications. While they were performing these tasks, their eye movements were recorded. The interviews were carried out with semi-structured interview method after participants completed the tasks.

2.3. Participants

Participants were selected with convenient method among Istanbul University students. The participants consist of 10 volunteer university students from the departments where the researcher had access. The average age was 22, and the information about their departments and social media accounts are listed in Table 1.

2.4. Experiment Laboratory: Human Computer Interaction Laboratory

The study was carried out in Human-Computer Interaction Lab of Open and Distance Education Faculty in Istanbul University. There are images taken from the lab below (See Figure 4).

2.4.1. Eye-Tracking Device

It is a device that provides information about where, what, how long and how many times the participant looks at the screen and records eye movements during the time that the user performs the test. The device is also connected to the observer computer that records screen image of the user (See Figure 5).

Table 1. Properties of participants

Participants	Department	Age	Sex	Facebook Account	Twitter Account	LinkedIn Account
User 1	Turkish Education	22	Woman	+	-	-
User 2	Turkish Education	21	Woman	+	+	-
User 3	Turkish Education	22	Woman	+	+	+
User 4	Business	24	Man	+	+	+
User 5	Psychology	22	Woman	+	+	-
User 6	Psychology	25	Woman	+	+	-
User 7	Math Education	23	Man	+	+	-
User 8	Social Science Education	23	Man	+	+	-
User 9	Computer Education	25	Man	+	+	+
User 10	Computer Education	22	Man	+	+	-

Figure 4. Human computer interaction laboratory

2.4.2. Observer Computer

The experiment was prepared and the experimental processes were carried out in the human-computer interaction lab, and the responses were tracked using a researcher machine (See Figure 6).

Figure 5. Eye-tracking device

Figure 6. Observer computer

2.4.3. Mobile Eye-tracking Devices

It is the device that provides information about the eye movement of the user in mobile test device. The device is connected to the observer computer and the places looked at with the glasses were tracked and recorded (see Figure 7).

Figure 7. Mobile eye-tracking devices

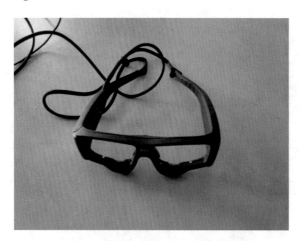

2.4.4. Software

iView X is the software that provides connection between eye tracking device and observer computer. Experiment Center is the software that enables to form eye tracking test, manage and control the test. The experiments created with Experiment center software is connected to the user's computer via iViewX software. In Experiment Center software, calibration settings are placed and when the user starts experiment via entering the website to be analyzed it is automatically brought against the user. Then, record is performed with BeGaze software. BeGaze is the software that keeps the records for evaluation of stored data.

- Easy to use design software for gaze tracking experiments and visual stimulus presentation
- Study design center and recording control.
- Variable calibration modes and themes incl. children module.
- Integrated validation tool.
- Instructions, text, image, video, web, screen recording, external video sources, questionnaires.
- Webpages with scroll compensation.
- Stimuli pre-play and study test mode visualizer.
- Various random groups, straight or nested sequences.
- Subject demographic import wizard.
- Online subject tracking monitor and position control.
- User video and sound.
- Keyboard and mouse event logging.
- Background screen recording.
- Optional remote control from separate stimulus PC.
- Live Viewer of current stimulus and gaze point.

SMI Experiment Center is an easy to operate experiment creation, planning and experiment execution environment. It is complemented by the SMI iView X for gaze tracking data acquisition and SMI BeGaze for gaze tracking data analysis.

The BeGaze eye tracking software allows analyzing and structuring information on experiments and subjects, as well as displaying the eye tracking data as meaningful graphs – all in one advanced application. Basic functionality can be extended by specific optional packages, e.g. for video analysis, reading analysis, observational studies etc. (SMI, 2016).

2.5. Data Collection

The data was obtained with eye tracking and semi-structured interview methods. In the study, Facebook, Twitter and LinkedIn social media websites and mobile applications were used. First, eye calibration was performed for the participants. Then, they were asked to carry out the tasks assigned by the researchers and their path, the time spent and whether the tasks were performed were recorded.

The tasks about Facebook, Twitter and LinkedIn websites:

1.   Hiding the pictures to friends on Facebook,
2.   Taking user confirmation for tag requests on Facebook,
3.   Blocking ads on behalf of those who share on Facebook,
4.   Deactivating Twitter profile,
5.   Searching for company on LinkedIn.

The tasks about Facebook, Twitter and LinkedIn applications:

1.   Blocking any application to take personal information on Facebook,
2.   Changing password on Twitter,
3.   Sharing a tweet already shared on Twitter on Facebook,
4.   Searching for job position on LinkedIn,
5.   Applying for a work on LinkedIn.

The study was carried out in Human-Computer Interaction Lab in Istanbul University. The participants were met in Human-Computer Interaction Lab in appointment time. The experiment was previously recorded as screen recording with "SMI Experiment" program in the test computer to which eye tracking device was connected. This process was performed only once during the research and each participant used this experiment. Participants were told that their heads should not move much during the test. The experiment was started by making eye calibration. Each point in the calibration screen appeared one by one and the user was asked to look at white space within the points. When the point was focused on for 2 seconds, the program automatically passed to the next point. At the end, calibration rate was given with x and y values and calibration process was repeated according to the values if necessary or the experiment was initiated. In addition to SMI Experiment program, the record of "Noldus Observer 9.0" program found in the observer computer providing video, audio, mouse, keyboard and screen recordings simultaneously was initiated. Eye calibration was tracked and the participant was warned when necessary. The eye movements, the time spent and whether the participants performed the tasks were recorded. Then, audio record was carried out by asking semi-structured interview questions to the participants.

2.6. Data Analysis

The recordings showing eye and mouse movements recorded with the Experiment program were analyzed with Be Gaze program. In the analyses, fixation numbers, Gridded Area of Interest, sequence, heat map and scan path values were obtained. The interview records were analyzed by the researcher.

3. FINDINGS

This section includes analysis of the users' data obtained from eye tracking device.

3.1. Data Analysis about Social Media Applications

3.1.1. The Time that Participants Spend in Mobile Applications

According to the results, all tasks except two of them were completed although completion of the tasks by participants took a long time (See Table 2). The reason for long time to complete tasks or not able to do tasks is due to the lack of having LinkedIn and Twitter accounts and making Facebook settings.

3.1.2. Task Completion Status on Social Media Mobile Applications

According to the data obtained, all tasks except two of them were completed although completion of the tasks by participants took a long time (See Table 3). The reason for long time to complete tasks or not be able to do tasks is due to the lack of having LinkedIn and twitter accounts and making Facebook settings.

Table 2. The time that participants complete the tasks in mobile applications (sec)

	Task 1	Task 2	Task 3	Task 4	Task 5	Total
User 1	58	60	45	16	25	204
User 2	48	48	110	7	13	226
User 3	60	60	45	5	17	187
User 4	26	11	36	7	9	89
User 5	52	24	5	10	10	101
User 6	60	34	60	12	14	180
User 7	120	33	20	15	23	211
User 8	23	15	5	10	13	66
User 9	60	60	53	10	32	215
User 10	23	9	12	9	9	62
Mean	53	28.6	39.1	10.1	16.5	1421

Table 3. Completed tasks in social media applications

	Task 1	Task 2	Task 3	Task 4	Task 5	Total
User 1	+	+	+	+	+	5
User 2	+	+	-	+	+	4
User 3	+	+	+	+	+	5
User 4	+	+	+	+	+	5
User 5	+	+	+	+	+	5
User 6	+	+	+	+	+	5
User 7	-	+	+	+	+	4
User 8	+	+	+	+	+	5
User 9	+	+	+	+	+	5
User 10	+	+	+	+	+	5
Total	9	10	9	10	10	48

Table 4. Steps of participants to complete tasks in mobile devices (click numbers)

	Task 1	Task 2	Task 3	Task 4	Task 5	Total
User 1	10	7	9	3	4	33
User 2	6	4	0	3	4	17
User 3	8	4	3	6	3	24
User 4	6	6	11	3	2	28
User 5	14	8	5	4	3	34
User 6	8	10	4	3	5	30
User 7	0	9	5	5	3	22
User 8	5	4	4	4	3	20
User 9	6	11	9	3	6	35
User 10	4	4	5	3	3	19
Mean	6.7	6.7	5.5	3.7	3.7	263

3.1.3. Step Numbers to Complete Tasks in Social Media Applications

It seems that participants make the most clicks at the first two tasks (See Table 4). This result shows parallelism with the time to complete task (See Table 3).

3.1.4. The Analysis of the Tasks given for Social Media Applications

3.1.4.1. First Task: To Prevent Any Application to Obtain Personal Information from Facebook

- **Usability:** Average time of the first task completed is 53 seconds (See Table 2).
- **Effectiveness:** Only one of 10 participants could not complete the task (See Table 3).

- **Productiveness:** It was completed in an average time of 53 seconds by all participants. The fastest participant completed the task in 23 seconds while the slowest participant completed in 60 seconds. The participant who could not complete the task asked to pass the task after 120 seconds (See Table 2). When we look at it as the task that the users performed with the maximum number of clicks, it can be said that the task has low productiveness (See Table 4).
- **Satisfaction:** When participant's comments about the task were evaluated, it was stated that they primarily searched at the security or privacy settings due to thinking that the task was at the security or privacy setting. One participant stated not to complete the task because he/she used this setting never before.

3.1.4.2. Second Task: To Perform Password Change Process on Twitter

- **Usability:** Average time of the second task completed is 28.6 seconds (See Table 2).
- **Effectiveness:** All 10 participants completed the task (See Table 3).
- **Productiveness:** It was completed in an average time of 28.6 seconds by all participants. The fastest participant completed the task in 9 seconds while the slowest participant completed in 60 seconds (See Table 2). The task is also one of the tasks performed with the most clicks (See Table 4). It is a task that can be done with only many clicks in a short time.
- **Satisfaction:** When participant's comments about the task were evaluated, the participants stated that they completed the task in a long time due to not using Twitter much and 'Settings' menu should be more attention-grabbing.

3.1.4.3. Third Task: To Share a Tweet Written on Twitter on Facebook

- **Usability:** Average time of the third task done is 39.1 seconds (See Table 2).
- **Effectiveness:** Only one of 10 participants could not complete the task (See Table 3).
- **Productiveness:** It was completed in an average time of 39.1 seconds by all participants. The fastest participant completed the task in 5 seconds while the slowest participant completed in 60 seconds. The task was completed at average 5 steps (See Table 4).
- **Satisfaction:** When participant's comments about the task were evaluated, it was revealed that the participants had no idea where they could perform the task and they found it after surfing in the main page.

3.1.4.4. Fourth Task: To Perform Search for Job Advertisement on LinkedIn

- **Usability:** Average time of the fourth task completed is 10.1 seconds (See Table 2).
- **Effectiveness:** All 10 participants completed the task (See Table 3).
- **Productiveness:** It was completed in an average time of 10.1 seconds by all participants. The fastest participant completed the task in 5 seconds while the slowest participant completed in 16 seconds (See Table 2). It is the task found in a short time with the least clicks (See Table 4).
- **Satisfaction:** When participant's comments about the task were evaluated, it was stated that although the participants did not have LinkedIn account, they performed the task in the main page easily.

3.1.4.5. Fifth Task: To Perform Job Application on LinkedIn

- **Usability:** Average time of the fifth task done is 16.5 seconds (See Table 2).
- **Effectiveness:** All 10 participants completed the task (See Table 3).
- **Productiveness:** It was completed in an average time of 16.5 seconds by all participants. The fastest participant completed the task in 9 seconds while the slowest participant completed in 32 seconds (See Table 2). It is one of the tasks found with the least clicks (See Table 4).
- **Satisfaction:** When participant's comments about the task were evaluated, it was stated that the participant had no difficulties to perform the task although they did not use LinkedIn much.

3.1.5. Data Analysis about Social Media Websites

3.1.5.1. First Task: To Hide Facebook Photos from Friends

- **Usability:** Average time of the first task completed is 39.1 seconds (See Table 5)
- **Effectiveness:** All 10 participants completed the task (See Table 6).
- **Productiveness:** It was completed in an average time of 28.6 seconds by all participants. The fastest participant completed the task in 8 seconds while the slowest participant completed in 58 seconds (See Table 5).
- **Satisfaction:** When the comments of the participants about the task were analyzed, the participants stated that it was easy to perform the task because they hid photos previously.

3.1.5.2. Second Task: To Get User Permission for Tag Request on Facebook

- **Usability:** Average time of the second task completed is 39.1 seconds (See Table 5).
- **Effectiveness:** Two of 10 participants could not complete the task (See Table 6).
- **Productiveness:** It was completed in an average time of 21.3 seconds by all participants. The fastest participant completed the task in 5 seconds while the slowest participant completed in 44 seconds (See Table 5).

Table 5. The time that participants complete the tasks in websites (sec)

	Task 1	Task 2	Task 3	Task 4	Task 5	Total
User 1	44	10	5	30	40	129
User 2	32	42	10	20	15	119
User 3	9	20	38	26	18	111
User 4	55	44	14	38	20	171
User 5	25	30	29	55	50	189
User 6	54	23	20	25	18	140
User 7	15	5	35	65	30	65
User 8	30	10	22	70	40	72
User 9	58	19	10	18	20	125
User 10	8	10	16	40	55	129
Mean	33	21.3	19.9	38.7	30.6	125

Table 6. Completed tasks in websites

	Task 1	Task 2	Task 3	Task 4	Task 5	Total
User 1	+	+	+	+	+	5
User 2	+	+	+	+	+	5
User 3	+	+	+	+	+	5
User 4	+	+	+	+	+	5
User 5	+	+	+	+	+	5
User 6	+	+	+	+	+	5
User 7	+	+	+	-	-	3
User 8	+	+	+	-	-	3
User 9	+	+	+	+	+	5
User 10	+	+	+	+	+	5
Total	10	10	10	8	8	46

- **Satisfaction:** When the participants' comments were examined, they said that it was a little bit hard to find 'Settings' menu and they performed the task in a short period when they found the menu.

3.1.5.5. Third Task: To Block Advertisements Performing Sharing on Facebook on Behalf of the Participants

- **Usability:** Average time of the third task completed is 19.9 seconds (See Table 5).
- **Effectiveness:** All 10 participants completed the task (See Table 6).
- **Productiveness:** It was completed in an average time of 19.9 seconds by all participants. The fastest participant completed the task in 5 seconds while the slowest participant completed in 38 seconds (See Table 5).
- **Satisfaction:** When the comments of the participants were analyzed, they stated that the task took some time because they did not use Twitter accounts a lot.

3.1.5.6. Fourth Task: To Make Twitter Profile Private

- **Usability:** Average time of the fourth task completed is 38.7 seconds (See Table 5).
- **Effectiveness:** All 10 participants completed the task (See Table 6).
- **Productiveness:** It was completed in an average time of 38.7 seconds by all participants. The fastest participant completed the task in 18 seconds while the slowest participant completed in 40 seconds (See Table 5).
- **Satisfaction:** When the participants' comments were examined, the participants pointed out that they did not perform a task like this before, but they would do after a little search.

3.1.5.7 Fifth Task: To Search for Company in LinkedIn

- **Usability:** Average time of the fifth task completed is 38.7 seconds (See Table 5).
- **Effectiveness:** All 10 participants completed the task (See Table 6).

- **Productiveness:** It was completed in an average time of 30.6 seconds by all participants. The fastest participant completed the task in 10 seconds while the slowest participant completed in 55 seconds (See Table 5).
- **Satisfaction:** When the comments of the participants were examined, they stated that it was easy to perform the task on main page although they did not have any LinkedIn accounts.

3.2. Eye-Tracking Data

When the eye-tracking data of the participants performing Facebook tasks is examined, it seems that they first start to look for the settings menu on the left side and their attentions focus on different parts during this process (See Figure 8). During interview, the participants stated that they had difficulties in finding the settings menu.

When the participants accessed to the settings menu, they easily reached the parts from the menu on left side to perform the task. As seen in Heat Map in Figure 9, it is observed that they mostly focus on the left side containing target buttons.

When the eye-tracking data of the Twitter tasks is examined, it seems that the users mostly focus on the left side for the settings menu. It is observed that they try to reach the settings menu via clicking on the profile picture found on the left (See Figure 10). It seems that the difficulty in finding the settings menu on Facebook is also present in Twitter.

Figure 8. Eye-tracking data of Facebook

Figure 9. Heat maps of settings page of Facebook

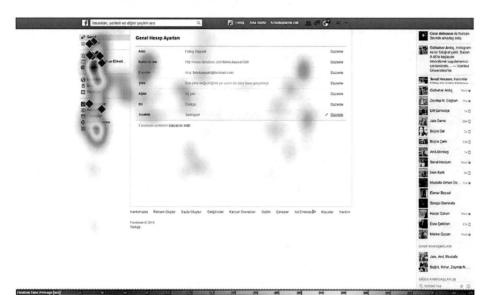

Figure 10. Heat maps of Twitter

Figure 11. Fixation numbers of settings page of Twitter

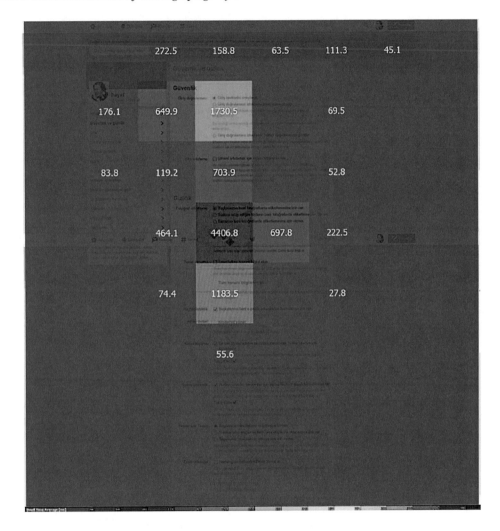

When the participants accessed to the settings menu, they easily completed the tasks from the menus on the left side (See Figure 11).

Although the users had no LinkedIn accounts, they easily performed the tasks. It is observed that the users mostly focused on search bar found on the top to perform the tasks (See Figure 12, 13). In addition, they accessed to the Settings menu easier than the Settings menus on Facebook and Twitter.

4. RESULTS

As a result of the analysis made with university students to obtain information about usability situation of social networks, it was observed that the participants completed most of the tasks. However, the completion time varied. While they easily performed the tasks related with general use, they had difficulties in the tasks related with settings which they do not use a lot. In the study carried out by Ozdener (2005), the participants who previously used the system was more successful than the participants did not. Be-

Figure 12. Eye-tracking data of Linkedin

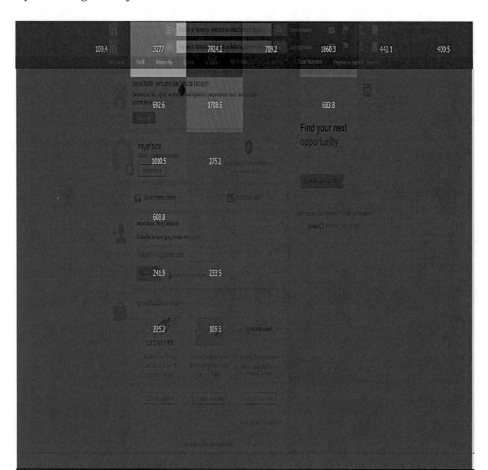

Figure 13. Heat map of display screen of Linkedin job advertisement

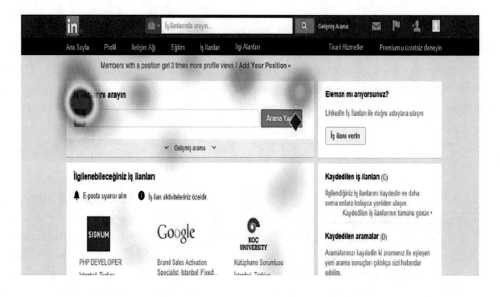

ing already familiar to environment which group will use provides positive results in terms of usability. Among the findings, Sennersten (2004) included that preliminary information and experiences affected the subjects' behaviors. In the study the participants stated that mobile applications were more useful than websites. This situation is resulted from the use of social media on mobile application. Sundar and Limperos (2013) suggested that motivation and satisfaction are also effective in the ease of use of social media.

The participants completing some tasks without any problem stated that they learned these settings as necessary because they previously faced with security threats on social media. The reason for not knowing these settings in social media networks can be due to insufficient informing.

According to the results obtained from the experiments in web-based and mobile-based environments which eye-tracking device was used, the users mostly focused on the upper left and middle sides of the screen. As a result of the research about eye-tracking, application usability and media carried out by Schiessl et al. (2003) in Berlin, it was revealed that the participants mostly focused on pictures and the left side of the sites.

When overall data was examined, LinkedIn was perceived more useful than Facebook and Twitter. Even the participants without LinkedIn accounts could complete the given tasks. According to analysis and the comments of the users, the reason is that menus on LinkedIn are on the upper side of the site and they are attractive. Nielsen (2000) emphasizes that a site map should be prepared during website preparation and this map should be a place where users access very easily. Menus on pages should be chosen according to page layout. If there are multiple sub-headings under a title, nested menus should be preferred. Preferred menus in this way help users to access information faster. However, 'the pop-up menus opening to the one side after clicking' should be used during the choice of these menus instead of 'the pop-up menus that are open to the one side when the mouse comes on it'.

In the study, it was observed in some tasks that the users scanned the area where they were supposed to perform the tasks, but they did not operate any function. This result is compatible with 'covert attention' defined by Wright and Ward (2008). It may vary with the cognitive process phases of eye tracking data.

As a result, performing necessary settings on setting page took time for the users although they use Facebook and Twitter the most. They performed the tasks in a short time even they did not have LinkedIn accounts. Based on these, it can be suggested that menu layout can be in a way that users predict and they would not be different from the structures that they are used to use.

When the data was analyzed, the users generally used the left or upper middle sides to perform the tasks. It seems that website can be more useful when menus are placed the upper left or upper middle sides. These sides are the places where users first look at and focus on (Byerly, 2007). Similarly, Goff (2004) stated that the upper left side of the website screens is the navigation center.

REFERENCES

Acartürk, C., & Çağıltay, K. (2006). İnsan bilgisayar etkileşimi ve ODTÜ'de yürütülen çalışmalar. *Akademik Bilişim*, 9-11.

Akcapinar, G., Altun, A., & Mentes, T. (2012). The Effect of Prior Knowledge on Navigational Profiles in Hypertext Environments. *Eğitim ve Bilim*, *37*(163), 143.

Andrzejczak, C., & Liu, D. (2010). The effect of testing location on usability testing performance, participant stress levels, and subjective testing experience. *Journal of Systems and Software, 83*(7), 1258–1266. doi:10.1016/j.jss.2010.01.052

Baser, A. (2014). *Sosyal Medya Kullanıcılarının Kişilik Özellikleri, Kullanım Ve Motivasyonlarının Sosyal Medya Reklamlarına Yönelik Genel Tutumları Üzerindeki Rolü: Facebook Üzerine Bir Uygulama.* (PhD Thesis). Marmara University.

Bayram, S., & Bayraktar, D. M. (2013). Using Eye Tracking to Investigate the Relationship Between Attention and Change Blindness. *World Journal on Educational Technology, 5*(2), 257–265.

Bayram, S., & Yeni, S. (2011). Web Tabanlı Eğitsel Çoklu Ortamların Göz İzleme Tekniği ile Kullanışlılık Açısından Değerlendirilmesi. *Ahi Evran Üniversitesi Eğitim Fakültesi Dergisi, 12*(2), 221–234.

Biedert, R., Buscher, G., & Dengel, A. (2010). The eyebook–using eye tracking to enhance the reading experience. *Informatik-Spektrum, 33*(3), 272–281. doi:10.1007/s00287-009-0381-2

Bostanci, M. (2010). *Development Of Social Media And Social Media Usage Habits Of Communication Faculty Students.* (Master Thesis). Erciyes University.

Boyd, D. (2007). Why youth (heart) social network sites: The role of networked publics in teenage social life. *MacArthur foundation series on digital learning–Youth, identity, and digital media*, 119-142.

Bryer, T. A., & Zavattaro, S. M. (2011). Social media and public administration: Theoretical dimensions and introduction to the symposium. *Administrative Theory & Praxis, 33*(3), 325–340. doi:10.2753/ATP1084-1806330301

Bucher, H. J., & Schumacher, P. (2006). The relevance of attention for selecting news content. An eye-tracking study on attention patterns in the reception of print and online media. *Communications, 31*(3), 347–368. doi:10.1515/COMMUN.2006.022

Byerly, G. (2007). Look in their eyes-eye tracking, usability, and children. *School Library Media Activities Monthly, 23*(8), 30.

Chen, G. M. (2011). Tweet this: A uses and gratifications perspective on how active Twitter use gratifies a need to connect with others. *Computers in Human Behavior, 27*(2), 755–762. doi:10.1016/j.chb.2010.10.023

Cooke, M., & Buckley, N. (2008). Web 2.0, Social Networks And The Future Of Market Research. *International Journal of Market Research, 50*(2), 267–292.

Dal, N. E., & Dal, V. (2014). Personality Traits And Social Network Sites Usage Habits: A Research On University Students. *Mehmet Akif Ersoy Üniversitesi Sosyal Bilimler Enstitüsü Dergisi, 6*(11), 144–162.

Davey, L. (1991). Çeviri: Tuba Gökçek (2009). *Elementary Education Online, 8*(2), 1–3.

Dix, A., Finlay, J., Abowd, G., & Beale, R. (2004). *Human-Computer Interaction*. Prentice Hal.

Facebook. (2011). *Statistics*. Palo Alto, CA: Facebook.

Fukuda, R., & Bubb, H. (2003). Eye tracking study on Web-use: Comparison between younger and elderly users in case of search task with electronic timetable service. *PsychNology Journal, 1*(3), 202–228.

Goff, C. (2004). Where, why, who? Some usability techniques reveal where users are looking, but knowing why they look is also useful, especially for niche audiences. *New Media Age*, 6-9.

Goldberg, H. J., & Kotval, X. P. (1999). Computer interface evaluation using eye movements: Methods and constructs. *International Journal of Industrial Ergonomics, 24*(6), 631–645. doi:10.1016/S0169-8141(98)00068-7

Goldberg, J. & Kotval, X.P. (1998). Eye Movement-Based Evaluation of the Computer Interface. *Advances in occupational ergonomics and safety*, 529-532.

Gonsalves, A. (2010). *Social Network Use By Smartphones Jumps*. Retrieved November 7, from http://www.informationweek.com/news/hardware/handheld/showArticle.jhtml?articleID=223101506

Gundogan, M. B. (2003). Kullanılabilirlik (Usability) Kavramı ve Egitim Teknolojileri; Yansımalar, Uygulamalar, International Educational Technologies Symposium and Fair, Vol:I. *Tojet*, 642-649.

Gursakal, N. (2009). *Sosyal Ağ Analizi*. Bursa: Dora Yayıncılık.

Ito, M., Horst, H., Bittanti, M., Boyd, D., Herr-Stephenson, B., Lange, P. G., & Robinson, L. (2008). Living and learning with new media: Summary of findings from the digital youth project. *The John D. and* Catherine T. *MacArthur Foundation Reports on Digital Media and Learning*. MIT Press.

Jacob, R. J. K., & Karn, K. S. (2003). Eye tracking in human-computer interaction and usability research: Ready to deliver the promises. *Mind, 2*(3), 4.

Jakob, N. (2000). *Why you only need to test with 5 users*. Norman Group Website. Retrieved from http://www.nngroup.com/

Josephson, S., & Holmes, M. E. (2002, March). Visual attention to repeated internet images: testing the scanpath theory on the world wide web. In *Proceedings of the 2002 Symposium on Eye tracking research & Applications* (pp. 43-49). ACM. doi:10.1145/507072.507081

Karn, K. S., Ellis, S., & Juliano, C. (1999, May). The hunt for usability: tracking eye movements. In CHI'99 extended abstracts on Human factors in computing systems (pp. 173-173). ACM. doi:10.1145/632716.632823

Kemp, S. (2014). *Social, Digital & Mobile in The Middle East*. Retrieved from http://wearesocial.com/blog/2014/07/social-digital-mobile-middle-east

Kennedy, A. (2009). *Whitepaper, The Global Facebook Phenomenon*. Retrieved from www.beyondink.com/Whitepaper-The-Global-Facebook-Phenomenon-by-Anne-Kennedy.pdf

Kırık, A. M., Arslan, A., Çetinkaya, A., & Mehmet, G. Ü. L. (2015). A quantitative research on the level of social media addiction among young people in Turkey. *International Journal of Science Culture and Sport, 3*(3), 108–122.

Lee, S., & Cho, M. (2011). Social Media Use in a Mobile Broadband Environment. Examination of Determinants of Twitter and Facebook Use. *International Journal of Mobile Marketing, 6*(2), 71–87.

Lee, S., & Koubek, R. J. (2010). The effects of usability and web design attributes on user preference for e-commerce web sites. *Computers in Industry, 61*(4), 329–341. doi:10.1016/j.compind.2009.12.004

Lefebvre, H. (2007). *Modern Dünyada Gündelik Hayat*. Istanbul: Metis Yayınları.

Liu, H. C., Lai, M. L., & Chuang, H. H. (2011). Using Eye-Tracking Technology to Investigate The Redundant Effect of Multimedia Web Pages on Viewers' Cognitive Processes. *Computers in Human Behavior*, 27(6), 2410–2417. doi:10.1016/j.chb.2011.06.012

MobileBeyond. (2010). *Smartphone consumer expectations driving industry crazy*. Retrieved May 7, 2015, from http://mobilebeyond.net/smartphone-consumer-expectations-driving-industry-crazy/#axzz14ZIJKAri

Mutlu Bayraktar, D., & Bayram, S. (n.d.). Evaluation Of Situations Causing Split Of Attention. In S. Hai-Jew (Ed.), *Design Strategies and Innovations in Multimedia Presentations* (pp. 320–344). IGI Global.

Namahn. (2000). *Using eye tracking for usability testing*. Brussels: Author.

Nielsen, J. (1999). *Designing web usability: The practice of simplicity*. New Riders Publishing.

Nielsen, J. (2003). *Usabilitiy 101: Introduction to Usability*. Retrieved from http://www.useit.com/alertbox/20030825.html

Nielsen, J., & Pernice, K. (2010). *Eyetracking web usability*. New Riders.

Ozcelik, E., Kursun, E., & Cagiltay, Y. D. D. K. (2006). *Göz Hareketlerini İzleme Yöntemiyle Üniversite Web Sayfalarının İncelenmesi*. Akademik Bilisim.

Ozdener, N. (2005). Use of simulation in experimental teaching methods. *The Turkish Online Journal of Educational Technology*, 4(4), 93–98.

Pentina, I., Zhang, L., & Basmanova, O. (2013). Antecedents and Consequences of Trust in A Social Media Brand: A Cross-Cultural Study of Twitter. *Computers in Human Behavior*, 29(4), 1546–1555. doi:10.1016/j.chb.2013.01.045

Quan-Haase, A., & Young, A. L. (2010). Uses And Gratifications Of Social Media: A Comparison of Facebook and Instant Messaging. *Bulletin of Science, Technology & Society*, 30(5), 350–361. doi:10.1177/0270467610380009

Radach, R., Hyona, J., & Deubel, H. (Eds.). (2003). *The Mind's Eye: Cognitive And Applied Aspects Of Eye Movement Research*. Elsevier.

Radach, R., & Underwood, G. (1998). *Eye guidance and visual information processing: Reading, visual search, picture perception and driving. Eye Guidance in Reading and Scene Perception*. Oxford, UK: Elsevier.

Russell, M. (2005). Using Eye-tracking Data to Understand First Impressions of a Website. *Usability News*, 7(1), 1–14.

Schiessl, M., Duda, S., Thölke, A., & Fıscher, R. (2003). *Eye Tracking and Its Application In Usability and Media Research*. Retrieved from http://www.smiling.club/assets/fileupload/eye_tracking_application_duda.pdf

Schneiderman, B., & Plaisant, C. (2005). *Designing the user interface: Strategies for Effective Human-Computer Interactions. The United States of America: Pearson Education* (4th ed.). Reading, MA: Addison-Wesley.

Sener, G. (2010). *Türkiye'de Facebook Kullanımı Araştırması, XIV. Türkiye'de İnternet Konferansı.* Bilgi University.

Sennersten, C. (2004). *Eye movements in an action game tutorial.* Department of Cognitive Science. Lund University.

Smi. (2016). *Smi Experiment Center Software.* Retrieved at March 2015 from http://www.smivision. com/en/gaze-and-eye-tracking-systems/products/experiment-center-software.html

Statista. (2015). Retrieved from http://www.statista.com/statistics/272014/global-social-networks-ranked-by-number-of-users/

Stratten, S. (2012). Unmarketing. *Education, 2.*

Sundar, S. S., & Limperos, A. (2013). Uses and grats 2.0: New gratifications for new media. *Journal of Broadcasting & Electronic Media, 57*(4), 504–525. doi:10.1080/08838151.2013.845827

Timisi, N. (2003). *Yeni iletişim teknolojileri ve demokrasi.* Ankara: Dost.

Tonbuloğlu, I., & Bayram, S. (2012). Usability Test: Using Eye Tracking Method in Educational Software Pop-Up Content. Journal of Research in Education and Teaching, 1(3), 324-332.

Uysal, A. (2013). *Meslek Lisesi Öğrencilerinin Sosyal Medya Kullanim Amaçlari İle Eğitsel Sosyal Medya Kullanımlarının Değerlendirilmesi.* (Master Thesis). Bahcesehir University.

Wright, R. D., & Ward, L. M. (2008). *Orienting of attention.* Oxford University Press.

ADDITIONAL READING

Andrzejczak, C., & Liu, D. (2010). The effect of testing location on usability testing performance, participant stress levels, and subjective testing experience. *Journal of Systems and Software, 83*(7), 1258–1266. doi:10.1016/j.jss.2010.01.052

Ballings, M., Van del Poel, D., & Bogaert, M. (2016). Social media optimization: Identifying an optimal strategy for increasing network size on Facebook. *Omega,* Volume 59, Part A, March 2016, Pages 15-25.

Bryer, T. A., & Zavattaro, S. M. (2011). Social media and public administration: Theoretical dimensions and introduction to symposium. *Administrative Theory and Praxis, 33*(3), 325–340. doi:10.2753/ ATP1084-1806330301

Lee, S., & Moonhee, C. (2011). Social Media Use in a Broadband Environment: Examination of Determinants of Twitter and FB Use. *International Journal of Mobile Marketing, 6*(2), 71–87.

Moffatt-Bruce, S. D. (2015). Using social media: A way for us to sit at the table, *The Journal of Thoracic and Cardiovascular Surgery,* In Press, Available online 30 October 2015.

Ngai, E. W. T., Tao, S. S. C., & Moon, K. K. L. (2015). Social media research: Theories, constructs, and conceptual frameworks. *International Journal of Information Management*, *35*(1), 33–44. doi:10.1016/j.ijinfomgt.2014.09.004

Quan-Haase, A., & Young, A. L. (2010). Uses and Gratifications of Social Media: A Comparison of Facebook and Instant Messaging. *Bulletin of Science, Technology & Society*, *30*(5), 350–361. doi:10.1177/0270467610380009

KEY TERMS AND DEFINITIONS

Eye-Tracking Method: It's an eye movement data collection method used for while individuals follow the content on-screen where pay attention to the areas, which elements are ignored, to determine what they are uncomfortable.

Social Media: Social media is used to share and discuss experiences and knowledge of internet tools and other people in electronic media.

Usability: It is a measure of how easy individuals can complete operations on a product or system according to given tasks.

Section 2
Analytics from the Online Crowd

Chapter 5
A Route Recommender System Based on Current and Historical Crowdsourcing

Marlene Goncalves
Universidad Simón Bolívar, Venezuela

Daniela Andreina Rodríguez
Universidad Simón Bolívar, Venezuela

Patrick Rengifo
Universidad Simón Bolívar, Venezuela

Ivette C. Martínez
Universidad Simón Bolívar, Venezuela

ABSTRACT

Due to the rise of the social networks it's possible to use techniques based on crowdsourcing to easily gather real-time information directly from citizens in order to create recommendation systems capable to employ knowledge that is shared from the crowd. Particularly, in Twitter, the users publish a big amount of short messages; however, to automatically extract useful information from Twitter is a complex task. In order to provide an informed recommendation of the current best route between two city points, this chapter introduces a workflow that integrates natural language techniques to build an vector of features for training two linear classifiers which obtain current information from Twitter, and integrates that information with historical information about possible routes using exponential smoothing; current and historical data to feed a route selection algorithm based on Dijkstra. The effectiveness of the proposed workflow is shown with routes between two interest points in Caracas (Venezuela).

INTRODUCTION

Over the last years, new ways of sharing information have been created with the purpose of the users be informed, and thereby provide users with more capacity to make a decision. Today, the Web allows to share any type of information about different subjects and events. Specifically, the social networks are utilized to share on real time events of great importance locally or globally.

The age of social networking has made possible to use techniques based on crowdsourcing in order to support recommendation systems able to utilize the knowledge that is shared on these social networks. In particular, the crowdsourcing consists in obtaining the collaboration of a great amount of people with

DOI: 10.4018/978-1-5225-0648-5.ch005

the objective of performing several tasks with their help. An example is reCAPTCHA (Von Ahn, Maurer, McMillen, Abraham, & Blum, 2008), which seeks to improve the optic system in charge of digitizing old books. In this system, the users help to recognize the words that are not correctly detected.

On the other hand, social networks represent a rich source of information to evaluate situations such as protests, traffic or natural disasters, because they are widely used to report events in real time. However, the automatic interpretation of this information is a difficult task. On the one hand, the information is expressed in natural language and on the other hand, the first step is to decide whether this information is relevant to the situation to be evaluated, and the second step is to determine what is actually saying about the situation.

In the Twitter social network, the users publish a good deal of tweets or short messages of 140 characters written in natural language. For this reason, automatically extract information from this social network is complex. First, the grammatical structure of the tweets is affected by the character restriction, which leads the user to use abbreviations and a particular lingo of the social network. On the other hand, the amount of tweets published daily makes difficult to detect if a tweet is relevant to a subject on which information is being sought. Finally, a tweet processing can be complicated, depending on what you want to measure. For example, in the case of traffic, a user may want to know, first, if there is traffic in a route and, then, quantify it.

Recently, several works have been realized about classifying text extracted from Twitter. In (Sriram, Fuhry, Demir, Ferhatosmanoglu & Demirbas, 2010), the tweets are classified in preselected categories, like News, Opinion and Events with the intention to simplify the information flow. Similarly, in (Lee, Palsetia, Narayanan, Patwary, Agrawal, & Choudhary, 2011), the tweets belonging to the Trending Topics are classified in their possible categories as these are hard to understand without previous knowledge of the subjects. Both attack the classification problem, but nevertheless, they not see the potential to use this classified information to make analysis and make predictions or recommendations.

The general objective of this chapter is to describe a recommendation system based on crowdsourcing with the purpose to collect documents from the Internet about some topic, process them and be capable to give recommendations on the subject in question. More specific, traffic is the selected topic, Twitter is the information source and the best route from a point to another is the recommendation.

Additionally, this work presents the traffic in Caracas as a case study. Caracas (Caracas, n.d.) is the capital of Venezuela and has more than 5,000,000 habitants on 1,820.5 square miles. Over the years, the city of Caracas has experienced significant population growth. This growth coupled with insufficient planning of expansion and maintenance of arterial roads and frequent accidents that occur have hampered the mobility of inhabitants and visitors who must drive through the city every day (Lizarraga, 2012). Particularly, the Simon Bolivar University is located on the periphery of the city and is isolated from the urban disturbance of Caracas. However, its access is limited due to the remoteness from the rest of the city and the routes to/from this university are not designed for vehicular traffic which owns the area. In addition, the travel to the university (or from the university) also includes the delays that can be found within the city, as well as problems from nearby roads. If to this we add unexpected variables such as protests which limit the free movement of the streets and avenues, then the arrival to the campus can be complicated such as we experienced in 2014 due to protests over the whole city (Buxton, 2014).

Currently, there are several mechanisms to know the traffic conditions in the city. One is Waze, a mobile application, which finds the quickest route from the current user's position to the desired destination. In addition to this data, in order to give directions to the chosen location, Waze utilizes user's GPS (Global Positioning System) data and reports. Nevertheless, Waze may not have enough users to report on all the routes, so that road recommendations may not be precise. Google Maps is a different tool that finds possible routes between an origin and destination and an estimated travel time for each route. Although Google Maps takes into account information on daily rush hours, it does not consider some incident (accidents on the way) affecting the movement of vehicles in the city. Another tool is Twitter, a popular microblogging social network (Java, Song, Finin, & Tseng, 2007). Twitter's users manually consult the state of routes by: i) searching and reading traffic specialized accounts or ii) using traffic related hashtags of the major roads such as #AFF for the Francisco Fajardo highway. This manual process can be slow and take time due to the numerous accounts to be checked for all traffic routes, without being able to have all the information in a single search. Moreover, a disadvantage of using Twitter for traffic is not having an estimated time to reach the destination.

Although there are tools for recommending routes, the proposed recommendation system works with Twitter as a traffic information source in Caracas because Twitter is a very popular social network in Venezuela (Ghosh, 2013). Unlike developed countries, in Venezuela there are no traffic cameras, red light cameras or speed cameras. In consequence, Venezuelans often use radio and TV programs, Waze, Google Maps or Twitter for information on city traffic. Radio programs as traffic center (FM_Center, n.d.) are also listened by Venezuelans to know the current traffic conditions. Several national TV programs post tweets about the current traffic. The common use of Twitter to check traffic has given rise to some accounts that are dedicated to collect and disseminate information on traffic of the city as @trafficaracas (806K followers), @TraficoCCS (242K followers), @fmcenter (993K followers), @eutrafico (1.09M followers), @traficovv (480K followers). Consequently, many people check one or more of these accounts to decide the best route that they will take to reach their destination. In order to make the best decision, people look at route segments which can be blocked by an accident. In Caracas, transit can become totally stopped because a vehicle completely blocked a road. Just at that moment, people often post tweets for helping others to take an alternative route.

Notice that we are only analyzing the text from tweets because there is no location information. Consider the following tweet "traffiCARACAS: vía @mahery21: CERRADA LA VALLE COCHE DESVÍAN TODOS LOS CARROS POR LOS TÚNELES #VALLECOCHE (hace un par de minutos)" extracted from Traficovc (2015, November 24) at 3:05 pm. The hashtag #VALLECOCHE refers to a locality, the Valle Coche Highway.

Twitter is already used for traffic issues. Planned closures of roads such as Carmageddon (Rosario, Kaing, Taylor, & Wachs, 2012) were reported by means of Twitter. Carmageddon was the name given by Los Angeles residents to a 10-mile stretch closure of the 405 Freeway where celebrities broadcasted messages through Twitter to notify people to stay away the roads. In this case, the information was broadcasted from celebrities' accounts to people while our proposal is to create a human sensor network based on Tweets. Thus, our goal is to build a system able to automatically recommend a route, saving time to people who otherwise have to manually search tweets to verify if any route segment is congested (usually the retrieved information is by route segment). When people read the traffic reports, they usually search by a route segment. Therefore, the system must join the information of each segment to finally recommend the route, i.e., the problem becomes the integration of the best segments for recommend the best route. Lastly, in order to avoid the process of reading Twitter by people to determine which is the current best route, in this chapter we propose a system that is able to read unstructured data from Twitter to inform if there is traffic or not, using techniques of machine learning, specifically a logistic regression classifier (Burns & Burns, 2008).

We summarize our contributions as follows:

- Use of natural language processing techniques to process documents, in particular, tweets.
- Generation of predictions using current and historic information from tweets.
- An algorithm that returns a route with less time to travel from point A to point B using the predictions that have been generated.
- An experimental study to evaluate proposed classifier's quality and performance.

This chapter is composed of five additional sections. Section 2 summarizes basic concepts required to understand the applied techniques. In Section 3, we define our system named R2C2 (Route Recommender on Current Crowd information). Section 4 reports experimental results. Finally, we give our conclusions and future work in the sections 5 and 6.

BACKGROUND

This section briefly describes theoretical concepts relevant to this chapter. It begins by explaining what crowdsourcing is and its opportunities to collect information. Subsequently, some techniques to be applied to texts collected from the crowd are introduced. Sentiment analysis, n-grams and binary classification are concepts used to create a system capable of generating recommendations in the context of a selected problem, e.g., to determine the route with less traffic from one point to another from tweets about the state of the roads.

Crowdsourcing

Crowdsourcing is the practice of obtain services, ideas or content from a numerous group of persons, known as the crowd, freely or for a minor price than a conventional employee. This allows to solve large scale problems, as the delimitation of areas where natural disasters occur. For example, the case of Nepal's earthquake, the Facebook Safety Check system allows users on the affected zones to inform their welfare (Gleit, Zeng, Cottle, 2014). Similarly, it allows to resolve multiple problems of small magnitude, such as Amazon's Mechanical Turk, from where individuals are responsible to categorize new products of the same page.

Furthermore, crowdsourcing based techniques allow to exploit the resources that are in the crowd. For example, crowdfunding is the practice to gather some amount of money to fund projects, where many people contribute with small amounts of money which allows to reach a bigger funding goal. Another example of this is the query system Qurk (Marcus, Wu, Karger, Madden, & Miller, 2011), Qurk provides an interface to pose queries over a database, and that same query will be answered by people over the Mechanical Turk system for an amount of money. Those answers are combined through an algorithm to give the final answer to the system user.

Over the last years, crowdsourcing has raised in popularity thanks to the availability of new services that allows easy contact with large crowds. Social networks like Twitter and Facebook make great amounts of available information through their web services that can be exploited for various purposes, e.g., recommendation systems (Ricci, Rokach, Shapira, & Kantor, 2011) capable of inferring specific situations taking place and make decisions about it.

Sentiment Analysis

"Sentiment analysis or opinion mining is the computational study of people's opinions, appraisals, attitudes, and emotions toward entities, individuals, issues, events, topics and their attributes" (Liu & Zhang, 2012, pp.415). The sentiment analysis uses natural language processing Techniques, statistics or machine learning methods to determine sentiments expressed on certain text unit. Sentiments include attitudes, emotions and opinions over a certain issue (Nasuwaka & Yi, 2003).

Social media, especially microblogging websites as Twitter, has become a great source of information since they are continuously fed with real time post on variety of subjects, from current political issues to opinions about daily use products. This fact added to the fact that sentiment analysis has been used on documents at many levels of granularity, from documents to phrases (Agarwal, Xie, Vovsha, Rambow, & Passonneau, 2011), made sentiment analysis on Tweeter data a natural match.

Even when Sentiment Analysis is a recent field of study, it has been applied to several domains as market prediction, box office prediction, business analytics, recommender systems for social advertising and marketing intelligence (Ravi & Ravi, 2015). As examples of these sentiment analysis applications we can mention: on market prediction, the "wisdom of the crowds" from Twitter is used by (Qiu, Rui, & Whinston, 2013) to enrich the prediction of the market. An intra-day market prediction using text mining of news-headlines for FOREX market prediction is done by (Li, Xie, Chen, L., Wang, & Deng, 2014). In order to measure customer satisfaction for a mobile service a combination of sentiment analysis and a ranking method for multi-criteria decision making, called VIKOR, was used over a collection of reviews from de AppStore (Kang & Park, 2014).

From the work presented by Go, Bhayani, and Huang (2009), sentiment analysis of Tweeter data has been used in several domains from the prediction of elections' outcomes (Tumasjan, Sprenger, Sandner, & Welpe, 2010; Choy, Cheong, Laik, & Shung, 2011; Wang, Can, Kazemzadeh, Bar, & Narayanan, 2012), to the evaluation if public mood is related to stock market fluctuations (Bollen, Mao, & Zeng, 2011).

While the use of Twitter as a source of information in sentiment analysis has become popular in various fields, its use for assessing situations of vehicular traffic is limited even though it may be valuable because "Twitter information is interesting because it is inexpensive, readily accessible, has broad geographic coverage, and provides a uniquely passenger-centric perspective" (Mai and Hranac, 2013). Some works that explore the use of sentiment analysis over Twitter data for traffic are Collins, Hasan and Ukkusuri (2013), Mai and Hranac (2013) and Cottrill et al. (2015). Collins et al. (2013) used Twitter to monitor users' sentiments about the rapid transit system of the Chicago Transit Authority. Mai and Hranac (2013) compared the records of incidents of the California Highway Patrol with tweets related to these events on the roads. In Cottrill et al. (2015) authors studied how twitter was used over the 2014 Commonwealth Games in Glasgow to share information related to transportation during those games.

Bag of Words

The bag-of-words model is a representation of the frequency of words in a phrase. It is used in natural language processing. The text to be processed is represented as a multiset of its words, keeping the multiplicity of these words. Thus, the text is represented in a structured way such that a classifier can understand it. Suppose a number of instances where each of them is a document in natural language. In this case, the set of feature vectors can be considered as a matrix where each row is one instance and each column represents a word found in any of the documents. Thus, each cell (i, j) represents the number of

Table 1. Example of bag of words model

Phrase	Choque	Panamericana	Nivel	Fuerte	Tiuna	Genera	Retraso	Últimos	Kilómetros	Lentitud	AFF
1	1	1	1	1	1	1	1	0	0	0	0
2	2	1	0	0	0	1	0	1	1	1	0

times a word appears in the text of the document. Table 1 illustrates this definition. The bag-of-words matrix for the texts "Choque en la panamericana a nivel Fuerte Tiuna genera retraso" and "Choque en la panamericana en sus últimos kilómetros genera lentitud. Choque en la AFF" is represented in Table 1. It can be noted that this model builds a matrix nxm where n is the number of phrases and m is the number of words without repetitions that appear in the n phrases. For reasons of space, we removed connectors and stop words in the matrix.

However, this model presents several problems because of its simplicity. First, the resulting matrix can become very scattered by the number of columns, and therefore, many cells will be represented by zeroes (not shown). This is a memory space problem for very large sets of text that will be represented as a very large matrix which cannot fit in memory. Additionally, those languages that have several conjugations for a verb, there will be multiple columns to represent the same meaning. Moreover, when considering each text as a set of words, the connectors will be repeated many times. Thus, it is necessary to normalize the weights assigned to each of the words since the classifier will assign a greater importance to the connectors.

The n-gram model is a generalization of the bag of words. Instead of considering independent words, this model considers sequences of n consecutive words. Depending on the number of adjacent words can be a unigram (one word), bigram (two words), trigram (three words), 4-gram (four words), and so on. Its main advantage over the bag-of-words model is that it allows us to consider the context in which the words appear. The n-grams have been used in various fields of information processing to estimate the semantic information between words in Web documents. However, space requirements will increase for n-grams with $n > 1$ due to there are $\begin{pmatrix} m \\ n \end{pmatrix}$ possible columns in the matrix for m words in all documents.

For example, the phrase "Colapsada la PDE por laguna subiendo a Altamira" contains the following trigrams:

- Colapsada, la, PDE,
- la, PDE, por,
- PDE, por, laguna,
- por, laguna, subiendo,
- laguna, subiendo, a,
- subiendo, a, Altamira.

Binary Classification

The classification problem, part of supervised learning, consists in identify to which category belongs a new observation x, namely, make the correspondence from x to y, where $y \in \{1,...,C\}$ and C is the

Table 2. Table of hypothesis testing

	A	¬A
Classified in A	True Positive	False Positive
Classified in ¬A	False Negative	True Negative

number of categories. If $C = 2$ the problem is a binary classification, but if $C > 2$ it is a multi-class classification. A classifier is a system whose input is a vector x of discrete or continuous values (feature vector) and has as output only one category C_x. In the context of machine learning, a classifier training consists in, given a set of examples $D = \{(x_i, y_i)\}$ where x_i is the feature vector and y_i the category of every example, determining a classifier that is capable to classify correctly new instances of x_j whose category are unknown.

In most cases, it's desired that the classifier obtained after the training may be capable to generalize as best as possible. Namely, when a new instance arrives, it will be capable to classify it correctly into the category to which belongs. For this reason, is necessary to determine the quality of the classifier resulting after the training.

The evaluation process uses several statistical measures to determine the capacity of the classifier in order to generalize new sets of instances never seen before. Table 2 shows a confusion matrix with the possible outputs of classifying a new instance in one of the possible categories (A and ¬A).

In general, the classifier must be in the diagonal of the matrix, that is to say, it classifies correctly to one of the two categories. Starting from this, the following statistical measures are defined to test the efficiency of a classifier:

- **Accuracy:** The accuracy a in Equation 1 tests if a classifier can correctly identify how far the predicted value from the real one is. In other words, it measures if there is a statistical bias in the results.

$$a = \frac{true\ positives + false\ negatives}{true\ positives + false\ positives + true\ negatives + false\ negatives} \tag{1}$$

- **Precision:** The precision p in Equation 2 is the proportion of recovered relevant material from the total set of documents. Intuitively, the precision is considered as the capacity of a classifier to correctly classify a True Positive instance.

$$p = \frac{true\ positives}{true\ positives + false\ positives} \tag{2}$$

- **Recall:** The recall r in Equation 3 is the proportion of relevant documents from the total of them, recovered or not. Intuitively, the recall is the capacity of given a True positive instance, the classifier detects it.

$$p = \frac{true\ positives}{true\ positives + false\ negatives} \qquad (3)$$

R2C2 (ROUTE RECOMMENDER ON CURRENT CROWD INFORMATION)

We will call our solution as R2C2 for Route Recommender on Current Crowd information. We propose a framework that divides this inference problem into two stages; a schematic representation of our framework is presented in Figure 1. The first stage is carried out by the Traffic Classifier which determines for a current tweet if it indicates whether there are or not traffic jams. The second stage is performed by the Route Recommender which integrates the information produced by the classifiers for each possible route segment and combines it with historical data for suggesting the fastest route between two locations. Lastly, in the following subsections, we will detail the steps for each of these stages.

Traffic Classifier

In the first stage of R2C2 the Traffic Classifier takes a set of tweets, performs natural language processing tasks over this set and generates a set of labeled tweets (traffic, no traffic) for the current situation. Also, these processed tweets are stored on an historical data repository. In this work, we propose to split the traffic classifying task into four steps. Figure 2 shows the proposed steps. The first step is the gathering of documents to be used by the system, like tweets or newspaper articles. As we are interested in real-time documents, a constant stream of new documents is needed. The gathered documents go through a pre-processing step, which largely depends of the domain and corpus of the documents. For example, the

Figure 1. R2C2 system architecture global view

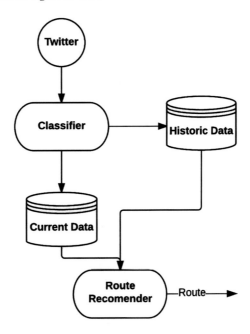

Figure 2. Traffic classifier

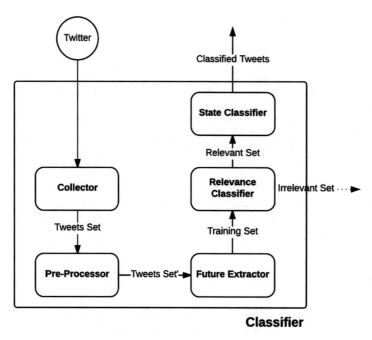

pre-processing that is needed for a set of tweets, which might have a lot of grammatical errors, is very different to the one needed for newspapers articles, which have a more rigid and well-defined structure. In general, documents are pre-processed to normalize their structure, remove or reduce ambiguity.

After pre-processing, a relevance analysis is performed to filter out documents that are unrelated or provide little to no substance to estimate the variables that we want to measure. We perform this task by generating an estimate of how relevant this document is. For example, a document that was written in English is probably not going to be very useful when used in a Spanish-based system. Similarly, a document talking about the long queues are during the Black Friday in the United States is not going to be very relevant to make an useful estimate about the queues to buy basic needs products in Caracas.

The final processing is done to estimate the variables we want to measure. In this chapter, we use a logistic classifier to carry on this task.

Collector

We are interested in documents related to car traffic in Caracas. To gather documents relating this topic, we used Twitter and its API to collect real time tweets. Manually, an account was set up on Twitter which follows users that constantly make traffic reports, and also followed other accounts to generate noise.

Also, we are interested on querying all the tweets that relate to a given road or highway. Due to the diverse ways to write about a road, we associate to each edge e a list of common and possible ways to refer to it. For example, in the Caracas city, a popular road is named "Carretera Panamericana". Twitter users generally refer to this as: Panamericana, PNM, and #PNM.

To gather all the documents that talk about "Carretera Panamericana" we simply query the store for all the documents where any of those words appear. After doing this, we proceed to perform the relevance analysis using our relevance classifier, and then proceed to perform the current/historical partitioning of the data.

Pre-Processing

In Twitter, users make short documents of up to 140 characters called tweets. This implies the existence of unique elements, like user mentions, hashtags and a high usage of word shortening for brevity. When pre-processing tweets, URLs are removed, common words that don't add much information, like "RT", are removed along with user mentions. Some hashtags that we noticed were being automatically appended to tweets were removed.

Additionally, since Caracas is a Spanish speaking city, documents were written in Spanish. This represents a challenge to process since Spanish has a more complex grammatical structure due to semantic rules, word ambiguities, and the use of verb conjugation. In consequence, some concepts end up being represented by multiple words. To diminish this effect, we remove accents, normalize verbs, and make textual substitution to correct common mistakes. Various techniques are used to achieve this, including a dictionary of common mistakes in tweets and a stemmer to normalize verbs down to its stem.

On the other hand, we use an n-gram model with $n = 1, 2, 3$. Note that $n = 1$ implies a simple bag of words model. Subsequently, we use TF-IDF to normalize the weights assigned to each column in the matrix. The general intuition is assigning higher weights to semantically richer n-grams, and to lower the weight of highly repeated n-grams that don't add much value.

According to Sriram, Fuhry, Demir, Ferhatosmanoglu, & Demirbas (2010), the bag of words model works reasonably well to capture underlying information present in documents like tweets. However, it is of interest to measure the behavior of this model when we consider $n > 1$.

Relevance Classification

We trained a logistic regression classifier using approximately 1000 tweets, half of which were positive examples, while the rest consisted of tweets regarding various topics. As previously stated, this stage is done to filter out noise that can make it to the stream of tweets being gathered. For example, the following tweet "Traffic jam down XYZ" is a relevant document, while "Someone on this plane has SUPER-strong perfume" is not relevant. The biggest challenge for this classifier is correctly classifying documents that seemingly talk about traffic but refer to another topic. For example, in native Caracas lingo, traffic jams are sometimes referred to "colas", which is also used to refer to queues to enter stores, or drugstores. Due to this, tweets referring to the long queues due to high scarcity of basic need products must be filtered out, and tweets talking about traffic jams must be classified as relevant.

State Classification

We trained another logistic regression classifier using 4500 tweets that were manually classified as relevant. The goal is to correctly classify the level of traffic that is being spoken in a tweet.

Due to the traffic status (no traffic, light traffic, moderate traffic, heavy traffic), measure is not objective, i.e., two people at the exact same situation can assign a different status to the situation. Thus, we treat the problem as a binary classification problem where Class 0 is "No Traffic" and Class 1 is "Traffic". An example of a tweet manually classified as "No Traffic" is: "Cota mil como la temporada de Caribes de oriente libre de punta a punta", and one classified as "Traffic" is: "Cola fuerte en la Autopista Valle-Coche de Longaray a Plaza Venezuela".

Route Recommender

The previous section focused on how an estimate is generated for a given document. However, in the context of this work, we want to aggregate the separate document estimations into a final estimate for one of the vertexes or edges of a graph G. For example, if we are estimating the traffic on a road e from a set of tweets T_e, we could process all the tweets in T_e as explained in the previous section and then return the median of all the generated tweet estimates.

In general, we want to consider prediction windows or horizons, which answer the question of what is the current state, along with historic data, which answer the question what has been the state in the past. We consider these separately for a number of reasons. Firstly, some behaviors are highly historical. For example, crime rates in a city don't change overnight, but are, rather, the consequence of slow variations that accumulate over time. Furthermore, even when current data is unavailable (i.e. no one is reporting), it is feasible to use our historic data to generate an estimate. Finally, when considered separately, we can control the effect each has on the final estimate.

Figure 3 shows the processing of documents to generate a final estimate over a graph G during a prediction window λ. The document store is simply where documents classified using the process described in the previous section are kept. When a prediction or an estimate is wanted, these documents are partitioned into two sets A and H. A represents the documents received in the current prediction window. For example, the tweets reporting the traffic state during the last $\lambda = 20$ minutes. H represents the historic data, and has the rest of the tweets that have been previously gathered.

Processing A and H is done separately and depends on the problem and variables that are to be estimated. However, the output of both process must be in the same domain R of possible results. Let V_A and V_H be the results of both processes, for A and H respectively. Then, we define the following function ϕ where $\alpha \in [0, 1]$ controls the weight that each estimate has in the final result. α is a parameter for ϕ since the value of α can dynamically change in some problems. Note that ϕ also generates a value in R. That is, ϕ is a function that takes two estimates and combines them to generate a final estimate for the variable that was to be measured.

Figure 3. The route recommender

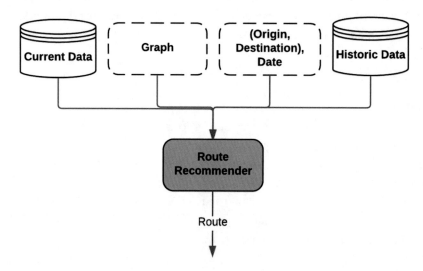

Historical Data

Historical data is used to generate an estimate even when current data might be unavailable (i.e. no tweets related to a road in the current window). Note that traffic, generally, follows a well-established pattern. During rush hour, usually early in the morning and late in the noon, high spikes in the traffic levels are observed, followed by a slow decrease down to normal, or below normal, levels. On the other hand, some events strongly affect roads, preventing it from returning to normal state quickly. For example, road maintenance or building of new infrastructure generally affect close by roads for the amount of time that it takes for it to be done.

Using historical data tries to exploit these two observations about the traffic distribution. However, note that not all data points carry the same weight onto the historical estimation. For example, a road maintenance that was undertaken a month ago doesn't carry the same weight as the closure of a road during the current week. For this reason, the historical data is partitioned into non-overlapping time-spans for which estimates are generated, and then those estimates are exponentially smoothed to generate the historical estimate.

We partition the historical data as follows: current week, past week, two weeks ago, a month ago, two months ago, and the rest of tweets. Inside each partition, estimates are generated by taking the mean of the separate tweet estimates.

Current Data

Current data is a picture of what is currently happening on a road. When we talk about traffic, small changes on the road have a major impact on the state of the same. Therefore, isolated events like car accidents and weather conditions are reflected in traffic. Likewise, historical events such as peak hours will be seen reflected in the estimate of the current data window. The estimate of the current window is simply an average of the estimates of each of the tweets in the current window.

Traffic Prediction

To calculate the time it takes to travel a route, it is desired that both the Historical Data and Current Data are considered. Let α be the value that controls the weight of the actual data estimate, it is restricted as follows: $\alpha \geq 0.6$. That is, the actual data estimate will always have at least 60% of influence in ϕ because it is desired that the historical data never dominates the actual data given that even though a path is usually not affected by traffic, roadblocks or major accidents can cause an immediate influx of tweets that indicate the path is not a good option at that moment.

Due to the dynamics of the paths, we wish to give the recommendation of which is the best (quickest) path to move from one point to another. For this reason, the selection of α must change according to the actual position on graph G, this way, if a person is too close to a road, in driving time, the estimate of the actual data must have more weight. On the other hand, if a person wants an estimate of how much traffic one will encounter in a road that takes 45 minutes to travel, the actual data estimate may have change considerably and can no longer be trusted which is why the historical data of that path at the approximate time that will take to arrive has more weight. Therefore, α varies according to a function $\alpha(t)$ where t is the time that it takes to arrive at a particular path.

$$\varphi(Va, Vh, t) = \alpha(t)Va + (1 - \alpha(t))Vh \tag{4}$$

where *Va* and *Vh* are the estimates of the actual data and historical data respectively, and *t* belongs to $\mathbb{R}$. There are infinite functions that comply with the first restriction; we have selected the Equation 5.

$$\alpha(x) = 1 - \min\left(\frac{2}{5}, \frac{1}{5} + \frac{2x}{1200}\right) \tag{5}$$

where *x* is the time travel in minutes.

Route Calculation

For the system to be able to give the best path based on the predictions, it is necessary to extend the information about the graph. Let $G = (V, E)$ be the graph to be worked on. To each (a, b) belonging to E, it is added:

- A cost. The time it takes to travel the path without traffic.
- A penalization function. $p_{a \to b}: R \to \mathbb{R}$. It assigns a cost in additional time associated to the state of the path that the system is able to estimate.

In the algorithm to calculate the best route from node *s* to node *t* on the graph *G*, considering windows of α time on a particular date. The algorithm makes an exhaustive search on the graph searching for the minimum cost path *s-> t*. On each iteration of the main cycle, it is selected the partial path with the minimum cost until that moment, and it expands using the traffic prediction process and it updates the estimate cost for each adjacent arc to the expanding node with the penalization function.

The search of the path is being done on a graph *G''* with dynamic cost arcs. In the literature, there are specialized algorithms like *D** (Allen, Underwood, & Scheding, 2007) and others based on it for the navigation with partial information where each time the cost of an arc changes, and the optimal path is recalculated. These results, in many cases, are much more efficient than constant recalculation of the minimum cost path. Nonetheless, in graphs where the changes of cost occur not on a few arcs but in the majority of the graph, like it's the case of traffic prediction, it can be observed a performance equal or inferior than find a minimum cost path each time the graph is updated. This is because when an updates occurs, the information that was previously saved on other runs is now obsolete and must be recalculated, which is slower than discard all information and start again. For this reason, we prefer to make the search of the minimum cost path each time it is needed, instead of modifying of adapting *D**.

EXPERIMENTAL STUDY

In this section, we describe an experimental study focused on the evaluation of three main tasks: (1) tweets' preprocessing, (2) classification task's performance, and (3) improvement due to exponential smoothing. To evaluate these tasks we have used three of the most common classification metrics: i) Accuracy (the fraction of correctly classified items); ii) Precision (the fraction of items classified as positive between all that actually are positive); iii) Recall (the fraction of items that belongs to class positive that are classified as positive). In addition, we made use of scikit-learn 0.16.0 as a tool for data mining and data analysis.

Corpus Collection

To gather texts related to car traffic in Caracas, we used Twitter API to collect real time tweets every 10 minutes. In order to feed our system we created a Twitter account, @r2c2_usb, and used it to follow 126 users that publish information about traffic status in Caracas (as well as some other accounts for getting negative examples), and extract the complete timeline of this account. This account follows all accounts of city traffic, traffic users who regularly report and accounts of any issue to generate noise. Subsequently, using the twitter APIs, we extracted timeline for this account until 8 months earlier. Then, the extracted tweets were stored in a PostgreSQL database. Finally, the historical is built by means of current date subtracting from 1 week to 3 weeks.

This procedure gave us a set of 990 tweets in order to train the relevance classifier. These tweets were read and classified as relevant or not. In this dataset there are 425 "relevant" tweets and 565 "irrelevant" tweets. Additionally, these tweets were manually labeled by at least two people that agreed on the assigned label.

For the traffic status' classifier we collected a set of 4159 tweets which were also manually labeled by at least two people. In this dataset, there are 3066 tweets on class "Traffic" and 1093 on class "No Traffic". This collection is available on (Rengifo, 2015) and the Twitter account is (R2C2_USB, 2015).

Classifiers' Performance

Our goal is to use Twitter information to decide if there is traffic between two points. We can split this task in two steps: i) deciding if a tweet is relevant for the situation; ii) establishing which traffic' state a relevant tweet indicates.

To develop and evaluate both classifiers a cross validation procedure was used in the learning process to ensure that the same training set is not always used and to give correct predictions. This is done by splitting the training set in k - 1 parts training with them, and then validating the results with the remainder part. The unused part is exchanged k times obtaining a different result which are weighted in order to produce the model final. All reported metrics are over test set of the best classifier obtained by a 10-fold cross validation procedure.

Relevance Classifier's Performance

The preprocessing is performed under combination of four filters in order to detect which is the combination that produces the best results. The filters to be combined are: i) basic filters, ii) basic dictionary (with words observed in the texts); iii) stemmer, and iv) spell checker. Subsequently, we present the results without the use of any filter, and increasingly we are adding filters until we use all filters together.

On the first part of this experiment we explore how different filter combinations affect the results of our initial classifier; the initial classifier is the one that separates tweets with relevant traffic information. A summary of these results can be observed in Table 3.

Table 3. Results of the relevance's classifier

Pre-Processing	Accuracy	Precision	Recall	Time (sec)
None	0.95	0.95	0.95	0.0585
Basic filters (B)	0.93	0.97	0.87	0.0843
Basic dictionary (D)	0.97	0.99	0.96	19.1542
Stemmer (S)	0.95	0.95	0.95	0.8491
Intelligent Dictionary (I)	0.95	0.96	0.93	262.4337
B+D+S	0.96	0.99	0.93	95.8587
B+D+I	0.96	0.99	0.93	288.9187
All	0.97	0.99	0.98	307.7974

In Table 3 it can be observed that the best combination of accuracy (97%), precision (99%), and recall (98%) was achieved using all filters, but this option is extremely slow (more than 5 minutes for the training set, which is 16 times the time used for D; and this difference can be extrapolated to the time that the system will use for new tweets). The classifier that involves a basic dictionary along with the basic filters (D) is second better with the same prediction an accuracy values that the one that uses all filters and a recall of 96%. Due to the big difference in time processing, we will choose D as our pre-processing set of filters.

Figure 4 presents the Confusion Matrix obtained for the test set of the best 10-fold crossfold for the best combination of preprocessing filters (D), i.e., basic filters plus dictionary. It can be observed that, even when the number of elements on each class is unbalance (113 negatives examples, 85 positives examples), the number of false positives and false negatives is the same (4). From 85 tweets that are relevant for a traffic situation our classifier detects 81 (95.29%), and from 113 that are not relevant it detects 109 (96.46%); which gave us an Accuracy of 96%, a Precision of 96%, and a Recall of 96%.

Traffic Status' Classification Performance

To evaluate the performance of our binary classifier for traffic status (traffic vs. no-traffic) we also tested several pre-processing filters. Now To complete this experiment, we explore the effects filter combinations over the traffic status. These results can be observed in Table 4.

Table 4. Results of the traffic status' classifier

Pre-Processing	Accuracy	Precision	Recall	Time (sec)
None	0.94	0.96	0.96	0.1663
Basic filters (B)	0.91	0.94	0.94	0.2363
Basic dictionary (D)	0.95	0.98	0.93	74.4848
Stemmer (S)	0.91	0.93	0.95	3.4115
Intelligent Dictionary (I)	0.91	0.93	0.96	888.1927
B+D+S	0.91	0.96	0.92	182.1936
B+D+I	0.92	0.94	0.95	1064.6841
All	0.93	0.95	0.93	1064.9591

Figure 4. Confusion matrix for the relevance classifier

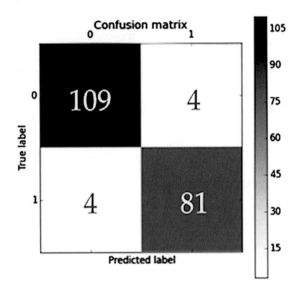

In Table 4, the main metrics for the traffic status' classifier are presented. It can be observed that the best combination of accuracy (95%), precision (98%), and recall (93%) was achieved using the basic dictionary along with the basic filters (D). Improvements on recalls (up to 96% for the Intelligent Dictionary are more than 10 times slower.

Figure 5 introduces the Confusion Matrix obtained for the test set of the best classifier for traffic status (of the 10-crossfold validation procedure). The number of false positives (the classifier indicates "traffic" when there is not traffic) is 11 (11.34%), while the number of false negatives (the classifier said "no traffic" when there is traffic) is 1 (0.92%). In consequence, we have an Accuracy of 94%, a Precision of 99% and a Recall of 89%.

Figure 5. Confusion matrix for the traffic' status classifier

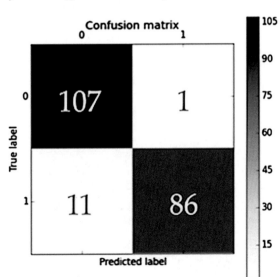

Evaluating the System Ability to Make Recommendations

Some proof of concept tests were performed in order to observe the system ability to detect incidents, build route's recommendations between the points of origin and destination, and to calculate an estimated travel time, based on the historical database and current information.

These tests were run using a normal day without incidents as a basis for normal times without traffic and two days in which a problem has occurred in the normal routes from the "Universidad Simón Bolívar" (our starting point) to "El Cafetal" (our ending point).

May 10, 2015 is chosen as the base day without traffic to take the time and route of reference. The two days of problems on the road are the May 7, 2015, the day on which the track by Seminario between El Hatillo and Los Naranjos was closed on April 14, 2015 when a truck got stuck in Piedra Azul - El Placer. The recommended routes resulting from these experiments can be seen in Table 5.

It is seen as the system detects when an incident in a route and thereby makes the decision to recommend another route.

Impact of Exponential Smoothing

To observe the effect of exponential smoothing in the system, several executions of the algorithm (with various α) were performed over two routes: AFF-La Rinconada and AFF-Los Ruices.

In Figures 6 and 7, the effect of several α values for exponential smoothing over the average scores (an estimate of the traveling time on a route' segment) for the aforementioned routes on 3 time periods (1 week, 2 weeks, and 3 weeks) are presented.

We can observe in Figure 6 the average scores, without the smoothing showed noticeable differences: 25% between 1 week and 2 weeks, and 50% between 2 weeks and 3 weeks. That difference can be attributable to incidents on the route (for example a car crash). The desirable behavior for our system is that the historic time' estimates do not be affected by casual incidents then we will use exponential smoothing to reduce those incidents influence over the scores.

It can be observed that the effect of smoothing the data is greater as a lower value of α, eliminating those outliers that may affect the calculation of the average.

In the route AFF-Los Ruices (Figure 7), differences between the timed averaged scores are less noticeable; but nevertheless exponential smoothing also reduces those differences (smaller alphas entail smaller differences).

With this technique, the system appears to be able to have a historic of information with priority to the most recent information, without the influence of outliers affecting a specific day, such as an accident or protest in any route by example.

Table 5. Results of the recommended routes

Scenery	Route
Normal day	USB ->El Placer ->Piedra Azul ->La Trinidad ->Los Samanes ->Vizcaya ->El Cafetal
Close road	USB ->El Placer ->Piedra Azul ->La Trinidad ->Los Samanes ->Vizcaya ->El Cafetal
Truck accident	USB ->El Placer ->El Volcan ->El Hatillo ->Los Naranjos ->El Cafetal

Figure 6. Impact of exponential smoothing on the route AFF-La Rinconada

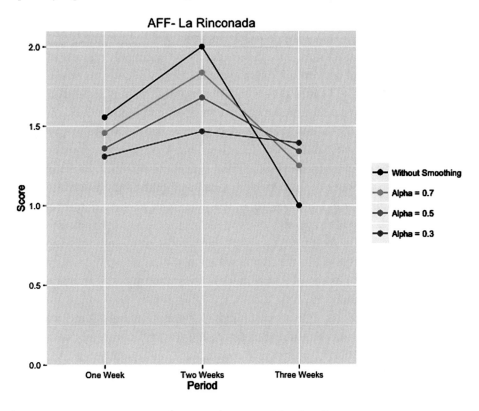

Figure 7. Impact of exponential smoothing on the route AFF-Los Ruices

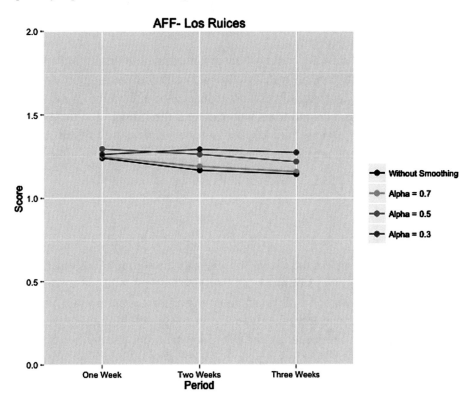

FUTURE RESEARCH DIRECTIONS

In the city of Caracas, Venezuela, there are no traffic cameras, red light cameras or speed cameras and due to characteristics of its arterial roads, unforeseen accidents can quickly congest traffic. On the other hand, Twitter is a popular social network in Venezuela and many Venezuelans read this social network to check daily traffic. Commonly, Twitter's users report any jam in the city to help others take alternate routes in order to reach their final destination. Although users can read Twitter, this process may be slow because users have to check several accounts dedicated to traffic. Therefore, we proposed in this chapter a system based on crowdsourcing able to collect and process texts from Twitter, and recommend the best route from a point to another considering tweets about traffic. Particularly, the routes to/from the Simon Bolivar University in Caracas were taken as a case study. Currently, our system does not contemplate the way direction. For example, a tweet can refer to there is traffic jam on Francisco Fajardo highway in the westbound direction. However, the system is unable to determine direction of the highway in which there is traffic and therefore, our recommendation system may suggest that there's a traffic jam in the eastbound direction. In the future, we are planning to expand the language processing work on the tweets to be able to extract the direction of a way and thus, the recommendation given by our system will be more accurate.

Additionally, the traffic intensity is not considered. Our classifier only determines whether or not there is traffic. Using a multi-class classifier can determine the traffic intensity with multiple classes: no traffic, light traffic, strong traffic, completely congested. Consequently, our system can suggest a better route with regards to the traffic intensity and therefore, we will explore the use of a multi-class classifier in order to compare results against the binary classifier used in this chapter.

Furthermore, the synonym file was built by means of abbreviations and misspelled words found in tweets. For a more accurate classifier, we plan to check what additional words can confuse the classifier in order to add them to the synonym file and thus increase the number of words in the synonym file used by the personal dictionary to improve its scope.

Finally, we want to increase the functionality of our recommendation system incorporating other tools like Google Maps to visually display suggested routes and enlarging the graph of routes to cover with more accuracy the city of Caracas manually or with an automatic alternative. We also want to validate routes suggested by our system with end users who can rank these suggested routes. We plan to look for validation methods for the system recommendations, for example, a web system to consult the users about the given information upon arrival their destination.

CONCLUSION

In this chapter we present a recommendation system based on crowdsourcing using natural language processing and machine learning techniques, with Twitter as the source of information, to give routes based on the traffic jam of the city of Caracas. This system receives as input a subset of tweets from Twitter which containing information in Spanish about traffic in a given period. This set of tweets is pre-processed to clean data, remove abbreviations and correct typos. The data is processed by means of scripts and/or python libraries. Subsequently, the relevance classifier selects the set of tweets relevant to traffic theme using learning machine techniques. Thereafter, the relevant tweets are processed by the binary classifier and thus the traffic areas are determined on a particular day and time. The relevance and status classifications are done using logistic regression. After identifying areas with traffic and given an origin and a destination, the Dijkstra's algorithm is executed to determine the most optimal route between the origin and the destination based on scores of current and historical traffic. Through Exponential Smoothing, the historical weighted score of traffic is calculated giving priority to areas with more recent unexpected events. Finally, the binary and relevance classifiers use filters to improve the understanding of the Spanish language in order to classify texts in their respective category. Caracas city was selected as a case study because it is an unpredictable city in terms of traffic and is very useful for drivers know in advance what is the best route to take since choosing a bad route can involve spent hours and stress.

In addition, an experimental study was conducted to determine the best filters in order to classifiers understand the texts in Spanish. Firstly, the precision and recall of classifiers were computed. The classifiers showed to have high precision and recall because they are at least 90%. To validate the results, a set of people validated that the tweets really contained valid information. In this context, during the experimental study we can observe that the best combination of processing tweets is to use Basic Filters with the Personal Dictionary with vectorization of a bag of words. Spite of the improvement that the use of an Intelligent Dictionary to correct the orthographic errors of the users that share the information could mean, the classifier didn't improve over the statistical measures and the execution time of the system increased significantly.

Secondly, the impact of Exponential Smoothing was also studied to determine how much influenced an outlier in the historical weighted score. Particularly, a traffic accident in Caracas can make a route is not good in a day but it can be good in another day. Using Exponential Smoothing, any outlier can be softened and thus avoid affecting the weighted average. Indeed, the results showed that if that outlier is softened, then makes the historical data are more accurate. Thirdly, it was studied the system effectiveness to identify the route between Cafetal and the Simon Bolivar University in three particular days: a normal day without incident, a day with enough traffic and one day with a closed way. The system effectiveness detects the event in the two days with traffic and recommended another route that is not normally identified in a normal day.

Also, with the exponential smoothing technique we can maintain a weighted historic record, with priority to the newest ones. In this manner, the system avoids to recommend a route that had traffic in recent days. Last, the system is capable of infer the amount of traffic through extracted information from the social network users. The precision of it depends on the use and accuracy of the shared information by the users and the penalization formulas from every path.

REFERENCES

Agarwal, A., Xie, B., Vovsha, I., Rambow, O., & Passonneau, R. (2011). Sentiment analysis of twitter data. In *Proceedings of the Workshop on Languages in Social Media* (pp. 30-38). Association for Computational Linguistics.

Allen, T. L., Underwood, J. P., & Scheding, S. J. (2007). A planning system for autonomous ground vehicles operating in unstructured dynamic environments. In *Proccedings of 2007 Australasian Conference on Robotics & Automation*.

Bollen, J., Mao, H., & Zeng, X. (2011). Twitter mood predicts the stock market. *Journal of Computational Science*, 2(1), 1–8. doi:10.1016/j.jocs.2010.12.007

Burns, R. P., & Burns, R. (2008). Business research methods and statistics using SPSS. *Sage (Atlanta, Ga.)*.

Buxton, J. (2014). *Venezuela: The Real Significance of the Student Protests*. Latin American Bureau. Retrieved August 31, 2015, from http://lab.org.uk/venezuela-%E2%80%93-student-protests

Caracas. (n.d.). Retrieved August 31, 2015, from the Wikipedia: https://en.wikipedia.org/wiki/Caracas

Choy, M., Cheong, M. L., Laik, M. N., & Shung, K. P. (2011). *A sentiment analysis of Singapore Presidential Election 2011 using Twitter data with census correction*. arXiv preprint arXiv:1108.5520

Collins, C., Hasan, S., & Ukkusuri, S. V. (2013). A novel transit rider satisfaction metric: Rider sentiments measured from online social media data. *Journal of Public Transportation*, *16*(2), 2. doi:10.5038/2375-0901.16.2.2

Cottrill, C., Yeboah, G., Gault, P., Nelson, J., Anable, J., & Budd, T. (2015). Tweeting transport: Examining the use of Twitter in transport events.*47th Annual UTSG Conference, At Collaborative Transport Hub. City University London.*

FM_Center. (n.d.). Retrieved August 31, 2015, from the Wikipedia: https://en.wikipedia.org/wiki/FM_Center

Ghosh, M. (2013). *Guess Which Country Uses Twitter More Than Anyone Else In The World?* Retrieved August 31, 2015, from http://trak.in/tags/business/2013/11/18/twitter-usage-country-max-penetration

Gleit, N., Zeng, S., & Cottle, P. (2014). *Introducing Safety Check*. Retrieved August 31, 2015, from http://newsroom.fb.com/news/2014/10/introducing-safety-check/

Go, A., Bhayani, R., & Huang, L. (2009). Twitter sentiment classification using distant supervision. CS224N Project Report. Stanford.

Java, A., Song, X., Finin, T., & Tseng, B. (2007, August). Why we twitter: understanding microblogging usage and communities. In *Proceedings of the 9th WebKDD and 1st SNA-KDD 2007 workshop on Web mining and social network analysis* (pp. 56-65). ACM. doi:10.1145/1348549.1348556

Lee, K., Palsetia, D., Narayanan, R., Patwary, M., Agrawal, A., & Choudhary, A. (2011). Twitter Trending Topic Classification. *2011 IEEE 11Th International Conference On Data Mining Workshops*. doi:10.1109/icdmw.2011.171

Li, X., Xie, H., Chen, L., Wang, J., & Deng, X. (2014). News impact on stock price return via sentiment analysis. *Knowledge-Based Systems*, *69*, 14–23. doi:10.1016/j.knosys.2014.04.022

Liu, B., & Zhang, L. (2012). A survey of opinion mining and sentiment analysis. In Mining text data (pp. 415-463). Springer US. doi:10.1007/978-1-4614-3223-4_13

Lizarraga, C. (2012). Expansión metropolitana y movilidad: el caso de Caracas. *EURE (Santiago)*, *38*(113), 99-125. Retrieved August 31, 2015, from http://www.scielo.cl/scielo.php?script=sci_arttext&pid=S0250-71612012000100005&lng=es&tlng=en

Luong, T. B. T., & Houston, D. (2015). Public opinions of light rail service in Los Angeles, an analysis using Twitter data. In *iConference 2015 Proceedings*. Retrieved from http://hdl.handle.net/2142/73771

Mai, E., & Hranac, R. (2013). Twitter Interactions as a Data Source for Transportation Incidents. *Proceedings of the 2013 Annual Meeting Transportation Research Record.*

Marcus, A., Wu, E., Karger, D., Madden, S., & Miller, R. (2011). Human-powered sorts and joins. *Proc. VLDB Endow.*, 5(1), 13-24. doi:10.14778/2047485.2047487

Nasukawa, T., & Yi, J. (2003, October). Sentiment analysis: Capturing favorability using natural language processing. In *Proceedings of the 2nd international conference on Knowledge capture* (pp. 70-77). ACM. doi:10.1145/945645.945658

Qiu, L., Rui, H., & Whinston, A. (2013). Social network-embedded prediction markets: The effects of information acquisition and communication on predictions. *Decision Support Systems*, 55(4), 978–987. doi:10.1016/j.dss.2013.01.007

R2C2_USB. (2015). Retrieved August 31, 2015, from https://twitter.com/r2c2_usb

Ravi, K., & Ravi, V. (2015). A survey on opinion mining and sentiment analysis: Tasks, approaches and applications. *Knowledge-Based Systems*, 89, 14–46. doi:10.1016/j.knosys.2015.06.015

Rengifo, P. (2015). *Datasets.* Retrieved August 31, 2015, from https://github.com/prengifo/r2c2usb/tree/master/datasets

Ricci, F., Rokach, L., Shapira, B., & Kantor, P. B. (Eds.). (2011). *Recommender Systems Handbook.* New York, NY: Springer-Verlag New York, Inc. doi:10.1007/978-0-387-85820-3

Rosario, Z. D., Kaing, E., Taylor, B. D., & Wachs, M. (2012). Why it wasn't "Carmageddon": An Analysis of the Summer 2011 Closure of the Interstate 405 Freeway in Los Angeles. A Report to the Mayor's Office Institute of Transportation Studies Ralph & Goldy Lewis Center for Regional Policy Studies, UCLA Luskin School of Public Affairs, City of Los Angeles.

Sriram, B., Fuhry, D., Demir, E., Ferhatosmanoglu, H., & Demirbas, M. (2010). Short text classification in twitter to improve information filtering. *Proceeding Of The 33Rd International ACM SIGIR Conference On Research And Development In Information Retrieval - SIGIR '10.* doi:10.1145/1835449.1835643

Stentz, A., & Mellon, C. (1993). Optimal and efficient path planning for unknown and dynamic environments. *International Journal of Robotics and Automation*, 10, 89–100.

Traficovc. (2015, November 24). *traffiCARACAS: vía @mahery21: CERRADA LA VALLE COCHE DESVÍAN TODOS LOS CARROS POR LOS TÚNELES #VALLECOCHE (hace un par de minutos)* [Twitter post]. Retrieved from https://twitter.com/traficovc

Tumasjan, A., Sprenger, T. O., Sandner, P. G., & Welpe, I. M. (2010). Predicting Elections with Twitter: What 140 Characters Reveal about Political Sentiment. In *Proceedings of the Fourth International AAAI Conference on Weblogs and Social Media* (pp. 178-185). Washington, DC: The AAAI Press.

Von Ahn, L., Maurer, B., McMillen, C., Abraham, D., & Blum, M. (2008). reCAPTCHA: Human-Based Character Recognition via Web Security Measures. *Science*, 321(5895), 1465–1468. doi:10.1126/science.1160379 PMID:18703711

Wang, H., Can, D., Kazemzadeh, A., Bar, F., & Narayanan, S. (2012, July). A system for real-time twitter sentiment analysis of 2012 us presidential election cycle. In *Proceedings of the ACL 2012 System Demonstrations* (pp. 115-120). Association for Computational Linguistics.

KEY TERMS AND DEFINITIONS

Binary Classification: The task of categorizing the elements belonging to a set into two groups based on a classification rule.

Crowdsourcing: Process outsource tasks traditionally performed employees or contractors, leaving them in charge of a large group of people or a community, through an open call.

Exponential Smoothing: The process that exponentially increases the weight of the observations as the observations increase their antiquity.

Machine Learning: A branch of artificial intelligence that aims to develop techniques that allow computers to learn.

Natural Language Processing: A field that is responsible for the development and research of computationally efficient mechanisms for communication between people and machines through the natural language.

Recommender System: A system that predicts the preference or rating that a user would give to an item.

Sentiment Analysis: A process that identifies and extracts subjective information in source materials.

Stemmer: A process for removing the commoner morphological and inflexional endings from words in order to reduce them to their roots.

Chapter 6
Customer Complaints in Social Networks in the Spanish Telecommunication Industry:
An Analysis Using 'Critizen'

Antonia Estrella-Ramón
University of Almeria, Spain

Alba Utrera-Serrano
University of Almeria, Spain

ABSTRACT

Nowadays social networks have a high potential to disseminate information, positive and negative, of any person, organization or product generating electronic word of mouth through customers' comments and complaints. Consequently, this paper proposes a novel research on the content related to the users' online complaints and seeks to understand the power of social networks as creating electronic word of mouth. For this task, the user-generated social network Critizen is used, especially critiques related to one of the most criticised sectors in Spain, that is, the telecommunication industry. The main results of this paper reveal that content analysis is an effective technique to extract business value from the vast amount of data available on the Internet, and especially in social networks.

INTRODUCTION

Social media have intensely changed our lives, how we interact with one another and the world around us (He, Zha, & Li, 2013). They offer what was never before thought possible, that is, constant connectivity between people (Jansen, Zhang, Sobel, & Chowdury, 2009). Although social networks have existed for a short while, they are evolving into an essential part of many businesses' marketing strategies. In this regard, companies are increasingly adopting social media tools (e.g., Twitter, Facebook, Instagram) to provide services, and more importantly, interact with customers (Woo, Lim, & Brymer, 2015). However, customers are also generating their own communities in order to give their opinions about products and

DOI: 10.4018/978-1-5225-0648-5.ch006

services they acquire and use every day (Jeong & Koo, 2015). The emergence of Web 2.0 has promoted the development of this user-generated content about companies, which creates electronic word of mouth (e-WOM) through customers' comments and complaints. E-WOM refers to any statement made by potential, actual, and former customers about products, services, and/or companies, which is made available to a multitude of people and institutions via the Internet (Henning-Thurau, Gwinner, Walsh, & Gremler, 2004). In this regard, e-WOM can be positive or negative, seriously improving (in case of positive comments) or harming (in case of negative comments) a company reputation in a short period of time. More specifically, the negative e-WOM is created by dissatisfying product or services customers' experiences (i.e., complaints), which can lead to consumer exit and have a detrimental effect on the reputation of companies (Clark, 2013).

Therefore, as a result of the rapid evolution of social networks, a large amount of user-generated content is available on the Internet. In order to benefit from this customer-generated content and increase the competitive advantage of business, companies need to monitor and analyse this information. In an effort to help companies understand how to perform social media competitive analysis and transform social media data into knowledge for decision making, this research describes a case study that applies content analysis methodology to evaluate unstructured text content on 'Critizen', a Spanish user-generated online community. This social network facilitates a platform for customers to write reviews about companies, brands, products and services from different industries (e.g., telecommunication sector, banks and insurance sectors, e-commerce, hotels, restaurants). As a social network, this website requires users to sign up to write a comment or a complaint. Users also have the opportunity to view, write comments and pass comments and complaints within this social network, generating the three types of e-WOM, that is, opinion seeking (i.e., the display level of a comment/critique), opinion giving (i.e., the level of comments received by a comment/critique) and opinion passing (i.e, the level of sharing of a comment/critique), respectively. For this study, we have analysed users' comments and critiques related to the telecommunication sector, because this is the leading sector on complaints for more than a decade in Spain. Telecommunication sector has received more than 37% of complaints handled by Facua[1] in 2014 (Facua, 2014), being more than seven points up the same period on 2013. Thus, these figures make this sector of particular interest for this study.

Some previous studies analyse customer complaints within the telecommunication companies (e.g., Edvardsson & Roos, 2003), but expressed in an offline context. Despite the fact that previous research shows that in the context of tourism and hospitality, the use of consumer rating, travel blogs, and review sites on the Internet (e.g., Tripadvisor) have received increasing attention from researchers in recent years (Leung, Law, van Hoof, & Buhalis, 2013), the use of this kind of customers' data from other sectors, such as telecommunications, is scarce. From a wider perspective, previous research about e-WOM has been mainly focused on review-generating factors (previous factors that cause consumers to write reviews), and impacts of e-WOM (impacts caused by online reviews) from a consumer perspective and a company perspective (Cantallops & Salvi, 2014). However, there is a certain lack of research analysing which information depicted in comments contributes more to increase the e-WOM of companies, and more specifically, about the role of social media platforms in generating public concerns and complaints against organizations (Clark, 2013).

The main goal of this research is focused on analyzing the power of social networks in creating e-WOM. In particular, this study seeks to show the relationship between the public response (i.e., the act of publicly expressing a complaint addressed to the company providing the service, and which cause dissatisfaction to customer) and the private and amplified response (because of the effect of spreading the message through social networks). For this task, we get a complaint classification based on the different dimensions of e-WOM (i.e., opinion seeking, opinion giving, opinion passing) and a set of independent variables that reflect all the information depicted in each comment or critique (i.e., company receiving the comment, service, topic, user's gender, user's state and whether the complaint has been solved) using Latent Class (LC) Regression methodology. In summary, this case study investigates two main research questions:

RQ 1: Which information depicted in a comment has greater effects on the creation of different types of e-WOM?

RQ 2: How we can classify customers' complaints in terms of e-WOM?

The main results of this study reveal that content analysis is an effective technique to extract business value from the vast amount of data available on the Internet, and especially on social networks. Recommendations are also provided to help companies develop better customer management using information from social media sites.

This research is structured as follows. Firstly, we review the relevant literature related to the present study. Secondly, we describe the methodology used to conduct the empirical study and present the results of the analysis. Finally, we discuss the implications of the research and identify several limitations and directions for future research.

LITERATURE REVIEW

In this Section, the most relevant literature related to the present study is reviewed, such as complaining behaviour of customers, word of mouth (WOM), electronic word of mouth (e-WOM), and the effect that Social Networks Sites (SNSs) exerts on the dissemination of electronic word of mouth.

Complaining Behaviour and Negative WOM

Dissatisfaction plays a key role in customers' complaint behaviour. It is an evaluative process whereby expectations are compared to actual performance. From the Theory of Complaining (Kowalski, 1996), a complaint can be defined as "an expression of dissatisfaction, whether subjectively experienced or not, for the purpose of venting emotions or achieving intrapsychic goals". Therefore, dissatisfaction is a frequent but not necessary antecedent of complaining. When customers experience dissatisfaction, the decision to complain implies an analysis of the subjective utility of complaining. In this process, customers decide about the effort involved in making the complaint and the benefit they will receive for doing so (Kim, Kim, Im, & Shin, 2003).

Complaints can be classified using two criteria: (i) media used to make a complaint (direct and indirect) (Sparks & Browning, 2011), and (ii) audience of the complaint (public and private) (Clark, 2013). On one hand, dissatisfied customers have traditionally make complaints to companies personally, face-to-face or even using the phone. They are called direct complaints (Sparks & Browning, 2011). Conversely, dissatisfied customers have also make complaints indirectly by writing, or done nothing but told friends and family of the incident (Sparks & Browning, 2011). On the other hand, public complaints are directed to the company by customers in order to get compensation. Therefore, public complaints reflect the fact of complaining (Clark, 2013). On the contrary, private complaints involve switching behaviour and spreading negative WOM, which sometimes remains largely undetected by the organisation (Clark, 2013). Despite the fact that some authors treat differently public and private complaints (e.g., Singh & Howell, 1985), other authors consider that both types of complaints can be developed simultaneously (e.g., Blodgett, Hill, & Tax, 1997). For example, if a dissatisfied customer decides to write a public complaint to the company, he/she can also practice negative WOM (i.e., through a private complaint).

As we have previously stated, complaints and negative WOM are related concepts. Until a few years ago, the cost of complaints and consequently, negative WOM that companies had to assume was limited to a small audience. Nowadays, with the development of Internet and information technology, online comments can now go viral, reach thousand and even millions of people, seriously improving (in case of positive comments) or harming (in case of negative comments) a company reputation in a short period of time.

Electronic Word of Mouth (e-WOM)

Customers often look for information and advice from their interpersonal relationships because one cannot easily evaluate products and services without previously hear a first-hand experience. This phenomenon is known in marketing communication as Word of mouth (WOM), and is defined as interpersonal communication about products and services among customers, which affects the message effectiveness and evaluations of reviewed goods (Hong & Park, 2012). Traditional WOM has been known as an effective marketing tool that has a major influence on customer behaviour. While advertising may increase recognition of products or services, information obtained from relatives (i.e., through WOM) has proven to have more impact on customers' decision making (Khammash & Griffiths, 2011).

WOM can be negative or positive, organic or amplified, and comes from a range of sources (Chatterjee, 2001). Word of Mouth Marketing Association (WOMMA) defines organic WOM as such which occurs naturally when customers become advocates because they feel happy with a product and have a natural desire to share their support and enthusiasm with others. On the contrary, amplified WOM occurs when marketers launch communication campaigns especially designed to encourage or accelerate WOM, which do not necessarily imply that customers use the product.

With respect to the WOM source, the development of the network technology of the Internet facilitates access to online product reviews and comments written by consumers. This fact has changed the traditional face-to-face WOM communication into computer-mediated WOM communication, generating the electronic word of mouth (e-WOM). More specifically, e-WOM refers to any statement made by potential, actual, and former consumers about a product, services, and/or companies, which is made available to a multitude of people and institutions via the Internet (Henning-Thurau *et al.*, 2004). WOM information accessible online is available in much larger quantity, in comparison to similar types of information that may be available offline (Chatterjee, 2001). Thus, there are diverse forms of user-generated e-WOM, which include short verbal depictions of customer experiences, rankings between different product elements, pictures, text, videos, etc. In addition, several types of electronic media have been used to spread e-WOM (see Table 1). Their typology is two-dimensional, which comprises level of interactivity and communication scope. In particular, the level of interactivity can be asynchronous (e.g., emails, review sites, blogs and micro blogs) and synchronous (e.g., chat rooms, newsgroups, instant messaging). On

Table 1. Typology of e-WOM

Communication Scope	Level of Interactivity	
	Asynchronous	Synchronous
Many-to-Many	Blogs and micro blogs	Newsgroups
	Virtual Communities	
One-to-Many	Websites	Chat Rooms
	Product Reviews	
	Hate Sites	
	Video-sharing sites, image-sharing sites, pinning sites, tagging sites	
One-to-One	E-mail	Instant Messaging

Source: Adapted from Jalilvand, Esfahani, & Samiei (2011).

the other hand, the communication scope ranges from one to one, connecting one customer with another (e.g., e-mails), one to many, connecting a single customer with many others (e.g., review sites), or many to many, connecting many customers with many others (e.g., virtual communities) (Jalilvand, Esfahani, & Samiei, 2011).

Conceptually, e-WOM in Social Network Sites (SNSs) can be examined through three main aspects, which include opinion seeking, opinion giving and opinion passing (Chu & Kim, 2011). As previous research has been mainly focused on offline WOM, opinion seeking and opinion giving dimensions have received more attention from academics. In this regard, customers with a high level of opinion seeking behaviour tend to search for information and advice from friends and relatives when making a purchase decision (Flynn, Goldsmith, & Eastman, 1996). However, there are also people more interested in disseminate information about products and brands that they test, that is, they have a high level of opinion-giving behaviour. They are considered opinion leaders and usually exert a big impact on other customers (Feick & Price, 1987).

The great level of fast interactivity provided by the Internet makes e-WOM a more dynamic communication tool than traditional WOM. Consequently, an online customer can take the different roles of opinion seeker (characterised by a high level of opinion seeking behaviour), opinion provider (as an opinion leader, with a high opinion giving behaviour), and more importantly within the online context, opinion transmitter (with a high level of opinion passing behaviour). Online opinion forwarding/passing is an important behaviour consequence of e-WOM, which facilitates the flow of information among customers (Sun, Youn, Wu, & Kuntaraporn, 2006). For example, online customers in addition to search for brand information and create content, they can feel the necessity to share contents with other customers, implying a high level of opinion passing behaviour. For this task, they can use their Social Networks in order to create and collect content to share with others, because Social Networks are configured as a credible and reliable source of information for purchases. Indeed, opinion passing behaviour is more likely to occur in online Social Networks, mainly because they are a multidirectional media and with a few clicks of the mouse, consumers can spread the word on a global scale (Norman & Russell, 2006).

E-WOM in Social Networks Sites (SNSs)

Organizations use the Integrated Marketing Communications (IMC) to communicate with their target markets (Mangold & Faulds, 2009). IMC is a concept under which a company systematically coordinates its multiple messages and many communications channels and integrates them into a cohesive and consistent marketing communication mix (Lee & Park, 2007). Therefore, IMC tries to manage and control the different elements of the promotional mix –advertising, personal selling, public relations, publicity, direct marketing, and sales promotion– to create a unified customer-focused message and, thus, get various organizational objectives (Boone & Kurtz, 2014). Consequently, IMC provides several brand outcomes, such as brand awareness, brand loyalty, and more sales (Reid, 2005). Nevertheless, as we have previously stated, the tools and strategies for communicating with customers have experienced a great change with the fact known as social media, also referred to as consumer-generated media (e.g., Critizen) (Mangold & Faulds, 2009). This kind of media describes a variety of new sources of online information that are created, initiated, circulated and used by consumers intent on educating each other about products, brands, services, personalities, and issues (Blackshaw & Nazzaro, 2004).

Social media is a hybrid element of the communication mix because it combines characteristics of traditional IMC tools (i.e., companies talking to customers) with a highly magnified form of WOM (i.e., customers talking to one another) whereby marketing managers cannot control the content and frequency of such information (Mangold & Faulds, 2009). This change in the information control (i.e., from controlled media to uncontrolled ones with the advent of social media) influences the way consumer perceive and respond to market information (Ramsey, 2006; Singh, Veron-Jackson, & Cullinane, 2008), feeling more free and unconstrained.

Nowadays, social media has augmented the power of consumer-to-consumer conversations in the marketplace by enabling one person to communicate with factually hundreds of other customers rapidly and almost without effort –as indicated earlier, generating e-WOM– (Mangold & Faulds, 2009). Due to the fact that managers cannot control these conversations, many companies are using their own SNSs to enhance customers' interest in their brands (e.g., Dove, Coca Cola, and Harley-Davidson), because they associate themselves with brands explicitly by becoming a friend or fan. These organizations have created communities of like-minded individuals through SNSs, such as Facebook and Twitter, where they can exert some control but cannot totally control what people says (Chu & Kim, 2011).

An important characteristic that makes SNSs distinctive from other e-WOM media is that social networks users are willingly available on these sites. SNSs contacts may be perceived as more trustworthy and credible than unknown strangers, which leads SNSs to get an important source of product information for customers, and enormously facilitates and accelerates e-WOM (Chu & Kim, 2011). As we have previously stated, WOM has been recognized as one of the most influential resources of information transmission. Therefore, despite the fact that traditional WOM communication is only effective within limited social contact boundaries, the advances of information technology and the emergence of online SNSs have expanded the way information is transmitted. The power of social media and e-WOM are enormous to help business to maintain competitiveness in the market (Racherla, Connolly, & Christodoulidou, 2013), especially because of the increasing availability of customer data: we are in the era of the big data (McAfee & Brynjolfsson, 2012).

METHODOLOGY

Research Context

The scope of the present study was restricted to the telecommunication sector, in particular telecommunication companies operating in Spain. As we have stated previously, telecommunication sector has received in this country a high number of customers' complaints over the last few years (Facua, 2014), thereby making this sector of particular interest for this study. More specifically, as secondary data provided by the Spanish Government we have included Table 2. These data can be used as baseline information indicating which telecommunication companies have received more claims throughout the year 2014.

This research was conducted through social network 'Critizen'. 'Critizen', as a user-generated social network, was created with a clear motivation, that is, it offers customers a new channel to share views/opinions about the services received or products purchased from different companies not controlled by these companies, thus providing citizens with a structured channel where they can feel free and unconstrained. In 'Critizen' we can find first-hand opinions from other customers (positive or negative), offer their positive opinions and critiques, and even sometimes get feedback from firms. However, 'Critizen' does not mediate customer complaints, it is only a place where users can share their opinions and companies can hear customers getting them a fast reply (i.e., companies can also log in to the social network as a standard user). 'Critizen' offers customers a number of advantages, such as they can complaint without having to wait in line or carry out complex processes (i.e., avoiding the bureaucracy of complaints made directly to companies) and feel that a complaint is not heard by anyone. When an individual wants to join 'Critizen', he/she can use his/her Facebook, Twitter or Google+ account in order to log in to the social network. Due to 'Critizen' is a Spanish social network, the main language is Spanish, but a user can write his/her opinions in a different language. When a user logs in to Critizen, he/she cannot find

Table 2. Percentage of critiques received by telecommunication companies in Spain in 2014

Telecommunication Companies	Fixed Line Telephony	Mobile Line Telephony	Internet (At Home)	Data Plan (Internet in Mobile Devices)	Package (Fixed Line Telephony and Internet at Home)	Package (Mobile Line Telephony and Data Plan)
Movistar	1.64%	1.90%	0.31%	0.43%	2.14%	0.19%
Vodafone	4.60%	4.51%	1.52%	0.46%	5.37%	0.36%
Orange	8.25%	3.20%	2.15%	0.26%	11.58%	0.44%
Ono	5.58%	NA	4.29%	NA	12.19%	NA
Jazztel	7.43%	NA	1.48%	NA	9.99%	NA
Pepe Phone	NA	NA	NA	NA	NA	NA
Amena	NA	NA	NA	NA	NA	NA
Yoigo	NA	1.53%	NA	0.15%	NA	0.10%
Simyo	NA	NA	NA	NA	NA	NA
NA: Not available						

Source: Spanish Government, Ministry of Industry, Energy and Tourism.

companies included in an index of industry sectors. On the contrary, he/she will find a list of institutions, famous people, companies and miscellanea. In case of companies, which is the section involved in this research, they are ordered in two different rankings: those companies receiving more critiques and those ones receiving more positive comments. When a user clicks on a company, a list of users' comments about this company is displayed on the screen, and he/she can click on a comment in order to read it (and increase the level of opinion seeking of this comment), leave a comment (and increase the level of opinion giving of this comment) or share this comment (and increase the level of opinion passing of this comment). In addition, users can write their own comments (positive or negative) about the existing companies (listed on Critizen) or include a new Company in the list (through the text included in the subject of the comment).

'Critizen' has been operating since January 4th, 2015 throughout the Spanish national level. This social network started operating through a website and a mobile application (i.e., app), but since July 2015 'Critizen' only operates through the mobile app. Despite its recent launch into the marketplace, 'Critizen' has already received a great deal of success among customers, who can make comments and critiques to companies of different sectors (e.g., telecommunication sector, banks and insurance sectors, e-commerce, hotels, restaurants). In this regard, the sector that has been mostly criticised also within 'Critizen' is the telecommunication sector. At the time of the data collection the number of comments towards this sector reached approximately 2,000 (more specifically, Movistar received 434 comments, Vodafone 314, Orange 499, Ono 222, Jazztel 388, Pepe Phone 44 and Amena 25).

Data Collection and Measures

Content analysis is a reputable and widely used tool for conducting objective, systematic and quantitative analysis of communication content (Kassarfian, 1977). It has been used in different fields of marketing, such as consumer behaviour, advertising, and international marketing to understand the characteristics and behaviour of the target market (Singh & Matsuo, 2004). Therefore, we use content analysis to systematically analyse and classify the level of customers' engagement in e-WOM depicted on the social network 'Critizen' regarding the telecommunication sector. In particular, the sample for this study consists of customers' reviews of men and women over 14 belonging to the Spanish population (because child under 14 cannot participate in 'Critizen' as is stated in the terms and conditions of the company policy), who have joined this social network site in order to make public their comments and complaints. We manually analyse the content of 880 customers' reviews published on Critizen accessed using a standard user account. The time period considered in order to collect the information is fixed to those customers' reviews posted on the website between January 18th and March 18th 2015. All the measures related to each comment/complaint were coded into a database during April 2015. A process of estimating the reliability of codification was performed. More specifically, two researchers have monitored the codification of some problematic cases.

Men represent 69% of the sample, whereas women represent 31% of the sample. As a social network specifically designed to host complaints, public information related to each user's profile comprises only the user's name, and consequently, in some cases customers' gender. However, we cannot measure customers' age. The only information available online about customers' age is described in the company policy, which states that children under 14 cannot participate in this social network. In addition, from each comment we have collected the following information: company receiving the comment, service, topic, user state, and whether the complaint has been solved. Moreover, the degree of depiction of each e-WOM type is evaluated as three continuous variables, which represent opinion seeking, opinion giving and opinion passing (Chu & Kim, 2011). The set of variables used in this study are described in Table 3.

Table 3. Variables included in this study

Dependent Variables	Description		Type of Variable
Opinion seeking	Number of displays per comment/complaint		Continuous
Opinion giving	Number of comments received per comment/complaint		Continuous
Opinion passing	Number of shared per comment/complaint		Continuous
Independent Variables	**Description**		**Type of Variable**
Company	Name of the company receiving the comment/critiques. Companies are ordered according to market share (in Spain):		Categorical
	1. Movistar	6. Pepe Phone	
	2. Vodafone	7. Amena	
	3. Orange	8. Yoigo	
	4. Ono	9. Simyo	
	5. Jazztel		
Service	We have considered as services the following categories, which receive comments/critiques:		Categorical
	1. Fixed-line telephony	4. Data plan (Internet in mobile devices)	
	2. Mobile line telephony	5. Package (comprises 1, 2, 3 and 4)	
	3. Internet (at home)	6. Others	
Topic	We have considered as topics the following categories, which receive comments/critiques:		Categorical
	1. Cancelation of contracts/ unsubscriptions	6. Coverage	
	2. New subscriptions	7. Device	
	3. Portability	8. Permanency	
	4. Billing	9. Telemarketing	
	5. Service conditions	10. Others	
User's state	'Critizen' proposes a number of states that users can choose when they are writing a comment/critique. In particular:		Categorical
	1. Happy	4. Outraged	
	2.Upset	5. Angry	
	3. Frustrated		
User's gender	1. Female; 2. Male		Binary
Whether the complaint has been solved	Using the information available in each comment, we have coded if the complaint has or has not solved by the company. Some complaints do not include this information:		Categorical
	1. Yes, the critique has been solved		
	2. No, the complaint has not been solved		
	3. Not available		

Data Analysis

This study seeks to get a complaint classification based on the different dimensions of e-WOM as dependent variables (i.e., opinion seeking, opinion giving, opinion passing) explained by a set of independent variables. The set of independent variables selected to explain and classify e-WOM behaviour of customers are described in Table 2. For this task, we have used LC regression methodology as implemented in the Latent Gold 4.5 software. Latent Gold is a powerful latent class and finite mixture software program, which contains separate modules for estimating three different model structures: LC Cluster models, Discrete Factor (DFactor) models and LC Regression models. The Latent Class Regression models module was used to perform the proposed analysis.

LC regression analysis is a powerful technique for marketing segmentation that has demonstrated its superior performance over other traditional methods (DeSarbo & Wedel, 1994). It provides a powerful probabilistic analysis especially flexible to deal with dependent and independent variables of mixed types (Kamakura & Wedel, 1995; Magidson & Vermunt, 2004). In particular, the regression model proposed in this research mainly includes continuous and categorical variables. Another advantage of the LC regression over other segmentation methods implies the creation of a posteriori segments by estimating utilities for each segment and the probability that each individual belongs to each segment (Wilson-Jeanselme & Reynolds, 2006). On the contrary, other techniques imply the creation of a priori segments, which may be distinct but may not behave differently with respect to the variables analysed in the study (DeSarbo, Jedidi, & Sinha, 2001).

Results

To check the existence of multicollinearity, we examined bivariate correlations (see Table 4) and VIF values. Correlations with values above 0.8 indicate multicollinearity. In our case, all correlations are below this value and all VIF values were below 2, which is the cut-off value recommended by Neter, Wasserman, & Kutner (1990). Thus, we can conclude that multicollinearity is not a problem in this study.

The segment membership is identified by applying LC regression analysis using Latent Gold 4.5 software. We have performed three different analyses, each one related to each dependent variable considered (i.e., opinion seeking, opinion giving and opinion passing). Firstly, in order to clarify the

Table 4. Correlation matrix (N = 880)

	1	2	3	4	5	6
1. Company	1					
2. Service	0.142**	1				
3. Topic	0.016	0.198**	1			
4. User's state	-0.144**	-0.094**	0.070*	1		
5. User's gender	-0.002	0.013	-0.046	-0.058	1	
6. Whether the complaint has been solved	0.097**	0.051	0.041	-0.139**	0.056	1

** $p < 0.01$; * $p < 0.05$

Table 5. Opinion seeking model: selection criteria for competing LC regression models

Number of Segments	BIC (LL)	Change in BIC [a]	AIC	Change in AIC [a]	CAIC (LL)	Change in CAIC [a]	Classification Error	R^2
1 cluster	16.048,96	-	15.900,78	-	16.079,96	-	0	0,13
2 clusters	**15.725,01**	**-2,02**	**15.423,87**	**-3,00**	**15.788,01**	**-1,82**	**0,0076**	**0,74**
3 clusters	15.814,26	0,57	15.360,16	-0,41	15.909,26	0,77	0,1391	0,79
4 clusters	15.976,22	1,02	15.369,17	0,06	16.103,22	1,22	0,2372	0,95
5 clusters	16.036,13	0,38	15.276,12	-0,61	16.195,13	0,57	0,2489	0,96
6 clusters	16.126,04	0,94	15.213,07	-1,02	16.317,04	1,33	0,2435	0,98

[a]Changes in BIC, AIC, and CAIC refer to the previous number of clusters.
[b]The values supporting the appropriateness of the *2-segment* solution are printed in boldface.

output (in terms of number of segments, goodness of fit and validation) of the selected technique (i.e., LC Regression analysis), we have included a brief description of the indicator BIC, AIC and CAIC, classification error and R^2 (Martínez-Guerrero, Ortega-Egea, & Román-González, 2007). In particular:

- Bayesian Information Criteria (BIC), Akaike Information Criteria (AIC) and Consistent AIC (CAIC) are very useful for comparing different model solutions in LC analysis. These indicators allow for comparisons between different models based on their model fit and parsimony (Magidson & Vermunt, 2004). Lower values of BIC, AIC or CAIC characterise optimal solutions.
- Classification error statistic reports information about the proportion of cases classified into an incorrect class or segment. This value should be as close to zero as possible.
- R^2 statistic represents the proportional reduction of errors of a concrete model, compared with a baseline model. This value should be as close to one as possible.

With respect to the first model (i.e., opinion seeking), among one to six possible class structures, the two-class solution has the lowest BIC (15,725.01), AIC (15,423.87) and CAIC (15,788.01) values (see Table 5). The entropy or proportional reduction of errors of a model R^2 (0.74) and the classification error (0.0076) also support the appropriateness of the two-segment solution. On the other hand, with respect to the second model (i.e., opinion giving), among one to six possible class structures, the two-class solution also has the lowest BIC (4,651.06), AIC (4,349.93) and CAIC (4,714.06) values (see Table 6). The entropy or proportional reduction of errors of a model R^2 (0.67) and the classification error (0.16) also support the appropriateness of the two-segment solution. Finally, with respect to the third model (i.e., opinion passing), the 2-class solution was also preferred over more complex models in terms of interpretability of the segment profiles, thus providing a higher practical value (see Table 7). Indeed, cluster solutions with more than two segments were not regarded as appropriate, owing to practically insignificant reductions in all segments retention criteria and excessive classification errors (Ortega-Egea, García-de-Frutos, & Antolín-López, 2014).

As detailed in Table 8, for each model latent class sizes and average value of dependent variables were unbalanced between the two differentiated segments. From the LC regression results, we are able to rank the mean level of opinion seeking, opinion giving and opinion passing associated to each model.

Table 6. Opinion giving model: selection criteria for competing LC regression models

Number of Segments	BIC (LL)	Change in BIC [a]	AIC	Change in AIC [a]	CAIC (LL)	Change in CAIC [a]	Classification Error	R²
1 cluster	4.699,99	-	4.551,81	-	4.730,99	-	0	0,11
2 clusters	**4.651,06**	**-1,04**	**4.349,93**	**-4,44**	**4.714,06**	**-0,36**	**0,1577**	**0,67**
3 clusters	4.709,31	1,25	4.255,21	-2,18	4.804,31	1,91	0,1446	0,87
4 clusters	4.794,68	1,81	4.187,63	-1,59	4.921,68	2,44	0,1712	0,92
5 clusters	4.881,20	1,80	4.121,19	-1,59	5.040,20	2,41	0,2385	0,92
6 clusters	5.045,46	5,23	4.132,49	-1,32	5.236,46	6,40	0,2171	0,97

[a]Changes in BIC, AIC, and CAIC refer to the previous number of clusters.
[b]The values supporting the appropriateness of the 2-segment solution are printed in boldface.

Table 7. Opinion passing model: selection criteria for competing LC regression models

Number of Segments	BIC (LL)	Change in BIC [a]	AIC	Change in AIC [a]	CAIC (LL)	Change in CAIC [a]	Classification Error	R²
1 cluster	1.507,50	-	1.349,77	-	1.540,50	-	0	0,05
2 clusters	1.644,30	9,07	**1.324,04**	**-1,91**	1.711,30	11,09	**0,1448**	**0,54**
3 clusters	1.818,94	10,62	1.336,16	0,92	1.919,94	12,19	0,3966	0,72
4 clusters	1.918,56	5,48	1.273,28	-4,71	2.053,56	6,96	0,4492	0,97
5 clusters	2.097,38	9,32	1.289,57	1,28	2.266,38	10,36	0,5709	0,99
6 clusters	2.319,37	20,89	1.349,05	5,95	2.522,37	22,83	0,6262	1,00

[a]Changes in BIC, AIC, and CAIC refer to the previous number of clusters.
[b]The values supporting the appropriateness of the 2-segment solution are printed in boldface.

With regard to the effect of independent variables inside each group, the following variables provide differentiated effects in each group for the first LC regression model: company (Wald (=) = 92.06; p < 0.05), service (Wald (=) = 72.18; p < 0.05), topic (Wald (=) = 86.68; p < 0.05), and whether the complaint has been solved (Wald (=) = 9.08; p < 0.05) (see Table 8). For the second LC regression model, only the variable company (Wald (=) = 27.35; p < 0.05) provide differentiated effects in each

Table 8. Description of the classes

	Opinion Seeking Model		Opinion Giving Model		Opinion Passing Model	
	Class 1	Class 2	Class 1	Class 2	Class 1	Class 2
Class size (%)	86.89%	13.11%	57.05%	42.95%	86.89%	13.11%
Class size (number of customers' reviews)	765	115	502	378	765	115
Mean dependent variable	6,388,35	1,467.62	1,654.56	-16,604.73	6,388.35	1,467.62
Class brief description	High opinion seeking	Low opinion seeking	High opinion giving	Low opinion giving	High opinion passing	Low opinion passing

Table 9. Independent variables associations with opinion seeking

Independent Variables		Parameter Estimates [a]		Wald	p-Value	Wald (=)	p-Value
		Class 1	Class 2				
Company	1. Movistar	**1,122.41**	-352.27	**245.4335**	**0.00**	**92.0595**	**0.00**
	2. Vodafone	**477.63**	-512.98				
	3. Orange	**-181.98**	-809.32				
	4. Ono	111.00	**245.37**				
	5. Jazztel	**-165.25**	-373.00				
	6. Pepe Phone	-598.09	**8.70**				
	7. Amena	-165.17	**2,340.13**				
	8. Yoigo	199.95	**275.52**				
	9. Simyo	**-800.51**	-822.14				
Service	1. Fixed-line telephony	218.84	**3,469.89**	**136.4376**	**0.00**	**72.1767**	**0.00**
	2. Mobile line telephony	**123.66**	-578.14				
	3. Internet (at home)	**55.75**	-676.12				
	4. Data plan (Internet in mobile devices)	**-221.53**	-766.95				
	5. Package	**78.63**	-956.95				
	6. Others	**-255.36**	-491.73				
Topic	1. Cancelation of contracts/ unsubscriptions	**58.54**	-120.12	**126.3417**	**0.00**	**86.6756**	**0.00**
	2. New subscriptions	**-7.49**	-632.27				
	3. Portability	-82.61	**-8.03**				
	4. Billing	**-78.02**	-634.90				
	5. Service conditions	**-52.73**	-389.52				
	6. Coverage	**-232.31**	-385.66				
	7. Device	**307.66**	-557.46				
	8. Permanency	-164.95	**3.740.78**				
	9. Telemarketing	**136.42**	-626.19				
	10. Others	**115.48**	-386.63				
Users' state	1. Happy	78.99	-73.32	11.4436	0.18	3.4279	0.49
	2.Upset	-8.33	-311.01				
	3. Frustrated	-7.46	132.96				
	4. Outraged	-77.63	34.79				
	5. Angry	14.43	216.59				
User's gender	1. Female	-7.65	-57.78	1.4601	0.48	0.571	0.45
	2. Male	7.65	57.78				
Whether the complaint has been solved	1. Yes, the critique has been solved	-230.64	**219.66**	**9.6755**	**0.046**	**9.0853**	**0.011**
	2. No, the complaint has not been solved	**-0.24**	-57.16				
	3. Not available	**230.88**	-162.51				

[a]Parameter estimates represent class-specific associations. of each independent variable with opinion seeking.
[b]The significant values are printed in boldface.

group. Finally, for the third LC regression model, the following variables provide differentiated effects between the two groups identified: company (Wald (=) = 17.05; p < 0.05), service (Wald (=) = 11.11; p < 0.05), user's gender (Wald (=) = 13.79; p < 0.05) and whether the complaint has been solved (Wald (=) = 5.76; p < 0.05) (see Table 9).

On the other hand, the first LC regression model suggests the existence of statistically significant influences of company (Wald = 245.43; p < 0.05), service (Wald = 136.44; p < 0.05), topic (Wald = 126.34; p < 0.05) and whether the complaint has been solved (Wald = 9.68; p < 0.05) on opinion seeking (see Table 9). Non-significant effects exist only for user's state and user's gender. More specifically, users' complaints in segment 1 are characterised by a high opinion seeking (i.e., receiving more views from other customers), they are related to companies such as Movistar, Vodafone, Orange, Ono, Jazztel and Symio, and services such as mobile line telephony, Internet (at home), data plan, packages and others. In addition, complaints in segment 1 are related to topics such as cancelation of contracts/unsubscriptions, new subscriptions, billing, service conditions, coverage, device, telemarketing and others.

The second LC regression model suggests the existence of statistically significant influences of company (Wald = 54.77; p < 0.05) on opinion giving (see Table 10). Non-significant effects exist for services, topic, user's state, user's gender and whether the complaint has been solved. In this case, users' complaints in segment 1 are characterised by a high opinion giving (i.e., receiving more comments from other customers) and they are related to companies such as Vodafone, Orange, Ono and Jazztel.

The third LC regression model suggests the existence of statistically significant influences of company (Wald = 36.40; p < 0.05), service (Wald = 26.38; p < 0.05), user's gender (Wald = 18.05; p < 0.05) and whether the complaint has been solved (Wald = 11.46; p < 0.05) on opinion passing (see Table 11). Non-significant effects exist only for topic and user's state. Users' complaints in segment 1 are characterised by a high opinion passing (i.e., receiving more shared from other customers), they are related to companies such as Movistar, Vodafone, Orange, Ono, Jazztel and Yoigo, and services such as mobile line telephony, Internet (at home) and data plan. Additionally, complaints in segment 1 are more depicted by women than men, and they are more related to complaints that have been solved by the company.

We conclude this section with a node-link diagram (see Figure 1) summarizing the main results of this research. Nodes represent variables included in this research, whereas links represents significant relationships between variables.

CONCLUSION

The main goal of this study was focused on analyzing the power of social networks in creating e-WOM. In particular, this study seeks to show the relationship between the public response (i.e., the act of publicly expressing a complaint addressed to the company providing the service, and which cause dissatisfaction to customer; public complaints reflect the fact of complaining) and the private and amplified response (i.e., involving switching behavior and spreading negative WOM, which sometimes remains largely undetected by the organization; this response is amplified by the effect of spreading the message through social networks). The main results of the LC regression analysis proposed offer enough information in order to achieve this goal, and thus, enhance the knowledge we have about the effect of social networks in creating e-WOM. In particular, regarding the first research question (i.e., RQ 1: Which information depicted in a comment has greater effects on the creation of different types of e-WOM?), the most influential variables defining opinion seeking are company, service, topic and whether the complaint

Table 10. Independent variables associations with opinion giving

Independent Variables		Parameter Estimates [a]		Wald	p-Value	Wald (=)	p-Value
		Class 1	Class 2				
Company	1. Movistar	-0.06	**0.19**	**54.7663**	**0.00**	**27.3472**	**0.00**
	2. Vodafone	**0.34**	0.22				
	3. Orange	**0.26**	-0.18				
	4. Ono	**0.01**	-0.96				
	5. Jazztel	**0.10**	-0.32				
	6. Pepe Phone	-0.34	**0.65**				
	7. Amena	-0.55	-3.89				
	8. Yoigo	0.95	**4.59**				
	9. Simyo	-0.71	**-0.29**				
Service	1. Fixed-line telephony	0.30	-1.74	11.4611	0.32	5.5629	0.35
	2. Mobile line telephony	-0.13	-0.14				
	3. Internet (at home)	-0.48	0.78				
	4. Data plan (Internet in mobile devices)	0.12	0.39				
	5. Package	0.09	0.30				
	6. Others	0.09	0.41				
Topic	1. Cancelation of contracts/unsubscriptions	-0.01	0.94	26.8385	0.082	12.5621	0.18
	2. New subscriptions	-0.74	-0.76				
	3. Portability	0.07	-0.51				
	4. Billing	0.28	-0.64				
	5. Service conditions	-0.13	-0.14				
	6. Coverage	-0.37	-1.94				
	7. Device	-0.33	0.01				
	8. Permanency	0.26	1.87				
	9. Telemarketing	0.82	2.11				
	10. Others	0.14	-0.95				
Users' state	1. Happy	-0.03	1.90	12.1961	0.14	6.0679	0.19
	2. Upset	0.30	-1.89				
	3. Frustrated	-0.07	-0.54				
	4. Outraged	-0.22	0.16				
	5. Angry	0.02	0.38				
User's gender	1. Female	-0.04	0.14	0.6193	0.73	0.5841	0.44
	2. Male	0.04	-0.14				
Whether the complaint has been solved	1. Yes, the critique has been solved	0.07	1.05	1.5963	0.81	0.8215	0.66
	2. No, the complaint has not been solved	0.02	-0.40				
	3. Not available	-0.09	-0.66				

[a]Parameter estimates represent class-specific associations. of each independent variable with opinion giving.
[b]The significant values are printed in boldface.

Table 11. Independent variables associations with opinion passing

Independent Variables		Parameter Estimates [a]		Wald	p-Value	Wald (=)	p-Value
		Class 1	Class 2				
Company	1. Movistar	**2.06**	-4.79	**36.4015**	**0.00**	**17.0548**	**0.03**
	2. Vodafone	**0.87**	-0.03				
	3. Orange	**1.33**	-2.47				
	4. Ono	**0.69**	-1.07				
	5. Jazztel	**2.37**	-7.63				
	6. Pepe Phone	0.77	**13.53**				
	7. Amena	-4.92	**2.00**				
	8. Yoigo	**1.62**	-4.50				
	9. Simyo	-4.80	4.96				
Service	1. Fixed-line telephony	-2.00	**2.72**	**24.3817**	**0.01**	**11.1125**	**0.04**
	2. Mobile line telephony	**0.94**	-3.48				
	3. Internet (at home)	**0.05**	-3.64				
	4. Data plan (Internet in mobile devices)	**0.86**	-3.79				
	5. Package	-0.19	**4.54**				
	6. Others	0.34	**3.65**				
Topic	1. Cancelation of contracts/unsubscriptions	1.73	-15.05	29.592	0.042	9.6458	0.38
	2. New subscriptions	1.71	-1.81				
	3. Portability	0.68	-2.19				
	4. Billing	0.16	2.35				
	5. Service conditions	0.58	1.81				
	6. Coverage	-5.38	9.73				
	7. Device	0.36	0.02				
	8. Permanency	0.22	7.99				
	9. Telemarketing	-0.35	-3.98				
	10. Others	0.30	1.15				
Users' state	1. Happy	1.53	-12.52	11.867	0.16	8.0903	0.08
	2.Upset	0.19	1.70				
	3. Frustrated	-4.26	7.01				
	4. Outraged	1.29	-0.15				
	5. Angry	1.25	3.96				
User's gender	1. Female	-0.28	**2.14**	**18.0532**	**0.00**	**13.789**	**0.00**
	2. Male	**0.28**	-2.14				
Whether the complaint has been solved	1. Yes, the critique has been solved	**0.85**	-9.30	**11.4613**	**0.02**	**5.7559**	**0.04**
	2. No, the complaint has not been solved	-0.26	**3.75**				
	3. Not available	-0.58	**5.54**				

[a]Parameter estimates represent class-specific associations. of each independent variable with opinion passing.
[b]The significant values are printed in boldface.

Figure 1. Main results of this research

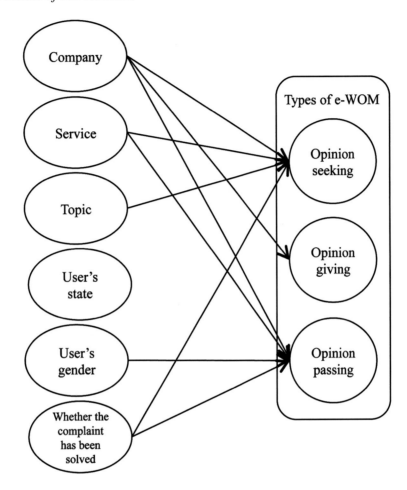

has been solved. On the other hand, the most influential variable defining opinion giving is mainly the company receiving the complaint. Finally, the most influential variables defining opinion passing are company, service, user's gender and whether the complaint has been solved. In addition, regarding the second research question (i.e., RQ 2: How we can classify customers' complaints in terms of e-WOM?), we have provided a significant classification of users' complaints according to the variables that exert more influence on opinion seeking, opinion giving and opinion passing.

The present study has important managerial implications for providers of customer goods and services, and more specifically, the telecommunication sector. In this regard, it has been demonstrated that e-business marketing and brand managers need to be aware of the benefits of observing online customer comments and critiques as sources of e-WOM, and consequently, they should carefully consider the influence of negative and positive reviews on the buying process. In particular, companies should consider information depicted in users' review platforms (such as 'Critizen') in order to introduce changes in their product development and innovation processes, which at the same time is going to improve customer satisfaction and customer retention. In this regard, using this information and on the basis of the performed analysis, companies generally should improve their orientation in order to develop better marketing strategies that do not generate dissatisfaction feelings to their customers, for example, meeting the agreements stated in contracts and providing better customer service. In addition, in the special case of the telecommunication companies, they should avoid unexplained charges on customers' bills. This fact can help companies to decrease the number of complaints or negative comments. Conversely, in case of the dissatisfaction is unavoidably generated, companies should try to make efforts to manage the situation in the best possible manner, for example, designing effective complaints-handling systems to facilitate and accelerate the process of processing claims. This could lead to changes in attitudes of users and would be good for both sides, customers and companies. For example, companies can improve aspects related to transparency in information and communication, such as track the status of complaints, act quickly and give equal responsibility to respond to all employees. The use of these strategies is suitable to see how users perceive the probability of success of complaints. As the positive reviews are also a powerful tool to disseminate information, companies have to be careful to make positive e-WOM grow among its customers. In this sense, companies should not be always focused in acquiring new customers, but also they should consider the implementation of retention strategies in order to improve the level of customer satisfaction and loyalty.

Finally, limitations and opportunities for further research are presented. Future research should consider customers' complaints from different sectors, a longer time period (comprising the analysis of more complaints), and further data about customers and their relationships with the companies receiving comments/critiques (even using other sources of information, such as a survey). In particular, further data about customers can include additional demographic variables, such as the user's age, education level and nationality. It would be also interesting to include variables related to the relationship between the customer and the company, for example reflecting the length of the relationship between the customer and the company, number of products or services acquired during this period or previous touch points. Finally, future research may be related to clarify whether e-WOM generated on Critizen is mainly a one-directional communication process devoted to put pressure on companies or whether it is more related to the communication among customers (and therefore affecting other customers to complain in terms of contagion).

REFERENCES

Blackshaw, P., & Nazzaro, M. (2004). *Consumer-Generated Media (CGM) 101: Word-of-mouth in the age of the Webfortified consumer*. Retrieved July 22, 2015, from http://www.nielsen-online.com/downloads/us/buzz/nbzm_wp_CGM101.pdf

Blodgett, J. G., Hill, D. J., & Tax, S. S. (1997). The effects of distributive, procedural and interactional justice on postcomplaint behavior. *Journal of Retailing, 73*(2), 185–210. doi:10.1016/S0022-4359(97)90003-8

Boone, L. E., & Kurtz, D. L. (2014). *Contemporary marketing* (16th ed.). Cengage Learning.

Cantallops, A. S., & Salvi, F. (2014). New consumer behavior: A review of research on eWOM and hotels. *International Journal of Hospitality Management, 36*, 41–51. doi:10.1016/j.ijhm.2013.08.007

Chatterjee, P. (2001). Online reviews: Do consumers use them? In M. C. Gilly, & J. Myers-Levy (Eds.), Advances in Consumer Research (129-134). Provo, UT: Association for Consumer Research.

Chu, S. C., & Kim, Y. (2011). Determinants of consumer engagement in electronic Word-of-mouth (eWOM) in social networking sites. *International Journal of Advertising, 30*(1), 47–75. doi:10.2501/IJA-30-1-047-075

Clark, J. (2013). Conceptualising Social Media as Complaint Channel. *Journal of Promotional Communications, 1*(1), 104–124.

DeSarbo, W. S., Jedidi, K., & Sinha, I. (2001). Customer value analysis in a heterogeneous market. *Strategic Management Journal, 22*(9), 845–857. doi:10.1002/smj.191

DeSarbo, W. S., & Wedel, M. (1994). A review of recent developments in latent class regression models. In Advanced methods of marketing research (pp. 352–388). Cambridge, MA: Basil Blackwell.

Edvardsson, B., & Roos, I. (2003). Customer Complaints and Switching Behavior - A Study of Relationship Dynamics in a Telecommunication Company. *Journal of Relationship Marketing, 2*(1-2), 43–68. doi:10.1300/J366v02n01_04

Facua. (2014). *Banks, telecom and energy companies are once again the 'kings of fraud' in FACUA's ranking 2014.* Retrieved July 22, 2015, from http://www.facua.org/es/noticia_int.php?idioma=1&Id=9065

Feick, L. F., & Price, L. L. (1987). The market maven: A diffuser of marketplace information. *Journal of Marketing, 51*(1), 83–97. doi:10.2307/1251146

Flynn, L. R., Goldsmith, R. E., & Eastman, J. K. (1996). Opinion leaders and opinion seekers: Two new measurement scales. *Journal of the Academy of Marketing Science, 24*(2), 137–147. doi:10.1177/0092070396242004

He, W., Zha, S., & Li, L. (2013). Social media competitive analysis and text mining: A case study in the pizza industry. *International Journal of Information Management, 33*(3), 464–472. doi:10.1016/j.ijinfomgt.2013.01.001

Henning-Thurau, T., Gwinner, K. P., Walsh, G., & Gremler, D. D. (2004). Electronic word-of-mouth via customer opinion platform: What motivates consumers to articulate themselves on the internet. *Journal of Interactive Marketing, 18*(1), 38–52. doi:10.1002/dir.10073

Hong, S., & Park, H. S. (2012). Computer-mediated persuasion in online reviews: Statistical versus narrative evidence. *Computers in Human Behavior, 28*(3), 906–919. doi:10.1016/j.chb.2011.12.011

Jalilvand, M. R., Esfahani, S. S., & Samiei, N. (2011). Electronic word-of-mouth: Challenges and opportunities. *Procedia Computer Science, 3*, 42–46. doi:10.1016/j.procs.2010.12.008

Jansen, B. J., Zhang, M., Sobel, K., & Chowdury, A. (2009). Twitter power: Tweets as electronic word of mouth. *Journal of the American Society for Information Science and Technology, 60*(11), 2169–2188. doi:10.1002/asi.21149

Jeong, H. J., & Koo, D. M. (2015). Combined effects of valence and attributes of e-WOM on consumer judgment for message and product. *Internet Research, 25*(1), 2–29. doi:10.1108/IntR-09-2013-0199

Kamakura, W. A., & Wedel, M. (1995). Life-style segmentation with tailoring interviewing. *JMR, Journal of Marketing Research, 32*(3), 308–317. doi:10.2307/3151983

Kassarjian, H. H. (●●●). Content analysis in consumer research. *The Journal of Consumer Research*, *4*(June), 8–18.

Khammash, M., & Griffiths, G. H. (2011). Arrivederci CIAO.com, Buongiorno Bing.com Electronic word-of-mouth (eWOM), antecedences and consequences. *International Journal of Information Management*, *31*(1), 82–87. doi:10.1016/j.ijinfomgt.2010.10.005

Kim, C., Kim, S., Im, S., & Shin, C. (2003). The effect of attitude and perception on consumer complaint intentions. *Journal of Consumer Marketing*, *20*(4), 352–371. doi:10.1108/07363760310483702

Kowalski, R. (1996). Complaints and complaining: Functions, antecedents, and consequences. *Psychological Bulletin*, *119*(2), 179–196. doi:10.1037/0033-2909.119.2.179 PMID:8851274

Lee, D. H., & Park, C. W. (2007). Conceptualization and Measurement of Multidimensionality of Integrated Marketing Communications. *Journal of Advertising Research*, *47*(3), 222–236. doi:10.2501/S0021849907070274

Leung, D., Law, R., van Hoof, H., & Buhalis, D. (2013). Social media in tourism and hospitality: A literature review. *Journal of Travel & Tourism Management*, *30*(1-2), 3–22. doi:10.1080/10548408.2013.750919

Magidson, J., & Vermunt, J. K. (2004). Latent class models. In The Sage handbook of quantitative methodology for the social sciences (pp. 175-198). Thousand Oaks, CA: Sage Publications. doi:10.4135/9781412986311.n10

Mangold, W. G., & Faulds, D. J. (2009). Social media: The new hybrid element of the promotion mix. *Business Horizons*, *52*(4), 357–365. doi:10.1016/j.bushor.2009.03.002

Martínez-Guerrero, M., Ortega-Egea, J. M., & Román-González, M. V. (2007). Application of the latent class regression methodology to the analysis of Internet use for banking transactions in the European Union. *Journal of Business Research*, *60*(2), 137–145. doi:10.1016/j.jbusres.2006.10.012

McAfee, A., & Brynjolfsson, E. (2012). Big Data: The Management Revolution. *Harvard Business Review*, *90*(10), 60–68. PMID:23074865

Neter, J., Wasserman, W., & Kutner, M. H. (1990). *Applied linear statistical models: Regression, analysis of variance, and experimental design*. Homewood, IL: Richard D. Irwin.

Norman, A. T., & Russell, C. A. (2006). The pass-along effect: Investigating word-of-mouth effects on online survey procedures. *Journal of Computer-Mediated Communication*, *11*(4), 1085–1103. doi:10.1111/j.1083-6101.2006.00309.x

Ortega-Egea, J. M., García-de-Frutos, N., & Antolín-López, R. (2014). Why Do Some People Do "More" to Mitigate Climate Change than Others? Exploring Heterogeneity in Psycho-Social Associations. *PLoS ONE*, *9*(9), 1–17. doi:10.1371/journal.pone.0106645 PMID:25191841

Racherla, P., Connolly, D. J., & Christodoulidou, N. (2013). What Determines Consumers' Ratings of Service Providers? An Exploratory Study of Online Traveller Reviews. *Journal of Hospitality Marketing & Management*, *22*(2), 135–161. doi:10.1080/19368623.2011.645187

Ramsey, G. (2006). *Digital marketing strategies in the age of consumer control.* Retrieved July 22, 2015, from http://www.emarketer.com/Article.aspx?id=1003886&src=article_head_sitesearch

Reid, M. (2005). Performance auditing of integrated marketing communication (IMC) actions and outcomes. *Journal of Advertising, 34*(4), 41–54. doi:10.1080/00913367.2005.10639208

Singh, J., & Howell, R. D. (1985). Consumer complaining behavior: a review and prospectus. In Consumer Satisfaction, Dissatisfaction and Complaining Behavior (pp. 59-66). Bloomington, IN: Indiana University.

Singh, N., & Matsuo, H. (2004). Measuring cultural adaptation on the Web: A content analytic study of U.S. and Japanese Web sites. *Journal of Business Research, 57*(8), 864–872. doi:10.1016/S0148-2963(02)00482-4

Singh, T., Veron-Jackson, L., & Cullinane, J. (2008). Blogging: A new play in your marketing game plan. *Business Horizons, 51*(4), 281–292. doi:10.1016/j.bushor.2008.02.002

Spanish Government, Ministry of Industry, Energy and Tourism. (2014). *Datos de la Oficina de Atención al Usuario de Telecomunicaciones.* Retrieved July 28, 2015, from http://www.usuariosteleco.es/Destacados/Datos%20oficina/Datos_OAUT_2014_ANUAL.pdf

Sparks, B. A., & Browning, V. (2011). Complaining in Cyberspace: The Motives and Forms of Hotel Guests' Complaints Online. *Journal of Hospitality Marketing & Management, 19*(7), 797–818. doi:10.1080/19368623.2010.508010

Sun, T., Youn, S., Wu, G., & Kuntaraporn, M. (2006). Online word-of-mouth (or mouse): An exploration of its antecedents and consequences. *Journal of Computer-Mediated Communication, 11*(4), 1104–1127. doi:10.1111/j.1083-6101.2006.00310.x

Wilson-Jeanselme, M., & Reynolds, J. (2006). The advantages of preference-based segmentation: An investigation of online grocery retailing. *Journal of Targeting. Measurement and Analysis for Marketing, 14*(4), 297–308. doi:10.1057/palgrave.jt.5740190

Woo, G. K., Lim, H., & Brymer, R. A. (2015). The effectiveness of managing social media on hotel performance. *International Journal of Hospitality Management, 44*, 165–171. doi:10.1016/j.ijhm.2014.10.014

ADDITIONAL READING

Atlikhan, A., Albadvi, A., & Ghapanchi, A. H. (2013). A conceptual model for proactive-interactive customer complaint management systems. *International Journal of Business Information Systems, 13*(4), 490–503. doi:10.1504/IJBIS.2013.055303

Fornell, C., & Wernerfelt, B. (1987). Defensive marketing strategy by customer complaint management: A theoretical analysis. *JMR, Journal of Marketing Research, 24*(4), 337–346. doi:10.2307/3151381

Garding, S., & Bruns, A. (2015). Conclusions for Organisational Complaint Management and Future Research. In Garding, S., & Bruns, A. (Eds.), Complaint Management and Channel Choice (75-82). Switzerland: Springer International Publishing. doi:10.1007/978-3-319-18179-0_5

Johnston, R., & Mehra, S. (2002). Best-practice complaint management. *The Academy of Management Executive*, *16*(4), 145–154. doi:10.5465/AME.2002.8951342

KEY TERMS AND DEFINITIONS

Content Analysis: A content analysis is a way to collect information manually or using computer-assisted techniques for contextualized interpretations of content of communication processes (any kind of text, written, multimedia, etc.) with the goal of the production of valid and trustworthy inferences.

Customer Complaint: A customer complaint is an expression of dissatisfaction on a consumer's behalf to a responsible party. It is also defined as a report from a customer, which provides documentation about a problem with a product or service.

Electronic Word of Mouth: Electronic Word of Mouth refers to any statement made by potential, actual, and former customers about products, services, and/or companies, which is made available to a multitude of people and institutions via the Internet, for example, through online social networks.

Latent Class Regression Analysis: Latent Class Regression Analysis is a powerful predictive technique (i.e., defines dependent and independent variables) for marketing segmentation. It provides a flexible probabilistic analysis to deal with dependent and independent variables of mixed types and implies the creation of a posteriori segments by estimating utilities for each segment and the probability that each individual belongs to each segment.

Opinion Giving: Opinion giving is one of three types of e-WOM that can be generated through online social networks. Opinion giving implies the act of giving the users' own opinion about a product, service or brand on a previously posted comment in a social network.

Opinion Passing: Opinion passing is one of three types of e-WOM that can be generated through online social networks. Opinion passing implies the act of sharing a previously posted comment in a social network (i.e., about a product, service or brand) in other social networks, blogs, etc.

Opinion Seeking: Opinion seeking is one of the three types of e-WOM that can be generated through online social networks. Opinion seeking implies the act of seeking the opinion of different comments depicted on social networks about a particular topic (e.g., a product, a service or a brand).

Social Network: A social network is a social structure consisting of a set of social actors, individuals or organizations, and a set of ties between these actors. A social network can be developed in an offline environment (implying personal interactions and relationships) and in an online environment (implying digital interactions and relationships).

ENDNOTE

[1]   'FACUA-Consumers in Action' is a Spanish non-profit organization dedicated to the defense of consumer rights.

Chapter 7
Applied Analytical "Distant Reading" using NVivo 11 Plus™

Shalin Hai-Jew
Kansas State University, USA

ABSTRACT

NVivo 11 Plus, a qualitative data analysis software tool, enables some types of "distant reading" albeit within the text data processing limits of the desktop machine. Some "distant reading" applications include the following: (1) word frequency counts (visualized as word clouds, tree maps, cluster analyses graphs, dendrograms, and ring graphs/circle graphs), (2) text searches (as word trees), (3) theme and sub-theme extractions (as bar charts), (4) matrix queries (as various types of data visualizations), (5) sentiment analyses (as bar charts, hierarchical treemaps, hierarchical sunburst diagrams, and text sets), (6) autocoding by existing pattern, and (7) geolocational mapping. While "distant reading" is still evolving, these unsupervised and semi-supervised machine reading approaches broaden the capabilities of researchers and may serve as a bridge to even more complex distant reading methods.

INTRODUCTION

I had come to see language as an almost supernatural force, existing between people, bringing our brains, shielded in centimeter-thick skulls, into communion. A word meant something only between people, and life's meaning, its virtue, had something to do with the depth of the relationships we form. It was the relational aspect of humans—i.e., 'human relationality'—that undergirded meaning. -- Paul Kalanithi, When Breath Becomes Air (2016)

Conventionally, reading is thought of as a uniquely human skill, which requires years to develop fluency. And writing is considered something set apart, something that people uniquely do for others—to entertain, to persuade, and to express care. Historically, writing has been used to capture human knowledge and to share it with peers and with those who come after in the future. As such, writing is used to understand the cultures and advancements of society. In people, in terms of learning and skills development, reading is a precursor to writing, and the skills in each co-develop and promote the advance of the other.

DOI: 10.4018/978-1-5225-0648-5.ch007

Reading is often an integrated part of earliest childhood for many in developed societies and evolves through adulthood and old age. There is a variety of reading matter over a lifetime, numerous genres and styles of writing, and reading content modes (print, multimodal electronic). Reading content may be experienced in different versioned and multisensory ways: text, audiobook, video, and live performance. People may read linearly or in a skipping around method; many will revisit texts for re-reading and re-exploration. Experientially, reading is an intimate experience between the text (as a representation of the author) and the reader, who draws on lived experiences and imagination to make meaning from the language-based symbols. Reading is integrated with the reader's lived life, and a person's memory of a work is often integrated with other sensory experiences: the physical feel of a print book with the irregular pulp or the weight of an e-book reader and the luminescent screen, the motion and sounds of a train car, the taste of an iced tea at a local coffee shop. There may be memories of conversations—in person and online—with other members of a book club. There may be a sense of emotional betrayal when a book character acts against expectations or when an author changes styles and explores different topical territory. People have very cherished and personal memories related to "close reading" or "natural reading" (and sometimes "active reading"). As an experience, reading requires mental concentration and uninterrupted space and time. Socially, for many, reading is a capability and a practice for those in higher social strata, and they indicate something of humanity ("what makes people human") and the advancement of society. How a person reads a work depends on not only his or her training and sophisticated de-coding capabilities but also his or her maturity, personality, and point-of-view. Because reading requires an investment of personal effort, a person generally has to select-in to reading a work from beginning to end and with a sufficient level of concentration to extract value; a published work may change the reader and his or her worldview and attitudes. Depending on training, lived experiences, and cognition, people can read in multiple languages.

Academic reading (a type of reading for learning), with its inherent complexity, is seen as requiring the slowest reading speeds for meaning acquisition, from 200 – 300 words per minute (wpm). "Full reading" or "active reading" (and analytical reading) require full human attention for comprehension; these approaches may include in-text annotations, cross-referencing, questioning, exploring, reflecting, and engaging deeply with the informational contents. There are several types of speed reading. Faster reading—such as "skimming" (reading a text at a high level to extract key concepts and capture a general sense of the information, but not to capture specific details) and "scanning" (glancing through a text for particular information, in a "search")—may be achieved at 800 – 1000 wpm but also with differing levels of accuracy. For example, readers may skim a chapter to capture the gist or the main idea. People may scan a phone book page to find a particular business or individual name. Fast reading tends to be cursory, superficial, and incomplete, as compared with a deeper and more thorough perusal of texts. People read for different reasons as well, and these differing reasons and expectations affect the experience. Reading for pleasure is different than reading analytically. Each person's reading diet is likely unique to the individual and based on his or her educational background, cultural influences, personal preferences, and textual availability. In human reading, the experience is informed not only by the text but also the lived experiences around and outside the text. Experientially, longer textual works are generally experienced as a sequence of reading moments, with culminating memories and impressions. The origins and genres of texts also affect the experiences of reading. While reading itself is often a solitary endeavor, there are many aspects of it which are social, including the literary taste:

To ask about literary excellence is to inquire about taste. Taste entails social expectations, which is to say audiences that are historically and culturally situated. Though the predilections and judgments of these audiences were of interest in traditional literary history, they were not conceptualized in a coherent fashion. Rather, those expectations that mirrored critics' sensibilities were valued, while other judgments were discarded. (Cohen, 2009, p. 52)

When people read, they share their opinions with others. They take part in reading groups. They hold and attend reading events.

The mode in which texts are offered—such as via print or electronic print or audiobook or Braille—also affect its consumption by people. In other words, texts may be consumed via visual, auditory, and tactual processing channels, either singly or in combination.

Reading by Human Means

There is nothing to limit how texts are interpreted and read once they are released to a broad public. For example, historical texts may be read to understand the origins of religious and social practices. Or novels (or poems or short stories or monographs) from a particular society may be read for sociological insights. Or the collected works of a particular author or authoring team may be studied for personality characteristics and the "author hand(s)." Or works based on particular domains may be studied to understand the evolution of new ideas and innovations. Languages evolve based on their usage by peoples over time, and the written materials are a part of that society's cultural residua for future generations. A crowd-sourced article on "reading" (as a process) captures some of the complexities of this practice:

Reading is a complex cognitive process of decoding symbols in order to construct or derive meaning (reading comprehension). It is a means of language acquisition, of communication, and of sharing information and ideas. Like all languages, it is a complex interaction between the text and the reader which is shaped by the reader's prior knowledge, experiences, attitude, and language community which is culturally and socially situated. The reading process requires continuous practice, development, and refinement. In addition, reading requires creativity and critical analysis. Consumers of literature make ventures with each piece, innately deviating from literal words to create images that make sense to them in the unfamiliar places the texts describe. Because reading is such a complex process, it cannot be controlled or restricted to one or two interpretations. There are no concrete laws in reading, but rather allows readers an escape to produce their own products introspectively. This promotes deep exploration of texts during interpretation, ("Reading_(process)," Jan. 7, 2016)

There are some easy ways to capture some evocations of close reading while using light machine reading processes. English Wikipedia features 5 million original articles and a total of 38 million wiki pages ("Wikipedia: Size_of_Wikipedia," Jan. 3, 2016). Its standards require writing to be cited and objective, and a slew of editors and approved robots work to ensure correct contents. Given the textual density and comprehensiveness of Wikipedia, it is a good place to explore article networks, which are interlinked pages based on content relationships. (There are fewer informational gaps in a go-to resource like Wikipedia.) The linkages are not machine created but human-created based on semantic ties. To capture an indirect sense of "close reading," an article network graph of the "Close_reading" page in Wikipedia was captured at one degree. Such a network shows the direct and visible ties between the

Figure 1. "Close Reading" article network on Wikipedia (1 deg.)

target page and all outgoing page links to related pages. These links are purposeful and defined ones. A quick glance over the article-article graph shows different evocations to "close reading" as a phenomena and as a practice. There are synonyms, the names of important figures related to close reading, objects which are read, and so on. This may be seen in Figure 1.

A one-degree article-article network based on "Reading_(process)" may be seen in Figure 2. This network has a larger number of nodes and more complex ties to other Wikipedia articles. Based on this visualization, reading has been a deeply studied topic. These pages refer to fields of study, language disorders, historical aspects, authors, publications, and other elements. The density of the graph means that some of the nodes overlap, leaving some of the vertex labels hidden. It is possible to redraw the graph for increased clarity or to physically move the nodes in the original visualization in order to read the contents. Or, people may peruse the data table underlying the article graph to output a full list of the nodes.

Both Figures 1 and 2 were created using Network Overview, Discovery and Exploration for Excel (NodeXL Basic), a free and open-source graphing add-on to Excel. An integrated third-party data extraction tool in NodeXL enabled data extraction from MediaWiki sites, the understructure to Wikipedia. The data visualizations were created using the Harel-Koren Fast Multiscale layout algorithm.

Figure 2. "Reading_(process)" article network on Wikipedia (1 deg.)

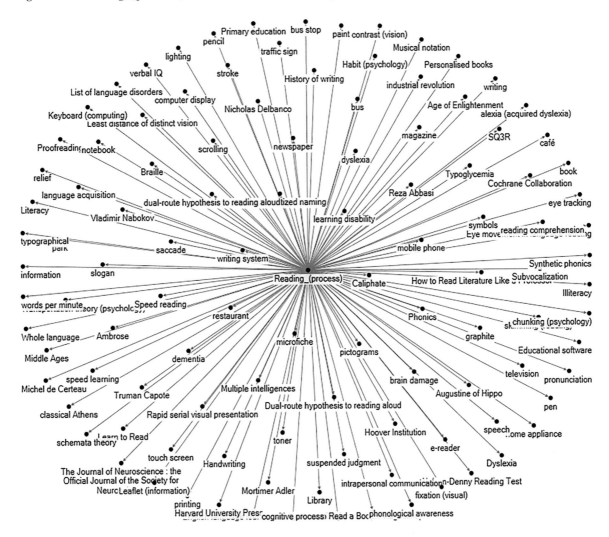

Another way to understand "reading" through social media is to use "distant reading" on a content-sharing site, Flickr. Flickr (owned by Yahoo, Inc.) has 112 million users and is used in 63 countries; in its holdings, it hosts 10 billion images, and an average of a million photos are shared daily (Smith, Aug. 10, 2015). Some 53 million tags have been added to its photo archives (Smith, Aug. 10, 2015). Tags are informal labels that are used to describe shared contents online. One common research method is to analyze co-occurring tags, or tags that appear together in the labeling of a digital object (above a certain threshold of times). The intuition is that the co-appearing works together to define a larger shared context. For example, "reading" and "book" are co-occurring tags in Figure 3, a one-degree related tags network (on Flickr) seeded with "reading" as the tag term. A one-degree network shows the entities with direct ties to a target or focal node. The tags are drawn here with related thumbnail images from Flickr although it is not clear how these thumbnails were selected (by human, computer, chance, or combination of means). These thumbnail images are static (non-dynamic or not changing each time the tags are called) and linked to the particular tag by Flickr.

Figure 3. "Reading" related tags network on Flickr (1 deg.)

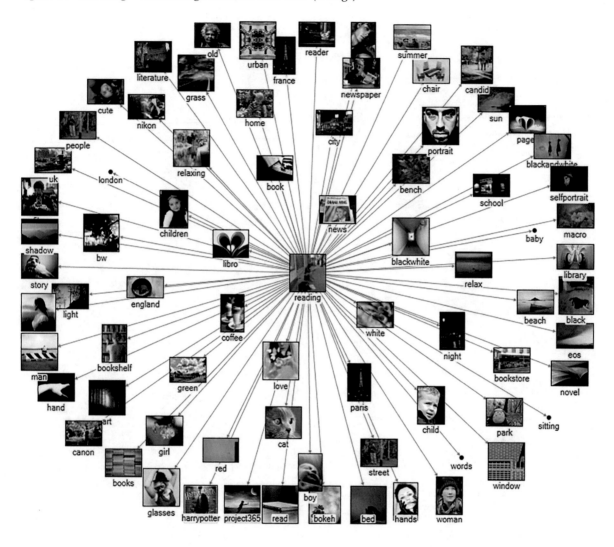

At 1.5 degrees, a "reading" related tags network on Flickr captures not only the ego neighborhood for "reading" (those with one-degree and direct ties to "reading") but also ties between the "alters" (the nodes or vertices with a direct tie to the focal node) in that network graph. A 1.5 degree network then shows the transitivity between alters or the likelihood of their also having a connection given that they are both connected to the focal node. The relatedness between the direct ties is represented as three groups based on the Clauset-Newman-Moore clustering algorithm. This may be seen in Figure 4. Roughly, the leftmost cluster may be something about the embodied experience of reading (with its evocations of parks, beaches, urban areas, and settings), the top right one about literature (with its evocation of fictional characters), and the third about the study of reading (with its evocations of children and school). Of course, there is a level of interpretation in the prior assertion, and others may well have much different insights. (This is a bit like interpreting computer-extracted factor analysis clusters.)

Figure 4. "Reading" related tags network on Flickr (1.5 deg.)

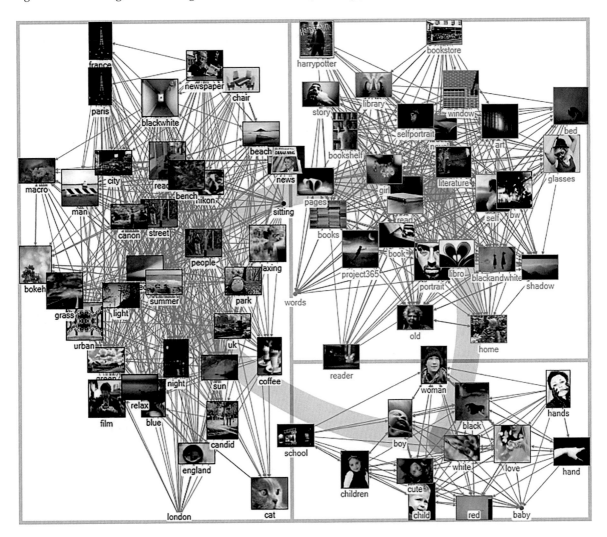

Both Figures 3 and 4 were extracted using NodeXL. The inclusion of the thumbnail imagery gives the sense of the richness of both text and also photos, drawings, videos, and other sorts of contents shared socially online and via other means.

A confluence of socio-technological affordances has enabled access to a wide range of digital text to the public for use in a variety of ways. There has been the low cost of digital storage of data. Analog contents are being digitized and archived digitally with Web-facing interfaces. In digital form, such contents are non-rivalrous, which means that virtually any number of users may access and use the contents simultaneously without using up the resource. Researchers today are awash in available texts: born-digital data, World Wide Web pages, social media datasets, digitized paper and analog artifacts, and a wide range of print and digital and digitized archives. There is a lower cost-of-entry to creating and maintaining digital archives (Purdy, 2011, p. 41), which means that many—professionals and amateurs and many in between—engage in digital archival. Even more traditional libraries are building professional digital archives:

But now the Library of Congress' print collection — something that has taken two centuries to gather — is dwarfed by their newest collection of archived born-digital sources, the vast majority only a matter of years old compared to the much wider date-range of nondigital sources in the traditional collection. The LOC has begun collecting its own born-digital Internet archive: multiple snapshots are taken of webpages, to show how they change over time. Even as a selective curated collection, drawing on governmental, political, educational, and creative websites, the LOC has already collected 254 TB of data and adds 5 TB a month. The Internet Archive, through its Wayback Machine, is even more ambitious. It seeks to archive every website on the Internet. While its size is also hard to put an exact finger on, as of late 2012 it had over 10 Petabytes of information (or, to put it into perspective, a little over 50 Library of Congresses if we take the 200 TB figure). (Milligan, 2012, p. 31)

Access to traditional analog archives often mediated by digital technology, and this increased access to information through "virtual proximity" has an effect on research; this effect demands awareness and reflection (Solberg, 2012, pp. 67 – 68, 69). Wider access to a variety of information through archives help researchers resist easy answers and facile conclusions (Wells, 2002). For researchers, digital archives do more than make informational contents more broadly available and also enable the engagement with "electronic textuality." Through their user interfaces and other tools, digital archives "allow writing and researching to occur together in the same virtual space, which frames these activities as integrated parts of knowledge production rather than as separate and separable steps" and promote collaborative "co-construction of meaning" through the easy connectivity to others (Purdy, 2011, pp. 37 - 39). Digital archives enable researchers to create "personalized research spaces and classification systems" and to tailor search aids based on unique needs often without using pre-defined categorical frameworks (Purdy, 2011, pp. 39-40).

The popularization of Web 2.0, the Social Web, has led to broad sharing (some would say over-sharing) through smart phones and mobile devices. Computational means are broadly used to disambiguate noisy social media data. These include content data (messaging, imagery, audio, video, slideshows, and others), metadata (tagging and labeling, content titles, profile names, and other data about data), and trace data (relational information, log-in information, locational information, and others).

A basic tenet of qualitative research is that information is everywhere, not just in traditionalist experimental designs and positivist assumptions. Text is a good point-of-entry for research exploration. As such, "distant reading" is common practice in fields like culturomics, media studies, communications studies, and the digital humanities. Up-and-coming "multimodal scholars" are conceptualized as engaging with content in various mediums as a core skillset:

This emergent breed, the multimodal humanist, brings together databases, scholarly tools, networked writing, and peer-to-peer commentary while also leveraging the potential of visual and aural media that so dominate contemporary life. This multimodal scholar complements rather than replaces other types of digital humanists, expanding the scope and reach of the field. She aims to produce work that reconfigures the relationships among author, reader, and technology while investigating the computer simultaneously as a platform, a medium, and a visualization device. She thinks carefully about the relationship of form to content, expression to idea. (McPherson, 2009, p. 120)

Figure 5. "Gray Literature" text search in the Google Books Ngram Viewer

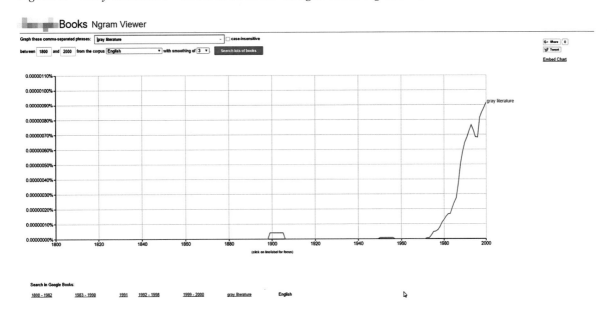

At the typical pace of a human reader, very little of this textual bounty could be consumed and analyzed. One early term pointing to the technology mediated interconnectivity and interrelatedness of online texts was "hypertextuality." "Hyper-reading" was coined in the late 1980s to describe reading online: unsequenced, fast, multi-medial, interlinked [in http networks (explicitly linked web pages)], and serendipitous. In Figure 5, the phenomenon of "hyperreading" originated in the late 1980s and truly sparked in the late 1990s. The wide availability contents online has enabled access to a wide range of "gray literature" documents which are produced by organizations but produced outside of formal publishing channels in addition to crowd-sourced user-generated contents which are usually wholly informal and un-curated.

The line graph in the prior figure (in Figure 5) was extracted from the Google Books Ngram Viewer (Michel, et al., Dec. 16, 2010), which enables users to non-consumptively read line charts representing ngrams (contiguous sequences of texts, counted as unigram or one-gram, bigram or two-gram, three-gram, four-gram, and so on) from the digitized books in the Google Books collection (ranging in the tens of millions of copies) as frequency counts per year. The Ngram Viewer may be accessed through a free web-based interface (located at https://books.google.com/ngrams), which enables some complex text-search queries including advanced ones (such as wildcard queries, inflection searches, case insensitive searches, part-of-speech tagged searches, setting sentence boundaries, comparatives, subtraction, and other features) ("What does the Ngram Viewer do?" 2015). Indeed, the Google Books Ngram Viewer is a common source for studies in culturomics or "the study of cultural and linguistic phenomena from large amounts of textual data distributed over a long timespan" (Tahmasebi, et al., 2015, p. 170). The screenshots in Figures 5, 6, and 7 are from the Ngram Viewer.

Non-consumptive reading refers to computational ways to engage source texts which are unavailable to the human researcher. The non-consumptive refers to the inability to download the original text sets for consumption even while being able to extract some statistical insights about those texts. Non-consumptiveness is a phenomenon which has come about in some cases because the textual collections

Figure 6. "Hyperreading" on the Google Books Ngram Viewer

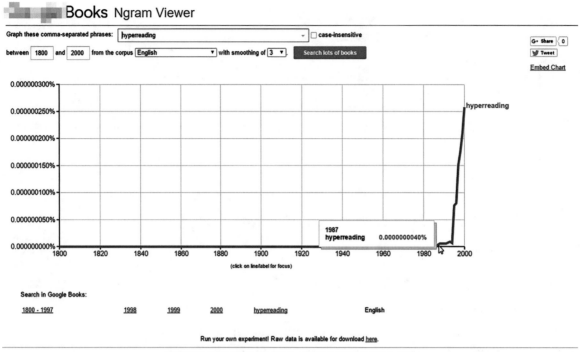

Figure 7. " Distant Reading" text search in the Google Books Ngram Viewer

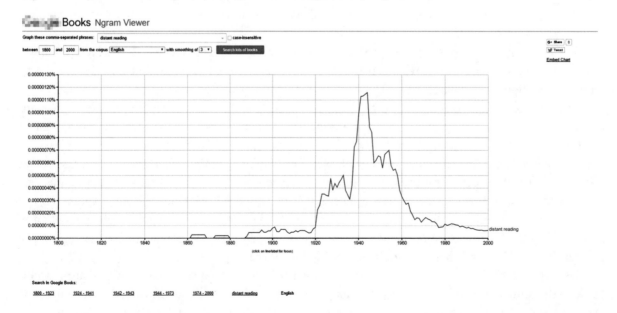

are sets of big data that are hosted on remote servers and not made directly available to users. In other cases, texts themselves are protected (such as under intellectual property rights protections or sensitivity strictures) and not available for public release and use. There are two basic approaches in terms of non-consumptive reading, a form of text analytics:

In the paradigm of non-consumptive reading, text data cannot be downloaded ("consumed") by a user and brought to the algorithms on the user's side for algorithmic distant reading for statistical analysis. Instead, non-consumptive reading can follow one of two strategies: the strategy of bringing the algorithms to the text, with the algorithms allowed to execute against the text in a secure, encapsulated environment in which the text is strictly isolated from the user; and the "feature-extraction" strategy, in which only certain notable or informative characteristics extracted from the text, but not the text itself, are brought to the algorithm. (Bhattacharyya, Organisciak, & Downie, 2015, p. 4)

The original source text data is "encapsulated" from the user even as the algorithms are allowed to run over the data for statistical insights (Bhattacharyya, Organisciak, & Downie, 2015, p. 3). The fact that non-consumptive distant reading disallows close reading at all by human readers is "likely to be especially anxiogenic" (anxiety causing) (Bhattacharyya, Organisciak, & Downie, 2015, p. 10). For a term (ngram or contiguous sequence of terms) to register on the Google Books Ngram Viewer, there must be at least 40 instances or more appearing in books in that particular year. There were an estimated 25 million books in Google Books as of October 2015 (Heyman, 2015). A number of researchers have published works based on data from the Google Books Ngram Viewer, including answering historical questions (empirically), exploring language use, and examining in-world phenomena like the social implications of censorship (Aiden & Michel, 2013). The extracted line graphs are drawn from a "shadow" data set of ngrams, not direct access to the scanned texts (Aiden & Michel, 2013). Accessing Google Books Ngram Viewer data is a form of non-consumptive reading, which enables access to a layer of information about the underlying texts but does not enable direct access to the source texts. In this light, some researchers have suggested that there is not sufficient information available about the massive text corpuses to draw certain types of conclusions (Heyman, 2015).

Hyper-reading referred to the act of engaging with hypermedia, including hypertexts (see Figure 6). What the terms do not refer to is "hyper" as in "hyper speed" or the increase of mental capabilities to read the many more texts that have become available. Even prior to the mass digitization of texts and the creation of born-digital texts, there were many texts that were part of "the great unread" which was a term originated by Margaret Cohen (1999, p. 23, as cited by Moretti, "Conjectures," 2009, p. 55). To enable the "reading" of texts at higher scale than human level, Franco Moretti proposed the application of computational means to read (decode text). This approach would align reading with some practices in computational research based on empirical data.

On a human scale, it seems that there are reasonable reasons for why certain works remain in the set of the "great unread". In a formal review context, critics select texts to review based on certain temporal fashions: "Problems range from the simple lack of time critics have to read closely all the texts that make up the great unread to the failure of some of these texts to signify in fashions that are meaningful using the criteria of close, formal analysis" (Cohen, 2009, p. 59).

Amir Khadem (2012) suggests that distant reading, as a "method of enquiry" (p. 409), may actually be doing a disservice to the literature in the "great unread". He writes:

Regarding the claim that distant reading covers "the great unread," a simple question of logic comes to mind, which may sound like petty quibble at first: If it is accepted that there is a vast body of literature that almost no one has yet covered, would it be adequate to use the works of other scholars—who, according to the predicate of our judgment, have not themselves included them in any critical reading—to cover them? Is it not a fallacy? If there is already some scholarship over a portion of literary works, then they are not "unread," and if they are unread, using other scholars' works will not shed any new light on the project. (Khadem, 2012, p. 414)

Khadem calls "distant reading" both "genuine and valuable" but also flawed (2012, p. 410). This researcher divides distant reading into "anatomical" and "epistemological." In the anatomical approach, a researcher does not study a literary work in its entirety but looks at a work in relation to other works and analyzes some "formal elements" that may be found in the range of works. Khadem (2012) explains: It is anatomically distant because the structural order of the work is to be ignored in favor of a simple device or generic feature" (p. 415). Of the epistemological distant reading approach, Khadem writes of researchers who rely heavily on others' work and not their own engagement with the literature:

But, in the latter, the method consists mainly of reading independent studies and treating them as mediating elements for a scholarly research. In this sense, the scholar's reading is epistemologically distant, since he is not equipped with the required epistemological tools (namely, linguistic and cultural proficiency) to cover a vast body of works. In this case, to uncover the general patterns, the scholar needs to put together literary works that are too diverse, thus he relies on studies of other scholars who, having enough time and knowledge, had each made their own contributions on a limited number of works. The distant reader collects those separated researches and tries to find their common denominator. In anatomical distant reading, the reason that the scholar is refraining from critical close reading is its uneconomical time-consuming quality and its deliberately narrow focus, but in the other case, distant reading is the only way for the scholar to extend the scope of his study without the anxiety of impossibility of an ideal knowledge. (2012, p. 415)

The reductionist and indirect nature of distant reading involves peril. Khadem's thoughtful critique follows:

As a consequence, in the former, the distant reader's inductive reasoning guides the direction of the study, but in the latter, it is the constellation of previous studies that directs the inductive reasoning. When the comparatist has attentively distanced his focus of study from a limited number of works, his mastership over those works is still preserved, thus he has the power to direct the path of his inferences. But in the other case, the scholar's access to the object of study is already funneled, and his only way through it is to pass the filter of others' researches...There is a huge difference between using other scholars' works as source of inspiration, influence, or acknowledgment, and treating them as "data." The inherent risk in this method is that, since works of other scholars were conducted independently, and naturally have their own irreducible multifaceted style, the distant reader would either reduce the stylistic complexity of those researches in order to wring out a straightforward remark to use as the raw material for his own research, or would go the other way: to maintain a malleable quality for his own inferences to assimilate works of other scholars without treating them as simplified statements. In the first case, the project would face the risk of outright misreading, and the second case can lead to indeterminate proclamations with little, if any, critical value, for the induction of the distant reader is inevitably twisted. (Khadem, 2012, p. 415)

Different researchers have weighed in on what "distant reading" means, and given advances in computational approaches to text analysis, this is likely a moving target. Some approaches assume an inherent structure in text sets. Data mining usually involves an open discovery-based approach to exploring data. There are also *a priori* definitions of particular formal elements of interest, which are explored computationally. One author describes a specific approach in a particular domain context: "Still, it is apparent that distant reading is a method of enquiry based on tracing a formal element through a vast body of works in a historical and geographical span, and then trying to build an explanatory model of the emergence, demise, or transformation of certain aspects of literature" (Khadem, 2012, p. 410).

Reading by Machine Means

People integrate new knowledge from reading into their own schemas and mental models; they are changed by the reading experience. This close interplay may explain, in part, the chagrin to the rise of computational methods of "reading". While "distant reading" is gaining a lot of attention currently, many of the text processing methods (such as k-means clustering) predate the origin of the term "distant reading". F. Moretti (2000) proposed the advent of "distant reading" (through computational means) in order to process more than the local canon but works of world literature, and the large amounts of digitized texts and born-digital contents in the Internet era.

Moretti (2000) uses a religious metaphor to evoke traditional reading, and in this context, portrays "distant reading" as, perhaps, heretical. He wrote:

At bottom, it's a theological exercise—very solemn treatment of very few texts taken very seriously—whereas what we really need is a little pact with the devil: we know how to read texts, now let's learn how not to read them. Distant reading: where distance, let me repeat it, is a condition of knowledge: it allows you to focus on units that are much smaller or much larger than the text: devices, themes, tropes—or genres and systems. And if, between the very small and the very large, the text itself disappears, well, it is one of those cases when one can justifiably say, Less is more. If we want to understand the system in its entirety, we must accept losing something. We always pay a price for theoretical knowledge: reality is infinitely rich; concepts are abstract, are poor. But it's precisely this 'poverty' that makes it possible to handle them, and therefore to know. This is why less is actually more. (Moretti, 2000, n.p.)

Moretti points to the heretical sense of going to machine reading with his reference to a "pact with the devil". Indeed, a person does not have to be a purist to argue against machine reading of texts, which is not analogical to the lived human experience of reading. No matter one's stance, there are not enough lifetime hours for people to engage all the available texts in the world. To engage larger text sets beyond human-readable domains, it is important to use computational means. He writes: "Inevitably, the larger the field one wants to study, the greater the need for abstract 'instruments' capable of mastering empirical reality" (Moretti, 2000, pp. 2 - 3). Human close-reading is necessarily limited, which leaves much of the world's literature unread. Into this human-to-human compact (between writers and readers) may be computers which provide "surface reading" or "non-reading" to extract characters, plots, concepts, and locations; to identify latent or hidden features; to identify author hands (through stylometry); to offer insights about human phenomena; to reveal changes over time, and other endeavors.

Some distant reading approaches build on "symptomatic reading," which focuses on latent and sub-surface level meanings in texts to attain the deep history (Best & Marcus, 2009, p. 3). In such approaches, what is not said also is relevant. When humans read for latency (hiddenness or covertness), they apply a range of tools for such understandings, including symbolic analysis, the application of psychological theories, author analysis, cultural analysis, and other approaches that may enable insights. The idea is that authors may be purposefully concealing information. It could also be that the particular insights are hidden to the authors, who may themselves be surprised or shocked or offended by others' analyses of their texts. The mark of a powerful researcher, in many fields, is the ability to see past surface understandings to what is non-obvious and maybe imperceptible. Researchers train for years to build their capabilities and skills to be able to attain such insights. "Distant reading" is also conceptualized as being able to surface latent insights, such as the "hidden tempo" of literary generations at 25 – 30 year intervals (Moretti, 2005, p. 90).

Such mechanistic approaches are currently conceptualized as occurring at some remove from human concerns, but still keeping humans somewhat in the loop—because such non-reading enables deeper insights that would not otherwise be easily observable (if at all) for human consideration and use. The premise is that if some insights may be observed in the text or text collections, assertions about the texts may be made independent of the respective author intention(s) or his / her points of view. While humans write for other humans, the intervention of a computer may seem highly alienating to some. The term "distant reading" has been in use since about the early 1860s as may be seen in Figure 7.

"Distant reading" techniques offer computational means to extract insights from text data. These machine "reading" techniques, also known as "surface reading" and "non-reading," tap into specific computational affordances: parsing text, pattern finding, statistical analysis, and data visualization. A computer "reads" by applying various functions to text as data.

Text sets are often pre-processed as part of the reading. For example, text may be broken up into word sets without any particular order; they may be treated as bags-of-words. Another approach may involve the automatic labeling of words based on their roles as parts-of-speech; more sophisticated approaches include tagging words based on named entities (pronouns of people, organizations, named phenomena, or other entities), action sequences, locations, and using this extracted data for analytical purposes. Once textual data are properly pre-processed, various types of patterns may be extracted from the text; in other terms, the data is "mined" for informative valuables. Once text has been cleaned and processed, that text is highly portable and may be processed in other software programs. Text sets may be processed with the identification of works in proxemic or close physical relationship to each other, such as words co-occurring within a certain size sliding window of text (such as windows of three words or n-words). There are, of course, other ways of creating text "slices" or "views" such as by sets of sentences containing certain terms to enable moving through a text (Muralidharan, Hearst, & Fan, 2013, pp. 2533 – 2534).

In word frequency counts, the words themselves may be counted (with words deemed of less interest placed in a stop words list). The text may be analyzed for co-occurrence, to better evoke the contexts in which target terms and phrases are used. The textual data may be analyzed for sentiment, emotion, or personality; how this is done depends on the methods applied, but one common method is comparing the target text set against sentiment / emotion / personality dictionaries of prelabeled terms. The textual data may be analyzed for themes and sub-themes, based on a variety of methods, which may include named entity tagging, word frequency counts, word clustering, and other algorithms. In qualitative research, theme identification is a critical part of the thinking work of researchers, but there are few explicit descriptions about how this is done; some common approaches—the identification of recurring patterns, line-by-line scrutiny, word counts, word co-occurrence, metacoding—have been cited in the literature, and these approaches are automatable (Ryan & Bernard, 2003, p. 85). There are various computational methods for extracting topics and themes from text sets. "Topic modeling," a form of statistics-based text mining enabled by machine learning, may be used to support researcher hypothesizing about the processed text data (Blei, 2012, p. 84). Topics are described as clusters of co-occurring words that appear in proximity to each other (such as within sentences or within paragraphs or other segments of text). Various functions may be applied to the text in various sequences and iterations for different data extractions.

The various capabilities of "distant reading" may be applied in a variety of sequences and ways, depending on the research method and the software tools. The extracted data may be visualized in a number of ways. Physical locations may be plotted on a 2D map. Frequency word counts may be depicted as related text-based cluster diagrams. Themes and subthemes may be depicted as bar charts. Focal named entities may be depicted as text graphs with links to other entities…or links to adjectives, with such relationships revealing some insights about the named entities.

Many who engage in distant reading go right to programming languages with language analysis packages and command line coding; they apply XML (extensible markup language) tags to texts—in both manual and automated ways—and then they run queries against the tagged text. The learning curve to process data that way is fairly high, and many experts in their respective fields will not choose that approach. A lower cost-of-entry involves the use of software with graphical user interfaces (GUIs) that enable some forms of distant reading. The software suite used in this chapter is one example of a **C**omputer **A**ssisted **Q**ualitative **D**ata **A**nalysi**S** tool (CAQDAS). NVivo 11 Plus is a qualitative data analysis software tool with some text mining capabilities that enable some types of distant reading: word frequency count (query), text search (query), theme and subtheme extraction (autocoding), matrix query (query), and sentiment analysis / opinion mining (autocoding). The extracted insights may be represented as data tables (with "structured" or labeled data), extracted text sets (with "semi-structured" or "unstructured" data), and data visualizations (such as bar charts, network graphs, and others). "Structured" data is conceptualized as data in data tables, with each cell labeled based on column headers and row labels. "Semi-structured" and "unstructured" data are data which are not labeled neatly in tables; such data include generic text sets from documents. Some have resisted the use of "unstructured" to describe freeform textual data because, as they rightly note, there is no such thing as unstructured data. Texts and language contain inherent structure. Only a truly random set of data is "unstructured."

In NVivo 11 Plus

A word frequency count involves the capture of semantic-laden terms and are represented from the most frequent to the least-frequent appearing term (above a certain threshold count). A built-in "stop words" list means that certain terms (usually those which are non-meaning-bearing) do not appear in the count. Interestingly, in most natural languages, Zipf's law applies: the frequency of a word is "inversely proportional to its rank in the frequency table." The most frequently occurring word occurs twice as often as the second most frequent word in this rank-frequency distribution. The most commonly used words tend to be syntactical ones which enable the structuring of language. The less commonly occurring words—in the long tail of the power law curve—tend to carry semantic meaning.

A text search enables the searching for certain words or phrases and represents the lead-up terms and lead-away terms to the target words or phrases, to provide a sense of the context in which the words are used. A theme and sub-theme extraction enables the unsupervised identification of concept terms in a text document or corpus. A matrix query enables various types of explorations of textual data. A sentiment analysis (opinion mining) feature codes text into one of four sentiment categories: "very negative," "moderately negative," "moderately positive," and "very positive"; a fifth assumed category is "neutral" (with that text not included in any of the four prior categories). "Unsupervised" distant reading refers to algorithmic sequences that are run on text without direct human input (except for the human hand in selecting the textual data and cleaning the text and setting parameters for certain types of extractions, in this case). "Supervised" distant reading refers to human-guided distant reading: one example of this may be the "autocoding by existing pattern" in NVivo 11 Plus, which enables a human coder (or a team of human coder) to first code a part of a text corpus or NVivo project and then has the software emulate that coding on the full set. This final example is also a form of distant reading because it is applying a "codebook" to text based on human direction (and machine emulation). There is also a mapping tool (which uses Mapquest maps as an understructure) for Twitter data; this enables mapping of representational pins to indicate the locations of the accounts of those which are a direct part of the focal Twitter account's ego neighborhood. (There are many ways to capture and map geolocational data using a variety of tools, but in NVivo 11 Plus, this seems to be the only application.)

The most common form of NVivo 11 Plus apparently is run off commercial desktops and laptops, which means that the text parsing is limited to what the local computer processors can handle. A server instantiation of NVivo 11 Plus may handle larger text datasets with more ease. All to say, this is not about large scale "big data" text analysis.

So far, the writing has given a broad overview of both close reading and distant reading and maybe provided a sense of the gist of each. Clearly, there are "humans in the loop" in both processes, but there is much more investment of the person in the first one. In all likelihood, researchers who engage with texts today will not merely use one to the exclusion of the other. The likelihood is that researchers will use one or the other depending on the context, or they may apply both to even the same text or text corpora in order to surface new insights. For example, if an individual wants to skim a large-scale set of texts in order see what he or she has and wants to know which texts to close-read from that set based on concepts, he or she may run a text search in order to identify mentions of a particular concept or a matrix query to identify the works which contain multiple mentions of particular concepts of interest. In other words, computers will do the heavy lifting of processing data, and people benefit by knowing which works should be read in depth.

If this chapter were to be represented using "distant reading," it might look like the following composite images. The following text queries are a mix of images from this chapter once it was initially drafted and includes the full citations list, appendix, key terms and definitions, and an index.

You can stop reading now. You know what you need to from the insights in this chapter. Well, not quite. What do these visuals show, and what don't they show? Would you trust your level of knowledge based on distant reading techniques alone? Would you trust a review of a work created by machine reading and machine writing? What gives? What this image does offer is the sense of the "and?" and the "so what?" to distant reading. This image in Figure 8 was created to provide an opening about the textual analysis affordances in NVivo 11 Plus; this figure was not actually created to be fully read or analyzed.

Figure 8. A composite image of this chapter acquired through "distant reading" processes and related data visualizations

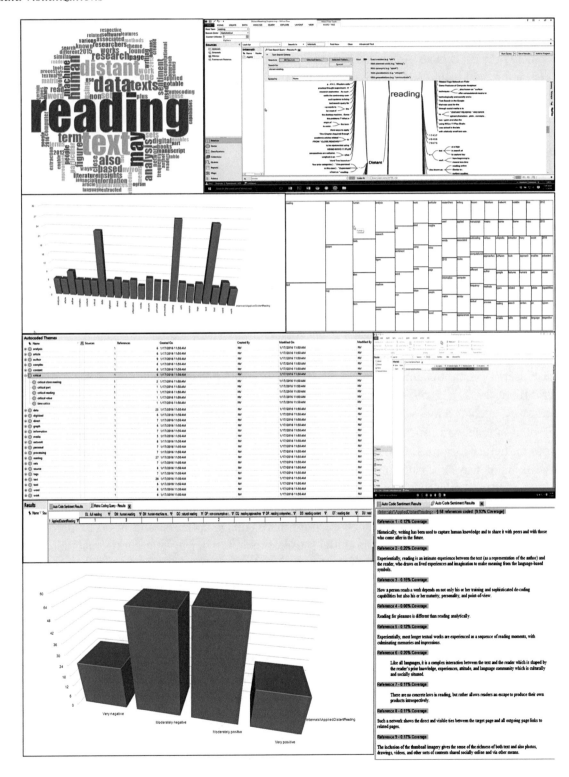

REVIEW OF THE LITERATURE

The rise of computational techniques in the humanities is set in the late 1940s and early 1950s. In 1951, Father Robert Busa of the Society of Jesus used punchcards and IBM computers to track concepts across the works of Thomas Aquinas to create a concordance (Winter, 1999). His approach is seen as "the beginning of humanities computing" (Winter, 1999, p. 4). In the intervening years, there have been advancements on the extraction of meaning from text sets using a variety of methods and applied to ever greater types of text sets.

Support for Human Reading and Thinking

Some of the computational tools in "distant reading" applications are applied in creative ways to assist in human reading. Sometimes, human readers only want summary data about a text: a research paper's main ideas, its executive summary, it supporting facts, its research methodologies, and its proposals; a novel's plots, characters, and main themes; a fictional character's (or a historical personage's) main dialogues and expressions of personality, and others. Unsupervised machine reading is sometimes applied to pre-process texts to identify potentially important concepts for further analysis (Müller-Birn, Schlegel, Klüwer, Benedix, & Breitenfeld, 2015).

Another approach uses semantic data extraction from websites and overlaying that site with "in-place translation" and other tools to enhance the accurate skimming of web pages for second-language readers (Yu & Miller, 2012); this tool also uses a method for spotlighting particular contents on a web page to increase user concentration and minimize distraction by making "non-salient sentences...transparent" (Yu & Miller, 2012, p. 2659). Some distant reading programs are built in a self-consciously human-mimetic way, such as a tool which enables machine-speed skimming of text, the extraction of entities represented in a network, and then interactive network exploration by users that enables them to drill down to particular locations in source documents (Nováček & Burns, 2013, p. 59). Researchers have been working on ways to create computer awareness of various types of textual layouts, which are often indicators of textual relevance (Kunze, Utsumi, Shiga, Kise, & Bulling, 2013).

In yet another approach, a keyword extraction engine outputs the descriptive keywords of a text and outputs four visualizations: tag clouds, mind maps, image collages, and in-text highlighting, to support pre-reading (to give readers an initial sense of the text), during-reading (to maintain a mental conceptualization of the overall structure of the text), and post-reading (to support memory of the text) (Angerbauer, Schmidt, Dingler & Kern, 2015, p. 1045). Not only may distant reading be used to test hypotheses against empirical data, but it may be used to originate hypotheses. The study of underlying text sets may be used to propose conjectures (Juola & Bernola, 2009, as cited in Juola, 2010).

Researchers are working on direct systems, too, to understand how readers are reading. One approach uses eye tracking to determine whether the reader is reading attentively or skimming based on various eye tracking features like "average forward speed" (Biedert, Hees, Denge, & Buscher, 2012, p. 123). Another system uses computational means to visually bookmark where a reader left off before they were interrupted, so a reader can pick up where he or she left off with ease (Jo, Kim, & Seo, 2015).

Table 1. Comparisons and contrasts between human analytical reading and computer analytical reading

Some Features of Human Analytical "Reading"	Some Features of Computer Analytical "Reading"
1. More subjective than objective; interpretive	1. More objective than subjective; non-interpretive
2. Contested, relative	2. Accuracy, somewhat contested
3. Requires domain expertise and prior training	3. Does not require prior domain expertise or prior training but may benefit the analysis with that
4. Clear author hand; personality and reputation filtering	4. Without necessarily an author hand or personality and reputation filtering (but possible to design)
5. Forgetting (vs. remembrance, memory)	
6. Serendipity; limited reproducibility; varying levels of control; different insights through mood and re-reading	5. No forgetting; long memory
	6. Low serendipity; reproducible; high levels of control; insight variance based on text set / algorithms / methods
7. Embodied, proprioception	7. Disembodied, non-proprioceptive
8. Canonical focus based on area of study or domain	8. May be targeted to particular canons and contexts…but may also be generalized
9. Not generally quantized	9. Quantized
10. Human speed	10. Machine speed
11. Human scale	11. Machine scale
12. "Supervised" (human directed)	12. Supervised, semi-supervised, and unsupervised methods (with and without human direction / coding)

APPLIED DISTANT READING USING NVIVO 11 PLUS

"Distant reading" is not a fully developed term, practice, or concept, and its definition is still highly fluid and dynamic. In the research literature (in English), there are currently a few dozen applied cases. Disambiguating the term is not as simple as exploring further but will require more years of others' publications and shared experiences.

In Table 1, it is possible to conceptualize a crossover point from the left column to the right at which the human reading transitions to machine reading. Table 1 data is represented in the spider chart in Figure 9. The underlying data represented in the spider chart is viewable in Table 2. The concepts of "close reading," "distant reading," and "human-machine reading" are broadly generalized here, and the representations here are to give a sense of each, not to fully describe each.

HOW THE TEXT SETS WERE ASSEMBLED

In order to see how the various distant reading tool features may work, several basic text sets were used. One was the set of academic articles related to "distant reading" that was used for the review of the literature section in this chapter. I wanted to use this because I had conducted a fairly close reading of this set of information, consisting of some 143 articles. (There were additional articles that were read and integrated into this chapter, but they were not included in the text set because of timing issues.) This main text set was used for most of the "distant reading" activities. The articles had to be integrated into one set so that the processing results would appear in one integrated set. First, a PDF Portfolio creation option was tried, but the file became too large and unwieldy. Then, I went from the PDF files to Word and also to ASCII text to try to have the fewest barriers to machine analysis of the texts as possible. In Figure 10, the screenshot shows what happened with one of the source files as it was being transcoded from PDF to Word format; the transcoding resulted in gibberish. In moving some contents from Word

Figure 9. Some features of close, distant, and human-machine reading process (a spider chart)

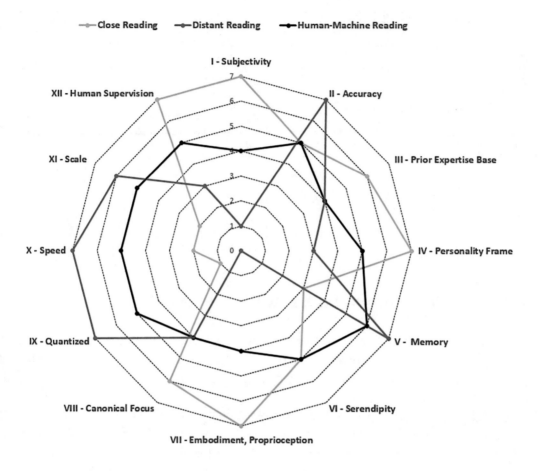

Table 2. Some features of close, distant, and human-machine reading process (a spider chart)

	I - Subjectivity	II - Accuracy	III - Prior Expertise Base	IV - Personality Frame	V - Memory	VI - Serendipity	VII - Embodiment, Proprioception	VIII - Canonical Focus	IX - Quantized	X - Speed	XI - Scale	XII - Human Supervision
Close Reading	7	5	6	7	3	5	7	6	1	2	2	7
Distant Reading	1	7	4	3	7	0	0	4	7	7	6	3
Human-Machine Reading	4	5	4	5	6	5	4	4	5	5	5	5

Figure 10. Some challenges with transcoding from PDF to Word to ASCII text

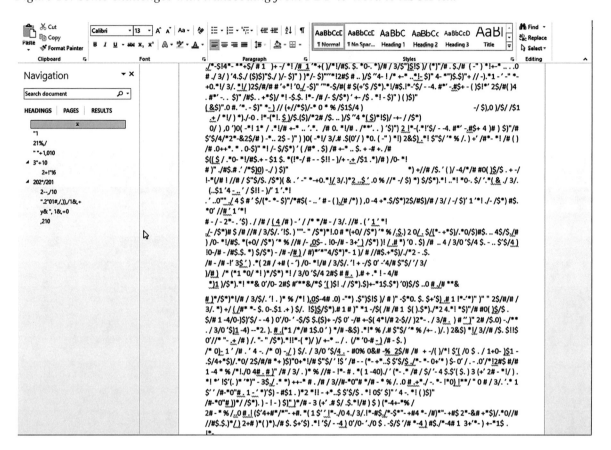

to ASCII text, the original formatting disappeared, and text spacing was not maintained in some cases, and paragraph breaks were not remembered. Some Unicode characters did not have a ready translation. Image data was lost. For easy reference, I called this the Combined Text set.

The text set worked for some of the distant reading processes but not others. A single article ("Close_reading") from Wikipedia was used to seed the sentiment analysis feature because the initial dataset was not able to be processed to attain sentiment. Also, a set of Tweets from @ReadingPartners was captured using NCapture (add-on to the Google Chrome web browser) of NVivo was used to seed a second sentiment analysis—to demonstrate some of the tool capabilities with larger datasets. The focus here is on the software tool and not on the text sets per se, so these were essentially convenience sets broadly selected based on topic and easy availability.

1. **Word Frequency Count Queries**: In Figure 11, the word cloud was drawn from a word frequency count (query) of the Combined Text set. No additional stopwords were added to the built-in stopwords list in NVivo.

In Figure 12, a treemap drawn from the same data as in Figure 11 is shown. The most frequently found words in the text set are in the left section and cover more space. Less frequent words are to the right part of the treemap.

Figure 11. Word cloud from a word frequency count of the combined text set

Figure 12. Tree map from a word frequency count

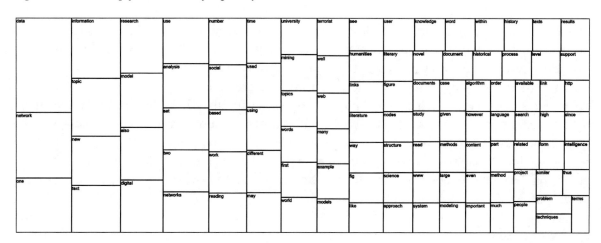

A cluster analysis was attempted on the articles, but there was insufficient text to conduct a cluster analysis. The lack of cluster data meant that using a cluster chart (2D or 3D), dendrogram, or ring lattice (circle) graph would not be feasible from this data. (It is helpful to review data visualization conventions to fully benefit from the data visualizations possible with distant learning.)

Figure 13. An interactive word tree based on "distant reading".

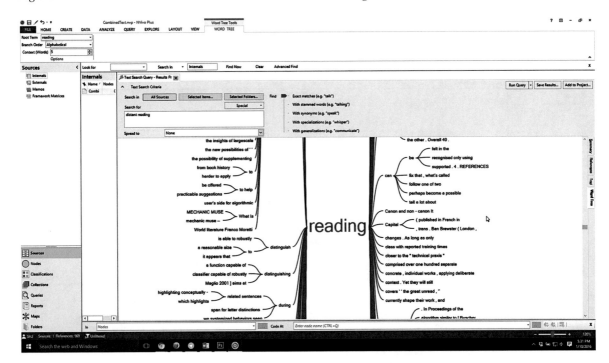

2. **Text Search Queries:** A text search query for "distant reading" from the Combined Text dataset resulted in the interactive word tree in Figure 13. The "distant" was in a higher part of the word tree…so that is not as easily viewable in the figure given the zoomed-in view (so that the text may be somewhat readable). The word tree is interactive. Users may double-click on a branch of the tree to access the underlying source file in which that part of a sentence was found. Highlighting a branch of the word tree shows both the lead-up words to the "distant reading" two-gram and also the lead-away text.

3. **Theme and Sub-Theme Autocoding Extractions:** An unsupervised theme and sub-theme extraction (autocoding) was conducted on the Combined Text set, and the results of the top-level themes may be seen in Figure 14. The theme and sub-theme autocoding was tried on three different computers multiple times before the extraction finally succeeded. That could have been a fact of the size of the text set or the differing capabilities of the respective machines.

The node outline of the theme and subtheme extraction may be seen in Figure 15. Note that one of the themes has been expanded, and the subthemes may be seen in the indented nodes.

4. **Matrix Queries:** Another "distant reading" approach involves using matrices (cross-tabulation analysis tables) to "read" a text. A matrix is essentially a rectangular array with column and row headers (which indicate matrix variables; "matrix indicators") and cell data. As such, the data in a matrix is generally structured data because the cells are essentially labeled.

Figure 14. Theme and subtheme extraction from the text set (as a bar chart).

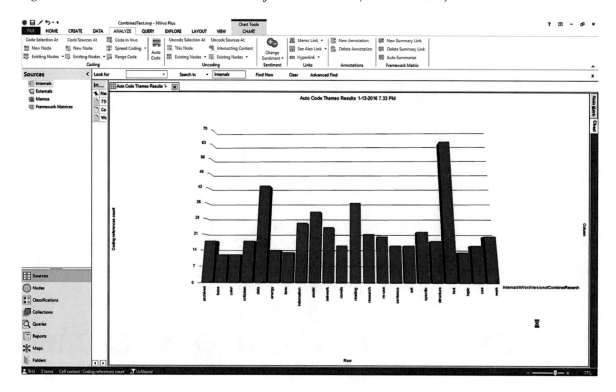

Figure 15. Theme and subtheme extraction from the text set (as a node outline)

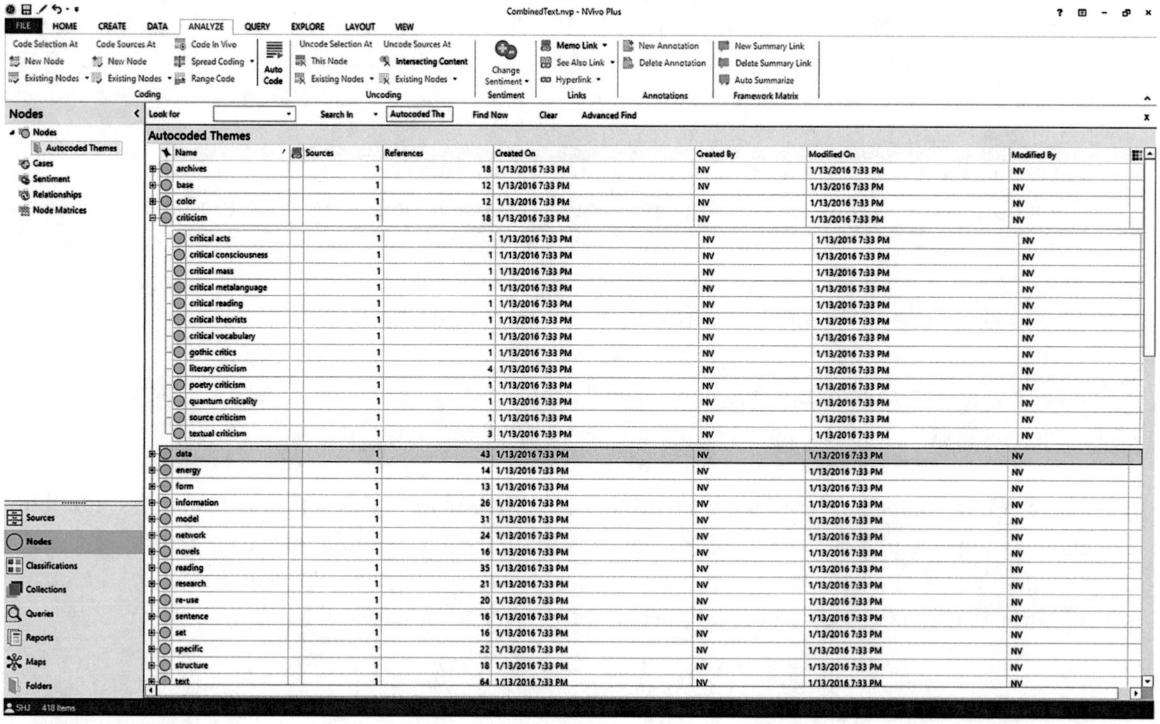

In qualitative research, the matrix contains both textual and numerical data. Matrices are used to identify anomalies in the empirical and observed data—such as unusual distributions that enable the rejection of the null hypothesis (such as through chi-square analysis). Or there may be data relationships and patterns; underlying all relational graphs are network matrices. There are matrices that use various indicators of relationship: binary 1s and 0s to show presence or absence of relationships, numbers indicating strength of relationship and in what direction (positive or negative), and so on.

In NVivo 11 Plus, there are a number of types of matrices that may be created based on how a user structures the respective matrices. Any sources, any coded nodes, any descriptive attributes of case nodes…may be used as matrix variables. NVivo 11 Plus also uses matrices to report out autocoded findings—such as from theme and subtheme autocoding, sentiment analysis autocoding, and so on. A few matrices will be shown here in simple format, and there will be some direct matrix extractions from NVivo 11 Plus as well.

In Table 3, a basic cross-tabulation analysis is depicted. In a classic cross-tabulation, the column headers are known as "banners," and row headers are known as "stubs." In a cross-tabulation analysis, the intersected cells contain data that show the overlap between the column and the row. One common type of comparison involves the observed counts (frequency distribution) vs. expected counts—in a contingency table. (A very common contingency table is a 2 x 2 one, but these can be much larger. Also the numbers of column and row variables do not have to necessarily match.) There is an assumption about what the counts would look like (based on the underlying data) if nothing (no other effect) was acting on the variables. If there is statistically significant differences between what is observed vs. what is expected, that may be grounds for hypothesizing about why there is such a discrepancy. Chi-square analysis does not offer sufficient power to assert causation, but it may show some associational relationships.

Table 4 shows a basic matrix that enables users to identify particular works to read from a large text set based on verbiage (themes, concepts, names, formulas, or others) that may be found in the particular article.

To visualize how this might look, a theme extraction was conducted on some 105 articles. The results of this may be seen in Figure 16. The intensity matrix based on theme extractions in Figure 16 was coded at the sentence level.

Table 3. A cross-tabulation analysis table

	Banner A	**Banner B**	**Banner C**	**Banner D**	**Banner E**	**Banner F**
Stub A						
Stub B						
Stub C						

Table 4. A matrix for identifying concepts in respective texts

	Concept	**Concept**	**Concept**	**Concept**
Text				
Text				
Text				

Table 5. A network matrix for relational terms

	Term A	**Term B**	**Term C**	**Term D**	**Term E**
Term A	--				
Term B		--			
Term C			--		
Term D				--	
Term E					--

Figure 16. A matrix for identifying concepts in respective texts

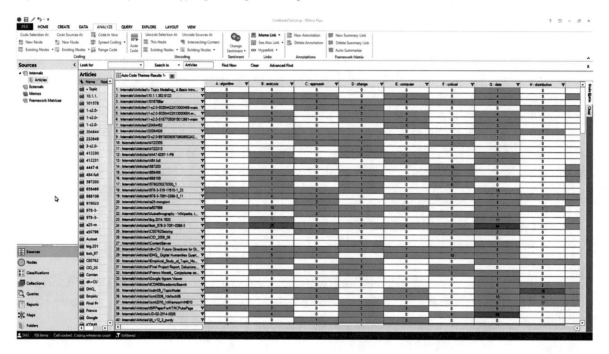

In Table 5, a network matrix that shows relationships between terms is depicted. The cells may consist of numbers showing presence of relationships based on binary coding (1 for present, 0 for non-present) or numbers indicating intensity of relationship. In qualitative analysis, the cells may be populated with overlapping texts from different documents or text sets (depending on how the matrix query is set up). Examples of network matrices would be what would be seen underlying sociograms as the underlying data. In other words, sociograms and sociographs are machine-drawn from underlying matrices.

The type of network depicted in Table 5 underlies Figure 17, which is a mapped sociogram.

5. **Sentiment Analysis Autocoding:** In terms of the sentiment analysis feature in NVivo 11 Plus, this was applied to the 1,382 page, 162-file, 592,781-word text set (as a .docx set and as a .txt set) multiple times on multiple machines and with multiple parameters (paragraph-level, sentence-level, or cell-level coding) without success. The text set was cut in half to see if it might be a size issue, but that also was still too large for the software and desktop / laptop computer to handle. Many

Figure 17. Mapped sociogram of the @ReadingPartners social network on Twitter

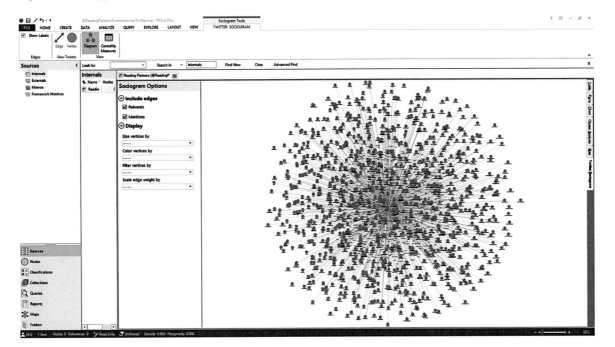

times, error messages were raised. Other times, the following message was raised: "The Auto Code Wizard could not find any sentiment coding references to create." The articles were then run individually, with the following sentiment-based intensity matrix as the result, as shown in Figure 18. (This is not shown as a bar chart because there are too many articles—in this case, 105.)

This sentiment analysis effort was applied to a Tweetstream from @literarylab, but that autocoding effort also failed. Finally, a Tweetstream set was extracted from the @ReadingPartners social media account on Twitter site for a larger text set (3,207 Tweets were extracted, including re-tweets). At the time of the data extraction, the account had 4,248 microblogging messages (Tweets), 885 following, 3,325 followers, 840 likes, and two lists. Apparently, Reading Partners is a national non-profit organization, and its Twitter profile reads: "Reading Partners is a national nonprofit empowering community volunteers to help students gain the reading skills they need to reach their full potential." This organization joined Twitter in April 2009. Their main website is at http://www.readingpartners.org. (The chapter author has no tie to the organization.)

Finally, the "Close_reading" article in Wikipedia was extracted for sentiment analysis. In Figure 19, the bar chart shows the breakdown of sentiment, from left bar to right bar: very negative, moderately negative, moderately positive, and very positive.

In Figure 20, the extracted text that was identified as "Moderately positive" may be seen. The intuition in sharing this screenshot is that the text may be "close read"; it may be further analyzed, with word frequency counts and text searches and other applications applied to that text set (particularly in cases where the text sets are longer).

Figure 18. A sentiment analysis of related standalone articles expressed in an intensity matrix

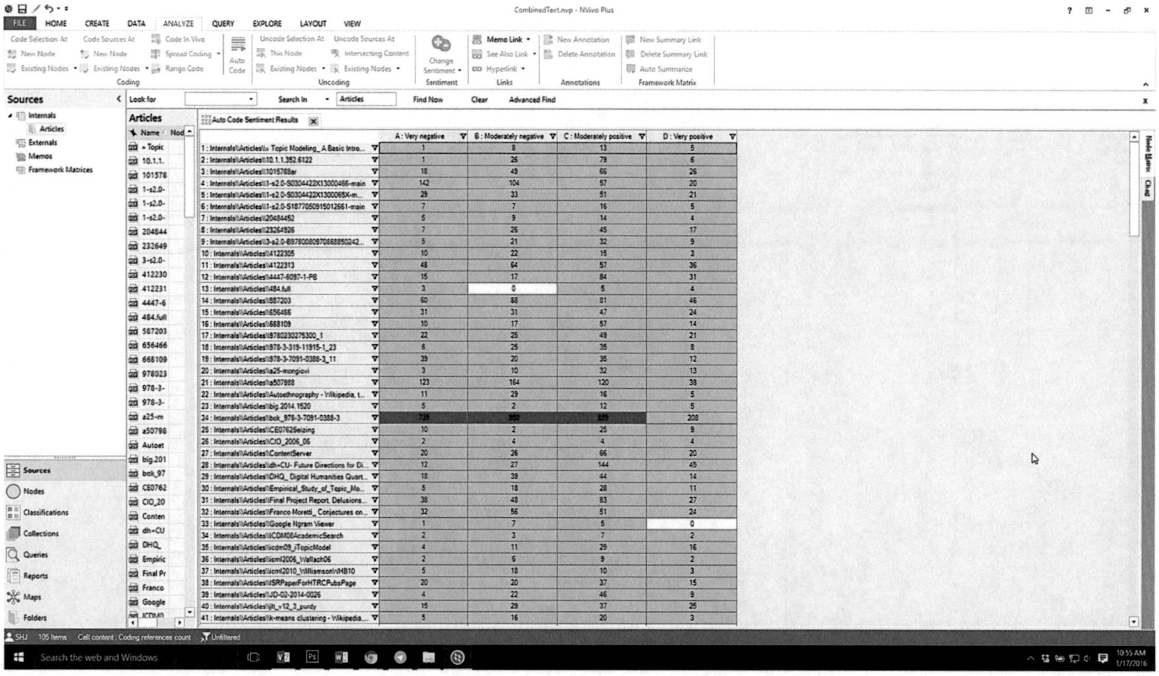

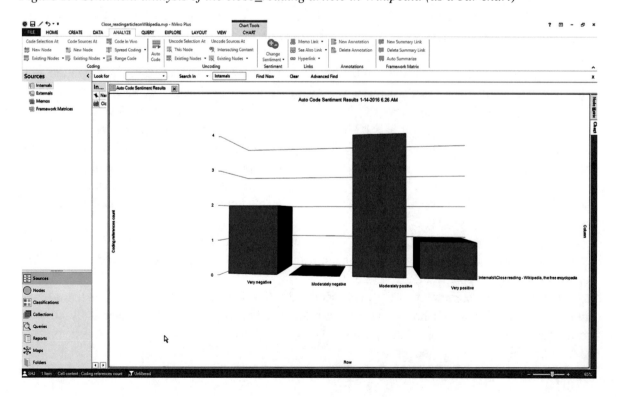

Figure 19. Sentiment analysis of the close_reading article in Wikipedia (as a bar chart)

Figure 20. Extracted text from the moderately positive sentiment category

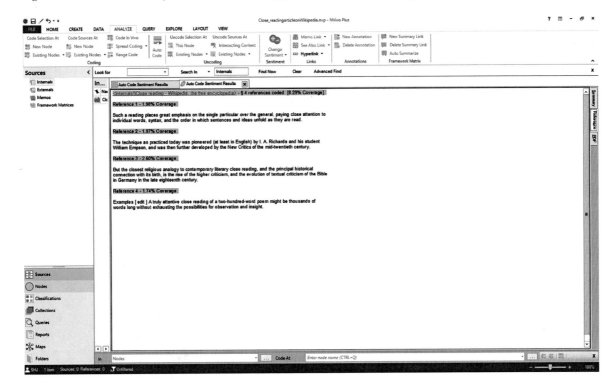

The sentiment analysis feature compares the target text(s) against a sentiment dictionary which has been precoded with various degrees of sentiment polarity (positive-negative). The sentiment analysis feature enables the analysis of multiple files and text sets at a time, but separated files and text sets are treated as separate objects even though the resulting sentiment matrix shows the objects in a combined sentiment matrix (with the four categories of sentiment as column headers and the respective text objects or sets as rows). NVivo 11 Plus's sentiment analysis tool seems to run better not with large-size sets but smaller unit ones (it is unclear where the limits of sentiment data processing are as-yet). The unit of analysis setting ranges from paragraph to sentence to cell, or coarser-grained units to more granular ones. It is possible to combine the "very negative" and "moderately negative" elements into a composite "negative" category and the "very positive" and "moderately positive" categories into a composite "positive" category for more of a traditional sentiment approach (which only labels positive and negative polarities). Finally, it helps to note that there is a hidden text set of "neutral" or at least non-sentiment text. These include not only syntactic (structural) terms but semantic (meaning-bearing) ones.

In Figure 21, the image shows the results of a sentiment analysis of the Tweetstream of the @ReadingPartners account on Twitter. In the background is the intensity matrix, and the inset shows the same data as a bar chart. The sentiment analysis was run based on cell-level data.

6. **Autocoding by Existing Pattern:** Another "distant reading" capability in NVivo 11 Plus involves semi-supervised autocoding. Here, a researcher sets up a coding structure and codes source content to that top-down coding structure…or conducts bottom-up emergent coding without an *a priori* coding structure. Either way (or using a combined approach), the researcher will have a coding

Applied Analytical "Distant Reading" using NVivo 11 Plus™

Figure 21. Sentiment analysis of @ReadingPartners Tweetstream as both an intensity matrix in the background and the bar chart in the foreground

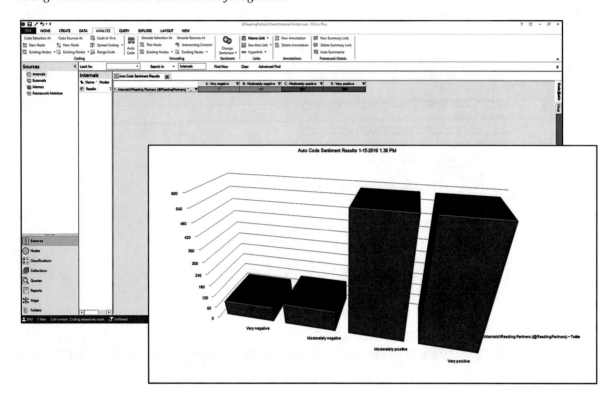

structure and some exemplars coded to each category (each coded node). NVivo 11 Plus, in its "autocoding by existing pattern" function, enables the computer to emulate the human coding to the rest of the source data. The researcher may set parameters for this emulated coding. The software indicates which codes have sufficient exemplars for the software to find other similar raw sources and which contain insufficient exemplars. This is an important semi-supervised text mining option, but since the original raw text was not coded in NVivo (but was done manually outside of the software), this type of autocoding example was not done in this case.

7. **Geolocation Mapping:** NVivo 11 Plus also enables geographical mapping of locations based on geotagged microblogging messages (and geotagged accounts) from Tweetsets that are downloaded through the related NCapture add-on to the Chrome web browser. XML tagging is used to manually label locations for mapping locations in literature, for example, but that is done with other tools and mapping tools.

Discussions

This work essentially surrounds the use of NVivo 11 Plus for applied "distant reading" with relatively small text sets. This summarized the application of the following features: word frequency count, text search, theme and sub-theme extraction, matrix query, sentiment analysis, autocoding by existing pattern, and mapping of geographical locations—from text sets. Autocoding by existing pattern could have

Figure 22. A map visualization of the @ReadingPartners social network on Twitter

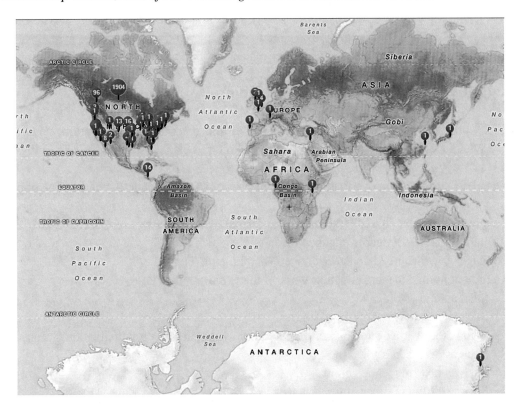

been applied to the research text set, if an actual coding schema had been created and applied, but this was not done for the particular chapter. These approaches are examples of consumptive reading because the researcher has access to the original source texts that were "distant read" in the software tool. One tool feature that is important to note is that textual imagery, cover images, maps, and other information-bearing contents may be included in the distant reading if those elements are summarized textually and informationally (since NVivo 11 Plus's query and autocoding processes are run over text only, not still images, audio files, and video files).

The idea behind "distant reading" is that it stands to benefit human researchers by helping them ask particular types of research questions, identify research leads, extract exploration-worthy themes, find unexpected relationships, and observe textual patterns. The impetus has not been to necessarily detract from human expertise or to remove the human from academic and research endeavors. In general, in terms of general "distant reading," humans are "in the loop" throughout the process. They do capture and select the textsets. They clean or pre-process the data. They choose the algorithms and programs to apply to the respective texts. They create the research design, and they follow through with the work. They output data visualizations. They apply their expert analysis to that. They conduct close readings of the parts of the text sets which are identified to be of particular interest or relevance to particular research questions or theoretical frameworks. They present their findings at conferences and in publications in ways that generally align with the rigorous standards of their respective fields and the assertability that may be made using distant reading. These approaches enable machine insights not otherwise attainable by humans; there are even capabilities to (partially) understand encapsulated texts explored with algorithms for the extraction of certain features in non-consumptive reading.

One researcher sees the mass digitization of texts and the affordances of data mining as the "remaking of reading" technologically and socially and a "provocation" but reading itself is not "at risk" (Kirschenbaum, 2007, p. 1, 5). "Digital reading," as a new reading modality and support to human readers, is part of a transformative shift in reading which will require readers to "think digital" (Dantas, 2013, p. 377 - 378).

A Thought Experiment about Distant Reading

Let's begin with a practical thought experiment: If "distant reading" is the solution, what is/are the problems? What is "distant reading" created to solve? So far, the answers have been as follows:

- To head off "information overload" with the masses of available data that have come online or are available electronically.
- To explore the "great unread" (the masses of formal literature, gray literature, and crowd-sourced information that is not deeply engaged by an audience).
- To engage crowd-sourced and user-created social media data.
- To augment human readers and their work in the exploration of large-scale texts;
  - Such as find leads,
  - Such as identify potential hypotheses.
- To provide other ways of text exploration and knowing that are reproducible and "objective":
  - Such as text search,
  - Such as text frequency counts,
  - Such as different types of text filtering,
  - Such as testing hypotheses with empirical data.
- To find information about texts and text sets/corpora/corpuses that would not be otherwise seeable:
  - Such as expressed sentiment, expressed emotions, and expressed personality (with varying degrees of accuracy),
  - Such as topic modeling,
  - Such as topic popularity,
  - Such as identifying locations in texts and mapping them.
- To allow algorithmic queries of encapsulated (non-downloadable) texts (through non-consumptive reading).
- To enable fast processing of texts for situational awareness (as with social media data).
- To identify the most active communicator in a #hashtag discussion network or online social network (follower-following networks) in a sociogram.
- …and others.

The above is a partial list, but it is fairly representative of the state-of-the-art. There are many areas in which this can move, such as using distant reading to inform machine writing, using distant reading to identify potential threats among communicators, and other applied uses.

Another question: What can't "distant reading" do currently? It cannot engage in embodied reading. It cannot read with the personae of a trained expert human. It cannot read for pleasure. It cannot "read socially" in a human sense. Yet. (This, too, is still a very partial list.)

Given the traditional "pride of place" given to reading in terms of human capabilities, the advancement of "distant reading" may be disruptive in respective domains and disconcerting for researchers. Psychologically, going to computers for reading feels like ceding ground and a diminishment of the writers and readers and their labors. It feels like an incursion and an affront. It is most certainly a challenge to reading orthodoxy. There is a psychic cost, and of course, there is resistance. At first glance, computer-based "distant reading" seems mechanistic, wooden, and literal; it seems awkwardly imitative; it seems insufficiently nuanced; it seems excessively stripped-down and reductionist. It takes a while before the eyes adjust, and the augmented analytical possibilities become clearer.

There are often implied ideologies inherent in technologies and their usage. While theories and theoretical frameworks are not explicitly tied to distant reading, these approaches seem to align more with positivist understandings of the world, with reproducible results. Distant reading techniques suggest empirical-based approaches to research. Distant reading, with its computational accuracy and statistical analysis, can provide objective measures related to texts that have and will challenge human interpretations (Aiden & Michel, 2013).

While computers enable fairly large-scale text analytics with macro-level summary statistics, they also enable very close-in view of texts based on search and mapping functions (such as text searches with contextual mapping around those particular search terms). In other words, computers enable zooming out from texts as well as zooming in, the 30,000 foot view and the close-in word-by-word view.

The sense of threat is multiplied given the uses of programs to create academic writing. For example, SCIgen, an automatic computer science paper generator, was created by graduate students at the Massachusetts Institute of Technology's (MIT) Computer Science and Artificial Intelligence Laboratory (CSAIL) in 2005 and has a web interface from which such papers may be generated (https://pdos.csail.mit.edu/archive/scigen/). Many dozens of its papers had been submitted and accepted into conferences and digital archival holdings (Van Noorden, 2014).

Sidestepping the Controversies

To suggest that distant reading only enables statistical analyses of texts and the creation of metadata about the source texts would be inaccurate. A superficial "read" and representation of "distant reading" might enable the dismissal of the set of computational and human-researcher-based techniques that may be loosely labeled under this term. A closer analysis may suggest helpful augmentations to human work efforts and objectives.

This chapter was *not* written to settle the controversy over "distant reading" as compared to "close reading". While there are very real human limits to reading speeds and comprehension and memory, humans are highly inventive and have powerful imaginations that can bring texts to life and that can contribute spinoff works and newly inspired creations from reading. Through reading, people who are highly trained and expert in respective fields may contribute to their respective fields and other proxemics fields and even highly distal fields. They bring unique interpretive insights in their subjective gaze to topics and writings that other people cannot even begin to emulate. Distant reading does not take away from any of those understandings.

Certainly, the two generalized types of reading are not able to be directly equated. Machine processing of text is a kind of "reading" in a broad sense because information is being extracted from a text or texts but in a way quite different than human processing of text as "reading." Distant reading is challenging to qualitative researchers because there are inherent claims to objectivity and reproducibility; there are possibilities of machine-based universalizing claims about bodies of work (such as: this literature is generally focused on "x" topic). Qualitative researchers generally do not assert any intrinsic features of reality but focus on social constructions of meaning. A machine does not read for "pleasure" in the way that humans may consume texts for pleasure, and comprehension by machine is different than human comprehension of text. The outcomes of meaning-making by machine and by human are also quite different, and while humans interpret the meanings of machine interpretations of text, there is a fair amount of effort required by the person to achieve this. From a human perspective, the extracted data tables, data sets, and data visualizations are engaging but are to reading as print recipes are to the actual dishes. Distant reading feels flat as compared to full-sensory reading, which engages the full imagination and the reader's history and the social company of those around the reader.

In "distant reading," humans are generally in the loop. Humans are creating the computer programs that "read" texts. People will decide how to apply the distant reading research methods to the original texts. They select the texts; they process the texts; they interpret the results; they use the data based on human interests. The importance of human interpretation is not diminished but augmented, in a sense. Language remains polysemic or multi-meaninged. The extracted facts may be used to build or challenge certain arguments and forward certain interpretations. Whenever certain lines of argumentation or interpretation are taken, there are counterfactuals (in this case, potential arguments and interpretations not made) and roads not taken.

While there is growing capability in "distant reading," most do not see a future in which this approach ever supplants human "close reading". "Distant reading" is seen as a research augmentation. In 1960, J.C.R. Licklider described the "man-computer symbiosis" and suggested cooperative interactions between human and machines, with each complementing the other's strengths. This concept applies to distant reading. And as machines are built to be ever more capable, it is all the more critical to align the work of people and ever-more capable machines by finding common ground (Markoff, 2015). The interdisciplinary collaborations that have contributed to the advances in computational text analysis may help dispel some of artificial divides between qualitative and quantitative analyses, particularly as the software tools are "able to dig into 'latent' meaning rather than counting surface observations" and "as long as they are able to keep the link between the qualitative input data and their quantified results" (Wiedemann, 2013, pp. 353 – 354).

FUTURE RESEARCH DIRECTIONS

One prediction is in order: the future has arrived in which "not reading" is reading. This chapter highlighted some of the affordances of NVivo 11 Plus which may enable general researchers to benefit from some of the affordances of "distant reading." This is by no means a full exploration of the tool's capabilities. This chapter provided a simple walk-through of the features without addressing other more complex combinations of the tool's affordances and query sequences. For example, it is possible to first conduct a sentiment analysis and then to conduct a text frequency count within the respective text sets to find out which the most common terms are that are labeled "very negative," "moderately negative," "moderately positive," and "very positive." As noted earlier, this is by no means about "big data" analytics because that requires the uses of different technologies, tools, and processes.

Related future research may proceed in any number of directions. New works may continue to build on the body of literature that shows practical and substantive research insights from distant reading. Each one of the features described here may be applied in different ways in different research contexts for extractable insights. There is high potential for the creation of different applied research cases. One particularly notable one involved an in-depth analysis of government discourse around national security. The researchers here show how human-machine readings of texts may be done in a theoretically sound way (in this case, based on Kenneth Burke's "grammar of motives" concept and "dramatistic pentad" including agent, agency, scene, purpose, and act). The authors explain:

We use Natural Language Processing methods (specifically, Named-Entity Recognition) to search the NSS texts in order to identify all of the probable examples of what Burke would describe as "Agents" (or, "Actors"). Second, using semantic grammar parsers, we identify "Acts" that are purported to be associated with these agents by pulling out all of the verbs that are semantically connected (within a sentence) to agents. Third, using Latent Dirichlet Allocation (LDA) topic model techniques, we identify each of the "Scenes" in which the identified agents act. Using these three legs of the pentad, we will then explore the utility of seeking to understand the NSS documents in terms of the grammar of motives that underlie the rhetorical form being employed in the NSS documents. (Mohr, Wagner-Pacifici, Breiger, & Bogdanov, 2013, p. 678)

Research method using distant reading is important. There may be different sequences in applying NVivo 11 Plus for distant reading. There are a number of complementary software tools that may be used to surface fresh insights. Also, researchers may develop fresh ways of combining human – and machine-reading for human ends.

Another approach may focus on ways that researchers and others adapt to distant reading. In another notable work, an author described how he integrated digital pedagogy in an English class. In English, the pedagogical approach is one of interrogative stances and questioning, not about finding discrete answers. In that light, the application of "not reading" produces disorientation for learners: "Digital pedagogy complements and complicates this familiar goal, as students are freed to imagine what they don't know and encouraged to invent and interrogate their own methods of finding out" (Fyfe, 2010, p. 5). It would help to know what scaffolding may encourage adjustments to distant reading.

Certainly, farther out from this limited application of distant reading, there are plenty of open challenges. It helps to acknowledge that there is the discomfiting specter of mass production of reading and writing by computers *without humans in the loop* and potentially with dubious benefits for people—unless those who design such systems and those who use them can make a clear research-based case for the benefits. There is something of the vision of the Semantic Web in this conceptualization—with computers collecting and collating data on the Web but in ways that benefit people. There is also the sense that human privacy will have disappeared when machines may read the collective output of humanity and interpret it for patterns that people would not see otherwise; to this end, people will likely have to revise what they think of as human personal space (and the intrusiveness of computers). Without awareness of how texts may be analyzed or used, it is hard for individual writers to set up defenses against computational text analysis in the wild; in the lab, there are ways to confuse various forms of text analysis (such as author attribution in stylometry applications), but these are *ceteris paribus* and controlled lab conditions.

Is it possible for those who design such systems to bring "distant reading" closer to the human reading experience? Would that make distant reading less agonistic and less conflictual? Are there ways to apply "distant reading" not only for analytical ends but aesthetic pleasure? (There are machine-created insights on what elements make for predictably popular songs, and that may be applied to predict which features in particular genres of books make for predictably viral reads. Does knowing what goes into the genre formula ruin the reading experience?) The human tendency to personify computers—to attribute to them personality and volition—may affect their readiness to work with programs that enable distant reading (although it is unclear in what ways at present). There are also automated applications that run continuously and with set "triggers" to notify people when some message requires expert human attention. It would be interesting to have more writing on those in the academic literature.

CONCLUSION

The old-school sense of reading as decoding text alone is no longer singularly valid (if it ever was) as people's reading capabilities have been augmented with expanded computational capabilities. For researchers to engage with ever larger sets of textual data, they will need to more fully incorporate computational research into their toolkits. While there are a number of approaches and software programs that may be applied to this task, the state of the art is still nascent. The learning curve is high to understanding various applied computer algorithms and machine learning approaches. For many, it is not clear how integrated human-machine research should be designed and where humans should come in to the research sequence and where machines should. There is not yet comfort with discovery learning by prospecting through text corpora. It is not clear whether fresh machine insights and perspectives are welcome.

What "distant reading" actually means is still being defined by researchers (as research methods) and those creating various software tools, algorithms, and scripts. At this point, it may be possible to suggest that there are distant reading applications in particular contexts and cases (with custom algorithms and coding) and those in more generalist applications. Distant reading was not designed to take the place of human reading; rather, it augments human capabilities in reading and text analysis. In most cases, humans will be "in the loop". At this time, it is hard to imagine programmers investing in the highly complex reading through interpretive lens and complex critical-analytical traditions (including moral, psychoanalytic, historical, semiotics, deconstructionist, Marxist, formalist, post-colonial, feminist, gender, sociological, biographical, and others. (Technically, there are challenges to creating computational expert systems.) Also, there are real challenges in computationally reading multi-lingually, which is also in the purview of human reading.

NVivo 11 Plus enables broadly new ways of exploring texts using computational affordances, including the following methods:

1. Word frequency counts,
2. Text searches,
3. Theme and sub-theme extractions,
4. Matrix queries,
5. Sentiment analyses,
6. "Autocoding by existing pattern," and
7. Mapping geographical locations.

These unsupervised and semi-supervised machine reading approaches broaden the capabilities of researchers. To actually harness the capabilities of distant reading, researchers will have to familiarize themselves with the related established methods and technologies. They will have to re-conceptualize reading as something that requires so much mental focus and effort to incorporate the computationally speedy and efficient text processing approaches.

While use of an off-the-shelf data analytics tool, NVivo 11 Plus, does not require scripting, it may serve as a bridge to even more complex distant reading methods that may require some developer work like coding, scripting using a high-level computer language, or command line work.

Regardless, research design, textual data capture, data analysis, data visualizations, research writing, and publishing, are all uniquely challenging and require highly developed skill sets. Various strategies at distant reading may be wielded to enhance the very human work of analytical reading and research.

ACKNOWLEDGMENT

QSR International puts out a dazzling software with plenty of enablements for data analytics for qualitative, mixed methods, and multi-methods research. NVivo 11 Plus has many value-added capabilities, of which "distant reading" is a part.

REFERENCES

Aiden, E., & Michel, J.-B. (2013). *Uncharted: Big Data as a Lens on Human Culture*. New York: Penguin Group.

Angerbauer, K., Schmidt, A., Dingler, T., & Kern, D. (2015). Utilizing the effects of priming to facilitate text comprehension. In *Proceedings of CHI 2015*.

Best, S., & Marcus, S. (2009, Fall). Surface Reading: An Introduction. *Representations, 108*(1), 1 – 21. Retrieved Jan. 3, 2016, from http://www.jstor.org/stable/10.1525/rep.2009.108.1.1

Bhattacharyya, S., Organisciak, P., & Downie, S. J. (2015). *A fragmentizing interface to a large corpus of digitized text: (Post)humanism and non-consumptive reading via features*. IDEALS Home. Graduate School of Library and Information Science. Retrieved Jan. 3, 2016, from https://www.ideals.illinois.edu/handle/2142/72732

Biedert, R., Hees, J., Dengel, A., & Buscher, G. (2012). A robust realtime reading-skimming classifier. In *Proceedings of ETRA 2012*. doi:10.1145/2168556.2168575

Blei, D. M. (2012). Probabilistic topic models. *Communications of the ACM, 55*(4), 77–84. doi:10.1145/2133806.2133826

Cohen, M. (2009). Narratology in the archive of literature. *Representations (Berkeley, Calif.), 108*(1), 51–75. doi:10.1525/rep.2009.108.1.51

Dantas, T. R. (2013). The digital reading as a product of the evolution of information: books between screens. In *Proceedings of the First International Conference on Technological Ecosystem for Enhancing Multiculturality* (TEEM '13). doi:10.1145/2536536.2536593

Fyfe, P. C. (2010). *How not to read a Victorian novel*. Diginole. Florida State University. Retrieved Jan. 4, 2016, from http://diginole.lib.fsu.edu/cgi/viewcontent.cgi?article=1002&context=eng_faculty_publications

Heyman, S. (2015, Oct. 28). Google Books: A complex and controversial experiment. *The New York Times*. Retrieved Jan. 12, 2016, from http://www.nytimes.com/2015/10/29/arts/international/google-books-a-complex-and-controversial-experiment.html?_r=1

Jo, J., Kim, B., & Seo, J. (2015). EyeBookmark: Assisting recovery from interruption during reading. In *Proceedings of CHI 2015*.

Juola, P. (2010). Distant reading and mapping genre space via conjecture-based distance measures. *Digital Humanities 2010*. Retrieved Jan. 3, 2016, from http://dh2010.cch.kcl.ac.uk/academic-programme/abstracts/papers/html/ab-669.html

Kalanithi, P. (2016). *When Breath Becomes Air*. New York: Random House.

Khadem, A. (2012). Annexing the unread: A close reading of 'distant reading'. *Neohelicon*, *39*(2), 409–421. doi:10.1007/s11059-012-0152-y

Kirschenbaum, M. G. (2007, Oct.). The remaking of reading: Data mining and the digital humanities. In *the National Science Foundation Symposium on Next Generation of Data Mining and Cyber-Enabled Discovery for Innovation* (NGDM '07). Retrieved Jan. 3, 2016, from http://citeseerx.ist.psu.edu/viewdoc/download?doi=10.1.1.111.959&rep=rep1&type=pdf

Kunze, K., Utsumi, Y., Shiga, Y., Kise, K., & Bulling, A. (2013). I know what you are reading—Recognition of document types using mobile eye tracking. In *Proceedings of ISWC '13*.

Licklider, J. C. R. (1960, March). Man-computer symbiosis. *IRE Transactions on Human Factors in Electronics*. Retrieved January 13, 2016, from http://groups.csail.mit.edu/medg/people/psz/Licklider.html

Markoff, J. (2015). *Machines of Loving Grace: The Quest for Common Ground between Humans and Robots*. New York: HarperCollins.

McPherson, T. (2009, Winter). Introduction: Media Studies and the Digital Humanities. *Cinema Journal*, *48*(20), 119–123. Retrieved from http://www.jstor.org/stable/20484452

Michel, J-B., Shen, Y.K., Aiden, A.P., Veres, A., Gray, M.K., Brockman, W., … Aiden, E.L. (2010, Dec. 16). Quantitative Analysis of Culture Using Millions of Digitized Books. *Science*.

Milligan, I. (2012). Mining the 'Internet Graveyard': Rethinking the historians' toolkit. *Journal of the Canadian Historical Association*, *23*(2), 21–64. doi:10.7202/1015788ar

Mohr, J. W., Wagner-Pacifici, R., Breiger, R. L., & Bogdanov, P. (2013). Graphing the grammar of motives in national security strategies: Cultural interpretation, automated text analysis and the drama of global politics. *Poetics*, *41*(6), 670–700. doi:10.1016/j.poetic.2013.08.003

Moretti, F. (2000, January – February). Conjectures on world literature. *New Left Review*, *1*, 1–13.

Moretti, F. (2005). Graphs, Maps, Trees: Abstract Models for Literary History – 1. *New Left Review*, *24*, 67–93.

Müller-Birn, C., Schlegel, A., Klüwer, T., Benedix, L., & Breitenfeld, A. (2015). Neonion—Combining human and machine intelligence. In *Proceedings of CSCS '15*.

Muralidharan, A., Hearst, M. A., & Fan, C. (2013). WordSeer: A knowledge synthesis environment for textual data. In *Proceedings of CIKM '13*. doi:10.1145/2505515.2508212

Nováček, V., & Burns, G. A. P. C. (2013). SKIMMR: Machine-aided skim-reading. In *Proceedings of IUI'13 Companion*.

Purdy, J. P. (2011). Three gifts of digital archives. *Journal of Literacy and Technology*, *12*(3), 24–49.

Reading (Process). (2016, Jan. 7). In *Wikipedia*. Retrieved January 10, 2016, from https://en.wikipedia.org/wiki/Reading_(process)

Ryan, G. W., & Bernard, H. R. (2003). Techniques to identify themes. *Field Methods*, *15*(1), 85–109. doi:10.1177/1525822X02239569

Size of Wikipedia. (2016, Jan. 3). In *Wikipedia*. Retrieved Jan. 12, 2016, from https://en.wikipedia.org/wiki/Wikipedia:Size_of_Wikipedia

Smith, C. (2015, Aug. 10). *By the numbers: 14 interesting Flickr stats*. DMR. Retrieved January 12, 2016, from http://expandedramblings.com/index.php/flickr-stats/

Solberg, J. (2012). Googling the archive: Digital tools and the practice of history. *Advances in the History of Rhetoric*, *15*(1), 53–76. doi:10.1080/15362426.2012.657052

Tahmasebi, N., Borin, L., Capannini, G., Dubhashi, D., Exner, P., Forsberg, M., & Risse, T. et al. (2015). Visions and open challenges for a knowledge-based culturomics. *International Journal on Digital Libraries*, *15*(2-4), 169–187. doi:10.1007/s00799-015-0139-1

Van Noorden, R. (2014). Publishers withdraw more than 120 gibberish papers. *Nature*. Retrieved January 7, 2016, from http://www.nature.com/news/publishers-withdraw-more-than-120-gibberish-papers-1.14763

Wells, S. (2002). Claiming the archive for rhetoric and composition. In *Rhetoric and Composition as Intellectual Work* (pp. 55–64). Carbondale, IL: Southern Illinois University Press.

What does the Ngram Viewer do? (2015). *Google Books Ngram Viewer*. Retrieved Jan. 16, 2016, from https://books.google.com/ngrams/info

Wiedemann, G. (2013). Opening up to big data: Computer-assisted analysis of textual data in social sciences. *Historical Social Research (Köln)*, *38*(4), 332–357.

Winter, T. N. (1999). Roberto Busa, S.J., and the invention of the machine-generated concordance. *The Classical Bulletin*, *75*(1), 3–20. Retrieved Jan. 3, 2016, from http://digitalcommons.unl.edu/cgi/viewcontent.cgi?article=1069&context=classicsfacpub

Yu, C.-H., & Miller, R. C. (2012). Enhancing web page skimmability. In *Proceedings of CHI 2012*. doi:10.1145/2212776.2223852

KEY TERMS AND DEFINITIONS

Affordance: Something that enables a particular capability or action (initially conceptualized "action possibilities" for particular agents in an environment, with both beneficial and detrimental possibilities to the agent, as per J.J. Gibson, 1979).

Autocoding: Using a computer to "code" data into particular categories (whether defined in an *a priori* way or dynamically).

Burstiness: Showing short and sudden spikes in popularity.

Close Reading (also "Natural Reading" and "Active Reading"): Acquiring knowledge and thinking critically while engaging with text; decoding text through careful mental processing.

Codebook: A reference that lists the names of codes and the descriptions for which types of raw data and processed information are coded to the particular label.

Corpora (also "Corpuses"): A collection of texts.

Digital Reading: Human decoding of texts using a range of computational and other methods.

Distant Reading (also "Remote Reading" and "Non-Reading"): Using computers to extract text patterns and other data from texts and text corpora.

Gray (Grey) Literature: Documents created by organizations but released outside of formal publishing channels (sometimes used to include less formal sources of information).

Hyper Reading: Reading online.

Ngram: A contiguous sequence of items (such as words) in a sequence of text or speech, such as uni-gram or one-gram, bigram or two-gram, three-gram, four-gram, and so on.

Non-Consumptive Reading: The application of various algorithms against text corpora for statistical analysis without researcher access to the underlying source texts (which are encapsulated and protected against direct access).

Objectivism: A focus on what is externally observable, independent of human observation

Parasocial: Relating to often-public figures in a one-sided followership relationship enabled by mediated communications.

Reading: The extraction of information / creation of meaning from written language or symbols; the interpretation of language.

Scanning: Reading a text to capture key concepts.

Sentiment Analysis (Opinion Mining): The extraction of human-expressed positive or negative sentiment.

Skimming: Reading a text in search of particular information.

Subjectivism: A focus on human-filtered or perceived experiences (often as a counterpoint to objectivism).

Tag: To label an object with a word, phrase, or hashtag (#) descriptor.

Unigram: A one-gram item.

APPENDIX: A REFLECTION: FROM "CLOSE READING" TO "DISTANT READING" AND BACK

Reading has something that has been daily practice for this author since childhood. As a part of common qualitative research practice, it would seem helpful to explore how the researcher stands in relation to this topic which has been such a part of her life for decades. This self-reflection is not being done as an indulgence or as insertion of subjectivity into a traditional research work. Rather, this is provided to provide insight about how a traditional reader has evolved to some acceptance of distant reading for analytical and research ends.

Real-World Scenario 1: Over a dozen years ago, when I was a writing professor at a small college, I received a request to work with a programmer who wanted to write a book. He was working on software to create writing, and he wanted to describe his work in a published text. While he had not written for publication in the past, he wanted to output a book in 10 weeks. The ambition of his plan was high-risk, and his project itself, then, was sufficiently offensive to me that I passed on taking on this potential student. Then and now, I have seen writing as painstaking and difficult work. I had sincere doubts about the value of the text that a machine could output, which I thought of as synthesis more than fresh creation. Then, and now, I consider writing a book as professionally sacrosanct. Publishing itself is something that academics aspire to; it is something deeply integrated with academic practice and ritual, a rite of passage. Publications show culmination of years of work. They offer something for both colleagues and others who pursue related studies in the future.

Real-World Scenario 2: Several university colleagues assigned video essay assignments, which are mash-ups of existing videos and fresh video footage brought together as short films that serve as "essays." In this scenario, student authors are not those who can write a coherent essay but those who may coalesce video snippets into a lucid piece of communications. In terms of actual writing, students had written up design plans for their video.

Real-World Scenario 3: Over the several months when this was a work-in-progress, I (as the author) engaged in self-conscious reading—maintaining meta-awareness of the reading process while enjoying various fiction works (mysteries, thrillers, and sci-fi works) and non-fiction works (technical books). The idea was to capture insights that would inform this work. While various insights have been interwoven into this work, there were some additional insights that bear mentioning. One insight is that people can get very involved in what they are reading, emotionally and cognitively. They care about characters as if they were real people; they care about plots and often have an internal sense of poetic justice. They have an animal sensibility for the dramatic moment. Human attention aligns with what is perceived as relevant for survival (sense of risk) and reproduction (attractiveness). They often like predictability in the respective genres that they read, and authors who break expectations do so at their own risk. There is sometimes rabid loyalty to a particular author and bursty expressions of excitement at the release of new works (partially fanned by expert promotion). ("Burstiness" refers to sudden spikes in popularity.) Readers have to commit to consuming a text in a highly competitive attentional economy, with all sorts of other media and activities competing for their attention. The time and attention invested in reading a work means less time for other activities; there is a very real opportunity cost. People have to anticipate some value in the text, whether it is pleasure or learning or other purpose. For nonfictional works, readers also have to be willing to suspend disbelief (based on their knowledge of the real world) and accept the artifice presented by the author. Texts are written programs used to hack humans. For many readers, there is a direct sense of relationship with authors, and it does not take much to break that trust. [Technically, these are one-way parasocial relationships, with readers feeling closeness to authors through mediated textual means.] Writers, as public figures (and often at the advice of publicists), often strive to maintain strategic ambiguity so as to maintain connections with a wide range of readers. This ambiguity allows readers to assume that writers are the way they imagine because there is no contradicting information otherwise. Revealing too much about themselves may be "TMI" and off-putting to readers. Another example of this sense of relationship is the resistance to having other authors "ghost" for a late author because it feels inauthentic and emulative.

Real-World Scenario Today: In the past few years, I have attended several day-long XML tagging workshops to learn from professionals how this is done. I have used NVivo 10 and NVivo 11 Plus for qualitative research and publishing. I have also supported the use of this software tool with colleagues on campus. I have also used the Google Books Ngram Viewer for years, for learning, amusement, training, and research. I have worked in publishing for decades and understands the importance of structure and context in writing, but I can also see value in decontextualized texts based on distant reading approaches. (There are machine ways to recontextualize information, too, such as broadening the captured text around search terms or bringing up the entire source document from which particular words or phrases were found. It is possible to capture overall summaries of context from mass text sets as well based on something as simple as a word frequency count—with the intuition that the more something is mentioned, the more of a focus it is for the creators of the texts in that text set.)

There are always tradeoffs in research processes. Every research effort brings up some new insights, but these efforts are all qualified and non-absolute. In terms of text processing, every aspect of the research sequence is important: where the source text comes from, how it was created, how it was acquired, how it was manually coded (if it was); the types of technology tools applied to that text and in what sequence; the actual functions of the technology tools under the hood (if available); how human expertise was applied to the research at every stage, and the research insights. As always, the process should be as transparent and fully disclosed as possible.

In terms of what I've read in the computer science literature and observed in the field, my sense is that the tools enabling text analysis will only develop further because the need to understand texts in all sorts of contexts and in all human languages is so critical. Now, so many years later, I wonder what I could have learned had I taken on this computer scientist as a writing student. (My standard for machine writing would be "that's something that I would write" on the one hand. On the other, the more likely standard is a coherent work that contains human-valuable insights and that draws from mass-scale data. The standards should be higher than human-created writing.) I also wonder if my attitude towards machine writing would have been somewhat different had I seen some of the current research and better understood applications for both machine writing and machine reading. If machine writing was the "bleeding edge" then years ago, it's likely "cutting edge" now.

Certainly, this chapter will not settle any disagreements about the respective applied uses of distant reading in any field. It does not make the topic less controversial. The uses of distant reading are not settled issues for any number of fields. The acceptance or non-acceptance of this approach and its respective methods will depend in part on how the tools are wielded by researchers and coders, how the research assertions are made (overstating? understating? coherence?), and the theoretical and research insights surfaced.

Chapter 8
Conducting Sentiment Analysis and Post–Sentiment Data Exploration through Automated Means

Shalin Hai-Jew
Kansas State University, USA

ABSTRACT

One new feature in NVivo 11 Plus, a qualitative and mixed methods research suite, is its sentiment analysis tool; this enables the autocoding of unlabeled and unstructured text corpora against a built-in sentiment dictionary. The software labels selected texts into four categories: (1) very negative, (2) moderately negative, (3) moderately positive, and (4) very positive. After the initial coding for sentiment, there are many ways to augment that initial coding, including theme and subtheme extraction, word frequency counts, text searches, sociogram mapping, geolocational mapping, data visualizations, and others. This chapter provides a light overview of how the sentiment analysis feature in NVivo 11 Plus works, proposes some insights about the proper unit of analysis for sentiment analyses (sentence, paragraph, or cell) based on text dataset features, and identifies ways to further explore the textual data post-sentiment analysis—to create coherence and insight.

INTRODUCTION

In a complex multimedia environment, the most common base form of data is still textual. Even common multimedia—audio and video—tend to have a textual component (the transcript) that captures some of the informational value of the digital file; likewise, imagery often have "alt-text" and metadata descriptors. In text may be found residuals of common human endeavors: inter-communications, record-keeping, research, and history-keeping. In this current age of social media, much of the outpouring of created data is in text form. In a time of informational plenty (in terms of certain topics), there are computational ways of "read" and "understand" information from various text sets.

DOI: 10.4018/978-1-5225-0648-5.ch008

The inherent structures of language and their common use for the encoding and decoding of shared interchanges and understandings have made it possibly to apply computational means (in scalable ways and at machine speeds) to extract insights from texts and text corpora (collections of texts). One capability involves classifying texts into sentiment polarities or valence (either a binary positive or a binary negative) or into sentiment categories (various gradations of sentiment based on both polarity and intensity/arousal). Sentiment analysis (also known as "opinion mining") is the identification of attitude, whether positive or negative, towards a particular issue, event or phenomenon, concept, product, service, person, organization, or another element. How sentiment is understood computationally varies, but one of the simplest approaches involves using a pre-defined sentiment dictionary or word set and comparing the terms of a target text or text corpus against that and classifying the target text based on identified sentiment. The number of opinion words found informs the sense of intensity of sentiment in that text corpus. Technically, the practice of sentiment analysis stems from work in natural language processing (NLP), artificial intelligence (AI), computational linguistics, data mining, and text analysis.

Sentiment or opinion analysis may be applied to a text and then the coded texts may be further machine queried and processed for insight. Themes and subthemes may be extracted to capture a summary view of what a text or a text corpus is "about." Word frequency counts are used as a proxy measure of the focus or emphasis of a particular text corpus. The more frequently words that are listed, the more mentions are being represented, and the greater interest there is in the group of documents around that topic. This approach has been applied to Tweetstream texts, #hashtag conversations texts, and formal article sets in particular domain fields, among other applications. Text searches may be applied to see every instantiation of selected words, n-grams (consecutive verbatim text sequences), phrases, names, formulas, or other textual elements…and the proximity text leading up to- and away- from the selected text presented in a word tree to show the contextual gist of the phrases. Content and messaging data that people share via social media platforms are thought to be highly opinion-laden data: think upvotes and downvotes, likes and dislikes, votes about hot-or-not, reviews about everything bought or sold (and the sellers besides), raging feuds, and people calling out each other. Data extracted from "social media"—broadly including email systems, social networking sites, content-sharing sites, microblogging sites, blogging sites, crowd-sourced encyclopedias, and others—may be depicted in sociograms (social networks displayed as graphs). Also, it is possible to capture textual data with various locational markers and to map those locations onto a two-dimensional geolocational map.

There are two basic hypotheses in this work:

Hypothesis 1: There is an optimal unit of analysis for sentiment analysis (sentence, paragraph, or cell) using the NVivo 11 Plus tool based on the dataset type (and how the textual data is structured in that corpus).

Hypothesis 2: There are data analytics benefits to defining a sequence of data analytics steps post-sentiment analysis to add value to the coded data (using NVivo 11 Plus).

One of the new features of NVivo 11 Plus, a qualitative and mixed methods research suite, is its sentiment analysis tool which enables the autocoding of text corpora against a sentiment dictionary (a listing of words and lexical elements which are seen to contain inherent sentiment or attitude). The software labels texts into four categories: very negative, moderately negative, moderately positive, and very positive. After the initial coding for sentiment, there are still a number of ways to augment that initial coding by using various query and related data visualization features in NVivo 11 Plus, including theme and subtheme extraction, word frequency counts, text searches, sociogram mapping, geolocational mapping, and others. This chapter provides a light overview of how the sentiment analysis tool in NVivo 11 Plus works and provides ways to further explore the textual data post-sentiment analysis—to create data coherence and insight (including some latent ones).

One caveat: It is not always possible to fully understand algorithmically what is going on under the hood of a software tool. Because of the newness of the tool's features and the lack of academic research documentation of the underlying algorithms, what is presented here is somewhat limited.

REVIEW OF THE LITERATURE

Sentiment—both within individuals and among groups—is of intense research interest because it may be a motivating factor in people's perceptions of the world, their decision-making, and their actions. In a 2013 article, Ronen Feldman noted that sentiment analysis was one of the "hottest" areas of research in computer science, and over 7,000 articles had been written on this topic (p. 82). Sentiment itself may be contagious, spreading among people, particularly those who are peers. Individuals, as social actors, may affect (reinforce or undercut) others' sentiments and resolve regarding particular issues. (Some researchers have looked at "sentiment homophily" or the attraction between people who have similar sentiments toward particular topics to create relationships. In such contexts, sentiment is one feature of like-mindedness. Others have used expressed sentiment to profile other egos and entities from social media, to understand their proclivities and classify personalities.) While sentiment has been studied for the past decade-and-a-half, there have been spinoffs of studies into automated emotion extraction and analysis and identification of objectivity or subjectivity features in text sets. Sentiment itself is often a critical variable in understanding various aspects of personality (Sarkar, Bhatia, Agarwal, & Li, 2014).

In terms of the state of the field, there are varying degrees of automated sentiment extraction for particular languages, with some researchers using language translators from one language into English in order to apply extant sentiment dictionaries from English. There are also dedicated domain-specific lexicons that are applied to specific text sets in particular fields.

To broadly over-simplify, it may help to review some standards of binary classifiers (such as sentiment analysis classifiers who evaluate textual data to determine whether that text is positive or negative). More on this is in Box 1.

In *Dataclysm: Who We Are When We Think No One's Looking,* Christian Rudder (2014) observed, "The era of data is here; we are now recorded." One of the main sources of such recording is from social media platforms: social networking sites, microblogging data streams, crowd-sourced online dictionaries, blogs, content-sharing sites, and others. As such, there are a range of content data, metadata (descriptors of that data), and trace data (recorded log information about interactions among those on social media). The Web itself is a rich source, with http networks and data-scrapable sites. Some social media datasets align fairly directly with classic formal articles while others have many of their own rules. Many others have their own rules of engagement and their own slang. Researchers have explored various methods for classifying sentiment in the short texts of microblogging messages by classifying sentiment found in #hashtags in Twitter datasets (Wang, Wei, Liu, Zhou, & Zhang, 2011) and the inherent sentiment in various emoticons given their role in self-expression, message emphasis, and clarification of sentiment (Hogenboom, Bal, Frasincar, Bal, de Jong, & Kaymak, 2013).

Box 1. A sidebar about the F-score and sentiment classifiers

The various tools and methods for the extraction of sentiment are tested and redesigned to increase their accuracy for identifying negative and positive sentiment. A typical measure involves the f-score (or f-measure) as applied to binary classification predictions (whether "positive" or "negative"). Simply put, there will be a set of correct predictions as "true negatives" and "true positives" and then incorrect predictions as "false negatives" and "false positives." This is often expressed as a four-celled confusion matrix (Table 1).

The f-score ranges between 0 and 1, and the higher the score, the more predictive the classification procedure; a score of 1 represents perfect classifier predictability (if the classifier identifies a particular object as positive or negative, then that is true-to-reality). The harmonic accuracy score is a representation of the predictive power of the classifier. This f-score takes into consideration both "precision" and "recall" and is said to capture the "harmonic mean" of precision and recall.

"Precision" (also known as "specificity" / "true negative rate") as the number of correctly identified positive results divided by the number of predicted positive results (or true positives divided by the sum of true positives and false positives). False positives are actual negatives that were falsely identified or labeled as positives. This means that the classifier wrongly labeled the contents and mistook noise for signal (in signals detection theory). Such misidentifications lower the level of trust in the accuracy of the tool when it labels a particular thing positive or negative. If a classifier has a low threshold to identify a term or phrase as "positive," it will capture a lot of true positives but also a lot of false positives.

Precision = TP / (TP + FP)

The precision of the tool refers to how accurately it can differentiate between an actual positive and a false one. This is a measure of the "true negative rate". An imprecise tool will over-reach and falsely label contents to a set which do not belong.

"Recall" (also known as "sensitivity" / "true positive rate") is the number of correct positive results divided by the sum of actual positive results as well as false negatives (or true positives divided by the sum of true positives and false negatives). If a classifier has a very high standard (threshold) to record a "positive," it capture some true positives but also miss many and misclassify many positives as false negatives. In this case, the tool is not sufficiently sensitive to identify all positives. This sort of tool will fail to capture the whole universe of actual positives. The captured subset will be a smaller percentage of the universe of positives that would be captured.

Recall = TP / (TP + FN)

The f-score strives to capture how well the classifying tool is able to identify positives from the universe of all actual positives in the dataset without mistaking actual negatives as positives. This is a measure of the "true positive rate." Conventionally, the f-score is known as the "harmonic mean of precision and recall" and is expressed as follows:

$$F = \frac{2}{\dfrac{1}{Recall} + \dfrac{1}{Precision}}$$

or

$$F = 2 \times \frac{Precision \times Recall}{Precision + Recall}$$

One visualization of the f-score is shown in Figure 1.

In information retrieval, the measures of precision and recall are "both independent of the number of true negatives, which is generally unknown and much larger than the actual numbers of relevant and retrieved documents" ("Sensitivity and specificity," Dec. 4, 2015).

Generally speaking, sentiment classifiers may work better within dedicated types of textual information sets than in a broadly generalized way. In dedicated contexts, the classifier may be "tuned" (manually and by data patterns) to the nuances of that text set.

Table 1. A classic confusion matrix

	Prediction Outcome: +	**Prediction Outcome: -**
Actual Value: +	(+,+) / true positive	(+,-) / false negative (Type 1 Error)
Actual Value: -	(-,+) / false positive (Type II Error)	(-, -) / true negative

205

Figure 1. A visualization of F-scores with varying levels of identification accuracy

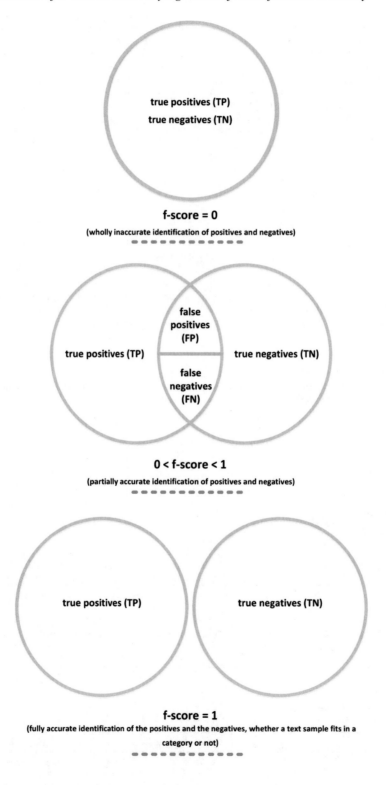

Twitter, a perennial favorite for data analysis, involves fast-evolving and dynamic interchanges among a global audience, with #hashtags, @user accounts, RT or retweeting of messages, URLs, elongated terms (with repeated characters, letters, symbols, and punctuation marks), emoticons, Internet slang, and a mix of languages (anything expressible with the UTF-8 set in Unicode). Researchers have observed that the communications in social media is a "sub-language" of natural language (Min, Lee, & Hsu, 2013, p. 203). There are various endeavors to create social media sentiment lexicons that are almost continually updated to capture human sentiment expressions accurately. Beyond text, there is a range of other multimedia-based data in social media, including imagery, audio files, and video files, which may require analysis for fuller understandings. How others are responding to the messaging of a particular user account on Twitter, whether the messages are trending positive or negative, has been assessed to evaluate the popularity or unpopularity of the individual (Bae & Lee, 2011). On Twitter, there tends to be one-to-many influence relationships which are one-way. In other words, Twitter is an environment with low levels of reciprocity: "Twitter shows a low level of reciprocity; 77.9% of user pairs with any link between them are connected one-way, and only 22.1% have reciprocal relationships between them" (Bae & Lee, 2011, p. 733). Messaging with sentiment tends to be retweeted more than neutral ones (Stieglitz & Dang-Xuan, 2011), which may align with cognition research which suggests that affect heightens message salience. "Neutrality" in sentiment analysis may suggest an absence of sentiment information, but there are nuances to this. In terms of online reviews, one research team interpreted positive sentiment as support for the target and negative sentiment as aversion for the target. They wrote: "Neutral tweets, on the other hand, are usually the ones that contain unbiased opinions or a purely informative content" (Bigonha, Cardoso, Moro, Goncalves, & Almeida, 2012, p. 172).

Popular events are associated with increases in negative sentiment strength in Twitter messaging and even that negative sentiment is "often the key to popular events in Twitter" (Thelwall, Buckley, & Paltoglou, Dec. 2010/ February 2011, p. 415). One research team found evidence that latent user characteristics may affect the sentiments of other users—based on "sentiment-based later user factors" defined as "influence," "susceptibility," and "cynicalness" (Lee & Lim, 2015, p. 411). In this research, "influence" refers to how easily a particular user may affect the sentiments of others on Twitter, "susceptibility" refers to how easily a user adopts the same sentiments diffused by others, and "cynicalness" refers to "how easy (sic) the user adopts opposing sentiments diffused by other users" in an interdependent and interactive model (Lee & Lim, 2015, p. 412). An empirical analysis of randomly curated Tweets found that approximately a third were positive, a fifth were negative, and a half were neutral in terms of sentiment (Han & Kavuluru, 2015). The authors explain:

Even in their effort, Agarwal et al. assume equal proportion for the three sentiment classes, which our manual analysis shows is not realistic. So in our current effort 1. We manually estimate the proportion of [positive: negative: neutral] tweets to be 29% (26–32%): 18% (16–21%): 53% (50–56%) from a sample of 1000 randomly selected tweets selected from a set of 20 million tweets collected through Twitter streaming API in 2013. We also estimate that only 10% (7–13%) of the tweets have named entities in them. (Han & Kavuluru, 2015, p. 183)

This chapter tests two hypotheses.

Hypothesis 1: There is an optimal unit of analysis for sentiment analysis (sentence, paragraph, or cell) using the NVivo 11 Plus tool based on the dataset type (and how the textual data is structured in that corpus).

Hypothesis 2: There are data analytics benefits to defining a sequence of data analytics steps post-sentiment analysis to add value to the coded data (using NVivo 11 Plus).

The chapter is set up in the following way. First, sentiment analysis is introduced broadly. Then, there is a proposed sequence for extracting sentiment analysis using NVivo 11 Plus followed by a range of other data analytics approaches to enhance the information value of the data extractions. A generalized method for characterizing the nature of text sets is introduced. Several datasets of texts are acquired using "healthcare" as a seeding phenomenon to extract real-world text sets of multiple types (from research databases, from the Web, and from Twitter). Then, the autocoded sentiment analysis and additional follow-on analytical approaches are applied.

STARTING WITH SENTIMENT ANALYSIS TO AUTOCODE DATA

The way sentiment analysis (opinion mining) is often conceptualized in the research literature is as a positive-negative polarity. In other words, sentiment may be conceptualized as a binary or either positive or negative (and the other uncoded text is "neutral" or neither "positive" nor "negative"). Another approach involves conceptualizing positivity and negativity on a "polarization strength" continuum and then separating out the continuum into respective categories. NVivo 11 Plus enables both approaches to the coding of sentiment data (see Figure 2).

In terms of the extracted texts, they are not mutually exclusive. In other words, the placement of a text into one sentiment category does not mean it is reserved and can only be used in that category and no other. Rather, a term may have various instantiations that are positive and others that are negative. There are some terms that may be very positive, moderately positive, moderately negative, and (not necessarily "or") very negative. A fairly common processing method involves using a pre-sentiment-labeled text set (dictionary) against which a collection of words is compared and the application of tags to the respective target terms. While certain semantic terms and certain parts-of-speech terms (nouns,

Figure 2. Sentiment analysis defined as a positive-negative polarity (and binaries or continuums)

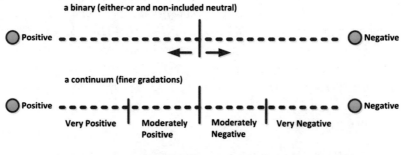

Sentiment Analysis Defined as a Positive-Negative Polarity
(and Binaries or Continuums)

verbs, adjectives, and adverbs) may be considered inherently loaded with particular pre-loaded meanings and sentiment, their computational extraction is not usually done by single words but by words in their close-in contexts (such as their respective positions in phrases and sentences). For example, certain negative words may reverse directionality of the sentiment; irony, humor, and other ways that people use language may change sentiment meaning.

The sentiment analysis tool in NVivo 11 Plus enables users to uncode text that has been autocoded to the respective sentiment categories. Or, users may recode text coded to certain categories. Also, users may manually review the raw source information and choose to code segments to particular sentiment categories, while attentively controlling for double-coding or multiple-coding (as it would not be good to echo machine coding that has already occurred). There is currently no direct way for users to customize how NVivo 11 Plus codes by changing the underlying sentiment dictionary. Also, the sentiment is based on the base language or "Text Content Language" selected by the user [Chinese, English (US), English (UK), French, German, Japanese, Portuguese, or Spanish]. In the future, customization of the sentiment dictionary may be a tool feature (Flett, Nov. 12, 2015). (Current options include ways to pre- and post-process the data in different ways outside of NVivo 11 Plus—to take into account various features of interest and to classify various parts of the texts in different ways.)

Semantic terms are often polysemic by nature, and they may mean different things in different contexts, and they may also have differing directionality, as well as shifting intensification or diminishment. This is not to say that a term is coded multiply but that a term in its various respective forms may be coded differently. (Also an individual may re-code text that has been miscoded to the wrong sentiment category. Human oversight is a critical element in virtually all sentiment analysis tools because errors may be quite easily introduced in the automated analysis.) If a word appears a fair amount in a text document or text corpus, it can easily appear across all four categories of sentiment based on the NVivo 11 Plus sentiment analysis functionality.

The basic premise of this work is that there is a way to sequence analytics using various tools in NVivo 11 Plus that may enable deeper insights from a sentiment analysis (which involves filtering data by machine-identified sentiment). The essential sequence begins with the capture of the textual information, preparation for its analysis, and running the sentiment analysis. The sentiment analysis provides a broad sense of positivity or negativity related to the target text set and the possible representation of an issue from that text set. At that point, in a very valid way, researchers may ask the two classic questions: "And?" and "So what?"

To push beyond sentiment (without losing the insights from the sentiment labeling), it is possible to analyze the extracted sentiment-categorized texts using a range of tools: automated and unsupervised theme and subtheme extraction, word frequency counts, text searches, sociogram mapping, and geolocational mapping—with all the attendant data visualizations and follow-on analyses. Throughout the process and at the end, the researcher is engaging the text for various types of analytics and the capture of "deep meaning" or gist. One author describes "deep structure":

Linguists recognize two types of language structure: surface structure and deep structure. Surface structure refers to the specific way an idea is expressed, such as the words used and their order. Deep structure refers to the gist of the idea. Most of us avoid the problems of clutter by retaining the gist but freely discarding details. As a result, although we can retain deep structure—the meaning of what was said—for long periods of time, we can accurately remember surface structure—the words in which it was said—for just eight to ten seconds. (Mlodinow, 2012, pp. 64 - 65)

In Figure 3, the sequence which is the core of this chapter is visualized. Even at this high level, there is sensitivity to sequencing because what is processed first affects the data that is processed in ensuing steps. If data is cleaned at a certain change, the dataset itself is different, and outcomes may vary. Those who would use this process should likely closely document the work at every step and include that documentation when sharing the research through publication or presentations.

Figure 3. A sentiment analysis and post-sentiment analysis "sequence" in Nvivo 11 plus

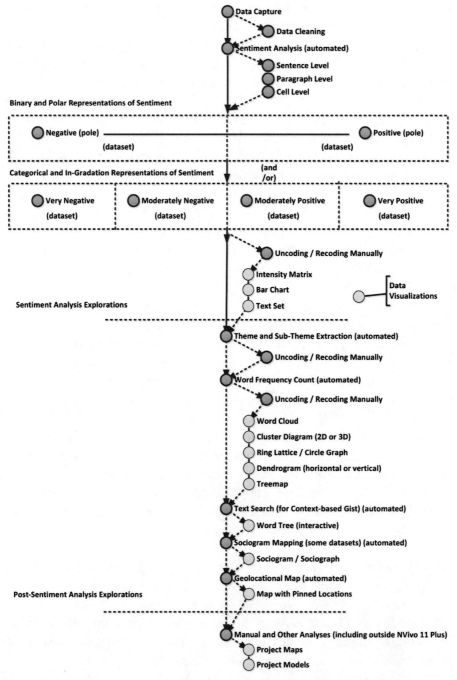

A Sentiment Analysis and Post-Sentiment Analysis "Sequence" in NVivo 11 Plus

Applied Sentiment Analysis

To clarify, sentiment alone has informational and applied value. For example, extracting sentiment from online conversations about a particular issue may shed light on public moods and public understandings on particular issues. Sentiment may inform researchers about whether an online crowd is in a "hot state" or a "cold state" and making decisions from that mental and emotional state, and these insights may provide crowd reactivity to information and some predictivity for the momentum of large-scale movements or events. It would be possible to have a sense of the relative size of subgroups with particular points-of-views on an issue by applying some additional network analysis. Having a layer of awareness will enable an entity to enter conversations and strive to clarify misunderstandings. If fluid situations that may turn violent, for example, law enforcement may track shared social media messages to see if an issue is trending negative and likely to spark and turn "ugly"; this enables the reading of the mood of crowds actively sharing on social media. Another angle is to use sentiment in messaging between public entities to understand interrelationships for understanding sentiment polarity of relations in "signed social networks" (those social networks in which relationships are revealed based on the messaging from each side to the other). The sentiment polarity of a network may be inferred through sentiment analysis to understand the latent sentiment in messaging among a particular social cluster or larger group. Awareness of sentiment may enhance decision-making and guide strategic actions in engaging a broader public.

Another example of applied sentiment analysis may be to less dynamic information streams than near-real-time social media in the prior example. For example, sentiment analysis may be applied to article text sets based on particular topics—from journalism publications, from academic publications, from databases, and from the Web. There may be particular questions posed such as the following:

- How has sentiment changed in terms of elite / researcher / public (and other) groups about a particular topic over time? Why?
- Are there differences in sentiment on particular issues between authors of particular time periods? Demographic characteristics (like gender, class, nationality, or other feature)?
  - What are potential causal factors that affect expressed sentiments in particular text sets? How may these causal factors be identified, and how may the respective effects of each be measured?
- If messaging (like ad campaigns, movie releases, public statements, and informational releases) and other interventions have been applied, what were the effects (pre- and post- event sentiment)?

In Figure 3, an early step in this process involves acquiring text sets. This is an important step in the process. Text sets may be broadly summarized based on various types of information: where the data is from, who created it, how it was vetted (if at all), how much text there is, the languages used in the text set, the various conventional applications of that data, how the data is structured, what percentage of a full set the selected text or dataset represents, the time span represented in the text, and so on. A subset of these descriptors may be helpful to identify, so as to broadly summarize features of the text set.

Some Conventions of Text Types and Text Sets

Texts may be understood as falling on particular axes as follows: informal to formal, non-structured to structured, objective to subjective, low voice to high voice, non-purposive to purposive, unoriginal data to original data, no informational value to having high informational value, and characterized by short texts to long texts. Informal texts are casual, unofficial, relaxed in terms of rules and conventions, and even off-the-cuff; formal texts, on the other hand, are pre-determined and official, often defined by set rules. Non-structured texts do not have a set structure while structured ones do (with required textual elements in certain orders and in certain formats). Objective texts show little of the individual author hand and are focused on facts and straight reportage; subjective texts show more of the individual author's personality, point-of-view, ego, style, and history. A low-voice piece (or set) has little sense of an author hand; in contrast, a high-voice text or text corpora has a sense of an authentic individual behind the work. Texts and text corpora may be understood to have texts that tend to be non-purposive (without a clearly defined purpose) as compared to those that are more clearly purposive and role-driven. There are text sets with unoriginal data, which means that the contents are widely available and common, as compared to those with highly original data, which means contents unavailable elsewhere and informative (in a particular domain or multiple domains). Low informational value texts are those which contain little applied or practical value while high informational value texts have application to knowledge and decision-making. By convention, "short texts" are microblogging messages, social networking site posts, brief product or movie reviews, instant messages, email messages, and the like. There are the lengths of texts, from "short" to "long." Finally, there is the speed-of-change of the language used in those types of texts.

While some of these variables may seem like they overlap, it is helpful to consider that texts may be original but of little value broadly speaking (such as Tweets of a unique person's lived day). Or a text may be generic but of high value (such as a bulk retweet of a trending issue which shows broad consensus and emotion on an issue). A work may be informal but highly structured, such as a casual letter which follows letter-writing conventions. Clearly, these textual variables will be context-sensitive to the cultures and audiences and practices in which the texts are used. For example, when texts are labeled as "non-purposive" or "purposive," that assumes an audience and a context (in which texts might have purpose). Table 2 captures these concepts as common variables, and these are later expressed as axes on a spider chart in Figure 4. One intuition here is that textual data (in documents and in sets) may have

Table 2. Selected common variables of text types in common text sets

0 (The Center of the Spider Chart)	1	2	3	4	5	6 (The Far Edge of the Spider Chart)
Informality						I - Formality
Unstructured						II - Structure
Objectivity (high)						III - Subjectivity
Voice (low)						IV - Voice (high)
Purpose (low)						V - Purpose
Data originality (low)						VI – Data originality (high)
Informational value (none to low)						VII -Informational value (high)
Text length (low)						VIII – Text length (high)
Speed of language change (low)						IX – Speed of language change (high)

Figure 4. Nine selected generalized features of various types of text sets (a spider chart)

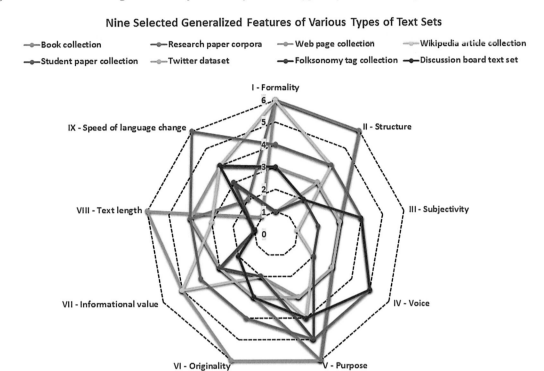

general over-arching characteristics. Another intuition is that these variables may vary in levels of presence / non-presence, and intensity. Other variables may certainly be selected to describe a work, but these were identified as some of the most common by the author.

To illustrate this point, eight types of fairly common corpora used in academia were identified, and some of their main features were extracted. The eight types are as follows: book collection, research paper corpora, web page collection, Wikipedia article collection, student paper collection, Twitter dataset, folksonomy tag collection, and discussion board text collection. The nine general features are used to broadly describe these text sets.

- **Book Collection:** Formal, structured, medium subjective, medium voice, semi-purposive, original data, semi-high data value, long, and slow speed of language change.
- **Research Paper Corpora**: Formal, structured, objective/ semi-objective, semi-voice, purposive, semi-original, semi-data value, medium length text, and slow speed of language change.
- **Web Page Collection:** Semi-formal, semi-structured, semi-subjective, medium voice, medium purposive, semi-original data, medium data value, medium length, and medium speed of language change.
- **Wikipedia Article Collection:** Formal, semi-structured, objective, low voice, purposive, unoriginal data, medium data value, medium length text, and medium speed of language change.
- **Student Paper Collection:** Semi-formal, semi-structured, semi-objective, high voice, semi-purposive, semi-original, mid informational value, mid-length, and medium speed of language change.

- **Twitter Dataset:** Informal, semi-structured, semi-subjective, semi-voice, semi-purposive, semi-original, some data value, short text length, and high speed of language change.
- **Folksonomy Tag Collection:** Informal, semi-structured, semi-objective, semi-voice, purposive, semi-original, semi-data value, short length text, and medium speed of language change.
- **Discussion Board Text Set:** Semi-formal, minimally structured, semi-subjective, high voice, semi-purposive, partially original, some informational value, short text length, and medium speed of language change.

In a spider chart (or "radar" or "star" chart), the respective axes are understood to begin at 0 in the center and rise in intensity as one moves farther to the periphery or outer ring. Figure 4 shows the representation of the prior eight types of text sets and their defining features.

The idea here is that if sentiment analysis is applied to a previously unlabeled textual dataset that has certain features, the extracted sentiment may be understood differently based on the characteristics of the underlying text set. Sentiment likely manifests differently in different types of textual data corpora (but exploring how those differ is beyond the purview of this current work).

An Applied Case with Various "Healthcare" Text Sets

To see how this process might work, a topic ("healthcare") was selected that would be a topic with some aspects of public interest, and it would not obviously trend necessarily positively or negatively only but would offer dispersed or various mixes sentiment. "Healthcare" was used as a seed or source term for data extractions. In all the social media-based text set extractions, the "http" and "https" were removed from the word frequency counts. What follows are analyses of a healthcare text collection from ProQuest, a healthcare academic article collection from multiple online sources, a small collection of healthcare articles from Wikipedia, a @HealthCareGov Tweetstream dataset, a @RedCross Tweetstream dataset, a #healthcare hashtag search on Twitter / basic network dataset, and a "healthcare" keyword search on Twitter / basic network dataset.

Combined "Healthcare" Text Collection from ProQuest

Some 280 articles related to healthcare were extracted from the ProQuest Research Library database. The articles were melded into one Word file for sentiment extraction. This combined file contained 387,696 words in 1,395 pages (see Figures 5 and 6).

The same information may be seen in an intensity matrix in Figure 6.

The initial version of the ProQuest articles were also run as separate files in one NVivo project. A bar chart of a sentiment analysis shows that most of the ideas expressed that contained sentiment were "moderately positive." This issue of running items individually shows that there may be specific insights extracted based on how the data is represented in the .nvp project.

Following the initial sentiment analysis, a general theme extraction was run over the research contents. Intriguingly, how the text was ingested affected the extracted themes, even though the underlying data was the same content-wise.

Figure 8 shows some differences between extracted themes from the same ProQuest dataset but the only difference being whether the information was in multiple PDF documents or one Word file.

Figure 5. Fused "healthcare" proquest article set sentiment analysis as a bar chart

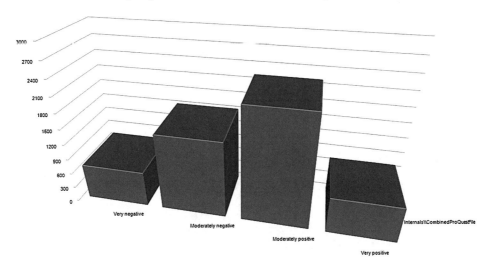

Figure 6. Fused "healthcare" proquest article set sentiment analysis as an intensity matrix

The top-level themes (see Figure 9) may be viewed as an intensity matrix (Figure 10) or a bar chart (Figure 11). The intensity matrix is from the data as multiple files, and the bar chart is from the data as a single Word file.

In Figure 12, there is a screenshot of the coded nodes at the level of subthemes under the top-level System coded theme.

Figure 7. A bar chart of extracted sentiments from the "healthcare" dataset from proquest

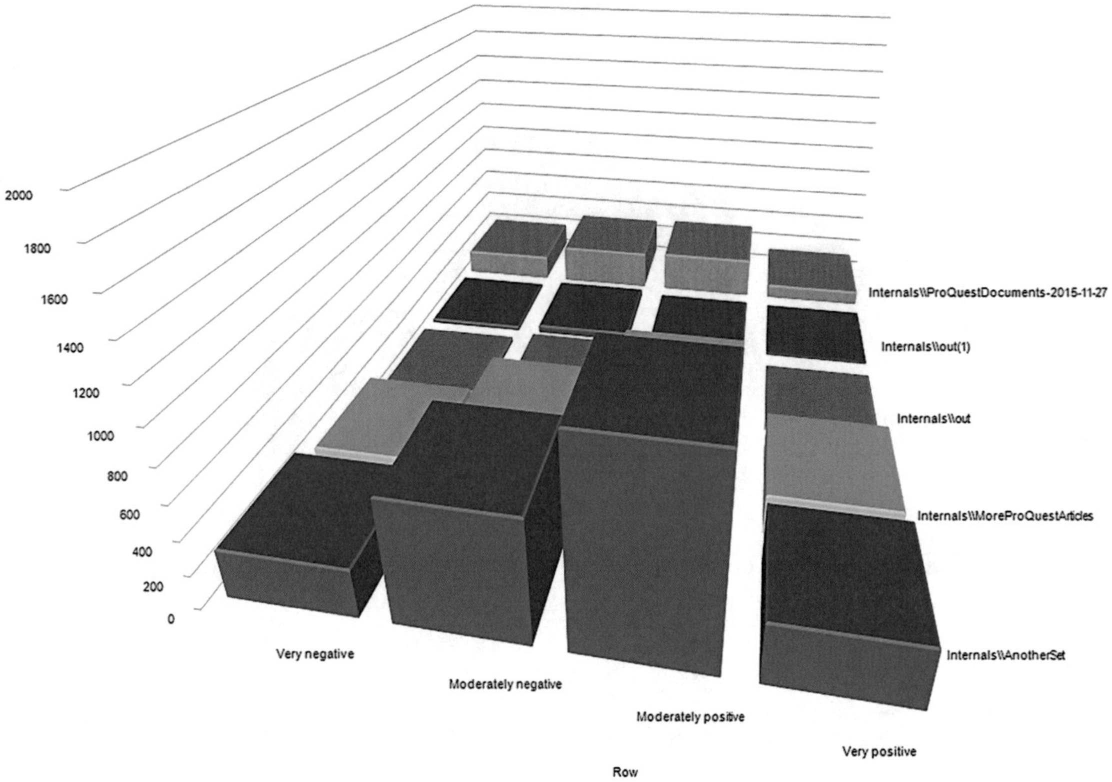

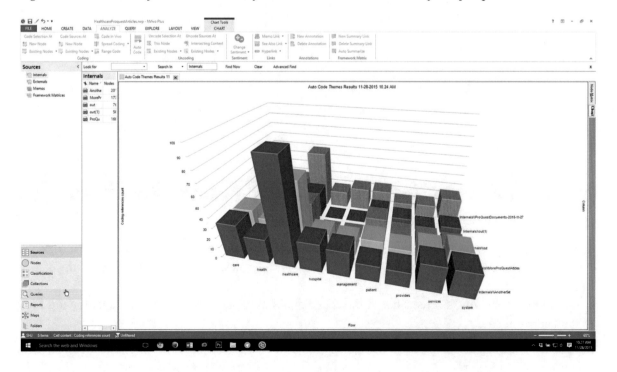

Figure 8. A bar chart of extracted themes from the "healthcare" dataset from proquest

Figure 9. Top-Level themes extracted from a "healthcare" dataset from proquest as separated files or as one integrated file

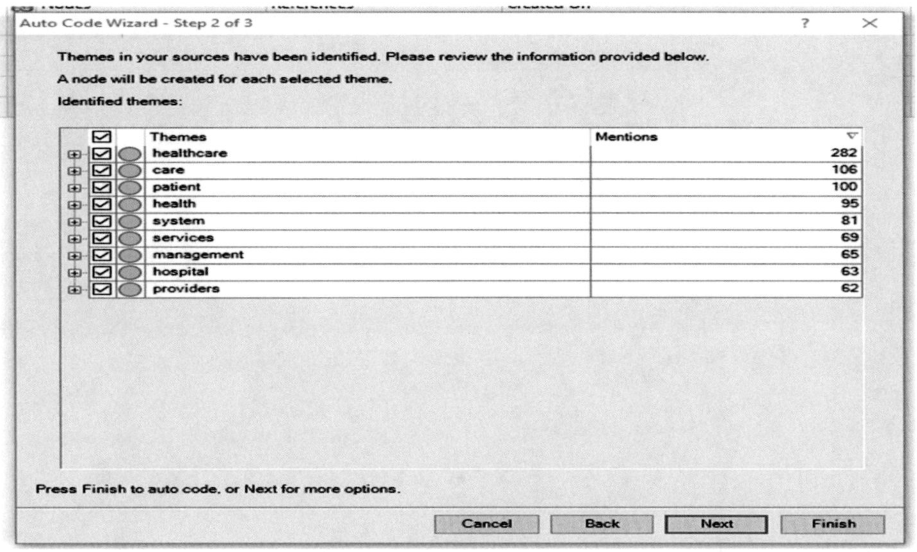

**Top-Level Themes from a
"Healthcare" Dataset from ProQuest in Several Individual Files**

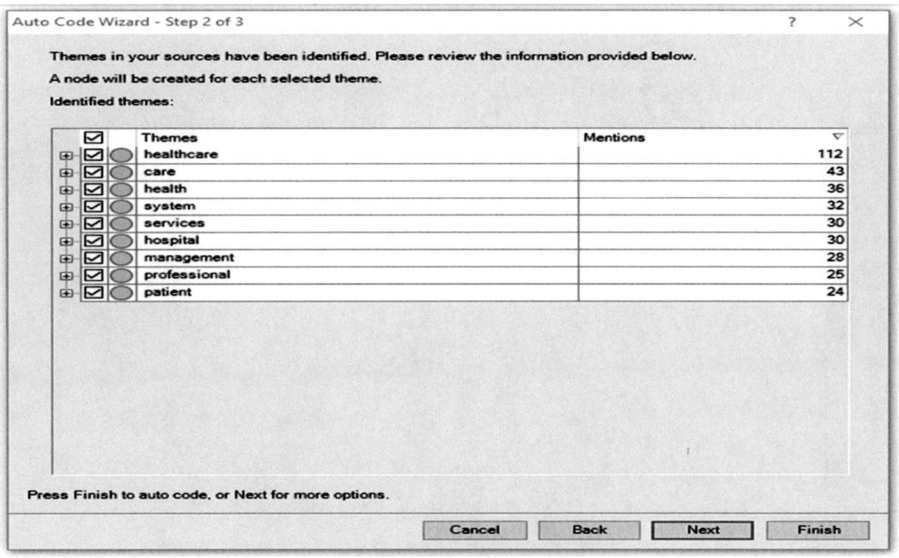

**Top-Level Themes from a
"Healthcare" Dataset from ProQuest in One Integrated File**

Figure 10. An intensity matrix of extracted themes from the combined "healthcare" dataset from ProQuest

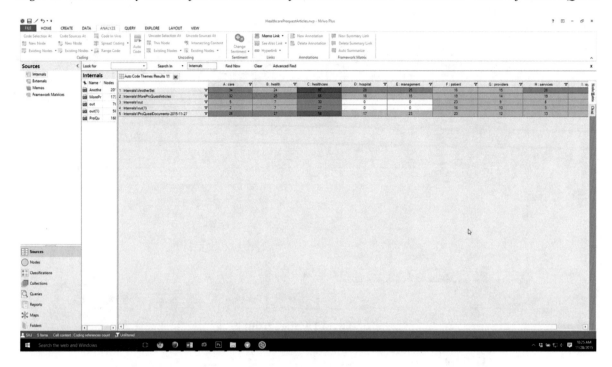

Figure 11. Fused "healthcare" ProQuest article set top-level theme extraction as a bar chart

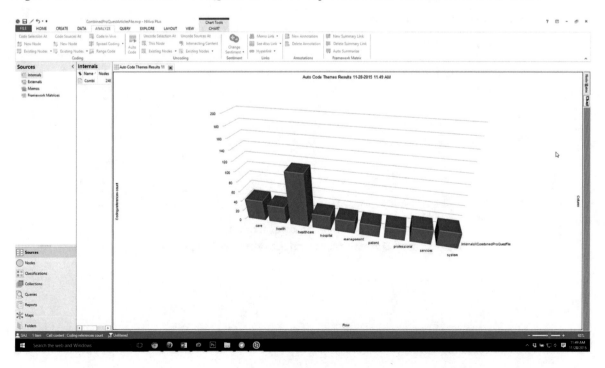

Figure 12. Autocoded themes and subthemes from the combined "healthcare" text collection from ProQuest

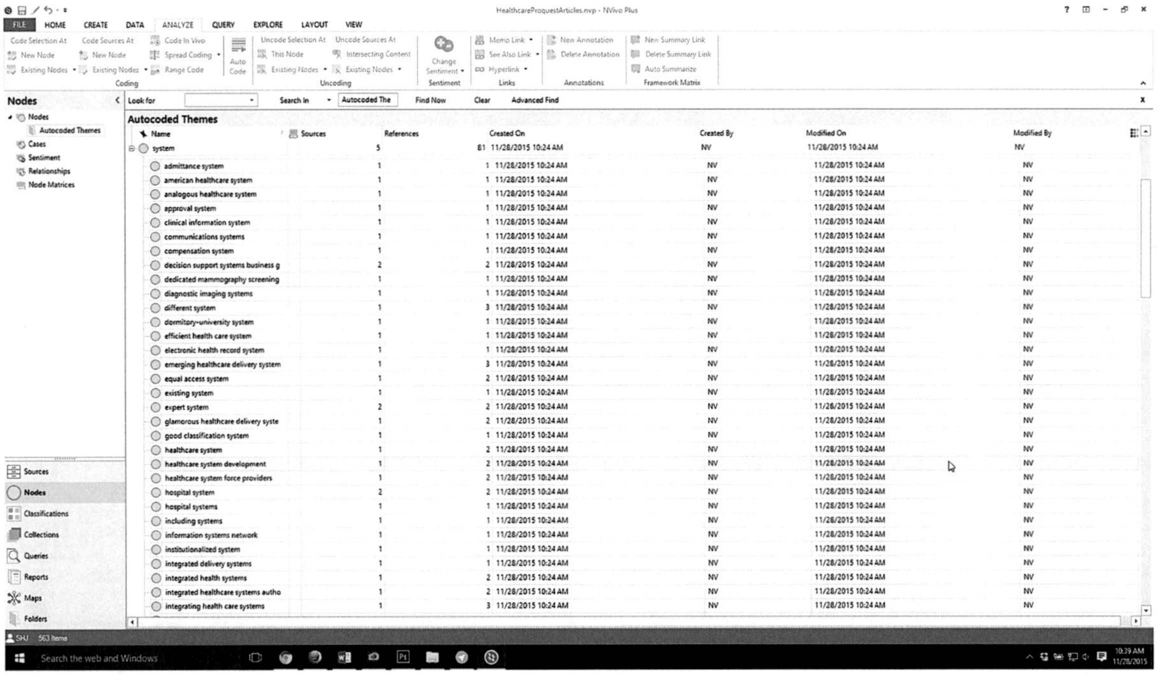

In Figure 13, the themes extraction was also run on a ProQuest dataset of individual articles, and this larger broadscale intensity matrix is possible to not only represent the themes…but to provide a map for which articles should be human-read through "close reading." In NVivo, there is a chartable maximum of 50 themes while maintaining visual coherence, and a bar chart was not able to be created for this. There were 563 items in the autocoded themes (as indicated at the bottom left of the NVivo workspace) in Figure 13.

Combined "Healthcare" Academic Article Set from Multiple Online Sources

A general "healthcare" academic article set was collected using Google Scholar and some subscription-only databases. This set is comprised of articles numbering 286,958 words and translated to 262 pp. single-spaced. In terms of sentiment analysis, this may be run across a set of texts with article-to-article comparisons possible across the four sentiment categories: very negative, moderately negative, moderately positive, and very positive. In Figure 14, the sentiment analysis was run on sentence level; in Figure 15, the sentiment analysis was run on paragraph level. The overall positivity and negativity patterns may be seen in both data runs, but there are some numerical differences. The more granular sentence level of coding meant there were more examples in the cells as compared to the paragraph level of sentiment coding.

In Figure 16, there are theme and subtheme extractions into respective nodes from the healthcare academic article set from mixed online sources.

Figure 13. An intensity matrix of extracted themes within items from the "healthcare" ProQuest dataset

Figure 14. "Healthcare" academic article set (from mixed online sources) with sentence-level coding for sentiment

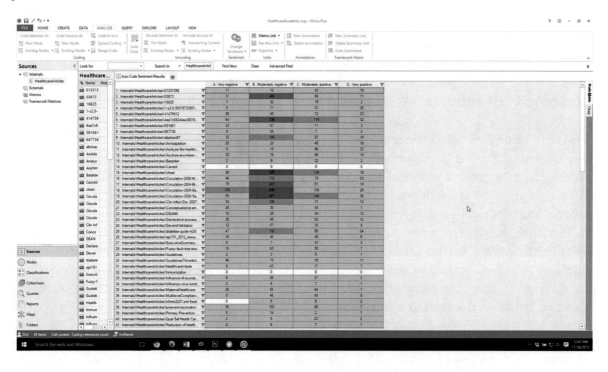

Figure 15. "Healthcare" academic article set (from mixed online sources) with paragraph-level coding for sentiment

Figure 16. Theme and subtheme extraction from the "healthcare" academic article set (from mixed online sources)

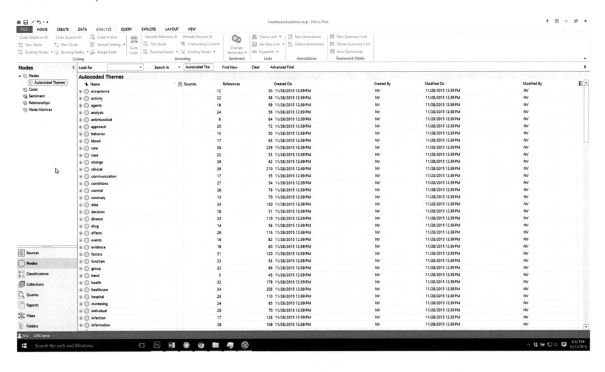

Figure 17. An Intensity matrix of the extracted sentiments from the small textset of "healthcare" articles from Wikipedia

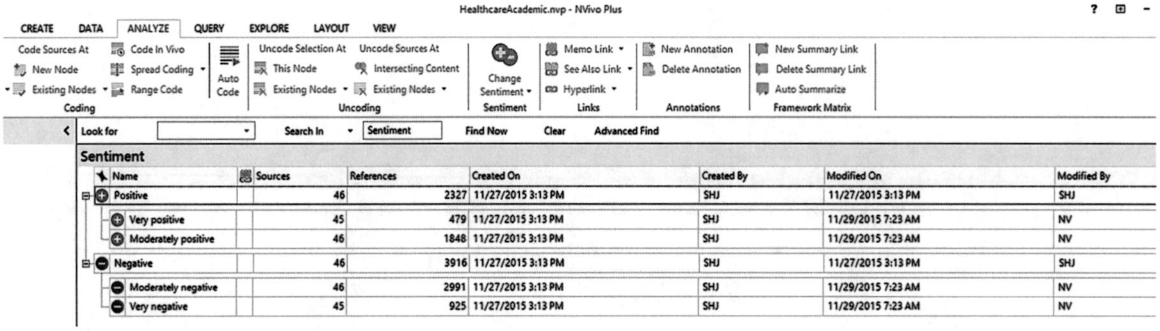

Wikipedia Article Collection

By definition, Wikipedia articles are supposed to be written in a neutral point-of-view and written objectively, with research sources actually cited ("Editing Wikipedia," 2015, p. 8). While many of the articles had few sentiment references, there was one article that stood out from the six articles: The "Public health" article (located at https://en.wikipedia.org/wiki/Public_health) had quite a few more references in the "very negative," "moderately negative," and "moderately positive" categories. This may be seen in the intensity matrix in Figure 17.

The "healthcare" related article collection from Wikipedia contained only four top-level themes: care, health, policy, and public health. Underlying those four were major subthemes—some 418 items.

Figure 18. Subthemes linked to "health" theme from the "healthcare" article set from Wikipedia

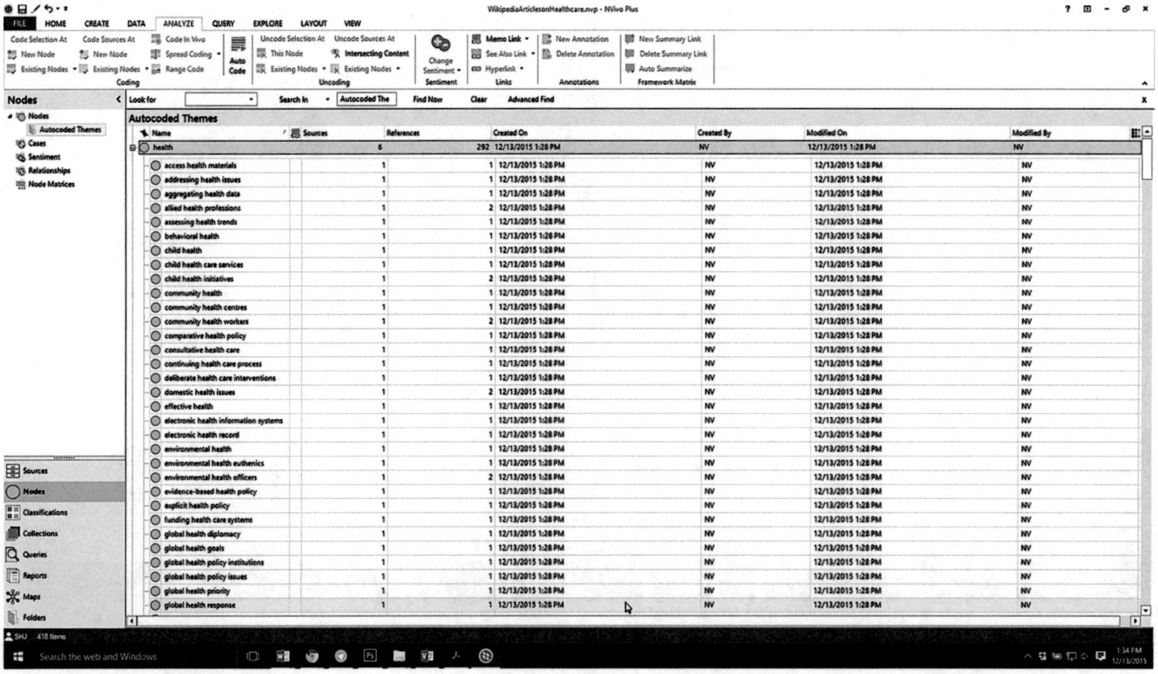

Figure 19. A bar chart of the sentiment analysis of the @HealthCareGov Tweetstream

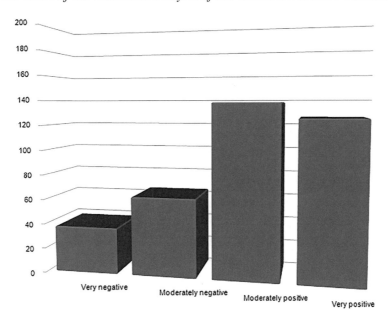

@HealthCareGov Tweetstream Dataset

In that spirit, the @HealthCareGov user account's Tweetstream (at https://twitter.com/HealthCareGov) was captured. The account was activated in November 2009; at the time of the extraction, the account had 2,702 Tweets, 125 following, 237,000 followers, and 629 likes. The extraction using NCapture of NVivo enabled the capturing of 2,033 messages including retweets. A sentence-level sentiment analysis on the dataset resulted in the following: Very Negative (37), Moderately Negative (63), Moderately Positive (138), and Very Positive (126). In other words, the Tweetstream generally trends positive versus negative. The resulting bar chart may be viewed in Figure 19.

When a word frequency count was run on each of the text sets labeled by sentiment, the top ten word counts were as follows for the three levels of analysis: sentence level, paragraph level, and cell level. Interestingly, the top-ten word lists were very similar across the data sets, probably because microblogging Tweetstreams are downloaded as datasets, and the data does not contain sentences nor paragraphs in the traditional senses. The results may be seen in Table 3.

In each of the four sentiment categories—very negative, moderately negative, moderately positive, and very positive—the text sets were visualized as word clouds, in Figures 20 to 23. There are some repeated words. Some #hashtag campaigns and events are identifiable. A perusal of the underlying text sets will readily show some weaknesses in this approach. For example, because the term "cancer" is seen as a net negative, it is often listed in the "very negative" category even if it refers to #worldcancerday and practical efforts to raise awareness, improve human health, raise resources, and ultimately treat and eradicate it in its many forms.

What may be less clear is why a certain word cloud has certain terms and the context of the reference. To better understand granular (fine-grained) context, it helps to run text searches in NVivo 11 Plus. A text search results in every found instance of the target term or phrase and enables the visualization

Table 3. Extracted sentiment categories from the @HealthCareGov account Twitter Tweetstream

	Very Negative	Moderately Negative	Moderately Positive	Very Positive
Sentence Level	Counts: 37 Top 10 Words in Category: cancer (11), health (10), @hhsgov(5), #aca (4), coverage (4), insurance (4), without (4), women (4), #breastcancer (3), #getcovered (3)	Counts: 63 Top 10 Words in Category: health (22), insurance (15), care (12), coverage (10), bit (9), #mycare (6), @hhsgov (6), breaking (6), law (6), new (6)	Counts: 138 Top 10 Words in Category: health (42), new (22), coverage (19), insurance (16), keep (13), #aca (11), excited (10), plans (10), @hhsgov (9), healthy (9)	Counts: 127 Top 10 Words in Category: health (36), happy (20), #getcovered (14), day (14), today (14), coverage (12), care (11), @hhsgov (9), plan (9), affordable (8)
Paragraph Level	Counts: 37 Top 10 Words in Category: (same as above)	Counts: 63 Top 10 Words in Category: (same as above)	Counts: 135 Top 10 Words in Category: (same as above)	Counts: 126 Top 10 Words in Category: (same as above)
Cell Level	Counts: 37 Top 10 Words in Category: (same as above)	Counts: 63 Top 10 Words in Category: (same as above)	Counts: 135 Top 10 Words in Category: (same as above)	Counts: 126 Top 10 Words in Category: (same as above)

Figure 20. Category 1: an extracted word cloud from the "very negative" text set from the @Health-CareGov Tweetstram

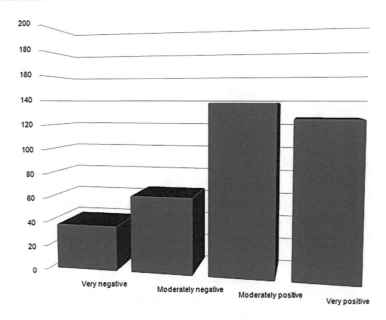

of that term with prior lead-up terms and lead-away terms. When a particular part of the data tree is highlighted, its correlating lead-up or lead-away sections are also highlighted, so readers may acquire a sense of how the target term is used. To demonstrate this, the @hhsgov account was selected as a target term. This word tree may be seen in Figure 24.

It is also possible to see extracted terms from the @HealthCareGov extracted Tweetstream in Figure 25. At the top level, the auto-extracted themes are the following (in alphabetical order): care, coverage, health, health coverage, insurance, and plan. In descending order, "health" was the most dominant theme, followed by "coverage" and "plan."

Figure 21. Category 2: An extracted word cloud from the "moderately negative" text set from the @ HealthCareGov Tweetstram

Figure 22. Category 3: An extracted word cloud from the "moderately positive" text set from the @ HealthCareGov Tweetstrea

Figure 23. Category 4: An extracted word cloud from the "very positive" text set from the @Health-CareGov Tweetstream.

Figure 24. @hhsgov word tree from the @HealthCareGov Tweetstream dataset

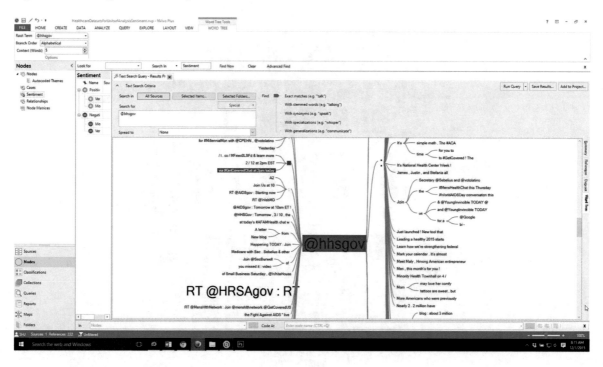

Figure 25. Extracted top-level topics in the @HealthCareGov Tweetstream

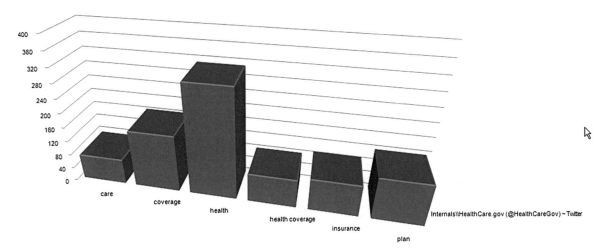

In Figure 26, a ring lattice graph (circle graph) may be seen of the respective user names from the @HealthCareGov Tweetstream clustered by word similarity. The clustering is indicated in part by proximity and by color (which is hard to see in b/w image renderings in the text version of the book). The edges or links show the fact of intercommunications between those user accounts in this particular extracted Tweetstream.

Another social-based type of data involves a Twitter sociogram of the @HealthCareGov ego neighborhood (a group of nodes with direct links to @HealthCareGov). This may be viewed in Figure 27.

Another type of data extraction involves the usage of geolocational information from the Tweetstream and the mapping of those points on a MapQuest map (integrated in NVivo 11 Plus). This map may be seen in Figure 28.

@RedCross Tweetstream Network and Dataset

The @RedCross user account on Twitter was created in June 2007 (shortly after Twitter started). The organization is based out of Washington, D.C. At the time of the data extraction, the account had 40,318 following, 2,582,877 followers, 4,347 Tweets, 2,812 likes, and 9 lists. The data extraction was conducted using NCapture and resulted in the recording of 2,646 messages.

A sentiment analysis of the @RedCross Tweetstream at the cell level resulted in the following: very negative (262), moderately negative (324), moderately positive (274), and very positive (207). The message in NVivo for the cell-level analysis reads: "Code entire cell for datasets, transcripts and logs. (Code paragraphs for other source types.)"

The same dataset was also run by sentence and paragraph levels. The results of this may be seen in Table 4.

In this case, sentiment coding by paragraph and cell levels were the same in terms of the numbers in each category (Table 5). However, the top-10 word counts were similar between the sentence and paragraph level coding but not for cell level. It is unclear to this author at this time why these results occurred, but she did run these processes multiple times to verify.

Figure 26. Users in the ego neighborhood/social network of @HealthCareGov on Twitter (in a ring lattice)

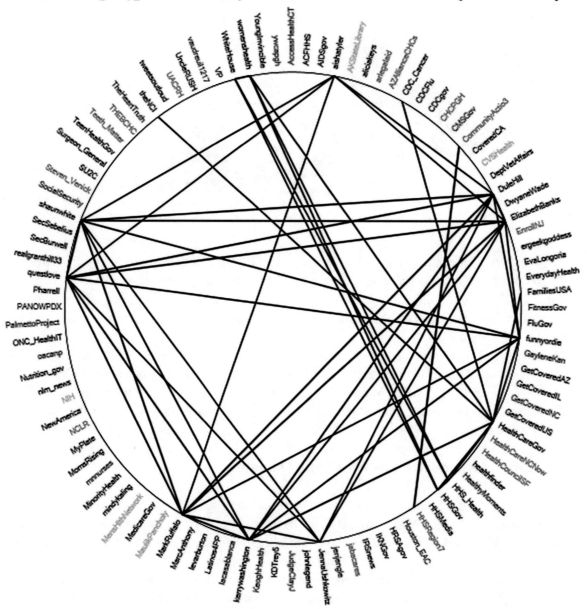

HealthCare.gov (@HealthCareGov) ~ Twitter - Usernames Clustered by Word similarity

It is also possible to run a word frequency count on a sentiment analysis construed as only a binary (comprised of two things only) polarity—either positive or negative. Here, the "Positive" category contains both the "Very Positive" and "Moderately Positive" sub-categories, and the "Negative" category contains both the "Very Negative" and "Moderately Negative" sub-categories. This may be seen in Figure 30, and Table 6 shows the actual top-10 most frequent words in each category.

Figure 27. The mapped sociogram of the @HealthCareGov ego neighborhood (direct social network)

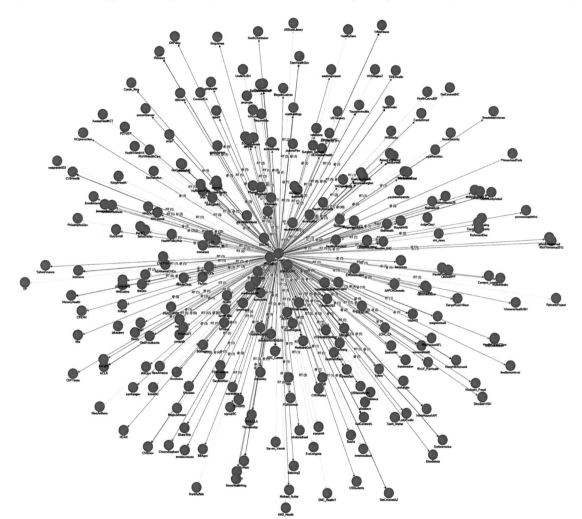

Figure 28. Geographical features of the user accounts of the @HealthCareGov Tweetstream

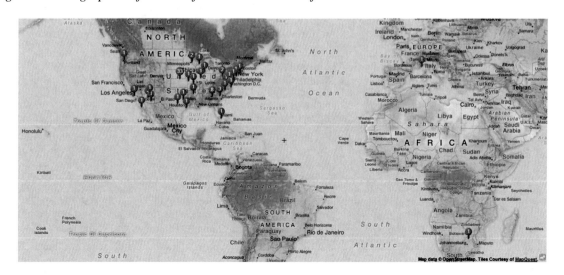

Figure 29. Bar chart of extracted sentiment from the @RedCross Tweetstream

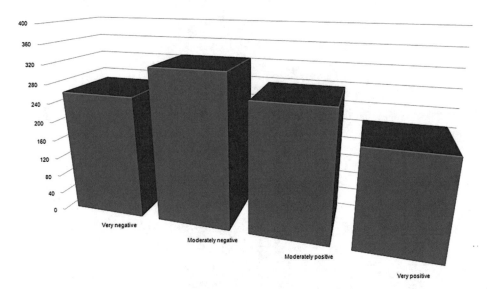

Table 4. Straight counts of sentiment categories of the same dataset with differing levels of granularity

	Very Negative	**Moderately Negative**	**Moderately Positive**	**Very Positive**
By Sentence Level	269	345	289	217
By Paragraph Level	262	324	274	207
By Cell Level	262	324	274	207

Table 5. Extracted sentiment categories from the @RedCross Tweetstream on Twitter

	Very Negative	**Moderately Negative**	**Moderately Positive**	**Very Positive**
Sentence Level	Counts: 269 Top 10 Words in Category: disaster (90), disasters (45), help (33), #redcross (28), @redcross (26), home (25), fire (24), affected (22), response (21), relief (19)	Counts: 345 Top 10 Words in Category: emergency (61), severe (56), #redcross (45), weather (42), flooding (36), @redcross (29), flood (27), damage (26), help (24), red (21)	Counts: 289 Top 10 Words in Category: safe (80), @redcross (37), stay (27), tips (27), #redcross (24), great (19), help (19), friends (15), red (13), cross (13)	Counts: 217 Top 10 Words in Category: thank (35), safe (22), happy (19), @redcross (17), today (15), #redcross (14), blood (13), stay (11), day (11), thanks (11)
Paragraph Level	Counts: 262 Top 10 Words in Category: (closely similar to the Sentence Level text set)	Counts: 324 Top 10 Words in Category: (closely similar to the Sentence Level text set)	Counts: 274 Top 10 Words in Category: (closely similar to the Sentence Level text set)	Counts: 207 Top 10 Words in Category: (closely similar to the Sentence Level text set)
Cell Level	Counts: 262 Top 10 Words in Category: disaster (99), disasters (45), help (33), #redcross (28), @redcross (26), home (25), fire (24), affected (22), response (21), relief (19)	Counts: 324 Top 10 Words in Category: emergency (56), severe (45), #redcross (45), weather (42), flooding (36), @redcross (29), flood (27), damage (26), help (24), red (21)	Counts: 274 Top 10 Words in Category: safe (80), @redcross (37), stay (27), tips (27), #redcross (24), great (19), help (19), friends (15), red (15), cross (13)	Counts: 207 Top 10 Words in Category: thank (35), safe (22), happy (19), @redcross (17), today (15), #redcross (14), blood (13), stay (12), day (11), thanks (11)

Figure 30. Using positive and negative categories by subsuming two sub-categories each

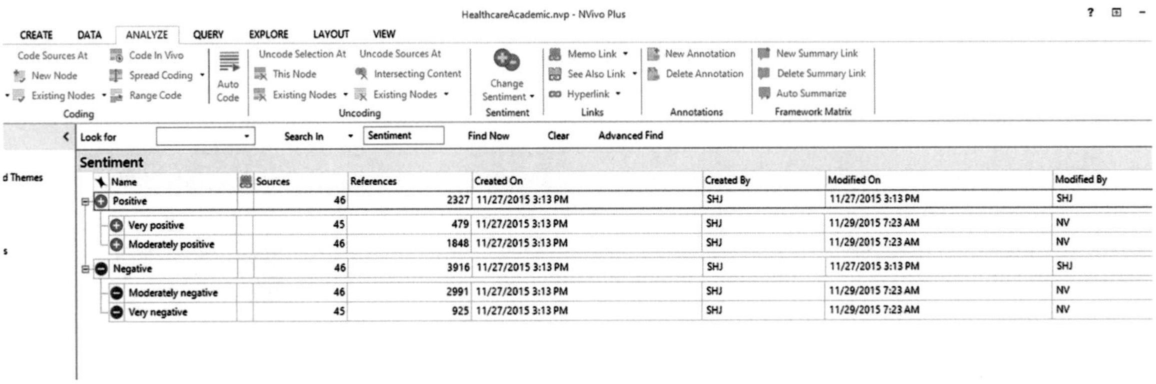

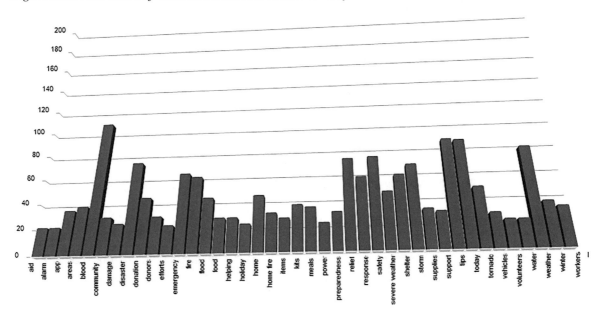

Figure 31. A bar chart of extracted themes and subthemes from the @redcross tweetstream text set

Table 6. Top word counts from the "positive" and "negative" text set extractions from the @RedCross Tweetstream

Positive	Negative
safe (102), @redcross (54), stay (39), #redcross (38), thank (38), tips (37), help (28), happy (26), blood (25), great (24), today (24), friends (21), good (21), love (21), red (21), day (18), prepared (18), cross (17), #givingtuesday (16), know (16), support (16), thanks (16)	disaster (100), emergency (74), #redcross (73), severe (69), help (57), @redcross (55), weather (55), disasters (45), flooding (41), response (41), affected (34), home (34), flood (33), red (33), fire (29), today (29), relief (28), tips (28), cross (27), damage (27), bit (25), shelters (24), prepared (23), #tornado (21)

Figure 32. #healthcare hashtag search network on Twitter (sentence level)

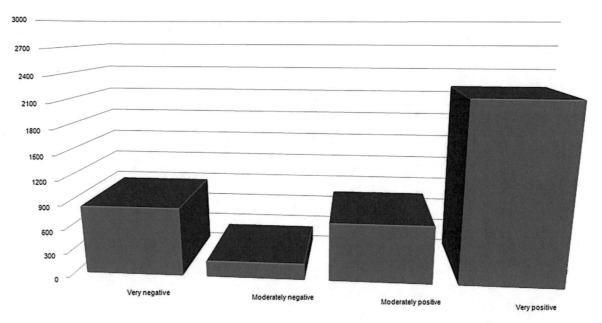

While the respective top-10 word counts are identified as single words, it is important to note that the sentiment analysis was not applied in a uni-gram or one-gram fashion. Rather, the context of the term matters, such as the "not" in front of a term changing its polarity (see Figure 31).

#Healthcare Hashtag Search on Twitter/Basic Network Dataset

A #hashtag search network captures the names of the user accounts and their exchanged microblogging messages in an online discussion of a particular #hashtagged topic. By practice, hashtags are labels applied by respective communicators. The hashtags themselves may refer to campaigns, concepts, trending issues, names, and other aspects. It is a common practice to identify the "mayors of the hashtag" or those who are high-influence communicators with high numbers of formally declared followers and also those who retweet their ideas (those who act as followers). The network graph contains 4,072 vertices (user accounts) and 3,665 unique edges (links or communications interchanges, such as replies or retweets). There were 15,618 self-loops, which suggests a fair amount of self-replies and follow-on messaging. The largest connected component in this network was comprised of 1,904 vertices, which suggests a fairly dominant cluster. The maximum geodesic distance (graph diameter) was 26, and the average geodesic distance or path between any two nodes was 8.2498. The number of clusters was 1,922 groups, which may show a fairly high number of very small groups (likely dyadic and triadic ones). The actual #healthcare tweetset was comprised of 292,058 words in 783 pp. single-spaced.

When the #healthcare hashtag search network set was analyzed for sentiment at the sentence level, the numbers came up: very negative (852), moderately negative (200), moderately positive (720), and very positive (2,187). (The sentence-level extraction may be seen in the bar chart in Figure 32). By comparison, a run of the same data at the coarser paragraph level resulted in the following numbers: very negative (705), moderately negative (204), moderately positive (834), and very positive (1506) (see

Table 7. A comparison of #healthcare hashtag search network as coded by sentence- or paragraph- level

	Very Negative	**Moderately Negative**	**Moderately Positive**	**Very Positive**
Sentence-Level Coding for Sentiment	852	200	720	2187
Paragraph-Level Coding for Sentiment	705	204	834	1506

Table 7). (The paragraph-level coding for sentiment of the #healthcare hashtag search network may be see in an intensity matrix in Figure 33 and a bar chart in Figure 34.) Intriguingly, it is not as if all the category numbers are somewhat lesson. In the "moderately positive" category, there are quite a few more examples. The way to apparently understand this side-by-side comparison is that particular elements in a sentence may be negative, but the overall paragraph may trend broadly positive.

Interestingly, a theme extraction of the #healthcare hashtag set resulted in only one top-level theme node—for "https". Some of the subthemes may be seen in Figure 35.

"Healthcare" Keyword Search on Twitter/Basic Network Dataset

"Healthcare" was used as a seeding term for a keyword search on Twitter using NodeXL Basic (Network Overview, Discovery, and Exploration for Excel). This network is comprised of 10,668 vertices and 10,504 unique edges. There were 10,565 self-loops. The largest connected component in this network

Figure 33. Intensity matrix of extracted sentiment for the #healthcare hashtag search network on twitter (paragraph level)

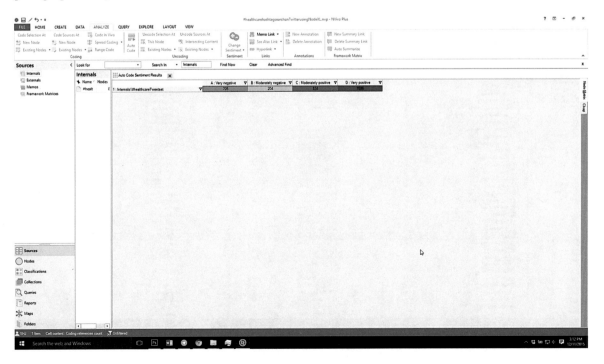

Figure 34. A bar chart of extracted sentiment for the #healthcare hashtag search network on twitter (paragraph level)

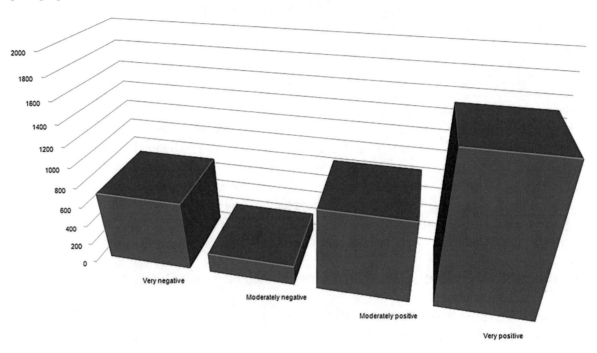

Figure 35. A node tree of extracted subthemes for the #healthcare hashtag search network on Twitter

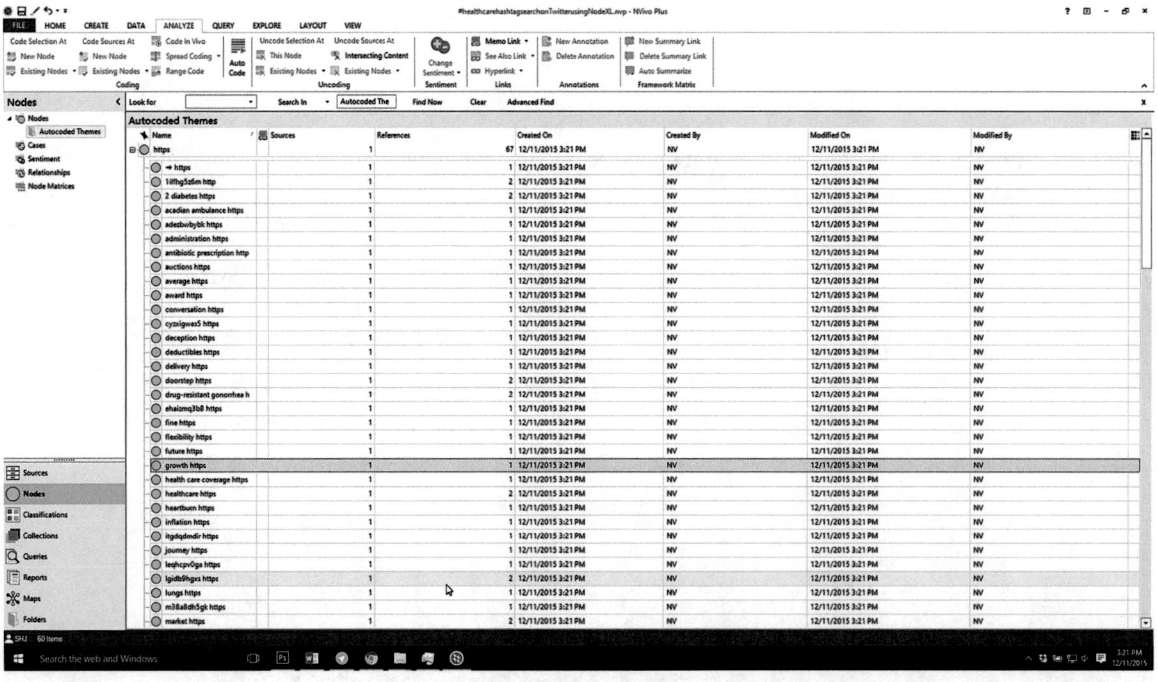

Figure 36. A bar chart of sentiment data from "healthcare" keyword search Tweetstream on Twitter

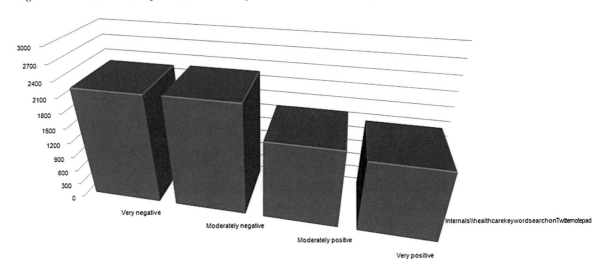

was 5,010 vertices. The maximum geodesic distance (graph diameter) of this network was 40, and the average geodesic distance was 8.1062. The network contained 3,451 clusters or groups based on the Clauset-Newman-Moore clustering algorithm. The resulting dataset of Tweets contained 326,050 words and was 421 pages single-spaced. In this context, the numbers were the same whether sentiment was coded by sentences, paragraphs, or cells. The numbers were: very negative (2238), moderately negative (2253), moderately positive (1594), and very positive (1447). In general, the dataset seems to be trending somewhat negative, as may be seen in the bar chart graph in Figure 36.

Figure 37. Theme and subtheme extraction from the "healthcare" keyword search text set from Twitter

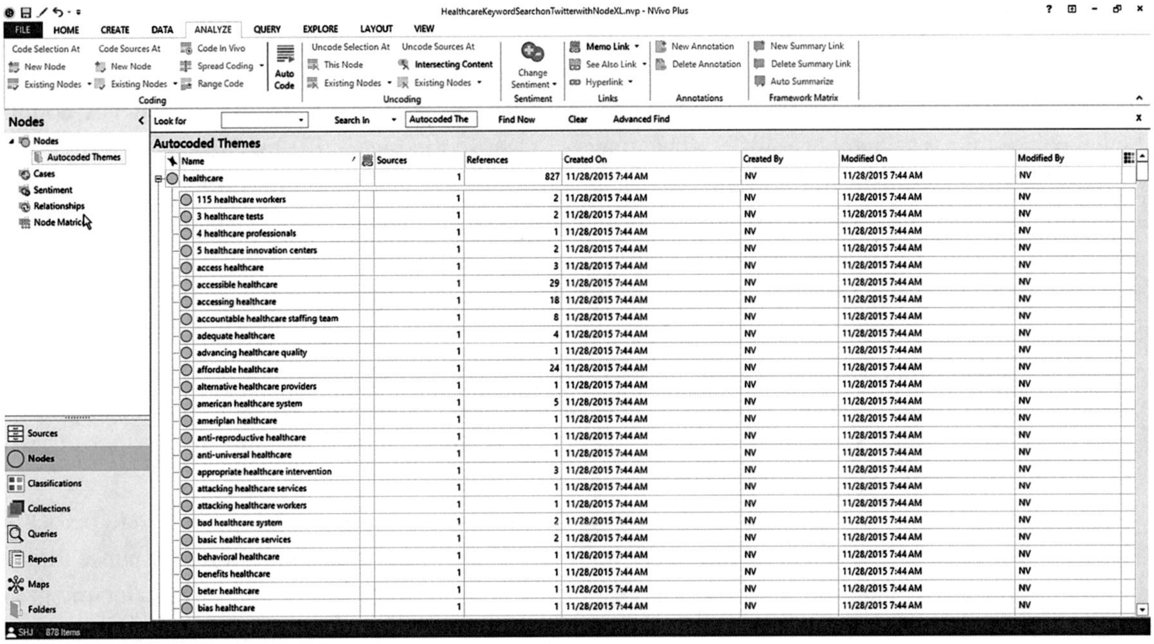

235

The node-level view of extracted themes from the "healthcare" keyword search network may be seen in Figure 37. A theme extraction of the "healthcare" keyword search Tweetstream on Twitter resulted in only two high-level themes, namely "healthcare" and "https." With the inclusion of subthemes, there were 878 themes and subthemes extracted.

DISCUSSION

While a number of data extractions, data analyses, and data visualizations were conducted for this chapter, it is important to note that various factors can affect sentiment outcomes: the size of text sets, the way text sets were acquired, the data processing, and others. The core nature of the text sets also should be taken into consideration in analyzing the extracted results, as noted in the spider diagram in Figure 4. Also, while the insights are generally broad data summarization ones, there are ways to explore outlier data (the diverse long tail extracted from the word frequency counts, for example), which may be revelatory in their own way. Also, as was noted before, many text sets contain non-lexical features, and to fully understand a text set, there will be a need for the analysis of related imagery, links, author names, and other features of texts.

There were two basic hypotheses in this work:

Hypothesis 1: There is an optimal unit of analysis for sentiment analysis (sentence, paragraph, or cell) using the NVivo 11 Plus tool based on the dataset type (and how the textual data is structured in that corpus).

Hypothesis 2: There are data analytics benefits to defining a sequence of data analytics steps post-sentiment analysis to add value to the coded data (using NVivo 11 Plus).

Findings Related to Hypothesis 1

Regarding Hypothesis 1, what was found is that the unit of analysis can have some small effects on the outcomes of the sentiment analysis—such as the counts of objects for each of the four sentiment categories, their relative size relationships to each other, and even the general top words in frequency counts of each of the four sentiment categories. This may be because the respective text sets used were all of a type, whether a Tweetstream or academic article collection. As such, by convention, the text lengths (within the datasets) and document types tend to follow certain conventions. It may help to try truly heterogeneous data sets to see what may be extracted. Also, the datasets were fairly comparable in size. Most Tweetstream extractions ranged from about 2,000 messages to about 3,200 messages (the top limit of message extractions given the Twitter API for those types of data extractions). The article collections were comprised of some 200 or so articles. It may be that there may be observable differences with datasets of differing sizes. It may be that the competitive advantage of going with a sentence-, paragraph-, or cell-level of analysis may be seen in much larger datasets (albeit within the limits of NVivo 11 Plus hosted on a commercial desktop computer or laptop).

Generally speaking, if a text set has a lot of insights at the sentence level, it would seem to be better to go with more granular analysis even though that has a slightly higher computational expense (and a more noticeable lag with larger datasets). If there are only general insights desired of a text document or corpus, and the generally unit of organization is in paragraph form, it would seem appropriate to go with paragraph-level autocoding of sentiment. In general, the relative amounts of "very negative," "moderately negative," "moderately positive," and "positive" categories seem fairly similar when running general article sets (with data in paragraph units).

Also, datasets with text in cells tend to come out with fairly similar sentiment analysis results across the units of analysis (and occasionally near-similar findings): sentence, paragraph, and cell. Such data has historically been identified as structured data (since the data are in labeled cells), even if the data may be multi-faceted such as extractions from Twitter (including scraped thumbnail imagery and URLs, for example).

One direct future research outcome of this work should be an impetus to combine mixed text datasets (in terms of types) in order to see if there are benefits to going with sentence, paragraph, or cell level analysis. At this point, the intuition is that sentence level coding would be more accurate and granular, even if computationally expensive. The cell option is available only when the data is a dataset with cellular-level information.

Findings Related to Hypothesis 2

As to the second hypothesis, that there are benefits to harnessing other aspects of this tool for further text analytics, this seems supported, too, by the initial findings. The insights here are that sentiment analyses are not the end step of an exploration sequence but one of a number of possible approaches to analyzing textual data using computational means. It is important not only to know about broad sentiments but the rationales behind those respective sentiments (as explorable through word frequency counts, text search queries, automated theme and subtheme extraction, and others). It is important to explore geospatial features of the text set because those offer another path to deeper understandings.

The proposed sequence—first extracting sentiment text sets and then applying further computationally-enabled analytics—may be transferred to other use cases and topics. However, the amount of data here is too limited to over-generalize. There are limits to using only one tool for the analytics. (More data on how the sentiment analysis tool works under the covers would need to be provided by QSR International, the makers of NVivo 11 Plus.)

The additional analytics are not without limitations. For example, the word frequency count works at the level of one-grams or unigrams. If that could be run with larger windows of consecutive text (two-grams, three-grams, and so on), then the word clouds could be more sensitive to on-ground meanings and would not treat words as individual isolates.

FUTURE RESEARCH DIRECTIONS

This work would suggest that there are a number of ways to ask other questions of text sets from a sentiment filtering point-of-view (and with NVivo 11 Plus). For example, it is conceivable to ask the following questions:

- Are there patterns to negativity or positivity based on data linked to particular locations? Is it possible to say that opinion on a certain topic is trending a particular way based on extracted social media data with geolocationally-labeled messaging and accounts?

- Based on selected social media user accounts, what sorts of personality insights may be understood based on the extraction of competing Tweetstreams?
- What are the various f-scores of the sentiment analysis tool in NVivo 11 Plus as applied to various analytical contexts and with differing text sets? And why are there differences in the performance of the tool?

In this work, eight basic types of text collections (book collection, research paper corpora, web page collection, Wikipedia article collection, student paper collection, Twitter dataset, folksonomy tag collection, and discussion board text collection) were broadly framed according to descriptive axes (formal, structured, subjective, voice, purposiveness, originality, informationally valuable, and length). Only a handful of these text types were explored in this work (several research paper corpora and several Twitter-based datasets—Tweetstreams, #hashtag networks, and keyword search networks). There may be work on the spider chart and the introduction of new axes (and proposed reductions by the removal of other axes). There are certainly other types of text collections that may be explored.

Even if none of the core elements of the text sets and text set descriptors are changed, it is possible to use other seeding concepts (beyond "healthcare") to base explorations. For that matter, "healthcare" itself could also be used to spawn other datasets for sentiment analysis and textual data exploration.

Also, in this chapter, a sequence of processes were proposed, with a basic categorization of sentiment preserved as a core part. It is wholly possible to apply the tool's functionalities in different ways for different insights. For example, it is possible to conduct a text search, which results in the capturing of other terms of proximity around the target terms, and then conduct a sentiment analysis on the results of that text extraction. Or all messages based on a particular location may be extracted and the sentiment extracted…and compared with the messages from other locations.

CONCLUSION

To conclude, this chapter summarizes the research conducted to capture some insights based on two hypotheses related to the latest version of the NVivo qualitative data analytics suite, NVivo 11 Plus. To these ends, two basic types of text corpora based on "healthcare" were captured from various sources—academic and web-based databases, and the Twitter microblogging platform. The findings of the research suggest that the basic unit of analysis for the sentiment analysis extraction may result in somewhat differing coding to the four sentiment categories and some difference in terms of the top terms in each coded category, but not highly different. Secondly, there do seem to be data analytics benefits to extending an automated sentiment orientation analysis by applying a range of other text data exploration tools.

In terms of the novel aspects of this work, the software tool's latest iteration was only released a few months prior to this research. The research sequence described is novel, particularly in terms of using a basic sentiment analysis first before the additional text queries, data explorations, and data visualizations. The conceptualization of features of text datasets in the spider chart is also original.

REFERENCES

Bae, Y., & Lee, H. (2011). A sentiment analysis of audiences on Twitter: Who is the positive or negative audience of popular Twitterers? In G. Lee, D. Howard, & D. Ślęzak (Eds.), *ICHIT 2011. LNCS 6935. 732 – 739.* doi:10.1007/978-3-642-24082-9_89

Bigonha, C., Cardoso, T. N. C., Moro, M. M., Goncalves, M. A., & Almeida, V. A. F. (2012). Sentiment-based influence detection on Twitter. *Journal of the Brazilian Computer Society, 18*(3), 169–183. doi:10.1007/s13173-011-0051-5

Feldman, R. (2013). Techniques and applications for sentiment analysis. *Communications of the ACM, 56*(4), 82–89. doi:10.1145/2436256.2436274

Hai-Jew, S. (2016, Spring/Summer). Extracting human sentiment from text sets with NVivo 11 Plus. *C2C Digital Magazine.* Retrieved November 26, 2015, from http://scalar.usc.edu/works/c2c-digi-magazine-spring-summer-2016/extracting-human-sentiment-from-text-sets-with-nvivo-11-plus

Han, S., & Kavuluru, R. (2015). On assessing the sentiment of *general* Tweets. In D. Barbosa & E. Milios (Eds.), *Canadian AI 2015. LNAI 9091. 181- 195.* doi:10.1007/978-3-319-18356-5_16

Hogenboom, A., Bal, D., Frasincar, F., Bal, M., de Jong, F., & Kaymak, U. (2013). Exploiting emoticons in sentiment analysis. In *Proceedings of SAC '13.* doi:10.1145/2480362.2480498

Lee, R. K.-W., & Lim, E.-P. (2015). Measuring user influence, susceptibility and cynicalness (sic) in sentiment diffusion. In A. Hansbury et al. (Eds.), *ECIR 2015, LNCS 9022. 411 – 422.*

Min, M., Lee, T., & Hsu, R. (2013). Role of emoticons in sentence-level sentiment classification. In M. Sun et al. (Eds.), *CCL and NLP-NABD 2013, LNAI 8202. 203 – 213.* doi:10.1007/978-3-642-41491-6_19

Mlodinow, L. (2012). *Subliminal: How your Unconscious Mind Rules your Behavior.* New York: Pantheon Books.

Sarkar, C., Bhatia, S., Agarwal, A., & Li, J. (2014). Feature analysis for computational personality recognition using YouTube personality data set. In *Proceedings of WCPR '14.* doi:10.1145/2659522.2659528

Sensitivity and Specificity. (2015, Dec. 4). In *Wikipedia.* Retrieved Dec. 13, 2015, from https://en.wikipedia.org/wiki/Sensitivity_and_specificity

Stieglitz, S., & Dang-Xuan, L. (2011). The role of sentiment in information propagation on Twitter—An empirical analysis of affective dimensions in political Tweets. In *Proceedings of ACIS 2011.22ⁿᵈ Australasian Conference on Information Systems.*

Thelwall, M., Buckley, K., & Paltoglou, G. (2010/2011). Sentiment in Twitter events. *Journal of the American Society for Information Science and Technology, 62*(2), 406–418. doi:10.1002/asi.21462

Wang, X., Wei, F., Liu, X., Zhou, M., & Zhang, M. (2011). Topic sentiment analysis in Twitter: A graph-based hashtag sentiment classification approach. In *Proceedings of the CIKM '11.* doi:10.1145/2063576.2063726

Webmedia. (2010). *Editing Wikipedia: A Guide to improving content on the online encyclopedia.* Wiki Education Foundation.

KEY TERMS AND DEFINITIONS

Autocoding: The use of a computer to code (textual—in this case) data.

Microblogging: The sharing of short blog messages through a microblogging site or service.

N-Gram: A contiguous sequence of terms in a sequence.

Polarity: Having opposite poles which capture the extremes of a continuum.

Recoding: The apply labeling or descriptive or other code to text.

Semi-Structured Data: Data that includes information in pre-labeled data tables and those without any pre-labeling.

Sentiment Analysis (Opinion Mining): The extraction of positive and negative polarity from a text set.

Sentiment Dictionary (or Set): A listing of words and lexical elements which are seen to contain inherent sentiment or attitude.

Structured Data: Data that is pre-labeled in formatted tables.

Theme Extraction: The identification of concepts and related sub-concepts from a text set.

Tweetstream: A collection of microblogging messages belonging to a particular social media user account.

Uncoding: Removing the coding from (manual or machine-coded) coded text.

Unstructured Data: Data that is not pre-labeled in formatted tables but may be heterogeneous like multimedia and textual datasets.

Word Set: A digital collection of words.

Section 3
Tapping Specific Social Media Platforms

Chapter 9

Exploring "User," "Video," and (Pseudo) Multi-Mode Networks on YouTube with NodeXL

Shalin Hai-Jew
Kansas State University, USA

ABSTRACT

Network Overview, Discovery and Exploration for Excel (NodeXL Basic) enables the extraction of "user" (entity), "video" (content), and pseudo multi-modal networks from YouTube. This open-source add-on to NodeXL captures a wide range of data, enables data processing for analysis, and then visualization in a variety of graphs (based on different layout algorithms). This chapter summarizes some of the "ask-able" questions using this approach. Various types of data extractions are shared to give a sense of the breadth of some approaches, including the following: (1) entities, (2) in-world phenomena, (3) imaginary phenomena, (4) themes, (5) reputations by name, (6) genres, (7) language-specific phenomena, and (8) location-specific phenomena.

INTRODUCTION

The work of this chapter overlapped with the ten-year anniversary of the start of YouTube. In the lore, the first YouTube video ever posted was titled "Me at the zoo" (by YouTube co-founder Jawed Karim); in the decade since, the historic video "in praise of elephants" as racked up almost 20 million views (Newcomb, Apr. 23, 2015). As a social media platform, YouTube is a formidable and dominant player, with billions of video views daily and presences across the globe. YouTube is "the world's second-largest search engine next to Google" (Rogers & Krishnan, 2014, p. 84). The functioning of the site depends in part on the collection of various text-based metadata about the videos, and the collection of user- and video- relationship data.

This metadata and trace data may be extracted and visualized through NodeXL (Network Overview, Discovery and Exploration for Excel), a free and open-source add-on to Excel. The structuring of user networks, video networks, and two-mode / multi-mode networks, enables insights about the users of the

DOI: 10.4018/978-1-5225-0648-5.ch009

social media platform, the video contents, and other information that would otherwise be latent or hidden. Various types of data extractions (based on topics that were contemporaneous at the time of the data extraction) are shared here to give a sense of the breadth of some approaches. This chapter will address some of the types of questions that may be asked using this research tool and some of the embedded methodologies. Real-world examples using empirical data were used and include some of the following types of seeding contents to extract the data and networks from YouTube, including the following:

1. Entities,
2. In-world phenomena,
3. Imaginary phenomena,
4. Themes,
5. Reputations by name,
6. Genres,
7. Language-specific phenomena, and
8. Location-specific phenomena.

This list is a partial one only and is meant to be used to potentially inspire reader ideas for research.

This chapter includes a selective summary of some of the academic research about YouTube, examples of "video," "user," and two-mode networks extracted from YouTube, some of the "askable" questions using this software add-on, and an overview of the two YouTube-based data extraction and modeling features of the NodeXL tool.

One Caveat about the Data Visualizations

The data visualizations here include the use of some colors that may be less readable when processed in black-and-white and in paper format. The electronic versions of this chapter will likely read much more clearly than the print version. The electronic version would also enable zooming in for close-in analysis.

A SELECTIVE REVIEW OF THE LITERATURE

Founded in February 2005 and purchased by Google in October 2006, YouTube was designed initially as a platform for people to broadcast themselves. Since then, it has become the premiere video-sharing site in the world, with localization in 75 countries and availability in 61 languages. Some 300 hours of video are uploaded to YouTube every minute (Newcomb, Apr. 23, 2015). This video-sharing platform itself is a sophisticated one. It has an automated and built-in system to detect contravening of copyright or intellectual property rights—in text, audio, visual, video, and multimedia forms. [Its Content ID program enables the protection of copyright for text, audio, and video—and the company has paid out $1 billion since 2007 to those who monetized their copyright claims ("Statistics," 2015)]. Since 2009, it has integrated a built-in machine-based speech-recognition tool to enable audio-to-text annotation (in ten different languages), which works in a complementary way to human corrected transcription for timed text captioning. YouTube uses owner-uploaded video transcripts to generate additional semi-supervised training data and deep neural networks acoustic models with large state inventories, according to Google researchers (Liao, McDermott, & Senior, 2013, p. 368).

At this moment, it has more than a billion users around the world. The broad public watches millions of hours of video on YouTube daily, and they generate billions of video views. Every hour, 18,000 hours of videos are uploaded. For video creators, some 60% of their views comes from outside their home country. Half of the video viewcounts are on mobile devices ("Statistics," 2015). YouTube itself has been widely used and broadly popular since its early days and through the years (Benevenuto, Duarte, Rodrigues, Almeida, Almeida, & Ross, 2008; Davidson, Liebald, Lu, Nandy, & Van Vleet, 2010; Liao, McDermott, & Senior, 2013, p. 368). Beyond the numbers that Google's YouTube has released broadly, there are some other targeted insights about the YouTube platform, based on the work of researchers.

In terms of video popularity, based on virality, a few videos capture mass attention (in the tens of millions range) and are broadly viewed (Brodersen, Scellato, & Wattenhofer, 2012), but a majority of videos receive just a few views—which suggests a power law video viewership distribution and a long tail (with many videos meeting the diverse interests of niche audiences) (Cha, Kwak, Rodriguez, Ahn, & Moon, 2009). One research team observed that 10% of the videos on YouTube garner about 80% of the views (Kruitbosch & Nack, 2008, p. 7), a small variation on the 80-20 rule (Pareto principle of factor sparsity) that suggests that 80% of effects come from 20% of the causes. On the user side, there is a power law distribution as well, with some users using YouTube intensively and a long tail of users watching just a small number of videos (Santos, Rocha, Rezende, & Loureiro, 2007). Widespread popularity eludes most user-generated videos (Brodersen, Scellato, & Wattenhofer, 2012, p. 243). This 80-20 rule also applies to uploaders, with the most active fifth of video uploaders contributing about 72.5% of the videos; for many video uploaders, they share videos infrequently, maybe a few videos at a time. "An uploader who uploads multiple videos may only upload once during its life time," they write (Ding, Du, Hu, Liu, Wang, Ross, & Ghose, 2011, p. 362). From a dataset of 83,769 uploaders that joined YouTube prior to 2010, "32.5%, 40.0%, and 56.1% of uploaders have been active for only one day, one month, and one year, respectively. Thus, less than half of the uploaders have been active for a period extending over one year" (Ding, Du, Hu, Liu, Wang, Ross, & Ghose, 2011, p. 362). Creating and uploading videos may be expensive in time, effort, and other costs; those who do contribute are motivated in no small part by "ego-involvement" as an antecedent to attitude and intent to share videos on a social media platform (with collective social norms much less of a factor) (Park, Jung, & Lee, 2011).

YouTube is not just a site for video viewing and sharing; it is itself a driver (and contributor) to various social phenomena—viral cat videos, flash mob weddings, GoPro feats, YouTube stars and performers (some of whom have crossed over to the mainstream), mass confessions, social displays and "selfies," and other social phenomena. As a destination point, YouTube has enabled video watching as one of the most popular user activities on the Web. It has also enabled broad-scale videoblogging.

The insights about YouTube vary in the research literature, in part, due to the limitations from the publicly available information, the types of research questions asked, the research methods used, and the questions ultimately answered. Researchers sometimes have access to sensitive datasets provided by the corporation. For most researchers, they can glean information using publicly accessible data extractable from some of YouTube's public-facing databases). A majority of the videos tend to be short-form or under 10 minutes in length (Davidson, Liebald, Lu, Nandy, & Van Vleet, 2010, p. 293). While YouTube was thought to demonstrate slower responsiveness to events (than, say, microblogging sites like Twitter), the ease of video creation using mobile devices and smart phones has made the cost of entry to sharing video on the site much less. The culture of just shooting video without worrying so much about video production values (such as lighting, sound quality, editing, and more sophisticated videography) has made it socially all right to just point-and-capture. Oftentimes, videos are shared as soon as they are captured (via smart phones, web cams, camcorders, and screen capture tools), which also means that the related descriptive metadata are applied on-the-fly. This also means that live events may be captured and shared on YouTube near instantaneously to their occurrence. To understand the "YouTube-ness" or particularisms of this content-sharing social media platform (to borrow Burgess and Green's observation, 2009), it may help to conduct *sousveillance* (surveillance from below, from a term coined by Steve Mann) from within the various social platforms for a deeper understanding of their history, their evolution, and their use before using these for more in-depth research.

Social media sites change quickly along with their respective cultures of use. There can be high variance in how various individuals or groups use the platform, such as narrow-casting to smaller and intended audiences (or even private networks by using unlisted channels for the videos and "friends only" networks for sharing) as well as broadcasting widely to the potential general public. Others have noted that people use sophisticated methods on YouTube to maintain their friendships online and to control who their audience is for their videos—such as by being "privately public" (Lange, 2008, p. 372), such as using "cryptic tagging practices" as a way to discourage others from finding and viewing certain videos (p. 370). Some use YouTube to videoblog and tell stories in video; others use it to deliver videos as parts of trainings, marketing, and games. People also come to YouTube for a variety of reasons:

...To watch a single video that they found elsewhere (direct navigation), to find specific videos around a topic (search and goal-oriented browse), or to just be entertained by content that they find interesting (Davidson, Liebald, Lu, Nandy, & Van Vleet. 2010, p. 293)

The sharing of video contents—which are non-rivalrous goods that are not dissipated by use—align with what Yochai Benkler termed "the wealth of networks" (Benkler, 2006, p. 446). While YouTube started out initially as "a personal video sharing service" (Paolillo, 2008, p. 1) with the tagline of "Broadcast Yourself" (from 2005 – 2009) ("YouTube," Logopedia), it has since broadened out beyond user-generated contents (UGC) to the sharing of commercial contents—television shows, training videos, music videos, commercial movies, repurposed newscasts, and others. User-generated contents also tend to be "considerably shorter than professionally edited content" (Kruitbosch & Nack, 2008, p. 8). Viewers (content consumers) tend to gravitate more towards professionally created video contents instead of (generally amateur) self-authored, the latter of which rarely appears on lists of most viewed videos (Kruitbosch & Nack, 2008, p. 7). Another research team observed that user-created contents tended to appear on lists that indicate social interactions: "User-created content makes up more than two-thirds of the content coded in both the Most Responded and Most Discussed categories, where it comprises 63 and 69 percent respectively—a dramatically higher percentage than traditional media content, especially when compared to the Most Viewed category, where the situation was reversed" (Burgess & Green, 2009, n.p.).

So why would people upload self-created videos to YouTube if there are so few views? One answer is that much of it is not actually user-generated contents (UGC) but rather user copied contents (UCC), particularly given the popularity of "mash-ups" or recombinations of digital contents. Analysis of videosets on YouTube resulted in the finding that there is "a high amount of redundancy, in the form of videos with overlapping or duplicated content" (San Pedro, Siersdorfer, & Sanderson, 2011, p. 13). To generalize, the duplication of contents means that the cost of entry is lower than the creation of wholly novel contents. Researchers have expressed surprise at the finding that much of the video on YouTube is not user-generated.

We found that 63% of the most popular uploaders are primarily uploading UCC content, and that UCC uploaders on average upload many more videos than UGC uploaders. The results and observations in Section 3 can be used as a first step towards an automatic algorithm for classifying UGC and UCC content. (Ding, Du, Hu, Liu, Wang, Ross, & Ghose, 2011, p. 366)

Some researchers suggest it is because YouTube works as a "social filter" to enable people to know where to spend their limited attentional resources; having a social network find relevant and entertaining information lowers the cost of self-discovery. Videos are contents that may work as conversation pieces around which people may laugh and talk, no matter how banal or kitschy. Kruitbosch and Nack (2008) explain that YouTube is more about social engagement and interaction than it is about promoting user creativity through the creation of user-generated video contents. As such, they point to the ability to respond to videos with videos and to post comments as promoting social interactions. They write:

It does not really matter whether they created this content themselves, or if they reuse something they found or captured somewhere else: it's a way to facilitate "watercooler" discussions, gossip, and other friendly chat. If someone missed the particular tv (sic) series episode, or the funny news item about a politician misbehaving, or the sports event, or your daughter's first steps, that you'd like to talk about - just upload it to YouTube, and everybody can join in. This enables the sharing of experiences within your social circle or for the general public. (Kruitbosch & Nack, 2008, p. 10)

The research work of Lange (2008) also suggests that the making and sharing of videos has a way of bringing people together socially—with people bonding and creating closeness around the shared experience around watching video contents and using videos as "emotional connection point(s)" (Lange, 2008, p. 368). In the same way that messaging may be animating for some people—to spark them to actions—videos likewise may serve as tools of mutual support or recruitment for particular endeavors (whether "mass social" or individual); they may encourage continuing commitments and actions. Lange (2008) observes some mechanisms for socializing on YouTube:

Conversely, interviewees reported that people who post comments of affinity or leave thoughtful comments may prompt the video maker to respond to the poster of the comment. Video makers may react to comments by: 1) reading them; 2) posting comments in response to the comments they received on a video; 3) posting a comment or question on the commenter's video or channel page; 4) extending a friend request to the commenter; or 5) viewing or subscribing to the commenter's videos.

Although further interaction is not guaranteed through comments, interviewees noted that these interactions were often the initial steps in broadening social connections through media circuits. (Lange, 2008, p. 369)

Researchers estimate that "roughly 60-80% of the YouTube comments do actually contain opinions" and so are a potential rich data source for sentiment analysis (Severyn, Moschitti, Uryupina, Plank, & Filippova, 2015, n.p., in process). Social uploaders (those who belong to social networks) are observed uploading more video contents than nonsocial ones. The intuition is that such individuals have social incentives to share (Ding, Du, Hu, Liu, Wang, Ross, & Ghose, 2011). The direct ability for creators of video to reach an audience, without working through formal media companies, enables an empowering disintermediation; this affordance enables access to a whole population of videographers outside of traditional video media (Burgess & Green, 2009, p. 45).

The social media platform features on YouTube go beyond the content sharing and commenting. Users may explicitly create private and public networks through following and being followed. YouTube enables to ability for users to restrict access to their respective video streams by making channels unlisted and available by invitation only. Individuals and groups may create multiple accounts. An example used was that of celebrities who have a broad fan account and then more private accounts for close-in friends and family (Lange, 2008). Users of social media platforms work to preserve some privacy, in what Lange calls a "fractalized pattern" with "different desired levels of informational and behavioral publicity and privacy" (Lange, 2008, p. 378).

Even with one email-verified account, individuals may create multiple video channels. Some will write cryptic tags to their videos to make them less findable (Lange, 2008, p. 369). Indeed, the site itself is undergoing constant redesign to enhance the user experiences. They may create groups of those with shared interests. They may interact in a multimedia way based on contents. They may engage around information based on extractable data from the YouTube platform (as will be shown here).

Google has also started sharing ad revenues with those who run highly popular and copyrighted video channels (Cheng, Fatourechi, Ma, Zhang, Zhang, & Liu, 2014). YouTube enables access to metrics of viewer access to owners' videos on the site. YouTube partners have access to "Insight Analytics" which offers even more in-depth information about video viewer traffic. YouTube touts more than a million channels from the YouTube Partner Program, with "thousands of channels are making six figures per year" ("Statistics," 2015). Some YouTube "partners" position their videos in order to drive traffic to other video contents within their own channels and their networks, particularly in the critical early time periods when new video contents have been uploaded and when most "viewing surges" are observed (Chang, Fatourechi, Ma, Zhang, Zhang, & Liu, 2014, p. 6). Most popular videos on YouTube do have a clear first "peak day," with over half of them receiving "between 33% and practically 100% of their views on a single (peak) day" when the video is highly popular and trending (Figueiredo, Benevenuto, & Almeida, 2011, pp. 749 - 750), and then "remaining attractive for a while" (p. 753) before the popularity fades. In terms of the mechanisms that bring individuals to videos, users tend to initially find their way to videos through "social links, search, other YouTube internal mechanisms or some external website, instead of receiving them via e-mail or viewing them on mobile devices" (Figueiredo, Benevenuto, & Almeida, 2011, p. 753). It is thought, too, that user interactions on YouTube, which tend to be "relatively short and noisy" may be used to offer up personalized sets of videos customized to the user: "The set of recommended videos is generated by using a user's personal activity (watched, favorited, liked videos) as seeds and expanding the set of videos by traversing a co-visitation based graph of videos. The set of videos is then ranked using a variety of signals for relevance and diversity" (Davidson, Liebald, Lu, Nandy, & Van Vleet, 2010, pp. 293 - 294).

The four evolutionary patterns of video viewership are typically attributed to user interactions within the YouTube platform and then external events, which may drive people's actions (so both endogenous factors and exogenous ones). Most videos have stable user patterns, usually with little activity, as contrasted to those that are popular or viral, which tend to be more dynamic and bursty. The patterns may be as follows: memoryless and hovering close to average; viral based on word-of-mouth propagation; a burst of popularity for quality videos based on external featuring of the video on a media platform, and junk videos with possibly a burst of popularity ("spam, chance") and generally a pattern of non-dissemination through social networks (Figueiredo, Benevenuto, & Almeida, 2011, p. 750). Internal YouTube mechanisms—YouTube search, lists of related videos—are important drivers of human traffic to different types of videos (Figueiredo, Benevenuto, & Almeida, 2011, p. 754). Others have suggested that YouTube's internal mechanisms may provide only "limited promotion efficiency" (Yan, Sang, & Xu, 2014, p. 557). [It is important to mention that publicity should not be conflated with actual follow-through on actions, as there is often a gap between expressed interests and actual actions.]

Critical Time for Video Viewing and Survival

On YouTube, most videos have "short active life span(s)", with most receiving half of their total views in the first six days of publication and diminishing views thereafter (Xu, Dale, & Liu, 2008, as cited in Yan, Sang, & Xu, 2014, p. 557). Once a video has been uploaded into YouTube, the clock has started ticking for it to either catch on, develop the momentum and word-of-mouth interest to move beyond its traditional audiences-of-interest silos, and go viral, as some of the few that gain broad popularity, or to merely be part of the "long tail" with a few niche viewers. Interestingly, where people post videos within YouTube may affect their popularity: "Our analysis shows that users posting videos under a specific category get a better recognition than those actively posting videos belonging to a large variety of categories" (Spathis & Gorcitz, 2011, p. 12). Users posting videos that are aligned with the topic draw attention to themselves and are recognized in the user-generated content communities and ultimately build their brand (Spathis & Gorcitz, 2011, p. 17). This would suggest that starting in a categorical space is preferable than scattering distribution across multiple categories. Rather, popularity by word-of-mouth may mean that powerful and bridging individuals may be the conduits through which video contents are disseminated across to other communities. The social standing and credibility of the respective individuals work as cues for a recommender system for the particular video. Users may engage more intensely on a few particular topics of interest and within smaller communities because their attention is less dispersed across multiple groups

This is not to say that all popular videos have one large peak and then lessening attention from there; there may be periods of popularity burstiness now and again for a video's viewership, but in general, high attention comes early and then dissipates. The ultimate popularity of an uploaded video is often determined early on after a video's upload (a young age of the video); said another way, it is rare for non-popular and older videos to become hits (Cha, Kwak, Rodriguez, Ahn, & Moon, 2009, p. 1369). Early viewer reactions may be indicative of how well a video will do over time. A later study found that "only 9% of the Top videos have their first referrer access (of any category) after 40% of their lifetimes" (Figueiredo, Benevenuto, & Almeida, 2011, p. 753). For a video to popularize, it has to get out of the orbits of its niche audience(s) and appeal more broadly to the public masses.

Our data show that attention in YouTube cannot be taken for granted as its audience is split into interest groups where users can manage their relationships and share their preferences. Due to the networked patterns of interactions within those online communities, there is a dispersal of the attention that prevents all videos posted online from competing on the same footing with regard to popularity. A first result concerns YouTube users' engagement as we showed that users are more engaged when they focus their interest on few specific topics. Our results also showed that users posting videos under a specific category get a high recognition which draws attention to themselves. This suggest that user recognition in UGC communities works in a similar way to brand building efforts taken by traditional companies. We believe that our work helps better understand the impact of UGC systems like YouTube on the Internet. The properties we observed are likely to be applicable in the design of efficient UGC systems and other applications for social networks. (Spathis & Gorcitz, 2011, p. 17)

Another approach is to examine messaging on multiple platforms to try to understand which videos may spark and start to trend based on the bursty and fast aspects of Tweeting on Twitter and the URL-based referral to YouTube videos from that platform (Deng, Yan, Sang, & Xu, 2014). One research team looks to Twitter messaging to understand short-term interests and YouTube profiles to understand user long-term interests "in the video domain" (Deng, Yan, Sang, & Xu, 2014, p. 31:20).

These findings suggest the criticality of setting up a "hard launch" early on leading up to and beyond the upload of a video. For some, a hard launch includes maximizing synergies between mainline media and social media—often using formal advertising campaigns on commercial mainline media and then also co-running a social media campaign (#hashtagged conversations and events) alongside. Various individuals, organizations, and businesses have tried to seed videos' "escape velocity" (into stratospheric virality) as part of a strategy to disseminate messaging through various communications channels. Mainstream media mentions and Twitter have long been known to drive YouTube video views, for example, by piquing broadscale interest. Twitter retweeting rates are linked to the popularity of YouTube videos (Abisheva, Garimella, Garcia, & Weber, 2014, p. 600). Researchers have long tapped cross-platform social media application programming interfaces (APIs) to profile individuals on multiple dimensions (Vu, Morizet-Mahoudeaux, & Abel, 2013). Another described a cross-network strategy of driving video traffic by identifying user accounts that overlap between Twitter and YouTube and which focus on particular topics or fields of interest and winning over such high centrality individuals. The authors summarize their approach:

Three stages are addressed: (1) heterogeneous topic modeling, where YouTube videos and Twitter followees are modeled in topic level; (2) cross-network topic association, where the overlapped users are exploited to conduct cross-network topic distribution transfer; and (3) referrer identification, where the query YouTube video and candidate Twitter followees are matched in the same topic space. Different methods in each stage are designed and compared by qualitative as well as quantitative experiments. Based on the proposed framework, we also discuss the potential applications, extensions, and suggest some principles for future heterogeneous social media utilization and cross-network collaborative applications. (Yan, Sang, & Xu, 2014, p.557)

Collective interests and attention are time-sensitive, with "correlated behavior concerning the time between video creation and sharing within certain timescales, showing the time onset for a coherent response, and the time limit after which collective responses are extremely unlikely" (Abisheva, Garimella, Garcia, & Weber, 2014, p. 593); further, the topic preferences of Twitter and YouTube are "largely aligned" based on a clustering analysis of topics on both social media platforms (Abisheva, Garimella, Garcia, & Weber, 2014, p. 601). Social network positioning and advocacy of certain products and services have long been related. There is a clear tie between popular positioning of a node in its local network and the "global diffusion of products seeded by it" (Yoganarasimhan, 2012, p. 111). Recent research has shown that it is not the direct ties alone to a high-centrality node that is important but the second-degree networks.

First-degree friends of a seed are essential for initial take-off, but second-degree friends are responsible for later spread. Moreover, both Clustering and Betweenness dampen later growth, but do not harm initial growth. Further, specific to our context, we find that lagged video attributes such as ratings and comments have no impact on video viewership in the long run, though they aid initial diffusion. (Yoga-narasimhan, 2012, p. 114)

This finding has been replicated by others in more recent work. Direct ego neighborhoods (raw numbers of direct followers) of influential users who communicated early videos shares on Twitter were not as effective predictors of video popularity as "second-order neighborhoods" (those of the initial ego neighborhood "alters") and "retweet rates" (Abisheva, Garimella, Garcia, & Weber, 2014, pp. 601 - 602).

Those trying to influence public opinion do not always use strategies that are considered appropriate. For example, some use socialbots (or "algorithmic agents") to Tweet on Twitter about a video to drive traffic, by capitalizing on the interaction effects and synergies between social media systems; still, others have created 'bots and cyborgs to do the same on YouTube. The fraudulent uses of social media platforms, including "astroturfing" and "content pollution" and misrepresentational accounts—which are explicitly against the end user license agreements (EULAs)—are considered anti-social, manipulative, and self-promoting. If left to proliferate, such dynamics can result in a decline in video contents and harm to the user experience. Researchers have been working on ways to identify fraudulent videos and robot profiles and faked reviews to promote those videos (Bulakh, Dunn, & Gupta, 2014, p. 1111); even with a mix of strategies to identify and remove such contents, researchers have found many of the faked profiles, faked reviews, and "fraudulent videos" left online (p. 1111). In one study, the researchers found that faked user accounts on YouTube "are relatively new in the system but (are) more active than legitimate profiles. They are more active in viewing and interacting with videos and rarely upload any videos"; "an average fraud video has shorter and fewer comments but is rated higher – 4.6 on a 5-point scale when an average legitimate video is rated only at 3.6" (Bulakh, Dunn, & Gupta, 2014, p. 1111). Researchers have been speculating on ways to raise a video's ranking within YouTube such as viewcounts, liking counts, favoriting counts, comments, and channel subscribers (Bulakh, Dunn, & Gupta, 2014, p. 1112).

For the company providing the video sharing service, there are benefits to knowing which video contents would popularize, so that the high-demand videos will be cached or pre-fetched to the particular localized servers for more efficient video delivery on-demand (Pinto, Almeida, & Goncalves, 2013). Prior researchers have suggested that there is a lack of correlation between the global popularity of a video and local popularity, and suggest that the global popularity metric "might not be used to support local caching mechanisms" (Zink, Suh, Gu, & Kurose, 2008, n.p.).

"Survival Analysis" of Videos through Viewing Popularity

One research team has created an analogical parallel between video popularity and the passing on of genetic material (biological survival):

Some of the parallels are straightforward. Videos follow grammar rules of good formation (genotypes), and have immediately observable differences by genre (phenotypes).

The sequences within and across short clips tend to be preserved, except for editorial inclusions (introns) and superfluous beginnings and endings (telomeres). Their relationships to each other can be traced by their reuse of near duplicate shots (phylogenetics), discoverable through time flexible matching algorithms (Smith-Waterman and Clustal).

Near-dups are sometimes dropped or interrupted (genetic gaps), but their basic patterns of repetition are indicative of structure, which can be displayed graphically (electrophoresis).

Competition for views can be enhanced by coexistence on playlists with related videos (symbiosis), or by copying (asexual reproduction) or by mashups (sexual reproduction), leading to evolution of content (genetic drift). (Kender, Hill, Natsev, Smith, & Xie, 2010, p. 1254)

In general, there is a tendency for uploaders to concentrate videos "in a small number of categories" (Ding, Du, Hu, Liu, Wang, Ross, & Ghose, 2011, p. 363), so there is a convergence of categories of topics. Some researchers have speculated that YouTube tends to drive traffic to less popular uploaders on the one hand but also to privilege popular uploaders on the other:

Specifically, more than 47% of uploaders attract more than 1,000 uploader views, implying that YouTube uploaders enjoy good visibility, even for those who upload a very small number of videos. Thus, YouTube's recommendation system (that is, related videos) seems to be somewhat biased towards less popular uploaders. On the other hand, among all uploaders, the most popular 20% of the uploaders attract 97.0% of views, which does not follow the 80-20 rule. Thus YouTube's recommendation system seems to be also biased to the very popular uploaders…We briefly remark that there are also many very unpopular uploaders in our random sample: 13.5% of the 100,000 uploaders have less than 100 views. (aggregated across all of the uploader's videos). (Ding, Du, Hu, Liu, Wang, Ross, & Ghose, 2011, pp. 363 - 364)

In this 2011 study, the researchers found in one dataset that there were three times more male uploaders than female ones; the male uploaders "contribute more than three times the number of videos and attract more than three times the number of views than female uploaders" (Ding, Du, Hu, Liu, Wang, Ross, & Ghose, 2011, p. 364), and the contributor population tended to trend younger, with those in their 20s and 30s contributing approximately 40% of YouTube videos in the sample.

Social Aspects of Video Sharing and Interacting around Video Contents

How do individuals arrive at particular YouTube videos? The identification of videos of interest for viewing does not usually occur in a social vacuum. People are not insensitive or indifferent to the enthusiasms of others, particularly those in their direct social network. Crowd-sourced opinions may also affect people's selectivity for video contents to consume. All online contents are in competition with other contents for people's attention, which when exercised entails a cost to finite time and energy.

"Social referral" and external sources of video referring are critical particularly in the first week of a video's upload on YouTube; channels that contain non-informative videos often depend on subscription to the channel to drive traffic, and such videos rely more on attractiveness to acquire human attention (Chang, Fatourechi, Ma, Zhang, Zhang, & Liu, 2014, p. 6). The prior research team describe five categories of referral sources for viewers of YouTube videos: suggestion from YouTube's "related video links" (the built-in recommender system, the outros that follow the playing of a video, for example); video search (YouTube referrals based on in-platform search results and Google search results), YouTube surfing (described as referrals from "any YouTube pages except related video links and search results, including annotation link, YouTube channel pages, subscriber links, paid and unpaid YouTube promotion, and other pages on YouTube"), social referral (links and embed text from external web pages), and "non-social direct" (direct navigation to the video such as "by copying and pasting the URL") (Chang, Fatourechi, Ma, Zhang, Zhang, & Liu, 2014, p. 5).

A research team studied whether there was correlation between objectively measured audio content quality and the popularity of viewed music videos on YouTube. Interestingly enough, researchers have found that the popularity of music videos is not associated with objectively and technically measured audio quality (Schoeffler & Herre, 2014). Music videos are a highly popular genre on the site. Prior work has observed complaints about the poor quality of some of the user-generated videos on YouTube, mostly around technical issues of poor editing, lighting, sound, or some combination of such factors (Lange, 2008, p. 368); there were also complaints about irrelevant contents, such as an excess of videos of people "sparring" (p. 368).

Early social network sites—beginning with usernets and bulletin board systems—started in 1997, and these have been growing in complexity since, for instant messaging, dating, live gaming, collaboration, content sharing, tagging, fund-raising, and other endeavors. YouTube also fits comfortably within the definition of a social networking site. The acts of creating and circulating videos "affectively enacts social relationships between those who make and those who view videos" (Lange, 2008, p. 368). As such, YouTube offers various features that enable individuals to create social media accounts, share videos through embed text and linking, interact with each other through text-messaging and videos, and create a sense of virtual community. As such, YouTube is known as a social media platform.

We define social network sites as web-based services that allow individuals to (1) construct a public or semi-public profile within a bounded system, (2) articulate a list of other users with whom they share a connection, and (3) view and traverse their list of connections and those made by others within the system. The nature and nomenclature of these connections may vary from site to site. (Boyd & Ellison, 2008, p. 211)

Once users have arrived at a site, there is interest also in what content they engage with and how, who they connect with in terms of other users, how they watch the videos (the pauses, when they may stop watching), how much time is spent on the site, behaviors like "scrubbing" over videos (by navigating a video using the slider bar), which transcripts are downloaded, and so on. Researchers have explored what makes a video-based conversation sufficiently interesting to encourage participation in a related discussion on YouTube and then the impacts of "interestingness" on "participation in related themes, participant cohesiveness and theme diffusion" (De Choudhury, Sundaram, John, & Seligmann, 2009, p. 331); this team has posited that understanding content interestingness to human users and the ensuing communications dynamics may help understand return and continuing visits to rich media social networking sites. External events were a main driver of high interest for participants, and mutual interest levels often resulted in "co-participation with other interesting participants" (De Choudhury, Sundaram, John, & Seligmann, 2009, pp. 339 – 340). While the idea of epidemic spreading between individuals in a network has some credence, many other researchers are looking to exogenous factors as drivers of human attention. Suffice it to say that there are a number of factors that affect video viewership.

Understanding Types of Relatedness

Researchers have asked whether YouTube is actually a "community" and whether its users explicitly experience "a sense of community." At its core, community is about relationships and interactions among members who share some common interests. After all, people may engage with the video contents and related messaging; there may be ways to engage with others based on the contents, the ideas, and the emotions evoked. People's ties may often be fleeting and ephemeral. One research team considered a range of potential relationships on YouTube:

- **User-User Friendship:** Two users mutually regard each other as a friend;
- **User-User Subscription:** A user subscribes to video feeds from another user;
- **User-Video Favoring:** A user adds a video to his/her list of favorites;
- **Video-Video Relatedness:** A video is regarded related to another one by the YouTube's search engine (Santos, Rocha, Rezende, & Loureiro, 2007).

For this particular study, they found user reputations on YouTube "strongly connected" to their uploaded videos and represented by the numbers of subscribers following a particular account. "Channel views" and videos are another indicator of reputation but may be less indicative of actual popularity at a given time since either a channel or a video may accrue a lot of views at some period in the past, but the actual channel or videos may have fallen out of favor (Santos, Rocha, Rezende, & Loureiro, 2007). Inclusion of videos on users' favorites lists is considered more reflective of "the current status of the video and not an old popularity" (Santos, Rocha, Rezende, & Loureiro, 2007). In terms of video (content) relationships, these were formed by (1) similarity of tags and keywords and (2) co-presence on the same favorite list. (Santos, Rocha, Rezende, & Loureiro, 2007). Users may have relationships with video contents, such as viewing a video in its entirety or only viewing a part and ultimately stopping partway through; users may comment on videos; users may create reply videos in response to uploaded contents on the site. Santos, Rocha, Rezende, and Loureiro (2007) found that content viewership as "extremely influenced by social relationships" and influenced "by human social behavior." They wrote, "Visualizations of videos, relations among users and others have statistical distributions that follow power-law functions, showing evidence of Small-World models and preferential attachment scenarios" (Santos, Rocha, Rezende, & Loureiro, 2007). A more recent work questions whether YouTube "communities" are actually structured as communities. Users may come to YouTube and subjectively perceive community when it may not be objectively perceivable. To capture possible gaps between subjective and objective senses of community on YouTube, a research team combined qualitative and quantitative research methods. They wrote:

To accomplish this, YouTube was examined using two different and complementing methods. Using Grounded Theory, we performed a detailed analysis of more than 30 videos and their corresponding textual comments, which discussed two topics: users' feelings about the YouTube community, and users' accounts of interaction within the community. We then performed a structural analysis on the ties these users display on their YouTube channels. This analysis showed that although users perceive YouTube to be a cohesive community, the explicit relationships in the friendship and subscription network are almost random. We suggest that users' sense of community is not necessarily related to the structure of the YouTube network, and may result from subjective affinity towards other users. (Rotman, Golbeck, & Preece, 2009, p. 41)

Using qualitative and quantitative research approaches, Rotman, Golbeck and Preece found that although individual users perceived that they were participating in a community, the social network formed by "friendships" or "subscriptions" did not necessarily indicate communal sorts of ties (or a "small world" social graph structure). The researchers do not deny that there is community participation but suggest that these may exist invisibly to the observed interaction structures. Structurally, online communities are viewed in the literature as a complex matrix of personal ties and fairly continuous communications (Rotman, Golbeck, & Preece, 2009, pp. 41 - 42). The authors found that the networks they studied on YouTube had a radically low clustering coefficient, which would suggest that the graphs they were studying were "almost entirely random" (Rotman, Golbeck, & Preece, 2009, p. 42).

Geographical "Locality of Interest" Effects on Video Consumption

One long-held assumption of the World Wide Web is that its global access has erased geographical boundaries and people differences. People's relationships could be mediated across distances, and foundational dynamics in human relationships would change. A number of studies have served to refute some of the more grandiose assertions of large-scale human changes in relationships. Researchers have found that geographical proximity is a factor in the formation of close human relationships and social ties. In YouTube, as with virtually all social media platforms, there are geographical, demographic, and linguistic factors in terms of participation and content consumption. Some of these limits are government-created. For example, China, Iran, Pakistan, and Turkmenistan ban access to YouTube ("YouTube," Apr. 20, 2015). Other countries have demanded that particular contents be banned in order for the service to be used in-country. On YouTube, the U.S. is the top country in terms of uploaders and accounts for nearly a third of the total number of uploaders; in terms of popularity. There are also differences between access patterns from different locales. YouTube is widely accessed in the U.S., Europe, and S. America, but it is less popular in Japan and Korea (Ding, Du, Hu, Liu, Wang, Ross, & Ghose, 2011, p. 364).

Based on a randomly selected 20-million video corpus (of vidoes uploaded to YouTube between September 2010 to August 2011), a research team found that YouTube videos do exhibit some localness effects on video preference vs. a global one. For example, they found that 50% of the videos studied had "more than 70% of their views in a single region" (with the unit-of-analysis at the country levels), and further, that social sharing of videos widen the geographic reach of a video beyond its main physical locales of interest before the video's popularity ultimately fades (Brodersen, Scellato, & Wattenhofer, 2012, p. 241). So even though YouTube is a global platform, with global access, it shows some of the traditional signs of regional markets and regional segmentation. Researchers suggest that there are various factors that create a "locality of interest" for online videos: namely, particular topics like "sports, politics, and news"; geographic proximity between users, given word-of-mouth sharing of videos; shared language and culture; the "geographic scope of a video" (Brodersen, Scellato, & Wattenhofer, 2012, p. 241), and others. YouTube videos do not show uniform popularity across the world but rather variations in popularity across geographical locations and strong localities of interest for particular videos. The authors describe their findings:

YouTube videos are local: we find that about 50% of videos have more than 70% of their total views in a single country (which holds even for popular videos);

Viral spreading traps videos: we analyze that the impact of social sharing on the geographic properties of video views is surprisingly non-trivial. As a video receives a larger fraction of views through social mechanisms Its geographic audience widens, but when the fraction of socially-generated views grows larger than 20% the videos experience a more focused popularity in fewer regions. (Brodersen, Scellato, & Wattenhofer, 2012, p. 242)

When a video popularizes, it moves beyond geographical locations, but as its popularity dissipates, the concentration of viewership reverts back to the focus location after peaking. This suggests that there are geographical patterns even over "temporal evolution" (Brodersen, Scellato, & Wattenhofer, 2012, p. 242), in the various phases of a video's lifespan on YouTube. YouTube videos attain most of their views from a small number of regions and demonstrate "highly localized interest" (Brodersen, Scellato, & Wattenhofer, 2012, p. 243). The top 10 regions of YouTube video consumers (listed in descending order: USA, Brazil, UK, Germany, Japan, Spain, France, Mexico, Canada, and Italy) account for 60% of the total views for popular videos (that transcend regional popularity for a time) and 80% of the total views for less popular videos (Brodersen, Scellato, & Wattenhofer, 2012, p. 243). Approximately 40% of YouTube videos receive 80% of their views from a single region (Brodersen, Scellato, & Wattenhofer, 2012, p. 243). A lot of the video traffic (more than a third) is generated in the U.S., showing the predominance of YouTube there; of the others in the top ten list, each generates less than 5% of the videos, besides Brazil.

Datamining Applications

Online data from social media platforms are also analyzed for data mining purposes. Researchers explore and measure societal happiness based on geolocated digital data (images, texts, videos, and others). For example, researchers have designed a method to use trimodal information streams (visuals, audio, and textual features of videos on YouTube) to infer sentiment in an automated way (Morency, Mihalcea, & Doshi, 2011). Subjectivity and sentiment analysis focuses on the automatic identification of video subjects' private states, such as their opinions, emotions, and beliefs. The researchers describe their work:

This is unlike most of the work done on multimodal emotion analysis, which often addressed only one or two modalities at a time (e.g., visual and audio cues). Second, we present a qualitative and statistical analysis that identifies five multimodal features that are found helpful to differentiate between negative, neutral, and positive sentiments: polarized words, smile, gaze, pauses, and voice pitch.

Finally, in our experiments we target and use real online data, which poses additional challenges with respect to the artificial datasets that have been typically used in the past in multimodal research. We introduce a new dataset consisting of video opinions, collected from the YouTube web site, which we analyse and annotate for sentiment. The results of our initial experiments show that the joint use of multiple modalities can improve significantly over classifiers that use only one modality at a time, thus demonstrating the potential of multimodal sentiment analysis. (Morency, Mihalcea, & Doshi, 2011, pp. 169 - 170)

This team identified polarized words. They observed that smiling tends to co-occur with positive utterances and looking away to co-occur with the expression of neutral or negative utterances. They observed that video subjects tend to pause less when expressing polarized speech. They identified that there is great variation in pitch when expressing polarized speech (Morency, Mihalcea, & Doshi, 2011, p. 173). In a fully scaled and applied context, this would mean that videos may be analyzed for expressed sentiment at machine speeds in the same way that text expressions are on social media platforms—to enable near real-time awareness of human expressions. A different study on partisan sharing tried to ascertain political leanings based on video consumption, but with the result that general YouTube videos are not polarized enough to be easily told apart. (Weber, Garimella, & Borra, 2013, p. 44). Another research team analyzed monologues on video blogs (vlogs) hosted on YouTube to predict personalities; based on linguistic analysis; the researchers found: "Coarse-grain emotional categories resulted in performance gains for Agreeableness and Neuroticism, while the inclusion of fine-grain emotional features had more positive effect on predicting Extroversion and Openness to Experiences" (Gievska & Koroveshovski, 2014, p. 19). Such research studies use publicly available information to extend what is knowable by what is fairly easily and publicly available.

Network Analysis from Metadata and Trace Data

Not only is there informational (and entertainment) value in the shared videos (the content), but the collected metadata (in this case, titles, descriptions, tags, author names, and other text-based information also has value) and also trace data (data that is a byproduct of the functioning of the system). For example, it is possible to map the social networks of various account holders (user) on YouTube (if their account is set to be publicly viewable). Online relationships are notoriously "weak" in linkage, with fleeting and often fast-decaying interactions, and little in the way of depth. Also, it is possible to map video (content) networks based on various types of relationships—such as videos with shared semantic labels, videos which are related based on commenting or on user accounts, and other connections. It is also possible to extract two-mode and multi-mode networks that consist of both video creators (users or "authors") and video titles, in combination, as well as other mixes. (Multi-mode networks are those in which the vertices represent multiple different types of entities.)

Network analysis itself, which includes the study of relational structural topology, involves a fair amount of complexity—in methods, in statistics, and in analysis; further, the nature of the social media platform itself, its user bases (the demographics of its users and their habits on the site), and the API will affect the types of data that are extractable and what may be asserted (in a controlled research context). The use of metadata (information about information) from a video content sharing site highlights the fact that text is mono-dimensional while video contents contain text, audio, still visuals, and moving images, in various sequences, and are multi-dimensional. The amateur or "folk" labeling of video contents introduces noise into the data (Davidson, Liebald, Lu, Nandy, & Van Vleet, 2010, p. 293). In other words, this analytical approach—as with all other research and analytical approaches—is powerful for some types of queries and understandings but not others. The resulting data visualizations also provide insights about the respective social and content networks (and the two-mode ones), in a way that the data captured in the extracted data tables may not show.

While this mapping may be done with direct command-line data scraping through YouTube's application programming interfaces (APIs), a somewhat easier way is to use a free and open-source add-on to Excel. Network Overview, Discovery and Exploration for Excel (NodeXL) is a network graphing tool that features a number of integrations with various social media platforms' APIs that enable data extractions, their data processing for network analysis, graph data visualizations (from a number of layout algorithms), and data analysis. Users may find that there are varying degrees of semantic coherence from the extracted networks.

EXPLORING YOUTUBE "USER," "VIDEO," AND MIXED-MODE NETWORKS

To demonstrate how this might work, a number of data extractions from social media platforms were conducted using NodeXL. This work was not done in an in-depth full analysis way; rather, this was done lightly and almost superficially to showcase the NodeXL technology and the network analysis research approach.

A YouTube User's Network

When importing from a YouTube user's network, there needs to be a seeding user account name, and then the following parameters: the degrees of the extracted network (1, 1.5, or 2), whether the researcher would like a statistics column and image files, and then whether there should be a top limit for the numbers of people included. What this data extraction captures will be the "person or channel subscribed to by the user," so the resulting network is a directed network in one direction (those whom the target user is following on the YouTube network). This enables the asking of some questions such as the following:

- Who is the target user following on YouTube? Who are the "alters" in this ego neighborhood? (1-degree network)
- What is the transitivity between the "alters" in the target user account's ego neighborhood? (1.5-degree network)
- What is the nature of the ego neighborhoods of the "alters" of the direct members of the ego neighborhood of the target user account on YouTube? What may be understood from the two-degree members of the two-degree network? (2-degree network)
- What are the videos in the videostream for the particular user? What does this content suggest about the nature of the particular YouTube account?

A YouTube Video Network

In terms of importing a YouTube video network, a user needs to begin with seeding text to start the search "for videos whose title, keywords, description, categories, or author's user name" contain the target text (alphanumeric letters, hashtags, words, phrases, and others). Such variables have to be passed to the YouTube API in order to define the search and evoke a "correct system and data response" (Rogers & Krishnan, 2014, p. 86). The user then has to decide when edges (relationships or links) should be added to show relationships: for each "pair of videos that have the same category" (dyadic relationship based on belongingness to a category); for each "pair of videos commented on by the same user" dyadic (relationship based on commenting by a particular user); and for each "pair of videos responded to with another video by the same user" (dyadic relationship based on video commenting by a particular user). A user may choose to check none of the boxes (in which case the listing will only be of the videos pulled based on the target term and its appearance in the various fields mentioned prior. Or, a particular relationship or combination of relationships may be selected for the data extraction. The identifying of videos connected by relationships result in the identifications of subsets from the larger set of videos culled based on the search term(s). Multiple data extractions may be pulled in sequence as well, for different aspects of the particular video network to be highlighted. Finally, a user may choose to limit the number of videos or not. The default video limit is pre-set at 100 videos, but it is possible to push the upper limit to 9,999 using the check-box and the up-arrow; if the box is unchecked, then there is no artificial limit of 100 videos, and the extraction may involve any number of videos that the YouTube API enables (and it is unclear where the limits then fall). There minimum number of videos is ten (10). Depending on how disambiguated the original seeding term is, this enables the asking of some questions such as the following:

- What are some of the basic titles linked to a particular video topic on YouTube? A particular location? A particular phenomenon? A particular theme or concept?
- What semantics may be extrapolated from the titling? The commenting?
- What are some of the basic titles linked to a particular YouTube account, and what does this say about the nature of the particular account? The sentiment? The main messages? The stances on particular issues? (based on a disambiguated search based on a particular account name)
- Who are the network members on the user account? (based on a disambiguated search based on a particular account name)
- Which accounts are interacting around a particular topic-based video network? Which of the accounts are the most active in this particular network? (The most prolific in presenting videos? The most prolific in commenting on videos?)
- What are the video (and messaging) contributions of various accounts?

Certainly, much more may be asked and ascertained based on the subject matter, based on further exploration methods, and researcher insights, among other aspects. NodeXL's capabilities are constantly changing, and the APIs of the various social media platforms are also changing. In other words, there are near-constant dynamic changes that change-up the data extraction capabilities. Within NodeXL, there are ways to cluster data by time zones, node features (such as in-degree, out-degree, betweenness centrality, degree centrality, and others), relationship features, and so on. The extracted data may be placed in other software tools for analysis—such as word frequency counts, text searches, cluster analyses, image analyses, video analyses, URL (uniform resource locators) analyses, and others. There are also various research and analytical methods that may enhance knowability.

The typical sequence of a data extraction using NodeXL to tap YouTube could go as follows: first, a researcher decides on whether to go with a targeted query or an open exploration. Next, he or she decides on the text-based seed for the data extraction from YouTube. The more disambiguated the seed text, the more direct the ties to particular contents. The higher the limit for the data extraction, the broader the range of diverse topic understandings (and fuller fleshing out of word meanings for the seed terms) as expressed or manifested in the uploaded videos (based on their textual labeling. From there, the parameters of the data extraction are set up in NodeXL, the data is extracted. There are clearly dependencies in the data extraction. What is extracted depends in part on the parameters set for the data extraction in NodeXL, but it also depends on the speed of connectivity to the Internet, the social media platform API and how busy it is, and other factors. Once the data has been captured, it is processed, the data visualization is created (for analytical and data clarity purposes), and the data is analyzed. The analysis part requires a fair amount of human insight, such as applying in-world knowledge about people's profiles or summarizing the related clusters of videos by title (to describe the topical clustering), and other minimally analytical approaches. The analysis may occur at three main levels: the granular micro level (nodes: user accounts, videos), meso level (clusters or motifs: groups of users; groups of related videos), and macro level (network: the entire extracted network). Close-reading of the extracted text may also provide other insights.

Within Excel, there are additional tools—that enable filtering, counting, and data organizing. It is also possible to start new columns for the addition of notes for each of the records. There are ways to cobble data to meld datasets for two-mode or multi-mode networks. Further analyses may be conducted based on the extracted data using other tools beyond Excel. An overview of this process is depicted in Figure 1, "Acquiring YouTube User and Video Networks: A Basic Sequence".

The prior portion highlighted some types of questions which may be asked and partially answered using NodeXL to explore YouTube networks. To introduce NodeXL further, it may help to show how specific topic categories may be explored. The various topic categories may range from the generic to the specific (or disambiguated). The network research from YouTube may be complementary to other streams of research, or it may be stand-alone. As a basic start, the various approaches may include the following:

1. **Entities:** Individual, persona, group, organization, company, or other extant being.

Figure 1. Acquiring YouTube user and video networks: a basic sequence

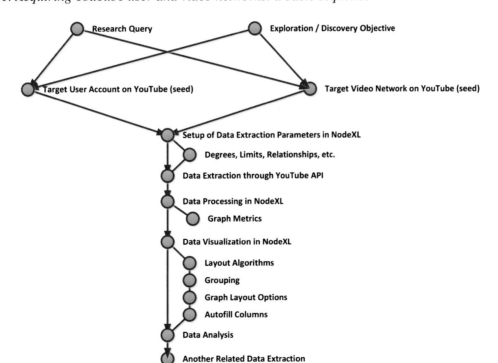

Acquiring YouTube Video Networks: A Basic Sequence

2. **In-World Phenomena:** Events, conferences, festivals; weather phenomena; longer-term occurrences.
3. Imaginary or fictional phenomena.
4. Themes (or concepts).
5. **Reputations:** Based on brands, company names, organizations.
6. **Genres:** Music, movies, games, and others.
7. Language-specific phenomena.
8. Location-specific phenomena.

This list is by no means exhaustive but may be a starting-off point in terms of shaping some queries. In terms of specific topic selection, some element of serendipity and convenience sampling came into play, depending in part on what issues were in the headlines in the American press. This work was capturing over a number of months in spring and summer 2015. These extractions are depicted through light data visualizations, without accessing the underlying data in the NodeXL worksheets or the other analytical and visualization tools within NodeXL. This tool is used at a basic level and in an introductory way. It is thought that this approach already involves a fairly high cognitive load and effort. As such, there is always a tradeoff between breadth and depth, and this approach will involve more of the first.

Figure 2. The NodeXL interface with the "import from YouTube user's network" window open

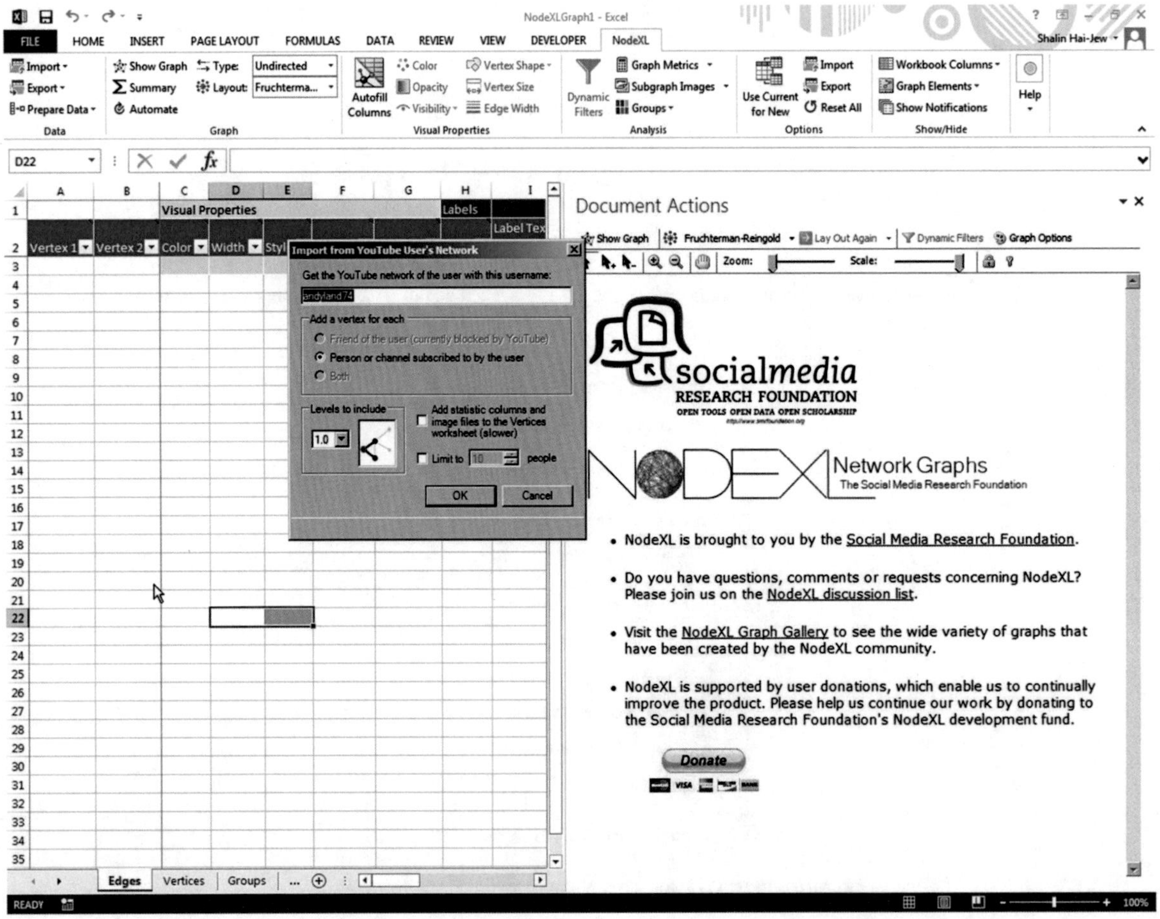

In NodeXL

As with many types of data extractions from social media platforms, the original query starts with a seed term, word, or phrase, in alphanumeric format. In NodeXL, the extraction starts with the NodeXL template. In the ribbon, go to the NodeXL tab. At the far left, in the Data area, go to the Import dropdown menu, and select either "From YouTube User's Network…" or "From YouTube Video Network…" The first tool involves the mapping of a one-directional graph of followees followed by the targeted YouTube social media account user. (The links are all formal outlinks to other YouTube accounts on the platform.) (see Figure 2)

The latter extraction enables the mapping of topically related networks based on information from the following text fields in YouTube: keywords, description, categories, or author's username. The seeding term is the topic. This captures relationships between video contents based on the "folk" (amateur) textual labeling applied to these contents. This latter approach is based on the video contents but also enables the capturing of some ad hoc social networks—of various accounts that are interrelated based on interactions and intercommunications around particular video contents (see Figure 3).

Figure 3. The NodeXL interface with the "import from YouTube video network" window open

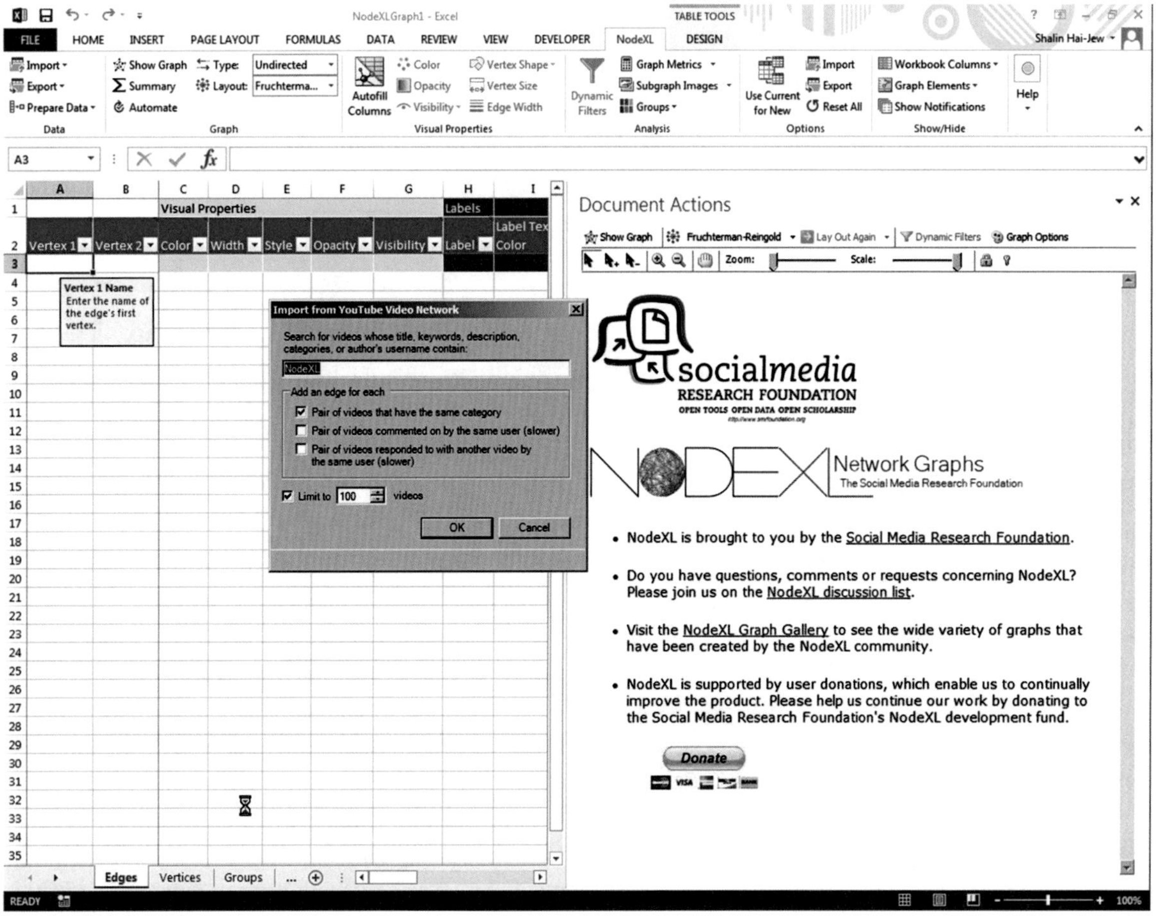

Data Extraction, Data Processing, and Data Visualization Parameters

In terms of the data extractions, the top limit of 9,999 vertices was used (although none of the data extractions came anywhere close to that). All the extracted data was processed for the full graph metrics data processing and extractions. The clusters were all extracted based on the Clauset-Newman-Moore clustering algorithm, and the graph layouts were generally created using the Harel-Koren Fast Multiscale layout algorithm. In some of the graphs, partitioning (placing each of the groups' vertices in their own respective boxes or partitions) was applied to make the graphs more easily viewable. In general, the same parameters were used to create a consistent look-and-feel. NodeXL enables a much wider range of data visualizations, which were not showcased in this work. Also, all data visualizations are interactive with the data; users may zoom and pan as well.

Before moving on to the use of real-world data to create examples, it is important to note that the tags applied to YouTube videos may be quite incomplete and noisy. By definition, they are free-form terms, so people may apply whatever they think may be relevant to their video contents. By definition, folk tagging results in noisy labeling data.

In the early days of YouTube, a set of a million videos with 517,008 distinct tags were studied to gain a sense of the tags' informational value. The research team described some of their findings:

In our sample of more than one million YouTube videos, a total of 517,008 distinct tags (without stemming or punctuation normalization) were used. The median number of tags applied per video was 6.0. A significant majority (66%) of tag terms applied were ones that did not appear in the tagged video's title, description, and author fields, suggesting that many of the tag terms applied to videos provide additional descriptors for submitted video. However, our sample also contained many examples of tagging behaviors that indicate tags are being used in ways that do not enhance the description of the video but are instead a result of system constraints and non-descriptive strategies for sharing video. (Geisler & Burns, 2007, p. 480)

A later study found that the tags for YouTube videos "generally quite small" and only capable of capturing "a small sample of the content" (Baluja, Seth, Sivakumar, Jing, Yagnik, Kumar, Ravichandran, & Aly, 2008, p. 895). Such limits may result in poorer findability of potentially relevant videos for users. In many cases, video metadata on YouTube is seen to have severe informational limits, in a research context, which almost always has higher standards than user requirements. One research team writes (2010):

In all cases, the data that we have at our disposal is quite noisy: Video metadata can be non-existent, incomplete, outdated, or simply incorrect; user data only captures a fraction of a user's activity on the site and only indirectly measures a user's engagement and happiness, e.g., the fact that a user watched a video in its entirety is not enough to conclude that she actually liked it. The length of the video and user engagement level all influence the signal quality. Moreover, implicit activity data is generated asynchronously and can be incomplete, e.g., the user closes the browser before we receive a long-watch notification. (Davidson, Liebald, Lu, Nandy, & Van Vleet, 2010, p. 294)

Still, for all the limits to the available data and the limited extrapolations that may be made from it, YouTube does offer a potent repository of shared videos for a broad range of human uses. It is a highly popular space for collaborative knowledge creation and sharing. Its members can be highly loyal and rabidly enthusiastic.

1. ENTITIES

An entity refers to an individual, persona, group, organization, company, or other extant being. The seeding term in this case involves Kaspersky Lab, a Russian software security company that has recently been in the news (see Figures 4 and 5).

Figure 4. "Kaspersky" video network on YouTube (with titled vertices)

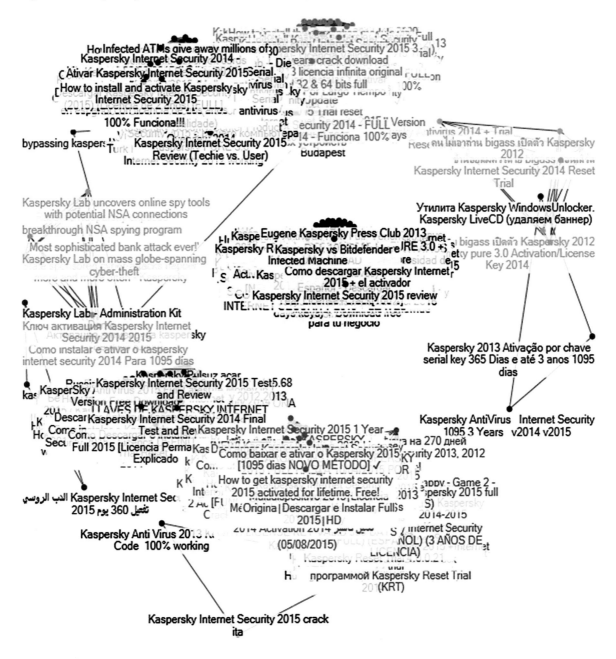

Figure 5. "Kaspersky" video network on YouTube (with authored vertices)

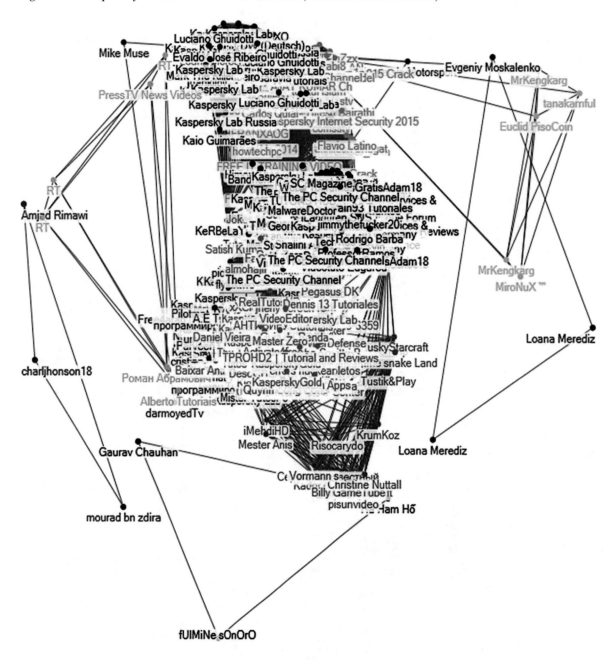

A video network with the term "Kaspersky" in its textual descriptors or name shows a range of video clusters in a variety of languages: English, Spanish, Arabic, Russian, and others. The general contents seem to be similar, in terms of dealing with Kaspersky products and computer security issues.

The same network may be viewed albeit with the social media accounts ("authors") listed. This view shows that the network is not only the company interacting but also a range of YouTube users. A perusal of the landing page for the Kaspersky Lab account does show wide viewership of some of their videos and lively interactive commentary. There are YouTube account names related to computer publications, cyber events, companies, groups, and individuals (see Figure 6).

Figure 6. "Kaspersky" user network (following) on YouTube

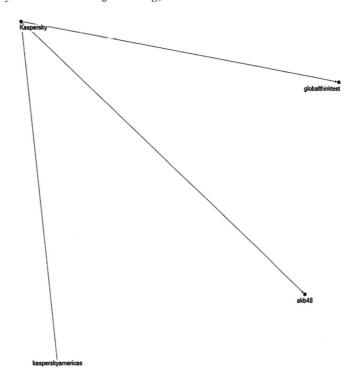

A user network search using "Kaspersky" as the seeding term extracted the various social media accounts followed by the verified Kaspersky account. This resulted in three accounts, one of which is obviously linked to the Kaspersky company; sometimes, organizations will subscribe to their own channels to create a sense of both self-awareness and of messaging reverberations. The other two accounts do not have an obvious tie: one is a channel for puzzle solving, and another is to an account that hosts telecast entertainment videos. The subscriptions to these various other channels may be a reflection of an employee's interests than a formal decision by the company to link to particular accounts on YouTube. There are some risks in following other accounts (unless they are a somewhat known quantity) because of the sense that an organization is partly identified by the company it keeps and the assumption of homophily (the preference for others who are similar to the self). Some companies also use their networks as an extension of their branding. The followership network here does not particularly show the Kaspersky account using its subscriptions to necessarily learn from other organizations. This is not to say that they don't but that if they do through YouTube it is not so obvious through their subscriptions to a few accounts. This account is a public-facing one; this is not to say that the organization does not have private channels, private networks, and private videos—potentially.

On the other hand, it would be interesting to see who follows Kaspersky, but that information is not currently easily extractable using these means and this tool (see Figure 7).

Another type of data extraction involves the extraction of the network of pairs of videos commented on by the same user (Kaspersky) and then placed in related clusters. This network shows a fair amount of relatedness and commenting, which may show that the account that has launched such videos will interact with those who comment on its channel and / or that it uses the commenting feature to add more information about the video contents (see Figure 8).

Figure 7. "Kaspersky" video network and pairs of videos commented on by the same user on YouTube

In terms of a network extraction of the pairs of videos responded to with another video by the same user, there were no relationships identified although a fairly large set of videos were extracted (as mentioning "Kaspersky"). This would make sense because of the relatively higher cost in creating another video as part of a video-based conversation.

Finally, another extraction involves the pulling of the "Kaspersky" video network with any incidence of "Kaspersky" in the title, in the keywords, in the description, in the category labels, or in the author's user name. Because none of the relational boxes were selected, the resulting graph in Figure 9 does not show any ties or relatedness. The graphs in this first section are all single-mode networks (as visualized), with the vertices (nodes) representing all items of a kind (all videos or all authors).

Within NodeXL, it is possible to re-output the various graphs with different information to create a sense of a two-mode or multi-mode network (with the vertices representing different information—either videos or authors or geographical locations or time zones, etc.). A classic two-mode or multi-mode network has multiple types of vertices simultaneously, so users and their respective videos. To achieve

Figure 8. "Kaspersky" Video network and pairs of videos responded to with another video by the same user on YouTube

this, it may take using the edges or links to carry additional information, which will be depicted below. From one data extraction, with full data processing in NodeXL, it is possible to extract a wide range of other data which is not depicted here. (The additional analytical capabilities of this tool are beyond the purview of this chapter.)

Figure 9. "Kaspersky" video network for videos with "Kaspersky" in the title, keywords, description, categories, or author's user name on YouTube

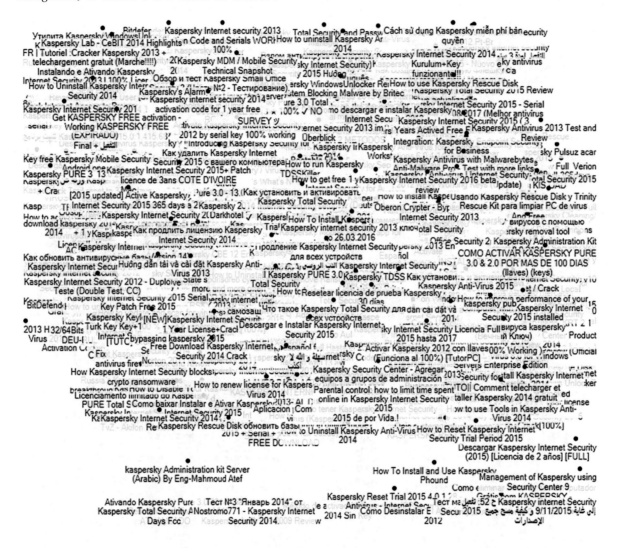

2. IN-WORLD PHENOMENA

In-world phenomena may be human-planned and executed events, conferences, and festivals; these may be weather phenomena; these may be longer-term occurrences. For this example, a very recent event was the "Nepal earthquake." A video network was extracted on April 25, 2015, based on the prior disambiguated term. An edge was extracted for each of the following dyadic relationships between the videos: "pair of videos that have the same category," "pair of videos commented on by the same user," and "pair of videos responded to with another video by the same user." In general, with YouTube video extractions, the top end of numbers for the vertices tend to be about 500, but there are often tens of thousands of ties or relationships.

Figure 10. "Nepal earthquake" video network on YouTube on April 25, 2015 (2:45 p.m. CST)

Figure 10 shows the 11 clusters or groups that were clustered based on similarity based on the text labels. This data extraction is re-visualized in the consecutive following figures (see Figure 11). This shows that, contrary to the idea that video networks are somewhat slower to respond to breaking world events, in this connected age, people can be fairly fast at responding to breaking events with video. In this case, it is telling that there is even video from camps on Mount Everest, where climbers were left stranded by avalanches caused by the earthquake and follow-on aftershocks.

Figure 11. "Nepal earthquake" video network on YouTube on April 25, 2015 (2:45 p.m. CST) (with some extracted screen grab imagery and video cluster partitioning)

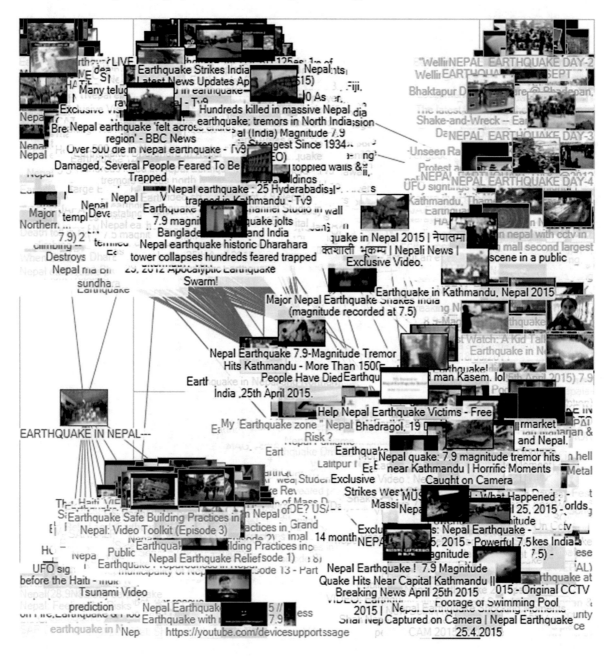

In Figure 12, the same network is depicted with the vertices representing the authors who uploaded the contents. The various authors here are a range: individuals, companies related to professional climbing, media organizations, entertainment companies, and others. It would be possible to extract the age of the respective extracted accounts on YouTube using the initial data extraction, in order to tell if an account was possibly created in response to the breaking event or if it had a prior account through which prior video contents may have been shared. It is also possible to see if locational information has been included—for either the authoring accounts or for the video itself (in the data sheets in NodeXL).

Figure 12. "Nepal earthquake" Video Network with Author Names on YouTube on April 25, 2015 (2:45 p.m. CST)

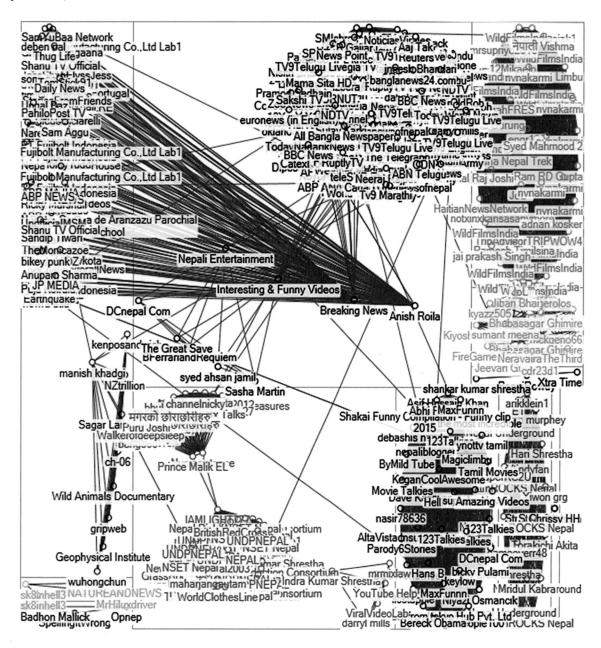

There is also the ability to place Group (clustering) numbering on the 11 groups in order to track the same groups across for cross-comparisons, as in Figure 13. The grouping enables cross-comparisons of data such as authors, titles, geography, time zones, and other data. Within the constraints of the tool, it is possible to label groups (beyond Group 1, Group 2…)by types of contents…and then to develop further insights about those groups. For example, if there are common terms in each cluster, it may be possible to extract those (through a basic word frequency count) and use those as labels for that cluster.

Figure 13. "Nepal earthquake" video network on YouTube on April 25, 2015 (2:45 p.m. CST) (with groups labeled and view counts per video as callouts at each vertex)

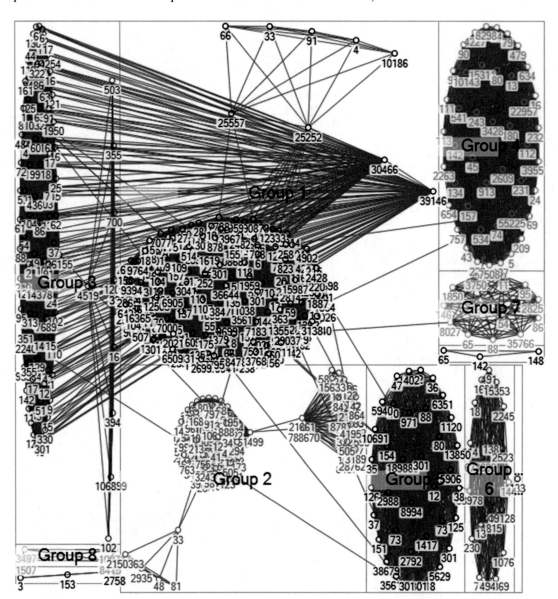

In Figure 13, the same data is visualized albeit showing the various views per video. Conceptualized in sequence, these may be understood as a form of sequential data querying and visualizing to attain deeper insights. Researchers may go straight to the data worksheets to examine the records individually. Various queries and filtering may be applied to the data in Excel (on which NodeXL rides). Or, the dataset may be exported to other software programs for word frequency counts, text searches and modeling in word trees, and so on.

3. IMAGINARY OR FICTIONAL PHENOMENA

Another approach to YouTube video networks is to pursue fictional phenomena. A large amount of video contents are based on fictional characters, worlds, and concepts. For this type of content, it is possible to seed a video network extraction. Figure 14 shows a video extraction based on "Cinderella"; it is helpful to note that the links show the type of category in each group (although the overlap covers up some of these). The nine (9) groups in the "Cinderella" video network was visualized with the authors indicated by the shape of the vertex, so all authors of a type with a particular color and shape as indicator (for

Figure 14. "Cinderella" video network on YouTube (with title callouts on the vertices and category callouts on the edges)

Figure 15. "Mickey Mouse" video network on YouTube (with title labels on the vertices and one high-lighted cluster)

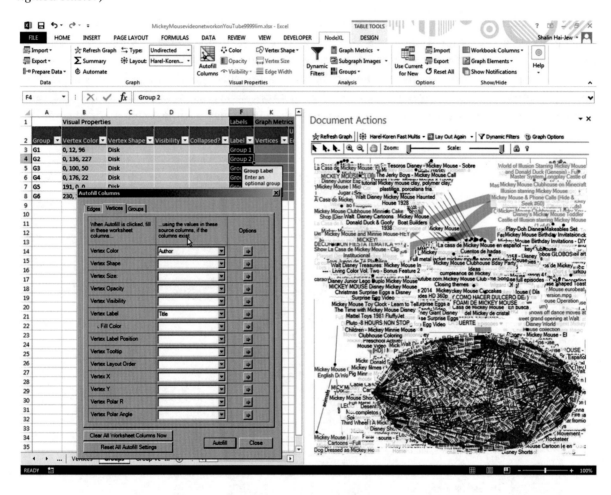

deeper exploration later on). This approach enables a kind of multi-mode graph network in the sense that the vertices are not one kind, but that is somewhat misleading since each node is both an author and a video title (in a kind of data shimmer).

Another example of an imaginary character is Mickey Mouse (see Figure 15). This video extraction resulted in six (6) groups. When a group is clicked in the data row, its corresponding part of the visualization is highlighted in the NodeXL graph pane.

In Figure 16, the same graph is extracted albeit with some of the thumbnails of the video screen grabs included, to give readers more of a visceral (albeit lightly so) sense of some of the videos.

Another sense of the imaginary may be captured in "Second Life" video networks on YouTube. The resulting graph may be seen in Figure 17. There were five groups in this data extraction.

As yet another extension of this, a "fantasy" video network was also captured on YouTube. The results may be seen in Figure 18. The term "fantasy" contains a wide range of polysemic (multiple) meanings that may be seen in the various clusters of video titles. The images were not inserted so as not to overlap with some of the titles.

Figure 16. "Mickey Mouse" video network on YouTube (with thumbnails of video screen grabs)

4. THEMES (CONCEPTS)

There are a wide range of themes and concepts that are expressed in videos online. One of the common ones is that of "DIY" or the "do it yourself" phenomena. YouTube has a useful repository of various types of videos for skills sharing by those who have varying levels of expertise in particular fields, practices, work, and hobbies.

Figure 17. "Second Life" video network on YouTube (with video titles at the vertices and some video screen grabs)

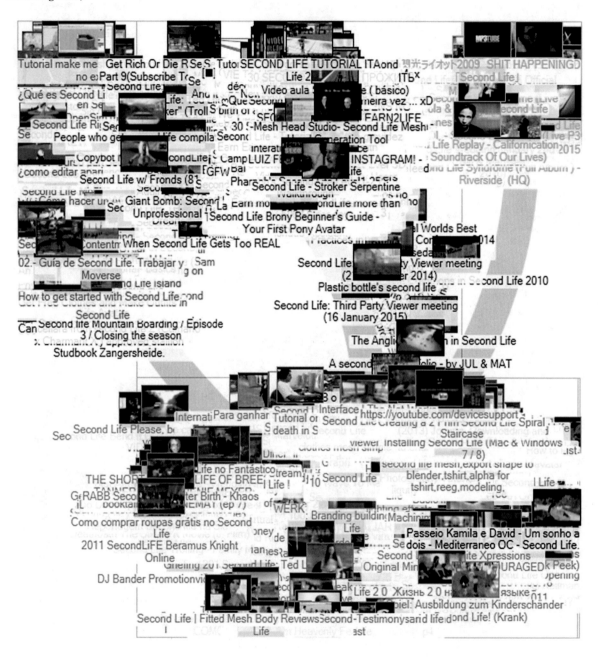

The "DIY" video network consists of five (5) groups. This network may be seen in Figure 19. At the time of the data extraction, a "diy" search in YouTube resulted in the following auto-complete terms: diy room décor, diy projects, diy crafts, diy clothes, diy phone case, diy makeup, diy bath bomb, and diy room decorating ideas for teenagers.

Figure 18. "Fantasy" video network on YouTube

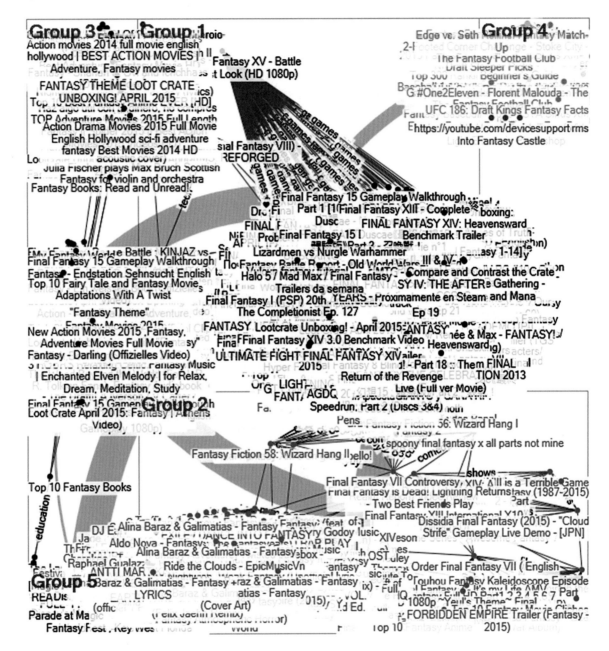

5. REPUTATIONS (BY NAME)

Another approach is to examine an entity with a public-facing side (or persona) to acquire a sense of its public reputation (via videos on YouTube). One approach is to map the user network for the entity to find out which other YouTube entities are being followed by the target social media account (in a one-degree directional graph, with other vertices as the "person or channel subscribed to by the user"). In this case,

Figure 19. "DIY" video network on Youtube

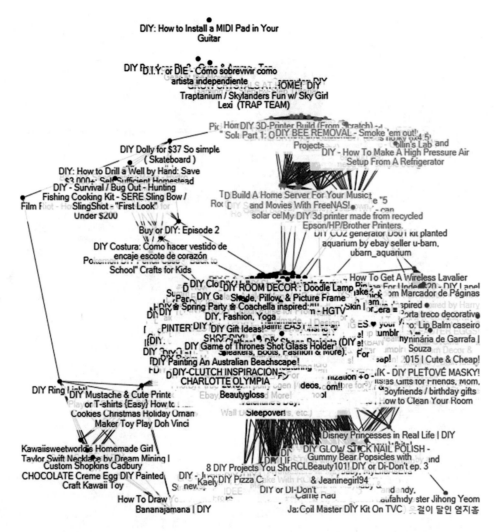

ABCNews was selected after a dozen or so other entities were found to have protected networks. A 1 degree extraction was done, with a listing of those being followed by the ABCNews account. In this case, the other entities may be those that are under the same corporate umbrella. (It should be noted that not all highly public media organizations have their YouTube accounts set so that their user networks may be extracted.) This graph may be seen in Figure 20.

A 1.5 degree network (shown in Figure 21) shows some level of "transitivity" or interrelationship between the alters of the ABCNews outlink network.

A two-degree network may be seen in Figure 22. This shows more complexity and more obvious groupness or clustering.

Figure 20. "ABCNews" user following network on YouTube (1 deg)

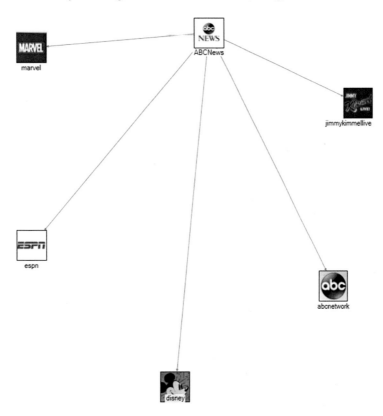

Figure 21. "ABCNews" user following network on YouTube (1.5 deg)

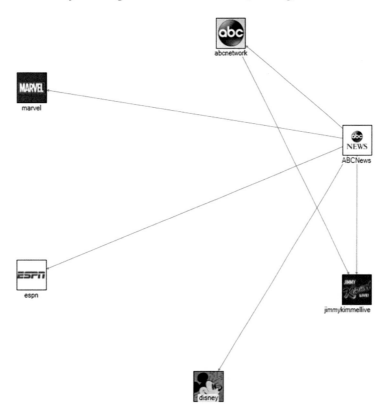

Figure 22. "ABCNews" user following network on YouTube (2 deg)

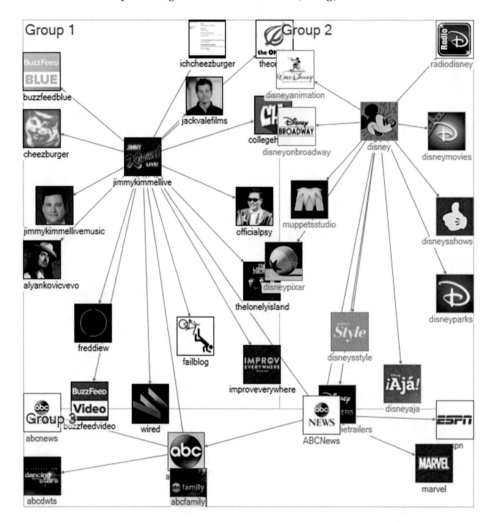

6. GENRES

A genre is a category of artistic expression, such as music, video game, movie, or some other form. This section uses those general categories as a seeding approach, with varying levels of depth. Figure 23 shows a "jazz" video network on YouTube, with 498 vertice sand 69,287 unique edges. The various groups or categories show different gists of the term "jazz": in reference to a basketball team, individuals, events, and the music, among others. The video network is separated into four (4) clusters; for the visualization, one cluster was highlighted (to show the interaction between the data and the graph pane visualization). There are different ways to mix information for multiple modes in the graph, using the Autofill feature. For example, the respective categories of contents may be seen in the edges (lines or links).

Figure 24 represents a video network for a popular massively multiplayer online (MMO) digital game, World of Warcraft. A few years ago, a headline in relation to this game involved a 1.3 million drop in subscribers in a 3-month period (Kenreck, May 9, 2013). The resulting graph contains 495 vertices and

Figure 23. "Jazz" video network on YouTube

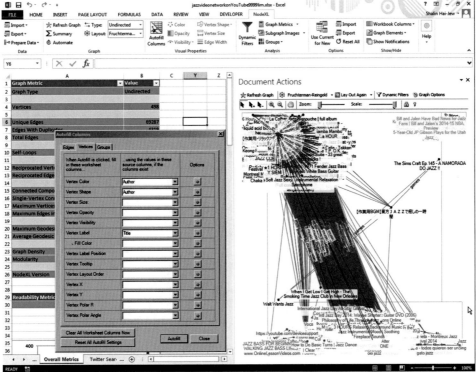

Figure 24. "WorldofWarcraft" video network on YouTube

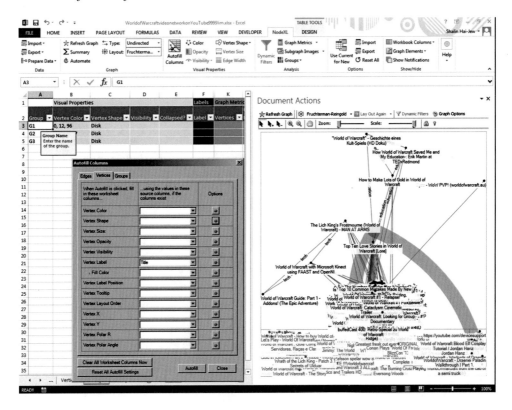

Figure 25. "Anime" video network on YouTube

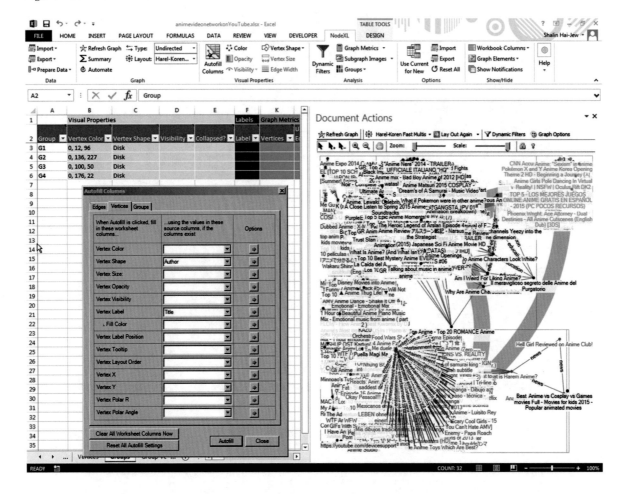

78,939 unique edges, in three (3) groups or clusters. Video titles are represented in the vertices, and category labels are represented in the edges or links.

Finally, in the genre category, a data extraction was done to capture a video network around the term "anime." This network consists of 499 vertices, 32,209 unique edges, and four (4) groups. In terms of categories, there were basic ones, including news, education, and entertainment (see Figure 25).

7. LANGUAGE-SPECIFIC PHENOMENA

Another approach involves video networks based on language-specific queries. To showcase this, the simplified Chinese characters "北京" were used to indicate "Beijing," or the capital city of the People's Republic of China. Not surprisingly, the video network was mostly comprised of Chinese characters. The network is comprised of seven (7) groups. The vertices are listed by titles (see Figure 26).

Figure 26. "北京"video network on YouTube (with titles listed)

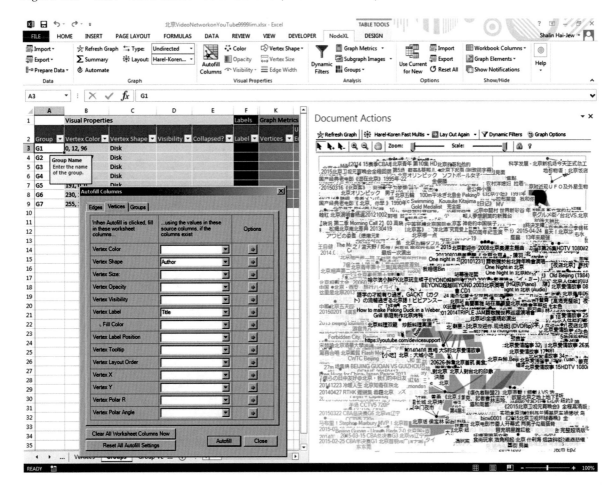

In Figure 27, the 北京 video network uploaders also often went with the simplified Chinese characters although there are some in English as well. The extracted networks would be different using pinyin or "Beijing" or the Wade-Giles system or "Peking." In a sense, it may be understood that the labeling of videos is an indicator for the targeted audiences for that content.

To test this supposition, data extractions of video networks were done for both "Beijing" and "Peking" video networks on YouTube. The resulting graphs are placed side-by-side above. The two networks clearly have differing contents. This may be seen in Figure 28 and Table 1.

Table 1. "Beijing" vs. "Peking" video networks on YouTube (some selective extracted graph metrics)

"Beijing" Video Network Metrics on YouTube	"Peking" Video Network Metrics on YouTube
499 vertices 17,803 unique edges 2.77 average geodesic distance 7 graph diameter	496 vertices 22,251 unique edges 2.71 average geodesic distance 7 graph diameter
8 groups	9 groups

Figure 27. "北京"video network on YouTube (with authors listed)

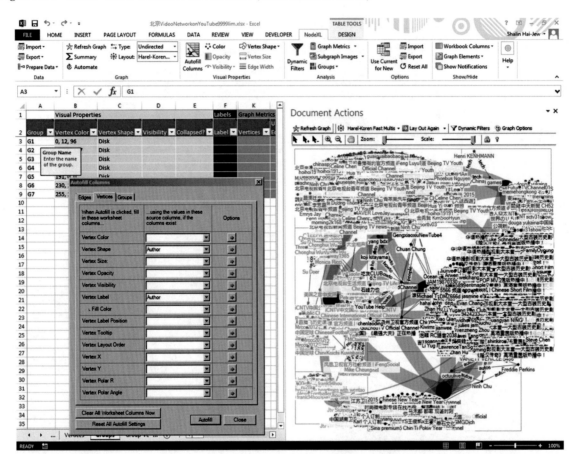

Figure 28. "Beijing" vs. "Peking" video networks on YouTube

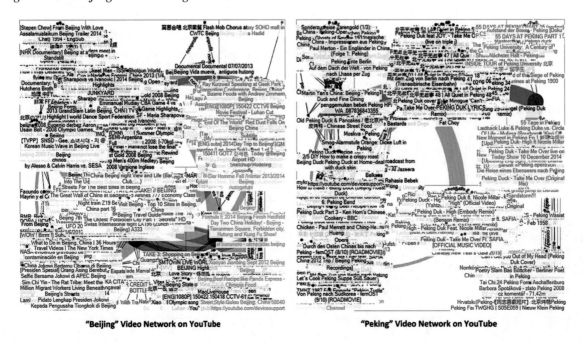

"Beijing" Video Network on YouTube   "Peking" Video Network on YouTube

Figure 29. "Dubai" video network on YouTube (9999 limit)

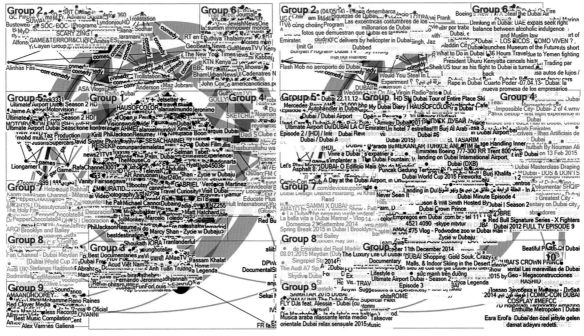

| Vertices Labeled by Author | Vertices Labeled by Title |

8. LOCATION-SPECIFIC PHENOMENA

It is also possible to capture video networks based on location-specific information. For this section, a handful of global cities were selected.

Dubai refers to one of the main cities of the United Arab Emirates (UAE). For the "Dubai" video network graphs in Figure 29, the graph visualizations from the data extractions are depicted in graph format. The graph on the left lists the authors of the videos in the vertices; the graph on the right lists the titles of the videos in the vertices. The ten (10) groups are labeled in the partitions. Some in-depth analysis would result in a topical summary of each group's contents (and maybe identify the main reasons for the clustering). It is also very possible to link the authors with the video contents in the data worksheets. Figure 30 shows the columns with the Title and Author respectively, just under the red arrow.

Hong Kong is another global city. In Figure 31, the Hong Kong video network on YouTube shows videos labeled using multiple languages.

Finally, "NYC" (as an acronym) refers to yet another global city. Nine (9) groups were extracted. The titles of the videos indicate events in the city, crime issues, documentaries and shorts, local locational footage, tours and performances, and ultimately, something of the life of this great city (see Figure 32).

Figure 30. "Dubai" video network data table on YouTube (9999 limit)

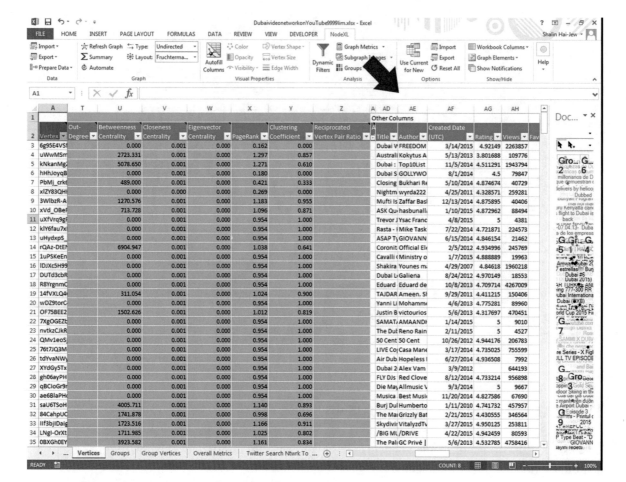

DISCUSSION

The above data extractions and visualizations from YouTube only show some light approaches and applications of this NodeXL tool and network analysis (both user- and video-based) method. While these methods may provide some helpful gists and leads for further analysis, it may help to further (dis) confirm the assertions by extending analyses beyond YouTube and onto other social media platforms and the Surface Web. As YouTube makes other types of data available (such as users' "view histories" and other internal data, for example), more may be ascertainable.

The extraction of "user," "video," and two-mode or multi-mode networks from YouTube using NodeXL provides insights about a variety of topics with a public-facing angle. Some questions that are askable from the respective types of networks include the following:

Figure 31. "Hong Kong" video network on YouTube

A YouTube User Network

- Who is the target user following on YouTube? Who are the "alters" in this ego neighborhood? (1-degree network)
- What is the transitivity between the "alters" in the target user account's ego neighborhood? (1.5-degree network)

Figure 32. "NYC" video network on YouTube

- What is the nature of the ego neighborhoods of the "alters" of the direct members of the ego neighborhood of the target user account on YouTube? What may be understood from the two-degree members of the two-degree network? (2-degree network)
- What are the videos in the videostream for the particular user? What does this content suggest about the nature of the particular YouTube account?

A YouTube Video Network

- What are some of the basic titles linked to a particular video topic on YouTube? A particular location? A particular phenomenon? A particular theme or concept?
- What semantics may be extrapolated from the titling? The commenting?
- What are some of the basic titles linked to a particular YouTube account, and what does this say about the nature of the particular account? The sentiment? The main messages? The stances on particular issues? (based on a disambiguated search based on a particular account name)
- Who are the network members on the user account? (based on a disambiguated search based on a particular account name)
- Which accounts are interacting around a particular topic-based video network? Which of the accounts are the most active in this particular network? (The most prolific in presenting videos? The most prolific in commenting on videos?)
- What are the video (and messaging) contributions of various accounts?

The sample data extractions—about entities, in-world phenomena, imaginary or fictional phenomena, themes (or concepts), reputations, genres, language-specific phenomena, and location-specific phenomena—provides some insights about how this approach may be applied to practical questions. For example, researchers may acquire a "text summarization" gist of particular entities. They may surface insights about in-world events and phenomena—through a sense of gist based on video titles and video title clusters and YouTube "uploaders." Likewise, there may be a capturing of the gist of fictional occurrences. A public sense of themes or concepts may be discovered. Public-facing reputations may be explored. For any of the topics, many of the most active uploaders and communicators may be extracted from the user networks. Personal user networks may be extracted as well to understand who is of interest to a particular social media account on YouTube. It is possible to get a glimpse of YouTube's holdings around particular genres. It is possible to explore a language-focused phenomenon given YouTube's global video holdings and the multi-lingual affordances of users in their annotations and tagging. Also, as demonstrated in this chapter, it is possible to extract information based on locations that are named ones—to gain a sense of the types of video contents surrounding particular regions.

It is possible to extract the main account names of those uploading videos and using other information from the Surface Web to link to the individuals or organizations behind the respective social media accounts. The analysis of social networks on YouTube may enable insights about information exchanged between user accounts and potential alliances dyadically (between two nodes), triadically (between three nodes), and across the network (on YouTube).

The basic description of a two-modal or multi-modal network is that the vertices represent two or more types of objects in a graph. In other words, some of the nodes may represent entities, and other nodes may represent objects. The graphs here cannot be said to fully display such tendencies for co-representation. That said, it is possible to manually create graphs with nodes representing social media user accounts linked to nodes representing videos. (This capability was not fully displayed here.)

- **Exploring Broadly:** It is hard to understand any sort of practical topic on one social media platform alone. While each social media platform may offer particular insights, combined insights offer a fuller sense of the topic and deeper understandings. Such cross-platform explorations may enable deeper insights from each respective social media platform. As suggested in other parts of this chapter, it may be too limiting to look at one social media platform alone, especially given the YouTube-ness of YouTube and the various "nesses" of other social media platforms. There are benefits to researching broadly and across a number of (social media) platforms (which is enabled by NodeXL and other tools) and across the Surface Web.

- **Using Additional Research Tools:** Programmers who can write their own programs to interact with the YouTube APIs may be able to capture a larger amount of data. In such contexts, those who can "roll their own" in the developer lingo may be able to ask different questions of their own uniquely extracted datasets.

- **Using Other Research Methods:** There are benefits to using other research methods than data extractions from a social media platform and then the application of structural network analysis. For example, additional data extractions in this context may include the downloading of some or all of the target videos and their analysis using formalized content analysis approaches. It is possible to explore video networks to understand the gists of the videos by titles and to infer gaps in the provided video information (as a form of gaps analysis).

Finally, it may be helpful to mention that the extracted data highlight a sample of video and user contents which may be examined to understand some aspects of society, social activism, human expression, the social constructions of particular phenomena, regionalisms, culture, or a range of other insights. In a sense, the works will be contingent on various factors (material such as access to video-capture and video-editing equipment; social, such as the sense of social appropriateness of the videotaped communications; legal, such as the openness / closedness of the respective nation-state to having citizen participation with the social media platform, and so on).

FUTURE RESEARCH DIRECTIONS

This approach of mapping "user," "video," and multi-mode networks from YouTube data using NodeXL has potential in surfacing insights about how video networks are being used, who is participating, what cultural uniquenesses there may be in certain societies, whether there is a global culture emergent from social media platforms and the Surface (and Deep / Hidden) Web, how regions and proximity may affect video creation and video consumption, and how collective ideas are socially constructed (in part) from social media.

There is a number of unique and special use cases in terms of how YouTube is (and may be) used to achieve particular endeavors around shared interests and affinities. Linking YouTube videos to broader connections on the Surface and Deep Webs may surface relational connections and identities that may not be visible otherwise. This social video-sharing platform features interactive videos, 3D videos, and other videos that enable higher levels of user interactivity. Exploring these advances may surface additional insights.

CONCLUSION

This chapter introduced the use of NodeXL to extract public data from the YouTube video-sharing social media platform. It introduced some "askable" questions using this software add-on, and an overview of this YouTube-based feature of the NodeXL tool. Various types of data extractions are shared here to give a sense of the breadth of some approaches, including the following:

1. Entities,
2. In-world phenomena,
3. Imaginary phenomena,
4. Themes,
5. Reputations by name,
6. Genres,
7. Language-specific phenomena, and
8. Location-specific phenomena.

ACKNOWLEDGMENT

This chapter has been through a number of iterations. The data extractions, the data processing, and the data visualizations all required a lot of attention, hard work, computational expense, and time. I am grateful to the Social Media Research Foundation (SMRF) for its support of Network Overview, Discovery and Exploration for Excel (NodeXL Basic). Also, I am grateful for Google's YouTube, which makes some of its vast holdings of information available for exploration and research.

To be fully candid, though, the third-party data extraction tool functionality for capturing data from YouTube using NodeXL has not been functioning for over a year at the time of publication. Efforts to bring this to the attention of the SMRF were not successful in achieving a fix. The various technological dependencies to achieve certain research aims are constantly changing, and the environment sometimes feels fragile, particularly in terms of the uses of open-source and free tools, like NodeXL Basic.

REFERENCES

Abisheva, A., Garimella, V. R. K., Garcia, D., & Weber, I. (2014). Who watches (and shares) what on YouTube? And when? Using Twitter to understand YouTube viewership. In *Proceedings of WSDM '14*.

Baluja, S., Seth, R., Sivakumar, D., Jing, Y., Yagnik, J., Kumar, S., . . . Aly, M. (2008). Video suggestion and discovery for YouTube: Taking random walks through the view graph. In *Proceedings of WWW 2008: Industrial Practice and Experience*.

Benevenuto, F., Duarte, F., Rodrigues, T., Almeida, V., Almeida, J., & Ross, K. (2008). Understanding video interactions in YouTube. In *Proceedings of MM '08*. doi:10.1145/1459359.1459480

Benkler, Y. (2006). *The Wealth of Networks: How Social Production Transforms Markets and Freedom*. New Haven, CT: Yale University Press.

Boyd, D. M., & Ellison, N. B. (2008). Social network sites: Definition, history, and scholarship. *Journal of Computer-Mediated Communication*, 210–230.

Brodersen, A., Scellato, S., & Wattenhofer, M. (2012). YouTube around the world: Geographic popularity of videos. In *Proceedings of WWW 2012—Session: Behavioral analysis and Content Characterization in Social Media*.

Bulakh, V., Dunn, C. W., & Gupta, M. (2014). Identifying fraudulently promoted online videos. In *Proceedings of WWW '14*. doi:10.1145/2567948.2578996

Burgess, J., & Green, J. (2009). *YouTube: Online video and participatory culture*. Cambridge, MA: Polity Press.

Cha, M., Kwak, H., Rodriguez, P., Ahn, Y-Y., & Moon, S. (2009). Analyzing the video popularity characteristics of large-scale user generated content systems. *IEEE / ACM Transactions on Networking, 17*(5), 1357 – 1370.

Cheng, X., Fatourechi, M., Ma, X., Zhang, C., Zhang, L., & Liu, J. (2014). Insight data of YouTube from a partner's view. In *Proceedings of NOSSDAV '14*.

Davidson, J., Liebald, B., Liu, J., Nandy, P., & Van Vleet, T. (2010). The YouTube video recommendation system. In *Proceedings of RecSys2010*. doi:10.1145/1864708.1864770

De Choudhury, M., Sundaram, H., John, A., & Seligmann, D. D. (2009). What makes conversations interesting? Themes, participants and consequences of conversations in online social media. In *Proceedings of WWW 2009*.

Deng, Z., Yan, M., Sang, J., & Xu, C. (2014). Twitter is faster: Personalized time-aware video recommendation from Twitter to YouTube. *ACM Transactions on Multimedia Computing, Communications, and Applications, 11*(2), 31:1-31:23.

Ding, Y., Du, Y., Hu, Y., Liu, Z., Wang, L., Ross, K. W., & Ghose, A. (2011). Broadcast yourself: Understanding YouTube uploaders. In *Proceedings of IMC '11*.

Figueiredo, F., Benevenuto, F., & Almeida, J. M. (2011). The Tube over Time: Characterizing popularity growth of YouTube videos. In *Proceedings of WSDM '11*.

Geisler, G., & Burns, S. (2007). Tagging video: Conventions and strategies of the YouTube community. In *Proceedings of JCDL '07*.

Gievska, S., & Koroveshovski, K. (2014). The impact of affective verbal content on predicting personality impressions in YouTube videos. In *Proceedings of WCPR14*. doi:10.1145/2659522.2659529

Kender, J. R., Hill, M. L., Natsev, A., Smith, J. R., & Xie, L. (2010). Video genetics: A case study from YouTube. In *Proceedings of MM'10*. doi:10.1145/1873951.1874198

Kenreck, T. (2013, May 9). In-game: "World of Warcraft" lost 1.3 million subscribers in three months. *MSNBC*. Retrieved April 26, 2015, from http://www.nbcnews.com/video/in-game/51831293/#51831293

Kruitbosch, G., & Nack, F. (2008). Broadcast yourself on YouTube—really? In Proceedings of HCC '08.

Lange, P. G. (2008). Publicly private and privately public: Social networking on YouTube. *Journal of Computer-Mediated Communication, 13*(1), 361–380. doi:10.1111/j.1083-6101.2007.00400.x

Liao, H., McDermott, E., & Senior, A. (2013). Large scale deep neural network acoustic modeling with semi-supervised training data for YouTube video transcription. In *Automatic Speech Recognition and Understanding (ASRU), 2013 IEEE Workshop*. Retrieved March 19, 2015, from http://static.googleuser-content.com/media/research.google.com/en/us/pubs/archive/41403.pdf. 368 – 373.

Morency, L.-P., Mihalcea, R., & Doshi, P. (2011). Towards multimodal sentiment analysis: Harvesting opinions from the Web. In *Proceedings of the ICMI '11*.

Newcomb, A. (2015, Apr. 23). The surprising topic of first YouTube video posted 10 years ago today. *ABC News*. Retrieved Apr. 23, 2015, from http://abcnews.go.com/Technology/surprising-topic-youtube-video-posted-10-years-ago/story?id=30524242

Paolillo, J. C. (2008). Structure and network in the YouTube core. In *Proceedings of the 41st Hawaii International Conference on System Sciences*. doi:10.1109/HICSS.2008.415

Park, N., Jung, Y., & Lee, K. M. (2011). Intention to upload video content on the internet: The role of social norms and ego-involvement. *Computers in Human Behavior, 27*(5), 1996–2004. doi:10.1016/j.chb.2011.05.006

Pinto, H., Almeida, J. M., & Goncalves, M. A. (2013). Using early view patterns to predict the popularity of YouTube videos. In *Proceedings of WSDM '13*. doi:10.1145/2433396.2433443

Rogers, S. P., & Krishnan, K. (2014). Social Platforms. Social Data Analytics: Collaboration for the Enterprise, 75 – 91.

Rotman, D., Golbeck, J., & Preece, J. (2009). The community is where the rapport is—on sense and structure in the YouTube community. In *Proceedings of C&T'09*.

San Pedro, J., Siersdorfer, S., & Sanderson, M. (2011). Content redundancy in YouTube and its application to video tagging. *ACM Transactions on Information Systems, 29*(3). Retrieved March 30, 2015, from http://www.l3s.de/~siersdorfer/sources/2011/TOIS-2011-youtube%28pre-print%29.pdf

Santos, R.L.T., Rocha, B.P.S., Rezende, C.G., & loureiro, A.A.F. (2007). *Characterizing the YouTube video-sharing community*. Retrieved March 22, 2015, from http://homepages.dcc.ufmg.br/~rodrygo/wp-content/papercite-data/pdf/santos2007report.pdf

Schoeffler, M., & Herre, J. (2014). The influence of audio quality on the popularity of music videos: A YouTube case study. In Proceedings of WISMM '14. doi:10.1145/2661714.2661725

Severyn, A., Moschitti, A., Uryupina, O., Plank, B., & Filippova, K. (2015). Multi-lingual opinion mining on YouTube. *Information Processing & Management*. doi:10.1016/j.ipm.2015.03.002

Spathis, P., & Gorcitz, R. A. (2011). A data-driven analysis of YouTube community features. In *Proceedings of AINTEC '11*.

Statistics. (2015). *YouTube*. Retrieved April 13, 2015, from https://www.youtube.com/yt/press/statistics.html

Vu, X. T., Morizet-Mahoudeaux, P., & Abel, M.-H. (2013). Empowering collaborative intelligence by the use of user-centered social network aggregation. In *Proceedings of the 2013 IEEE/WIC/ACM International Conferences on Web Intelligence (WI) and Intelligent Agent Technology (IAT)*. doi:10.1109/WI-IAT.2013.60

Weber, I., Garimella, V. R. K., & Borra, E. (2013). Inferring audience partisanship for YouTube videos. In *Proceedings of WWW 2013*. doi:10.1145/2487788.2487803

Yan, M., Sang, J., & Xu, C. (2014). Mining cross-network association for YouTube video promotion. In *Proceedings of MM'14*. doi:10.1145/2647868.2654920

Yoganarasimhan, H. (2012). Impact of social network structure on content propagation: A study using YouTube data. *Quantitative Marketing and Economics*, *10*(1), 111–150. doi:10.1007/s11129-011-9105-4

YouTube. (2015, Apr. 20). In *Wikipedia*. Retrieved April 23, 2015, from http://en.wikipedia.org/wiki/YouTube

YouTube. (2015). *Logopedia. Wikia*. Retrieved April 14, 2015, from http://logos.wikia.com/wiki/YouTube

Zink, M., Suh, K., Gu, Y., & Kurose, J. (2008). *Watch Global, Cache Local: YouTube Network Traffic at a Campus Network - Measurements and Implications*. Computer Science Department Faculty Publication Series. Paper 177. http://scholarworks.umass.edu/cs_faculty_pubs/177

ADDITIONAL READING

Hansen, D. L., Schneiderman, B., & Smith, M. A. (2011). *Analyzing Social Media Networks with NodeXL: Insights from a Connected World*. Amsterdam: Elsevier.

KEY TERMS AND DEFINITIONS

Application Programming Interface (API): Tools that enable developers to access data from social media platforms.

Content Network: Mapped interrelationships between concepts and contents.

Edge: A link.

Geolocation: The relating of online information to a physical location on Earth.

Multi-Mode Network: A network which contains nodes which represent multiple different types of vertices.

Network Graph: A representation of entities and relationships in a system.

Network Topology: The graphed or mapped representation of entities and (inter)relationships.

Node-Link (Vertex-Edge): The visual representation of an entity and a relationship through a vertex and an edge (a circle and a line, typically).

Profiling: The description of an entity and its characteristics.

Relationship: A connection.

Social Media Platform: An online service that enables people to create profiles and interact with others.

Structure Analysis: The study of interrelationships between entities to understand dynamics; may include interrelationships between contents.

Text Summarization: The capturing of broadscale ideas from texts and text corpuses using a variety of computational approaches (such as text frequency counts, content networks, and others) at machine-scale.

User Network: The ego neighborhood of direct ties to a focal node at 1 degree (and larger networks based on higher levels of degree of ties).

Vertex: A node representing an entity (in a network).

Video Network: The collection of related videos based on the textual descriptions linked to the respective videos.

Videostream: The collection of videos linked to a particular account.

Chapter 10

Flickering Emotions:
Feeling–Based Associations from Related Tags Networks on Flickr

Shalin Hai-Jew
Kansas State University, USA

ABSTRACT

Using the emotion words of Robert Plutchik's "Wheel of Emotions" (based on his multidimensional emotion model) as seeding terms to extract related tags networks (and related thumbnail imagery) from Flickr (at 1 deg., 1.5 deg., and 2 deg.), it is possible to formulate (1) insights about emotions and their interrelationships (through the lens of collective folksonomic tagging), (2) understandings about what the related tags in the networks may suggest about the image item holdings on Flickr, and (3) awareness of the collective mental models of the Flickr users regarding particular emotions, and (4) fresh methods of research to folk tagging through the extraction and analysis of related tags networks and related thumbnail imagery. This chapter introduces this case of analyzing related tags networks to more deeply understand public conceptualizations of emotions through data labels.

INTRODUCTION

A by-the-numbers summary of Flickr shows a social media platform with 112 million users from 63 countries. Since its founding in February 2004, Flickr has amassed some 10 billion shared images and averages about a million photos shared daily. As a social media platform, Flickr hosts some two million groups. A hundred institutions participate in the Flickr Commons digital collection (with a total of 4 million images shared through the Flickr Commons). Flickr users have shared some 53 million tags and nearly a quarter million comments (Smith, Aug. 10, 2015).

Informal tagging by the users who share their digital contents online tends to be egocentric and localized. Such users are generally thinking in a localized and personalized way, and their applied labels (described as "lightweight descriptions") may reflect that mindset. The tagging structures that are extracted from such informal amateur-labeled digital contents are known as folksonomies—or "folk" "taxonomies," as termed by Thomas Vander Wal in 2005. Folksonomies are also known as "social classifications" or

DOI: 10.4018/978-1-5225-0648-5.ch010

"ethnoclassification" or what one author himself calls "communal categorization" (Sturtz, 2004, p. 1). Social tagging has long been seen as a "collaboration tool" (Begelman, Keller, & Smadja, 2006, p. 1) that enables interactive browsing of shared contents.

Broadly speaking, folksonomies consist of users, digital resources, and tags (freeform keywords). These classification hierarchies reflect the organic, bottom-up, and evolving nature of such metadata labels. A "broad folksonomy" is one which has "many people tagging the same object and every person can tag the object with their own tags in their own vocabulary," according to Vander Wal (Feb. 21, 2005). With so many people tagging in a collective way, the tags may be seen to fall into a power law curve (with highly popular terms and many lesser used ones which fall into a long tail), observes Vander Wal. A "narrow folksonomy," by contrast, is one in which objects are tagged by the individual who uploaded the contents and (potentially) others within his or her friend network. This self-indexing was seen as a way to help re-find contents placed on the Web and Internet. Colloquially, this is referred to as "self-tagging" vs. "free-for-all" tagging. The goal of a narrow folksonomy is to help the individual user re-find the object on the Web or Internet and may be more elusive to analyze because of idiosyncratic usage (Vander Wal, Feb. 21, 2005). Auray (2007) sees narrow folksonomies as being "less casual" than broad folksonomies in the labeling of an object, but these features may prove to be its strength, enabling "more open, more random, exploration of content" in the wild (Auray, 2007, p. 74).

'Narrow' folksonomy, however, because it is less casual as regards the attachment of a key word to a piece of content, reveals its strength in finding precise content from a key word search. It is particularly useful when it comes to building databases on content, which cannot be easily found by text-based searches using the standard tools. An indirect advantage is that it allows for the grouping of content on a basis of the co-occurrence of key words within the groups by ascending classification methods 3. A high level of importance is attributed to grouping by Flickr, for example, allowing photographs with a similar content to be tracked down by ascending classification. (Auray, 2007, p. 73)

The folk tags tend to be more "novel" and dynamically "volatile" (Auray, 2007, p. 68). Other researchers highlight the subjectivity of tags as a form of self-expression (Gupta, Li, Yin, & Han, 2011, p. 452). Such collectively-created folk tags also tend to be "noisy," without the professional discipline of a pre-made disambiguated label and data structure. Those created user-generated contents are writing in the vernacular, in the "comfort vocabulary of everyday usage" (Vander Wal, Feb. 21, 2005). With the advent and popularization of social sharing on social media platforms, initially, there were no taxonomies that fully captured the dynamism and lingo of the Web and Internet, with the #hashtagged words, run-together terms, abbreviations, non-words, and other aspects.

Taxonomies (with controlled vs. free-text vocabularies), while authoritative for the respective fields within which they are used, tend to be expensive to create both in terms of human hours and time. Such structured data labels did not actually exist for the freeform data when content sharing sites were popularized. Folksonomies have been compared with selected structured taxonomies of pre-labeled data to understand the differences. Folksonomies have been studied for a variety of applications—such as improving online social media services by understanding users' better by analyzing their tagging streams. There have been automated suggestions for creating candidate tags (keywords) and tag sets for particular digital images. In recent years, computer scientists and programmers have been developing ways to deploy artificial intelligence (AI) to auto-tag multimedia contents, to "recognize" objects in the image frame, and to identify specific people in an image.

Researchers have been developing ways to analyze and use the collected metadata from social media platforms. One approach involves creating related tags networks from "folk" tags that site users apply to the image and short video contents they upload to Yahoo's Flickr. Network analysis has been used to study folksonomies, and typical graph metrics like degree distribution, clustering coefficient, average path length, and other details have been applied to understand tag networks; tag networks have been found to have features of complex small world and scale-free networks (Shen & Wu, 2005).

Related tags networks (in this research) are tags that co-occur in application to respective digital resources. Researchers have used graphs to portray related tags in folksonomies (Papadopoulos, Kompatsiaris, & Vakali, 2010). For example, when a particular photo is uploaded to Flickr, the user may apply up to 75 tags per digital object; those in the user's social network (who have been accepted into the user's social circle on Flickr) may also tag the digital object. On Flickr, the tagging system used is termed "viewable tagging," which means that other users are able to see the tags associated with a particular digital resource (Auray, 2007, p. 84); further, Flickr enables the extraction of related tags linked to any tag through its web-based application programming interfaces (API). As a platform, Flickr has enabled various ways to access their content data and metadata:

Flickr has Flickr clusters, which, provided a popular tag, give related tags grouped into clusters. For example, looking at the clusters for the word Jaguar14, we see that the clusters neatly fall into several semantic categories of Jaguars: animal, car and plane. The hereby presented guidepost is what makes the difference. Clustering makes it possible to present a guidepost, to provide the means that allow the user to explore the information space. In addition, Flickr also has an interestingness exploration technique which they define as a factor of several parameters including the pageviews, the comments left by users, the specific users, etc. (Begelman, Keller, & Smadja, 2006, p. 3)

A related tags network involves the extraction of a particular tag (or seeding /source term) and finding all the other tags that tend to co-occur with it directly (at one degree in the direct "ego neighborhood"), the transitivity between "alters" (nodes directly connected to the target node) in the "ego neighborhood" of the seeding tag (at 1.5 deg), and the broader tag relationships by including the "ego neighborhoods" of the "alters" (2 deg.). The "relationship" in a related tags network can be one of co-occurrence, but there are other types of tag relationship (such as co-reference to a particular person or location or event; semantic relatedness, language origin, and others) as well. Some describe "subsumption-based models" to create hierarchical relationships between tags (Specia & Motta, 2007). One research team identifies three measures of tag relatedness: "tag co-occurrence, cosine similarity of co-occurrence distributions, and FolkRank, an adaptation of the PageRank algorithm to folksonomies" (Cattuto, Benz, Hotho, & Stumme, 2008, p. 1). Another approach involves the identification of denser subgraph clusters within a tag network (Papadopoulos, Kompatsiaris, & Vakali, 2010).

One tool that enables the capturing of related tags networks from Flickr's application programming interface (API) is Network Overview, Discovery and Exploration for Excel (NodeXL Basic), which is a free and open-source add-on to Excel and downloadable from Microsoft's CodePlex site.

To see what may be achieved with analyses of related tags networks from Flickr, Robert Plutchik's "Wheel of Emotions" (1960, 1962, 1965, and 1982) was used to extract tags related to emotions, with the understanding that emotions are a large part of universal human experience. These tags were used as seeding terms for related tags networks at 1, 1.5, and 2 degrees. At each graph size, one network involved only the extraction of the tagged terms, and a second one involved the additional extraction of thumbnail imagery.

Four basic research questions were asked:

1. What may be learned about emotions and their interrelationships through the lens of collective folksonomic tagging based on the Plutchik Wheel of Emotions?
2. What may be understood about the image item holdings on Flickr based on the extracted related tags (as well as those emotion words without any tags)?
3. What may be understood about the collective mental models of Flickr users regarding particular emotions based on the related tags networks?
4. Finally, what are some research capabilities in the analysis related tags networks and the related thumbnail imagery?

A "Review of the Literature" follows, and then a description of the research and initial research findings in "Exploring Senses of Collective Emotions as Embodied in Related Tags Networks on Flickr Contents".

REVIEW OF THE LITERATURE

Emotions are seen as a fundamental aspect of human perception, cognition, and intelligence. A person's state-of-mind is said to affect decision-making as well as performance on certain tasks. A person's level of arousal (such as whether low or high) also affects how an individual interacts with his or her environment, the others in it, and his or her actions. A person's emotional response to information helps them decide how relevant that issue is and how they should respond (Frijda, 1986, as cited in Scherer, 2000, p. 138). Transitory and episodic, emotions are conceptualized broadly as part of the human experience and as a core impetus for human actions. More long-term primary emotions (in varying measures) are seen as part of a person's disposition or personality. Robert Plutchik's three-dimensional model of emotion portrays emotions in concentric circles. In the center are core emotions, and each step out indicates a descending dilution of the core emotion. Each spoke of the wheel (or "blade") is connected by similar semantic meaning. This model is fairly popularly used in computer science. From the eight primary emotions represented in the center—ecstasy, admiration, terror, amazement, grief, loathing, rage, and vigilance, the Plutchik model suggests that personality traits form based on interactive influences between the mixes of primary emotions. For example, ecstasy and admiration become love; admiration and terror become submission; terror and amazement become awe; amazement and grief become disapproval; grief and loathing become remorse; loathing and rage become contempt; rage and vigilance become aggressiveness; vigilance and ecstasy become optimism. Here, the primary emotions in the center are like primary colors which may be mixed to create different shades of emotions and traits (see Figure 1).

Various dimensional psychological models of emotion differentiate between feeling dimensions based on "valence and activation" (Scherer, 2000, p. 151), or direction (positive or negative) and strength of the emotion (intensity). Emotions are not only internal states for individuals but socially affected, with people's emotions transmitting to those around them and moving through social networks. Emotions are thought to affect how people interact, with one individual's emotion-based signaling used to inform others how to behave around him or her.

Figure 1. Robert Plutchik's "Wheel of Emotions"
By Machine Elf 1735, public domain.

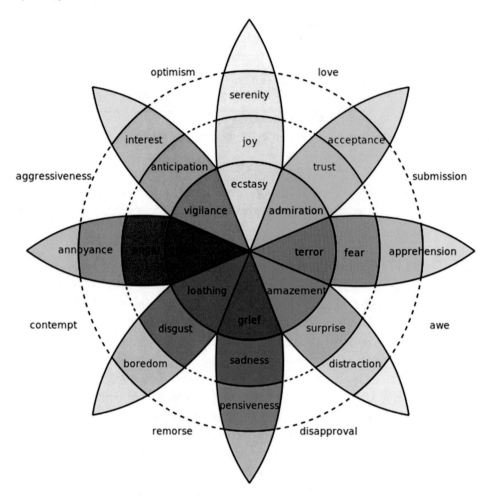

EXPLORING SENSES OF COLLECTIVE EMOTIONS AS EMBODIED IN RELATED TAGS NETWORKS ON FLICKR CONTENTS

On-ground, the tagging inside Flickr may be experienced piecemeal, based on the original digital object. The tag itself may be used to search for other objects that are labeled with that same manual tag. Studying related tags networks based on aspects of the Wheel of Emotions may be understood on various units of analysis. At a base level, each seeding term may be studied as the focal node of its own "ego neighborhood" at the 1, 1.5, and 2 degree networks (see Figure 2).

A single node may also be studied based on its related tags and the related tags thumbnail imagery (see Figure 3).

It is helpful to understand the graphs as data for analysis by zooming in and out from the networks and re-visualizing the underlying data using a range of layout algorithms. Beyond the visuals, there are also the underlying datasets with the linked tags (as text). Also, there are the graph metrics for each of the graphs: the numbers of nodes, the links, the graph diameter, average geodesic distances,

Figure 2. A focal node triptych: "interest" personality trait in the outer rim (1, 1.5, and 2 degrees)

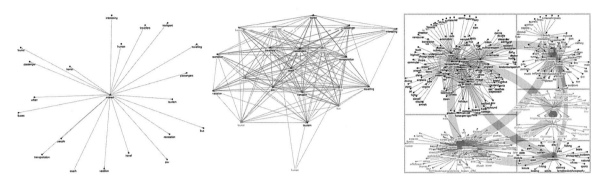

A Focal Node Triptych: "Interest" Personality Trait in the Outer Rim (1, 1.5, and 2 degrees)

Figure 3. A focal node triptych: "interest" personality trait in the outer rim (1, 1.5, and 2 degrees) with thumbnail imagery

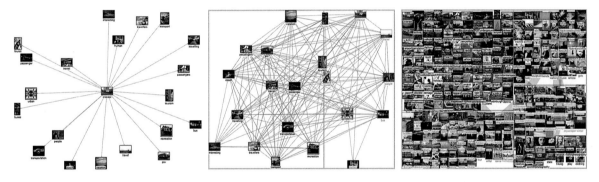

A Focal Node Triptych: "Interest" Personality Trait in the Outer Rim (1, 1.5, and 2 degrees) with Thumbnail Imagery

various types of node centralities, graph densities, and extracted clusters. For these elements to have informational value, it is important to set baseline metrics for related tags networks from Flickr, and as such, no additional elaboration will be added here. Another important point is that there are very few (if any) formalized and generalist models for image content analysis; there are some for specific contexts and use cases. How to approach the analysis of related tags thumbnail imagery from Flickr would be helpful. (It is unclear how the thumbnail images were selected by Flickr, but a particular image represents one or more tags. During this research, the author found one image used in over a half-dozen tags in multiple graphs. Some thumbnail images were so fitting that one might have guessed that there was a human-in-the-loop in the selection of the image; others seem not to relate to the tagging term at all. It is possible that the images selected were initially randomized and then checked by a human. That said, some extracted thumbnail imagery seemed so risqué and potentially offensive especially in some parts of the world that it is hard to imagine that they had human eyes on every thumbnail image. At this point, these are all speculations.)

Some basic questions that may be asked at the node level include the following:

- What are the tags linked to the particular seeding terms? Are there relations between and among the tags? Are there some seeding terms without any tags (like "vigilance" in this particular study)? Are there anomalous tags that may be incisive or insightful?
    - What sorts of physical objects are cited? What non-physical objects are cited?
    - What sorts of other emotions are evoked?
    - What phenomena are mentioned?
    - What events are mentioned?
    - What values are mentioned?
    - What identifiable personas / personalities are there (if any)?
    - What cultural angles may be observed (if any)?
    - What identifiable geographical regionalisms are there (if any)?
    - What languages are used in the tagging?
- Based on what is observed from the texts and the extracted thumbnail images, what are the differences between the text and image sets?
    - How do the images inform the tags? How do the tags inform the imagery?
    - What other semantic senses may be extracted from the thumbnail imagery?
    - Are there understood moods from the imagery?
    - What sorts of informational value is there in the imagery?
- What are the sentiments (if extractable) in the respective extracted text sets?
- What are similarities between the degree networks (1, 1.5, and 2 degrees)? What are the dissimilarities?
- How do the one-degree, 1.5 degree, and 2 degree networks differ based on a particular seeding term?
- What may be seen in terms of the respective tag clusters?

The initial research approach here is based on the "Wheel of Emotions" depiction. The columnar approach in Table 1 shows a focus on the different layers of the concentric circles, from the primary emotions outwards towards the personality traits layer. The rows represent the "spokes" or the "blades" of the emotions, with diminishing emotional intensity in the outer edges. Each of the blades (rows) are conceptualized as related.

Figure 4 depicts an analysis of the eight emotions in the inner core as one-degree related tags networks, with related datasets, for analysis. It would be possible to analyze the inner core, Tier 2, Tier 3, and the outer rim to see what differences there may be.

- Are there differences in intensity between those in the inner core (the first word) and those further out from the core?

Another approach involves the different emotion-based spokes or blades. The various blades are understood to have intensity in the core and diminishing concentration or force as one moves to the outer rim in the Plutchik Wheel of Emotions. It would be beneficial to analyze each of the eight spokes or blades as follows:

Table 1. Reconfiguring the "Wheel of Emotions" into separate related "blades"

	Inner Core (Primary Emotions)	Tier 2	Tier 3	Outer Rim (Personality Traits Layer)	
Wheel Spoke / Blade 1	Ecstasy	Joy	Serenity	love	
Wheel Spoke / Blade 2	Admiration	Trust	Acceptance		submission
Wheel Spoke / Blade 3	Terror	Fear	Apprehension	awe	
Wheel Spoke / Blade 4	Amazement	Surprise	Distraction		disapproval
Wheel Spoke / Blade 5	Grief	Sadness	Pensiveness	remorse	
Wheel Spoke / Blade 6	Loathing	Disgust	Boredom		contempt
Wheel Spoke / Blade 7	Rage	Anger	Annoyance	aggressiveness (aggression)	
Wheel Spoke / Blade 8	Vigilance	Anticipation	Interest		optimism
			Serenity (continued from Blade 1		

1. Ecstasy/joy/serenity,
2. Admiration/trust/acceptance,
3. Terror/fear/apprehension,
4. Amazement/surprise/distraction,
5. Grief/sadness/pensiveness,
6. Loathing/disgust/boredom,
7. Rage/anger/annoyance,
8. Vigilance/anticipation/interest.

Figure 5 shows the "Amazement, Surprise, and Distraction" blade, with related tags network graphs at one degree. The same thing may be done for the 1.5 degree networks and the 2 degree networks.

The same thing may be done for each emotion blade at the 1.5-degree and 2-degree networks levels. This should also be followed through with the graphs with thumbnail imagery.

In moving from local to global details, it may also help to analyze the entire graph—representing all the related tags networks and related thumbnail imagery based on the Plutchik's Wheel of Emotions.

- For example, which parts of the Wheel of Emotions had more terms, and what were those terms?
- Are there certain related tags which should be "nulled" in a tag set, such as the generic ones that include camera technologies (unrelated to the seeding focal tag) and recurring descriptors like blackandwhite?
- What were the related tags thumbnail images? What were the gists of the imagery?
- How well did the tags and images line up with a psychological understanding of emotions per Plutchik's model and Wheel of Emotions?

Figure 4. Related tags networks (1 deg.) of the inner core emotions

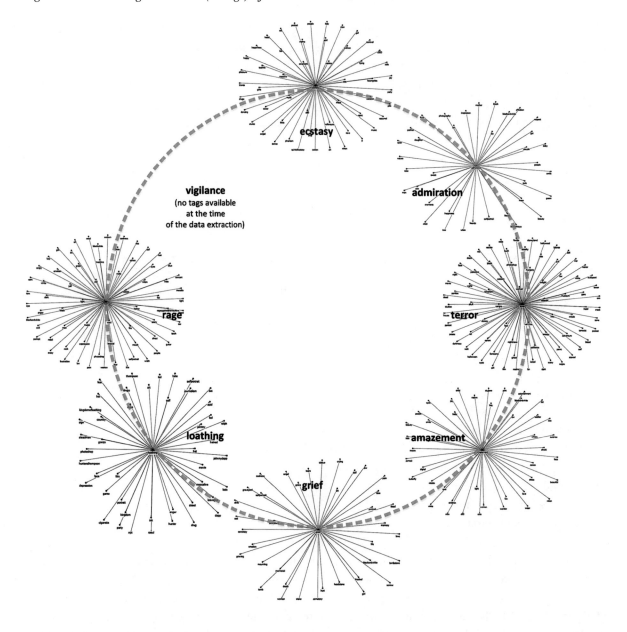

This initial "proof of concept" approach involved the extraction of three related tags network graphs for each seeding term (of which there were 32, 8 in each concentric circle of the Wheel of Emotions model), for a total of 96. Each data extraction is dependent on the local computer's connectivity to the Internet, its data processing speed, the performance of NodeXL (also with its limited degrees of 1, 1.5, and 2), the responsiveness of the Flickr API, and so on. Related tags networks from narrow folksonomies, in practice, tend to be sparse, with fewer co-occurring tags that appear in the small tag sets with each digital item. As compared to other types of networks from social media platforms (like those from microblogging sites), related tags networks tend to be relatively stable. Some related tags networks on Flickr remain virtually unchanged for a year or longer, as observed by this author. The focal tags tend to

Figure 5. Amazement, surprise, distraction emotion "blade" in one-degree related tags networks

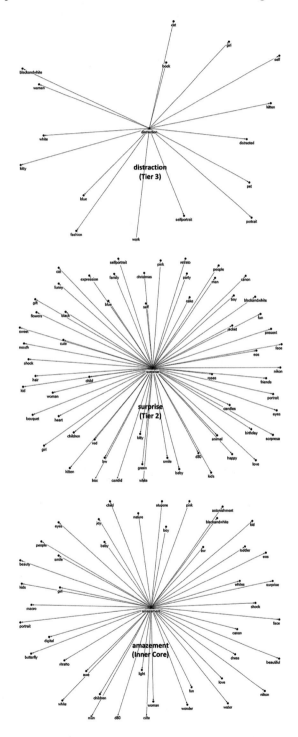

be case sensitive. Some terms from the model ("pensiveness" and "aggressiveness") did not have verbatim equivalents, so other word forms from the base one had to be substituted in. In terms of "vigilance," there was not a direct word form version that returned any related tags.

Each extracted related tags network dataset had to have data processed for graph metrics and for clustering (Clauset-Newman-Moore clustering algorithm, for all these graphs). Multiple graphs had to be visualized for each dataset for optimal clarity and readability. In addition, there had to be visualizations with the thumbnail images extracted and presented. The data visualizations in this chapter, of course, had to be created using a mixture of Adobe Photoshop and Microsoft Visio. Work combining datasets for each of the concentric circles and emotion blades would require additional data processing and human- and computer-based work.

DISCUSSION

It is important to revisit the initial four questions in order to see what was actually knowable about these.

1. What may be learned about emotions and their interrelationships through the lens of collective folksonomic tagging based on the Plutchik Wheel of Emotions?
2. What may be understood about the image item holdings on Flickr based on the extracted related tags (as well as those emotion words without any tags)?
3. What may be understood about the collective mental models of Flickr users regarding particular emotions based on the related tags networks?
4. Finally, what are some research capabilities in the analysis related tags networks and the related thumbnail imagery?

In terms of direct learning about emotions and their interrelationships, the extracted related tags networks did suggest some ways emotions instantiate through shared contents on Flickr. For example, the "submission" (from this outer rim) related tags network at one degree showed tags linked to bondage, mixed martial arts, MMA fighters, BDSM, fighting, socks, boots, latex, and designs and contests.

To question 2, the related tags are suggestive of what is not mentioned in the Flickr tags related to a particular word. This work suggests that people share a lot of language and meanings, and it may be that if a tag should be suggestive of certain contents but do not show those contents, that certain types of contents may not have been shared on the Flickr content sharing site (or that they were tagged with other terms).

As to the third question, the "collective mental models" of Flickr uses do show certain cultural tendencies and connections that might be indicative of certain points-of-view or cultural contexts.

Fourth, some of the research capabilities of this approach may be farther reaching that what this initial work might suggest. This chapter showed some basic inferences that may be made but did not offer huge depth of insights. Of course, the author purposefully stopped short since this work is about a fresh approach and not about an actual exploration of the Plutchik Wheel of Emotions or his model. To do a full-fledged analysis would require more analysis of the model and then more analytical work of the related tags networks and the related thumbnail imagery. While much data were captured, and some observations were made, these are highly preliminary.

FUTURE RESEARCH DIRECTIONS

One observation that is generally supportable is that related tags networks, applied in this context, may offer various types of inferences and suggestions but not definitive research without additional in-depth analysis. After all, what is directly shared are contents (the images), metadata (the tags), and trace data (commenting and interactivity around the image contents. Tags are somewhat indirect and "noisy," with tags that may be batch-applied or not directly related to the specific image contents of a particular image.

It may help to collect a full image set of images linked to a particular focal tag and to analyze that image set systematically. The tags may also be studied. Also, the communications around the social media accounts interacting around a particular focal tag, its imagery, its co-occurring tags, and such, may be analyzed. If there are inferences made about digital image item holdings on Flickr, there should be ways to test and possibly verify.

Also, it may help to acquire full tag sets instead of just those in the related tags networks. There are machine-based ways to extend the usability of related tags network data, such as broadly available sentiment analysis tools, emotion analysis tools, semantic relatedness analysis tools, and others. For example, do co-occurring tags signal particular sentiments (positive or negative)? Particular emotions? Certain types of meaning-based relationships?

Also, there may be interest in looking at the embodiment of emotions on social media platforms—based on various types of given information. It may be helpful to set a baseline of the roles of emotions on social media platforms broadly speaking and then more specially on image-sharing platforms. Also, researchers may be interested in looking at the issue of the changing expressions of related emotions over time on the Flickr platform along with the differing tag evocations linked to those emotions.

CONCLUSION

Using the emotion words of Robert Plutchik's "Wheel of Emotions" (based on his multidimensional emotion model) as seeding terms to extract related tags networks (and related thumbnail imagery) from Flickr (at 1 deg., 1.5 deg., and 2 deg.), it is possible to formulate (1) insights about emotions and their interrelationships (through the lens of collective folksonomic tagging), (2) understandings about what the related tags in the networks may suggest about the image item holdings on Flickr, and (3) awareness of the collective mental models of the Flickr users regarding particular emotions, and (4) fresh methods of research to folk tagging through the extraction and analysis of related tags networks and related thumbnail imagery. This chapter introduces this case of analyzing related tags networks to more deeply understand public conceptualizations of emotions through data labels.

ACKNOWLEDGMENT

I am grateful to the peer reviewers who critiqued this work and through their insights made it better.

REFERENCES

Auray, N. (2007). Folksonomy: The new way to serendipity. *Communications & Stratégies, 65*, 67–89.

Begelman, G., Keller, P., & Smadja, F. (2006). Automated tag clustering: Improving search and exploration in the tag space. In *Proceedings of the WWW 2006*.

Cattuto, C., Benz, D., Hotho, A., & Stumme, G. (2008). *Semantic analysis of tag similarity measures in collaborative tagging systems.* arXiv:0805.2045v1

Gupta, M., Li, R., Yin, Z., & Han, J. (2011). An overview of social tagging and applications. *Social Network Data Analytics, 447 – 497.*

Machine Elf 1735. (2011, Feb. 12). *Robert Plutchik's Wheel of Emotions.* Retrieved November 8, 2015, from https://commons.wikimedia.org/wiki/File:Plutchik-wheel.svg

Papadopoulos, S., Kompatsiaris, I., & Vakali, A. (2010). *A graph-based clustering scheme for identifying related tags in folksonomies.* Academic Press.

Scherer, K. R. (2000). Psychological models of emotion. New York: Oxford University Press.

Shen, K., & Wu, L. (2005). *Folksonomy as a complex network.* arXiv:cs/0509072v1

Smith, C. (2015, Aug. 10). *By the numbers: 14 interesting Flickr stats.* Digital Marketing Stats / Strategy / Gadgets. Retrieved Nov. 10, 2015, from http://expandedramblings.com/index.php/flickr-stats/

Specia, L., & Motta, E. (2007). Integrating folksonomies with the Semantic Web. In E. Franconi, M. Kifer, & W. May (Eds.), *The Semantic Web: Research and Applications. 4th European Semantic Web Conference, ESWC 2007.* Springer. doi:10.1007/978-3-540-72667-8_44

Sturtz, D.N. (2004, Dec.). *Communal categorization: The folksonomy.* INFO622. Content Representation.

Vander Wal, T. (2005). Folksonomy. In Proceedings of Online Information 2005.

Vander Wal, T. (2005, Feb. 21). *Explaining and showing broad and narrow folksonomies.* Retrieved Nov. 9, 2015, from http://www.vanderwal.net/random/entrysel.php?blog=1635

KEY TERMS AND DEFINITIONS

Clustering: The bringing together of data points with similar numerical values.

Folk: Relating to common people.

Folksonomy: A data structure consisting of informally applied tags or keywords applied to digital resources.

Related Tags Network: A network graph showing various types of interrelationships between tags used to describe digital objects.

Seeding Term (Source Term): A target keyword used to extract a related tags network.

Tag: A free-form keyword.

Taxonomy: A formalized classification data structure.

User-Generated Contents (UGC): The various types of digital files and information that are created by the broad public and shared broadly through social media platforms.

APPENDIX

The appendices here contain six-packs of graphs. The top two graphs in each are 1degree (with the right graph inclusive of thumbnail graphs). The middle two graphs are 1.5 degrees. The bottom two graphs are two degrees. For the 1.5 and 2-degree graphs, some of them are "partitioned" into their respective groups for easier identification of the groups. In some cases where thumbnail images are included in the graph, those are laid out in grid form for less overlap between the graph nodes (for readability of the label and viewing of the thumbnail image). The graphs are presented in the following order:

1. Inner Core (Primary Emotions): ecstasy, admiration, terror, amazement, grief, loathing, rage, and vigilance (no tags).
2. Second Tier: joy, trust, fear, surprise, sadness, disgust, anger, and anticipation.
3. Third Tier: serenity, acceptance, apprehension, distraction, pensiveness ("pensive"), boredom, annoyance, and interest.
4. Outer Rim (personality trait layer): love, submission, awe, disapproval, remorse, contempt, aggressiveness ("aggression"), and optimism.

INNER CORE

Figure 6. Inner core: "ecstasy" related tags networks on Flickr (1, 1.5, to 2 degree networks, without and with linked thumbnail imagery)

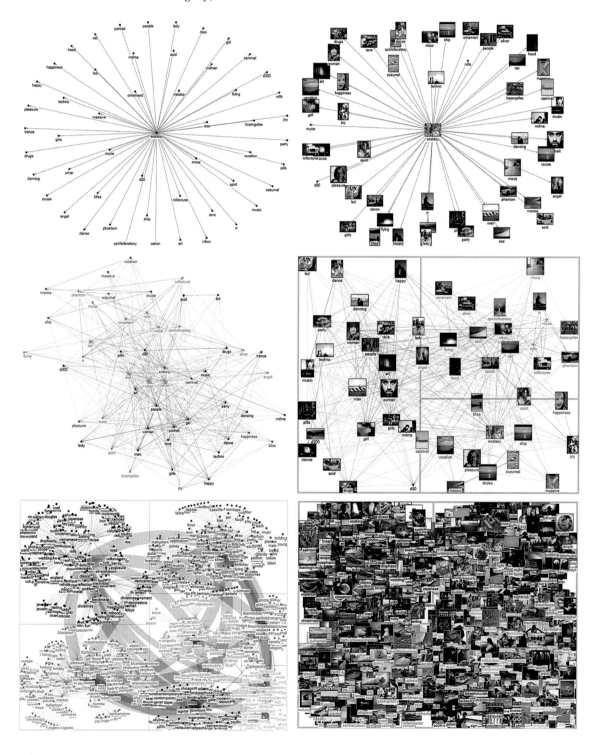

Figure 7. Inner core: "admiration" related tags networks on Flickr (1, 1.5, to 2 degree networks, without and with linked thumbnail imagery)

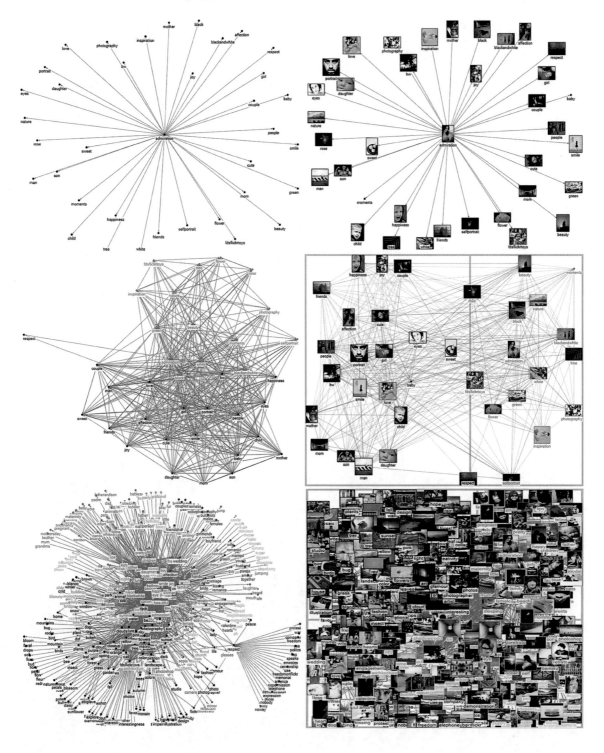

Figure 8. Inner core: "terror" related tags networks on Flickr (1, 1.5, to 2 degree networks, without and with linked thumbnail imagery)

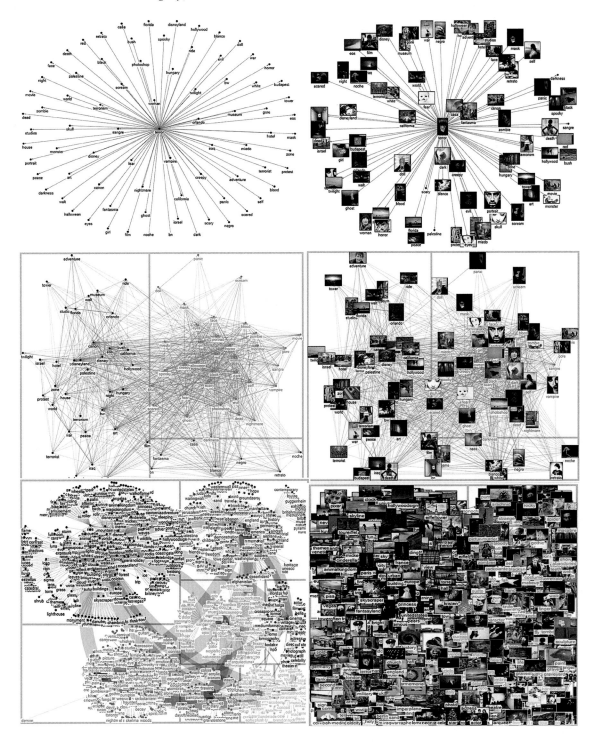

Figure 9. Inner core: "amazement" related tags networks on Flickr (1, 1.5, to 2 degree networks, without and with linked thumbnail imagery)

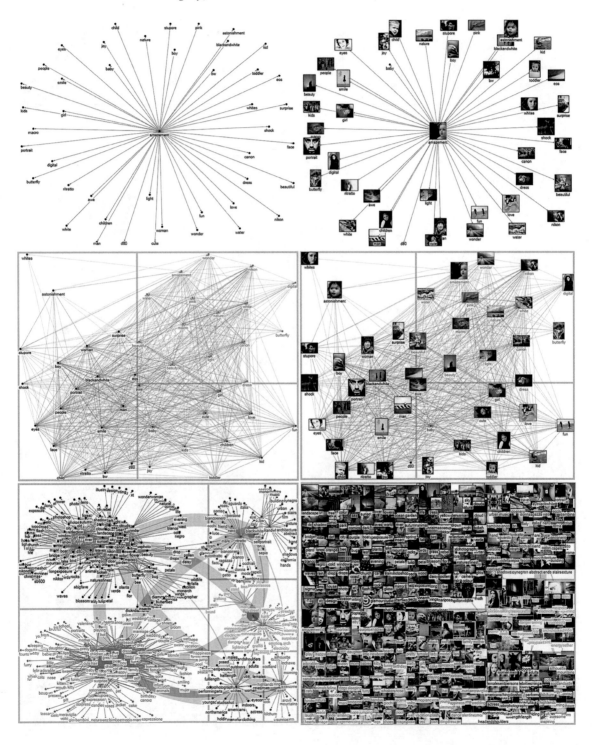

Figure 10. Inner core: "grief" related tags networks on Flickr (1, 1.5, to 2 degree networks, without and with linked thumbnail imagery)

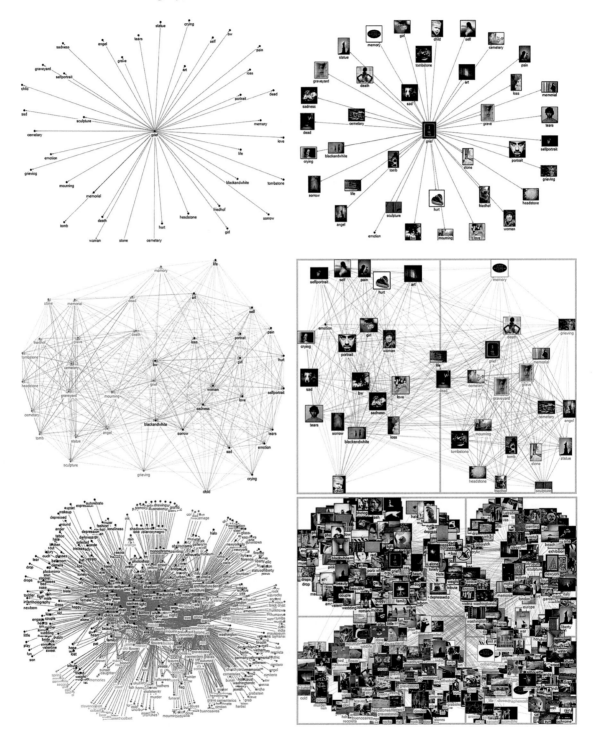

Figure 11. Inner core: "loathing" related tags networks on Flickr (1, 1.5, to 2 degree networks, without and with linked thumbnail imagery)

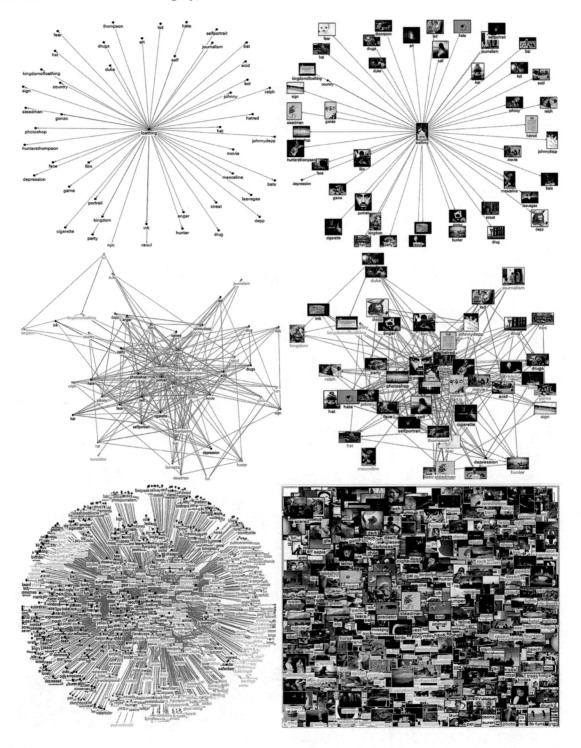

Figure 12. Inner core: "rage" related tags networks on Flickr (1, 1.5, to 2 degree networks, without and with linked thumbnail imagery)

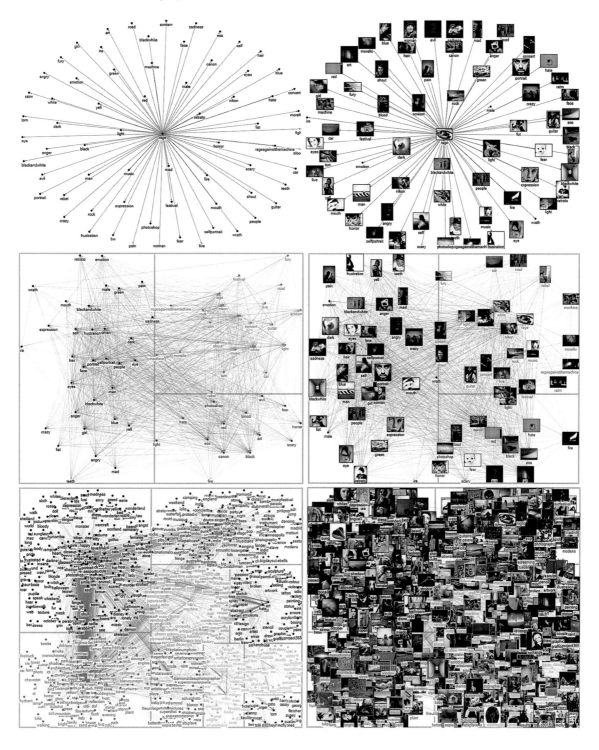

SECOND TIER

Figure 13. Second tier: "Joy" related tags networks on Flickr (1, 1.5, to 2 degree networks, without and with linked thumbnail imagery)

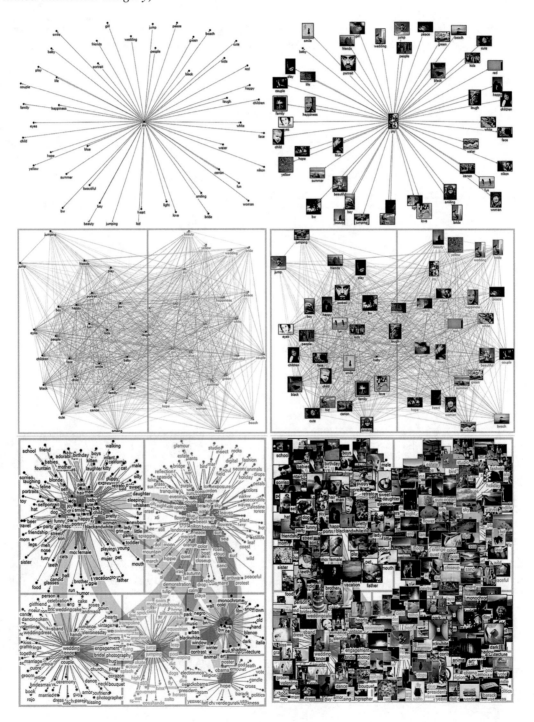

Figure 14. Second tier: "trust" related tags networks on Flickr (1, 1.5, to 2 degree networks, without and with linked thumbnail imagery)

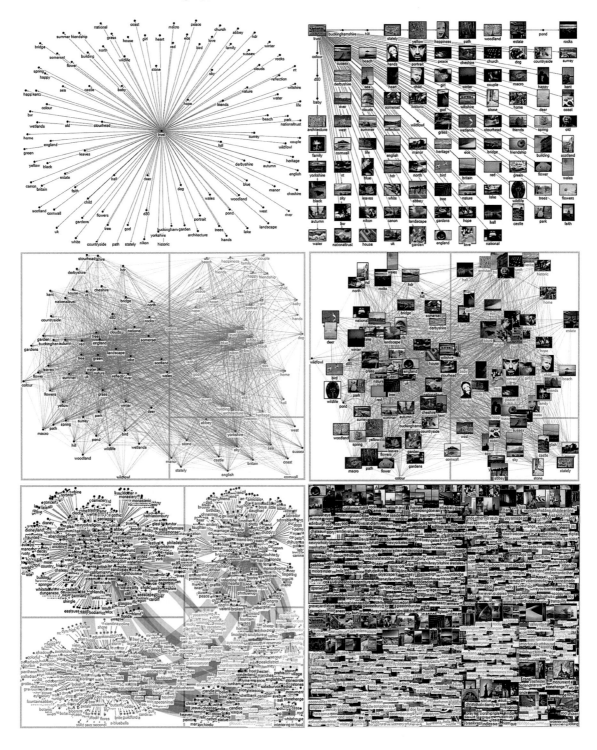

Figure 15. Second tier: "fear" related tags networks on Flickr (1, 1.5, to 2 degree networks, without and with linked thumbnail imagery)

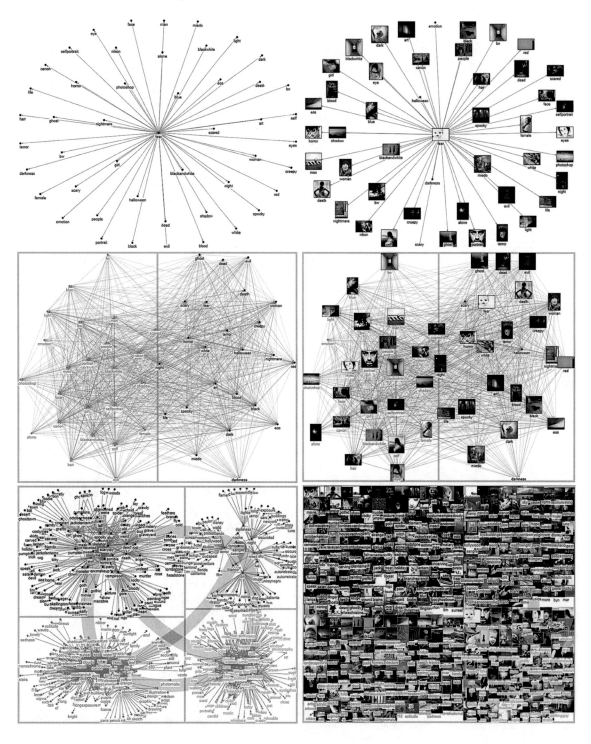

Figure 16. Second tier: "surprise" related tags networks on Flickr (1, 1.5, to 2 degree networks, without and with linked thumbnail imagery)

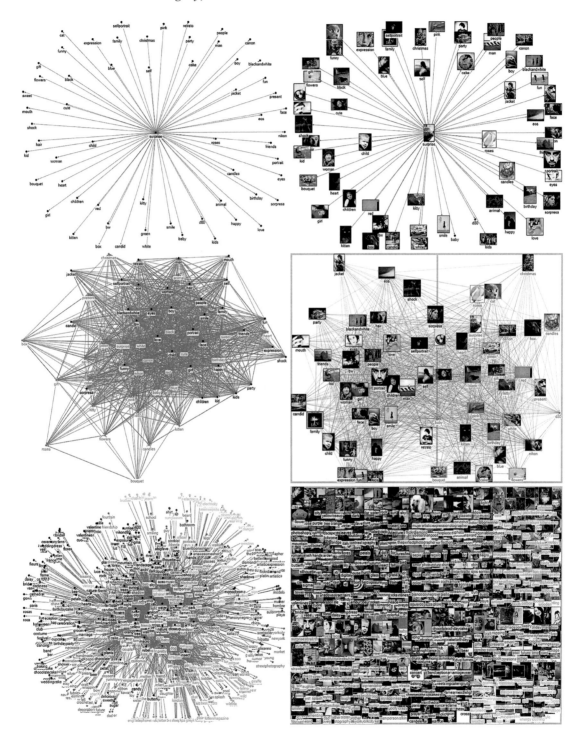

Figure 17. Second tier: "sadness" related tags networks on Flickr (1, 1.5, to 2 degree networks, without and with linked thumbnail imagery)

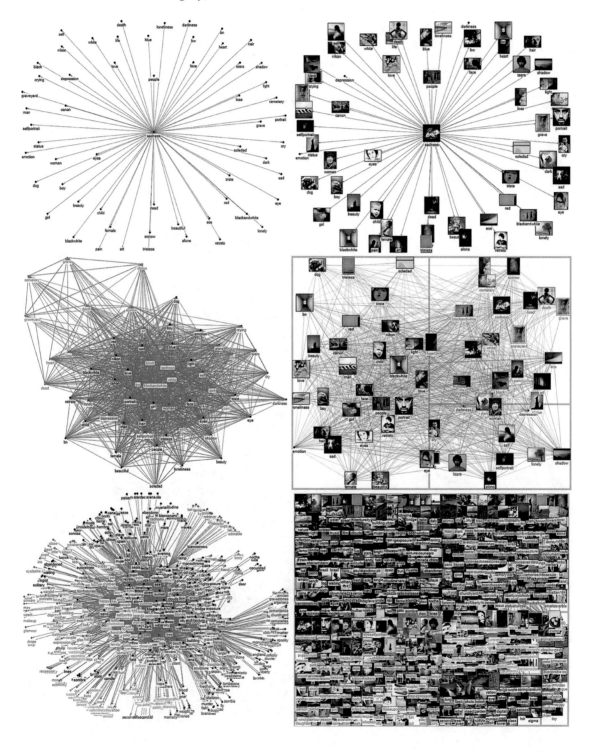

Figure 18. Second tier: "disgust" related tags networks on Flickr (1, 1.5, to 2 degree networks, without and with linked thumbnail imagery)

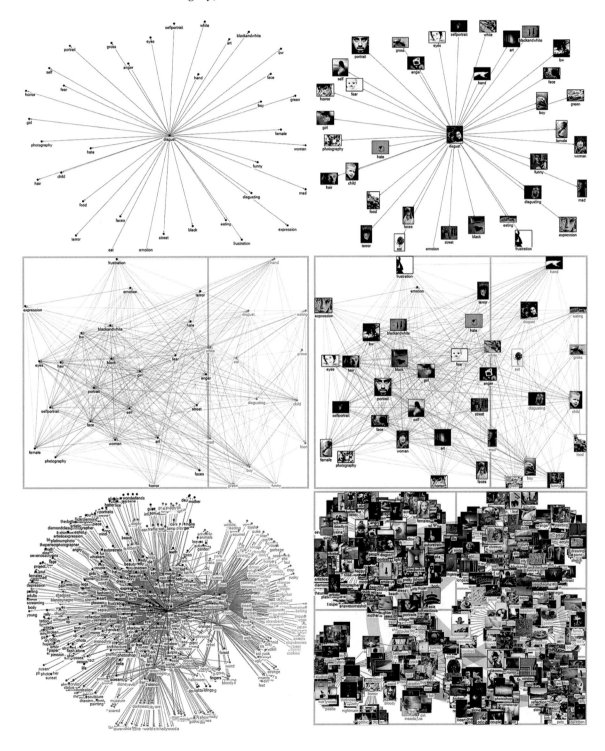

Figure 19. Second tier: "anger" related tags networks on Flickr (1, 1.5, to 2 degree networks, without and with linked thumbnail imagery)

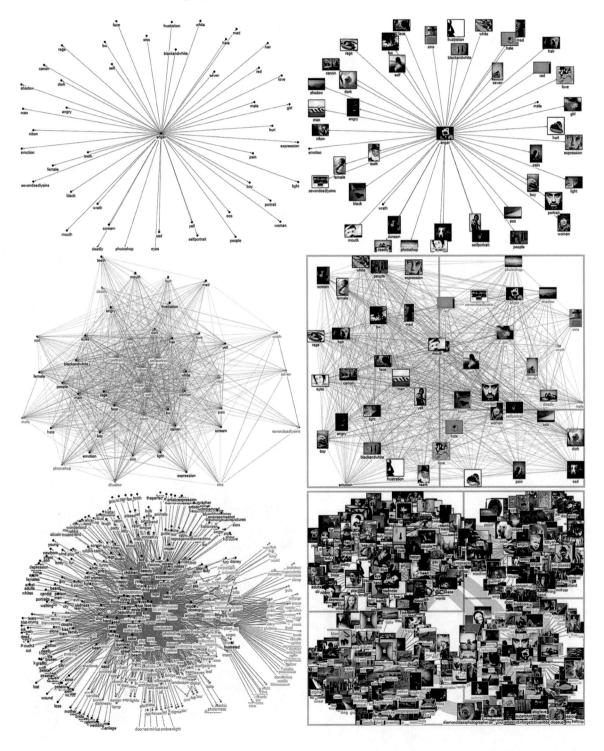

Figure 20. Second tier: "anticipation" related tags networks on Flickr (1, 1.5, to 2 degree networks, without and with linked thumbnail imagery)

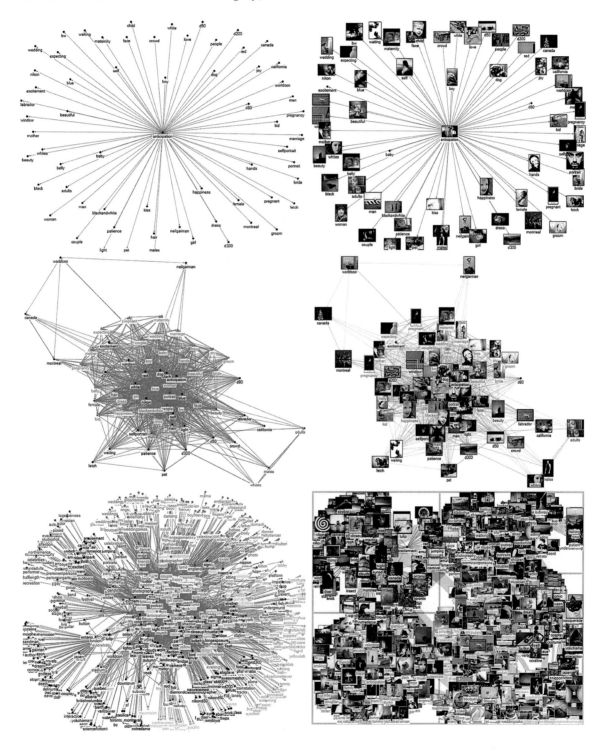

THIRD TIER

Figure 21. Third tier: "serenity" related tags networks on Flickr (1, 1.5, to 2 degree networks, without and with linked thumbnail imagery)

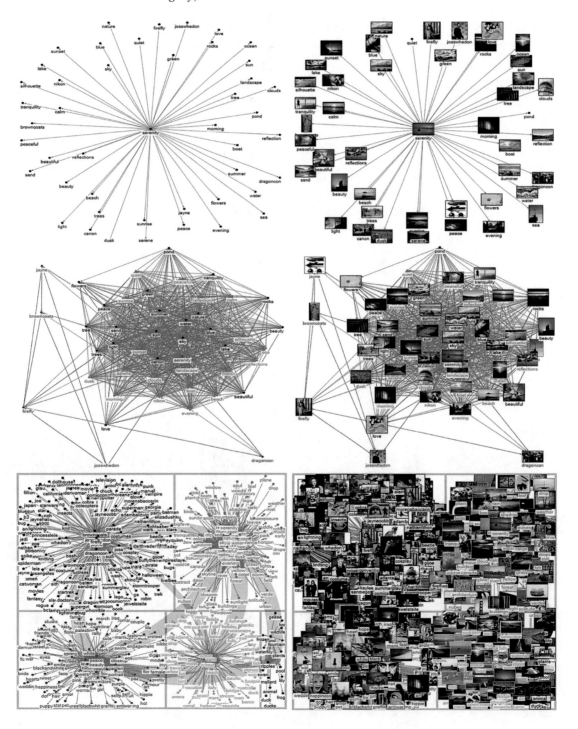

Figure 22. Third tier: "acceptance" related tags networks on Flickr (1, 1.5, to 2 degree networks, without and with linked thumbnail imagery)

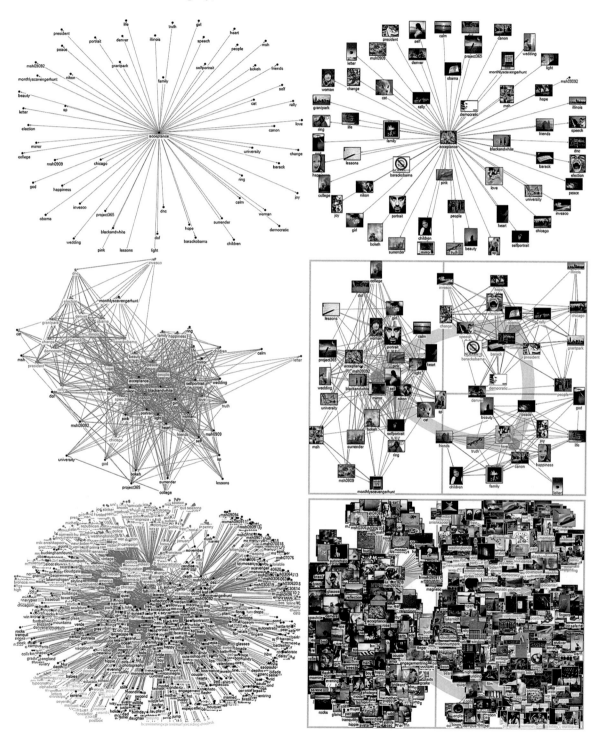

Figure 23. Third tier: "apprehension" related tags networks on Flickr (1, 1.5, to 2 degree networks, without and with linked thumbnail imagery)

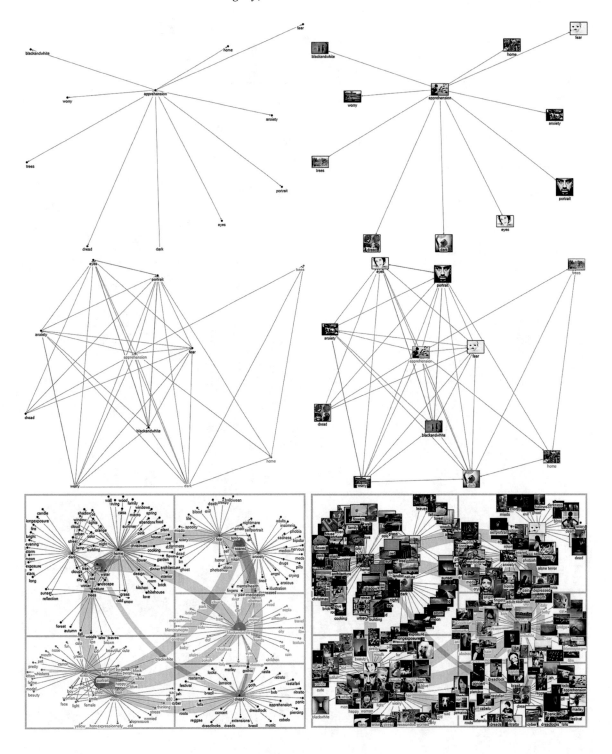

Figure 24. Third tier: "distraction" related tags networks on Flickr (1, 1.5, to 2 degree networks, without and with linked thumbnail imagery)

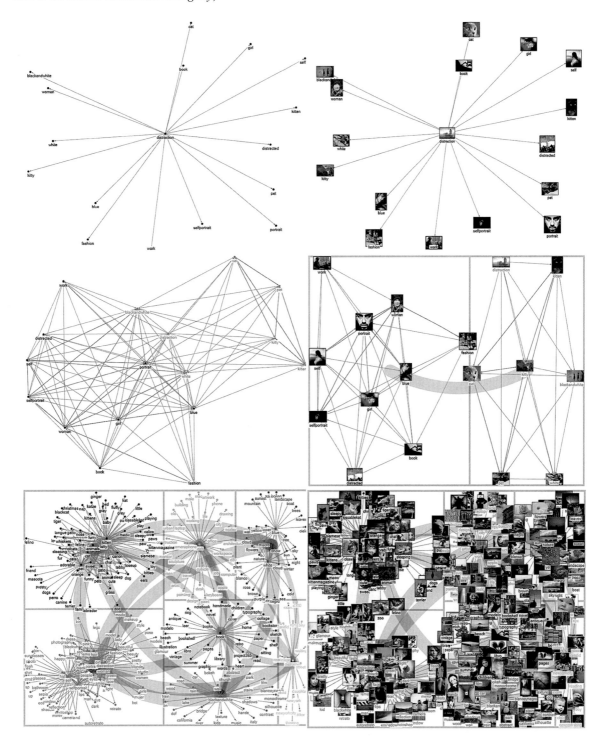

Figure 25. Third tier: "pensive" related tags networks on Flickr (1, 1.5, to 2 degree networks, without and with linked thumbnail imagery)

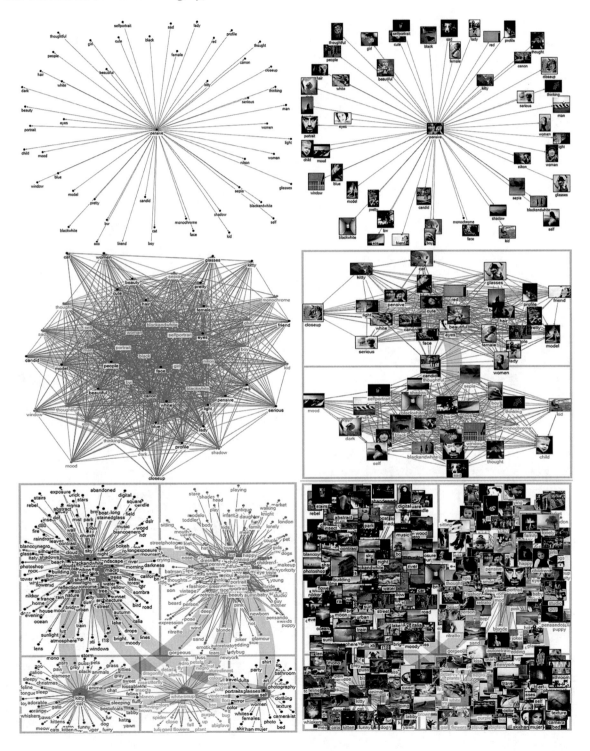

Figure 26. Third tier: "boredom" related tags networks on Flickr (1, 1.5, to 2 degree networks, without and with linked thumbnail imagery)

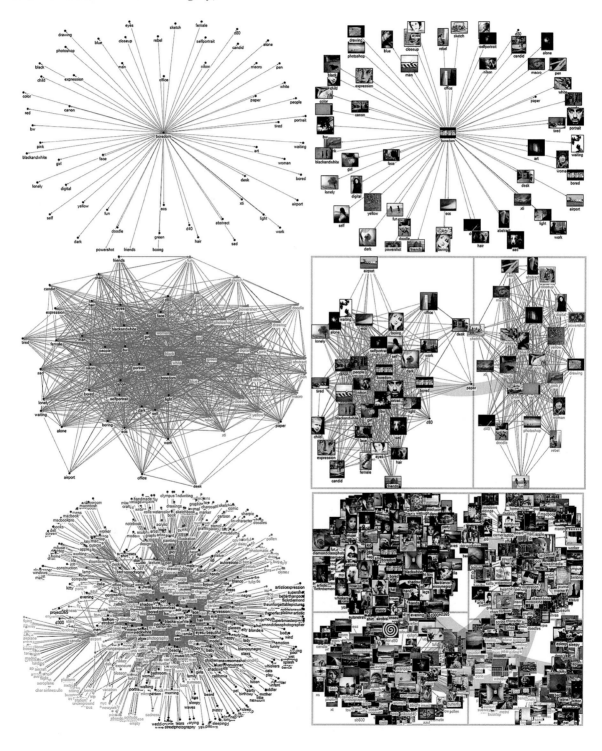

Figure 27. Third" tier: "annoyance related tags networks on Flickr (1, 1.5, to 2 degree networks, without and with linked thumbnail imagery)

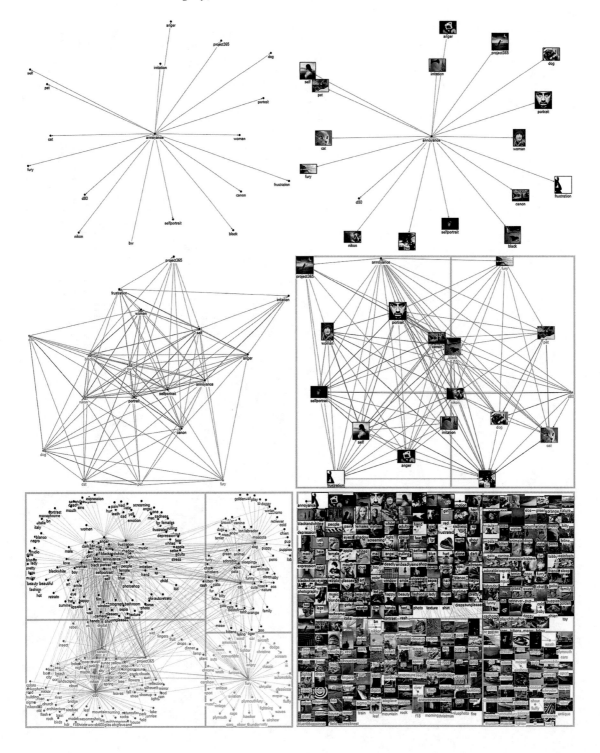

Figure 28. Third tier: "interest" related tags networks on Flickr (1, 1.5, to 2 degree networks, without and with linked thumbnail imagery)

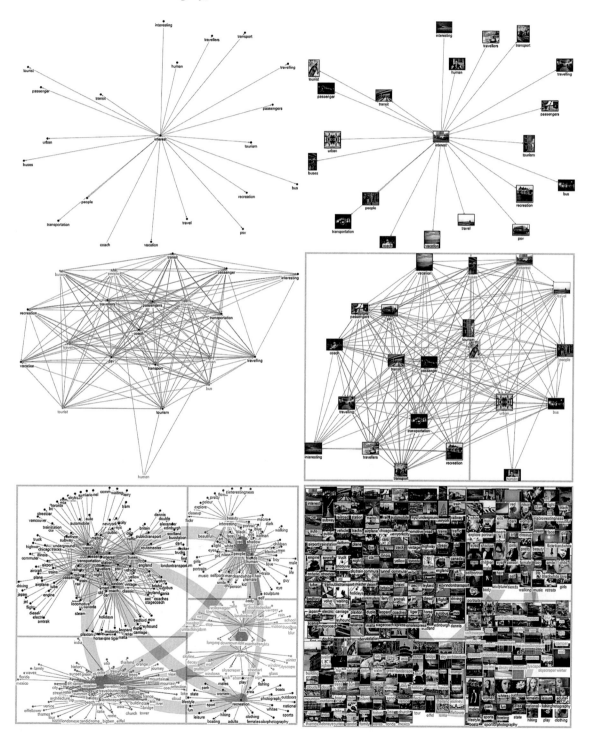

OUTER RIM

Figure 29. Outer rim: "love" related tags networks on Flickr (1, 1.5, to 2 degree networks, without and with linked thumbnail imagery)

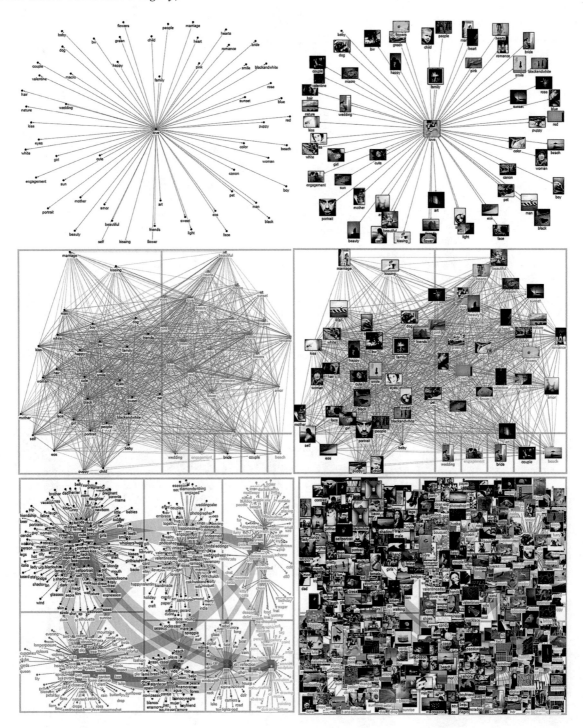

Figure 30. Outer rim: "submission" related tags networks on Flickr (1, 1.5, to 2 degree networks, without and with linked thumbnail imagery)

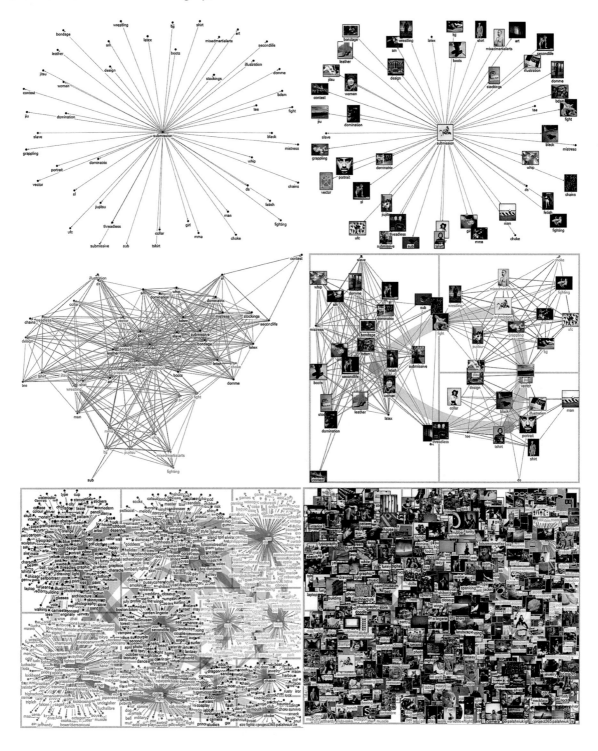

Figure 31. Outer rim: "awe" related tags networks on Flickr (1, 1.5, to 2 degree networks, without and with linked thumbnail imagery)

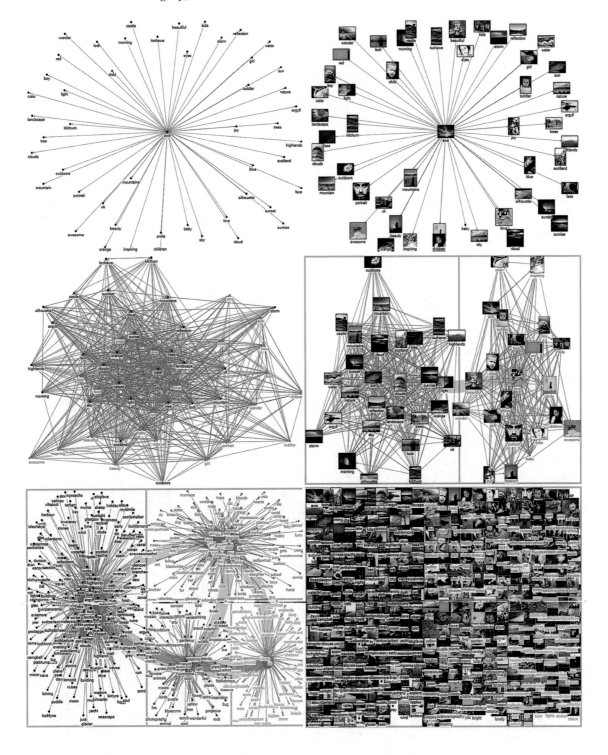

Figure 32. Outer rim: "disapproval" related tags networks on Flickr (1, 1.5, to 2 degree networks, without and with linked thumbnail imagery)

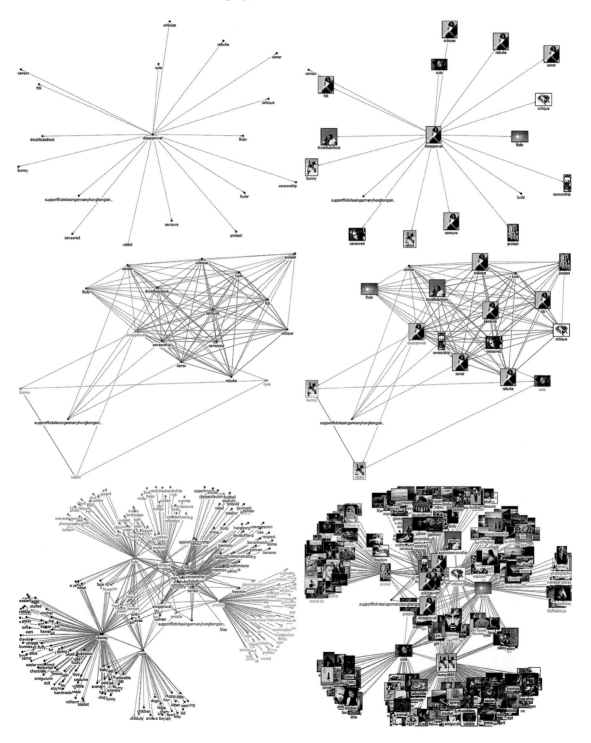

Figure 33. Outer rim: "remorse" related tags networks on Flickr (1, 1.5, to 2 degree networks, without and with linked thumbnail imagery)

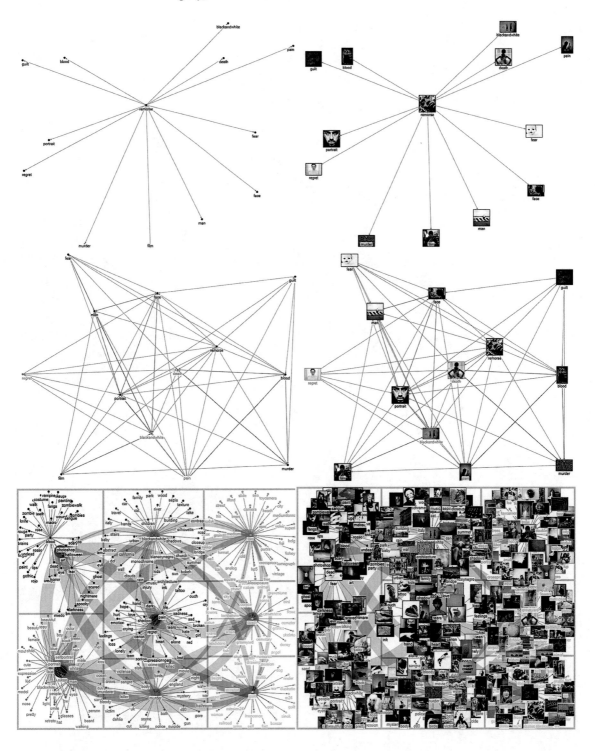

Figure 34. Outer rim: "contempt" related tags networks on Flickr (1, 1.5, to 2 degree networks, without and with linked thumbnail imagery)

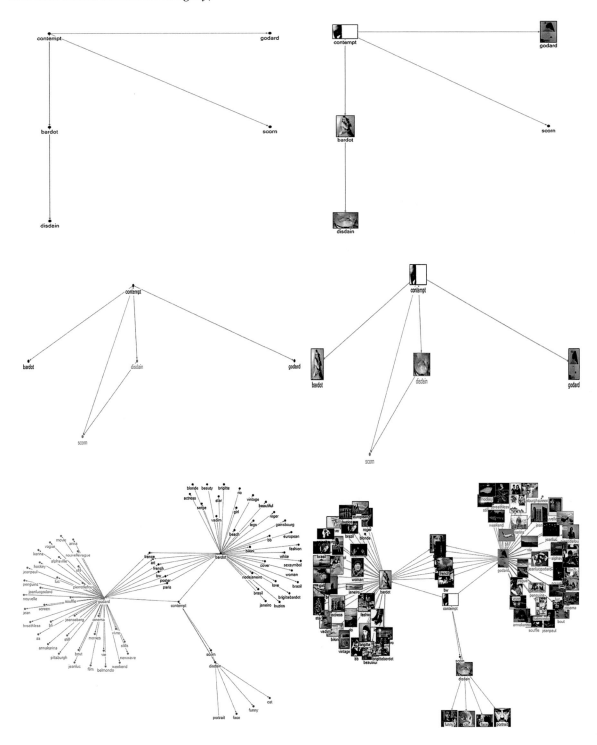

Figure 35. Outer rim: "aggression" related tags networks on Flickr (1, 1.5, to 2 degree networks, without and with linked thumbnail imagery)

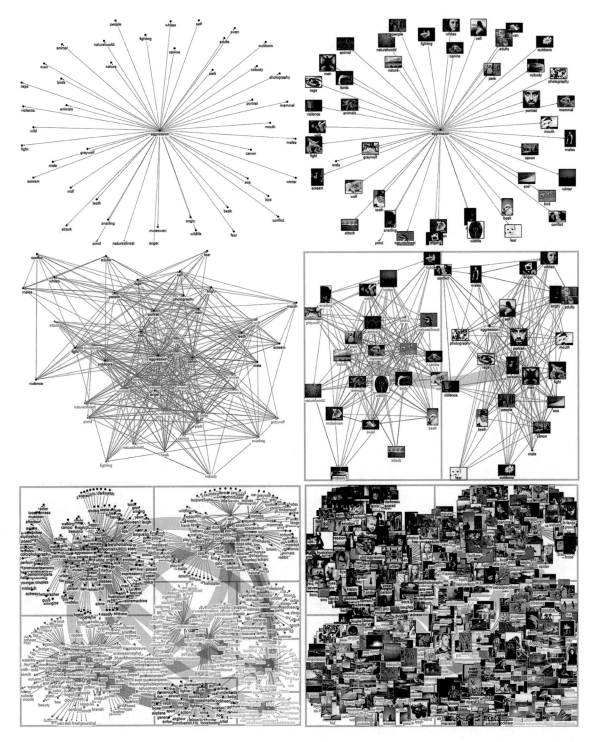

Figure 36. Outer rim: "optimism" related tags networks on Flickr (1, 1.5, to 2 degree networks, without and with linked thumbnail imagery)

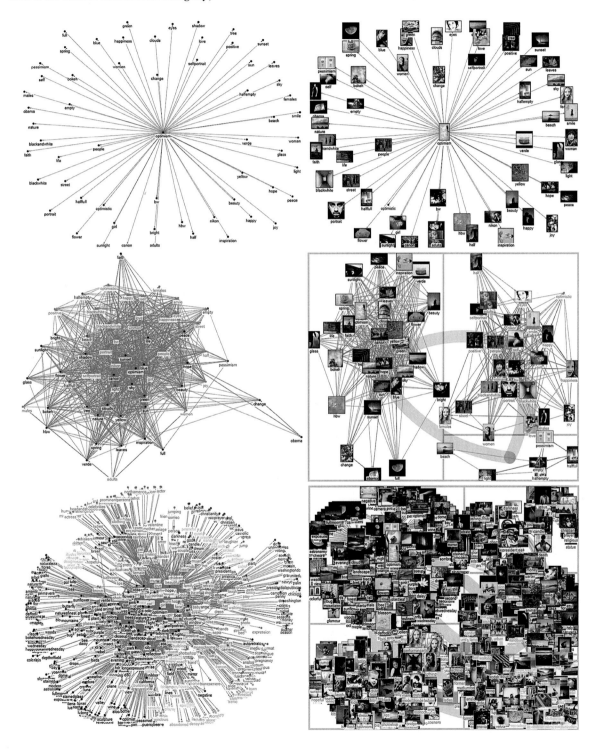

Chapter 11
Creating "(Social) Network Art" with NodeXL

Shalin Hai-Jew
Kansas State University, USA

ABSTRACT

If human-created objects of art are historically contingent, then the emergence of (social) network art may be seen as a product of several trends: the broad self-expression and social sharing on Web 2.0; the application of network analysis and data visualization to understand big data, and an appreciation for online machine art. Social network art is a form of cyborg art: it melds data from both humans and machines; the sensibilities of humans and machines; and the pleasures and interests of people. This chapter will highlight some of the types of (social) network art that may be created with Network Overview, Discovery and Exploration for Excel (NodeXL Basic) and provide an overview of the process. The network graph artwork presented here were all built from datasets extracted from popular social media platforms (Twitter, Flickr, YouTube, Wikipedia, and others). This chapter proposes some early aesthetics for this type of electronic artwork.

INTRODUCTION

In the same way that human eyes are pre-attentively drawn towards color, movement, novelty, and threat, so too, they are drawn towards objects of beauty. Evolutionary biologists suggest that this appreciation for beauty is part of biological instinct and evolutionary advantage—to select for health and biological survival. Beauty seduces; it captures human attention and draws them in. Brain research has suggested a specialized neural network to process visual stimuli related to erotic content and suggests selectivity for such contents (Anokhin, Golosheykin, Sirevaag, Kristjansson, Rohrbaugh, & Heath, 2006). The gravitation towards pleasure is not only an ancient brain or unthinking sort of function; it is also something pursued consciously and cognitively. Jeremy Bentham (1789) suggested that people pursue the greatest happiness possible (through his idea of utility) and said that humans served "two sovereign masters, pain and pleasure."

DOI: 10.4018/978-1-5225-0648-5.ch011

The concept of "panhedonism" (all + pleasure-seeking) suggests that people pursue pleasure universally; this concept is backed up by the more modern concept of "psychological hedonism" which asserts that pleasure is prized. All human endeavors are "directed towards pleasure; others do not exist" (Tatarkiewicz, 1947, 1950-51, p. 409). This pursuit of pleasure does not have to be a blatant one but masked in layers of complexity, based on one iteration of this theory:

It asserts instead that it is their original object. Originally man strives only for pleasure, but having once learnt by experience that certain things give him pleasure, he associates them with it and indirectly makes it also the object of his desires and actions. These associations become stabilized, inherited, (and) mechanical. Different things which attract us, do so in consequence of their associative connexion with pleasure. Pleasure may sometimes vanish from our consciousness, replaced by things associated with it, but nevertheless does not cease being the original and real aim of our desires. (Tatarkiewicz, 1947, 1950-51, p. 414)

The sense of pleasure is not a purely selfish (psychologically egoistic) one but may be social—with a desire for the pleasure of others. Emile Durkheim (1912) alluded to this in his classic work *Elementary Forms of the Religious Life* in which he described the sense of exaltation that may occur of people in the presence of others that may lead to a heady religiosity and ultimately a shared understanding of socially normed values. An idea of pleasure as "the basic ethical or normative value" still is defensible into the present even as it has resonated for centuries (Mendola, 2006, pp. 441 - 442).

One pleasure-giving artifact that has been a "cultural universal" through all known human societies and cultures is art, which both entrances the senses and the mind. Art is thought to inspire people to creativity. "High-quality, beautiful physical objects act as an ongoing, stimulating background against which intellectual growth can take place," particularly with the enablements of computers (Eisenberg & Buechley, 2008, p. 3). Aesthetics refers to concepts of beauty and art. According to various philosophical concepts, aesthetics comes in part from biology, from acculturation, and (individually and collectively) lived experiences. Modern aesthetics draw in yet other features of "art" such as a diversity of philosophies, sensibilities, cognitive and sensory evocations, and language (Koren, 2010, as cited in McCormack, 2013, pp. 7 – 8). Aesthetics is experiential and comes from an attentively and appreciatively lived life.

If art is a universal, it is also comprised of some universal features. Dutton (2002) lists some features of art that appear cross-culturally: expertise or virtuosity (of craft), non-utilitarian pleasure (enjoyment beyond its usefulness), style (some following of rules of form and composition), criticism (some context of appreciation and critique), imitation (albeit with "notable exceptions being abstract painting and music"), "special" focus of the art separate from "ordinary life", and appeal to the "imaginative experience" (Dutton, 2002). People through time have had an appreciation for novelty (Dutton, 2002, p. 5/13). Other thinkers have taken exception to Dutton's conceptualization of art and its universal features, with debate over artworks that prove to be exceptions to the concepts (such as artworks that do not fit a particular style or those that purposefully disavow any technical virtuosity), and debate over societies that did not apparently have a critical stance towards art (and in some, not even the apparent conceptualization of "art"). Dutton writes:

Art is not a technical field governed and explained by a theory, but a rich, scattered, and variegated realm of human practice and experience that existed before philosophers and theorists. It is a natural, evolved category, which means that it should not surprise anyone that it can have such a wide-ranging and comparatively open definition. (Dutton, 2006, p. 376)

Held lightly, Dutton's concepts of universal features of art are useful to contextualize (social) network art in part because these graph drawings "tick the boxes" of art. This definition also helps delimit the sense of graph visualizations discussed—to enable the exclusion of network graphs used more for utilitarian purposes like explanation, problem-solving, analysis, and research.

Data Visualizations as Information and Art

A data visualization is a figure which represents underlying data. The drawing of a data visualization is a three-step process: "the collection of data to be visualized, the visual display of data, (and) the human perception of the visualization" (Görg, Pohl, Qeli, & Xu, 2010, p. 164). Network graphs are a kind of data visualization. To over-simplify, most (social) network graphs are described, foundationally, as node-link diagrams (whether 2D or 3D); they show entities and (inter)relationships as "vertices" and "edges". [The "social" in social network art refers to the fact that the underlying data come from representations of human interactions--often in the contexts of social media platforms. Network art is "social" also in the sense that this art is shared, discussed, co-created, and part of shared culture; however, that is not the direct sense in the title or elsewhere in this chapter.] Human sensory capabilities are considered in the creation of data visualizations, particularly sight.

Humans have different senses to receive data: vision, acoustic, haptic/tactile, smell, and taste. With 100 MB per second, vision has the highest bandwidth of all of these senses. Furthermore, human vision is fast, works in parallel preattentively, is very suitable for pattern recognition, and is closely connected to the human's memory and cognitive capacity. People also often tend to think visually and therefore it makes sense to use this impressive sense to convey data. (Görg, Pohl, Qeli, & Xu, 2010, p. 171)

Sight and hearing are known as far senses, able to capture information from a spatial distance, as compared to smell, taste, and touch. The typical "aesthetics" (in the way the term is used) related to network graph consumption involves graph features that enhance their use in human viewing and analysis, or their "computational efficiency" and usability. Effective graph layouts help people "perceive the embedded information quickly and correctly, while poor layouts may confuse people, even convey misleading information" (Huang, 2011, p. 93). Automated graph layout algorithms take into account the research on how humans read and interpret graphs:

Many automatic graph layout algorithms have been implemented to display relational data in a graphical (usually node-arc) manner. The success of these algorithms is typically measured by their computational efficiency and the extent to which they conform to aesthetic criteria (for example, minimising the number of crossings, maximising symmetry). Little research has been performed on the usability aspects of such algorithms: do they produce graph drawings that make the embodied information easy to use and understand? (Purchase, Carrington, & Allder, 2000, p. 498)

Maximum symmetry enhances the use of the two-dimensional planar space, which enhances clarity (Purchase, Allder, & Carrington, 2001). Effective graph layouts enable people to "perceive the embedded information quickly and correctly" (Huang, 2013, p. 93), and the factors that lead to graph effectiveness are labeled "aesthetic criteria." The management of edge crossings (link overlaps with other elements of the graph) have been found to have an outsized effect on graph diagram legibility (Purchase, 1997).

While there have been a number of studies on human interpretations of graphs, one team found that the human perception of visual complexity, while consistent both for individuals and groups, do not necessarily relate to "computational metrics" (Purchase, Freeman, & Hamer, 2012, p. 200); what people see as visually complex may not be so from a computational point-of-view. The perception of complexity though is being researched to understand "its effect on user's aesthetic judgments, preference, performance, or perceived usability" (Purchase, Freeman, & Hamer, 2012, p. 200). Edge crossings affect eye movements over a graph:

1. When there were no crossings, eye movements were smooth and fast.
2. When edges crossed with large angles, eye movements were slower, but remained smooth.
3. When edges crossed with small angles, eye movements were very slow and no longer smooth (back-forth moves at the crossing points). (Huang, 2013, p. 103)

Ninety degree (90°) angles were postulated to be more readable on a graph than acute angles, although the research findings on that hypothesis have been mixed. Another core aesthetic in the utilitarian sense is that the "embodied information" in the graph should be accurately conveyed and perceived (Purchase, Allder, & Carrington, 2001, p. 5); as an example, semantic data underlying a graph differs from syntactic underlying data because the first has meaning in the world and application in a domain (p. 6). Another researcher echoes the idea of the importance of understanding the full data collection process and data handling to fully understand the resulting network graph (Kolaczyk, 2009). A graph needs to maintain users' "mental model" coherence (Purchase, Hoggan, & Görg, 2007). Plenty of underlying design work has been written into the layout algorithms for graphs (Harel, 1998). The various choices made within each layout algorithm involves the consideration of competing priorities and trade-offs:

The field of graph drawing has codified a number of 'graph drawing aesthetics,' which are typically measurable attributes of the visualization. These aesthetics include line crossings, node overlaps, drawing area, and drawing aspect ratio. Although codified as such, many aesthetics are contradictory and cannot be achieved in one drawing (except for the smallest examples). (Quigley, 2006, p. 318)

Of special difficulty are the visual depictions of "large scale, dense multivariate graphs" without them devolving into "hairballs" or "snowy wastes" (Jankun-Kelly, Dwyer, Holten, Hurter, Nöllenburg, Weaver, & Xu, 2014, pp. 207 - 208). Effective graph layout algorithms are built on "pre-specified aesthetic criteria" and are designed to lighten the cognitive load required for sensemaking (Huang, 2014, pp. 376 - 377). These challenges only multiply with the extraction of multi-dimensional and multi-modal relational data, which must be rendered visually for understanding and data coherence. Network graphs are essentially abstract mathematical objects. Meanings are embedded in all aspects of the visualization, such as the use of Euclidean distance between two nodes to convey graph-theoretic distance (Huang, 2014, p. 374).

The authors of one of the most engaging layout algorithms in Network Overview, Discovery and Exploration in Excel (NodeXL) explained the importance of both clarity and aesthetics, writing that a graph's usefulness "depends on its readability, that is, the capability of conveying the meaning of the diagram quickly and clearly" (Harel & Koren, 2001, p. 183); they add, further, "The intuition...for beauty in graph layout is that the graph should be nice on all scales" (Harel & Koren, 2001, p. 184). This means that when looking at a node, a motif structure, a subgraph, or the entire graph, every part should not only convey information but be aesthetically pleasing. [This may be in part why their algorithm for drawing graphs is the Harel-Koren Fast *Multiscale* layout algorithm (author italics).]

There are varying stances about how much post-processing should occur to finalize a graph after the initial output visualizations. At least one researcher suggests that reading graphs requires both a mix of science and art; he asserts further:

On a final practical note, we point out that graph drawing – like statistics itself, perhaps – involves not only 'science' but also some 'art.' Few automatically generated graph drawings cannot be improved upon through post-processing 'by hand'. (Kolaczyk, 2009, p. 59)

Most of the publicly available software tools that enable graph drawing enable a wide range of artistic updates to any rendered network graphs, both to enhance informational communications and attention-drawing aesthetic pleasure.

An Art for This Electronically Social Age

In 2008, in a prescient work, Christodoulou and Styliaras anticipated the meeting of art with the Social Web or Web 2.0, and they posited a digital art taxonomy; this categorization included the following: digital vector images and animations, digital painting, digital photography, 3D modeling, digital video, digital music, algorithmic/generative art, digital literature and storytelling, and art installations (pp. 158 – 159). The practice of social media graphing to express interrelationships seems somewhat tailor-made to the current age of the Social Web, particularly in the category of algorithmic or generative art.

People can draw or, rather, thread their social relationships using web-media platforms, embroidering elaborate identities with texts, artefacts, nodes and connectors, woven into the surfaces of media, communications and gaming platforms. Socio-spatial identities also are materialized in web-mapping, geographic information and positioning systems. Participation in digital media depends increasingly on touch-sensitive interfaces, serving to restage the gestural line as a means of digital threading. The embroidering of identifications forms as enmeshed surfaces of social domains. (O'Brien, 2014, p. 147)

Those hosting social media platforms have enabled broad access to their data (and metadata) through application programming interfaces (APIs). This extracted information may be extracted and visualized in social network graph formats.

This chapter is set up first with the basic introduction. Then, a sampler of (social) network art created by the author (and displayed on the NodeXL Graph Gallery) will be presented with some light commentary. An overview of the network graph creation process follows each graph. Then, there is a brief discussion and a look to the future.

A SAMPLER OF (SOCIAL) NETWORK ART FROM NODEXL

This sampler of (social) network art created in NodeXL focuses on a subset of network graphs, as explained in Figure 1. Network graphs may be organized in the following general sections. Generally, graphs are shown from the most "natural" (those showcasing the layout algorithms in NodeXL without much in

Figure 1. (Social) network art as a subset of network graphs

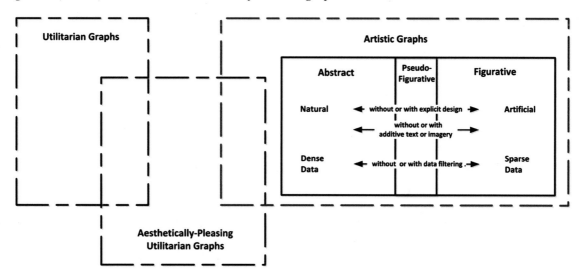

the way of external inputs) to the most artificial. Artifice here is understood as inputs to the graphs such as the addition of text or images, the changing up of the edges or backgrounds, data filtering, and layout options. Another way to categorize the graphs involves whether the visualization is abstract or figurative.

While creating a taxonomy of network graphs is well beyond the purview of this chapter, the sample graphs in this section were organized along a general continuum. The graphs in each section fit the label for the section. The earlier sections tend to be those in which the author extracted data and essentially made a few small feature selections within NodeXL in order to create the graph visualizations. Even the pseudo-figurative graphs were actually created by the data, happenstance, and the layout algorithms. As the graphs involved more human intervention and artifice, such as the adding of text, symbols, and thumbnail images, the sample graphs depict those interventions.

- In Mostly "Natural" States,
- Using Data Density as a Forcing Function,
- Filtering or Hiding Information,
- Going with Glitches,
- Going Pseudo-Figurative,
- *A Priori* Data Structures,
- An Overlay of Text and Symbols,
- The Addition of Thumbnail Images,
- Changing Up the Background,
- More Artifice.

The network art in this chapter were all created within NodeXL, from the initial data capture from a social media platform to the visualization uploaded to the NodeXL Graph Gallery. (Only one was created with outside data. There are integrations in NodeXL with outside graphing tools that enable the ingestion of data from UCINET, GraphML, Pajek—and in other data formats.) Every visualization is unique because of the uniqueness of every dataset. The same query run on two different computers with the exact same query parameters will result in different datasets because of the changing information, the application programming interfaces on the various social media platforms, the connectivity to the Internet, the local machine processing capabilities, and other factors. The data processing involves extracting the graph metrics that help define the network and extracting the sub-graphs (whether as groups, motifs, connected elements, or some other structure). Most expressed graphs tend to be abstract and non-figurative. The visuals are highly structured and based on layout algorithms. The underlying datasets used in this chapter were all real-world datasets extracted from social media platforms. No synthetic data was used; likewise, no manually created data was used.

A selection of network-graphs-as-art were selected in part because of their visual appeal and in part because of what these may show of the layout algorithms integrated within NodeXL. Some of the visualizations look like mapped constellations. Some who have seen the graphs have noted some light evocations of Piet Mondrian, Jackson Pollock, Mark Rothko, M.C. Escher, and Victor Vasarely. Some evoke mosaics and tiling; others Hollywood senses of "code" and "tech"; others are reminiscent of sidewalk chalk art.

IN MOSTLY "NATURAL" STATES

To set some ground-level understandings, the first and largest group of such graphs are presented pretty much as natural drawings of data using particular layout algorithms. The parameters of the data extractions will not be mentioned here in order to let the visuals display without too much of the background.

Suffice it to say that this particular visualization shows something of the clarity of some types of group clustering but also the criticality of the center here in connecting disparate groups. Each of the dots represents an account on Twitter. EDUCAUSEEditor is the focal node at the center of this social network which is drawn based on interactions and following relationships. Figure 2 was drawn using the Harel-Koren Fast Multiscale layout algorithm.

Star chef Alton Brown has quite the following, with 14,820 vertices in his direct Twitterverse. Figure 3 was only a partial extraction of his network on the Twitter microblogging site. The thicknesses of the connectivity serves as a strong backdrop to the nodes, which form visual patterns based on their closeness or distance in relation to each other. While this graph is essentially grayscale, it is difficult to go without color once one has used it. Another iteration of this same type of visual may be achieved with extracted groups as in Figure 4: usagov user network on Twitter.

A force-based layout algorithm (Fruchterman-Reingold force-based layout algorithm) enables increasing clarity on the various groups that are part of a social network. The force-based aspect refers to a repelling force that help nodes separate from each other for more white space. Figure 5 is the first iteration of this layout. Several iterations in, each of the groups would separate out into their own group, almost like petals of a flower.

Collecting datasets with large numbers of nodes (or vertices) enable users to test some of the limits of the layout algorithms because there is a limit to how much information may be condensed on a limited two-dimensional plane. Dense data has a forcing function. In Figure 6, there are a number of groups that may be identified based on the strips of color; there is also some clear interactivity with nodes of different colors integrated within other more apparently monolithic groups.

Figure 2. @EDUCAUSEEditor ego neighborhood on Twitter
General Sequence: *NodeXL Tab > From Twitter Users Network > Overall Graph Metrics > Grouped by Cluster (Clauset-Newman-Moore) > Harel Koren Fast MultiScale Layout Algorithm*

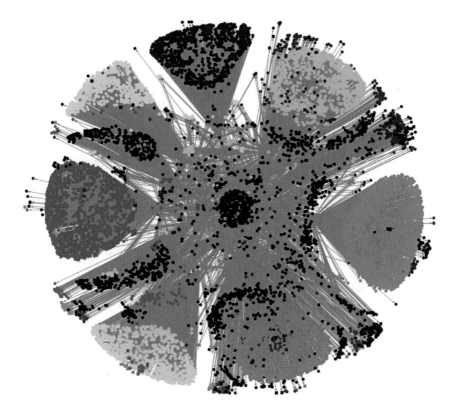

Figure 3. Alton Brown's Twitterverse @altonbrown
General Sequence: *NodeXL Tab > From Twitter Users Network (followers) > Overall Graph Metrics > (no grouping) > Harel-Koren Fast MultiScale Layout Algorithm*

Figure 4. @usagov user network on Twitter
General Sequence: *NodeXL Tab > From Twitter Users Network > Overall Graph Metrics > Grouped by Cluster (Clauset-Newman-Moore) > Harel-Koren Fast MultiScale Layout Algorithm*

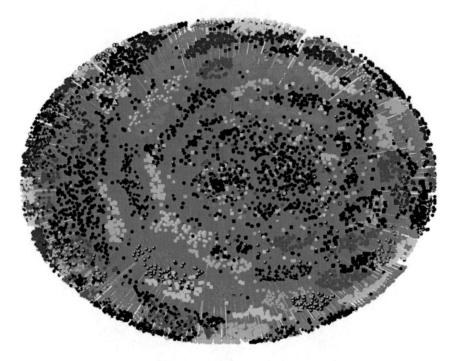

Figure 5. @mandiant user network on Twitter
General Sequence: *NodeXL Tab > From Twitter Users Network > Overall Graph Metrics > Grouped by Cluster (Clauset-Newman-Moore) > Fruchterman-Reingold Force-Based Layout Algorithm (one iteration only)*

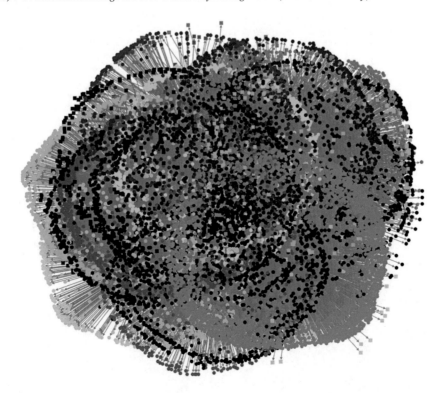

Figure 6. @EPICprivacy user network on Twitter
General Sequence: *NodeXL Tab > From Twitter Users Network > Overall Graph Metrics > Grouped by Cluster (Clauset-Newman-Moore) > Grid Layout Algorithm*

Sometimes, a particular mix of colors may be especially engaging, as in Figure 7. The default presets for visualizations in NodeXL gives the sense of forethought and visual sophistication. One way to experience this is to start changing up the visualization settings in the NodeXL graph pane only to return to "Reset All" with a greater appreciation for the simple pre-sets.

In Figure 8, the graph visualization shows a user network that has groups with disparate interests based on sparse clustering. Scaled-down graph visualizations may be used to highlight different overlapping groups of networks connected to the seeding user network, as in Figure 9. The scaling down creates a pointillist feel.

Figure 10 shows an ad hoc network based on social media accounts which are interacting around a particular hashtag in a particular point-in-time. It may be assumed that some of these discussants have interacted before and may have a prior relationship. For others, the interactions around a topic of interest may be a first-time event. Relationships may be fleeting and thin in online microblogging services.

Figure 11 gives a sense of organic connections and nature. This could read visually almost like a natural found object. The inclusion of text labels would likely ruin the visual spell. (In a research context, the text labeling is critical for analysis and understanding. In a research context, the underlying dataset may be partially or fully presented. There will likely be labeling through symbology or legends.

Figure 7. @NatGeo user network on Twitter
General Sequence: *NodeXL Tab > From Twitter Users Network > Overall Graph Metrics > Grouped by Cluster (Wakita-Tsurumi cluster algorithm) > Fruchterman-Reingold Layout Algorithm*

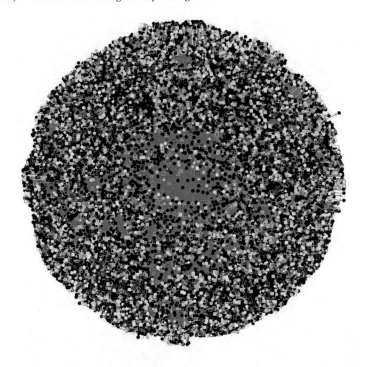

Figure 8. @comiccon user network on Twitter
General Sequence: *NodeXL Tab > From Twitter Users Network > Overall Graph Metrics > Grouped by Cluster (Clauset-Newman-Moore) > Fruchterman-Reingold Layout Algorithm*

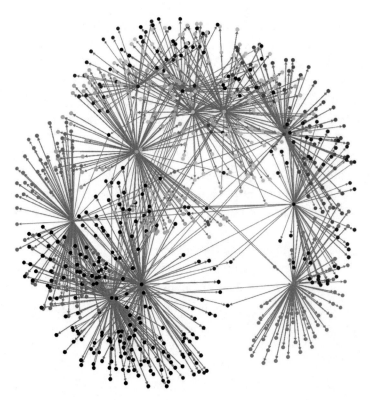

Figure 9. @groupon user network on Twitter
General Sequence: *NodeXL Tab > From Twitter Users Network > Overall Graph Metrics > Grouped by Cluster (Clauset-Newman-Moore) > Scaled-Down Visualization in the NodeXL Graph Pane > Fruchterman-Reingold Layout Algorithm*

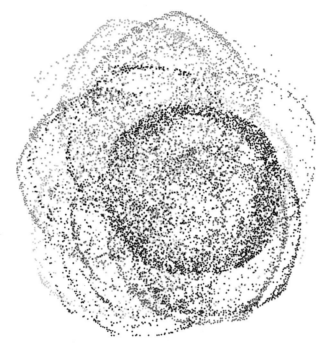

Figure 10. #DC hashtag search network on Twitter
General Sequence: *NodeXL Tab > From Twitter (#hashtag) Search Network > Overall Graph Metrics > Grouped by Cluster (Clauset-Newman-Moore) > Harel-Koren Fast MultiScale Layout Algorithm*

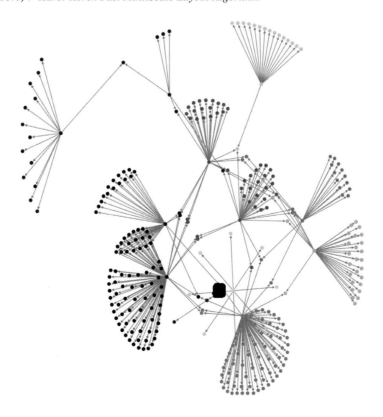

Figure 11. @AlprgAsari user network on Twitter
General Sequence: *NCapture on NVivo (data extraction) > Overall Graph Metrics > Grouped by Cluster (Clauset-Newman-Moore) > Harel-Koren Fast MultiScale Layout Algorithm*

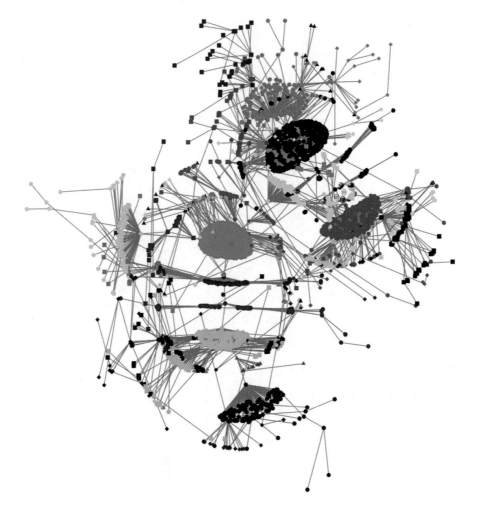

A discussion on the public NodeXL Discussion list resulted in the data extraction for Figure 12. A particular individual was collecting Tweets in Arabic that a person on the discussion list wanted to access. This individual had tried using a URL decoder / encoder to access the requisite application programming interface using NodeXL. On a whim, the author used a different tool and was able to extract the data and to post it to the Gallery.

Figure 13 offers an example of a graph created with sparse data, only 709 vertices in a two-degree network. Such top-down restrictions in a data extraction may result in incomplete information for research, but the data sparseness results in an engaging visual.

Some graph visualizations give the sense of movement and texture, as in Figure 12. Others seem like they could be organic if they weren't so fully patterned, but then, fractals do occur in nature. Figure 13 gives the sense of repeating patterns.

Some figures emerge as near-total surprises, at least the first time. Such images as Figure 14 are more satisfying maybe because of the expensive processing time.

Figure 12. @iaeaorg user network on Twitter
General Sequence: *NodeXL Tab > From Twitter Users Network > Overall Graph Metrics > Grouped by Cluster (Clauset-Newman-Moore) > Fruchterman-Reingold Layout Algorithm*

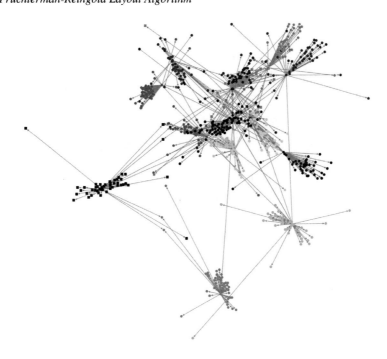

Figure 13. @unity3d user network on Twitter
General Sequence: *NodeXL Tab > From Twitter Users Network > Overall Graph Metrics > Grouped by Cluster (Clauset-Newman-Moore) > Layout Options with Groups in Own Boxes and a Force-Directed Layout > Harel-Koren Fast MultiScale Layout Algorithm*

Figure 14. @realtordotcom user network on Twitter
General Sequence: *NodeXL Tab > From Twitter Users Network > Overall Graph Metrics > Grouped by Cluster (Clauset-Newman-Moore) > Layout Options with Groups in Own Boxes and a Force-Directed Layout > Circle Layout Algorithm*

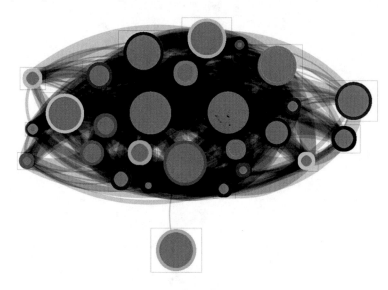

Figure 15 evokes an innate sense of form along with visual interest. For those interested in social networks, there are often some important clusters to explore.

Figure 15. @googlebooks user network on Twitter
General Sequence: *NodeXL Tab > From Twitter Users Network > Overall Graph Metrics > Grouped by Cluster (Clauset-Newman-Moore) > Layout Options with Groups in Own Boxes and a Force-Directed Layout > Harel-Koren Fast MultiScale Layout Algorithm*

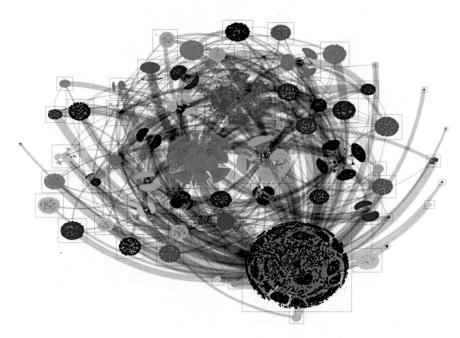

Figure 16. "Invisible web" keyword search network on Twitter
General Sequence: *NodeXL Tab > From Twitter (keyword) Search Network > Overall Graph Metrics > Grouped by Cluster (Clauset-Newman-Moore) > Layout Options with Groups in Own Boxes and a Force-Directed Layout > Harel-Koren Fast MultiScale Layout Algorithm*

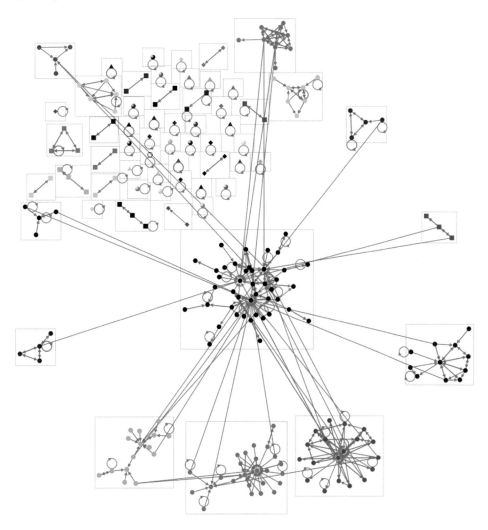

The layout algorithms seem informed by an inherent need for balance and some degree of symmetry (see Figure 16 and 17).

The rollout of the ability to "box" certain groups within which groups are laid out a particular way enabled sudden new complexity and visual enjoyment (in 2013).

Social network art evokes entities, connectivity, and dynamism, even though the dataset may be hidden on background or are not shared.

How edges are handled affect the look-and-feel of a social network graph, as may be seen between Figure 18 and Figure 19. Curved lines are often seen as more organic and naturally occurring, but direct lines may convey a sense of dynamism and energy that curved ones lack (see Figure 20).

Figure 17. @MickJagger user network on Twitter

General Sequence: *NodeXL Tab > From Twitter Users Network > Overall Graph Metrics > Grouped by Cluster (Clauset-Newman-Moore) > Layout Options with Groups in Own Boxes and a Force-Directed Layout > Sugiyama Layout Algorithm*

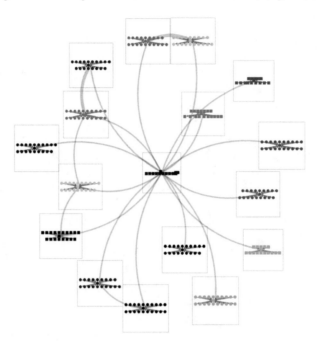

Figure 18. #hack hashtag network on Twitter

General Sequence: *NodeXL Tab > From Twitter (#hashtag) Search Network > Overall Graph Metrics > Grouped by Cluster (Clauset-Newman-Moore) > Layout Options with Groups in Own Boxes in a Force-Directed Layout > Harel-Koren Fast MultiScale Layout Algorithm*

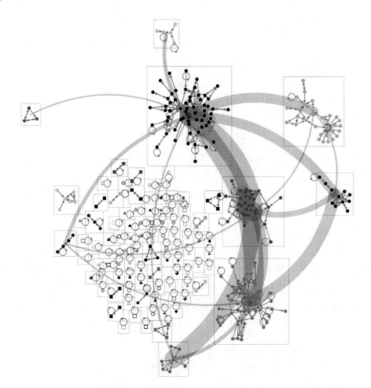

Figure 19. #trend hashtag network from a Twitter search
General Sequence: *NodeXL Tab > From (#hashtag) Search on Twitter > Overall Graph Metrics > Grouped by Cluster (Clauset-Newman-Moore) > Layout Options with Groups in Own Boxes > Harel-Koren Fast MultiScale Layout Algorithm*

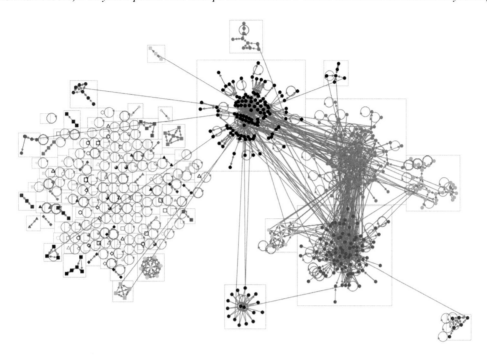

Figure 20. #patent hashtag search network on Twitter
General Sequence: *NodeXL Tab > From Twitter (#hashtag) Network > Overall Graph Metrics > Grouped by Cluster (Clauset-Newman-Moore) > Fruchterman-Reingold Layout Algorithm*

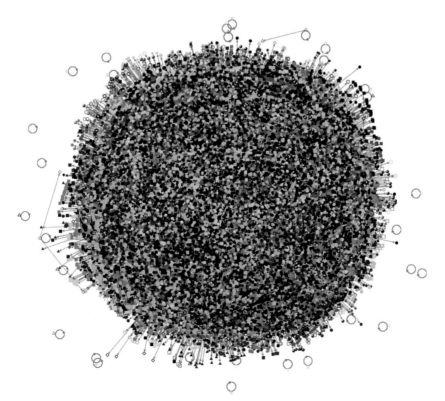

Figure 21. @yahoo ego neighborhood on Twitter
General Sequence: *NodeXL Tab > From Twitter Users Network > Overall Graph Metrics > Grouped by Cluster (Clauset-Newman-Moore) > Layout Options with Groups in Own Boxes > Fruchterman-Reingold Layout Algorithm*

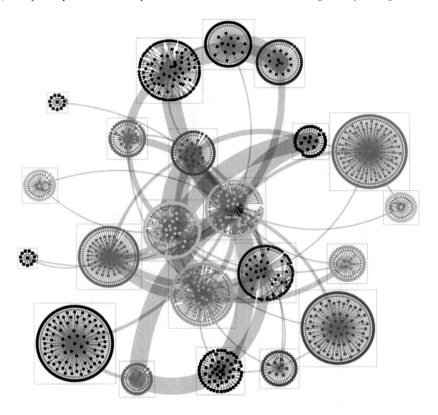

In the network of individuals that recently (in the past week) used #patent to label their microblogging messages, the center mass is of strong visual interest. So too are the free-floating isolates floating on the periphery in self-referential connection. There are some pendant nodes as well, connected only by one tie to the issue.

Some network graphs evoke a sense of playfulness and whimsy, as in Figure 21.

The outer edge on this graph of those recently discussing #travelban may already be seen in Figure 22. There are also clusters and coalescences among certain related nodes. In a sense, this is what an electronic conversation looks like; in another sense, this is just an evocative visual.

Figure 23 integrates the uses of motifs. Motifs are smaller connected elements or subnetworks. Motif censuses are run on larger social networks to "structure mine" the group in order to understand something of interactivity, communications, power, and resource sharing among that group. In NodeXL, the relationships are indicated by various types of fan, connector, and clique glyphs. The idea is that substituting motif simplifications for the underlying nodes and connectors would make the relationships more directly viewable in the graph visualization.). Motif simplifications…

(1) require less screen space and layout effort, (2) are easier to understand in the context of the network, (3) can reveal otherwise hidden relationships, and (4) preserve as much underlying information as possible. (Dunne & Schneiderman, 2013, p. 3247)

Figure 22. #travelban hashtag search network on Twitter
General Sequence: *NodeXL Tab > From Twitter (#hashtag) Search Network > Overall Graph Metrics > Grouped by Cluster (Clauset-Newman-Moore) > Fruchterman-Reingold Layout Algorithm*

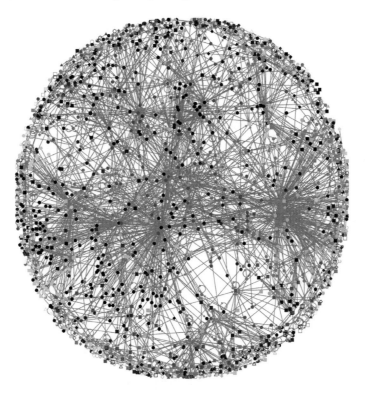

Figure 23. #swarm hashtag search network on Twitter
General Sequence: *NodeXL Tab > From (#hashtag) Search on Twitter Network > Overall Graph Metrics > Grouped by Motif (fan, D-connector, and clique motifs) > Fruchterman-Reingold Layout Algorithm (multiple centrifugal iterations)*

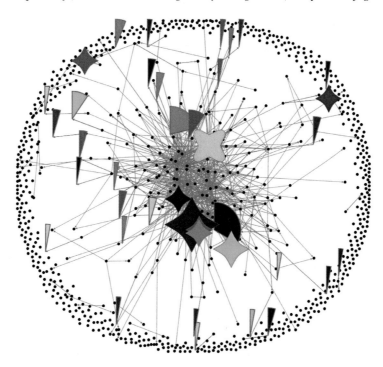

Figure 24. #pin Hashtag Search Network on Twitter
General Sequence: *NodeXL Tab > From (#hashtag) Search on Twitter Network > Overall Graph Metrics > Grouped by Cluster (Clauset-Newman-Moore) > Layout Options with Groups in Own Boxes in a Force-Based Layout > Sugiyama Layout Algorithm (see Figure 24).*

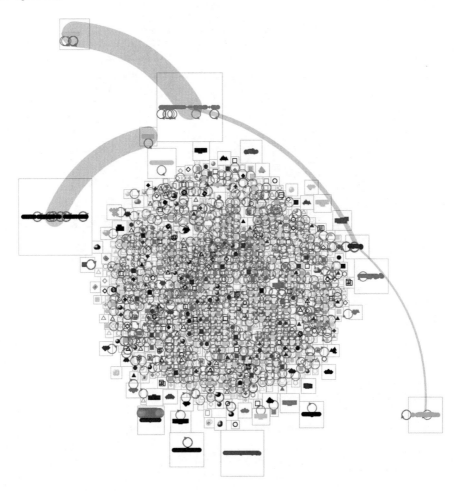

Words comprise all sorts of word senses or meanings, and conversations are numerous around the topic of #pin.

USING DATA DENSITY AS A FORCING FUNCTION

In some ways, having a large dataset of nodes and links enables people to hide the node-link relationships in some artistic network graphs.

In Figure 25, this visualization involves 316,518 vertices with 533,821 unique edges. This visualization came from one of the larger datasets used.

Figure 26 involved a graph with 163,826 vertices and 238,714 unique edges. The data is so thick that there is quite a bit of "over-plotting"; underneath are layers and layers of motif structures. Zooming in and moving the top-layer motifs will reveal some of the lower-level ones.

Figure 25. @reuters user network on Twitter
General Sequence: *NodeXL Tab > From Twitter Users Network > Overall Graph Metrics > Grouped by Motif (fan, D-connector, and clique motifs) > Grid Layout Algorithm*

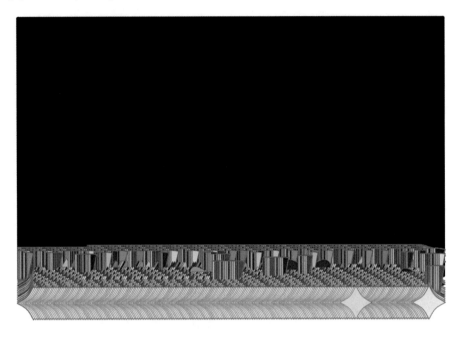

Figure 26. "CDC" keyword search network on Twitter
General Sequence: *NodeXL Tab > From Twitter Keyword Search Network > Overall Graph Metrics > Grouped by Motif (fan, D-connector, and clique motifs) > Random Layout Algorithm*

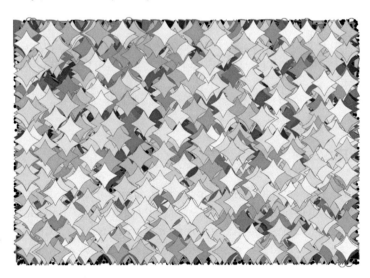

Figure 27. "Iraq" keyword search network on Twitter
General Sequence: *NodeXL Tab > From Twitter Keyword Search Network > Overall Graph Metrics > Grouped by Motif (fan, D-connector, and clique motifs) > Harel-Koren Fast MultiScale Layout Algorithm*

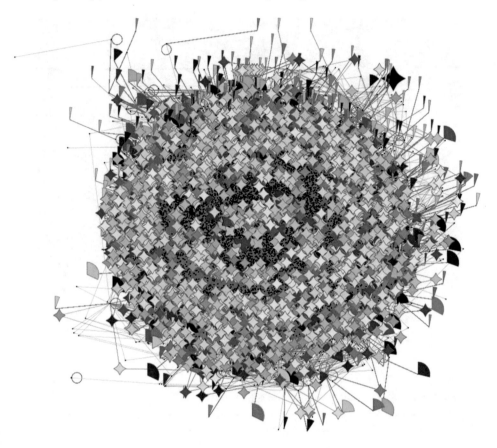

Figure 27 is a scaled-down view of a graph with motif connections highlighted.

Some data structures begin with a pre-set structure. In Figure 28, the extracted information is placed in a Treemap structure.

In Figure 29, this visualization is informed by a large and dense network.

FILTERING OR HIDING INFORMATION

Another strategy involves filtering or hiding information, which may be done in multiple ways. One way is to manually delete data from the spreadsheets in the .xl file. (To not actually lose the deleted information, it's a good idea to have a backed-up pristine copy of the file.) Another option is to use the "Dynamic Filters" feature in the NodeXL graph pane. Figure 30 shows an editing of data on the x-axis.

Figure 28. "MOOC" keyword search network on Twitter
General Sequence: *NodeXL Tab > From Twitter Keyword Search Network > Overall Graph Metrics > Group by Cluster (Wakita-Tsurumi) > Layout Options with Groups in Own Boxes > Sugiyama Layout Algorithm*

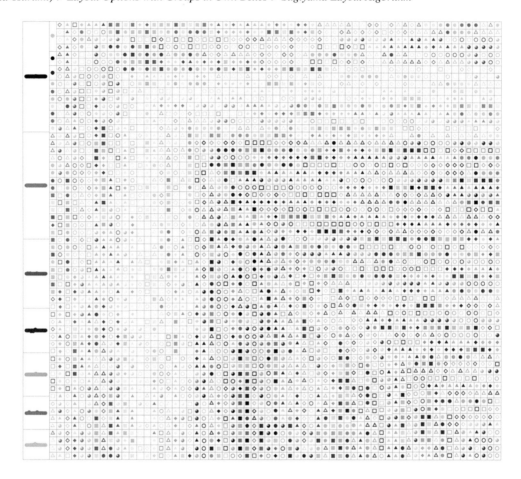

Figure 29. "Elon Musk" keyword search network on Twitter
General Sequence: *NodeXL Tab > From Twitter (keyword) Search Network > Overall Graph Metrics > Grouped by Cluster (Clauset-Newman-Moore) > Layout Options with Groups in Own Boxes > Circle Layout Algorithm*

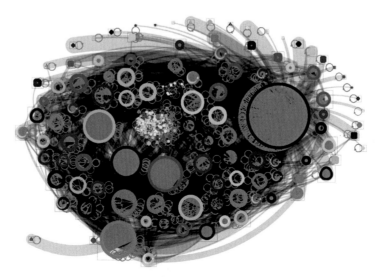

Figure 30. #offline hashtag search network on Twitter
General Sequence: *NodeXL Tab > From Twitter (#hashtag) Search Network > Overall Graph Metrics > Grouped by Cluster (Clauset-Newman-Moore) > Grid Layout Algorithm > Dynamic Filtering (on the x-axis)*

Figure 31. @qualtrics user network on Twitter
General Sequence: *NodeXL Tab > From Twitter Users Network > Overall Graph Metrics > Grouped by Cluster (Clauset-Newman-Moore) > Harel-Koren Fast MultiScale Layout Algorithm*

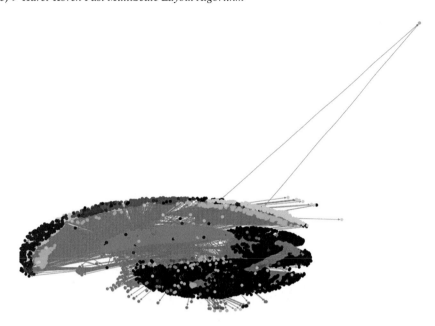

GOING WITH GLITCHES

Sometimes, some of the most memorable network art visualizations are those that occur from glitches or digital malfunctions. While datamoshing and other techniques purposefully create visual effects by purposefully interleaving video frames or transcoding videos from one lossy format to another, the "glitch art" approach here is more incidental and happenstance. One glitch involves the visualization in Figure 31. After a work is laid out again, the pulling out of one node to separate out so far from the others is not generally re-creatable. Chance elements are ephemeral and have to be captured as they happen. Sometimes, the white spaces in an image add to the drama, in this case of implied distance and positional dominance (which misrepresents the underlying information but which is visually engaging nonetheless).

Going Pseudo-Figurative

Another strategy for network art may be to go pseudo-figurative. Such an approach involves the identification of certain visual elements that look like a representation of something else—a flower, a human figure, a house—and to use that to advantage, particularly if the visualization aligns with the text used in the data extraction from the social media platform. Such emergent figures are artifacts of the data and the visualization process. They may be highlighted or partially created by adjusting some of the (data processing and data visualization) settings in NodeXL.

Figure 32 shows a visual evocation which might indicate the #berries of the Twitter hashtag search. Oftentimes, this only occurs by serendipity.

Figure 32. #berries hashtag search network on Twitter
General Sequence: *NodeXL Tab > From Twitter (#hashtag) Search Network > Overall Graph Metrics > Grouped by Cluster (Clauset-Newman-Moore) > Harel-Koren Fast MultiScale Layout Algorithm*

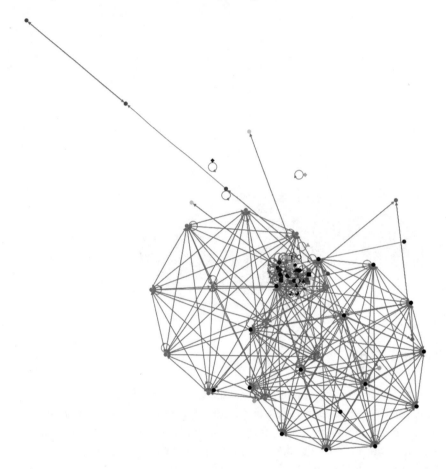

Figure 33 evokes butterflies, at least from a sufficient distance, but these are actually just horizontal sine waves depicted in boxes. For more realism, the boxes could have been disappeared as well as the vertices. Hiding information sometimes helps create a more effective illusion.

Every so often, a visualization seems to fit the topic. Figure 34 was created from an extraction of Tweets based on a keyword search for "Fiscal Cliff" at a time when this was a trending topic, with 1,199 vertices. The grid layout evoked the sense of "gridlock" simultaneously. Every so often, an alignment of a data extraction, an issue, and the visualization aligns.

Figure 35 is suggestive of an insect maybe focusing on a box of nibbles.

Figure 36 is somewhat reminiscent of a tree structure.

Figure 37 offers an organic floral sense, of flowers and leaves.

Figure 33. @UoPeople user network on Twitter
General Sequence: *NodeXL Tab > From Twitter Users Network > Overall Graph Metrics > Grouped by Cluster (Clauset-Newman-Moore) > Layout Options with Groups in Own Boxes > Horizontal Sine Wave Layout Algorithm*

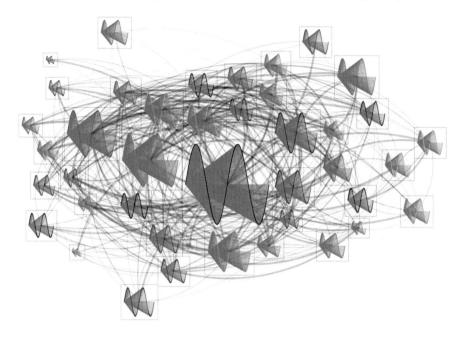

Figure 34. A grid(lock) of "fiscal cliff" tweets
General Sequence: *NodeXL Tab > From Twitter (Keyword) Search Network (directed graph) > Overall Graph Metrics > Vertices Grouped by Connected Component > Grid Layout Algorithm*

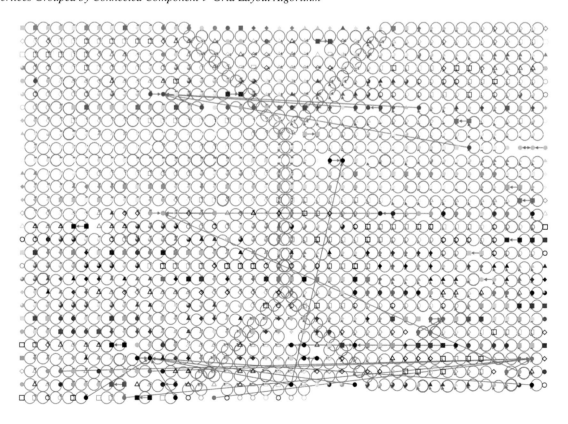

Figure 35. #breaking hashtag search network on Twitter
General Sequence: *NodeXL Tab > From Twitter (#hashtag) Search Network > Overall Graph Metrics > Grouped by Cluster (Girvan-Newman cluster algorithm) > Layout Options with Groups in Own Boxes > Sugiyama Layout Algorithm >*

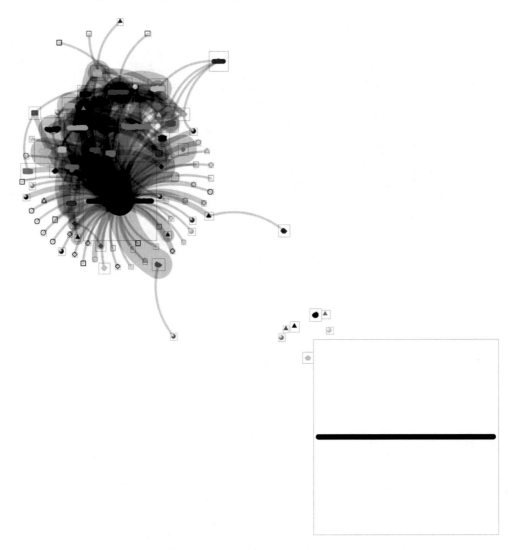

A PRIORI DATA STRUCTURES

In terms of layout algorithms, many already come with a priori structures. In other words, the data is placed in familiar ways. A few examples follow in this section.

Ring lattice graphs are always circular, with nodes on the circle and links inside the circle. Figure 38 is an example of a circle layout.

A vertical sine wave has a preset structure (as does the related horizontal sine wave). In Figure 39, the diaphanous look of the links is created by scaling down the visual.

Another structured layout is achieved using the Sugiyama layout algorithm, which places both the nodes and the links in a line. The structure is somewhat masked here with the uses of glyphs representing various motif relationships. This may be viewed in Figure 40.

Figure 36. #training hashtag search network on Twitter
General Sequence: *NodeXL Tab > From Twitter (#hashtag) Search Network > Overall Graph Metrics > Grouped by Motif (fan, D-connector, and clique motifs) > Grid Layout Algorithm > Curved Edges > Highlighted Rows at the Top > Scaled Down Visualization in the Graph Pane*

Figure 37. #thanks hashtag search network on Twitter
General Sequence: *NodeXL Tab > From Twitter (#hashtag) Search Network > Overall Graph Metrics > Grouped by Motif (fan, D-connector, and clique motifs) > Grid Layout Algorithm > Curved Edges > Vertices Placed on a Grid with Maximum Grid Size*

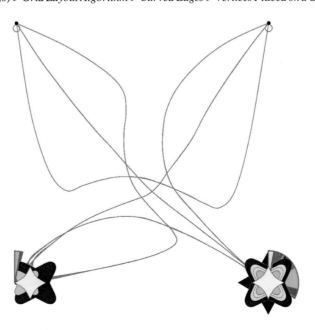

Figure 38. @samsung user network on Twitter
General Sequence: *NodeXL Tab > From Twitter (#hashtag) Search Network > Overall Graph Metrics > Grouped by Cluster (Wakita-Tsurumi cluster algorithm) > Circle Layout Algorithm*

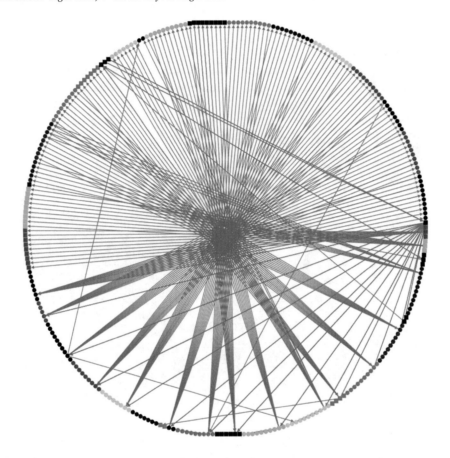

Figure 39. @NASAVoyager user network on Twitter
General Sequence: *NodeXL Tab > From Twitter Users Network > Overall Graph Metrics > Grouped by Cluster (Clauset-Newman-Moore) > Scaling Down of the Graph in the NodeXL Graph Pane > Vertical Sine Wave Layout Algorithm*

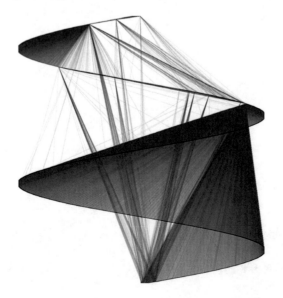

Figure 40. @cigital user network on Twitter
General Sequence: *NodeXL Tab > From Twitter Users Network > Overall Graph Metrics > Grouped by Motif (fan, D-connector, and clique motifs) > Sugiyama Layout Algorithm*

Figure 41 shows a spiral network graph, with the nodes on the spiral itself and the links in between the whorls.

Figure 42 was created in part by placing nodes on a grid. The inherent symmetry of this visualization, set up in quadrants, is not very common.

Another form of the grid involves grid elements that are spaced farther out. A sparse network's inner workings may be seen more clearly when the relationships are simplified in a grid format; however, such a data summarization loses information (as all summaries will). This may be viewed in Figure 43.

Figure 44 is built off of a grid layout.

Figure 45 was created from a grid-based understructure.

Figure 41. @S_C_ user network on Twitter
General Sequence: *NodeXL Tab > From Twitter Users Network > Overall Graph Metrics > Grouped by Cluster (Clauset-Newman-Moore) > Spiral Layout Algorithm*

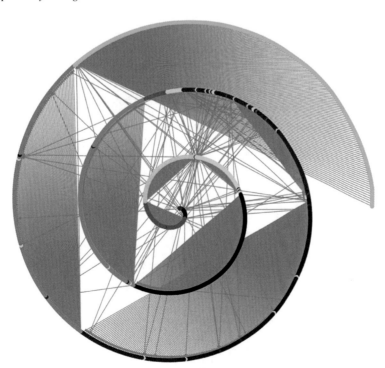

Figure 42. @UNDP user network on Twitter
General Sequence: *NodeXL Tab > From Twitter Users Network > Overall Graph Metrics > Grouped by Cluster (Clauset-Newman-Moore) > Fruchterman-Reingold Layout Algorithm > Snapping of Vertices to a Small-Cell Grid*

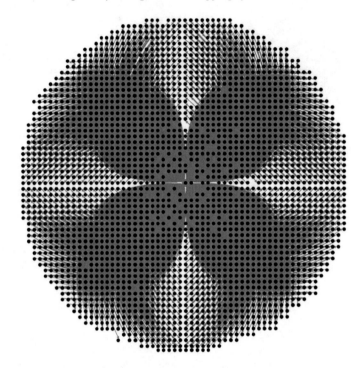

Figure 43. #syria hashtag search network on Twitter
General Sequence: *NodeXL Tab > From Twitter (#hashtag) Search Network > Overall Graph Metrics > Grouped by Cluster (Clauset-Newman-Moore) > Grid Layout Algorithm > Lay Out Again by Connecting Vertices to Grid*

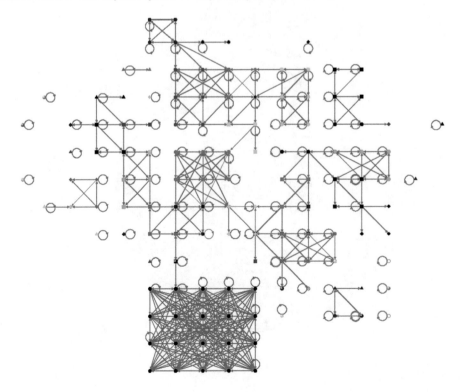

Figure 44. @vtnews user network on Twitter
General Sequence: *NodeXL Tab > From Twitter Users Network > Overall Graph Metrics > Grouped by Cluster (Clauset-Newman-Moore) > Layout Options with Groups in Own Boxes in a Force-Directed Layout > Grid Layout Algorithm*

Figure 45. @_AfricanUnion user network on Twitter
General Sequence: *NodeXL Tab > From Twitter Users Network > Overall Graph Metrics > Grouped by Cluster (Clauset-Newman-Moore) > Vertices Snapped to the Grid > Resized Edges*

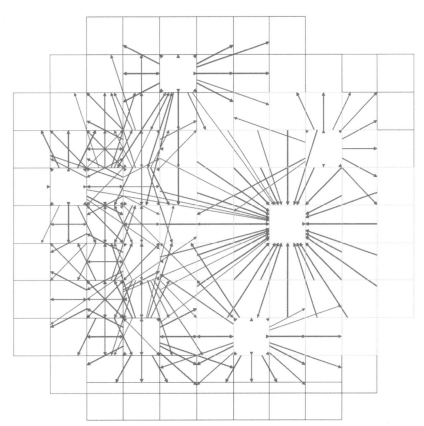

Figure 46. @avantgame user network on Twitter
General Sequence: *NodeXL Tab > From Twitter Users Network > Overall Graph Metrics > Grouped by Cluster (Wakita-Tsurumi cluster algorithm) > Layout Options with Groups in Packed Rectangles > Sugiyama Layout Algorithm*

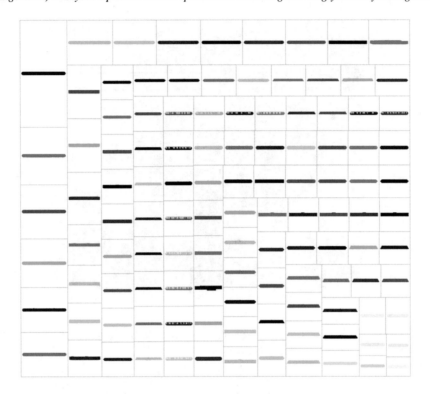

Another type of structured visualization involves putting all elements in a fitted boxes. Both Figure 46 and Figure 47 use this overarching layout, but the layout within each group (in each box) is different between the two.

AN OVERLAY OF TEXT AND SYMBOLS

Another way to add value to a visualization is to integrate text and symbols, but too much labeling detracts from the visual charms of the network art. Related tags networks from Flickr, article networks from Wikipedia, video networks from YouTube, all benefit from text labeling. Some #hashtag conversation networks on Twitter also benefit from having labeled vertices and even labeled edges (such as Tweets on the edges), but while many of these were created during the learning process for learning NodeXL, they were not really seen as sufficiently aesthetically pleasing to qualify as art. Text-based network art is beyond the purview of this chapter.

Figure 48 integrates the use of some textual information in the design.

Figure 49 also involves a condensed graph with symbology integrated.

Figure 47. "sony" keyword search network on Twitter
General Sequence: *NodeXL Tab > From (#hashag) Twitter Search Network > Overall Graph Metrics > Grouped by Cluster (Clauset-Newman-Moore) > Layout Options with Groups in Packed Rectangles > Sugiyama Layout Algorithm*

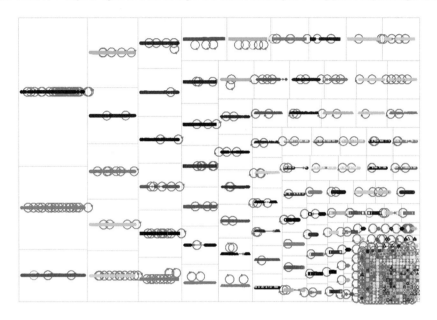

Figure 48. @DeptVetAffairs user network on Twitter
General Sequence: *NodeXL Tab > From Twitter Users Network > Overall Graph Metrics > Grouped by Cluster (Clauset-Newman-Moore) > Autofill Columns > Harel-Koren Fast MultiScale Layout Algorithm*

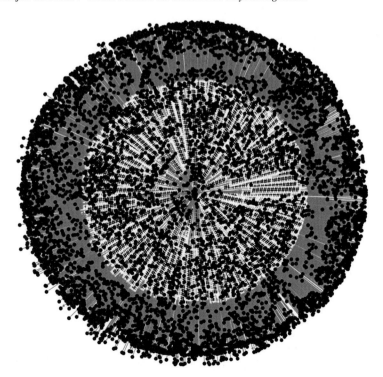

Figure 49. #morning hashtag search network on Twitter
General Sequence: *NodeXL Tab > From Twitter (#hashtag) Search Network > Overall Graph Metrics > Grouped by Cluster (Clauset-Newman-Moore) > Collapse Groups > Autofill Columns > Harel-Koren Fast MultiScale Layout Algorithm*

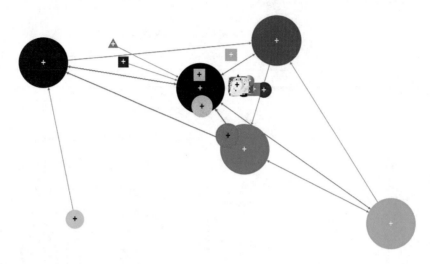

The Addition of Thumbnail Images

Another form of (social) network art includes graph visualizations with added thumbnail images. (These are only available in some types of data extractions.) The inclusion of photos may be analogical to the importing of photo-based textures in virtual worlds. A resulting network graph may be seen in Figure 50. (This was created for visual effect, not direct informational value, but many such graphs that are less dense have extractable value.)

Changing Up the Background

A type of "network art" visualization that may be quite entertaining involves the illusion of three dimensions by changing the color of edges and the color of the background. In such a situation, especially if the nodes are drawn in a circular shape and if the nodes are sufficient in number, it'll look like the nodes are a kind of snow globe under water.

Figure 51 creates an illusion of virtual 3D, especially on a computer monitor. Changing up the background color in other ways enables a person to more purposefully "foreground" and "background" particular parts of the visualization. Cool colors recede, and warm colors advance. On a computer monitor, which emits light, there are various special effects that capitalize on luminescence; this is especially so with a black or darker background and then the uses of lighter and more deeply saturated colors on that background.

Figure 52 contains a dramatic network with its edges melded into a black background. Another variation on the play on color involves going to black-and-white, in order to use extracted shapes as silhouettes. Figure 53 is an example.

Figure 50. @PSBJ user network on Twitter grid with thumbnail images
General Sequence: *NodeXL Tab > From Twitter Users Network > Overall Graph Metrics > Grouped by Cluster (Clauset-Newman-Moore) > Account-Based Thumbnail Images Swapped out for Vertices > Grid Layout Algorithm*

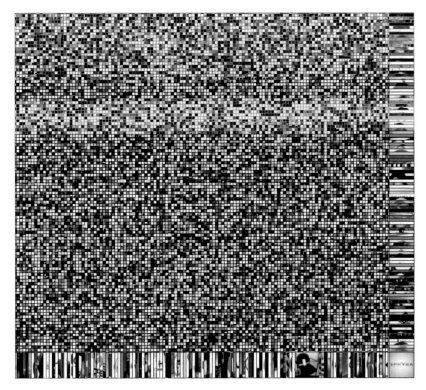

Figure 51. @bartongellman user network on Twitter
General Sequence: *NodeXL Tab > From Twitter Users Network > Overall Graph Metrics > Grouped by Cluster (Clauset-Newman-Moore) > Harel-Koren Fast MultiScale Layout Algorithm > Recolorizing the Edges and the Background (in the Graph Pane)*

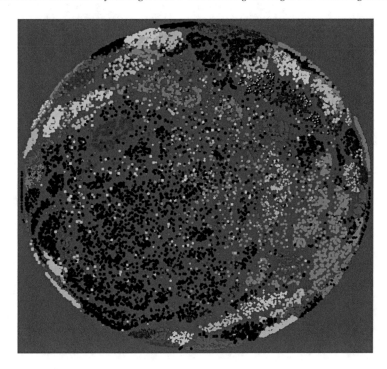

Figure 52. "Iraq" keyword search network on Twitter
General Sequence: *NodeXL Tab > From Twitter Keyword Search Network > Overall Graph Metrics > Grouped by Motif (fan, D-connector, and clique motifs) > Harel-Koren Fast MultiScale Layout Algorithm > Vertices and Background Blacked Out*

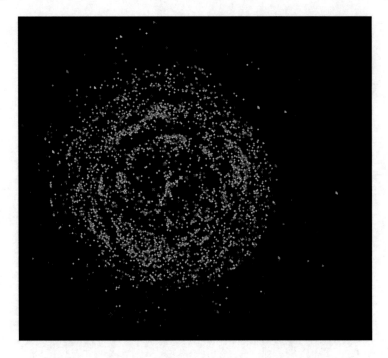

Figure 53. #DHS hashtag search network on Twitter
General Sequence: *NodeXL Tab > From Twitter Keyword Search Network > Overall Graph Metrics > Grouped by Cluster (Wakita-Tsurumi) > Sugiyama Layout Algorithm > Layout Options with Groups in Own Boxes and a Force-Directed Layout > Black Background > Whited-Out Vertices and Edges*

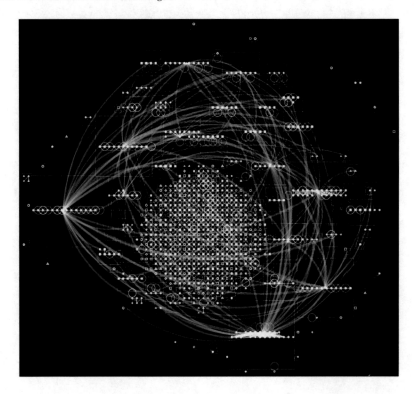

Figure 54. "GCHQ" keyword search network on Twitter
General Sequence: *NodeXL Tab > From Twitter Keyword Search Network > Overall Graph Metrics > Grouped by cluster (Clauset-Newman-Moore) > Spiral Layout Algorithm > Vertices Invisible > Background Blacked Out > Edges Curved > Select Vertices Highlighted to Evoke the Edges (with the Ctrl Key held down for multiple selections)*

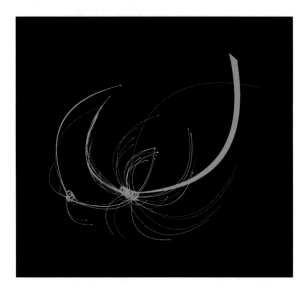

Besides changing their colors to a background color, vertices may also be hidden by reducing their opacity to 0. This may be used to hide an underlying structure which is used to highlight curved edges. Figure 54 is structured with a hidden spiral layout in the background.

MORE ARTIFICE

Other effects are possible with small changes like raising the width of links and arrows, and introducing some serious link curvature as well. Again, though, it's important to have an essential dataset to work with which might be amenable to such manipulations. Figure 55 provides a barbed wire look.

Another approach may involve drawing thick-edged boxes around particular subgraphs and then scaling down to turn the node colors into faded pastels (Figure 56). In one effort, the author went into the dataset and changed the colors of the nodes to various fluorescent colors based on hex color numbers used online.

In the captions for the images, the original seeding terms were integrated for disclosure purposes. In most cases, the words and the images do not necessarily relate, but such alignments can only enhance the power of the network graphs, their aesthetic enjoyment, and their potential messaging. The social and time-based (whether contemporaneous or historical) aspects of social media contents also add depth to network graphs. In this chapter, words themselves were not integrated into the labels for the vertices or edges, but such integrations may be another approach as well.

Ultimately, beauty is its own *raison d'etre*. This form of network-based machine art contributes to a modern aesthetic of data, form, expression, and accent.

Figure 55. @euro_pet_travel user network on Twitter
General Sequence: *NodeXL Tab > From Twitter Users Network > Overall Graph Metrics > Grouped by Cluster (Clauset-Newman-Moore) > Circle Layout Algorithm > Increased Edge Curvature > Increased Edge and Arrow Sizes*

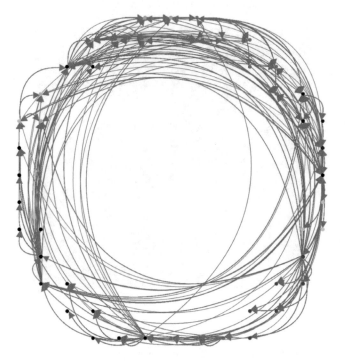

Figure 56. @cholick user network on Twitter
General Sequence: *NodeXL Tab > From Twitter Users Network > Overall Graph Metrics > Grouped by Cluster (Clauset-Newman-Moore) > Layout Options with Groups in Own Boxes and a Force-Directed Layout > Random Layout Algorithm*

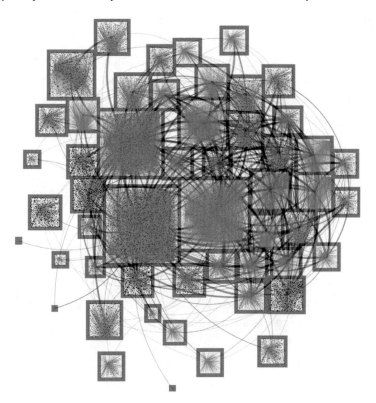

BUILDING (SOCIAL) NETWORK ART WITH NODEXL

There are three basic steps to building (social) network art with NodeXL:

1. Data extraction from a particular social media platform;
2. Data processing, and
3. Graph drawing.

These steps are all performed within Network Overview, Discovery and Exploration for Excel (NodeXL). A network graph at its most elemental and simple is a two-dimensional node-link diagram that shows entities and relationships. Behind these graphs are a complex of understandings stemming from early sociology as well as statistics, computer science, and other fields. An overview of the process is available in Figure 57. This partially specified decision tree starts at the top and moves down. This is conceptualized as a recursive, 9-step process, broadly conceptualized:

1. Conceptualization,
2. Data extraction,
3. Data processing,
4. Algorithm-based layout,
5. Visual presentation adjustments,
6. Data reduction (for visualization),
7. Layout iteration,
8. Labeling, and
9. Layout versioning and finalization.

The purpose of this visualization is to provide an overview of the processes and to be able to identify critical decision junctures when decisions may be made to affect the intermediate and ultimately final graph outputs. The conceptualization of the process may stem from any range of initial motivations, whether research-based or not.

Major decision junctures in this decision tree may be seen as the following moments: data extraction (2), data processing (3), and layout and finalization (9), because what is decided at these main points have an outsized impact on the resulting network graph. Steps 5, 6, 7, and 8 all may affect the final results in terms of editing at the margins, in a sense. These steps can affect overall look-and-feel, but they do not change up the underlying structure in the way underlying data structure and a selected layout algorithm will.

Future Graph Visualizations and Explorations

For future exploration, it helps to probe other types of visualizations that may be artfully created in NodeXL. At one level, the numbers of vertices and links may be pre-set in the parameters of the data extraction for sparseness or density of various types. Data structures from the different social media platforms also vary, and their variances may be exploited to create certain visual effects. Synthetic data—such as randomized data—may be created for certain types of visualizations. The data processing—such

Figure 57. A partially specified decision flow for creating "network art" in NodeXL

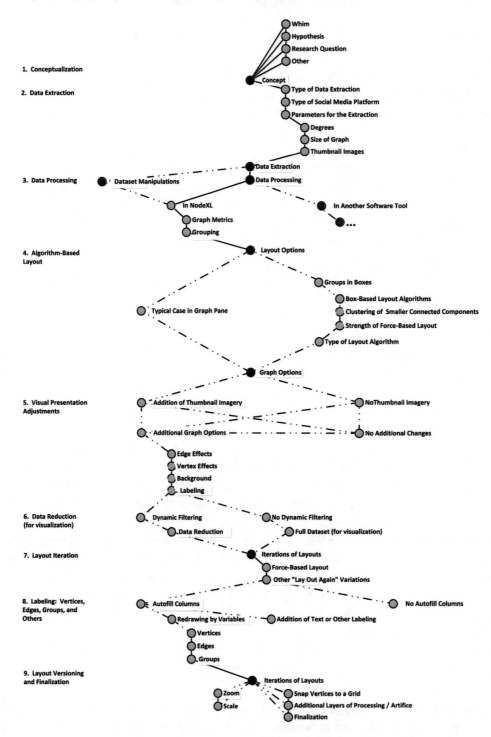

A Partially Specified Decision Flow for Creating "Network Art" in NodeXL

Figure 58. A "leaf": defining graph aesthetics

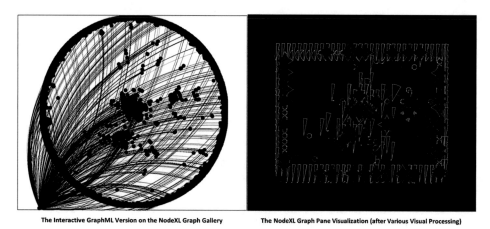

The Interactive GraphML Version on the NodeXL Graph Gallery   The NodeXL Graph Pane Visualization (after Various Visual Processing)

as the extraction and definition of particular relationships (such as content similarity ties only) but not others—may also be defined for certain data-level effects.

Other approaches involve changing up the actual output visualizations. Textual, symbolic, time, and other elements may be integrated with the network graph visualizations through the Autofill tool. Customized colors may be applied to the graphs (by inputting different RGB or "red, green, blue" codes in the color columns). Different shape forms may be interchanged. Another approach that was only tried superficially here involved applying varying sequences of processes to the extracted graph; some steps leave residual effects which may be carried on to other intermediate and ultimate visual effects. Graphs (with or without alpha channels) may also be overlaid on other images, such as maps or other visuals in the background. NodeXL is a complex tool, and it has levers that have not yet been exploited in the creating of data visualizations (in this chapter).

Various iterations of a graph may be presented as a diptych, triptych, quadtych, or other, for example, to create a sense of sequentiality, movement, or comparison and contrast. The force-based Fruchterman-Reingold layout algorithm is a natural for this because of the iterated force-based visualizations which gradually push the vertices to the edges (as if the elements were in a digital centrifuge). Network graphs may be grouped as similar images on a "proof sheet" or "contact sheet" (visual presentation methods back from the print age). Various visual overlays may be placed on a graph for other visual effects.

As some of the data extractions become dynamic, it may be that this process of data visualization is simply automated for real-time understandings of social networks as individuals interact in a mediated way online; indeed, some preliminary work has been completed in this direction (Khurana, Nguyen, Cheng, Ahn, Chan, & Schneiderman, 2011).

The aesthetic aspect of graph visualizations has always been a critical part of their appeal, with graphs informing about the underlying data while appealing to the senses. This chapter was the result of a two-year tour of NodeXL's graph visualization capabilities as aesthetic pleasure.

ACKNOWLEDGMENT

Thanks to Dr. Marc A. Smith, Director of the Social Media Research Foundation (SMRF) for his encouragement of this work. Your project was my first choice.

REFERENCES

Anokhin, A. P., Golosheykin, S., Sirevaag, E., Kristjansson, S., Rohrbaugh, J. W., & Heath, A. C. (2006). Rapid discrimination of visual scene content in the human brain. *Brain Research*, *1093*(1), 167–177. doi:10.1016/j.brainres.2006.03.108 PMID:16712815

Christodoulou, S. P., & Styliaras, G. D. (2008). Digital art 2.0: Art meets Web 2.0 trend. In the proceedings of DIMEA 2008. In *Proceedings of the 3rd International Conference on Digital Interactive Media in Entertainment and Arts.*

Dunne, C., & Schneiderman, B. (2013). Motif simplification: Improving network visualization readability with fan, connector, and clique glyphs. In *Proceedings of CHI 2013: Changing Perspectives.*

Dutton, D. (2002). Aesthetic universals. In *The Routledge Companion to Aesthetics.* Retrieved November 12, 2014, from http://www.denisdutton.com/universals.htm

Dutton, D. (2006). A naturalist definition of art. *The Journal of Aesthetics and Art Criticism, 65*(3), 367 – 377. Retrieved from http://www.jstor.org/stable/3700568

Eisenberg, M., & Buechley, L. (2008). Pervasive fabrication: Making construction ubiquitous in education. *Journal of Software*, *3*(4), 62–68. doi:10.4304/jsw.3.4.62-68

Görg, C., Pohl, M., Qeli, E., & Xu, K. (2010). Visual representations. In *Advances in Visual Computing: 6th International Symposium, ISVC 2010.* doi:10.1007/978-3-540-71949-6_4

Harel, D. (1998). *On the aesthetics of diagrams (summary of talk).* Springer Link. Retrieved Nov. 9, 2014, from http://download.springer.com/static/pdf/217/chp%253A10.1007%252FBFb0054280.pdf?auth66=1415578223_a51f9b36e41305ce52a357413fbbc1da&ext=.pdf

Harel, D., & Koren, Y. (2001). A fast multi-scale method for drawing large graphs. In GD 2000, LNCS. doi:10.1007/3-540-44541-2_18

Huang, W. (2013). Establishing aesthetics based on human graph reading behavior: Two eye tracking studies. *Personal and Ubiquitous Computing*, *17*(1), 93–105. doi:10.1007/s00779-011-0473-2

Huang, W. (2014). Evaluating overall quality of graph visualizations indirectly and directly. In Handbook of Human Centric Visualization. New York: Springer Science + Business. doi:10.1007/978-1-4614-7485-2_14

Jankun-Kelly, T. J., Dwyer, T., Holten, D., Hurter, C., Nöllenburg, M., Weaver, C., & Xu, K. (2014). Scalability considerations for multivariate graph visualization. In A. Kerren et al. (Eds.), *Multivariate Network Visualization.* Springer International Publishing. doi:10.1007/978-3-319-06793-3_10

Khurana, U., Nguyen, V.-A., Cheng, H.-C., Ahn, J.-W., Chen, X., & Schneiderman, B. (2011). Visual analysis of temporal trends in social networks using edge color coding and metric timelines. In *Proceedings of Privacy, Security, Risk and Trust (PASSAT) and 2011 IEEE Third International Conference in Social Computing* (SocialCom). doi:10.1109/PASSAT/SocialCom.2011.212

Kolaczyk, E. D. (2009). Mapping networks. In *Statistical Analysis of Network Data.* Springer Science. Retrieved from http://download.springer.com/static/pdf/560/chp%253A10.1007%25 2F978-0-387-88146-1_3.pdf?auth66=1415657155_389a8f9c38c4330d7eebb4cf76dfa5dd&ext=.pdf

McCormack, J. (2013). Aesthetics, art, evolution. EvoMUSART 2013, LNCS. Springer-Verlag. doi:10.1007/978-3-642-36955-1_1

Mendola, J. (2006). Intuitive hedonism. *Philosophical Studies, 128*(2), 441–477. doi:10.1007/s11098-004-7810-5

O'Brien, J. (2014). Reasoning with graphs. In Shaping Knowledge: Complex Social-Spatial Modelling for Adaptive Organizations. Oxford, UK: Elsevier.

Purchase, H. (1997). *Which aesthetic has the greatest effect on human understanding?* Berlin: SpringerLink. Retrieved from http://www.dcs.gla.ac.uk/publications/PAPERS/6453/gd97.pdf

Purchase, H. C., Allder, J.-A., & Carrington, D. (2001). User preference of graph layout aesthetics: A UML study. In J. Marks (Ed.), *GD 2000, LNCS 1984* (pp. 5–18). Berlin: Springer-Verlag. doi:10.1007/3-540-44541-2_2

Purchase, H. C., Carrington, D., & Allder, J.-A. (2000). Experimenting with aesthetics-based graph layout. In P. Cheng & V. Haarslev (Eds.), *Diagrams 2000, LNAI 1889* (pp. 498–501). Springer-Verlag Berlin Heidelberg.

Purchase, H. C., Freeman, E., & Hamer, J. (2012). An exploration of visual complexity. N Diagrams 2012, LNAI 7352. Berlin: Springer-Verlag.

Purchase, H. C., Hoggan, E., & Görg, C. (2007). How important is the 'mental map'? An empirical investigation of a dynamic graph layout algorithm. GD 2006. Berlin: Springer-Verlag.

Quigley, A. (2006). Aesthetics of large-scale relational information visualization in practice. In P. A. Fishwick (Ed.), *Aesthetic Computing* (pp. 315–334). Cambridge, MA: The MIT Press.

Tatarkiewicz, W. (1947). Psychological hedonism. From: *On Happiness. Synthese, 8*(8/9), 409 – 425.

ADDITIONAL READING

Hai-Jew, S. (2015). Beauty as a Bridge to NodeXL. Slideshare. Retrieved Oct. 27, 2015, from http://www.slideshare.net/ShalinHaiJew/beauty-as-a-bridge-to-nodexl

Hansen, D. L., Schneiderman, B., & Smith, M. A. (2011). *Analyzing Social Media Networks with NodeXL: Insights from a Connected World.* Amsterdam: Elsevier.

KEY TERMS AND DEFINITIONS

Algorithmic Art: An aesthetically pleasing visual-based object (usually in two-dimensions) created by computer.

Network Graph: A node-link diagram that represents entities and relationships.

Social Media Platform: Any number of types of online spaces where people may interact and collaborate in a mediated way.

APPENDIX

SIDEBAR: A Personal Journey in Social Network Graphs through the NodeXL Graph Gallery

My first interaction with Network Overview, Discovery and Exploration for Excel (NodeXL) came about in early December 2012. I had already been acquainted with UCINET, a software tool that enables the drawing of graphs with manually input data among other functions, and some rudimentary statistics behind network graphs. I had already drawn maybe a dozen or two graphs using UCINET for various publications. Figure 59 is my first graph on NodeXL, and at that time, I'm quite certain that I did not know much if anything about groups. The graph was uploaded into the NodeXL Graph Gallery (http:// nodexlgraphgallery.org/Pages/Default.aspx). That first graph was the start of "weak ties" engaging with the virtual community surrounding the gallery and learning from the uploaded work of others. The sense of audience was instrumental in this author's ultimately learning the tool because of the appeal of a sense of audience to see the various visualizations. [While the data extractions from the respective social media platforms may have seemed like a "shout-out" in some ways, they were not intended as much. Often, keyword topics or hashtags were selected only on whimsy.] The experimental and interactive GraphML (file format) version for the various graphs were also engaging and eye-opening; the interactive version encouraged zooming and panning; the simplified structure enabled visualization of the underlying structural dynamics without the aesthetic overlay; the named vertices really emphasized the fact of the underlying dataset based on real people and their communications. Figure 60 shows the drawn graph to the left and the interactive zoomable version on the right (see also Figure 61).

Two Years and 3,500 Graphs Later

Now, almost two years later, and more than 3,200 published graphs later on the Gallery and hundreds in various publications (which did not appear in the gallery), I have versioned graphs in lots of different ways and from all available social media platforms, but can also attest that there are still many other options and combinations that have not yet been tried. Even though I try not to pattern, I can see the tendencies in my graph visualizations. I tend to capture as large a dataset as possible because the research background says that more information is usually better, and if I wanted to depict something smaller, I can always filter out information (without loss to the underlying data). For a researcher, "knowability" is important. I try to put the software through its paces because my instructional design training has me constantly testing out software tools and assessing their applicability across a range of possible projects. Of special interest has been how a social network graph may be analyzed at virtually every level of analysis: node, motif, sub-cluster, sub-clusters, and network. Such graphs may be considered "big data"—relatively speaking—and share that characteristic of being analyzable at a number of different levels. If there was any sense of taste brought to this, it was a discovered one based on interactions within the tool, not an *a priori* one. In general, the preference was for naturally drawn graphs with as few changes as possible.

I also experimented with how changing up the parameters of a data extraction can radically change the types and amounts of data extracted: how you ask the question affects what you can know. Then, too, in my workplace, I have a number of computers for my use (at least two of which are hand-me-downs), and it takes little to be running a data extraction on several of them while I am using a main laptop for my development work.

Figure 59. The author's first network graph using NodeXL

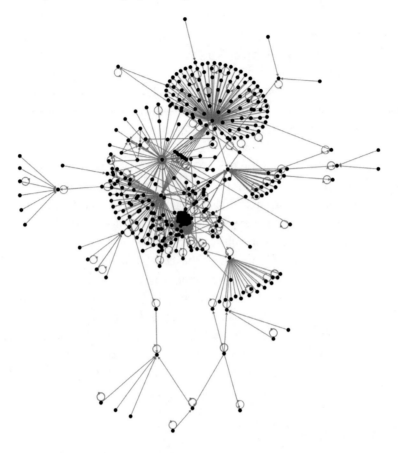

Figure 60. The drawn version vs. the interactive version

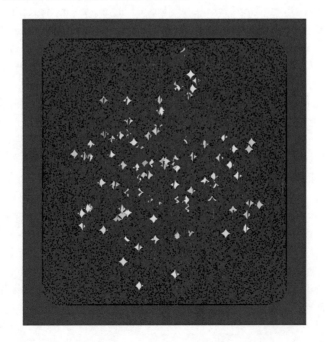

Figure 61. The drawn graph (left) beside the interactive graphml experimental version on the NodeXL site

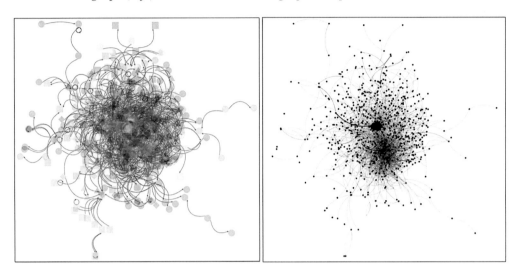

The graph samples in this chapter came from the published set of network graphs but are only 1.5% of the full set. I have extracted graphs based on multiple different languages. I've drawn graphs using NodeXL with imported datasets extracted with other software tools.

Sui Generis Visualizations

Every graph is *sui generis* based on the uniqueness of each dataset extracted from across the dozens of social media platforms accessible by NodeXL. I've learned about the peculiar structures that emerge from content networks such as from video networks on YouTube (relatively fewer vertices and lots of links and some basic stability over time) and related tags networks on Flickr (typical clusters found on that platform, which enables sharing of photo and video contents). I've extracted article networks from Wikipedia and seen how ideas interrelate. I've noticed how hashtag (#) conversations and eventgraphs flood into broad public awareness and then dissipate like so much (actually permanent) ephemera on Twitter. I've seen how there are "forbidden" (blocked) queries on various social media platforms and also the stony silence from protected or private accounts. I've seen how there may be moments of silence or near-silence even as large-scale scientific phenomena are discovered and revealed. I've extracted http (web) networks to see how various presences appear on the Surface Web using the Virtual Observatory for the Study of Online Networks (VOSON). I've extracted a few Facebook networks to look at social connectivity through this social networking site. I've mapped wikis that have been part of my professional projects. I've mapped eventgraphs for conferences that I've organized or attended. I've mapped a work-based email network. I've seen how social media echoes events trending in mainline media, with mainline media also tapping social media platforms and channels for news leads and accents to the news. I've learned some basics about application programming interfaces (APIs) and the types of information accessible through NodeXL (as well as site scraping). Throughout, I've kept in mind the phenomena of strategic messaging, social performance, and "folk" sensibilities.

The initial inchoate sense of bedazzlement at the beauty of the graphs created in NodeXL has never left me. I've played with virtually all the layout algorithms available through NodeXL and drawn graphs with one node all the way to 320,000 nodes (which my computer processed but was unable to extract groups or to depict visually except in a very condensed way). Pushing the limits of the layout algorithms with extremes of sparseness and density of nodes and links produces various types of visual surprises—from spirals or ring lattices that do not coalesce recognizably with sparse networks to glorious pops of visceral color in multilayered grids with dense networks. Then, too, there have been colorful visualizations of motif censuses. The ability to add thumbnail images from Flickr content networks enabled a whole other look-and-feel. The ability to scale down a graph visualization and change the color sense from bolds to pastels to pure black-and-white was another moment of visual insight. The ability to create word art by extracting captured microblogging messages between individual accounts was yet another moment of memorable discovery. In terms of revelatory moments in these past two years, there have been a number of them.

I've attained a sense of which layout algorithms are demanding of scratch memory and which can snarl a quad-core video rendering computer. I have lost days and days of processing in pursuit of a particular data extraction only to have my machine reboot as part of a Windows update. I've learned how to be patient to attain a full data extraction and then to process the information (such as for full graph metrics) in small pieces and parts (saving the .xl file at every possible juncture) in order to protect the work and ultimately emerge with a usable graph. I understand viscerally what computational expense may be involved through both (1) the experience of using NodeXL to extract social media platform data, process it, and output graphs, and (2) some light academic readings about layout algorithms and network analysis. There are days when I think I can look at the numbers in the graph metrics table and pre-see what a particular layout algorithm will look like if it is selected.

In terms of network graph aesthetics, it helps to first understand some of the inherent characteristics of graphs themselves and the rules for their drawing. Most are non-figurative in the classic sense but may evoke a hint of figure now and again. Aesthetics are often personal, and this sensibility often diverges from what is more purely analytically valuable and informative. Part of the charm of graphs comes from a sense of happenstance—of the fact that the extracted data is likely accurate for the particular slice-in-time alone. While graphs may be drawn and re-drawn and materialized in different ways, there is something of the need to preserve the sanctity of the underlying data that limits the amount of artifice that may be applied to the visualization (at least for this author). This is so even for the drawings that are totally unmoored from the underlying data and used for purely illustrative purposes (such as to illustrate an abstract idea in a fictional work). There is something of the sense of "found art" to network graphs that discourages from too much tampering.

Now that I'm trying to recreate the sense of "new eyes" in terms of looking at graphs, I have the sense that someone who has not experienced such graphing might assume that some of these are very easy to create. Indeed, NodeXL can work in a blisteringly fast way for some data extractions… but not others depending on the size of the data extraction, the social media platform, whether the individual has "whitelisted" or not, and a range of other factors. Then, too, the data processing and other work may be highly computationally demanding, and with larger data sets, such processing may take days (or NodeXL may crash out before the full extraction or data processing is achieved). At heart, the real elegance is in the data, the underlying math and the layout algorithms, and the people behind the data.

For the small piece that people bring to the visualizations, it helps generally to experiment broadly and to avoid having a few "go-to" methods. Even today, it surprises me that a software tool can be designed with such complexity (most software designers would default to making decisions for their users and then hiding the potential for options) and yet be so easy to learn and to use in some ways. I appreciate that the team that has made and evolved NodeXL works hard to ensure that the layout algorithms and network analysis ideas are not "black box" but acquirable for the users who want to learn.

Committing to a software tool is non-trivial because this requires a large investment for the learning and its use, and there are opportunity costs and tradeoffs in going with one vs. another. The market is constantly changing, and there is a transitory aspect to some tools, which may have little support, little improvement over time, and a lack of stability. In such an environment, it is always *caveat emptor*, even if the tool is free.

The chapter addresses the happenstance aspect of some artistic graphs by lauding the chance factors in data extractions, the power of some glitches in data visualization, and other senses that contribute to the sense of ephemera. There are other methods such as deforming the graph pane by resizing the Excel window and letting the image respond by re-drawing…and pushing that image out. The range of discovery is enormous in ways intended and unintended. I look at new graphs posted on the Gallery that zoom in on particular parts of a social network map, and I smile in recognition because there are times even now when I zoom in and out of graphs to analyze particular aspects and relationships, and the magic of how lovely graphs are at virtually every level is still with me.

Learning about "network art" experientially has been a partial byproduct of the visual explorations of these past two years. Part of the charm of network art is the superficial sense that a graph is understandable through the visual-cognitive channel alone. Each graph stands alone as its own digital entity, but it also is suggestive of the underlying data. Each is a puzzle and a mystery with varying degrees of complexity. A graph leaks data even as it somewhat obscures it in dazzle. And when the back-end data is brought into play along with the wealth of metrics, a range of other substantive understandings may be brought into play beyond the machine-created beauty.

Section 4
Applied Uses of Social Media Data for Awareness and Problem-Solving

Chapter 12
Social Network Synthesis:
A Dynamic Approach for Building Distance Education Programs

E. Pınar Uça-Güneş
Anadolu University, Turkey

Gülsün Eby
Anadolu University, Turkey

ABSTRACT

Distance Education is more preferable by both learners and institutions in the 21st century. The technology, teaching-learning and communication processes are in a change that each stakeholder should comply with. One up-to-date form of these processes is social networking. Social networks have the potential of providing access to more resources and improving the quality of communication and interaction. Social Network Analysis and Network Weaving approaches are useful to determine the social network structure and improve it. Further to that, in this chapter, "Social Network Synthesis" approach is introduced, obtained by applying synthesis process on Social Network Theory. The approach is thought to allow for the establishment of optimum relationships between the concerned actors in a newly configured goal-directed social network. An illustrative framework that can be used for building Distance Education programs is also presented.

INTRODUCTION

Developments in Information Communication Technologies within the changes on views of education and teaching has lead Distance Education to be gradually preferable for both institutions and learners. The Distance Education Programs' superiorities can be effective on this choice like learners' providing a workforce while learning (Macdonald & Poniatowska, 2011), avoiding a possible job loss because of living in another place, removing the problems like accommodation which can cause a negativity on time and cost (Burgess & Russell, 2003). According to Sloan-C's data in 2011, the number of students joining at least one (online) distance education class is 6,7 million outnumbering the previous year with

DOI: 10.4018/978-1-5225-0648-5.ch012

an increase of 570 thousand more students (Allen & Seaman, 2013). In mostly young populated Turkey, to meet the demand for increasing capacity in higher education without making large investments, developing distance education was concluded as one of the solutions (YÖK, 2007).

Developments occurring in the field should be reflected as well as running particularly field related notional and practical knowledge and skills on process of management, implementation and design of Distance Education Programs. In Distance Education, learners and teachers are connected to a technology to transfer information and communicate with each other as a result of being in different places on most part of the educational activities (Moore & Kearsley, 2005). Therefore, researches should be done on the developments and changes of technologies by following them closely to determine their active availability in Distance Education. In development of Distance Education when it is closely taken into consideration, it is observed that application usage changes depending on the technology. In Distance Education, different approaches from philosophy and pedagogy are also adopted as there are changes in technological perspective.

Distance Education even when considered as a system, it is inevitable not to see existence of relationship affecting each other between its components (Moore & Kearsly, 2005). For instance, the change in technology has played a role in shaping the pedagogical dimension in Distance Education. The system approach must be adopted while designing a Distance Education Program, so; the relationship among dimensions (learning, technology, communication, management, evaluation) should not be ignored. Within the framework of system approach, a communication structure depending on technology might be designed and learning-teaching activities built on that communication structure might be planned while configuring Distance Education Programs.

Taylor (2001) explained Distance Education models and distribution technologies depending on technology in five generations as for Caladine (2008) mentioned the requirement of a sixth generation subjecting to changes in technology and learning point of views (Table 1). In this context, e-learning 2.0 concept comes forward related to Web 2.0 technology. While providing their contribution in configuration of knowledge, Web 2.0 enables users to interact with each other. Social software, resources created by students, sharing experiences and resources, media richness are the elements giving clues about learning method of the generation. These elements can be interpreted as distance education learners learn by taking part in online social networks or the Distance Education program is or should be designed accordingly.

Although in the 21st century social network concept is mostly used in terms of online social networking, it can be said that the social networks exists since human does. Since the very beginning of its existence, human beings have been making different kinds of connections with other people and in this way, various social networks being built. Social network can be described as *actors*, in general, showing different existence such as individuals, groups, companies, nations and within *the relations (ties)* showing resource flows can be related to situations such as control, dependence, cooperation, information interchange, and competition (Carrasco, J. A.; Hogan, B.; Wellman, B. & Miller, E. J., 2006). In 21st century, the term Social Network is mostly used to define online social networking. This way, individuals also appear to have social networks in virtual environments. This matter happens to be more considering in Distance Education in which interaction and learning is provided via technologies and most frequently the Internet. Social Networks could increase the quality of interaction and communication in Distance Education System. In addition to this, providing learners to reach more resources may contribute to their critical thinking.

Table 1. Models of distance education: a conceptual framework

Models of Distance Education and Associated Delivery Technologies	
First Generation The Correspondence Model	Print
Second Generation The Multimedia Model	• Print • Audiotape • Videotape • Computer-based learning (e.g. CML/CAL/IMM) • Interactive video (disk and tape)
Third Generation The Telelearning Model	• Audio tele-conferencing • Video-conferencing • Audiographic Communication • Broadcast TV/Radio and audio- teleconferencing
Fourth Generation The Flexible Learning Model	• Interactive multimedia (IMM) online • Internet-based access to WWW resources • Computer-mediated communication
Fifth Generation The Intelligent Flexible Learning Model	• Interactive multimedia (IMM) online • Internet-based access to WWW resources • Computer-mediated communication, using automated response systems • Campus portal access to institutional processes and resources
Sixth Generation Web 2.0 and e-Learning 2.0	• Social software • Student creation of resources • Sharing of experiences and resources • Media rich

Source: Taylor, (2001); Caladine, (2008)

On the other hand, Siemens (2006) claims that distinctions of physical and virtual existences are rapidly changing as physical and virtual realities are blurring. Whether physical or virtual, social network is considered to take an important role in determining effectiveness and quality of Distance Education system and program. The social network's structure will change depending on the field in Distance Education programs. For example, the social network, actors of the network, relationships and properties that is Social Network's Structure will be different in marketing and health field. But the actors could take place in a social network for a program being conducted from distance can be individuals such as administrators, instructors, learners, technical, administrative and social support staff, consultants, field experts; organizations as the communities, associations and foundations related to the field; resources as learning management systems, libraries, online information sources, websites and online groups; tools like software and equipment. The relationship among actors can be described in variations as guidance, information exchange, feedback and membership. In this manner, actors and relationships determine the social structure.

Social Network Analysis takes social structure as a network of sets of actors and relationships uniting them into pairs, and examines the effects with the structure (Tindall & Wellman, 2001). Studies, about social networking, conducted after 2000s especially focuses on social network analysis (Ethier, 2006). Analysis of existing social networks in physical and virtual environment can make contributions for renewing it by revisions. Social network analysis studies can also be used to clarify the existing situations for ongoing programs about Distance Education. So, decision makers can detect any deficiencies with the program, and solution oriented intervention can be made.

Another approach is the Network Weaving Approach. According to network weaving approach, *an actor* (network weaver) that is not included in the network connects not related actors by getting involved to the network. For this reason, in solving problems detected by social network analysis and correcting possible deficiencies, the network weaving approach can be used. When it comes to configuring a Distance Education program for the first time both of these approaches are not sufficient enough about how to reach the desired goal of building a proper social network.

Within coherence of what's discussed above, it can be said that by using Social Network Synthesis Approach for a Distance Education program, optimum relationships between individuals, organizations, resources and tools can be built. The social network synthesis term is used as the meaning in from time to time i) work of programs which provides access to different applications by one single username and password at a mutual time period in online environments ii) synthesis of different networks which is one of the aims of network science. But, in this study, the term is used to mean as; "the design to form a goal directed social network determining what the actors (individuals, organizations, resources and tools) and how the relationships among them should be." (Uça-Güneş, 2014). In this context, benefiting from social network theorem to build a Distance Education Program the required actors taking place and the properties of relationships among them can be demonstrated.

Later in this chapter, social network approaches are explained in more detail. Afterwards, it is stated how Social Network Synthesis Approach can be used in building Distance Education Programs. Accordingly, a framework is built by illustrating the steps taken toward implementation of the approach.

BACKGROUND

Distance Education Programs and System Approach

Moore and Kearsly (2012, p. 2) claims that "Distance Education is teaching and planned learning in which teaching normally occurs in a different place from learning, requiring communication through technologies as well as special institutional organization." The system can generally be described as a structure of which component pieces provides the whole system work effectively. It is essential for pieces to work compatible with each other. Distance Education has been seen as a system for the first time in the late 1960's and early 1970's. The following elements should take place in a Distance Education system (Moore & Kearsley, 2012):

- A source of teaching and content knowledge (An institution with instructors and other resources that provide content).
- A course design subsystem structures this into materials and activities for students.
- A subsystem conveys courses to learners by means of media and technologies.
- Instructors and support staff that interact with learners while using the materials.
- Learners in their different environments.
- A sub-management system that organizes politics, needs analysis and resource distribution, evaluates outcomes and coordinates other subsystems.

On the base of that it can be said that components of Distance Education System are learning, teaching, interaction, design, technology, management. Moore and Kearsly (2005) points out that although those subsystems could work separately, it is also required understanding interrelations between them. Distance education institutions should be considered as a system of which subsystems are knowledge sources, design, distribution, interaction, learning and management. Also, the better these subsystems are integrated in practice, the greater will be the effectiveness of distance education institution. When organizations adapt a system approach to distance education, there will be an impact on teachers, learners, administrators, and policy makers; and significant changes in the way that education is conceptualized, funded, designed, and delivered (Moore & Kearsley, 2005, pp. 22-23).

The System Approach is the point of view that studies and explains the addressed problem considering it as a system. In System Approach, unlike focusing on component or parts, the focus is on analysis and design of the whole. In this approach, the problem is examined in its entirety considering all aspects and parameters. It is tried to be comprehended how they interact with each other and how they will be formed in a proper relationship scheme for the optimum solution of the problem. The system approach prepares a ground for system to be automatically applied by showing different aspects of a problem with its connections and making the compromises and the optimizations. Application of system approach on an existing problem is making plans with thinking on the application for a solution of the problem after analysis and synthesis (Ramo & St.Clair, 1998). Moore and Kearsley (2012) denotes that a distance education program can be understood and delivered best by using the system approach.

Network Science and Social Networks

Networks can be defined as a structure formed with objects, that can be called as nodes, such as molecules, individuals, organizations, entities and cities and connections representing the relationship between nodes. Network science is an emerging, highly interdisciplinary research area which aims to develop theoretical and practical techniques and approaches in order to increase the understanding of natural and man-made networks (Börner vd.; 2007).

The aims of Network Science can be listed as follows (Gürsakal, 2009, pp. 49-50):

- Understanding the relationships between the architecture and functions of networks.
- Producing necessary means and concepts for modelling and analyzing very large networks.
- Producing the required techniques for design and synthesis of networks.
- Analyzing resistance and safety of networks.
- Doing measurements and experiments related to networks.
- Developing required mathematical structure about networks.

Three major steps can be mentioned about Network Science to come on the scene. First step is the article Euler (1736) wrote about seven bridges on Pregel River. The purpose of the article was to answer the question whether it is possible to build a path to cross all seven bridges without using any of them more than once or not. Euler's drawing, which he took lands as nodes and bridges as connections leading the passage between them, can be accepted as first network drawing. The origin of Graph Theory in maths has also happened by this drawing. Second step can be sum up as in 1933 Jacob Moreno's using sociogram to describe social structure of primary school students; Paul Erdös and Alfréd Rényi's bringing random networks model up; in 1967, Steve Milgram's small world hypothesis; in 2006 Eric Horvitz and

Jure Leskovec's showing six-degrees hypothesis was eligible. Third step was Albert Lazsio Barabasi's paying attention to Internet Network's measuring, mapping and modeling and in this context, Hawong Jeoung from research group's writing a program that maps by determining connections among documents in Web electronically; that program was applied in the internet domain of Notre Dame University (Gürsakal, 2009; Lewis, 2009).

The term "Social Network" has put forward by Barnes in 1954 (Marin & Wellman, 2012). Marin and Wellman (2012) defines social network as a set of nodes connected to each other with socially interrelated and in one and more relationships. In this definition, coherent with the definition of network, nodes' connecting to each other with 'social relations' comes into prominence. In social networks, nodes, in general, show the actors (individuals, groups, organizations). Actors can be connected in terms of similarities, social relationships, interactions or flows.

In 21st century, online social networks are commonly used within the opportunities supplied by Web 2.0. In Web 2.0 period, the user orientation and depending upon that participation and interaction has increased. Online social networks are contexts that make access to other individuals and resources easier for individuals in the network and intensify their interaction with the others. There are many social network sites built tending to various purposes such as friendship, finding job opportunities, sharing writings about particular subjects (food, travelling, economy, photos etc.), following up-to-date matters.

When evaluated in terms of Distance Education, it can be said that socials networks affect learning in terms of communication-interaction, information processing, learners' features and roles. In social networks, learners can access to more resources, organization and people faster and easier, communication-interaction can be provided just-in-time, more focused communication (the contact with the desired expert or the subject) can be done. In terms of information processing, social networks can take a part in comparing, comfirming and verifying a large number of and different knowledge, and also synthesis and reconstruction of information. In terms of learners' features and role, it is thought for them to take a more involved, conscious and critical role (Uça-Güneş, 2014).

Ties in social networks can be classified in two basic types as states and events. Being a friend of someone or having a talent etc. are examples of state-type ties. And phone calls, selling goods can be given as an example of event-type ties. Connections can be considered like pipes or roads that enable a kind of flow between nodes (Borgatti & Halgin, 2011). Borgatti and Lopez-Kidwell (2012) classifies state-type ties as role-based, event-type ties as cognitive/affective. According to their connection types, networks are dealt on the basis of different models.

In flow model, the focus is on social relations or interactions, by using these connections, backcloth (boundaries of network traffic) is diagnosed and then the flows are determined. According to this model, the actual flow of resources between nodes is subjected as in the flow of money from one person to another (Borgatti & Lopez-Kidwell, 2012). The flow model is the most developed platform in the network theorem. However, there is phenomenon that cannot be reduced to flow model and also improved theoretical explanations in the field. Power (authority) is one of these areas (Borgatti & Halgin, 2011). Another model for similar situations, like this one, is the model named as "Bond or Coordination Model" (Borgatti & Halgin, 2011), and sometimes "Network Architecture" (Borgatti & Lopez-Kidwell, 2012). In this model, the power (authority) or knowledge isn't directly transmitted; the work is done in the name of someone or with somebody. For instance, a judge can decide in favor of his friend on a case. In this situation, the friend benefits from it; but unlike flow model, the authority of judge isn't transferred to his friend (Borgatti & Lopez-Kidwell, 2012, p.45).

In studies of social networks, it is put emphasis on three types of networks: ego-centric, socio-centric and open-system networks. Ego-centric networks are networks related to only one individual or organization. Socio-centric networks can be considered as closed-system networks like the connection between students in a classroom. Boundaries in open-system network are not that clear as in the chain of influencers of a particular decision (Kadushin, 2004, p.4).

In order to compare, to determine their types and to analyze them, network measures are used (Gür-sakal, 2009). The network measures defining features of networks can be studied in three groups as network orientated, actor orientated and relationship orientated measures. Brass (2011) classifies social network studies into four groups according to their approaches or foci as a) structure, b) relationships, c) resources, d) cognition and he adds traditional organizational behavior focus to the actor attributes. Network measures are listed that are typically used in organizational research related to each approach.

- **The Approach Focusing on Structure:** It is the approach in which nodes and connections are evaluated (regardless of their other features) on only their structural positions in the network. Table 2 and Table 3 adapted from Brass (1995) respectively show typical structural social network measures aimed for network and actors. The point to note in Table 3 is that the measures in here showing actor's relationships with network and any change in the network can affect this relationship (Brass, 2011).

Table 2. Typical structural social network measures used to describe entire network

Measure	Definition
Size	Number of actors in the network
Inclusiveness	Total number of actors in a network minus the number of isolated actors (not connected to any other actors). Also measured as the ratio of connected actors to the total number of actors.
Component	Largest connected subset of network nodes and links. All nodes in the component are connected (either direct or indirect links) and no nodes have links to nodes outside the component. Number of components or size of the largest component are measured.
Connectivity (Reachability)	Minimum number of actors or ties that must be removed to disconnect the network. Reachability is 1 if two actors can reach each other, otherwise 0. Average reachability equals connectedness.
Connectedness/ fragmentation	Ratio of pairs of nodes that are mutually reachable to total number of pairs of nodes
Density	Ratio of the number of actual links to the number of possible links in the network.
Centralization	Difference between the centrality scores of the most central actor and those of other actors in a network is calculated, and used to form ratio of the actual sum of the differences to the maximum sum of the differences.
Core-peripheriness	Degree to which network is structured such that core members connect to everyone while periphery members connect only to core members and not other members of the periphery.
Transitivity	Three actors(A, B, C) are transitive if whenever A is linked to B and B is linked to C, then C is linked to A. Transitivity is the number of transitive triples divided by the number of potential transitive triples (number of paths of length 2). Also known as the weighted clustering coefficient.
Small-worldness	Extent to which a network structure is both clumpy (actors are clustered into small clumps) yet having a short average distance between actors.

Source: Brass, (2011)

Table 3. Typical structural social network measures assigned to individual actors

Measure	Definition
Degree	Number of direct links with other actors
In-degree	Number of directional links to the actor from other actors (in-coming links)
Out-degree	Number of directional links form the actor to other actors (out-going links)
Range (Diversity)	Number of links to different others (others are defined as different to the extent that they are not themselves linked to each other, or represent different groups or statuses)
Closeness	Extent to which an actor is close to, or can easily reach all the other actors in the network. Usually measured by averaging the path distances (direct and indirect links) to all others. A direct link is counted as 1, indirect links receive proportionately less weight.
Betweenness	Extent to which an actor mediates, or falls between any other two actors on the shortest path between those two actors. Usually averaged across all possible pairs in the network.
Centrality	Extent to which an actor is central to a network. Various measures (including degree, closeness, and betweenness) have been used as indicators of centrality.
Prestige	Based on asymmetric relationships, prestigious actors are the object rather than the source of relations. Measures similar to centrality are calculated by accounting for the direction of the relationship (i.e., in-degree).
Structural Holes	Extent to which an actor is connected to alters who are not themselves connected. Various measures include ego-network density and constraint as well as betweenness centrality.
Ego-network density	Number of direct ties among other actors to whom ego is directly connected divided by the number of possible connections among these alters. Often used as a measure of structural holes when controlling for the size of ego's network.
Constraint	Extent to which an actor (ego) is invested in alters who are themselves invested in ego's other alters. Burt's (1992, p. 55) measure of structural holes; constraint is the inverse of structural holes.
Liaison	An actor who has links to two or more groups that would otherwise not be linked, but is not a member of either group.
Bridge	An actor who is a member of two or more groups.

Source: Brass, (2011)

- **The Approach Focusing on Relationships:** While ties are studied as binary (present or absent) and directional in the structural approach, values are typically assigned to ties in the approach focusing on relationships. With regard to this, as well as describing a certain connection between two actors each measurement in Table 4 adapted from Brass (1995), the measurements combined to assign for a particular actor or used to describe the whole of the network (Brass, 2011).

Focusing on relationships in social networks gained greater emphasis with Granovetter's (1973) "The Strength of Weak Ties" theory. Granovetter found that weak ties were more often the source of helpful job information than strong ties. He claimed that the strong ties show tendency to be themselves connected (to be a part of the same social circle) and provide redundant information to the job seeker; on the other hand, weak ties provide useful information on finding a job by connecting with disconnected social circles (bridge) (Brass, 2011).

- **The Approach Focusing on Resources:** Instead of assuming all nodes (especially alters) being the same, it focuses on others' resources.

Table 4. Typical relational social network measures of ties

Measure	Definition	Example
Indirect links	Path between two actors is mediated by one or more others	A is linked to B, B is linked to C, thus A is indirectly linked to C through B
Frequency	How many times, or how often the link occurs	A talks to B 10 times per week
Duration (stability)	Existence of link over time	A has been friends with B for 5 years
Multiplexity	Extent to which two actors are linked together by more than one relationship	A and B are friends, they seek out each other for advice, and work together
Strength	Amount of time, emotional intensity, intimacy, or reciprocal services (frequency or multiplexity sometimes used as measures of strength of tie)	A and B are close friends, or spend much time together
Direction	Extent to which link is from one actor to another	Work flows from A to B, but not from B to A
Symmetry (reciprocity)	Extent to which relationship is bi-directional	A asks for B for advice, and B asks A for advice

Source: Brass, (2011)

- **The Approach Focusing on Attributes:** It includes the matters of how individual characteristics effect the network structure or how they interact with the opportunities and constraints presented by network structures (Brass, 2011:17).
- **The Approach Focusing on Cognition:** In cognitive approach, networks are considered like 'prisms'; focus is individuals' cognitive interpretations of the network (Brass, 2011:17).

Social network data may be collected from archival records, observations, informant perceptions or a combination of these methods. Researchers can collect ego network data or whole network data (Brass, 2011). Borgatti implies that the ego-centric network includes the ego, his direct-link alters, and ties among those alters (as cited in Brass, 2011, p.19).

In network studies, specifying boundaries according to the research question has a great importance. The problem like specifying number of different type networks, the number of links removed from ego (indirect links) should be taken into consideration in both conceptual and methodological aspects. Relationships can express different things (friendship, business relationships, positive-negative opinions) and a connection can include different types of relationships at the same time (Brass, 2011).

Wellman mentions social networks are touted for their ability to integrate micro and macro approaches (as cited in Brass, 2011, p.23). The effects of network's features on group or individuals or how a characteristic belonging to an individual affects the features of group can be studied. In this context, also in Distance Education, it is considered that doing social network research can present results that could contribute in aspects of both distance education institutions and learners.

SOCIAL NETWORK APPROACHES

In this part, respectively Social Network Analysis, Network Weaving and Social Network Synthesis are mentioned.

Social Network Analysis

Social Network Analysis can be described as an approach that has the following four features (Freeman, 2012, p. 26):

- It involves the intuition of relations among social actors are important.
- It's based on the collection and analysis of data related to relations that connects the actors.
- It uses mostly the graphic imagery to show structure of the connections.
- It develops models based on mathematical and computations to describe and clarify the structure.

Social Network Analysis, may be, dates back to 13th century; the use of four features mentioned at the same time has not been an issue until 1930s. Modern social network analysis has been introduced by a psychologist named Jacob J. Moreno and a psychiatrist named Helen Jennings. Moreno and Jennings named their approach as sociometry. Around the same time, a group led by an anthropologist named W.Loyd Warner being unaware of this approach and independently has also used social network approach. In the process till 1970, social network studies were applied on various fields and in 1970s, social network analysis has become worldwide known among social scientists. (Freeman, 2012). It can be said that there are three factors in the increase of Social Network Analysis studies in 2000s: i) applications' making it possible to conceptualize new perceptions about interactions, ii) its focusing on complexity and understanding systems and developing on this matter, iii) the availability of software which makes analyzing the data and forming sociograms easier (Durland & Fredricks, 2005, pp. 5-6). There are plenty of software developed to make Social Network Analysis. (UCINET, Pajek, Gephi etc.). These software differentiates on their concept and aims, data types and functions.

With Social Network Analysis, inferences on the inspected social structure can be made; in this way, required actions can be implemented by using the gathered information. It provides a viewpoint on matters like why a problem happened, on what a good application depend; by obtaining information about the position of actors, how relationships affect a situation etc., whereby, policies can be determined related to solve the problem or to increase the number of good applications.

Network Weaving

Krebs and Holley (2006) put Network Weaving notion forth aiming to make the network better and to develop it. Ingram and Torfason (2010), who state that most organizations' mission is to provide a context for continuing or regularly repeated relationships between actors over time, talk about the interaction being encouraged via Network Weaving, a common understanding being created and an institutional frame being provided to keep relations going. Krebs and Holley (2006), referring to networks growing most of the time without depending on a plan, state that it is possible to reach the success with an active network management. In this context, they mention about weaving networks to create productive individuals and smart communities. According to this approach, Network Weaver combines the actors who aren't connected to each other. To make this, it is necessary for network weaver to own a vision, energy and social skills to direct the flow in the network. Krebs and Holley (2006) explain the purposes of Network Weaving as preparing ground for collaborations with mutual benefits as much as building

Table 5. Pyramid of network weaving involvement

Level	Activity
7	Introducing A to B in person and offering a collaboration opportunity to get A and B off to a successful partnership
6	Introducing A to B in person and following up with A and B to nurture connection
5	Introducing A to B in person
4	Introducing A to B in a conference call
3	Introducing A to B in an email
2	Suggesting A talk to B and calling B to look for a contact
1	Suggesting to A that A should talk to B

Source: (Krebs & Holley, 2006 - developed by Jack Ricchiuto)

relationships in the network. So, it is mentioned the community and the network developing as well. It is also emphasized the necessity that there should be a transition from network weaver to network facilitator for continuation of improvement.

According to Krebs and Holley (2006), weaving a network requires two iterative and continuous steps:

1. **Know the Network:** Take regular x-rays of the network and evaluate the progress.
2. **Knit the Network:** Follow the 4 phase network knitting process:
    a. Scattered Fragments,
    b. Single Hub-and-Spoke,
    c. Multi-Hub Small-World Network,
    d. Core/Periphery.

Each phase has its own distinct topology and builds a more adaptive and resilient network structure than the prior phase. Network mapping can be used to track the progress through these four stages revealing what is known about the network and uncover possible next steps for the weaver (Krebs & Holley, 2006).

In this context, Table 5 includes the examples of activities can be done in a network for business sector. In the table, while first level shows network type interaction, 6th and 7th levels are related to build a high level community (Table 5).

Also Network Weaving Approach takes an existing social network; but adding actors (network weaver, network facilitator) into the network to serve the purpose of building new relationships or strengthening them is in question.

Social Network Synthesis

Synthesis is re-forming a whole that is divided into its elements by analyzing. The purpose of synthesis is making a whole by bringing simple elements together. The two conditions to be carefully considered about in the synthesis are; i) the separation of actual elements of a whole that comprise it, ii) combining the elements or parts collected by separating from a whole based on a true and correct order. Uça-Güneş (2014) has taken the notion Synthesis to mean *"Combining the components in an appropriate manner to create a whole"* and named it as "Social Network Synthesis" by applying it into Social Network Theorem.

Network and Network components (parts) are defined based on network measures by using the data related to an existing social network (whole) in Social Network Analysis. But in Social Network Synthesis, this process is operated inversely; network components (parts) are determined and defined, on the base of that the social network (whole) is formed. In other words, it is aimed to form "Social Network" by combining "Actors" and "Relationships" which are the components of social network in Social Network Synthesis Approach in an appropriate way. In this context, Social Network Synthesis is defined as *The design of what the actors (individuals, organizations, resources and tools) and how the relationships between them should be to form a goal directed social network* (Uça-Güneş, 2014).

Social Network Synthesis can be performed by different research patterns in accordance with the aim. Uça-Güneş (2014) defines the general steps to be followed as:

Step 1: Define the goal.
Step 2: Define the network type and boundaries.
Step 3: Define actor groups (or determine them on the research process).
Step 4: Define relationships (or determine them on the research process).
Step 5: Determine the actors (whom or what they should be).
Step 6: Determine the relationships and the properties of the relationships between actors (how they should be).
Step 7: Put the outcomes related to actors and relationships forth in Social Network structure.

Uça-Güneş (2014), using Social Network Synthesis approach, aimed to develop a model for structuring the technology dimension of Distance Education Graduate Programs which will be distance programs themselves. She also considered learning and communication dimensions in this process via related theories, respectively by Transformative Learning Theory and by Social Network Theory. The study was a qualitative case study that used Delphi method to benefit from the experts' opinions and experiences in Distance Education field. For this purpose, a theoretical matrix was developed considering both the theories to collect data and questions were generated according to the matrix. The focus was 'identifying the Actors which should be taken place in the Social Network that will be developed relating to provide Transformative Learning' in the first two rounds of Delphi, and 'how the Relationships between the Learner and the Actors, and properties of each relationship should be' in the following two tours. Based on the findings, an ego-network type of Social Network structure is presented where the Learner was in the centrum. In addition, regarding the suggestions for providing the Social Network structure that is found, a Social Network Synthesis Model was developed.

Social Network Approach is thought to make it possible to build optimum relationships between individuals, institutions, resources and tools in a newly configured network and thus, represents a method for determined purpose to happen. This approach also coincides with the system approach.

Comparison of Social Network Approaches

Social Network Approaches are shown in Table 6 on the basis of aim and functions with the questions that they're seeking answers for.

Table 6. Social network approaches and their functions

Social Network Approach	Aim/Function	Questions to Answer
Social Network Analysis	Making inferences by examining Social network structure	How is an existing social network structure?
Network Weaving	Making Social network structure better and improving it	How can an existing social network be improved (adding by which relationships)?
Social Network Synthesis	Designing optimum social network structure	How should a newly built social network structure be?

Source: Uça-Güneş & Eby, (2014)

For an existing Distance Education Program, it is possible to use Social Network Analysis and Network Weaving Approaches and in this way to reach some information and to intervene the Social Network. But when it comes to configuring a Distance Education Program for the first time and building a social network, these two approaches won't respond the needs. Social Network Synthesis Approach is thought to make it possible in a newly configured network to build optimum relationships between individuals, organizations, resources and tools and thus, represents a method for determined purpose to happen.

AN EXAMPLE FRAMEWORK FOR BUILDING DISTANCE EDUCATION PROGRAMS

In this section, an example framework for building Distance Education Programs by using Social Network Synthesis Approach is presented. The steps of social network synthesis with general suggestions and examples are shown in Table 7.

Uça-Güneş & Eby (2014) makes the following reminders about the last step. The strength and stability may not be digitized. It should be taken into consideration that the frequency can be variable in time depending on purpose and actors, and it may not be put forth very clearly on the research process. Similarly, it should be kept in mind that relationship between two actors can affect the relationships between other actors in different aspects. After this kind of situations are evaluated, it is suggested to do plans and then applying.

The institutions offering distance education should fulfill the duties and responsibilities set out in relation to the realization of the social network. In this context, activities should be arranged to inform the learners when needed. In addition, it should provide relations with other institutions, roles of instructors and design and management of learning environment to be regulated in this context; it should carry out the access to related resources and tools and their sustainability, up-to-dateness and maintenance should be provided in this direction.

Table 7. An example framework for building distance education programs

Steps	Explanations and Suggestions	Examples
1. Goal	It is suggested to be determined by the decision makers depending on the expert viewpoints. If the institution's presenting programs only in specific branches more specific purposes can be determined.	• Developing learners' problem solving skills. • Providing collaborative learning. • Increasing learners' capability about using the technology.
2. Network Type and Boundaries	In the aspect of Social Network Management, it is suggested to take institution's capacity and experience into consideration.	• **Ego-Centric Network:** The actors with whom the learners are in relation with; boundaries: learner's only direct connections. • **Socio-Centric Network:** The network which is created by all the learners in the institution and the relationships between them; boundaries: all the connections in the network.
3. Actor Groups	It can be determined in different forms based on the aim and applicability, also an expert's opinion can be utilized.	• Individual. • Individual, organization, resource and tool.
4. Relationships	It might be necessary to take institution's mission and vision or its capabilities into consideration. Experts' opinion can be referable. The relationship can be expressed generally or specifically. More than one relationship can be defined for the same purpose.	Any action that can improve learner's technological competence.
5. Actors	It is suggested to be determined by taking opinions of experts or stakeholders.	• **Individuals:** Administrators, instructors, learners; technical, administrative and social support staff, consultants, content experts, learning designers. • **Organizations:** Distance Education, R&D, mass communication institutions. • **Resource:** Academic publications, informal learning environments. • **Tool:** Distance Education Software, mobile devices.
6. Relationships and Their Properties	One or more properties on relationships can be taken into account. It is suggested to be determined by taking opinions of experts or stakeholders.	• Direction and Frequency. • Direction, Symmetry, Strength, Frequency, Duration (Stability).
7. Social Network Structure	It is important to evaluate the actors and relationships determined in the previous two steps with a holistic approach.	(Representation by expressions/formulation/graphic imagery)

Adapted from Uça-Güneş & Eby, (2014)

FUTURE RESEARCH DIRECTIONS

The study, providing an example framework of how to use social networks in the configuration phase of the program, can be improved in the future. Supported by other social network approaches, interventions such as addition of actors and relationships to the network or removal of them may be in question, providing an effective social network management.

Benefiting from social network analysis software, 'requested' features and values can be taken into consideration as they are 'existing', therefore social network structure can be visualized, other measures related to the network and actors can be calculated. The social network of a specific subject can be mathematically formulated.

The approach can be applied for the design of distance education system components separately as well as for whole of it. Furthermore, Social Network Synthesis can be used in different fields from distance education similarly like other social network approaches.

CONCLUSION

Distance Education is based on learner's being physically apart from instructor and educational institution. In such systems communication is provided via technology. Today, due to advances in technology, the structure of communication and interaction can be said to take form as social network. Thus, social networks can be considered as a suitable ground for the construction of distance education programs. Distance education should be dealt with system approach and social network approaches may be used supportively in this manner. Therefore, the social network approaches are examined and a comparison of them is presented in terms of aim and function. The Social Network Synthesis approach -a new one- is also introduced in this chapter. And a framework to use it for building distance education programs and designing distance education system is presented. Using this approach to design a program for the first time, a social network appropriate to the purpose could be configured and also be useful for decision makers.

ACKNOWLEDGMENT

A part of this work has been supported within the scope of a project (1103E056) accepted by Anadolu University Scientific Research Projects Commission.

REFERENCES

Allen, I. E., & Seaman, J. (2013). *Changing course: ten years of tracking online education in the United States*. Babson Survey Research Group and Quahog Research Group, LLC.

Borgatti, S. P., & Halgin, D. S. (2011). On Network Theory. *Organization Science*. Retrieved October 20, 2015, from http://steveborgatti.com/papers/orsc.1110.0641.pdf

Borgatti, S. P., & Lopez-Kidwell, V. (2012). Network Theory. In The SAGE handbook of social network analysis. SAGE Publications.

Börner, K., Sanyal, S., & Vespignani, A. (2007). Network science. *Annual Review of Information Science & Technology*, *41*(1), 537–607. doi:10.1002/aris.2007.1440410119

Brass, D. J. (2011). *A social network perspective on industrial/organizational psychology*. Retrieved October 21, 2015, from http://ejournal.narotama.ac.id/files/A%20Social%20Network%20Perspective%20On%20Industrial%20Organizational%20Psychology.pdf

Burgess, J. R. D., & Russell, J. E. A. (2003). The effectiveness of distance learning initiatives in organizations. *Journal of Vocational Behavior*, *63*(2), 289–303. doi:10.1016/S0001-8791(03)00045-9

Caladine, R. (2008). *Enhancing e-learning with media-rich content and interactions.* Hershey, PA: Information Science. doi:10.4018/978-1-59904-732-4

Carrasco, J. A., Hogan, B., Wellman, B., & Miller, E. J. (2006). *Collecting social network data to study social activity-travel behavior: an egocentric approach.* Presented at the 85th Transportation Research Board Meeting, Washington, DC. Retrieved October 21, 2015, from http://groups.chass.utoronto.ca/netlab/wp-content/uploads/2012/05/Collecting-Social-Network-Data-to-Study-Social-Activity-Travel-Behavior-An-Egocentric-Approach.pdf

Durland, M. M., & Fredericks, K. A. (2005, Fall). An Introduction to Social Network Analysis. *New Directions for Evaluation, 107*(107), 5–13. doi:10.1002/ev.157

Ethier, J. (2006). Current Research in Social Network Theory. *Social Network Theory.* Retrieved October 22, 2015, from http://www.ccs.neu.edu/home/perrolle/archive/Ethier-SocialNetworks.html

Freeman, L. C. (2012). The development of social network analysis – with an emphasis on recent events. In The SAGE handbook of social network analysis. SAGE Publications.

Gürsakal, N. (2009). *Sosyal ağ analizi. (1.baskı).* Bursa: Dora Yayıncılık.

Ingram, P., & Torfason, M. T. (2010). Organizing the in-between: The population dynamics of network-weaving organizations in the global interstate network. *Administrative Science Quarterly, 55*(4), 577–605. doi:10.2189/asqu.2010.55.4.577

Kadushin, C. (2004). Some Basic Network Concepts and Propositions. *Introduction to Social Network Theory.* Retrieved October 20, 2015, from http://melander335.wdfiles.com/local--files/reading-history/kadushin.pdf

Krebs, V., & Holley, J. (2006). *Building smart communities through network weaving.* Appalachian Center for Economic Networks. Retrieved October 24, 2015, from http://www.orgnet.com/BuildingNetworks.pdf

Lewis, T. G. (2009). *Network science: theory and practice.* Hoboken, NJ: John Wiley & Sons, Inc. doi:10.1002/9780470400791

Macdonald, J., & Poniatowska, B. (2011). Designing the professional development of staff for teaching online: An OU (UK) case study. *Distance Education, 32*(1), 119–134. doi:10.1080/01587919.2011.565481

Marin, A., & Wellman, B. (2012). Social network analysis: an introduction. In The SAGE handbook of social network analysis. SAGE Publications.

Moore, G. M., & Kearsley, G. (2005). *Distance education: a systems view* (2nd ed.). Thomson Wadsworth.

Moore, M. G., & Kearsley, G. (2012). *Distance education: a systems view of online learning* (3rd ed.). Belmont: Wadsworth.

Ramo, S., & St. Clair, R. K. (1998). *The systems approach: Fresh solutions to complex problems through combining science and practical common sense.* Retrieved October 24, 2015, from http://oldsite.incose.org/ProductsPubs/DOC/SystemsApproach.pdf

Siemens, G. (2006). *Knowing Knowledge.* Retrieved October 29, 2015, from http://www.elearnspace.org/KnowingKnowledge_LowRes.pdf

Taylor, J. C. (2001). *Fifth generation Distance education.* Retrieved October 12, 2015, from http://www. c3l.uni-oldenburg.de/cde/media/readings/taylor01.pdf

Tindall, D. B., & Wellman, B. (2001). Canada as social structure: Social network analysis and Canadian sociology. *Canadian Journal of Sociology, 26*(3), 265. doi:10.2307/3341889

Uça-Guneş, E. P. (2014). *Structuring the technology dimension of distance education graduate programs: Transformative social network synthesis.* (Doctoral Dissertation). Anadolu University, Turkey.

Uça-Güneş, E. P., & Eby, G. (2014). An Approach For Structuring Distance Education Programs: Social Network Synthesis. *Journal of Research in Education and Teaching, 3*(3). Retrieved from http://www. jret.org/FileUpload/ks281142/File/23.uca_gunes.pdf

Yükseköğretim Kurulu (YÖK). (2007). *Türkiye'nin yükseköğretim stratejisi.* Retrieved October 14, 2015, from http://www.yok.gov.tr/documents/10279/30217/yok_strateji_kitabi/27077070-cb13-4870-aba1-6742db37696b

KEY TERMS AND DEFINITIONS

Distance Education: The education type in which the learner, other individuals which take part in learning activity and the institution are in different physical environments; various technologies are used to provide communication for access to information, support, guidance, etc.

Network Weaver: The actor added into a social network for the purpose of combining actors who doesn't have a connection between by creating interaction.

Network Weaving: The Social Network Approach aiming to make the network better via a network weaver that provides relationships between the actors.

Social Network: Actors group combined to each other with social relationships.

Social Network Analysis: The Social Network Approach studying the social network's structure -that are formed by the actors and the relation groups combining them to each other- and effects.

Social Network Synthesis: The design to form a goal directed social network determining the actors (individuals, organizations, resources and tools) and the relationships between them.

Chapter 13

Facebook Content Analysis:
A Study into Australian Banks' Social Media Community Engagement

Vindaya Senadheera
Deakin University, Australia

Shona Leitch
RMIT University, Australia

Matthew Warren
Deakin University, Australia

Graeme Pye
Deakin University, Australia

ABSTRACT

Understanding the motives that encourage users to adopt social media to communicate with businesses is very important. This research study was conducted with Australian banks and adds to the development of empirically tested social media adoption model consisting of technological and social communication aspects (Senadheera, 2015). This chapter presents the findings of the research study based on analysis of wall posts gathered from Australian banks' Facebook presence in the year 2013. The research study involves a thematic analysis of frequently used words by Australian banks in their respective Facebook wall posts following an outcome of a word frequency test conducted using NVivo. This analysis was conducted with the proposed adoption model as the basis to determine whether banks' Facebook content addresses the basic user requirements driving them to adopt social media to communicate with Australian banks. The results strengthens the robustness and the applicability of the social media adoption model.

INTRODUCTION

When millions of social media users are provided with the capabilities to create and share content, businesses are increasingly focusing on ways to accurately understand the business value of this content by applying various strategies to analyse the content and report outcomes. The number of businesses adopting social media, such as Facebook, Twitter, and YouTube continue to grow (Harrison, Rintel, & Mitchell, 2014) in spite of privacy and ethical concerns raised by sections of the public (Braun, 2013). Acknowledging this trend, social media technology developers have improved social media technologies by continuously addressing public concerns to alleviate their fears of using this technology.

DOI: 10.4018/978-1-5225-0648-5.ch013

Even though there is a considerable user interest in various social media technologies, user participation in social media based communities formed by businesses depends upon the incentives available for them as participants that drive their motivation. The non-reciprocal nature of the relationships formed within these communities (Pentina, 2015) makes it challenging for businesses to keep their community interested in continued participation. This creates a challenging environment for businesses expecting to achieve business objectives through cost-effective direct access to a wider-section of the social media community.

In addressing these challenges, it is imperative for businesses to capture the expectations of their respective audience that have chosen to become participants of their respective social media-based online communities. In this regard, it is necessary to understand and address the motivating factors that draw people towards using social media to communicate and engage with businesses. Furthermore, the need to take a proactive strategy towards social media engagement is also driven by research findings that indicate not all businesses are privy to implementing engagement strategies that increase their reputational risk (Ott & Theunissen, 2015).

Australian banks could find greater potential in social media as a method to get direct and near-instantaneous access to potential customers to overcome increased competition in the banking sector. The competition within the Australian banking sector continues to increase following the release of the Australian Senate economics reference committee, "Competition within the Australian banking sector" report (2011) that had recommended to identify credit unions as banks. To a greater extent, this recommendation has contributed towards the increase in the number of banks identified as 'Australian-owned' from fourteen in 2010 to twenty seven in 2015 (APRA, 2015). The Australian banking sector is ranked 21st in the world out of 148 economies. (Schwab, 2013). The four largest Australian banks, namely ANZ bank, the Commonwealth bank, NAB, and the Westpac bank are among the worlds' banks with AA credit rating or above, they control around 67% of the Australian market share (Joshi, Cahill, & Sidhu, 2010). As a result, the smaller Australian banks may find social media an attractive method to reach out to a wider audience as they attempt to increase their market share. Hence, Australian banks provide a unique study sample that could rely more upon social media for enhanced public engagement.

The intention of this chapter is to focus on Australian banks. This is due to a number of reasons, more specifically their emphasis on the adoption of new technologies as business enablers and to gain greater value through their investment (Bielski, 2008). Likewise, the banking customers are also adopting new mobile and smart technologies, through which they could access services such as Internet Banking (Martins, Oliveira, & Popovič, 2014). This combination has the potential to distance banks from their customers and risk losing personal relationships with their customers (Ahmad, 2005). In this scenario, the ubiquitous nature of online social networks (Kane, Alavi, Labianca, & Borgatti, 2014) provides an antidote to re-energise that diminishing personal relationships and allows banks to consider social media as an vital tool in their communication strategic mix. With a growing number of Australians embracing social media (Lee, 2010), it provides an effective medium for Australian banks to engage directly with participants within their respective social media-based online communities.

The broader objective of this chapter is to use content published by Australian banks on Facebook to analyse and determine their effectiveness in attracting participants to social media-based online communities. As Facebook content holds insightful data generated by large volume of users, a process that goes beyond mere monitoring and capable understanding hidden insights is required. Therefore, the content analysis is informed by the CUP (Collect, Understand, Present) framework, identified as lifecycle analysis framework (Fan & Gordon, 2014) and uses the social media adoption model for Australian banks to communicate with the public (Senadheera, 2015).

REVIEW OF LITERATURE

During the period when many of the popular social media technologies, such as Twitter and Facebook were still at their infancy (2006-2010), businesses found it difficult to appropriately create a presence for themselves on social media due often to many legitimate reasons. These reasons included privacy concerns (Leitch & Warren, 2011), presenting themselves as a credible source of information (Westerman, Spence, & Van Der Heide, 2012), or as a result of inappropriate terminology available at the time (Knight, 2010). The situation had been more disadvantageous for banks because they are at the forefront of the economy as publicly listed companies and therefore highly regulated to maintain public confidence and faith in them and the services they offer.

Meanwhile, an exploratory longitudinal study conducted by Senadheera, Warren, and Leitch (2011) with Australian banks has observed that their social media presence was beginning to grow, albeit with an intensified social media activity (tweets, posts, followers etc.) and use strategies that are markedly vary notwithstanding their homogeneous nature. These strategies at times, displayed a lack of knowledge of the technologies they employed and the difficulty in keeping up with the growth of social media technologies. The study also observed that intensities of social media discussions/participation varies with the significance of the topic to the user-community that at times created 'discussion spikes'.

Definitions

This chapter uses several keys terms, the definition of which are provided here for greater clarity of the content and better understanding of the underlying research study.

Social Media Technology *is a specific technology, such as Facebook, and is defined as a website that provides space for interested users to make their presence and connect with others to engage in meaningful communications using functionalities inherent to each such website to create, share, and consume content. Social Media meanwhile is a broad term used to describe one or more social media technologies* (Senadheera, 2015).

Social media technologies facilitates the formation of social media-based online communities. They are defined as *online communities formed when social media users elect to connect with businesses' social networks formed on one or more social media technologies* (Senadheera, 2015).

Social media analytics "is concerned with developing and evaluating informatics tools and frameworks to collect, monitor, analyse, summarise, and visualise social media data ... to facilitate conversations and interactions ... to extract useful patterns and intelligence..." (Zeng, Chen, Lusch, & Li, 2010, pp. 14).

Theoretical Foundations of Communicating with Social Media

At the heart of the social media communication shift is the desire to use wide-ranging social media technologies to connect with others using similar technologies and broaden their social networks (Lipschultz, 2014), the composition of which has the potential to drive changes to social network analyses as scholars refine methods (Butts, 2008). In particular, the methods used to define social network centrality and boundaries are open to discussion and debate. As additional events are analysed, it should be possible to begin to predict participation behaviour (Howard, 2008). Importantly, social networks built around online social networking paradigms have introduced new communication options about leadership, behaviour and online social influence that enforce researchers to extend existing communication theories. By performing future systematic content analyses of language used in online interaction and engagement, research should strengthen understanding about the nature of popularity, opinion diffusion, and social network leadership (Huffaker, 2010, Greenhow & Robelia, 2009).

Similarly, the capabilities that social media inherit from its novel functionalities, offer nearly an unlimited range of potential uses that may or may not meet user-expectations for new gratification (Sundar & Limperos, 2013) and have the potential to drive changes to communication theories formed around traditional mass-media. For example, communications theory relating to traditional mass media suggests that, "open and easy communication as a basis for social solidarity between peoples become *more difficult* because of social differentiation, impersonality and distrust due to psychological alienation, the breakdown of meaningful social ties, and increasing anomie among the members" (Lowery & DeFleur, 1995, pp. 12). As users embrace various social media technologies to form their own social networks, they offer the hope of breaking-down such traditional social barriers thereby encouraging the formation of meaningful online communities, relationships, and social movements. These changes also encourage new theory formation or enforce changes to existing theories, application of which provide support to social media practitioners.

However, recent developments associated with social media technologies that facilitated businesses to create a reliable and credible online presence (Bates, 2011; Taintor, 2013) have expanded the context within which communication theories involving social media thus complicating the task of theory development. The complexities emanate from the complicated socio-technological nature of communications within social media-based online communities (Senadheera, 2015). In this environment, businesses are required to implement best practices to attract participants to their respective social media-based online communities while negotiating appropriate solutions to resolve the challenges posed by the evolving technologies.

Social media best practices involve first and foremost building relationships, that convert to followers, viewers, or '*like*'rs who would come to the defence of the given business during a crisis (Lipschultz, 2014). In this sense even though social media best practices align with traditional mass-media relations that use the power of celebrities and the excitement of events. It is essential for businesses to embrace social media with a clear strategy, formulated to address pre-defined business objectives. This proactive approach is necessary to engage in timely communication with online community participants to address their social media expectations in a timely manner and to avoid them leaving your community in search for another community that addresses their needs more directly. If appropriately exploited the possibilities offered by various social media technologies, businesses have the opportunity to create a conducive environment to drive discussions within their respective social media-based online community, as opinion leaders.

When users adopt a mediated communication technology they make judgements concerning the applicability of their perceived abilities or gain benefits through such adoption, and are presented with a scenario to confront situations derived from circumstances of their adoption (Lin, 2003). When social media is the preferred as the mediated communication technology, adopters do not possess total control or authority they had over conventional mass media. They do however have the capacity and authority to moderate communications within their own network. The challenge for businesses therefore, is to consider adequate provisions to make a concerted effort to meet the expectations of those who join the community as creators or consumers of communicated content.

Social media adoption model for Australian banks to communicate with the public (Senadheera, 2015) with its wide-ranging adoption factors supported by established theoretical foundations provides a framework to capture multitude of scenarios governing the communication technology adoption. This research study embedded in this chapter has used this model as the basis to inform the discussion enabling it to arrive at outcomes benefitting the theory building and social media strategy formation.

Social Media Adoption Model for Australian Banks

The social media adoption model for Australian banks to communicate with the public introduces an empirically tested framework for Australian banks when considering social media to communicate with the public. It encompasses technological and social communication aspects governing the social media adoption and simplifies an otherwise complex scenario. With the considering that Facebook had been identified as the technology to be explored, this chapter will discuss the social communication aspects of the model and discuss their implications for Australia banks when conducting effective communications with the public.

The social communication aspects of the model is a grouping of similar theoretical foundations identified as factors that drive the adoption of social media as a communication medium. These factors are:

- Use factors;
- Audience factors;
- Social factors; and,
- Contextual factors.

The factors are now discussed in detail.

Use Factors

In the context of using social media for communication, it is understandable that the public expects values such as communication efficiency, especially considering the easier access to the medium through mobile technologies. Use factors, drive users' desire to achieve a specific outcome and explain how and why people use social media to communicate. They encompass established theories such as communication flow, expectancy value theory, and uses and gratifications. For businesses expecting to maximise business benefits through their social media adoption, knowledge of use factors is important in devising appropriate strategies, such as using one or more social media technology to articulate messages differently for different demographic sectors.

Lin (2003, pp. 357) identifies use factors as a "cumulative use experience" that will come into effect post-implementation of the adoption decision and explains how such an experience would create a range of responses. Use factors bring together other theoretical underpinnings and include self-evaluation to seek: 1) an understanding of the perceived ability to control the use experience (communication flow);

2) the user attention generated by the use experience (expectancy value theory); and 3) whether expected rewards associated with the technology's use is realised and the gratifications received through such use (uses and gratifications theory).

Communication Flow

Perceived communication flow as described by Trevino and Webster (1992) in Lin's (2003, pp. 357) research consists of constructs such as a perceived sense of control, attentiveness, curiosity, and interest as experienced through their interaction with the technology which can influence how the audience evaluates a technology. Trevino and Webster (1992) have gone beyond previous understandings of the flow in computer-mediated technologies to include motivational aspects, such as enjoyment derived from the use of the technology. In confirming this, they have identified that respondents to their survey perceived greater communication flow with the use of email than voice mail, primarily driven by users' enjoyment in using the technology that goes beyond the process of communicating the message. However, Lin (2003) explains the possibility of such favourable perception and attitude being changed due to the unsatisfactory experiences of the participants.

With regard to social media, Lu, Lin, Hsiao, and Cheng (2010) discussed the importance of satisfaction and flow in using Web-based systems in relation to blogs, and interactivity was considered one of the antecedents of communication flow. Their research confirmed the significant impact of flow and satisfaction of using blogs and sharing behaviours within them.

Expectancy Value Theory

Conducting their research based on the expectancy value theory, LaRose and Atkin (1991) claimed that technology adopters are likely to develop positive attitudes towards the technology concerned if they can be convinced of the ability of the technology to improve their communication efficiency. For example, ease of use, while avoiding potential negatives such as adverse privacy or security issues.

Johnson and Yang's (2009) research explored the possibility of applying expectancy value theory in the social media context. They investigated the social and information motives of Twitter users. The study determined the absence of any relationship between Twitter use variables and social motives; however, it identified the existence of relationships between Twitter use variables and information motives, thus highlighting the informative nature of Twitter. They also measured the extent of their satisfaction with Twitter use by measuring the gratifications sought and gratification obtained, and determined that they were satisfied. This explains the need to consider the use of more than one social media technology in order to capture a broader picture of using social media to communicate, rather than just using a single technology.

Uses and Gratifications

Uses and gratification theory assumes that people use media to satisfy underlying needs or interests and emphasises how and why people use media (Klapper, 1963). Lin (2003) explains that a positive attitude towards the adoption of a technology is dependent upon the audience's expectancy values and it can be further mediated by the audience's gratification with their technological experience.

According to an explanation provided by Rubin (1994, pp. 419) on the uses and gratification perspective, media use is determined by a group of key elements including "people's needs and motives to communicate, the psychological and social environment, the mass media, functional alternatives to media use, communication behaviour, and the consequences of such behaviour". Wang, Tchernev and Solloway (2012b) have determined the gratification of only some of the categories of needs that drive social media use, namely emotional, cognitive, social and habitual. They have confirmed that any subsequent social media use is driven by those accumulated ungratified needs.

Audience Factors

Audience factors compel communication driven by individual users' personal characteristics. Considering the social impact created as a result of users' social memberships and the public nature of their social relationships, audience factors can be considered as an important social communication aspect in the context of this research discussion. Furthermore, by grounding the theoretical underpinnings that group together as audience factors, businesses will be able to derive key decision-support information to determine their own social media adoption strategies. This information will include why certain members of the public tend to prefer a particular social media technology over others for their social media-based communication. Audience factors, as a whole, are important in identifying insightful information relating to the actions of the public driven by their individual capabilities and confidence in self-evaluating innovative technologies for their own benefit.

Lin (2003) identifies that the audience factor contains four constructs. They are individual innovative attributes that according to Lin can be identified by a particular user's social membership to determine why, how, when, and which communication product may be adopted. These can be categorised to predisposed personality traits that make an audience receptive to the idea of innovation adoption (i.e. being venturesome, novelty seeking, sensation seeking, and willingness to take risks), innovative need (i.e. work or pleasure), and self-efficacy defined as belief in one's ability to adopt and use a technological innovation. Audience factors also encompass the construct of the theory of reasoned action that is understood to be the beliefs and attitudes about the rationale for innovation adoption.

Innovative Attributes

A research study by Amichai-Hamburger and Vinitsky (2010) describes people as increasingly transferring their offline activities and interaction with friends to online environments. This gives rise to the notion of applying the findings of previous research relating to other forms of technological innovation, such as the findings of Nov and Ye (2008), that some innovators are more open to new experiences than others. This is especially significant for creating a successful presence on social media because in the physical world communities, innovators, lead users, opinion leaders and those with a large number of offline connections, are being encouraged to participate in online communities too.

The theory is also applicable to social media. According to research by Correa, Hinsley, & De Zúñiga et al. (2010) innovative and creative people have the propensity to use social media more frequently than others. Hence they may prove important for the longevity of an online community based on social media.

Need for Innovativeness

The need for innovativeness is considered by Lin (2003, pp. 350) as "an indicator of an individual's need to satisfy their novelty-seeking drive". In their study, Hughes, Rowe, Batey, and Lee (2012) confirm that personality is an influential factor in the use of social media; however, they have identified different personality traits driving the use of different types of social media technologies. Meanwhile, taking this discussion further, Correa et al. (2010) observed that greater openness to experience is reflected in the curiosity and novelty-seeking tendency of the users.

Even though the above research was conducted in the context of person-person relationships on social media technologies such as Facebook, it can be logically concluded that openness to experience could also be associated with the communities formed around businesses, brands and personalities.

Self-Efficacy Theory

Lin (2003) describes self-efficacy as the self-belief about one's ability to adopt a mediated communication technology and determines how people make judgements concerning the applicability of their perceived abilities to confront situations derived from various circumstances. However, in relation to social media as a method of communication, adopters do not possess the same control or authority they had over conventional mediums, even though they have the authority and capacity to moderate communications within their own network. The challenge for users therefore is to take adequate precautions to make a concerted effort to meet the expectations of those who join the community as creators or consumers of communicated content.

Applying this to social media, the multi-item scale developed by Chandra (2011) primarily explored the self-efficacy of customers to use the services offered via social media. Most importantly, the scale confirms the importance of understanding one's self-confidence in evaluating technological innovations and adoption decisions. The study has also confirmed lesser susceptibility towards potential barriers of adoption, leading to adoption decisions being taken more confidently.

Social Factors

Social factors describe adoption driven by a particular user's need to participate in online social activities, to interact, share or collaborate with others.

Social media technologies facilitate the creation and maintenance of complex social networks consisting of millions of users. These users, with their diverse levels of technological capabilities and individual expectations of adopting social media as a form of communication, do influence others within their own networks.

Lin (2003) sees opinion leadership in a social or organisational setting, the availability of the critical mass of adopters, which enables a sufficient level of communication applications associated with technology use, and social symbolic meaning attached to the medium, as the key constructs of the social adoption factor. Pedersen (2005) discussed the relationship between social reasons for use, adoption and the need for integration of the two. Thereby drawing the conclusion that social networks and the position of the adopter in social networks are important determinants of adoption.

Opinion Leadership

The importance of opinion leadership in an environment where communication is conducted in a social setting was identified by Lin's (2003) model as a potential driver of adoption. The importance attached to opinion leaders in a social media environment has risen exponentially and opinion leaders with a larger social following have become influencers (Choudhary, Hendrix, Lee, Palsetia, & Liao, 2012), over and above their conventional role of disseminating information to a larger audience of followers. Metzgar and Marugi (2009) believe the opinion leadership role previously held by conventional media outlets has now been vested with the social media users who possess simple tools provided by various social media technologies to create and disseminate information. Here, the diffusion of information occurs with the flow of information from mass media to opinion leaders who in turn disseminate amongst online social networks to reach a wider population. This description has become more relevant in social media.

Two-Step Flow of Information

Two-step-flow of communication (Wu, Hofman, Mason, & Watts, 2011) in the theoretical sense is identified when individuals (opinion leaders) who pay close attention to the mass media and its messages pass on that information with their own interpretations in addition to the actual media content. Two-step flow and opinion leadership operate in a similar manner; however, the two can be differentiated by the fact that in two-step flow the person who pays close attention to information attaches 'personal influence' to the reprocessed message in addition to the content. It can be considered as the process intervening between the media's direct message and the audience's ultimate reaction to that message.

Social Impact

The term social impact was initially proposed by Latane (1981) that to describe the effect of other persons on an individual that later developed into a dynamic theory of social impact "to account for how coherent structures of cultural elements emerge from the interactions of people located in space. In this conception, social structure is seen to result from individuals, differing in their ability to influence each other in their spatial location" (Latané, 1996, pp. 13). This theory was later applied in research involving social media as a communication medium outcome of which indicated the positive impact of number of users on the perceived credibility of user-generated content.

Contextual Factors

Contextual factors explain situations where adopting social media is driven by specific situations that arise in a given context, for example problems relating to public-facing technologies providing banking services.

Senadheera's (2015) research study that proposed and validated the social media adoption model identified contextual factors in the context of promotions of banking products undertaken by Australian banks as a potential driver to adopt social media by the public to communicate with banks. Meanwhile, communications that occur during situational crises, such as Internet banking and ATM (Automated Teller Machines) outages, have also been identified as specific contextual issues and potential predictors of social media adoption (Coombs, 2007).

As previously explained, this book chapter encompasses a research study that undertakes the analysis of data obtained from Facebook wall posts of Australian banks and how the social media adoption model was to be used as the basis to facilitate this analysis. The methodology chapter explains this research process further.

METHODOLOGY

The broader process involving the methodology that facilitated the gathering of content, understanding their overall value that aligns with the primary aim of the analysis and presenting the overall findings are encapsulated in the Capture, Understand, and Present (CUP) framework proposed by Fan and Gordon (2014). The following sections further describes the capture, understand, and present components of the CUP process used in this study.

Capture

The component of capturing content to be analysed included the following steps.

Step 1: This study has considered the list of Australian banks maintained by Australian Prudential and Regulatory Authority (APRA, 2015) to search and identify their corresponding official Facebook pages. The search was conducted through both Google search and Facebook search.

Step 2: Once an official Facebook page is identified, they were then 'liked' by using the researcher's own Facebook profiles.

Step 3: Captured wall posts published on Facebook pages of respective Australian banks using NVivo nCapture software utility, an add-on function available for Internet Explorer to download streaming data and saved them in PDF format.

Understand

The component of understanding the content included the following five (5) steps.

Step 1: The files saved in PDF format were then edited using PDF editor to remove words that are irrelevant to wall posts thereby minimising their effect on word searches. These included information relating to Facebook profile of the researcher as well as the words 'like', 'comment', and 'share' that followed every Facebook wall post. This can be described as removing 'noisy' data described in the CUP framework.

Step 2: The edited PDF documents containing wall posts were then imported into NVivo qualitative analysis software as 'source' files.

Step 3: The NVivo software was then used to undertake a 'word frequency' analysis that led to the identification of ten (10) most frequently used words by all Australian banks with a Facebook presence. To enable the selection of a list of meaningful words, the words such as days of the week, months of the year, numbers, names of the respective banks and words containing less than three (3) characters were identified as 'stop' words. The word 'http' was not considered as a "stop word"

Table 1. Most commonly used words by Australian banks on Facebook wall posts

Word	No. of Banks Using the Word	Count
http	13	316
shared	13	287
link	13	244
day	13	209
home	13	160
new	13	160
year	13	154
photo	13	146
today	13	119
now	13	116

in this instance even though it is not a semantic or meaning-bearing term because in the context of this study it implies sharing of information using a web link. The words were not considered by the software when undertaking the word frequency analysis. The ten most commonly used words by all Australian banks are listed in Table 1.

The outcome of this word frequency analysis is also illustrated as a Word Cloud (Figure 1) and Dendrogram (Figure 2). Dendrogram illustrates word clusters that together with the Word Cloud enables analysis of the context upon which each of the words are used.

Step 4: An advanced analytics exercise was undertaken to qualitatively analyse each instance of the word used to determine the context in which they are used.

Step 5: Finally, a comparison of the context in which the words are used with the themes that subscribe to various theoretical foundations relating to communication technology adoption. The social media adoption model for Australian banks to communicate with the public proposed by Senadheera (2015) was applied to the coding process. As described earlier, the 'social communication' aspects of the model that groups together established theoretical foundations has enabled coding to be organised in manner that accommodated the determination of the extent to which Australian banks have prepared their Facebook wall posts to encourage users to maintain their community involvement or to encourage others to join.

Present

The presenting component will summarise and present the findings in the form of a discussion supported by theory and presented at the end of the discussion on the findings.

Figure 1. Word cloud

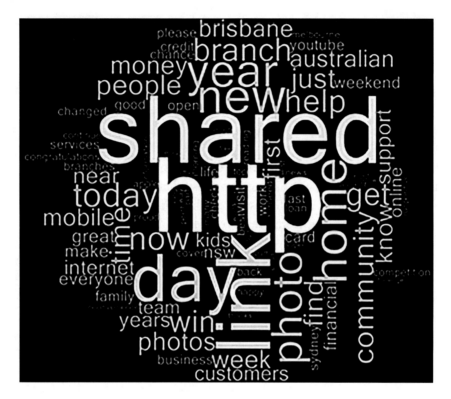

Figure 2. Dendrogram

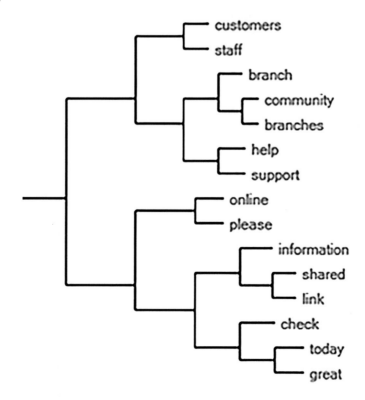

RESULTS

The analysis of the data collected as explained in the earlier section was conducted using NVivo, a commonly used software when undertaking qualitative research that contains capabilities that provide researchers the ability to interrogate data, revise conceptualisations through enhanced search and retrieve categorised data. As a result it introduces flexibility as well as rigour into qualitative analysis (Leech & Onwuegbuzie, 2007). These capabilities have only increased in its latest version (10) with the addition of more data visualisation capabilities, such as word charts, word clouds (Figure 1), and *Dendrogram* (Figure 2).

Information and Knowledge sharing – By sharing useful information and knowledge that could potentially be beneficial for online community participants, Australian banks endeavour to create a perception amongst community participants as a credible source of information and opinion leader. The depth and breadth of information varies from providing details of their respective bank locations to informing them of why's and how's of financial planning or renovation guidance to house buyers.

The importance of source credibility has gained importance with the growth of the online diffusion of information as users were compelled to undertake self-verification of source credibility by becoming their own gatekeepers (Haas & Wearden, 2003). The proliferation of social media where millions of users have become creators and publishers of content has further heightened the need to identify credible sources of information and knowledge and users of social media may utilise specific components of a source's profile, which are unavailable in traditional media, in order to make such credibility judgments (Westerman et al., 2012). With a concentrated effort on content creation, Australian banks have the potential to build trust amongst their Facebook community participants to establish themselves as opinion leaders for their respective community.

While the sharing of web-based knowledge and information can be attributed to opinion leadership, an established theory grouped under social factors, Australian banks as a credible source of information also address uses and gratification associated with the use of social media as a communication medium. As credible source of information and knowledge, Australian banks address emotional, cognitive, social or habitual gratification (Wang, Woo, Quek, Yang, & Liu, 2012a) relating to social media use, thereby addressing use factors of the social media adoption model.

To add to the significance of establishing themselves as a credible source of information and knowledge, Australian banks, the second most used word is 'shared' that is generally used in conjunction with a link to a web-based resource, The same word is also used when videos or photos get embedded to a Facebook wall post. Unsurprisingly, the word 'link' is the third most used word with the most common Wall Post sentence being "i.e. … bank shared a link – http://…" The sharing of knowledge that is available in the form of web-based content using content URL (Unified Resource Locator) is practiced by all Australian banks. Koh's and Kim's (2004) study outcomes explain this the advantages of this form of knowledge sharing where community knowledge sharing activity was identified as significantly related to both community participation and community promotion.

The word 'day' is also used by all thirteen Australian banks that have posted on Facebook in the year 2013. The word is primarily used in conjunction with a particular day of a calendar year, i.e. Remembrance, New Year, International Women's or Australia Day, but the word is also used to describe community events organised by an Australian bank. By sharing information of such community days, i.e. 'staff dress-up day' or a particular day important for a certain bank in a historical sense, the respective Australian bank aims to develop a closer online relationship with their online community participants.

While this activity has no direct bearing on the previously discussed online credibility, such action could have a positive effect on strengthening of the community relationships as members actively participate in discussions around those topics that tends to develop lasting relationships (Iriberri & Leroy, 2009).

These theories around innovative attributes and innovativeness were previously been confirmed in Correa et al. (2010) study in a social media setting. The study found innovative and creative people have the propensity to use social media more frequently than others. These wall posts that invite them to participate pay attention to innovative attributes of people to contribute in an online community setting or to attract people with novelty seeking tendencies to the community. These aspects of communication technology adoption grouped into Audience factors (Lin, 2003).

The word 'home' is another word frequently used in Wall Posts of all Australian banks with a Facebook presence. The perceived 'Australian dream' of owning one's own home is extensively applied to gain the attention of Australian banks' Facebook-based online communities. The word is used in conjunction with words such as 'loan(s)', 'first', 'owner', and 'your', indicating banks' inclination to address information motives. The outcomes of Johnson's and Yang's (2009) research study indicated the existence of a relationship between the technology (Twitter) use and information motives. This inclination of users to receive up to date information about their single biggest investment of life can be categorised with the expectancy value theory that groups with use factors of social media adoption model to communicate with the public.

The word 'new' is another highly used word in Facebook wall posts and highlights the tendency of banks to share news that matters to their respective community. In this instance, Australian banks are expecting to take advantage of the capabilities embedded in social media to harness relationships between news and participants of the community (Lee & Ma, 2012), such as 'like' 'comment' or 'share' that distributes news across a wider online community (Szabo & Huberman, 2010). The types of news varied from sharing non-banking information ranges from new mobile or smart technologies to new anti-bullying programs introduced by relevant charitable organisations to new national recycling programs. There are banking related news as well that cover issues pertaining to opening of new bank branches. Another key aspect is the 'tacit' knowledge sharing (Panahi, Watson, & Partridge, 2015) whereby Australian banks introduce for example results of new home loan surveys that carries the potential to drives new customer leads to relevant home loan products. In the context of ubiquitous nature of the social media technology, news can be considered as a value expected by users from their social media use and therefore can be subscribed to expectancy value theory.

The word 'year' meanwhile is used in Facebook wall posts primarily to describe events that occur in an annual basis or part of it. They include events that have implications to banks and evidently to their online community participants, such as new financial year, bank of the year, credit card products with 'honeymoon' rated fixed for 1-2 years, or events related with the new near. They frequently provide information that are either linked to an annual banking or finance related event that could generate community participants' personal interest or to describe a community events such as highlighting the need to reduce rubbish that people throw out every year that could generate online community-wide discussions. Hence they can be categorised under both use factors (expectancy value) and social factors (opinion leadership).

Sharing of visual information related to activities associated with banks' day-to-day is a common occurrence when Australian banks publish their Facebook wall posts. Yates et al. (2011, pp. 10) research associated with knowledge diffusion using social media has found the effectiveness of visual presentation of information as "visual medium can be constructed by layering different sources successively onto a common context or orientation". The significance of the visual presentation is further highlighted by the fact that the majority of the Facebook wall posts contain a relevant image even when the word 'photo' was not explicitly mentioned. On visual cursory inspection of online community engagement associated with wall posts attracts online community engagement through likes, comments and shares. However the online communities of the larger Australian banks, such as, the National Australia bank, the Commonwealth bank, Westpac banks and the ANZ bank attract greater participant engagement. For its capability generated online social engagement, the word photo is categorised under social factors.

The word 'today' is another frequently used word containing time specific information similar to the previously discussed word 'year'. The wall posts published by banks include reminders to their respective participants about importance of particular dates, a beginning of an activity, new entries added to the respective banks' blog, or the beginning of a special offer or a competition. In comparison to the use of the word of the 'year', the word 'today' provide information that invites immediate responses from the viewers/readers. Participants that use smart phones can be benefitted from these wall posts as they are more geared to provide an immediate response even while travelling. These wall posts also tend to get shared by the community participants as they would like inform those who are in their own social media-based online community. As a result of commonalities with the word 'year', this word will also be categorised under both use factors (expectancy value) and social factors (opinion leadership).

The frequent use of the word 'now' indicates how Australian banks use social media to inform their online community participants about the need to take an urgent action or to provide an up to date information. This includes information about the respective banks' technology maintenance work (planned 'outage' is now on), resolved issues concerning their technology ('EFTPOS terminal issues are now resolved') or submit an application relating to a special bank offer or a competition ('apply now'). By inviting for immediate action, primarily via links provided in wall posts Australian banks are targeting those who have developed a self-efficacy of the technology or 'reasoned action' leading to achieving an outcome form their use of social media as a communication media. Hence, classified under Audience factors.

As mentioned, the word 'now' is used in wall posts to inform online community participants about timely updates about scheduled maintenance or ad-hoc repair work conducted on customer-facing banking technologies. They are used to engage with online community participants who use social media as a medium to communicate with banks ubiquitously at a time when they are faced with problems accessing customer-facing banking services. As a consequence such engagement can also be categorised under contextual factors. This content analysis, undertaken with actual data has partly validated the useability of the CUP framework. The task of its validation will be completed with the presentation of the findings in the following section. Meanwhile this content analysis has further strengthened the significance of the social media adoption model for Australian banks to communicate with the public that encompass established theoretical foundations as a framework to undertake social media content analysis.

DISCUSSION

Themes presented in Table 2 reflect the context identified through the analysis of content around the commonly words used by Australian banks as a homogeneous group on their Facebook posts. In retrospection, these wall posts address every social communication aspect of the social media adoption

Table 2. Commonly used themes on Facebook wall posts by Australian banks

Adoption Factor	Theoretical Foundation	Common Themes of Australian Bank Facebook Wall Posts
Use Factors	Expectancy Value	Update information relating to banking products
		Provide assistance with investment protection
		Inform community events
		Keep participants informed of news that are relevant to them in the banking/finance context
	Uses & Gratifications	Create community discussion around uses/gratification
Audience Factors	Reasoned Action	Request participant responses to undertake further action
	Self-Efficacy	Improve user- manoeuvraebility of Facebook functions
Social Factors	Opinion Leadership	Strengthen the community as a credible information source
	Social Impact	Nurture events that concern the online community
		Share information that is worthwhile re-sharing
		Encourage discussion through visual infromation
Contextual Factors	Situational Crisis	Provide situational updates about customer-facing banking technologies

model that drive social media users to adopt the technology to communicate with Australian banks that explain growing social media maturity of Australian banks.

The themes identified alongside established theoretical foundations and presented in Table 2 explain the range of discussion possibilities available for Facebook Page users, in this instance the Australian banks when they engage users using social media. These findings extend the current discussion around the topic to include social media as a method of communication and add to the existing technology adoption theories. From the practitioners' point of view, they can formulate and publish wall posts around four adoption factors to stimulate vitality within the community and measure the success or failure by comparing them with the intended business objectives. As a result, practitioners as hosts of the respective online community' will be able to identify and comprehend the motivating factors that drive users to adopt social media to communicate with businesses. The overall findings has the potential to drive more effective and efficient use of wall posts with greater clarity to attract more participants to the respective online community and thereby broaden the communication reach.

FUTURE RESEARCH

The primary outcome of the using of theoretical frameworks in the analysis of Facebook wall posts was achieved. The outcome will have implications for theory by generating further research discussions and characterise practice by presenting practitioners with empirically tested frameworks leading to an informed development of a social media strategy.

However, this content analysis has also opened up possibilities for future research. Firstly, it is possible to explore the possibility using the frameworks in a different geographical and organisational setting. Secondly, the content analysis can be further expanded to include the levels of online community participant engagement to determine intrinsic value attached to wall posts. This can be achieved by quantifying the likes, comments and shares attached to each wall posts. Thirdly, this content analysis was conducted to identify and analyse commonly used words by all Australian banks with a Facebook presence. This content analysis can be further expanded to include how these findings compare with each individual banks to identify differences and similarities.

CONCLUSION

This chapter has explored the outcome of a research study that explored the general patterns of the contents created by homogenous group of businesses in Australian banks on their respective wall posts. In the process, this study has also evaluated the effectiveness of such contents in terms of possibility of attracting participants to their respective social media-based online community. The social communication aspects of the social media adoption model was used to determine whether the content created on wall posts are compatible with the community participants' expectations that encourage them to engage in communications with the banks.

The ensuing discussion has generated a deeper understanding of Australian banks Facebook engagement and explored whether they meet social media-based online community participants' expectations upon which their own social media adoption decisions were made. This was facilitated through a detailed and deeper analysis of most frequently used words has indicated that Australian banks have used in their respective wall posts. The findings have strengthened the significance of the social media adoption model as a capable tool that can be used for the benefit of improving social media engagement. The wide-ranging issues governing the adoption of social media to communicate that were condensed into a simple model structure by grouping similar theoretical foundations has enhanced model's feasibility and applicability.

REFERENCES

Ahmad, R. (2005). A conceptualisation of a customer-bank bond in the context of the twenty-first century UK retail banking industry. *International Journal of Bank Marketing*, *23*(4), 317–333. doi:10.1108/02652320510603942

Amichai-Hamburger, Y., & Vinitzky, G. (2010). Social network use and personality. *Computers in Human Behavior*, *26*(6), 1289–1295. doi:10.1016/j.chb.2010.03.018

Apra. (2015). *List of authorised deposit-taking institutions*. Retrieved April 29 2015, from http://goo.gl/rJ8kK

Australian Senate, Economics Reference Committee. (2011). *Inquiry into the competition within the Australian banking sector*. Canberra: Senate Printing Unit.

Bates, C. (2011). Facebook tightens privacy controls and gives users the option not to be tagged in photos. *Daily Mail*. Retrieved February 24, 2015, from http://goo.gl/qKnIZ

Bielski, L. (2008). Eight Tech innovations that took banking into the 21st Century. *ABA Banking Journal*, *100*, 84–89.

Braun, M. T. (2013). Obstacles to social networking website use among older adults. *Computers in Human Behavior*, *29*(3), 673–680. doi:10.1016/j.chb.2012.12.004

Butts, C. T. (2008). Social network analysis: A methodological introduction. *Asian Journal of Social Psychology*, *11*(1), 13–41. doi:10.1111/j.1467-839X.2007.00241.x

Chandra, N. (2011). Social media as a touch point in reverse logistics: Scale development and validation. *International Journal of Business Research*, *11*, 76–83.

Choudhary, A., Hendrix, W., Lee, K., Palsetia, D., & Liao, W.-K. (2012). Social media evolution of the egyptian revolution. *Communications of the ACM*, *55*(5), 74–80. doi:10.1145/2160718.2160736

Coombs, T. (2007). Protecting organisation reputations during a crisis: The development and application of situational crisis communication theory. *Corporate Reputation Review*, *10*(3), 163–176. doi:10.1057/palgrave.crr.1550049

Correa, T., Hinsley, A. W., & De Zúñiga, H. G. (2010). Who interacts on the web?: The intersection of users' personality and social media use. *Computers in Human Behavior*, *26*(2), 247–253. doi:10.1016/j.chb.2009.09.003

Fan, W., & Gordon, M. D. (2014). The power of social media analytics. *Communications of the ACM*, *57*(6), 74–81. doi:10.1145/2602574

Greenhow, C., & Robelia, B. (2009). Old communication, new literacies: Social network sites as social learning resources. *Journal of Computer-Mediated Communication*, *14*(4), 1130–1161. doi:10.1111/j.1083-6101.2009.01484.x

Haas, C., & Wearden, S. T. (2003). E-credibility: Building common ground in web environments. *L1-Educational Studies in Language and Literature*, *3*(1/2), 169–184. doi:10.1023/A:1024557422109

Harrison, J., Rintel, S., & Mitchell, E. (2014). Australian Social Media Trends. In C. Litang & M. H. Prosser (Eds.), *Social Media in Asia*. Dignity Press.

Howard, B. (2008). Analyzing online social networks. *Communications of the ACM*, *51*(11), 14–16. doi:10.1145/1400214.1400220

Huffaker, D. (2010). Dimensions of leadership and social influence in online communities. *Human Communication Research*, *36*(4), 593–617. doi:10.1111/j.1468-2958.2010.01390.x

Hughes, D. J., Rowe, M., Batey, M., & Lee, A. (2012). A tale of two sites: Twitter vs. Facebook and the personality predictors of social media usage. *Computers in Human Behavior*, *28*(2), 561–569. doi:10.1016/j.chb.2011.11.001

Iriberri, A., & Leroy, G. (2009). A life-cycle perspective on online community success. *ACM Computing Surveys*, *41*(2), 1–29. doi:10.1145/1459352.1459356

Johnson, P. R., & Yang, S. (2009). Uses and Gratifications of Twitter: An examination of user motives and satisfaction of Twitter use. In *Proceedings of the Communication Technology Division of the Annual Convention of the Association for Education in Journalism and Mass Communication*.

Joshi, M., Cahill, D., & Sidhu, J. (2010). Intellectual capital performance in the banking sector: An assessment of Australian owned banks. *Journal of Human Resource Costing & Accounting*, *14*(2), 151–170. doi:10.1108/14013381011062649

Kane, G. C., Alavi, M., Labianca, G. J., & Borgatti, S. P. (2014). What's different about social media networks? A framework and research agenda. *MIS Quarterly Theory & Review, 38,* 1–68.

Klapper, J. T. (1963). Mass communication research: An old road resurveyed. *Public Opinion Quarterly, 27*(4), 515–527. doi:10.1086/267201

Knight, A. (2010). FB friends with your bank? *The Age.* Retrieved July 14, 2010, from http://goo.gl/yV1YQL

Koh, J., & Kim, Y. G. (2004). Knowledge sharing in virtual communities: An e-business perspective. *Expert Systems with Applications, 26*(2), 155–166. doi:10.1016/S0957-4174(03)00116-7

Larose, R., & Atkin, D. (1991). Attributes of movie distribution channels and consumer choice. *Journal of Media Economics, 4*(1), 3–17. doi:10.1080/08997769109358200

Latane, B. (1981). The Psychology of Social Impact. *The American Psychologist, 36,* 343–356. doi:10.1037/0003-066X.36.4.343

Latané, B. (1996). Dynamic social impact: The creation of culture by communication. *Journal of Communication, 46*(4), 13–25. doi:10.1111/j.1460-2466.1996.tb01501.x

Lee, C. S., & Ma, L. (2012). News sharing in social media: The effect of gratifications and prior experience. *Computers in Human Behavior, 28*(2), 331–339. doi:10.1016/j.chb.2011.10.002

Lee, J. (2010). 10 million Australians on Facebook. *The Age.* Retrieved December 10 2010, from http://goo.gl/CEWXA

Leech, N. L., & Onwuegbuzie, A. J. (2007). An array of qualitative data analysis tools: A call for data analysis triangulation. *School Psychology Quarterly, 22*(4), 557–584. doi:10.1037/1045-3830.22.4.557

Leitch, S., & Warren, M. (2011). The ethics of security of personal information upon Facebook. *ICT Ethics and Security in the 21st Century: New Developments and Applications.*

Lin, C. A. (2003). An interactive communication technology adoption model. *Communication Theory, 13*(4), 345–365. doi:10.1111/j.1468-2885.2003.tb00296.x

Lipschultz, J. H. (2014). *Social Media Communication: Concepts, Practices, Data, Law, and Ethics.* Routledge.

Lowery, S., & Defleur, M. L. (1995). *Milestones in mass communication research.* Media Effects.

Lu, H.-P., Lin, J. C.-C., Hsiao, K.-L., & Cheng, L.-T. (2010). Information sharing behaviour on blogs in Taiwan: Effects of interactivities and gender differences. *Journal of Information Science, 36*(3), 401–416. doi:10.1177/0165551510363631

Martins, C., Oliveira, T., & Popovič, A. (2014). Understanding the Internet banking adoption: A unified theory of acceptance and use of technology and perceived risk application. *International Journal of Information Management, 34*(1), 1–13. doi:10.1016/j.ijinfomgt.2013.06.002

Metzgar, E., & Maruggi, A. (2009). Social Media and the 2008 US Presidential Election. *Journal of New Communications Research, 4,* 141–165.

Nov, O., & Ye, C. (2008) Personality and Technology Acceptance: Personal Innovativeness in IT, Openness and Resistance to Change. In *Proceedings of the 41st Annual Hawaii International Conference on System Sciences*. IEEE. doi:10.1109/HICSS.2008.348

Ott, L., & Theunissen, P. (2015). Reputation at risk: Engagement during social media crises. *Public Relations Review*, *41*(1), 97–102. doi:10.1016/j.pubrev.2014.10.015

Panahi, S., Watson, J., & Partridge, H. (2015). Information encountering on social media and tacit knowledge sharing. *Journal of Information Science*, 1–12.

Pedersen, P. E. (2005). Adoption of mobile Internet services: An exploratory study of mobile commerce early adopters. *Journal of Organizational Computing and Electronic Commerce*, *15*(3), 203–222. doi:10.1207/s15327744joce1503_2

Pentina, I., Covault, A., & Tarafdar, M. (2015). Exploring The Role of Social Media in News Consumption. In K. Kubacki (Ed.), *Ideas in marketing: Finding the new and polishing the old* (pp. 577–587). Springer. doi:10.1007/978-3-319-10951-0_209

Rubin, A. M. (1994). Media uses and effects: A uses-and-gratifications perspective. In B. Jennings & D. Zillamann (Eds.), *Media Effects: Advances in Theory and Research. LEA's Communication Series* (p. 505). Hillsdale, NJ: Lawrence Erlbaum Associates, Inc.

Schwab, K. (2013). *Global Competitiveness Report 2013-2014*. World Economic Forum.

Senadheera, V. (2015). *The adoption of social media by Australian banks to communicate with the public.* (Doctoral dissertation). Retrieved March 30, 2016, from http://goo.gl/cQcZ0C

Senadheera, V., Warren, M., & Leitch, S. (2011). A Study into How Australian Banks use Social Media. In *Proceedings of the Pacific Asia Conference on Information Systems (PACIS '11)*.

Sundar, S. S., & Limperos, A. M. (2013). Uses and grats 2.0: New gratifications for new media. *Journal of Broadcasting & Electronic Media*, *57*(4), 504–525. doi:10.1080/08838151.2013.845827

Szabo, G., & Huberman, B. A. (2010). Predicting the popularity of online content. *Communications of the ACM*, *53*(8), 80–88. doi:10.1145/1787234.1787254

Taintor, D. (2013). Facebook Introduces Verified Accounts. *ADWEEK*. Retrieved August 7, 2014, from http://goo.gl/kf5kkB

Trevino, L. K., & Webster, J. (1992). Flow in computer-mediated communication: Electronic mail and voice mail evaluation and impacts. *Communication Research*, *19*, 539–573.

Wang, Q., Woo, H. L., Quek, C. L., Yang, Y., & Liu, M. (2012a). Using the Facebook group as a learning management system: An exploratory study. *British Journal of Educational Technology*, *43*, 428–438.

Wang, Z., Tchernev, J. M., & Solloway, T. (2012b). A dynamic longitudinal examination of social media use, needs, and gratifications among college students. *Computers in Human Behavior*, *28*(5), 1829–1839. doi:10.1016/j.chb.2012.05.001

Westerman, D., Spence, P. R., & Van Der Heide, B. (2012). A social network as information: The effect of system generated reports of connectedness on credibility on Twitter. *Computers in Human Behavior*, *28*(1), 199–206. doi:10.1016/j.chb.2011.09.001

Wu, S., Hofman, J. M., Mason, W. A., & Watts, D. J. (2011). Who says what to whom on twitter. In *Proceedings of the 20th International Conference on World Wide Web*. ACM. doi:10.1145/1963405.1963504

Yates, D., & Paquette, S. (2011). Emergency knowledge management and social media technologies: A case study of the 2010 Haitian earthquake. *International Journal of Information Management*, *31*(1), 6–13. doi:10.1016/j.ijinfomgt.2010.10.001

Zeng, D., Chen, H., Lusch, R., & Li, S.-H. (2010). Social media analytics and intelligence. *IEEE Intelligent Systems*, *25*(6), 13–16. doi:10.1109/MIS.2010.151

Chapter 14
Code Reuse

Donna Bridgham
DARS, USA

ABSTRACT

The reuse of code can be used to add or update functionalities with little or no modifications to new or existing software applications. Developers have reused sections of code when the code is available but have been hindered by finding the code that is needed for an application. By creating a code repository, code would be available to developers in a systemic method. The code would be available for functional and nonfunctional uses in applications. Since the code has already be written, during the discovery phase of projects the developers involved should be able to search the repository for the code that is needed for strategies and problems that have already been successfully been implemented. Quality, cost, and time should be the focus of code reuse. To maximize code reuse, a code repository that is properly categorized and indexed would add to the software development lifecycle by making code available to developers that they can use with confidence. The code repository will improve the application process.

INTRODUCTION

The reuse of code can be used to add or update functionalities with little or no modifications to new or existing software applications such as including media in the development. Developers have reused sections of code when the code is available but have been hindered by finding the code that is needed for an application or specific action. By creating a code repository, code would be available to developers in a systemic method.

With the use of web applications this makes the use of a repository useful for all types of media. Since many web applications reuse the same style sheets, classes and modules they can be held in a repository. Since many languages are used, code libraries are no longer enough. A code repository would solve the problem by have the code available.

The code would be available for functional and nonfunctional uses in applications. Since the code has already been written, during the discovery phase of software projects the developers involved should be able to search the repository for the code that is needed for strategies and problems that have already been successfully been implemented. Quality, cost, and time should be the focus of code reuse.

DOI: 10.4018/978-1-5225-0648-5.ch014

To maximize code reuse, a code repository needs to be properly categorized and indexed so it would add another dimension to the software development lifecycle. If the code is made available to developers through the organizations own secure web site and the code is monitored the code repository can used by the developers with confidence. The developers will be able to share code from previous applications and media designed by previous developers that has already been tested and used in existing applications so there will a higher confidence level. This would be a strong start to creating a code repository.

Since the code had already been implemented in previous releases, the code will be available for the developers to find since it will be catalogued and indexed. Also by sharing code, developers will be encouraged to write comments in their code which will help other developers understand the purpose of the code. The code repository will improve the application process for the research purpose.

After implementation, all developers will be able to access the Code Repository through a web interface. It will have authentication so only approved personnel can look at the repository. There will be a screen where the developer can look for the category they need, the problem or action they are looking for and then a snippet will appear for them to use. All associated bugs, fixes and additional data will be included. This will enable the developer to understand previous testing, previous uses and the actual intent of the code.

BACKGROUND

Code reuse is not a new idea but moving it into a code repository is a new concept. Code reuse has been a practice for developers since it can be more effective, has fewer bugs and has been tested in previous versions of applications. If code is used on one application and then another application has the need for the same type of action or event then the code can be reused if other developers know the code is available (National Instruments, 2010). Since the code has already been tested, consolidated and meets the organizational standards the code should be reused. The more the code is reused and tested the less probability for bugs or errors (National Instruments, 2010). If code is reused it may also benefit the user since the action or event will be familiar. Researchers will enjoy new features but will also identify with familiarity that will help with improving research. Since developers already reuse code, the next logical step is to build a code repository.

When a developer is writing code for an application and they are able to find code that has already been used and tested, it will reduce the risk of error and speed up the development and research process making an efficient process. The risk therefore is not in the code that is reused since the probability of bugs or failure will most likely be in the new lines of codes so it will be easier to find the errors (National Instruments, 2010). It is important to find a place to store and use code in an area that all developers can access. A repository would be an efficient place to store the code. The repository can be a web application frontend with a file server backend or database backend. This can be secured so only authorized personnel can access the repository.

There are problems with reusing codes and this also must be addressed. When integrating code it should always be analyzed before integrating it into the project (Schmidt, 2012). The code should be evaluated on several levels, such as which code is the best solution, have all previous bugs or errors been addressed, and will any modifications cause a change in the integrity of the code. The reuse of the code should save money and not cost more money so an evaluation should be done to ensure that the reuse is the best investment (Schmidt, 2012). This includes whether or not the code makes sense technically for the rest of the application. This process would be part of the software development life cycle for each application.

Over ten years ago Schmidt wrote an article on how reuse would lead to failure (2012). In 2012, Schmidt reviewed his article and proposed some basic ideas for success that would lead to cost savings and a good model for reuse. In the IT industry, many years ago developers were rewarded for how many lines of code they wrote. An organization can simply change this policy to reward the developers who reuse efficient components and make an effort to keep projects within budget by reusing the software components. The developer would be rewarded for reusing code or implementing objects that have been previously used that can be used again for the next release of a game.

Since each project should have its own framework and documentation which includes the code, it is essential that each member of the development team review the aforementioned items. It is critical to developers to recognize frameworks and components that have already been used so they will be able to reuse code with confidence on new projects or upgrades (Schmidt, 2012). By doing this, the developers will have a familiarity with the existing components, know that the components have already been tested and any errors or bugs will most likely be from new code. This will also reduce risk by not repeating past mistakes.

MAIN FOCUS OF THE CHAPTER

With the advances of the web, advances in teleconferencing and other forms of communication, projects are being built on a global level. The issue with the cost of projects is the cost of communicating with each team and team member if the team is not on the same site. If the code is in a repository and is reviewed before each project then projected code that is to be used for a project can be mapped to the code repository. Developers will have rights to the code repository and will have access to the code no matter where they are located. In research, communicating with others is imperative and having access to all code is an important part of the process.

The key to communication is that all developers must access the code. With the code repository this will not be a problem since all developers can access the code through a secure web interface. Organizations find it is beneficial if smaller teams of developers are used since they can produce a higher quality of software than a larger group with less effort and expense through code reuse (Schmidt, 2012). In order to do this, the smaller teams must be able to access the code from previous projects. Being able to coordinate the work amongst the developers and being able to communicate how the work is done and coded will solve some many of the problems of having to recode each piece of an application when the work has already been done.

Since many organizations do not have a framework for code or code reuse a Code Repository would solve this problem. In some organizations just a class library is used but that does not include all the code for all the projects that are being built for the organization or include the common pieces of code that are needed for certain functions on applications. Building a framework that would include all code to be categorized and indexed would improve performance. This would save time, money and improve the software process (Bloch, 2008).

Each application will have its own framework based on its design; therefore the code repository has to be flexible enough to contain code based on the framework of the application. The developers as Schmidt has pointed out in his article on code reuse, must have confidence in the code repository by recognizing the framework that the code will support the applications and the media that are being developed (2012). This will reduce risk on existing as well as new projects and will enhance the Software Development Life Cycle.

Languages

Since there are so many different languages that can be used for research and media, there is an increased need for a code repository. These include software languages such as JAVA, C++ and other languages as well as many web languages that may reuse codes for classes and objects from application to application. As a developer it is important to know where the code is located and how it has been identified in the various applications or media that is being developed. This will reduce the amount of code that has to be written and will improve the development process. A code repository would be the place where this code could be stored and filed for future use.

When using code to recreate an object the idea is not to recreate an object because creating a new object may be expensive but because it is effective. When reengineering small objects which do little work but are used on many applications it is cheaper to reuse the code in each application than to recreate the code and class each time it is needed. By reusing code additional code can be added to an application to build additional objects that will enhance the application by its clarity, giving the user more power and making the application easier to use (Bloch, 2008).

Code libraries have been used for code reuse but the code is only available if it is added to the library. The other issue is that the code is only available to developers who are using the same language or are working on the same project. Code libraries depend on either the environment or the language they are working in such as .NET, JAVA or other languages that have developed class libraries. A code repository would be set up to allow for all languages including mark-up languages and templates that are used for web sites.

Agile

With the progression of different types of programming methodologies code reuse is being used in different ways. Agile Programming is one of the methods that use code reuse as a process to speed up programming time. The process only reuses code that has been tested and has gone through a quality check. There was an article written for AmbySoft in 2013 about the strategic use of code as part of its application development process.

After starting an initiative to reuse code, AmbySoft improved their software process. AmbySoft created a strategic way for developers to develop ways to use code reuse to improve the software process by centralizing the existing code. If developers are encouraged to share code and make it readily available to others, it will save the organization money, time and an improved product. That was the goal at AmbySoft which was achieved by centralizing the code.

Tools

There are tools such as GIT, which was developed by Apple. GIT develops its own code repository. For developers who use Apple products, GIT is a tool that is easy to use but is limited to Apple users. The tool will publish the code from the application to the repository and it is available as soon as it is released. GIT is similar to tools like Microsoft SourceSafe but all code is not available to all users and can be application dependent (Apple, 2014). Each developer needs access to the tool and has to be able to view the latest release of the code. One developer should not have the ability to overwrite the code of another developer until there has been a meeting of the minds. There are different theories such as first in and last out that will need to be identified as the process the organization will use, otherwise code that has been updated may be deleted. All code in the repository should be backed up on a regular basis.

Code libraries have been used for code reuse but the code is only available if it is added to the library. The other issue is that the code is only available to developers who are using the same language or are working on the same project. Code libraries depend on either the environment or the language they are working in such as .NET, JAVA or other languages. For today's software systems it may be difficult to share code because many applications may also be using web technology. When applications are written for the web there is also the use of mark-up languages or other languages designed exclusively for the web.

When developing for the web many objects are repeated. These objects would be stored in the code repository. As we had mentioned above, most likely a web interface would be used that would talk to a database back end. The object would be added, evaluated, categorized and then be available for use as time goes on. Many of the classes, pages, modules also would be repeated and would be placed in the code repository. This would speed up application development.

When software code is placed in a repository it needs to be reviewed on a constant basis. There are IT shops that build applications in-house, outsource software or use combination third party software and write additional code to meet standards. The code may be put in a repository but it may be difficult to maintain the repository. Schmidt wrote that code needs to be reliable to be reused, so in order to use third party software; it must be validated before it is placed in a Code Repository (2012).

Example of Code Reuse

Shin, Choi, and Lee wrote in 2013 that fields like the medical profession need to have the ability to turn over code quickly. Some fields of software development have not had the urgency for reuse code but the medical field is one field that is growing so quickly that developers need to reuse code. Standards are needed to ensure that the code that is being reused has been tested and has been quality checked. The code that is reused also has to be placed in an area so it can be found and reused quickly by developers. In the medical field, developers cannot afford to make mistakes so code reuse and the quality of the code is essential to the development process (Shin, Choi, and Lee, 2013). Also by using code reuse the developers will reduce risk, will produce applications that will be cost effective and have a higher quality. This will improve the ability for medical research through applications, patient record applications and Medical Groups to share development.

Since developers may work on several projects at a time, sharing code will help to expedite application development. In the airline industry it is a common practice to share code and organizations within the airline industry make the code available to all developers. It is placed in a directory so it can be shared. The code is commented so that developers know the purpose of the code and how to use it. Since safety is at the utmost priority in the airline industry the code needs to be written quickly but there is little room for risk so if the code is already tested and has there is zero tolerance for faults in the code reuse. By giving developers access to all the code and having the code in an order that is intuitive to the developers they waste little time and they can fetch the code and start to use it immediately which serves the airline industry well (Ascend, 2013).

Failure of Code Reuse

Mariani, Pastore, and Pezze wrote in 2011 why the reuse of code in software systems is still not working and why organizations still do not find it a feasible option when building software applications. One of the first areas they looked at is off the shelf components and plug-ins that usually have little or no code that can be rewritten by in-house developers. If developers use the components without testing the code and do not look for specific faults the software may fail. This will also limit the developer's ability to debug the code so the developer is left to write the code without exploring code reuse. The developer needs a way to analyze the functions.

Mariani, Pastore, and Pezze therefore suggested that there still may be a way to test the code for faults before it is used and still save time and money. If the code is tested properly then the developer can use the components or plug-ins without having to write the code (2011). There needs to be a process in place so there is a positive trade-off in time and money by using code that has been already been developed by someone else and the time it takes to test the code.

Mariani, Pastore, and Pezze suggested a Behavior Capture Test that can be used to build a model of components interactions for the components and plug-ins (2011). The test is based on the successful executions of the application and executions that satisfied the user expectations. Failure executions are based on when the program is aborted or the test fails. The test would be one way to evaluate off the shelf or third party code before it could be added to the code Repository.

The Behavior Capture Test (BCT) can be used to show the concept which the code may be reused in a project if there is a way to test the validity of it without reading every line of code. There needs to be a model in place and a set percentage of failure based upon the action of the code and the application. If the developer can quickly identify the reason for the failure they have reduced the amount of time that is used to write the code and then test the code (Mariani, Pastore, and Pezze, 2011). Once the code has been thoroughly tested through the BCT model it can be added to the Code Repository so it can be used in the future.

The reason Schmidt wrote that software reuse did not work was it was expected to reduce development time and save money but the code was not shared across the business units and organizations so there was not a logical way to find and reuse the code. The systemic way to reuse software and software components was the industries way to try to reduce the development life cycle, improve the quality, and apply multi-uses to design (2012). Therefore there needed to be steps in reusing code.

The idea was considered promising but did not materialize since organizations did not make reuse a part of their software development process. The organizations recognized the reward but did not understand how to make reuse a reality that all developers could use. Non-technical people were making decisions and therefore did not have the understanding of what types of tools, architecture and initiative it would take for reuse to become part of the software development plan.

Limitations/Delimitations

In a study done by Ercim it was found that reused components had a lower defect incidence than non-reused ones. The conclusions were drawn by looking at the defect density which was calculated by dividing the number of defects by the number of lines of code. On the other hand, the reused components had more defects with a higher level of severity but at delivery these defects decreased after delivery because the developers knew how to work with the code (Ercim News, 2005). The reused code has fewer defects but the developers need to know how to use it and test it before delivery.

The other limitation is using code that was not developed in-house. Code that is in the repository has been tested and used by applications by organizational teams. Code that is used that has been found online has to be customized and fit into the application. By using in-house code there is a lower risk. If other code is used, tested and found to be low risk then it can be added to the repository. In order to use the code in the repository in development it has to be catalogued and indexed before the project starts so the project team has access to it during the discovery phase.

Diffusion of Innovation

Wainwright and Waring address Roger's theory of the Diffusion of Innovation (DOI) in the field of Information Technology (2007). DOI research is practiced in many fields and is not a new concept. Rogers has worked and adopted his research so the framework has become refined. Diffusion is defined as the process in which innovation can be communicated through channels over time to members of a social system. Innovation is an idea, practice or object that is perceived as new by individuals or units. Rogers has divided the innovation decision process into five steps: relative advantage, compatibility, complexity, trialability and observability (2007). These lead to the five steps in the innovation decision process: knowledge, persuasion, decision, implementation and confirmation (2007).

Rogers goes further into his process to say that there are "five adopter categories based on innovativeness are identified: innovators, adopters, early majority, late majority and laggards, where the rate of adoption is the relative speed at which an innovation is adopted by members of a social system" (Wainwright and Waring, p. 3, 2007). Therefore the social and communication structure of system would either help or hinder diffusion where there are already norms, leadership in place, a change in or any set variables. In order to balance the process there are four types of innovation decisions. The decisions are independent choices, consensus, enforced by a few, or a choice made after a prior decision.

Wainwright and Waring wanted a way to improve health care through technology so they used Roger's approach to create a framework using the DOI (2007). When using innovations or discussing diffusion experiences it was important to discuss all experiences so they can be evaluated for future development. Wainwright and Waring divided their interviewees into three groups (2007). The conclusion they drew from their study was that the higher up in the hierarchy the more you knew about the processes and the decisions that impacted the system. The people who were more likely to use the system had little knowledge or input into the system and had little decision making power.

Developers needed a place to share, store and identify code. Like in the studies using the DOI Model people were put in position to create ideas for usage of applications without understanding the knowledge or input needed to create code and what the significance of code reuse is to developers. Therefore it was not assumed that a code repository would be an innovative idea. The five steps in the innovation process would lead to an improvement in development if the developers were part of the process.

If Wainright and Waring's writings were placed into a project that was written for IT and was to use Roger's DOI theory it would have to be modeled correctly so all users thought they were stakeholders (2007). The application would have to have technical complexity, ease of use and perceived use. When using the perceived use, the developers would need to know what the use of the application was, why the application was built and what the advantages of the application are to their development.

When designing the code repository it was important to follow a project plan so when it was completed it could be included in the Software Development Life Cycle for other Projects. A project plan template was used to write up the requirements for the project. The DOI model could be used to ensure that the repository was meeting the needs of the developers. The reason why the DOI was added is that code reuse has been an arguable point in Information Technology. It is important that the use of the code repository adds to the development of applications and not deters from it. It was found by taking the DOI model and incorporating this theory into the application of building a Code Repository, it strengthens the need for including code reuse in the SDLC by having a centralized area where categorized code can be found for projects.

Solutions and Recommendations

Since building a code repository will be a project itself it needs to follow a software development life cycle. There should be a project lead that understands the need for the code repository and the purpose for the application. They will need to go through the project plan and build the application to the specifics and see if any organizational standards need to be added or addressed.

There will need to be a full test process of the application before it can be released to the developers. This process will include test scripts that can be turned into training manuals for the users. This will be updated as needed. There should be someone assigned to make sure that all projects are updated and archived as needed.

Database

The relational database uses specific structure to locate the data and then display the data values. If a relational database is designed correctly it will be easy to query data to display it in a simple and meaningful way so the developers can find the code need quickly (Business Dictionary, 2012). In designs of other databases this was not possible.

The other limitation is the security. The SQL Server database allows the administrator of the application to set up the security based on role. If the user is authenticated as a user they will be able to access the application.

After implementation, all developers will be able to access the Code Repository through a web interface. It will have authentication so only approved personnel can look at the repository. There will be a screen where the developer can look for the category they need, the problem or action they are looking for and then a snippet will appear for them to use. All associated bugs, fixes and additional data will be included. This will enable the developer to understand previous testing, previous uses and the actual intent of the code.

Figure 1. Basic outline of tables for the code repository

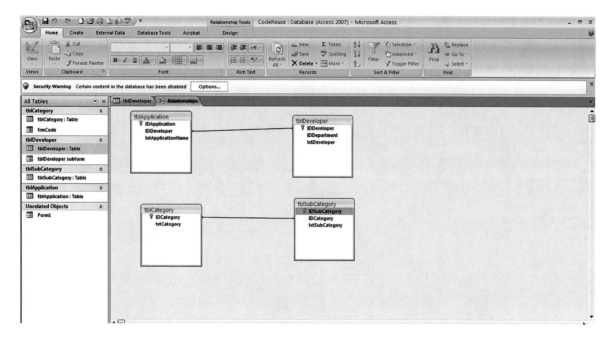

Once again the limitation here is that each developer must record any bugs or additional testing that they have done to the code. This will enhance the ease of use. A person must be assigned to the Code Repository External Interface will be a web based application. The form will be authentication based on the user role. Microsoft Visual Studio 2010 will be used to build the interface since it will be able to connect to a database and security can be controlled within the database server (for the prototype it will be Access 2007).

The database needs to start with simple design such as tblApplication, tblDeveloper, tblCategory, tblSubCategory as illustrated in Figure 1.

The internal Structure of the Project will be built by database developers who have an expertise in SQL Server technology. The internal structure will be a relational database so that there will be data integrity and will not leave any orphaned data during the conversion. The developers will be in house developers who will follow the organizational database naming and data conventions. The database must go through an approval process by the DBA before this piece can be signed off on. This is illustrated in Figure 2.

Wainwright and Wright wrote that by using the Diffusion of Innovation better applications could be built (2007). There are five steps that need to be included in the design. The developers need to use the knowledge of the previous developers to understand what the previously written code is about, developers need to be persuaded to write their code so it can be placed in a repository, the decision needs to be made that the repository will be used as part of the software development life cycle, the code repository needs to be implemented as a working application and a Process must be used to ensure that it is working as well as it can and then the IT department must confirm that the code repository will work and will be one for the applications used in the SDLC. Then at the implementation there will be an evaluation of technical compatibility, technical complexity and relative advantage (see Figure 3).

Figure 2. Database schema for relational data

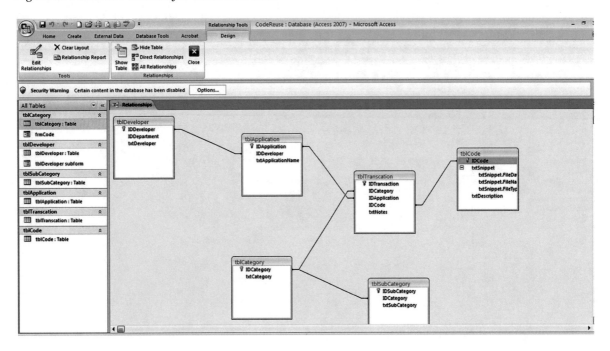

Figure 3. Basic work flow of the new system captured through the needs of the basic system to search the sub categories

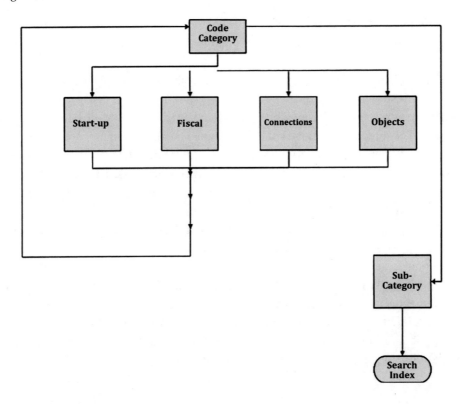

Building the System

A system will be built to allow all developers to review code from all applications. The database will start with 5 major functions that will need to be identified and carried over to the system.

Function 1: All applications must be entered into the system through a web form creating an identity key for each application; all code related to this application will carry this ID throughout the lifecycle of this project.

Function 2: All code associated with an application will be tracked through a web form and stored in a transaction table. The code will either be stored in a binary field or will be uploaded in a documented if it has extensive comments and fits the requirements (see Figure 4).

Function 3: All risks must be tracked and evaluated for each project through a web interface and stored in tables. This will be achieved through keying in the data and evaluating it based on the scale developed by the team.

Function 4: All Changes must be tracked through a web interface and stored in tables by the project name.

Function 5: All Analysis and Approvals need to be entered into the system through web interfaces and stored in tables per project. The approvers must have their names and ID's in the tables so that a clear and concise record of the code can be kept (see Figure 5).

Function 6: The next screen will show all the Internet and Intranet applications based on an application process. This will help the developers choose or look at code that has already been written. The developer will only be able to look at code that they have access to. This is illustrated in Figure 6.

Function 7: The next screen as illustrated in Figure 7 will show how to set up the category and subcategory for the code. This will distinguish where the code will placed in the repository. The reviewer will make sure that the proper categories were chosen and may change then if needed. This will all be accomplished through the interface.

Figure 4. Example of homepage

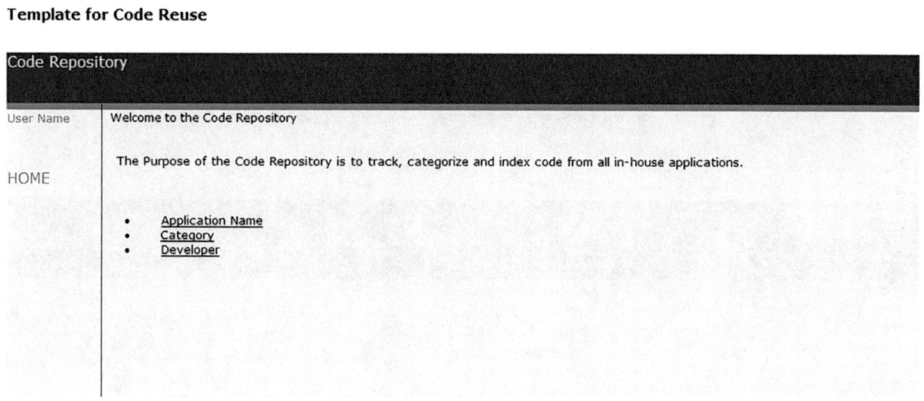

Template for Code Reuse

Figure 5. Overview of application

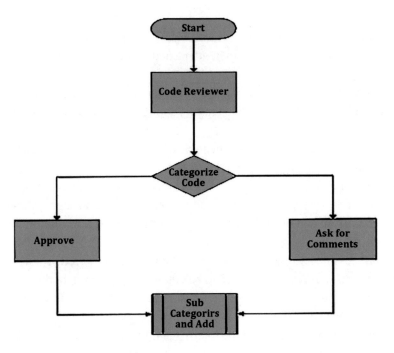

Figure 6. Data selection for developers

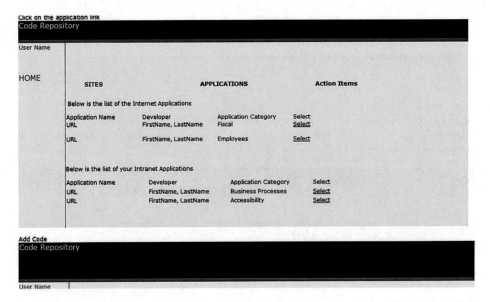

Figure 7. Screen for adding categories

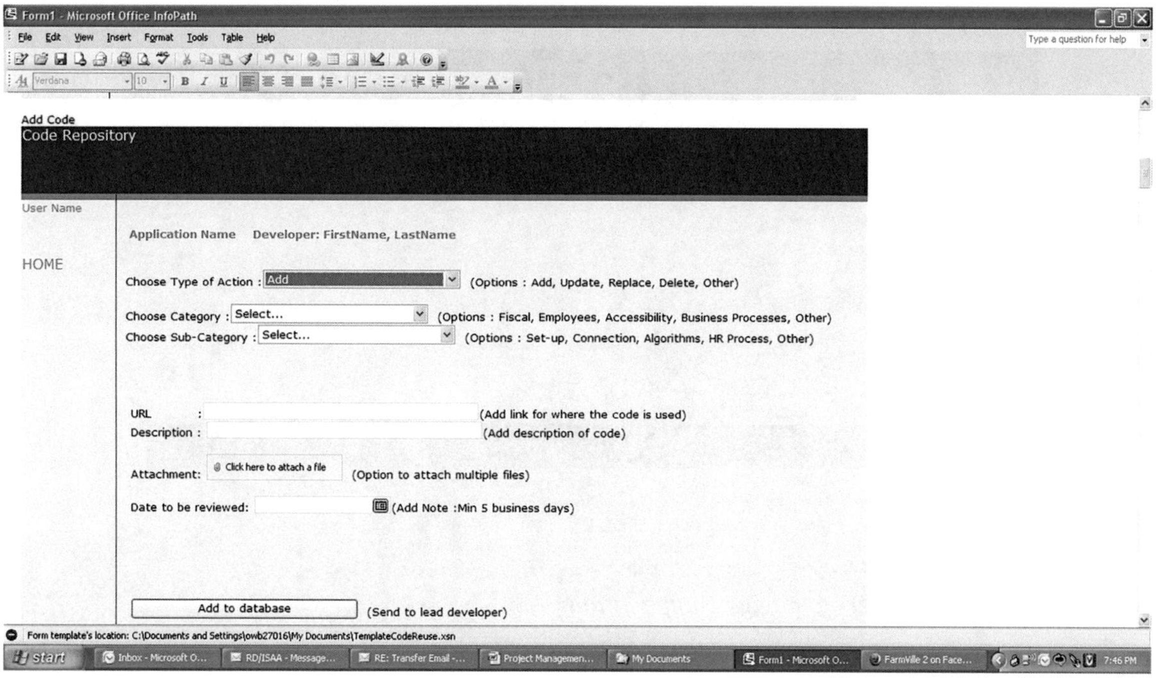

Applications

As mentioned above the applications would be listed on the Home Page based on Access. There would be a list of all the applications based on whether they were Intranet or Internet so the code could be found easily. The Home page will have links that gives the developer access to different sections of the application. Figure 8 is an example of a home page.

The developers can go to the site page to find the application the developer and the URL for the application. The developer can find the code based on the category. Figure 9 is an example of a site page for code reuse.

Action Screen

The action screen would allow the developers to add the code based on a category, sub-category, and whether the action is an update, new or other. A URL to the page will be included along with a description. A review date is also included to ensure that it is using the latest version if that is applicable (see Figure 10).

Move to Review

Each piece of code will need to be reviewed before it can be added permanently to the repository. The administrator of the repository may want to change the category or description before it is moved to production. The administrator will have the final say on all reviews (see Figure 11).

Figure 8. Home page with links for each section of the application

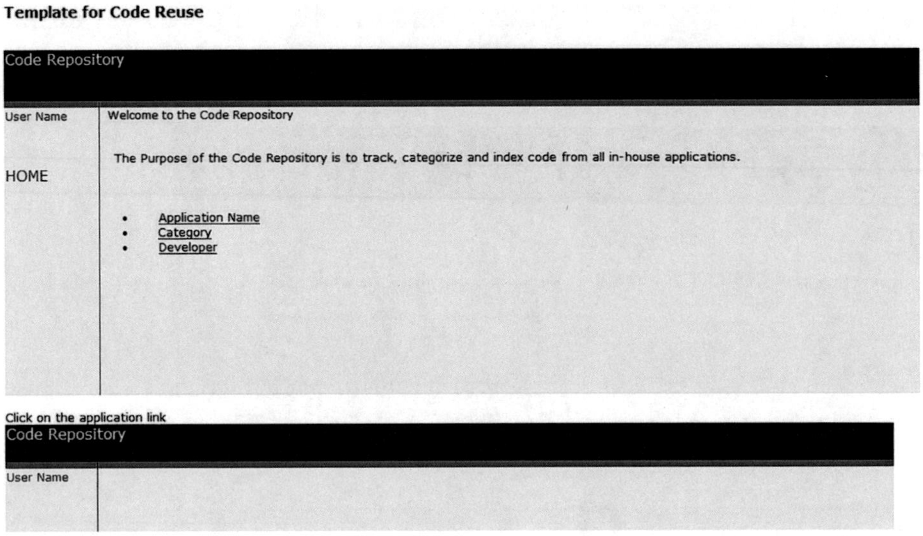

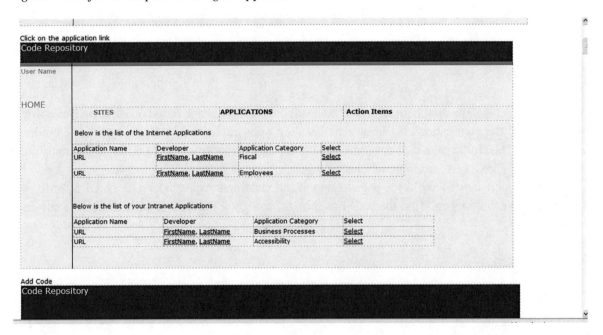

Figure 9. List for developers to navigate application

Administrator Status Screen

The administrator will need a screen to view all the actions that have taken place in the database. The screen will show if there are requests that are waiting review, the latest reviews that were made and who made them. This allows the administrator to keep the code up to date and to keep the repository clean. In building the repository it is instrumental that the code is identified, categorized, indexed and kept up to date (see Figure 12).

Figure 10. Screen to add new code based on category and sub category

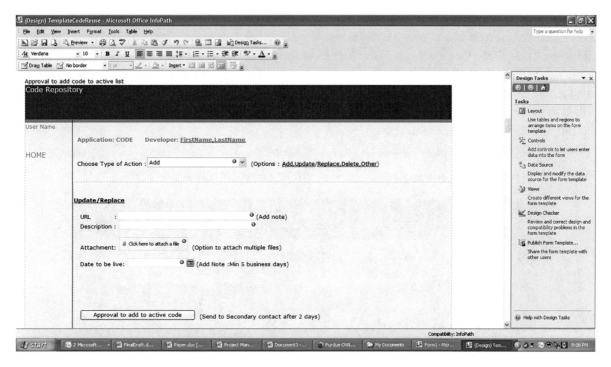

Figure 11. Interface to send code to reviewer

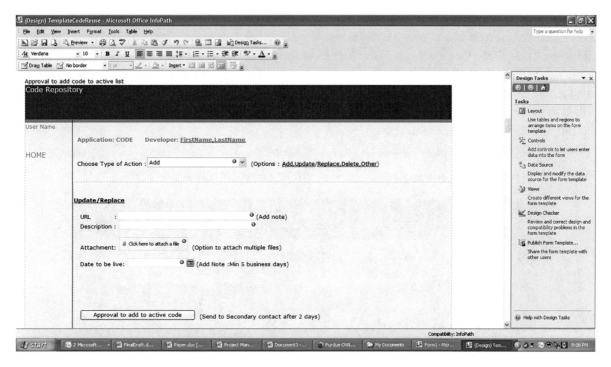

Figure 12. Screen for administrator to keep of actions

Code Repository

User Name						
HOME						
	SITES		**APPLICATIONS**		**Action Item**	
	Your Requests					
	Application Name	Developer	Type of Request	Date Requested	Status	
	URL	FirstName, LastName	Add	08/27/2014	Waiting for Review!	
	URL	FirstName, LastName	Replace	08/25/2014	Waiting for update on questions	
	Requests Waiting for your Approval					
	Application Name	Site Owner	Type of Request	Date Requested	Status	View
	URL	FirstName.LastName	Update	08/28/2014	Waiting to be added to active code	View
	URL	FirstName.LastName	Delete	08/23/2014	Waiting to be added to active code	View

Code Questions for Review

Code for Review

There will be a screen that allows the developer to add snippets of code. The code is added through a file format that SQL Server accepts. The Web form through SQL authentication will pick up the user name and will process the name, the department, and any other pertinent information. Once the code is added a button is click and then a request is sent to the administrator to review the code so it can be added to the repository. It can be new, updated or even deletion and replaced code. Figure 13 shows the simple web form to allow this function.

Figure 13. Screen to add code snippets to code repository base on simple function

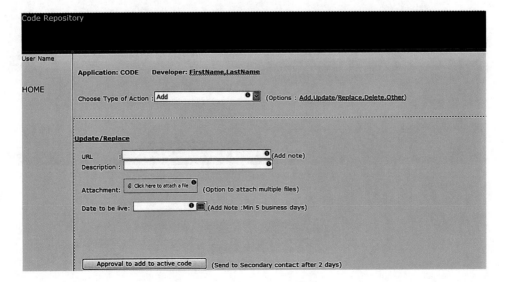

Figure 14. Screen to show code snippets

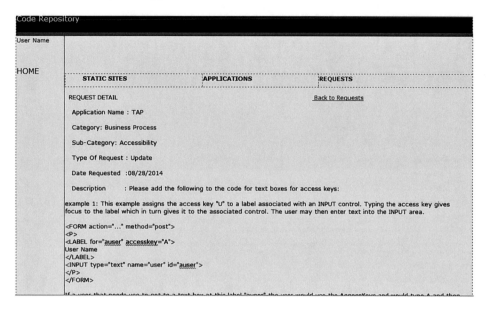

If a developer wants to review a snippet of code before they download a file they can use the web interface to accomplish this task. With web technology it is important that information can be accessed quickly and then downloaded easily. The web interface allows easy access to the code repository. Figure 14 shows a screen with the code that shows on the interface.

Accepted Request

Once a request is accepted into the repository an email is sent to all developers that a new entry has been added to the code repository. It will have the category, subcategory, name of developer and application code was used for. It may also have the name of a class or object if applicable. This will allow developers to look at the code and see if they will be able to look at it immediately. With application development that uses such tools as .NET, CSS, and other web languages these may be useful right away (see Figure 15).

FUTURE RESEARCH DIRECTIONS

The future of development relies on the ability of developers to develop applications as quickly, efficiently and professionally as possible. As Schmidt had written, the idea of code reuse can either be beneficial if done correctly or a disaster if everyone on a team or in an organization does their own thing. As pointed out in the DOI example the correct people within an organization are never asked for feedback for important projects. If the developers had the ability to have a voice in the development of the code repository and helped to index and categorize it could be a valuable tool

Figure 15. Interface to add accepted code to database and notify all developers of added code

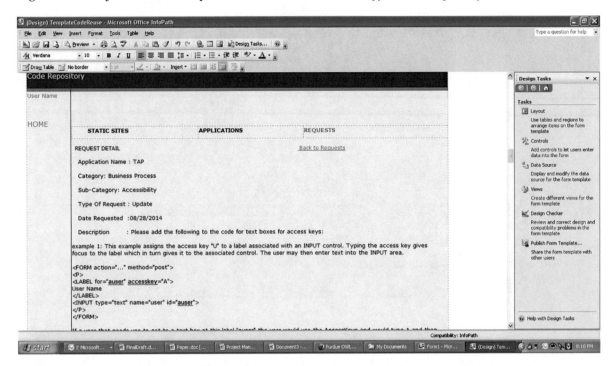

CONCLUSION

Once an application is built, it can be reengineered for extends for the present application or for a new application if the code is made available to all the developers. There needs to be a consistent process in place in order for the reengineering to be successful. By building a web repository, sharing code will become a reality. The code that will be in the repository will have already been through a business process, testing, a quality process and an implementation plan. Organizations need to be able to reproduce existing code and improve on it as technology evolves in order to be successful.

REFERENCES

AmbySoft. (2013). *Enterprise agile: Strategic reuse*. Retrieved from http://www.enterpriseunifiedprocess.com/essays/strategicReuse.html

Apple. (2014). *Integration guide*. Retrieved from https://developer.apple.com/library/ios/documentation/IDEs/Conceptual/xcode_guide-continuous_integration/PublishYourCodetoaSourceRepository/PublishYourCodetoaSourceRepository.html

Ascend. (2013). *Codeshare success*. Retrieved from http://www.ascendforairlines.com/2013-issue-no-3/codeshare-success

Bloch, J. (2008). *Creating and destroying Java objects*. Retrieved from http://www.informit.com/articles/article.aspx?p=1216151&seqNum=5

Ercim News. (2005). *The advantages of reused software components*. Retrieved from http://www.ercim.eu/publication/Ercim_News/enw60/mohagheghi.html

Mariani, L., Pastore, F., & Pezze, M. (2011). Dynamic analysis for diagnosing integration faults. *IEEE Transactions on Software Engineering*, *37*(4), 486–508. doi:10.1109/TSE.2010.93

National Instruments. (2010). *Weighing the cost and benefits of code reuse*. Retrieved from ftp://ftp.ni.com/pub/newsimages/2010/LabVIEW2010_OnlinePressKit/QandAs/IP%20Integration%20Q&A.pdf

Schmidt, D. (2012). *Why software reuse has failed and how to make it work for you*. Retrieved from http://www.dre.vanderbilt.edu/~schmidt/reuse-lessons.html

TechTarget. (2014). *Relational database*. Retrieved from http://searchsqlserver.techtarget.com/definition/relational-database

Wainwright, D. W., & Waring, T. S. (2007). The application and adaptation of a diffusion of innovation framework for information systems research in NHS general medical practice. *Journal of Information Technology*, *22*(1), 44–58. doi:10.1057/palgrave.jit.2000093

452

Compilation of References

Abisheva, A., Garimella, V. R. K., Garcia, D., & Weber, I. (2014). Who watches (and shares) what on YouTube? And when? Using Twitter to understand YouTube viewership. In *Proceedings of WSDM '14*.

Acartürk, C., & Çağıltay, K. (2006). İnsan bilgisayar etkileşimi ve ODTÜ'de yürütülen çalışmalar. *Akademik Bilişim*, 9-11.

Adamic, L. A., Huberman, B. A., Barabási, A.-L., Albert, R., Jeong, H., & Bianconi, G. (2000). Power-law distribution of the world wide web. *Science*, *287*(5461), 2115–2115. doi:10.1126/science.287.5461.2115a

Adamic, L. A., Lukose, R. M., Puniyani, A. R., & Huberman, B. A. (2001). Search in power-law networks. *Physical Review E: Statistical, Nonlinear, and Soft Matter Physics*, *64*(4), 046135. doi:10.1103/PhysRevE.64.046135 PMID:11690118

Agarwal, A., Xie, B., Vovsha, I., Rambow, O., & Passonneau, R. (2011). Sentiment analysis of twitter data. In *Proceedings of the Workshop on Languages in Social Media* (pp. 30-38). Association for Computational Linguistics.

Aggarwal, C. C. (2003). Towards systematic design of distance functions for data mining applications. In *Proceedings of the Ninth ACM SIGKDD International Conference on Knowledge Discovery and Data Mining*. doi:10.1145/956750.956756

Aggarwal, C. C., & Zhai, C. X. (2012). A survey of text clustering algorithms. In C. C. Aggarwal & C. X. Zhai (Eds.), *Mining Text Data* (pp. 77–128). Springer. doi:10.1007/978-1-4614-3223-4_4

Ahmad, R. (2005). A conceptualisation of a customer-bank bond in the context of the twenty-first century UK retail banking industry. *International Journal of Bank Marketing*, *23*(4), 317–333. doi:10.1108/02652320510603942

Aiden, E., & Michel, J.-B. (2013). *Uncharted: Big Data as a Lens on Human Culture*. New York: Penguin Group.

Ajjan, H., & Hartshorne, R. (2008). Investigating faculty decisions to adopt Web 2.0 technologies: Theory and empirical tests. *The Internet and Higher Education*, *11*(2), 71–80. doi:10.1016/j.iheduc.2008.05.002

Akcapinar, G., Altun, A., & Mentes, T. (2012). The Effect of Prior Knowledge on Navigational Profiles in Hypertext Environments. *Eğitim ve Bilim*, *37*(163), 143.

Albert, R., Jeong, H., & Barabási, A. L. (2000). Diameter of the World Wide Web. *Nature*, (401): 130–131.

Alexander, B. (2006). Web 2.0. A New Wave of Innovation for Teaching and learning. *EDUCAUSE Review*, (March/April), 33–44. Retrieved from http://www.educause.edu/ir/library/pdf/erm0621.pdf

Allen, T. L., Underwood, J. P., & Scheding, S. J. (2007). A planning system for autonomous ground vehicles operating in unstructured dynamic environments. In *Proccedings of 2007 Australasian Conference on Robotics & Automation*.

Allen, I. E., & Seaman, J. (2013). *Changing course: ten years of tracking online education in the United States*. Babson Survey Research Group and Quahog Research Group, LLC.

Alzouma, G. (2014). Between flaming and laudation: Political websites, social media, and democratic participation in niger. *The International Journal of Internet Trolling and Online Participation, 1*(1), 29–61.

AmbySoft. (2013). *Enterprise agile: Strategic reuse.* Retrieved from http://www.enterpriseunifiedprocess.com/essays/strategicReuse.html

Amichai-Hamburger, Y., & Vinitzky, G. (2010). Social network use and personality. *Computers in Human Behavior, 26*(6), 1289–1295. doi:10.1016/j.chb.2010.03.018

Andrzejczak, C., & Liu, D. (2010). The effect of testing location on usability testing performance, participant stress levels, and subjective testing experience. *Journal of Systems and Software, 83*(7), 1258–1266. doi:10.1016/j.jss.2010.01.052

Andzulis, J. M., Panagopoulos, N. G., & Rapp, A. (2012). A review of social media and implications for the sales process. *Journal of Personal Selling & Sales Management, 32*(3), 305–316. doi:10.2753/PSS0885-3134320302

Angeli, C., & Valanides, N. (2009). Epistemological and methodological issues for the conceptualization, development, and assessment of ICT–TPCK: Advances in technological pedagogical content knowledge (TPCK). *Computers & Education, 52*(1), 154–168. doi:10.1016/j.compedu.2008.07.006

Angerbauer, K., Schmidt, A., Dingler, T., & Kern, D. (2015). Utilizing the effects of priming to facilitate text comprehension. In *Proceedings of CHI 2015.*

Anokhin, A. P., Golosheykin, S., Sirevaag, E., Kristjansson, S., Rohrbaugh, J. W., & Heath, A. C. (2006). Rapid discrimination of visual scene content in the human brain. *Brain Research, 1093*(1), 167–177. doi:10.1016/j.brainres.2006.03.108 PMID:16712815

Apple. (2014). *Integration guide.* Retrieved from https://developer.apple.com/library/ios/documentation/IDEs/Conceptual/xcode_guide-continuous_integration/PublishYourCodetoaSourceRepository/PublishYourCodetoaSourceRepository.html

Apra. (2015). *List of authorised deposit-taking institutions.* Retrieved April 29 2015, from http://goo.gl/rJ8kK

Arakji, R. Y., & Lang, K. R. (2007). Digital consumer networks and producer-consumer collaboration: Innovation and product development in the digital entertainment industry. In *System Sciences, 2007. HICSS 2007. 40th Annual Hawaii International Conference on* (pp. 211c-211c). IEEE.

Ascend. (2013). *Codeshare success.* Retrieved from http://www.ascendforairlines.com/2013-issue-no-3/codeshare-success

Ashley, C., & Tuten, T. (2015). Creative strategies in social media marketing: An exploratory study of branded social content and consumer engagement. *Psychology and Marketing, 32*(1), 15–27. doi:10.1002/mar.20761

Auray, N. (2007). Folksonomy: The new way to serendipity. *Communications & Stratégies, 65*, 67–89.

Australian Senate, Economics Reference Committee. (2011). *Inquiry into the competition within the Australian banking sector.* Canberra: Senate Printing Unit.

Azevedo, R., & Feyzi-Behnagh, R. (2011). Dysregulated learning with advanced learning technologies. *Journal of e-Learning and Knowledge Society-English Version, 7*(2).

Azevedo, R. (2005). Computer environments as metacognitive tools for enhancing learning. *Educational Psychologist, 40*(4), 193–197. doi:10.1207/s15326985ep4004_1

Azevedo, R. (2008). The role of self-regulation in learning about science with hypermedia. In D. Robinson & G. Schraw (Eds.), *Recent innovations in educational technology that facilitate student learning* (pp. 127–156). Charlotte, NC: Information Age Publishing.

Azevedo, R., & Aleven, V. (2013). Metacognition and learning technologies: An overview of the current interdisciplinary research. In R. Azevedo & V. Aleven (Eds.), *International handbook of metacognition and learning technologies* (pp. 1–16). Amsterdam: Springer. doi:10.1007/978-1-4419-5546-3_1

Azevedo, R., & Cromley, J. G. (2004). Does training on self-regulated learning facilitate students' learning with hypermedia? *Journal of Educational Psychology, 96*(3), 523–535. doi:10.1037/0022-0663.96.3.523

Bae, Y., & Lee, H. (2011). A sentiment analysis of audiences on Twitter: Who is the positive or negative audience of popular Twitterers? In G. Lee, D. Howard, & D. Ślęzak (Eds.), *ICHIT 2011. LNCS 6935. 732 – 739.* doi:10.1007/978-3-642-24082-9_89

Baker, R. S. J. D., & Yacef, K. (2009). The state of educational data mining in 2009: A review and future visions. *Journal of Educational Data Mining, 1*(1), 3–16.

Baluja, S., Seth, R., Sivakumar, D., Jing, Y., Yagnik, J., Kumar, S., . . . Aly, M. (2008). Video suggestion and discovery for YouTube: Taking random walks through the view graph. In *Proceedings of WWW 2008: Industrial Practice and Experience.*

Barabási, A. L., & Albert, R. (1999). Emergence of scaling in random networks. *Science, 286*(5439), 509–512. doi:10.1126/science.286.5439.509 PMID:10521342

Barnes, J. A. (1979). Network analysis: orienting notion, rigorous technique or substantive field of study? In P. W. Holland & S. Leinhardt (Eds.), *Perspectives on Social Network Analysis* (pp. 403–423). New York: Academic. doi:10.1016/B978-0-12-352550-5.50024-9

Bartelt, A., & Lamersdorf, W. (2001). A multi-criteria taxonomy of business models in electronic commerce. *International Conference on Distributed Systems Platform*, Heidelberg, Germany. doi:10.1007/3-540-45598-1_18

Barton, B. (2006). *Stripped: Inside the lives of exotic dancers.* New York, NY: New York University Press.

Barua, A., Pinnel, J., Shutter, J., & Whinston, A. B. (1999). Measuring the internet economy. Center for Research in Electronic Commerce, University of Texas.

Baser, A. (2014). *Sosyal Medya Kullanıcılarının Kişilik Özellikleri, Kullanım Ve Motivasyonlarının Sosyal Medya Reklamlarına Yönelik Genel Tutumları Üzerindeki Rolü: Facebook Üzerine Bir Uygulama.* (PhD Thesis). Marmara University.

Bastian, M., Heymann, S., & Jacomy, M. (2009). Gephi: An open source software for exploring and manipulating networks.*Proceedings of the 3rd International AAAI Conference on Weblogs and Social Media.*

Bates, C. (2011). Facebook tightens privacy controls and gives users the option not to be tagged in photos. *Daily Mail.* Retrieved February 24, 2015, from http://goo.gl/qKnIZ

Bayram, S., & Bayraktar, D. M. (2013). Using Eye Tracking to Investigate the Relationship Between Attention and Change Blindness. *World Journal on Educational Technology, 5*(2), 257–265.

Bayram, S., & Yeni, S. (2011). Web Tabanlı Eğitsel Çoklu Ortamların Göz İzleme Tekniği ile Kullanışlılık Açısından Değerlendirilmesi. *Ahi Evran Üniversitesi Eğitim Fakültesi Dergisi, 12*(2), 221–234.

Begelman, G., Keller, P., & Smadja, F. (2006). Automated tag clustering: Improving search and exploration in the tag space. In *Proceedings of the WWW 2006.*

Benevenuto, F., Duarte, F., Rodrigues, T., Almeida, V., Almeida, J., & Ross, K. (2008). Understanding video interactions in YouTube. In *Proceedings of MM '08.* doi:10.1145/1459359.1459480

Benkler, Y. (2006). *The Wealth of Networks: How Social Production Transforms Markets and Freedom*. New Haven, CT: Yale University Press.

Berger, P. L., & Luckmann, T. (1991). *The social construction of reality: A treatise in the sociology of knowledge*. Penguin.

Best, R. S. (2014). *Social media and criminal offences* (First Report). London: House of Lords.

Best, S., & Marcus, S. (2009, Fall). Surface Reading: An Introduction. *Representations, 108*(1), 1 – 21. Retrieved Jan. 3, 2016, from http://www.jstor.org/stable/10.1525/rep.2009.108.1.1

Bhattacharyya, S., Organisciak, P., & Downie, S. J. (2015). *A fragmentizing interface to a large corpus of digitized text: (Post)humanism and non-consumptive reading via features*. IDEALS Home. Graduate School of Library and Information Science. Retrieved Jan. 3, 2016, from https://www.ideals.illinois.edu/handle/2142/72732

Biedert, R., Hees, J., Dengel, A., & Buscher, G. (2012). A robust realtime reading-skimming classifier. In *Proceedings of ETRA 2012*. doi:10.1145/2168556.2168575

Biedert, R., Buscher, G., & Dengel, A. (2010). The eyebook–using eye tracking to enhance the reading experience. *Informatik-Spektrum, 33*(3), 272–281. doi:10.1007/s00287-009-0381-2

Bielski, L. (2008). Eight Tech innovations that took banking into the 21st Century. *ABA Banking Journal, 100*, 84–89.

Bigonha, C., Cardoso, T. N. C., Moro, M. M., Goncalves, M. A., & Almeida, V. A. F. (2012). Sentiment-based influence detection on Twitter. *Journal of the Brazilian Computer Society, 18*(3), 169–183. doi:10.1007/s13173-011-0051-5

Bishop, J. (2011b). *The role of the prefrontal cortex in social orientation construction: A pilot study*. Poster Presented to the BPS Welsh Conference on Wellbeing, Wrexham, UK.

Bishop, J. (2004). *The potential of persuasive technology for educating heterogeneous user groups. (Unpublished MSc)*. Pontypridd, UK: University of Glamorgan.

Bishop, J. (2008). Increasing capital revenue in social networking communities: Building social and economic relationships through avatars and characters. In C. Romm-Livermore & K. Setzekorn (Eds.), *Social networking communities and eDating services: Concepts and implications* (pp. 60–77). Hershey, PA: IGI Global.

Bishop, J. (2011a). *The equatrics of intergenerational knowledge transformation in techno-cultures: Towards a model for enhancing information management in virtual worlds. (Unpublished MScEcon)*. Aberystwyth University, Aberystwyth, UK.

Bishop, J. (2012). Cooperative e-learning in the multilingual and multicultural school: The role of 'Classroom 2.0' for increasing participation in education. In P. M. Pumilia-Gnarini, E. Favaron, E. Pacetti, J. Bishop, & L. Guerra (Eds.), *Didactic strategies and technologies for education: Incorporating advancements* (pp. 137–150). Hershey, PA: IGI Global. doi:10.4018/978-1-4666-2122-0.ch013

Bishop, J. (2013). The art of trolling law enforcement: A review and model for implementing 'flame trolling' legislation enacted in great britain (1981–2012). *International Review of Law Computers & Technology, 27*(3), 301–318. doi:10.1080/13600869.2013.796706

Bishop, J. (2014). Representations of 'trolls' in mass media communication: A review of media-texts and moral panics relating to 'internet trolling'. *International Journal of Web Based Communities, 10*(1), 7–24. doi:10.1504/IJWBC.2014.058384

Bishop, J. (2015). Using 'on-the-fly corpus linguistics' to systematically derive word definitions using inductive abstraction and reductionist correlation analysis: Considering seductive and gratifying properties of computer jargon. In J. Bishop (Ed.), *Psychological and social implications surrounding internet and gaming addiction* (pp. 153–170). Hershey, PA: IGI Global. doi:10.4018/978-1-4666-8595-6.ch009

Bissessar, C. S. (2014). Facebook as an informal teacher professional development tool. *Australian Journal of Teacher Education, 39*(2), 121–135. doi:10.14221/ajte.2014v39n2.9

Biswas, G., Kinnebrew, J. S., & Mack, D. L. C. (2013). How do students' learning behaviors evolve in scaffolded open-ended learning environments?*Proceedings of the 21st International Conference on Computers in Education.*

Blackshaw, P., & Nazzaro, M. (2004). *Consumer-Generated Media (CGM) 101: Word-of-mouth in the age of the Webfortified consumer.* Retrieved July 22, 2015, from http://www.nielsen-online.com/downloads/us/buzz/nbzm_wp_CGM101.pdf

Blei, D. M. (2012). Probabilistic topic models. *Communications of the ACM, 55*(4), 77–84. doi:10.1145/2133806.2133826

Bloch, J. (2008). *Creating and destroying Java objects.* Retrieved from http://www.informit.com/articles/article.aspx?p=1216151&seqNum=5

Blodgett, J. G., Hill, D. J., & Tax, S. S. (1997). The effects of distributive, procedural and interactional justice on post-complaint behavior. *Journal of Retailing, 73*(2), 185–210. doi:10.1016/S0022-4359(97)90003-8

Blondel, V. D., Guillaume, J. L., Lambiotte, R., & Lefebvre, E. (2008). Fast unfolding of communities in large networks. *Journal of Statistical Mechanics, 2008*(10), P10008. doi:10.1088/1742-5468/2008/10/P10008

Bollen, J., Mao, H., & Zeng, X. (2011). Twitter mood predicts the stock market. *Journal of Computational Science, 2*(1), 1–8. doi:10.1016/j.jocs.2010.12.007

Boone, L. E., & Kurtz, D. L. (2014). *Contemporary marketing* (16th ed.). Cengage Learning.

Borgatti, S. P., & Halgin, D. S. (2011). On Network Theory. *Organization Science.* Retrieved October 20, 2015, from http://steveborgatti.com/papers/orsc.1110.0641.pdf

Borgatti, S. P., & Lopez-Kidwell, V. (2012). Network Theory. In The SAGE handbook of social network analysis. SAGE Publications.

Börner, K., Sanyal, S., & Vespignani, A. (2007). Network science. *Annual Review of Information Science & Technology, 41*(1), 537–607. doi:10.1002/aris.2007.1440410119

Bostanci, M. (2010). *Development Of Social Media And Social Media Usage Habits Of Communication Faculty Students.* (Master Thesis). Erciyes University.

Boyd, D. (2007). Why youth (heart) social network sites: The role of networked publics in teenage social life. *MacArthur foundation series on digital learning–Youth, identity, and digital media*, 119-142.

Boyd, D. M., & Ellison, N. B. (2008). Social network sites: Definition, history, and scholarship. *Journal of Computer-Mediated Communication*, 210–230.

Brass, D. J. (2011). *A social network perspective on industrial/organizational psychology.* Retrieved October 21, 2015, from http://ejournal.narotama.ac.id/files/A%20Social%20Network%20Perspective%20On%20Industrial%20Organizational%20Psychology.pdf

Braun, M. T. (2013). Obstacles to social networking website use among older adults. *Computers in Human Behavior, 29*(3), 673–680. doi:10.1016/j.chb.2012.12.004

Brinck, T., Gergle, D., & Wood, S. D. (2002). *Usability for the web: Designing web sites that work.* London: Morgan Kaufmann Publishers.

Bristow, D. N., & Mowen, J. C. (1998). The consumer resource exchange model: An empirical investigation of construct and predictive validity. *Marketing Intelligence & Planning, 16*(6), 375–386. doi:10.1108/02634509810237587

Brodersen, A., Scellato, S., & Wattenhofer, M. (2012). YouTube around the world: Geographic popularity of videos. In *Proceedings of WWW 2012—Session: Behavioral analysis and Content Characterization in Social Media.*

Bryer, T. A., & Zavattaro, S. M. (2011). Social media and public administration: Theoretical dimensions and introduction to the symposium. *Administrative Theory & Praxis, 33*(3), 325–340. doi:10.2753/ATP1084-1806330301

Bryman, A., & Bell, E. (2003). *Business research methods.* Oxford, UK: Oxford University Press.

Buchanan, M. (2003). *Nexus: small worlds and the groundbreaking theory of networks.* WW Norton & Company.

Bucher, H. J., & Schumacher, P. (2006). The relevance of attention for selecting news content. An eye-tracking study on attention patterns in the reception of print and online media. *Communications, 31*(3), 347–368. doi:10.1515/COMMUN.2006.022

Bulakh, V., Dunn, C. W., & Gupta, M. (2014). Identifying fraudulently promoted online videos. In *Proceedings of WWW '14.* doi:10.1145/2567948.2578996

Burgess, J. R. D., & Russell, J. E. A. (2003). The effectiveness of distance learning initiatives in organizations. *Journal of Vocational Behavior, 63*(2), 289–303. doi:10.1016/S0001-8791(03)00045-9

Burgess, J., & Green, J. (2009). *YouTube: Online video and participatory culture.* Cambridge, MA: Polity Press.

Burns, R. P., & Burns, R. (2008). Business research methods and statistics using SPSS. *Sage (Atlanta, Ga.).*

Butts, C. T. (2008). Social network analysis: A methodological introduction. *Asian Journal of Social Psychology, 11*(1), 13–41. doi:10.1111/j.1467-839X.2007.00241.x

Buxton, J. (2014). *Venezuela: The Real Significance of the Student Protests.* Latin American Bureau. Retrieved August 31, 2015, from http://lab.org.uk/venezuela-%E2%80%93-student-protests

Byerly, G. (2007). Look in their eyes-eye tracking, usability, and children. *School Library Media Activities Monthly, 23*(8), 30.

Cahill, L., McGaugh, J. L., & Weinberger, N. M. (2001). The neurobiology of learning and memory: Some reminders to remember. *Trends in Neurosciences, 24*(10), 578–581. doi:10.1016/S0166-2236(00)01885-3 PMID:11576671

Caladine, R. (2008). *Enhancing e-learning with media-rich content and interactions.* Hershey, PA: Information Science. doi:10.4018/978-1-59904-732-4

Cantallops, A. S., & Salvi, F. (2014). New consumer behavior: A review of research on eWOM and hotels. *International Journal of Hospitality Management, 36*, 41–51. doi:10.1016/j.ijhm.2013.08.007

Caracas. (n.d.). Retrieved August 31, 2015, from the Wikipedia: https://en.wikipedia.org/wiki/Caracas

Carrasco, J. A., Hogan, B., Wellman, B., & Miller, E. J. (2006). *Collecting social network data to study social activity-travel behavior: an egocentric approach.* Presented at the 85th Transportation Research Board Meeting, Washington, DC. Retrieved October 21, 2015, from http://groups.chass.utoronto.ca/netlab/wp-content/uploads/2012/05/Collecting-Social-Network-Data-to-Study-Social-Activity-Travel-Behavior-An-Egocentric-Approach.pdf

Carson, S., Kanchanaraksa, S., Gooding, I., Mulder, F., & Schuwer, R. (2012). Impact of OpenCourseWare publication on higher education participation and student recruitment. *International Review of Research in Open and Distance Learning, 13*(4), 19–32.

Carter, M., & Wright, J. (1999). Interconnection in network industries. *Review of Industrial Organization, 14*(1), 1–25. doi:10.1023/A:1007715215394

Cassidy, W., Jackson, M., & Brown, K. N. (2009). Sticks and stones can break my bones, but how can pixels hurt me? students' experiences with cyber-bullying. *School Psychology International, 30*(4), 383–402. doi:10.1177/0143034309106948

Castells, M. (2000). The information age: economy, society and culture.: Vol. 1. *The rise of the network society*. Oxford, UK: Blackwell.

Castells, M. (2003). The power of identity: The information Age: Economy, society and culture: Vol. 2. *The information age*. Oxford, UK: Blackwell.

Castells, M. (2007). Communication, power and counter power in the network society. *International Journal of Communication*, 238–266.

Catanese, S. A., De Meo, P., Ferrara, E., Fiumara, G., & Provetti, A. (2011). Crawling Facebook for social network analysis purposes. In *Proceedings of the international conference on web intelligence, mining and semantics* (p. 52). ACM. doi:10.1145/1988688.1988749

Cattuto, C., Benz, D., Hotho, A., & Stumme, G. (2008). *Semantic analysis of tag similarity measures in collaborative tagging systems*. arXiv:0805.2045v1

Cha, M., Kwak, H., Rodriguez, P., Ahn, Y-Y., & Moon, S. (2009). Analyzing the video popularity characteristics of large-scale user generated content systems. *IEEE / ACM Transactions on Networking, 17*(5), 1357 – 1370.

Chandra, N. (2011). Social media as a touch point in reverse logistics: Scale development and validation. *International Journal of Business Research, 11*, 76–83.

Chatterjee, P. (2001). Online reviews: Do consumers use them? In M. C. Gilly, & J. Myers-Levy (Eds.), Advances in Consumer Research (129-134). Provo, UT: Association for Consumer Research.

Cheng, X., Fatourechi, M., Ma, X., Zhang, C., Zhang, L., & Liu, J. (2014). Insight data of YouTube from a partner's view. In *Proceedings of NOSSDAV '14*.

Chen, G. M. (2011). Tweet this: A uses and gratifications perspective on how active Twitter use gratifies a need to connect with others. *Computers in Human Behavior, 27*(2), 755–762. doi:10.1016/j.chb.2010.10.023

Chesbrough, H., & Rosembloom, R. (2002). The role of the business model in capturing value from innovation: Evidence from Xerox Corporation's technology spin-off companies. *Industrial and Corporate Change, 11*(3), 529–555. doi:10.1093/icc/11.3.529

Chong, S. (2014). Business process management for SMEs: An exploratory study of implementation factors for the Australian wine industry. *Journal of Information Systems and Small Business, 1*(1-2), 41–58.

Choudhary, A., Hendrix, W., Lee, K., Palsetia, D., & Liao, W.-K. (2012). Social media evolution of the egyptian revolution. *Communications of the ACM, 55*(5), 74–80. doi:10.1145/2160718.2160736

Choy, M., Cheong, M. L., Laik, M. N., & Shung, K. P. (2011). *A sentiment analysis of Singapore Presidential Election 2011 using Twitter data with census correction*. arXiv preprint arXiv:1108.5520

Christodoulou, S. P., & Styliaras, G. D. (2008). Digital art 2.0: Art meets Web 2.0 trend. In the proceedings of DIMEA 2008. In *Proceedings of the 3rd International Conference on Digital Interactive Media in Entertainment and Arts*.

Chu, S. C., & Kim, Y. (2011). Determinants of consumer engagement in electronic Word-of-mouth (eWOM) in social networking sites. *International Journal of Advertising, 30*(1), 47–75. doi:10.2501/IJA-30-1-047-075

Clark, J. (2013). Conceptualising Social Media as Complaint Channel. *Journal of Promotional Communications, 1*(1), 104–124.

Cohen, M. (2009). Narratology in the archive of literature. *Representations (Berkeley, Calif.), 108*(1), 51–75. doi:10.1525/rep.2009.108.1.51

Collins, C., Hasan, S., & Ukkusuri, S. V. (2013). A novel transit rider satisfaction metric: Rider sentiments measured from online social media data. *Journal of Public Transportation, 16*(2), 2. doi:10.5038/2375-0901.16.2.2

Cooke, M., & Buckley, N. (2008). Web 2.0, Social Networks And The Future Of Market Research. *International Journal of Market Research, 50*(2), 267–292.

Coombs, T. (2007). Protecting organisation reputations during a crisis: The development and application of situational crisis communication theory. *Corporate Reputation Review, 10*(3), 163–176. doi:10.1057/palgrave.crr.1550049

Correa, T., Hinsley, A. W., & De Zúñiga, H. G. (2010). Who interacts on the web?: The intersection of users' personality and social media use. *Computers in Human Behavior, 26*(2), 247–253. doi:10.1016/j.chb.2009.09.003

Cottrill, C., Yeboah, G., Gault, P., Nelson, J., Anable, J., & Budd, T. (2015). Tweeting transport: Examining the use of Twitter in transport events.*47th Annual UTSG Conference, At Collaborative Transport Hub. City University London.*

Couldry, N., Markham, T., & Livingstone, S. (2005). *Media consumption and the future of public connection.* London: London School of Economics and Political Science.

Cui, G. (1997). Marketing strategies in a multi-ethnic environment. *Journal of Marketing Theory and Practice, 5*(1), 122–134. doi:10.1080/10696679.1997.11501756

Cunliffe, D., & Elliott, G. (2005). *Multimedia computing. Newcastle under Lyme.* Lexden Publishing Ltd.

Dal, N. E., & Dal, V. (2014). Personality Traits And Social Network Sites Usage Habits: A Research On University Students. *Mehmet Akif Ersoy Üniversitesi Sosyal Bilimler Enstitüsü Dergisi, 6*(11), 144–162.

Dalton, M. (1959). *Men who manage New York.* John Wiley and Sons.

Dantas, T. R. (2013). The digital reading as a product of the evolution of information: books between screens. In *Proceedings of the First International Conference on Technological Ecosystem for Enhancing Multiculturality* (TEEM '13). doi:10.1145/2536536.2536593

Davey, L. (1991). Çeviri: Tuba Gökçek (2009). *Elementary Education Online, 8*(2), 1–3.

Davidson, J., Liebald, B., Liu, J., Nandy, P., & Van Vleet, T. (2010). The YouTube video recommendation system. In *Proceedings of RecSys2010.* doi:10.1145/1864708.1864770

De Choudhury, M., Sundaram, H., John, A., & Seligmann, D. D. (2009). What makes conversations interesting? Themes, participants and consequences of conversations in online social media. In *Proceedings of WWW 2009.*

De Laat, M. (2002). *Network and content analysis in online community discourse.Third International Conference on Networked Learning.*

De Laat, M., & Lally, V. (2003). Complexity, theory and praxis: Researching collaborative learning and tutoring processes in a networked learning community. *Instructional Science, 31*(1-2), 7–39. doi:10.1023/A:1022596100142

De Laat, M., & Lally, V. (2005). Investigating group structure in CSCL: Some new approaches. *Information Systems Frontiers, 7*(1), 13–25. doi:10.1007/s10796-005-5335-x

De Laat, M., Lally, V., Lipponen, L., & Simons, P. (2005). *Patterns of interaction in a networked learning community: Squaring the circle.* Manuscript Submitted for Publication.

De Meo, P., Ferrara, E., Fiumara, G., & Provetti, A. (2014). On Facebook, most ties are weak. *Communications of the ACM, 57*(11), 78–84. doi:10.1145/2629438

Demirkan, I., Leeds, D. L., & Demirkan, S. (2012). Exploring the role of network characteristics, knowledge quality and inertia on the evolution of scientific networks. *Journal of Management, 39*(6), 1462–1489. doi:10.1177/0149206312453739

Deng, Z., Yan, M., Sang, J., & Xu, C. (2014). Twitter is faster: Personalized time-aware video recommendation from Twitter to YouTube. *ACM Transactions on Multimedia Computing, Communications, and Applications, 11*(2), 31:1-31:23.

DeSarbo, W. S., & Wedel, M. (1994). A review of recent developments in latent class regression models. In Advanced methods of marketing research (pp. 352–388). Cambridge, MA: Basil Blackwell.

DeSarbo, W. S., Jedidi, K., & Sinha, I. (2001). Customer value analysis in a heterogeneous market. *Strategic Management Journal, 22*(9), 845–857. doi:10.1002/smj.191

Desmarais, M. C., & Baker, R. S. (2012). A review of recent advances in learner and skill modeling in intelligent learning environments. *User Modeling and User-Adapted Interaction, 22*(1-2), 9–38. doi:10.1007/s11257-011-9106-8

Ding, Y., Du, Y., Hu, Y., Liu, Z., Wang, L., Ross, K. W., & Ghose, A. (2011). Broadcast yourself: Understanding YouTube uploaders. In *Proceedings of IMC '11.*

Dix, A., Finlay, J., Abowd, G., & Beale, R. (2004). *Human-Computer Interaction.* Prentice Hal.

Doerr, L. S., & Powell, W. W. (2005). Networks and economic life. In The Handbook of economic sociology. Russell Sage foundation and Princeton University Press.

Domingos, P., & Richardson, M. (2001). Mining the network value of customers. In *Proceedings of the seventh ACM SIG-KDD international conference on Knowledge discovery and data mining* (pp. 57-66). ACM. doi:10.1145/502512.502525

Dominici, G. (2012). E-business Model: a content based taxonomy of literature. *International Journal of Management and Administrative Sciences, 1,* 10-20.

Duff, A. S., Craig, D., & McNeill, D. A. (1996). A note on the origins of the information society. *Journal of Information Science, 22*(2), 39–45. doi:10.1177/016555159602200204

Dunne, C., & Schneiderman, B. (2013). Motif simplification: Improving network visualization readability with fan, connector, and clique glyphs. In *Proceedings of CHI 2013: Changing Perspectives.*

Durland, M. M., & Fredericks, K. A. (2005, Fall). An Introduction to Social Network Analysis. *New Directions for Evaluation, 107*(107), 5–13. doi:10.1002/ev.157

Dutton, D. (2002). Aesthetic universals. In *The Routledge Companion to Aesthetics.* Retrieved November 12, 2014, from http://www.denisdutton.com/universals.htm

Dutton, D. (2006). A naturalist definition of art. *The Journal of Aesthetics and Art Criticism, 65*(3), 367 – 377. Retrieved from http://www.jstor.org/stable/3700568

Ebner, M., Lienhardt, C., Rohs, M., & Meyer, I. (2010). Microblogs in higher education – A chance to facilitate informal and process-oriented learning? *Computers & Education, 55*(1), 92–100. doi:10.1016/j.compedu.2009.12.006

Edvardsson, B., & Roos, I. (2003). Customer Complaints and Switching Behavior - A Study of Relationship Dynamics in a Telecommunication Company. *Journal of Relationship Marketing, 2*(1-2), 43–68. doi:10.1300/J366v02n01_04

Efimova, L. (2009). Weblog as a personal thinking space. In *Proceedings of the 20th ACM Conference on Hypertext and Hypermedia.* doi:10.1145/1557914.1557963

Eisenberg, M., & Buechley, L. (2008). Pervasive fabrication: Making construction ubiquitous in education. *Journal of Software*, *3*(4), 62–68. doi:10.4304/jsw.3.4.62-68

Elavsky, C. M., Mislan, C., & Elavsky, S. (2011). When talking less is more: Exploring outcomes of Twitter usage in the large-lecture hall. *Learning, Media and Technology*, *36*(3), 215–233. doi:10.1080/17439884.2010.549828

Ellison, N. B., & Lampe, C. (2008). Social, capital, self-esteem and use of online social network sites: A longitudinal analysis. *Journal of Applied Developmental Psychology*, *29*(6), 434–445. doi:10.1016/j.appdev.2008.07.002

Ellison, N. B., Steinfield, C., & Lampe, C. (2007). The benefits of Facebook "friends:" Social capital and college students' use of online social network sites. *Journal of Computer-Mediated Communication*, *12*(4), 1143–1168. doi:10.1111/j.1083-6101.2007.00367.x

Ercim News. (2005). *The advantages of reused software components.* Retrieved from http://www.ercim.eu/publication/Ercim_News/enw60/mohagheghi.html

Erdos, P., & Renyi, A. (1961). On the strength of connectedness of a random graph. *Acta Mathematica Hungarica*, 152–163.

Escobar, M. L., Kommers, P., & Beldad, A. (2014). Using narratives as tools for channeling participation in online communities. *Computers in Human Behavior*, *37*, 64–72. doi:10.1016/j.chb.2014.04.013

Ethier, J. (2006). Current Research in Social Network Theory. *Social Network Theory.* Retrieved October 22, 2015, from http://www.ccs.neu.edu/home/perrolle/archive/Ethier-SocialNetworks.html

Facebook. (2011). *Statistics.* Palo Alto, CA: Facebook.

Facua. (2014). *Banks, telecom and energy companies are once again the 'kings of fraud' in FACUA's ranking 2014.* Retrieved July 22, 2015, from http://www.facua.org/es/noticia_int.php?idioma=1&Id=9065

Fan, W., & Gordon, M. D. (2014). The power of social media analytics. *Communications of the ACM*, *57*(6), 74–81. doi:10.1145/2602574

Farrell, H. (2012). The consequences of the internet for politics. *Annual Review of Political Science*, *15*(1), 35–52. doi:10.1146/annurev-polisci-030810-110815

Feick, L. F., & Price, L. L. (1987). The market maven: A diffuser of marketplace information. *Journal of Marketing*, *51*(1), 83–97. doi:10.2307/1251146

Feldman, R. (2013). Techniques and applications for sentiment analysis. *Communications of the ACM*, *56*(4), 82–89. doi:10.1145/2436256.2436274

Festinger, L. (1957). *A theory of cognitive dissonance.* Evanston, IL: Row, Peterson.

Figueiredo, F., Benevenuto, F., & Almeida, J. M. (2011). The Tube over Time: Characterizing popularity growth of YouTube videos. In *Proceedings of WSDM '11.*

Fink, D. (2006). The professional doctorate: Its relativity to the PhD and relevance for the knowledge economy. *International Journal of Doctoral Studies*, *1*(1), 35–44.

Flynn, L. R., Goldsmith, R. E., & Eastman, J. K. (1996). Opinion leaders and opinion seekers: Two new measurement scales. *Journal of the Academy of Marketing Science*, *24*(2), 137–147. doi:10.1177/0092070396242004

FM_Center. (n.d.). Retrieved August 31, 2015, from the Wikipedia: https://en.wikipedia.org/wiki/FM_Center

Fortunato, S. (2010). Community detection in graphs. *Physics Reports*, *486*(3-5), 75–174. doi:10.1016/j.physrep.2009.11.002

Freeman, L. C. (2012). The development of social network analysis – with an emphasis on recent events. In The SAGE handbook of social network analysis. SAGE Publications.

Freud, S. (1933). *New introductory lectures on psycho-analysis*. New York: W.W. Norton & Company, Inc.

Fuchs, C. (2009). Information and communication technologies and society a contribution to the critique of the political economy of the internet. *European Journal of Communication, 24*(1), 69–87. doi:10.1177/0267323108098947

Fuentelsaz, L., Garrido, E., & Maicas, J. P. (2015). A strategic approach to network value in network industries. *Journal of Management, 41*(3), 864–892. doi:10.1177/0149206312448399

Fukuda, R., & Bubb, H. (2003). Eye tracking study on Web-use: Comparison between younger and elderly users in case of search task with electronic timetable service. *PsychNology Journal, 1*(3), 202–228.

Fyfe, P. C. (2010). *How not to read a Victorian novel*. Diginole. Florida State University. Retrieved Jan. 4, 2016, from http://diginole.lib.fsu.edu/cgi/viewcontent.cgi?article=1002&context=eng_faculty_publications

Geisler, G., & Burns, S. (2007). Tagging video: Conventions and strategies of the YouTube community. In *Proceedings of JCDL '07*.

Ghosh, M. (2013). *Guess Which Country Uses Twitter More Than Anyone Else In The World?* Retrieved August 31, 2015, from http://trak.in/tags/business/2013/11/18/twitter-usage-country-max-penetration

Gibson, J. J. (1986). *The ecological approach to visual perception*. Lawrence Erlbaum Associates.

Gievska, S., & Koroveshovski, K. (2014). The impact of affective verbal content on predicting personality impressions in YouTube videos. In *Proceedings of WCPR14*. doi:10.1145/2659522.2659529

Gilinsky, A. Jr, Thach, E. C., & Thompson, K. J. (2015). Connectivity & Communication: A Study of How Small Wine Businesses Use the Internet. *Journal of Small Business Strategy, 14*(2), 37–57.

Gleit, N., Zeng, S., & Cottle, P. (2014). *Introducing Safety Check*. Retrieved August 31, 2015, from http://newsroom.fb.com/news/2014/10/introducing-safety-check/

Go, A., Bhayani, R., & Huang, L. (2009). Twitter sentiment classification using distant supervision. CS224N Project Report. Stanford.

Goff, C. (2004). Where, why, who? Some usability techniques reveal where users are looking, but knowing why they look is also useful, especially for niche audiences. *New Media Age*, 6-9.

Goldberg, J. & Kotval, X.P. (1998). Eye Movement-Based Evaluation of the Computer Interface. *Advances in occupational ergonomics and safety*, 529-532.

Goldberg, H. J., & Kotval, X. P. (1999). Computer interface evaluation using eye movements: Methods and constructs. *International Journal of Industrial Ergonomics, 24*(6), 631–645. doi:10.1016/S0169-8141(98)00068-7

Gonsalves, A. (2010). *Social Network Use By Smartphones Jumps*. Retrieved November 7, from http://www.informationweek.com/news/hardware/handheld/showArticle.jhtml?articleID=223101506

Goode, M. M. H., Moutinho, L. A. C., & Chien, C. (1996). Structural equation modelling of overall satisfaction and full use of services for ATMs. *International Journal of Bank Marketing, 14*(7), 4–11. doi:10.1108/02652329610151331

Goodwyn, A., & Stables, A. W. (2004). Learning to read critically in language and literacy. *Sage (Atlanta, Ga.).*

Görg, C., Pohl, M., Qeli, E., & Xu, K. (2010). Visual representations. In *Advances in Visual Computing: 6th International Symposium, ISVC 2010*. doi:10.1007/978-3-540-71949-6_4

Graham, C. R. (2011). Theoretical considerations for understanding technological pedagogical content knowledge (TPACK). *Computers & Education*, *57*(3), 1953–1960. doi:10.1016/j.compedu.2011.04.010

Granovetter, M. (1973). The strength of weak ties. *American Journal of Sociology*, *78*(6), 1360–1380. doi:10.1086/225469

Granovetter, M. (1983). The strength of weak ties: A network theory revisited. *Sociological Theory*, *1*, 201–233. doi:10.2307/202051

Greene, J. A., & Azevedo, R. (2007). A theoretical review of Winne and Hadwin's model of self-regulated learning: New perspectives and directions. *Review of Educational Research*, *77*(3), 334–372. doi:10.3102/003465430303953

Greenhow, C., & Robelia, B. (2009). Old communication, new literacies: Social network sites as social learning resources. *Journal of Computer-Mediated Communication*, *14*(4), 1130–1161. doi:10.1111/j.1083-6101.2009.01484.x

Grosseck, G. (2009). To use or not to use web 2.0 in higher education? *Procedia: Social and Behavioral Sciences*, *1*(1), 478–482. doi:10.1016/j.sbspro.2009.01.087

Gross, J. L., & Yellen, J. (2005). *Graph theory and its applications*. CRC Press.

Gundogan, M. B. (2003). Kullanılabilirlik (Usability) Kavramı ve Egitim Teknolojileri; Yansımalar, Uygulamalar, International Educational Technologies Symposium and Fair, Vol:I. *Tojet*, 642-649.

Gupta, M., Li, R., Yin, Z., & Han, J. (2011). An overview of social tagging and applications. *Social Network Data Analytics*, 447 – 497.

Gürsakal, N. (2009). *Sosyal ağ analizi. (1.baskı)*. Bursa: Dora Yayıncılık.

Gursakal, N. (2009). *Sosyal Ağ Analizi*. Bursa: Dora Yayıncılık.

Haas, C., & Wearden, S. T. (2003). E-credibility: Building common ground in web environments. *L1-Educational Studies in Language and Literature*, *3*(1/2), 169–184. doi:10.1023/A:1024557422109

Hai-Jew, S. (2016, Spring/Summer). Extracting human sentiment from text sets with NVivo 11 Plus. *C2C Digital Magazine*. Retrieved November 26, 2015, from http://scalar.usc.edu/works/c2c-digi-magazine-spring-summer-2016/extracting-human-sentiment-from-text-sets-with-nvivo-11-plus

Hannafin, M. J., Hall, C., Land, S., & Hill, J. (1994). Learning in open-ended environments: Assumptions, methods, and implications. *Educational Technology*, *34*(8), 48–55.

Han, S., & Kavuluru, R. (2015). On assessing the sentiment of *general* Tweets. In D. Barbosa & E. Milios (Eds.), *Canadian AI 2015. LNAI 9091. 181- 195*. doi:10.1007/978-3-319-18356-5_16

Harel, D. (1998). *On the aesthetics of diagrams (summary of talk)*. Springer Link. Retrieved Nov. 9, 2014, from http://download.springer.com/static/pdf/217/chp%253A10.1007%252FBFb0054280.pdf?auth66=1415578223_a51f9b36e41305ce52a357413fbbc1da&ext=.pdf

Harel, D., & Koren, Y. (2001). A fast multi-scale method for drawing large graphs. In GD 2000, LNCS. doi:10.1007/3-540-44541-2_18

Harris, L. C., & Goode, M. M. (2004). The four levels of loyalty and the pivotal role of trust: A study of online service dynamics. *Journal of Retailing*, *80*(2), 139–158. doi:10.1016/j.jretai.2004.04.002

Harris, L. C., & Goode, M. M. H. (2010). Online servicescapes, trust, and purchase intentions. *Journal of Services Marketing*, *24*(3), 230–243. doi:10.1108/08876041011040631

Harrison, J., Rintel, S., & Mitchell, E. (2014). Australian Social Media Trends. In C. Litang & M. H. Prosser (Eds.), *Social Media in Asia*. Dignity Press.

Hendler, J., & Golbeck, J. (2008). Metcalfe's law, Web 2.0, and the Semantic Web. *Web Semantics: Science, Services, and Agents on the World Wide Web, 6*(1), 14–20. doi:10.1016/j.websem.2007.11.008

Henning-Thurau, T., Gwinner, K. P., Walsh, G., & Gremler, D. D. (2004). Electronic word-of-mouth via customer opinion platform: What motivates consumers to articulate themselves on the internet. *Journal of Interactive Marketing, 18*(1), 38–52. doi:10.1002/dir.10073

He, W., Zha, S., & Li, L. (2013). Social media competitive analysis and text mining: A case study in the pizza industry. *International Journal of Information Management, 33*(3), 464–472. doi:10.1016/j.ijinfomgt.2013.01.001

Heyman, S. (2015, Oct. 28). Google Books: A complex and controversial experiment. *The New York Times*. Retrieved Jan. 12, 2016, from http://www.nytimes.com/2015/10/29/arts/international/google-books-a-complex-and-controversial-experiment.html?_r=1

Hoffman, D. L., & Fodor, M. (2010). Can you measure the ROI of your social media marketing. *MIT Sloan Management Review, 52*(1), 41–49.

Hogenboom, A., Bal, D., Frasincar, F., Bal, M., de Jong, F., & Kaymak, U. (2013). Exploiting emoticons in sentiment analysis. In *Proceedings of SAC '13*. doi:10.1145/2480362.2480498

Hollensen, S. (2015). *Marketing management: A relationship approach*. Pearson Education.

Holmes, B. (2013). School teachers' continuous professional development in an online learning community: Lessons from a case study of an eTwinning learning event. *European Journal of Education, 48*(1), 97–112. doi:10.1111/ejed.12015

Hong, S., & Park, H. S. (2012). Computer-mediated persuasion in online reviews: Statistical versus narrative evidence. *Computers in Human Behavior, 28*(3), 906–919. doi:10.1016/j.chb.2011.12.011

Hou, H.-T., Chang, K.-E., & Sung, Y.-T. (2009). Using blogs as a professional development tool for teachers: Analysis of interaction behavioral patterns. *Interactive Learning Environments, 17*(4), 325–340. doi:10.1080/10494820903195215

Howard, B. (2008). Analyzing online social networks. *Communications of the ACM, 51*(11), 14–16. doi:10.1145/1400214.1400220

Huang, W. (2014). Evaluating overall quality of graph visualizations indirectly and directly. In Handbook of Human Centric Visualization. New York: Springer Science + Business. doi:10.1007/978-1-4614-7485-2_14

Huang, A. (2008). Similarity measures for text document clustering.*Proceedings of the Sixth New Zealand Computer Science Research Student Conference* (pp. 49-56).

Huang, T.-C., Cheng, S.-C., & Huang, Y.-M. (2009). A blog article recommendation generating mechanism using an SBACPSO algorithm. *Expert Systems with Applications, 36*(7), 10388–10396. doi:10.1016/j.eswa.2009.01.039

Huang, W. (2013). Establishing aesthetics based on human graph reading behavior: Two eye tracking studies. *Personal and Ubiquitous Computing, 17*(1), 93–105. doi:10.1007/s00779-011-0473-2

Huffaker, D. (2010). Dimensions of leadership and social influence in online communities. *Human Communication Research, 36*(4), 593–617. doi:10.1111/j.1468-2958.2010.01390.x

Hughes, D. J., Rowe, M., Batey, M., & Lee, A. (2012). A tale of two sites: Twitter vs. Facebook and the personality predictors of social media usage. *Computers in Human Behavior, 28*(2), 561–569. doi:10.1016/j.chb.2011.11.001

Ingram, P., & Torfason, M. T. (2010). Organizing the in-between: The population dynamics of network-weaving organizations in the global interstate network. *Administrative Science Quarterly, 55*(4), 577–605. doi:10.2189/asqu.2010.55.4.577

Iriberri, A., & Leroy, G. (2009). A life-cycle perspective on online community success. *ACM Computing Surveys, 41*(2), 1–29. doi:10.1145/1459352.1459356

Ito, M., Horst, H., Bittanti, M., Boyd, D., Herr-Stephenson, B., Lange, P. G., & Robinson, L. (2008). Living and learning with new media: Summary of findings from the digital youth project. *The John D. and* Catherine T. *MacArthur Foundation Reports on Digital Media and Learning.* MIT Press.

Jacob, R. J. K., & Karn, K. S. (2003). Eye tracking in human-computer interaction and usability research: Ready to deliver the promises. *Mind, 2*(3), 4.

Jakob, N. (2000). *Why you only need to test with 5 users.* Norman Group Website. Retrieved from http://www.nngroup.com/

Jalilvand, M. R., Esfahani, S. S., & Samiei, N. (2011). Electronic word-of-mouth: Challenges and opportunities. *Procedia Computer Science, 3*, 42–46. doi:10.1016/j.procs.2010.12.008

Jamal, A., & Goode, M. M. (2001). Consumers and brands: A study of the impact of self-image congruence on brand preference and satisfaction. *Marketing Intelligence & Planning, 19*(7), 482–492. doi:10.1108/02634500110408286

Jankun-Kelly, T. J., Dwyer, T., Holten, D., Hurter, C., Nöllenburg, M., Weaver, C., & Xu, K. (2014). Scalability considerations for multivariate graph visualization. In A. Kerren et al. (Eds.), *Multivariate Network Visualization.* Springer International Publishing. doi:10.1007/978-3-319-06793-3_10

Jansen, B. J., Zhang, M., Sobel, K., & Chowdury, A. (2009). Twitter power: Tweets as electronic word of mouth. *Journal of the American Society for Information Science and Technology, 60*(11), 2169–2188. doi:10.1002/asi.21149

Java, A., Song, X., Finin, T., & Tseng, B. (2007, August). Why we twitter: understanding microblogging usage and communities. In *Proceedings of the 9th WebKDD and 1st SNA-KDD 2007 workshop on Web mining and social network analysis* (pp. 56-65). ACM. doi:10.1145/1348549.1348556

Jeong, H. J., & Koo, D. M. (2015). Combined effects of valence and attributes of e-WOM on consumer judgment for message and product. *Internet Research, 25*(1), 2–29. doi:10.1108/IntR-09-2013-0199

Jo, J., Kim, B., & Seo, J. (2015). EyeBookmark: Assisting recovery from interruption during reading. In *Proceedings of CHI 2015.*

Johnson, F., & Gupta, S. K. (2012). Web content mining techniques: A survey. *International Journal of Computers and Applications, 47*(11), 44–50. doi:10.5120/7236-0266

Johnson, P. R., & Yang, S. (2009). Uses and Gratifications of Twitter: An examination of user motives and satisfaction of Twitter use. In *Proceedings of the Communication Technology Division of the Annual Convention of the Association for Education in Journalism and Mass Communication.*

Josephson, S., & Holmes, M. E. (2002, March). Visual attention to repeated internet images: testing the scanpath theory on the world wide web. In *Proceedings of the 2002 Symposium on Eye tracking research & Applications* (pp. 43-49). ACM. doi:10.1145/507072.507081

Joshi, M., Cahill, D., & Sidhu, J. (2010). Intellectual capital performance in the banking sector: An assessment of Australian owned banks. *Journal of Human Resource Costing & Accounting, 14*(2), 151–170. doi:10.1108/14013381011062649

Jullien, N. (2012). *What we know about Wikipedia: A review of the literature analyzing the project (s).* Available at SSRN, 2053597.

Juola, P. (2010). Distant reading and mapping genre space via conjecture-based distance measures. *Digital Humanities 2010*. Retrieved Jan. 3, 2016, from http://dh2010.cch.kcl.ac.uk/academic-programme/abstracts/papers/html/ab-669.html

Kadushin, C. (2004). Some Basic Network Concepts and Propositions. *Introduction to Social Network Theory*. Retrieved October 20, 2015, from http://melander335.wdfiles.com/local--files/reading-history/kadushin.pdf

Kalakota, R., & Robinson, M. (2001). *E-business 2.0: Roadmap for Success*. Addison-Wesley Professional.

Kalanithi, P. (2016). *When Breath Becomes Air*. New York: Random House.

Kamakura, W. A., & Wedel, M. (1995). Life-style segmentation with tailoring interviewing. *JMR, Journal of Marketing Research, 32*(3), 308–317. doi:10.2307/3151983

Kane, G. C., Alavi, M., Labianca, G. J., & Borgatti, S. P. (2014). What's different about social media networks? A framework and research agenda. *MIS Quarterly Theory & Review, 38*, 1–68.

Karn, K. S., Ellis, S., & Juliano, C. (1999, May). The hunt for usability: tracking eye movements. In CHI'99 extended abstracts on Human factors in computing systems (pp. 173-173). ACM. doi:10.1145/632716.632823

Kassarjian, H. H. (●●●). Content analysis in consumer research. *The Journal of Consumer Research, 4*(June), 8–18.

Kemp, S. (2014). *Social, Digital & Mobile in The Middle East*. Retrieved from http://wearesocial.com/blog/2014/07/social-digital-mobile-middle-east

Kender, J. R., Hill, M. L., Natsev, A., Smith, J. R., & Xie, L. (2010). Video genetics: A case study from YouTube. In *Proceedings of MM'10*. doi:10.1145/1873951.1874198

Kennedy, A. (2009). *Whitepaper, The Global Facebook Phenomenon*. Retrieved from www.beyondink.com/Whitepaper-The-Global-Facebook-Phenomenon-by-Anne-Kennedy.pdf

Kenreck, T. (2013, May 9). In-game: "World of Warcraft" lost 1.3 million subscribers in three months. *MSNBC*. Retrieved April 26, 2015, from http://www.nbcnews.com/video/in-game/51831293/#51831293

Khadem, A. (2012). Annexing the unread: A close reading of 'distant reading'. *Neohelicon, 39*(2), 409–421. doi:10.1007/s11059-012-0152-y

Khammash, M., & Griffiths, G. H. (2011). Arrivederci CIAO.com, Buongiorno Bing.com Electronic word-of-mouth (eWOM), antecedences and consequences. *International Journal of Information Management, 31*(1), 82–87. doi:10.1016/j.ijinfomgt.2010.10.005

Khan, M. N. A. A., & Omar, N. A. (2013). A Study of Importance Items of Internet Financial Reporting: A Case of Malaysian Auditors. *Middle-East Journal of Scientific Research, 17*(3), 395–406.

Khribi, M. K., Jemni, M., & Nasraoui, O. (2008). Automatic recommendations for e-learning personalization based on web usage mining techniques and information retrieval. *Proc. IEEE Int. Conf. Adv. Learning Technol.* (pp. 241-245). doi:10.1109/ICALT.2008.198

Khurana, U., Nguyen, V.-A., Cheng, H.-C., Ahn, J.-W., Chen, X., & Schneiderman, B. (2011). Visual analysis of temporal trends in social networks using edge color coding and metric timelines. In *Proceedings of Privacy, Security, Risk and Trust (PASSAT) and 2011 IEEE Third International Conference in Social Computing* (SocialCom). doi:10.1109/PASSAT/SocialCom.2011.212

Kil, S. H. (2010). Telling stories: The use of personal narratives in the social sciences and history. *Journal of Ethnic and Migration Studies, 36*(3), 539–540. doi:10.1080/13691831003651754

Kim, C., Kim, S., Im, S., & Shin, C. (2003). The effect of attitude and perception on consumer complaint intentions. *Journal of Consumer Marketing*, *20*(4), 352–371. doi:10.1108/07363760310483702

Kırık, A. M., Arslan, A., Çetinkaya, A., & Mehmet, G. Ü. L. (2015). A quantitative research on the level of social media addiction among young people in Turkey. *International Journal of Science Culture and Sport*, *3*(3), 108–122.

Kirschenbaum, M. G. (2007, Oct.). The remaking of reading: Data mining and the digital humanities. In *the National Science Foundation Symposium on Next Generation of Data Mining and Cyber-Enabled Discovery for Innovation* (NGDM '07). Retrieved Jan. 3, 2016, from http://citeseerx.ist.psu.edu/viewdoc/download?doi=10.1.1.111.959&rep=rep1&type=pdf

Klapper, J. T. (1963). Mass communication research: An old road resurveyed. *Public Opinion Quarterly*, *27*(4), 515–527. doi:10.1086/267201

Knight, A. (2010). FB friends with your bank? *The Age*. Retrieved July 14, 2010, from http://goo.gl/yV1YQL

Koehler, M. J., & Mishra, P. (2009). What is technological pedagogical content knowledge? *Contemporary Issues in Technology & Teacher Education*, *9*(1).

Koellinger, P. (2008). The relationship between technology, innovation, and firm performance—Empirical evidence from e-business in Europe. *Research Policy*, *37*(8), 1317–1328. doi:10.1016/j.respol.2008.04.024

Kogut, B. (2003). Is there global convergence in regulation and electronic markets? The global internet economy. MIT Press.

Koh, J., & Kim, Y. G. (2004). Knowledge sharing in virtual communities: An e-business perspective. *Expert Systems with Applications*, *26*(2), 155–166. doi:10.1016/S0957-4174(03)00116-7

Kolaczyk, E. D. (2009). Mapping networks. In *Statistical Analysis of Network Data.* Springer Science. Retrieved from http://download.springer.com/static/pdf/560/chp%253A10.1007%252F978-0-387-88146-1_3.pdf?auth66=1415657155_389a8f9c38c4330d7eebb4cf76dfa5dd&ext=.pdf

Kommers, P. A. M., Ferreira, A., & Kwak, A. (1998). *Document management for hypermedia design.* Berlin: Springer-Verlag. doi:10.1007/978-3-642-95728-4

Kovarik, B. (2015). *Revolutions in communication: Media history from Gutenberg to the digital age.* Bloomsbury Publishing.

Kowalski, R. (1996). Complaints and complaining: Functions, antecedents, and consequences. *Psychological Bulletin*, *119*(2), 179–196. doi:10.1037/0033-2909.119.2.179 PMID:8851274

Kramarski, B., & Michalsky, T. (2015). Effect of a TPCK-SRL Model on Teachers' Pedagogical Beliefs, Self-Efficacy, and Technology-Based Lesson Design. In Technological Pedagogical Content Knowledge (pp. 89-112). Springer US.

Kramarski, B. (2008). Promoting teachers' algebraic reasoning and self-regulation with metacognitive guidance. *Metacognition and Learning*, *3*(2), 83–99. doi:10.1007/s11409-008-9020-6

Kramarski, B., & Gutman, M. (2006). How can self-regulated learning be supported in mathematical E-learning environments? *Journal of Computer Assisted Learning*, *22*(1), 24–33. doi:10.1111/j.1365-2729.2006.00157.x

Kramarski, B., & Michalsky, T. (2009). Three metacognitive approaches to training pre-service teachers in different learning phases of technological pedagogical content knowledge. *Educational Research and Evaluation*, *15*(5), 465–485. doi:10.1080/13803610903444550

Kramarski, B., & Michalsky, T. (2010). Preparing preservice teachers for self-regulated learning in the context of technological pedagogical content knowledge. *Learning and Instruction*, *20*(5), 434–447. doi:10.1016/j.learninstruc.2009.05.003

Kramarski, B., & Mizrachi, N. (2006). Online discussion and self-regulated learning: Effects of instructional methods on mathematical literacy. *The Journal of Educational Research*, *99*(4), 218–231. doi:10.3200/JOER.99.4.218-231

Krebs, V., & Holley, J. (2006). *Building smart communities through network weaving*. Appalachian Center for Economic Networks. Retrieved October 24, 2015, from http://www.orgnet.com/BuildingNetworks.pdf

Kruitbosch, G., & Nack, F. (2008). Broadcast yourself on YouTube—really? In Proceedings of HCC '08.

Kumar, V., Bhaskaran, V., Mirchandani, R., & Shah, M. (2013). Practice prize winner-creating a measurable social media marketing strategy: Increasing the value and ROI of intangibles and tangibles for hokey pokey. *Marketing Science*, *32*(2), 194–212. doi:10.1287/mksc.1120.0768

Kunze, K., Utsumi, Y., Shiga, Y., Kise, K., & Bulling, A. (2013). I know what you are reading—Recognition of document types using mobile eye tracking. In *Proceedings of ISWC '13*.

Lajoie, S. P., & Azevedo, R. (2006). Teaching and learning in technology-rich environments. In P. Alexander & P. Winne (Eds.), *Handbook of educational psychology*. Mahwah, NJ: Erlbaum.

Land, S. M. (2000). Cognitive requirements for learning with open-ended learning environments. *Educational Technology Research and Development*, *48*(3), 61–78. doi:10.1007/BF02319858

Lange, P. G. (2008). Publicly private and privately public: Social networking on YouTube. *Journal of Computer-Mediated Communication*, *13*(1), 361–380. doi:10.1111/j.1083-6101.2007.00400.x

Larose, R., & Atkin, D. (1991). Attributes of movie distribution channels and consumer choice. *Journal of Media Economics*, *4*(1), 3–17. doi:10.1080/08997769109358200

Latane, B. (1981). The Psychology of Social Impact. *The American Psychologist*, *36*, 343–356. doi:10.1037/0003-066X.36.4.343

Latané, B. (1996). Dynamic social impact: The creation of culture by communication. *Journal of Communication*, *46*(4), 13–25. doi:10.1111/j.1460-2466.1996.tb01501.x

Lee, J. (2010). 10 million Australians on Facebook. *The Age*. Retrieved December 10 2010, from http://goo.gl/CEWXA

Lee, K., Palsetia, D., Narayanan, R., Patwary, M., Agrawal, A., & Choudhary, A. (2011). Twitter Trending Topic Classification. *2011 IEEE 11Th International Conference On Data Mining Workshops*. doi:10.1109/icdmw.2011.171

Lee, C. S., & Ma, L. (2012). News sharing in social media: The effect of gratifications and prior experience. *Computers in Human Behavior*, *28*(2), 331–339. doi:10.1016/j.chb.2011.10.002

Leech, N. L., & Onwuegbuzie, A. J. (2007). An array of qualitative data analysis tools: A call for data analysis triangulation. *School Psychology Quarterly*, *22*(4), 557–584. doi:10.1037/1045-3830.22.4.557

Lee, D. H., & Park, C. W. (2007). Conceptualization and Measurement of Multidimensionality of Integrated Marketing Communications. *Journal of Advertising Research*, *47*(3), 222–236. doi:10.2501/S0021849907070274

Lee, R. K.-W., & Lim, E.-P. (2015). Measuring user influence, susceptibility and cynicalness (sic) in sentiment diffusion. In A. Hansbury et al. (Eds.), *ECIR 2015, LNCS 9022. 411 – 422*.

Lee, S., & Cho, M. (2011). Social Media Use in a Mobile Broadband Environment. Examination of Determinants of Twitter and Facebook Use. *International Journal of Mobile Marketing*, *6*(2), 71–87.

Lee, S., & Koubek, R. J. (2010). The effects of usability and web design attributes on user preference for e-commerce web sites. *Computers in Industry*, *61*(4), 329–341. doi:10.1016/j.compind.2009.12.004

Lefebvre, H. (2007). *Modern Dünyada Gündelik Hayat*. Istanbul: Metis Yayınları.

Leitch, S., & Warren, M. (2011). The ethics of security of personal information upon Facebook. *ICT Ethics and Security in the 21st Century: New Developments and Applications*.

Leung, D., Law, R., van Hoof, H., & Buhalis, D. (2013). Social media in tourism and hospitality: A literature review. *Journal of Travel & Tourism Management*, *30*(1-2), 3–22. doi:10.1080/10548408.2013.750919

Leung, L. (2003). Impacts of net-generation attributes, seductive properties of the internet, and gratifications-obtained on internet use. *Telematics and Informatics*, *20*(2), 107–129. doi:10.1016/S0736-5853(02)00019-9

Lewis, T. G. (2009). *Network science: theory and practice*. Hoboken, NJ: John Wiley & Sons, Inc. doi:10.1002/9780470400791

Leyton Escobar, M., Kommers, P. A. M., & Beldad, A. (2014). The key is not to forget to be awesome: Identifying narratives in an online community. *International Journal of Web Based Communities*, *10*(4), 490–505. doi:10.1504/IJWBC.2014.065396

Liao, H., McDermott, E., & Senior, A. (2013). Large scale deep neural network acoustic modeling with semi-supervised training data for YouTube video transcription. In *Automatic Speech Recognition and Understanding (ASRU), 2013 IEEE Workshop*. Retrieved March 19, 2015, from http://static.googleusercontent.com/media/research.google.com/en/us/pubs/archive/41403.pdf. 368 – 373.

Licklider, J. C. R. (1960, March). Man-computer symbiosis. *IRE Transactions on Human Factors in Electronics*. Retrieved January 13, 2016, from http://groups.csail.mit.edu/medg/people/psz/Licklider.html

Li, F., & Du, T. C. (2011). Who is talking? An ontology-based opinion leader identification framework for word-of-mouth marketing in online social blogs. *Decision Support Systems*, *51*(1), 190–197. doi:10.1016/j.dss.2010.12.007

Lin, C. A. (2003). An interactive communication technology adoption model. *Communication Theory*, *13*(4), 345–365. doi:10.1111/j.1468-2885.2003.tb00296.x

Lipschultz, J. H. (2014). *Social Media Communication: Concepts, Practices, Data, Law, and Ethics*. Routledge.

Liu, B., & Zhang, L. (2012). A survey of opinion mining and sentiment analysis. In Mining text data (pp. 415-463). Springer US. doi:10.1007/978-1-4614-3223-4_13

Liu, H. C., Lai, M. L., & Chuang, H. H. (2011). Using Eye-Tracking Technology to Investigate The Redundant Effect of Multimedia Web Pages on Viewers' Cognitive Processes. *Computers in Human Behavior*, *27*(6), 2410–2417. doi:10.1016/j.chb.2011.06.012

Li, X., Luo, Q., & Yuan, J. (2007). Personalized recommendation service system in e-learning using web intelligence. *Proceedings 7th Int. Conf. Comput. Sci.* (pp. 531-538). doi:10.1007/978-3-540-72588-6_86

Li, X., Xie, H., Chen, L., Wang, J., & Deng, X. (2014). News impact on stock price return via sentiment analysis. *Knowledge-Based Systems*, *69*, 14–23. doi:10.1016/j.knosys.2014.04.022

Lizarraga, C. (2012). Expansión metropolitana y movilidad: el caso de Caracas. *EURE (Santiago)*, *38*(113), 99-125. Retrieved August 31, 2015, from http://www.scielo.cl/scielo.php?script=sci_arttext&pid=S0250-71612012000100005&lng=es&tlng=en

Lowery, S., & Defleur, M. L. (1995). *Milestones in mass communication research*. Media Effects.

Lu, F., Li, X., Liu, Q., Yang, Z., Tan, G., & He, T. (2007). Research on personalized e-learning system using fuzzy set based clustering algorithm. *Proc. Int. Conf. Comput. Sci.* (pp. 587-590). doi:10.1063/1.2747485

Lu, H.-P., Lin, J. C.-C., Hsiao, K.-L., & Cheng, L.-T. (2010). Information sharing behaviour on blogs in Taiwan: Effects of interactivities and gender differences. *Journal of Information Science*, *36*(3), 401–416. doi:10.1177/0165551510363631

Luong, T. B. T., & Houston, D. (2015). Public opinions of light rail service in Los Angeles, an analysis using Twitter data. In *iConference 2015 Proceedings*. Retrieved from http://hdl.handle.net/2142/73771

Macdonald, J., & Poniatowska, B. (2011). Designing the professional development of staff for teaching online: An OU (UK) case study. *Distance Education*, *32*(1), 119–134. doi:10.1080/01587919.2011.565481

Machine Elf 1735. (2011, Feb. 12). *Robert Plutchik's Wheel of Emotions*. Retrieved November 8, 2015, from https://commons.wikimedia.org/wiki/File:Plutchik-wheel.svg

Magidson, J., & Vermunt, J. K. (2004). Latent class models. In The Sage handbook of quantitative methodology for the social sciences (pp. 175-198). Thousand Oaks, CA: Sage Publications. doi:10.4135/9781412986311.n10

Mahadevan, B. (2000). Business models for Internet-based e-commerce. *California Management Review*, *42*(4), 55–69. doi:10.2307/41166053

Mai, E., & Hranac, R. (2013). Twitter Interactions as a Data Source for Transportation Incidents. *Proceedings of the 2013 Annual Meeting Transportation Research Record*.

Mangold, W. G., & Faulds, D. J. (2009). Social media: The new hybrid element of the promotion mix. *Business Horizons*, *52*(4), 357–365. doi:10.1016/j.bushor.2009.03.002

Mann, C., & Stewart, F. (2000). *Internet communication and qualitative research: A handbook for research online*. London: Sage Publications.

Mantovani, G. (1996a). *New communication environments: From everyday to virtual*. London: Taylor & Francis.

Mantovani, G. (1996b). Social context in HCI: A new framework for mental models, cooperation, and communication. *Cognitive Science*, *20*(2), 237–269. doi:10.1207/s15516709cog2002_3

Marcus, A., Wu, E., Karger, D., Madden, S., & Miller, R. (2011). Human-powered sorts and joins. *Proc. VLDB Endow.*, *5*(1), 13-24. doi:10.14778/2047485.2047487

Mariani, L., Pastore, F., & Pezze, M. (2011). Dynamic analysis for diagnosing integration faults. *IEEE Transactions on Software Engineering*, *37*(4), 486–508. doi:10.1109/TSE.2010.93

Marin, A., & Wellman, B. (2012). Social network analysis: an introduction. In The SAGE handbook of social network analysis. SAGE Publications.

Markoff, J. (2015). *Machines of Loving Grace: The Quest for Common Ground between Humans and Robots*. New York: HarperCollins.

Martindale, T., & Wiley, D. A. (2005). An introduction to teaching with weblogs. *TechTrends*, *49*(2), 55–61. doi:10.1007/BF02773972

Martínez-Guerrero, M., Ortega-Egea, J. M., & Román-González, M. V. (2007). Application of the latent class regression methodology to the analysis of Internet use for banking transactions in the European Union. *Journal of Business Research*, *60*(2), 137–145. doi:10.1016/j.jbusres.2006.10.012

Martins, C., Oliveira, T., & Popovič, A. (2014). Understanding the Internet banking adoption: A unified theory of acceptance and use of technology and perceived risk application. *International Journal of Information Management*, *34*(1), 1–13. doi:10.1016/j.ijinfomgt.2013.06.002

Maslow, A. H. (1943). A theory of motivation. *Psychological Review, 50*(4), 370–396. doi:10.1037/h0054346

Maxwell, J. A., & Miller, B. A. (2008). Categorizing and connecting strategies in qualitative data analysis. Handbook of Emergent Methods, 461-477.

Mbakwe, C., & Cunliffe, D. (2002). *Towards systematically engineered seductive hypermedia.* Unpublished manuscript.

Mbakwe, C., & Cunliffe, D. (2003). *Conceptualising the process of hypermedia seduction.* The 1st International Meeting of Science and Technology Design: Senses and Sensibility – Linking Tradition to Innovation through Design, Lisbon, Portugal.

McAfee, A., & Brynjolfsson, E. (2012). Big Data: The Management Revolution. *Harvard Business Review, 90*(10), 60–68. PMID:23074865

McCormack, J. (2013). Aesthetics, art, evolution. EvoMUSART 2013, LNCS. Springer-Verlag. doi:10.1007/978-3-642-36955-1_1

McPherson, T. (2009, Winter). Introduction: Media Studies and the Digital Humanities. *Cinema Journal, 48*(20), 119–123. Retrieved from http://www.jstor.org/stable/20484452

Mendola, J. (2006). Intuitive hedonism. *Philosophical Studies, 128*(2), 441–477. doi:10.1007/s11098-004-7810-5

Metcalfe, B. (1995). Metcalfe's law: A network becomes more valuable as it reaches more users. *InfoWorld,* (October), 2.

Metzgar, E., & Maruggi, A. (2009). Social Media and the 2008 US Presidential Election. *Journal of New Communications Research, 4,* 141–165.

Michel, J-B., Shen, Y.K., Aiden, A.P., Veres, A., Gray, M.K., Brockman, W., … Aiden, E.L. (2010, Dec. 16). Quantitative Analysis of Culture Using Millions of Digitized Books. *Science.*

Milgram, S. (1967). The small-world problem Psychology Today. Sussex Publishers LLC.

Milligan, I. (2012). Mining the 'Internet Graveyard': Rethinking the historians' toolkit. *Journal of the Canadian Historical Association, 23*(2), 21–64. doi:10.7202/1015788ar

Min, M., Lee, T., & Hsu, R. (2013). Role of emoticons in sentence-level sentiment classification. In M. Sun et al. (Eds.), *CCL and NLP-NABD 2013, LNAI 8202. 203 – 213.* doi:10.1007/978-3-642-41491-6_19

Minor-Cooley, D. O., Bush, A., & Madupu, V. (2015). How Consumers are Searching: The Importance of the Internet to the Healthcare Industry. In *Proceedings of the 2008 Academy of Marketing Science (AMS)Annual Conference* (pp. 176-176). Springer International Publishing.

Mishra, P., & Koehler, M. (2006). Technological pedagogical content knowledge: A framework for teacher knowledge. *Teachers College Record, 108*(6), 1017–1054. doi:10.1111/j.1467-9620.2006.00684.x

Mlodinow, L. (2012). *Subliminal: How your Unconscious Mind Rules your Behavior.* New York: Pantheon Books.

MobileBeyond. (2010). *Smartphone consumer expectations driving industry crazy.* Retrieved May 7, 2015, from http://mobilebeyond.net/smartphone-consumer-expectations-driving-industry-crazy/#axzz14ZIJKAri

Mohr, J. W., Wagner-Pacifici, R., Breiger, R. L., & Bogdanov, P. (2013). Graphing the grammar of motives in national security strategies: Cultural interpretation, automated text analysis and the drama of global politics. *Poetics, 41*(6), 670–700. doi:10.1016/j.poetic.2013.08.003

Moore, G. M., & Kearsley, G. (2005). *Distance education: a systems view* (2nd ed.). Thomson Wadsworth.

Moore, M. G., & Kearsley, G. (2012). *Distance education: a systems view of online learning* (3rd ed.). Belmont: Wadsworth.

Morency, L.-P., Mihalcea, R., & Doshi, P. (2011). Towards multimodal sentiment analysis: Harvesting opinions from the Web. In *Proceedings of the ICMI '11*.

Moretti, F. (2000, January – February). Conjectures on world literature. *New Left Review*, *1*, 1–13.

Moretti, F. (2005). Graphs, Maps, Trees: Abstract Models for Literary History – 1. *New Left Review*, *24*, 67–93.

Morsillo, R. (2011). One down, two to go: Public policy in service of an available, affordable and accessible national broadband network for people with disability. *Telecommunications Journal of Australia*, *61*(2)

Müller-Birn, C., Schlegel, A., Klüwer, T., Benedix, L., & Breitenfeld, A. (2015). Neonion—Combining human and machine intelligence. In *Proceedings of CSCS '15*.

Muralidharan, A., Hearst, M. A., & Fan, C. (2013). WordSeer: A knowledge synthesis environment for textual data. In *Proceedings of CIKM '13*. doi:10.1145/2505515.2508212

Mutlu Bayraktar, D., & Bayram, S. (n.d.). Evaluation Of Situations Causing Split Of Attention. In S. Hai-Jew (Ed.), *Design Strategies and Innovations in Multimedia Presentations* (pp. 320–344). IGI Global.

Namahn. (2000). *Using eye tracking for usability testing*. Brussels: Author.

Nasukawa, T., & Yi, J. (2003, October). Sentiment analysis: Capturing favorability using natural language processing. In *Proceedings of the 2nd international conference on Knowledge capture* (pp. 70-77). ACM. doi:10.1145/945645.945658

National Instruments. (2010). *Weighing the cost and benefits of code reuse*. Retrieved from ftp://ftp.ni.com/pub/newsimages/2010/LabVIEW2010_OnlinePressKit/QandAs/IP%20Integration%20Q&A.pdf

Neter, J., Wasserman, W., & Kutner, M. H. (1990). *Applied linear statistical models: Regression, analysis of variance, and experimental design*. Homewood, IL: Richard D. Irwin.

Newcomb, A. (2015, Apr. 23). The surprising topic of first YouTube video posted 10 years ago today. *ABC News*. Retrieved Apr. 23, 2015, from http://abcnews.go.com/Technology/surprising-topic-youtube-video-posted-10-years-ago/story?id=30524242

Nielsen, J. (2003). *Usabilitiy 101: Introduction to Usability*. Retrieved from http://www.useit.com/alertbox/20030825.html

Nielsen, J. (1993). *Usability engineering*. London: Academic Press.

Nielsen, J. (1999). *Designing web usability: The practice of simplicity*. New Riders Publishing.

Nielsen, J., & Pernice, K. (2010). *Eyetracking web usability*. New Riders.

Norman, A. T., & Russell, C. A. (2006). The pass-along effect: Investigating word-of-mouth effects on online survey procedures. *Journal of Computer-Mediated Communication*, *11*(4), 1085–1103. doi:10.1111/j.1083-6101.2006.00309.x

Norman, D. A. (2013). *The design of everyday things: Revised and expanded edition*. Basic books.

Norris, G., Balls, J. D., & Hartley, K. M. (2000). *E-business and ERP: Transforming the Enterprise*. John Wiley and Sons, Inc.

Nováček, V., & Burns, G. A. P. C. (2013). SKIMMR: Machine-aided skim-reading. In *Proceedings of IUI '13 Companion*.

Nov, O., & Ye, C. (2008) Personality and Technology Acceptance: Personal Innovativeness in IT, Openness and Resistance to Change. In *Proceedings of the 41st Annual Hawaii International Conference on System Sciences*. IEEE. doi:10.1109/HICSS.2008.348

O'Brien, J. (2014). Reasoning with graphs. In Shaping Knowledge: Complex Social-Spatial Modelling for Adaptive Organizations. Oxford, UK: Elsevier.

Odlyzko, A., & Tilly, B. (2005). *A refutation of Metcalfe's Law and a better estimate for the value of networks and network interconnections.* Manuscript.

Oliveira, T., & Martins, M. F. (2009). Firms' Patterns of e-Business Adoption: Evidence for the European Union-27. In *Proceedings of the 3rd European Conference on Information Management and Evaluation.* Academic Conferences Limited.

Ortega-Egea, J. M., García-de-Frutos, N., & Antolín-López, R. (2014). Why Do Some People Do "More" to Mitigate Climate Change than Others? Exploring Heterogeneity in Psycho-Social Associations. *PLoS ONE, 9*(9), 1–17. doi:10.1371/journal.pone.0106645 PMID:25191841

Ott, L., & Theunissen, P. (2015). Reputation at risk: Engagement during social media crises. *Public Relations Review, 41*(1), 97–102. doi:10.1016/j.pubrev.2014.10.015

Ozcelik, E., Kursun, E., & Cagiltay, Y. D. D. K. (2006). *Göz Hareketlerini İzleme Yöntemiyle Üniversite Web Sayfalarının İncelenmesi.* Akademik Bilisim.

Ozdener, N. (2005). Use of simulation in experimental teaching methods. *The Turkish Online Journal of Educational Technology, 4*(4), 93–98.

Panahi, S., Watson, J., & Partridge, H. (2015). Information encountering on social media and tacit knowledge sharing. *Journal of Information Science,* 1–12.

Paolillo, J. C. (2008). Structure and network in the YouTube core. In *Proceedings of the 41st Hawaii International Conference on System Sciences.* doi:10.1109/HICSS.2008.415

Papadopoulos, S., Kompatsiaris, I., & Vakali, A. (2010). *A graph-based clustering scheme for identifying related tags in folksonomies.* Academic Press.

Park, N., Jung, Y., & Lee, K. M. (2011). Intention to upload video content on the internet: The role of social norms and ego-involvement. *Computers in Human Behavior, 27*(5), 1996–2004. doi:10.1016/j.chb.2011.05.006

Pedersen, P. E. (2005). Adoption of mobile Internet services: An exploratory study of mobile commerce early adopters. *Journal of Organizational Computing and Electronic Commerce, 15*(3), 203–222. doi:10.1207/s15327744joce1503_2

Pentina, I., Covault, A., & Tarafdar, M. (2015). Exploring The Role of Social Media in News Consumption. In K. Kubacki (Ed.), *Ideas in marketing: Finding the new and polishing the old* (pp. 577–587). Springer. doi:10.1007/978-3-319-10951-0_209

Pentina, I., Zhang, L., & Basmanova, O. (2013). Antecedents and Consequences of Trust in A Social Media Brand: A Cross-Cultural Study of Twitter. *Computers in Human Behavior, 29*(4), 1546–1555. doi:10.1016/j.chb.2013.01.045

Peppard, J., & Rylander, A. (2006). From value chain to value network: Insights for mobile operators. *European Management Journal, 24*(2), 128–141. doi:10.1016/j.emj.2006.03.003

Peters, L. H., O'Connor, E. J., & Eulberg, J. R. (1985). Situational constraints: Sources, consequences, and future considerations. *Research in Personnel and Human Resources Management, 3*, 79–114.

Phan, M., Thomas, R., & Heine, K. (2011). Social media and luxury brand management: The case of Burberry. *Journal of Global Fashion Marketing*, *2*(4), 213–222. doi:10.1080/20932685.2011.10593099

Pinto, H., Almeida, J. M., & Goncalves, M. A. (2013). Using early view patterns to predict the popularity of YouTube videos. In *Proceedings of WSDM '13*. doi:10.1145/2433396.2433443

Porter, M. F. (1980). An algorithm for suffix stripping. *Program*, *14*(3), 130–137. doi:10.1108/eb046814

Prajogo, D., & Olhager, J. (2012). Supply chain integration and performance: The effects of long-term relationships, information technology and sharing, and logistics integration. *International Journal of Production Economics*, *135*(1), 514–522. doi:10.1016/j.ijpe.2011.09.001

Preece, J., Nonnecke, B., & Andrews, D. (2004). The top 5 reasons for lurking: Improving community experiences for everyone. *Computers in Human Behavior*, *2*(1), 42.

Pritchett, J. E. (2009). *Identification of situational constraints in middle school business information technology programs*. (Doctor of Education Dissertation). The University of Georgia in Partial.

Purchase, H. (1997). *Which aesthetic has the greatest effect on human understanding?* Berlin: SpringerLink. Retrieved from http://www.dcs.gla.ac.uk/publications/PAPERS/6453/gd97.pdf

Purchase, H. C., Freeman, E., & Hamer, J. (2012). An exploration of visual complexity. N Diagrams 2012, LNAI 7352. Berlin: Springer-Verlag.

Purchase, H. C., Hoggan, E., & Görg, C. (2007). How important is the 'mental map'? An empirical investigation of a dynamic graph layout algorithm. GD 2006. Berlin: Springer-Verlag.

Purchase, H. C., Allder, J.-A., & Carrington, D. (2001). User preference of graph layout aesthetics: A UML study. In J. Marks (Ed.), *GD 2000, LNCS 1984* (pp. 5–18). Berlin: Springer-Verlag. doi:10.1007/3-540-44541-2_2

Purchase, H. C., Carrington, D., & Allder, J.-A. (2000). Experimenting with aesthetics-based graph layout. In P. Cheng & V. Haarslev (Eds.), *Diagrams 2000, LNAI 1889* (pp. 498–501). Springer-Verlag Berlin Heidelberg.

Purdy, J. P. (2011). Three gifts of digital archives. *Journal of Literacy and Technology*, *12*(3), 24–49.

Qiu, L., Rui, H., & Whinston, A. (2013). Social network-embedded prediction markets: The effects of information acquisition and communication on predictions. *Decision Support Systems*, *55*(4), 978–987. doi:10.1016/j.dss.2013.01.007

Quan-Haase, A., & Young, A. L. (2010). Uses And Gratifications Of Social Media: A Comparison of Facebook and Instant Messaging. *Bulletin of Science, Technology & Society*, *30*(5), 350–361. doi:10.1177/0270467610380009

Quigley, A. (2006). Aesthetics of large-scale relational information visualization in practice. In P. A. Fishwick (Ed.), *Aesthetic Computing* (pp. 315–334). Cambridge, MA: The MIT Press.

R2C2_USB. (2015). Retrieved August 31, 2015, from https://twitter.com/r2c2_usb

Racherla, P., Connolly, D. J., & Christodoulidou, N. (2013). What Determines Consumers' Ratings of Service Providers? An Exploratory Study of Online Traveller Reviews. *Journal of Hospitality Marketing & Management*, *22*(2), 135–161. doi:10.1080/19368623.2011.645187

Radach, R., Hyona, J., & Deubel, H. (Eds.). (2003). *The Mind's Eye: Cognitive And Applied Aspects Of Eye Movement Research*. Elsevier.

Radach, R., & Underwood, G. (1998). *Eye guidance and visual information processing: Reading, visual search, picture perception and driving. Eye Guidance in Reading and Scene Perception*. Oxford, UK: Elsevier.

Ramo, S., & St. Clair, R. K. (1998). *The systems approach: Fresh solutions to complex problems through combining science and practical common sense.* Retrieved October 24, 2015, from http://oldsite.incose.org/ProductsPubs/DOC/SystemsApproach.pdf

Ramsey, G. (2006). *Digital marketing strategies in the age of consumer control.* Retrieved July 22, 2015, from http://www.emarketer.com/Article.aspx?id=1003886&src=article_head_sitesearch

Ranieri, M., Manca, S., & Fini, A. (2012). Why (and how) do teachers engage in social networks? An exploratory study of professional use of Facebook and its implications for lifelong learning. *British Journal of Educational Technology*, *43*(5), 754–769. doi:10.1111/j.1467-8535.2012.01356.x

Ransbotham, S., Kane, G. C., & Lurie, N. H. (2012). Network characteristics and the value of collaborative user-generated content. *Marketing Science*, *31*(3), 387–405. doi:10.1287/mksc.1110.0684

Rao, A. S., & Georgeff, M. P. (1998). Decision procedures for BDI logics. *Journal of Logic and Computation*, *8*(3), 293–342. doi:10.1093/logcom/8.3.293

RapidMiner. (2015). *RapidMiner 6 Operator Reference Manual.* RapidMiner GmbH.

Ravi, K., & Ravi, V. (2015). A survey on opinion mining and sentiment analysis: Tasks, approaches and applications. *Knowledge-Based Systems*, *89*, 14–46. doi:10.1016/j.knosys.2015.06.015

Reading (Process). (2016, Jan. 7). In *Wikipedia.* Retrieved January 10, 2016, from https://en.wikipedia.org/wiki/Reading_(process)

Reed, E. P. (1999). *The sneaky exponential- beyond Metcalfe's law to the power of community building.* Context Magazine.

Reed, E. P. (2001). The law of the pack. *Harvard Business Review*, (March), 63–78. PMID:11213694

Reid, M. (2005). Performance auditing of integrated marketing communication (IMC) actions and outcomes. *Journal of Advertising*, *34*(4), 41–54. doi:10.1080/00913367.2005.10639208

Reiss, S. (2004). Multifaceted nature of intrinsic motivation: The theory of 16 basic desires. *Review of General Psychology*, *8*(3), 179–193. doi:10.1037/1089-2680.8.3.179

Rengifo, P. (2015). *Datasets.* Retrieved August 31, 2015, from https://github.com/prengifo/r2c2usb/tree/master/datasets

Ricci, F., Rokach, L., Shapira, B., & Kantor, P. B. (Eds.). (2011). *Recommender Systems Handbook.* New York, NY: Springer-Verlag New York, Inc. doi:10.1007/978-0-387-85820-3

Roblyer, M. D., McDaniel, M., Webb, M., Herman, J., & Witty, J. V. (2010). Findings on Facebook in higher education: A comparison of college faculty and student uses and perceptions of social networking sites. *The Internet and Higher Education*, *13*(3), 134–140. doi:10.1016/j.iheduc.2010.03.002

Rogers, S. P., & Krishnan, K. (2014). Social Platforms. Social Data Analytics: Collaboration for the Enterprise, 75 – 91.

Romero, C., & Ventura, S. (2007). Educational data mining: A survey from 1995 to 2005. *Expert Systems with Applications*, *33*(1), 125–146. doi:10.1016/j.eswa.2006.04.005

Romero, C., & Ventura, S. (2010). Educational data mining: A review of the state-of-the-art. *IEEE Transactions on Systems, Man and Cybernetics. Part C, Applications and Reviews*, *40*(6), 601–618. doi:10.1109/TSMCC.2010.2053532

Rosario, Z. D., Kaing, E., Taylor, B. D., & Wachs, M. (2012). Why it wasn't "Carmageddon": An Analysis of the Summer 2011 Closure of the Interstate 405 Freeway in Los Angeles. A Report to the Mayor's Office Institute of Transportation Studies Ralph & Goldy Lewis Center for Regional Policy Studies, UCLA Luskin School of Public Affairs, City of Los Angeles.

Rosenbaum, J. E., Kariya, T., Settersten, R., & Maier, T. (1990). Market and network theories of the transition from high school to work: Their application to industrialized societies. *Annual Review of Sociology, 16*(1), 263–299. doi:10.1146/annurev.so.16.080190.001403

Rosenfield, L., & Morville, P. (2002). *Information architecture for the world wide web.* Sebastopol, CA: O'Reilly & Associates, Inc.

Rotman, D., Golbeck, J., & Preece, J. (2009). The community is where the rapport is—on sense and structure in the YouTube community. In *Proceedings of C&T'09.*

Rowley, D. E. (1994). Usability testing in the field: Bridging the laboratory to the user. Boston, MA: Academic Press.

Roy, D. (1954). Efficiency and 'the fix': Informal intergroup relations in a piecework machine shop. *American Journal of Sociology, 60*(3), 255–267. doi:10.1086/221535

Rubin, A. M. (1994). Media uses and effects: A uses-and-gratifications perspective. In B. Jennings & D. Zillamann (Eds.), *Media Effects: Advances in Theory and Research. LEA's Communication Series* (p. 505). Hillsdale, NJ: Lawrence Erlbaum Associates, Inc.

Russell, M. (2005). Using Eye-tracking Data to Understand First Impressions of a Website. *Usability News, 7*(1), 1–14.

Rutherford, C. (2010). Facebook as a source of informal teacher professional development. *Education, 16*(1), 60–74.

Ryan, G. W., & Bernard, H. R. (2003). Techniques to identify themes. *Field Methods, 15*(1), 85–109. doi:10.1177/1525822X02239569

San Pedro, J., Siersdorfer, S., & Sanderson, M. (2011). Content redundancy in YouTube and its application to video tagging. *ACM Transactions on Information Systems, 29*(3). Retrieved March 30, 2015, from http://www.l3s.de/~siersdorfer/sources/2011/TOIS-2011-youtube%28pre-print%29.pdf

Sanders, N. R. (2007). An empirical study of the impact of e-business technologies on organizational collaboration and performance. *Journal of Operations Management, 25*(6), 1332–1347. doi:10.1016/j.jom.2007.01.008

Santos, R.L.T., Rocha, B.P.S., Rezende, C.G., & loureiro, A.A.F. (2007). *Characterizing the YouTube video-sharing community.* Retrieved March 22, 2015, from http://homepages.dcc.ufmg.br/~rodrygo/wp-content/papercite-data/pdf/santos2007report.pdf

Sarkar, C., Bhatia, S., Agarwal, A., & Li, J. (2014). Feature analysis for computational personality recognition using YouTube personality data set. In *Proceedings of WCPR '14.* doi:10.1145/2659522.2659528

Scherer, K. R. (2000). Psychological models of emotion. New York: Oxford University Press.

Schiessl, M., Duda, S., Thölke, A., & Fischer, R. (2003). *Eye Tracking and Its Application In Usability and Media Research.* Retrieved from http://www.smiling.club/assets/fileupload/eye_tracking_application_duda.pdf

Schiller, F., Penn, A. S., & Basson, L. (2014). Analyzing networks in industrial ecology–a review of Social-Material Network Analyses. *Journal of Cleaner Production, 76*, 1–11. doi:10.1016/j.jclepro.2014.03.029

Schmidt, D. (2012). *Why software reuse has failed and how to make it work for you.* Retrieved from http://www.dre.vanderbilt.edu/~schmidt/reuse-lessons.html

Schneiderman, B., & Plaisant, C. (2005). *Designing the user interface: Strategies for Effective Human-Computer Interactions. The United States of America: Pearson Education* (4th ed.). Reading, MA: Addison-Wesley.

Schoeffler, M., & Herre, J. (2014). The influence of audio quality on the popularity of music videos: A YouTube case study. In Proceedings of WISMM '14. doi:10.1145/2661714.2661725

Schwab, K. (2013). *Global Competitiveness Report 2013-2014.* World Economic Forum.

Segedy, J. R., Biswas, G., & Sulcer, B. (2014). A model-based behavior analysis approach for open-ended environments. *Journal of Educational Technology & Society, 17*(1), 272–282.

Senadheera, V. (2015). *The adoption of social media by Australian banks to communicate with the public.* (Doctoral dissertation). Retrieved March 30, 2016, from http://goo.gl/cQcZ0C

Senadheera, V., Warren, M., & Leitch, S. (2011). A Study into How Australian Banks use Social Media. In *Proceedings of the Pacific Asia Conference on Information Systems (PACIS '11).*

Sener, G. (2010). *Türkiye'de Facebook Kullanımı Araştırması, XIV. Türkiye'de İnternet Konferansı.* Bilgi University.

Sennersten, C. (2004). *Eye movements in an action game tutorial.* Department of Cognitive Science. Lund University.

Sensitivity and Specificity. (2015, Dec. 4). In *Wikipedia.* Retrieved Dec. 13, 2015, from https://en.wikipedia.org/wiki/Sensitivity_and_specificity

Severyn, A., Moschitti, A., Uryupina, O., Plank, B., & Filippova, K. (2015). Multi-lingual opinion mining on YouTube. *Information Processing & Management.* doi:10.1016/j.ipm.2015.03.002

Shapiro, C., Varian, H. R., & Becker, W. E. (1999). Information rules: A strategic guide to the network economy. *The Journal of Economic Education, 30*(2), 189–190. doi:10.2307/1183273

Shen, K., & Wu, L. (2005). *Folksonomy as a complex network.* arXiv:cs/0509072v1

Shulman, L. S. (1986). Those who understand: Knowledge growth in teaching. *Educational Researcher, 15*(2), 4–14. doi:10.3102/0013189X015002004

Shute, V. J., & Zapata-Rivera, D. (2012). Adaptive educational systems. In P. Durlach (Ed.), *Adaptive technologies for training and education* (pp. 7–27). New York, NY: Cambridge University Press. doi:10.1017/CBO9781139049580.004

Siemens, G. (2006). *Knowing Knowledge.* Retrieved October 29, 2015, from http://www.elearnspace.org/Knowing-Knowledge_LowRes.pdf

Siemens, G. (2008). *A World without courses.* Retrieved from http://www.elearnspace.org/media/worldwithoutcourses/player.html

Singh, J., & Howell, R. D. (1985). Consumer complaining behavior: a review and prospectus. In Consumer Satisfaction, Dissatisfaction and Complaining Behavior (pp. 59-66). Bloomington, IN: Indiana University.

Singh, N., & Matsuo, H. (2004). Measuring cultural adaptation on the Web: A content analytic study of U.S. and Japanese Web sites. *Journal of Business Research, 57*(8), 864–872. doi:10.1016/S0148-2963(02)00482-4

Singh, T., Veron-Jackson, L., & Cullinane, J. (2008). Blogging: A new play in your marketing game plan. *Business Horizons, 51*(4), 281–292. doi:10.1016/j.bushor.2008.02.002

Size of Wikipedia. (2016, Jan. 3). In *Wikipedia.* Retrieved Jan. 12, 2016, from https://en.wikipedia.org/wiki/Wikipedia:Size_of_Wikipedia

Slegers, K., & Donoso, V. (2012). The impact of paper prototyping on card sorting: A case study. *Interacting with Computers, 24*(5), 351–357.

Smi. (2016). *Smi Experiment Center Software*. Retrieved at March 2015 from http://www.smivision.com/en/gaze-and-eye-tracking-systems/products/experiment-center-software.html

Smith, C. (2015, Aug. 10). *By the numbers: 14 interesting Flickr stats*. Digital Marketing Stats / Strategy / Gadgets. Retrieved Nov. 10, 2015, from http://expandedramblings.com/index.php/flickr-stats/

Smith, C. (2015, Aug. 10). *By the numbers: 14 interesting Flickr stats*. DMR. Retrieved January 12, 2016, from http://expandedramblings.com/index.php/flickr-stats/

Smith, A. N., Fischer, E., & Yongjian, C. (2012). How does brand-related user-generated content differ across YouTube, Facebook, and Twitter? *Journal of Interactive Marketing, 26*(2), 102–113. doi:10.1016/j.intmar.2012.01.002

Solberg, J. (2012). Googling the archive: Digital tools and the practice of history. *Advances in the History of Rhetoric, 15*(1), 53–76. doi:10.1080/15362426.2012.657052

Solo, A. M. G., & Bishop, J. (2015). Avoiding adverse consequences from digital addiction and retaliatory feedback: The role of the participation continuum. In J. Bishop (Ed.), *Psychological and social implications surrounding internet and gaming addiction* (pp. 62–77). Hershey, PA: IGI Global. doi:10.4018/978-1-4666-8595-6.ch005

Sottilare, R., Graesser, A., Hu, X., & Holden, H. (Eds.). (2013). *Design recommendations for intelligent tutoring systems: Learner modeling* (Vol. 1). Orlando, FL: Army Research Laboratory.

Spanish Government, Ministry of Industry, Energy and Tourism. (2014). *Datos de la Oficina de Atención al Usuario de Telecomunicaciones*. Retrieved July 28, 2015, from http://www.usuariosteleco.es/Destacados/Datos%20oficina/Datos_OAUT_2014_ANUAL.pdf

Sparks, B. A., & Browning, V. (2011). Complaining in Cyberspace: The Motives and Forms of Hotel Guests' Complaints Online. *Journal of Hospitality Marketing & Management, 19*(7), 797–818. doi:10.1080/19368623.2010.508010

Spathis, P., & Gorcitz, R. A. (2011). A data-driven analysis of YouTube community features. In *Proceedings of AINTEC '11*.

Specia, L., & Motta, E. (2007). Integrating folksonomies with the Semantic Web. In E. Franconi, M. Kifer, & W. May (Eds.), *The Semantic Web: Research and Applications. 4th European Semantic Web Conference, ESWC 2007*. Springer. doi:10.1007/978-3-540-72667-8_44

Sriram, B., Fuhry, D., Demir, E., Ferhatosmanoglu, H., & Demirbas, M. (2010). Short text classification in twitter to improve information filtering. *Proceeding Of The 33Rd International ACM SIGIR Conference On Research And Development In Information Retrieval - SIGIR '10*. doi:10.1145/1835449.1835643

Statista. (2015). Retrieved from http://www.statista.com/statistics/272014/global-social-networks-ranked-by-number-of-users/

Statistics. (2015). *YouTube*. Retrieved April 13, 2015, from https://www.youtube.com/yt/press/statistics.html

Stelzner, M. A. (2011). Social media marketing industry report. *Social Media Examiner*, 41.

Stentz, A., & Mellon, C. (1993). Optimal and efficient path planning for unknown and dynamic environments. *International Journal of Robotics and Automation, 10*, 89–100.

Stieglitz, S., & Dang-Xuan, L. (2011). The role of sentiment in information propagation on Twitter—An empirical analysis of affective dimensions in political Tweets. In *Proceedings of ACIS 2011.22nd Australasian Conference on Information Systems*.

Štogr, J. (2011). Surveillancebased mechanisms in MUVEs (MultiUser virtual environments) used for monitoring, data gathering and evaluation of knowledge transfer in VirtuReality. *Journal of Systemics, Cybernetics & Informatics, 9*(2), 24-27. Retrieved from http://libezproxy.open.ac.uk/login?url=http://search.ebscohost.com/login.aspx?direct=true&db =a9h&AN=83259035&site=eds-live&scope=site

Stratten, S. (2012). Unmarketing. *Education, 2*.

Sturtz, D.N. (2004, Dec.). *Communal categorization: The folksonomy*. INFO622. Content Representation.

Sumuer, E., Esfer, S., & Yildirim, S. (2014). Teachers' Facebook use: Their use habits, intensity, self-disclosure, privacy settings, and activities on Facebook. *Educational Studies, 40*(5), 537–553. doi:10.1080/03055698.2014.952713

Sundar, S. S., & Limperos, A. (2013). Uses and grats 2.0: New gratifications for new media. *Journal of Broadcasting & Electronic Media, 57*(4), 504–525. doi:10.1080/08838151.2013.845827

Sun, T., Youn, S., Wu, G., & Kuntaraporn, M. (2006). Online word-of-mouth (or mouse): An exploration of its antecedents and consequences. *Journal of Computer-Mediated Communication, 11*(4), 1104–1127. doi:10.1111/j.1083-6101.2006.00310.x

Su, Z., Song, W., Lin, M., & Li, J. (2008). Web text clustering for personalized e-learning based on maximal frequent item sets.*Proc. Int. Conf. Comput. Sci. Softw. Eng.* (pp. 452-455).

Szabo, G., & Huberman, B. A. (2010). Predicting the popularity of online content. *Communications of the ACM, 53*(8), 80–88. doi:10.1145/1787234.1787254

Szewczyk, J. (2003). Difficulties with the novices' comprehension of the computer-aided design (CAD) interface: Understanding visual representations of CAD tools. *Journal of Engineering Design, 14*(2), 169–185. doi:10.1080/0954482031000091491

Tahmasebi, N., Borin, L., Capannini, G., Dubhashi, D., Exner, P., Forsberg, M., & Risse, T. et al. (2015). Visions and open challenges for a knowledge-based culturomics. *International Journal on Digital Libraries, 15*(2-4), 169–187. doi:10.1007/s00799-015-0139-1

Taintor, D. (2013). Facebook Introduces Verified Accounts.*ADWEEK*. Retrieved August 7, 2014, from http://goo.gl/kf5kkB

Tang, T., & McCalla, G. (2005). Smart recommendation for an evolving elearning system. *International Journal on E-Learning, 4*(1), 105–129.

Tatarkiewicz, W. (1947). Psychological hedonism. From: *On Happiness. Synthese, 8*(8/9), 409 – 425.

Taylor, J. C. (2001). *Fifth generation Distance education*. Retrieved October 12, 2015, from http://www.c3l.uni-oldenburg. de/cde/media/readings/taylor01.pdf

TechTarget. (2014).*Relational database*. Retrieved from http://searchsqlserver.techtarget.com/definition/relational-database

Thelwall, M. (2008). Social networks, gender, and friending: An analysis of MySpace member profiles. *Journal of the American Society for Information Science and Technology, 59*(8), 1321–1330. doi:10.1002/asi.20835

Thelwall, M., Buckley, K., & Paltoglou, G. (2010/2011). Sentiment in Twitter events. *Journal of the American Society for Information Science and Technology, 62*(2), 406–418. doi:10.1002/asi.21462

Thyer, B. (2009). *The handbook of social work research methods*. Sage.

Timisi, N. (2003). *Yeni iletişim teknolojileri ve demokrasi*. Ankara: Dost.

Tindall, D. B., & Wellman, B. (2001). Canada as social structure: Social network analysis and Canadian sociology. *Canadian Journal of Sociology, 26*(3), 265. doi:10.2307/3341889

Tonbuloğlu, I., & Bayram, S. (2012). Usability Test: Using Eye Tracking Method in Educational Software Pop-Up Content. Journal of Research in Education and Teaching, 1(3), 324-332.

Traficovc. (2015, November 24). *traffiCARACAS: vía @mahery21: CERRADA LA VALLE COCHE DESVÍAN TODOS LOS CARROS POR LOS TÚNELES #VALLECOCHE (hace un par de minutos)* [Twitter post]. Retrieved from https://twitter.com/traficovc

Travers, J., & Milgram, S. (1969). An experimental study of the small world problem. *Sociometry*, 425–443.

Trevino, L. K., & Webster, J. (1992). Flow in computer-mediated communication: Electronic mail and voice mail evaluation and impacts. *Communication Research, 19*, 539–573.

Tumasjan, A., Sprenger, T. O., Sandner, P. G., & Welpe, I. M. (2010). Predicting Elections with Twitter: What 140 Characters Reveal about Political Sentiment. In *Proceedings of the Fourth International AAAI Conference on Weblogs and Social Media* (pp. 178-185). Washington, DC: The AAAI Press.

Turner, S. M., Johnson, M. R., Beidel, D. C., Heiser, N. A., & Lydiard, R. B. (2003). The social thoughts and beliefs scale: A new inventory for assessing cognitions in social phobia. *Psychological Assessment, 15*(3), 384–391. doi:10.1037/1040-3590.15.3.384 PMID:14593839

Uça-Guneş, E. P. (2014). *Structuring the technology dimension of distance education graduate programs: Transformative social network synthesis.* (Doctoral Dissertation). Anadolu University, Turkey.

Uça-Güneş, E. P., & Eby, G. (2014). An Approach For Structuring Distance Education Programs: Social Network Synthesis. *Journal of Research in Education and Teaching, 3*(3). Retrieved from http://www.jret.org/FileUpload/ks281142/File/23.uca_gunes.pdf

Uysal, A. (2013). *Meslek Lisesi Öğrencilerinin Sosyal Medya Kullanim Amaçlari İle Eğitsel Sosyal Medya Kullanımlarının Değerlendirilmesi.* (Master Thesis). Bahcesehir University.

Van Noorden, R. (2014). Publishers withdraw more than 120 gibberish papers. *Nature*. Retrieved January 7, 2016, from http://www.nature.com/news/publishers-withdraw-more-than-120-gibberish-papers-1.14763

Vander Wal, T. (2005). Folksonomy. In Proceedings of Online Information 2005.

Vander Wal, T. (2005, Feb. 21). *Explaining and showing broad and narrow folksonomies.* Retrieved Nov. 9, 2015, from http://www.vanderwal.net/random/entrysel.php?blog=1635

VanLehn, K. (2006). The behavior of tutoring systems. *International Journal of Artificial Intelligence in Education, 16*(3), 227–265.

Von Ahn, L., Maurer, B., McMillen, C., Abraham, D., & Blum, M. (2008). reCAPTCHA: Human-Based Character Recognition via Web Security Measures. *Science, 321*(5895), 1465–1468. doi:10.1126/science.1160379 PMID:18703711

Vu, X. T., Morizet-Mahoudeaux, P., & Abel, M.-H. (2013). Empowering collaborative intelligence by the use of user-centered social network aggregation. In *Proceedings of the 2013 IEEE/WIC/ACM International Conferences on Web Intelligence (WI) and Intelligent Agent Technology (IAT)*. doi:10.1109/WI-IAT.2013.60

Vygotsky, L. S. (1930). *Mind in society*. Cambridge, MA: Harvard University Press.

Wainwright, D. W., & Waring, T. S. (2007). The application and adaptation of a diffusion of innovation framework for information systems research in NHS general medical practice. *Journal of Information Technology*, 22(1), 44–58. doi:10.1057/palgrave.jit.2000093

Wang, X., Wei, F., Liu, X., Zhou, M., & Zhang, M. (2011). Topic sentiment analysis in Twitter: A graph-based hashtag sentiment classification approach. In *Proceedings of the CIKM '11*. doi:10.1145/2063576.2063726

Wang, F. H., & Shao, H. M. (2004). Effective personalized recommendation based on time-framed navigation clustering and association mining. *Expert Syst. Appl. J.*, 27(3), 265–377. doi:10.1016/j.eswa.2004.05.005

Wang, H., Can, D., Kazemzadeh, A., Bar, F., & Narayanan, S. (2012, July). A system for real-time twitter sentiment analysis of 2012 us presidential election cycle. In *Proceedings of the ACL 2012 System Demonstrations* (pp. 115-120). Association for Computational Linguistics.

Wang, Q., Woo, H. L., Quek, C. L., Yang, Y., & Liu, M. (2012a). Using the Facebook group as a learning management system: An exploratory study. *British Journal of Educational Technology*, 43, 428–438.

Wang, V., Tucker, J. V., & Rihll, T. E. (2011). On phatic technologies for creating and maintaining human relationships. *Technology in Society*.

Wang, Z., Tchernev, J. M., & Solloway, T. (2012b). A dynamic longitudinal examination of social media use, needs, and gratifications among college students. *Computers in Human Behavior*, 28(5), 1829–1839. doi:10.1016/j.chb.2012.05.001

Watson, J. B. (1913). Psychology as the behaviorist views it. *Psychological Review*, 20(2), 158.

Watson, J. B., & Rayner, R. (1920). Conditioned emotional reactions. *Journal of Experimental Psychology*, 3(1), 1–14. doi:10.1037/h0069608

Watts, D. J., & Strogatz, S. H. (1998). Collective dynamics of small world networks. *Nature*, 393(6684), 440–442. doi:10.1038/30918 PMID:9623998

Weber, I., Garimella, V. R. K., & Borra, E. (2013). Inferring audience partisanship for YouTube videos. In *Proceedings of WWW 2013*. doi:10.1145/2487788.2487803

Webmedia. (2010). *Editing Wikipedia: A Guide to improving content on the online encyclopedia*. Wiki Education Foundation.

Wells, S. (2002). Claiming the archive for rhetoric and composition. In *Rhetoric and Composition as Intellectual Work* (pp. 55–64). Carbondale, IL: Southern Illinois University Press.

Welser, H. T., Cosley, D., Kossinets, G., Lin, A., Dokshin, F., Gay, G., & Smith, M. (2011, February). Finding social roles in Wikipedia. In *Proceedings of the 2011 iConference* (pp. 122-129). ACM. doi:10.1145/1940761.1940778

Westerman, D., Spence, P. R., & Van Der Heide, B. (2012). A social network as information: The effect of system generated reports of connectedness on credibility on Twitter. *Computers in Human Behavior*, 28(1), 199–206. doi:10.1016/j.chb.2011.09.001

What does the Ngram Viewer do? (2015). *Google Books Ngram Viewer*. Retrieved Jan. 16, 2016, from https://books.google.com/ngrams/info

Wiedemann, G. (2013). Opening up to big data: Computer-assisted analysis of textual data in social sciences. *Historical Social Research (Köln)*, 38(4), 332–357.

Wilson-Jeanselme, M., & Reynolds, J. (2006). The advantages of preference-based segmentation: An investigation of online grocery retailing. *Journal of Targeting. Measurement and Analysis for Marketing, 14*(4), 297–308. doi:10.1057/palgrave.jt.5740190

Winne, P., & Hadwin, A. (2008). The weave of motivation and self-regulated learning. In D. Schunk & B. Zimmerman (Eds.), *Motivation and self-regulated learning: Theory, research, and applications* (pp. 297–314). Mahwah, NJ: Erlbaum.

Winter, T. N. (1999). Roberto Busa, S.J., and the invention of the machine-generated concordance. *The Classical Bulletin, 75*(1), 3 – 20. Retrieved Jan. 3, 2016, from http://digitalcommons.unl.edu/cgi/viewcontent.cgi?article=1069&context=classicsfacpub

Wodtke, C. (2003). *Information architecture: Blueprints for the web*. Indianapolis, IN: New Riders.

Woo, G. K., Lim, H., & Brymer, R. A. (2015). The effectiveness of managing social media on hotel performance. *International Journal of Hospitality Management, 44*, 165–171. doi:10.1016/j.ijhm.2014.10.014

Wright, R. D., & Ward, L. M. (2008). *Orienting of attention*. Oxford University Press.

Wu, S., Hofman, J. M., Mason, W. A., & Watts, D. J. (2011). Who says what to whom on twitter. In *Proceedings of the 20th International Conference on World Wide Web*. ACM. doi:10.1145/1963405.1963504

Xie, X., Wang, Q., & Chen, A. (2012). Analysis of competition in chinese automobile industry based on an opinion and sentiment mining system. *Journal of Intelligence Studies in Business, 2*(1).

Yan, M., Sang, J., & Xu, C. (2014). Mining cross-network association for YouTube video promotion. In *Proceedings of MM'14*. doi:10.1145/2647868.2654920

Yang, F., Han, P., Shen, R., & Hu, Z. (2005). A novel resource recommendation system based on connecting to similar e-learners.*Proc. Int. Conf. Web-Based Learning* (pp. 122-130). doi:10.1007/11528043_12

Yates, D., & Paquette, S. (2011). Emergency knowledge management and social media technologies: A case study of the 2010 Haitian earthquake. *International Journal of Information Management, 31*(1), 6–13. doi:10.1016/j.ijinfomgt.2010.10.001

Yoganarasimhan, H. (2012). Impact of social network structure on content propagation: A study using YouTube data. *Quantitative Marketing and Economics, 10*(1), 111–150. doi:10.1007/s11129-011-9105-4

YouTube. (2015). *Logopedia. Wikia*. Retrieved April 14, 2015, from http://logos.wikia.com/wiki/YouTube

YouTube. (2015, Apr. 20). In *Wikipedia*. Retrieved April 23, 2015, from http://en.wikipedia.org/wiki/YouTube

Yu, C.-H., & Miller, R. C. (2012). Enhancing web page skimmability. In *Proceedings of CHI 2012*. doi:10.1145/2212776.2223852

Yuan, L., Zhongfeng, S., & Yi, L. (2010). Can strategic flexibility help firms profit from product innovation? *Technovation, 30*(5), 300–309. doi:10.1016/j.technovation.2009.07.007

Yukawa, J. (2005). Story-lines: A case study of online learning using narrative analysis. In *Proceedings of the 2005 Conference on Computer Support for Collaborative Learning: Learning 2005: The Next 10 Years!*. doi:10.3115/1149293.1149389

Yükseköğretim Kurulu (YÖK). (2007). *Türkiye'nin yükseköğretim stratejisi*. Retrieved October 14, 2015, from http://www.yok.gov.tr/documents/10279/30217/yok_strateji_kitabi/27077070-cb13-4870-aba1-6742db37696b

Zeng, D., Chen, H., Lusch, R., & Li, S.-H. (2010). Social media analytics and intelligence. *IEEE Intelligent Systems, 25*(6), 13–16. doi:10.1109/MIS.2010.151

Zikmund, W. G., & Scott, J. E. (1973). A multivariate analysis of perceived risk, self-confidence and information sources. *Advances in Consumer Research. Association for Consumer Research (U. S.)*, *1*(1), 406–416.

Zink, M., Suh, K., Gu, Y., & Kurose, J. (2008). *Watch Global, Cache Local: YouTube Network Traffic at a Campus Network - Measurements and Implications*. Computer Science Department Faculty Publication Series. Paper 177. http://scholarworks.umass.edu/cs_faculty_pubs/177

About the Contributors

Shalin Hai-Jew works as an instructional designer at Kansas State University (K-State). She has taught at the university and college levels for many years (including four years in the People's Republic of China) and was tenured at Shoreline Community College but left tenure to pursue instructional design work. She has Bachelor's degrees in English and psychology, a Master's degree in Creative Writing from the University of Washington (Hugh Paradise Scholar), and an Ed.D in Educational Leadership with a focus on public administration from Seattle University (where she was a Morford Scholar). She reviews for a number of publications and is editor of several IGI Global titles. Hai-Jew was born in Huntsville, Alabama, in the U.S. She has worked under the auspices of several federal grants, most recently to analyze complex survey data for publication, for principal investigators (PIs) in multiple countries.

* * *

Jonathan Bishop is an information technology executive, researcher and writer. He founded the Centre for Research into Online Communities and E-Learning Systems in 2005, now part of the Crocels Community Media Group. Jonathan's research and development work generally falls within human-computer interaction. He has over 75 publications in this area, including on Internet trolling, cyber-stalking, gamification, cyberlaw, multimedia forensics, Classroom 2.0 and Digital Teens. In addition to his BSc(Hons) in Multimedia Studies and various postgraduate degrees, including in law, economics and computing, Jonathan serves in local government as a councillor, and has been a school governor and contested numerous elections, including to the UK Parliament. He is a fellow of numerous learned bodies, including BCS, CILIP, the InstAM, the RAI, the RSS and the RSA. Jonathan has won prizes for his literary skills and been a finalist in national and local competitions for his environmental, community and equality work, which often form part of action research studies. In his spare time Jonathan enjoys listening to music, swimming and chess.

Donna Bridgham is Project Analyst with the Commonwealth of Virginia with the Division of Aging and Rehabilitative Services. Donna is proficient in breaking down high level information into details and distinguishing user requests from true needs. She also has a technical expertise in data analytics. She has an MBA from NCU and a MS in Information Technology from APUS.

Negar Fazeli Dehkordi is a PhD student in Cognition and Learning Science program in the Department of Educational Psychology at the University of Utah. After obtaining bachelor degree in Library and Information Science from University of Isfahan, Iran, she graduated in Master of Science in the same major from Ferdowsi University of Mashhad, Iran. Since working to complete her Master in Library and Information Science, her main interest has been focused on implementing information technologies, theories, and services in educational environments. Collaboration in a large scale-teamwork project about web portal design at Ferdowsi University of Mashhad, developing a bilingual E-library for Physics students and researchers, instructing in training workshops for teachers and school librarians about using information resources in teaching-learning processes, and creating guidelines for school librarians to acquire and develop required information literacy competencies in school system were her primary focuses in Master program. As PhD student, Negar Fazeli Dehkordi has been dedicated more to apply data mining, web mining, network analysis and visualization techniques as well as using potentials of Information Science theories (such as collection development, information evaluation and organization, and semantic relationship analysis) to develop databases of educational resources (especially on-line collaborative resources). Implementing adaptive instructional systems and intelligent tutoring systems to support teachers' self-regulated learning abilities and their professional development in open ended learning environments and using instructional scaffolds in augmented reality applications to aid students' learning in the field of science are her main research focuses as PhD student.

Gülsün Eby is a professor in Distance Education at the College of Open Education of Anadolu University. Dr. Eby undertook graduate studies at Anadolu University, Turkey (MA. Educational Technology) and the University of Cincinnati, USA (Ed.D. Curriculum & Instruction), and also has worked a post-doctoral fellow at the College of Education at New Mexico State University, USA (2001-2002). Dr. Eby earned her B.S. degree in Computer Engineering from the College of Informatics Technologies and Engineering of Hoca Ahmet Yesevi International Turk-Kazakhstani University in the year 2012-2013. Also, she is currently a graduate student in the Department of Computer and Instructional Technologies. Dr. Eby has over twenty-nine year experience in focusing on the egalitarian and ecological aspects of distance education; finding new answers, viewpoints and explanations to online communication problems through critical pedagogy; and improving learner critical thinking skills through project-based online learning. Dr. Eby is the Group Coordinator of R&D and International Relations of College of Open Education, Anadolu University. She continues to manage and provide pedagogical support for distance learning programs.

Davide Di Fatta is a PhD Student in Ecnomics at Messina University. Research Interests: web marketing, digital marketing, social media. Marketing Consultant and web strategist in Palermo.

Antonia Estrella-Ramón, PhD in Economics, Business and Legal sciences from the University of Almeria (Spain) and Hasselt University (Belgium), Assistant professor of Marketing at the University of Almeria (Spain). Her research interests include prediction of time series, data analysis applied to customer value modelling and online maketing.

Marlene Goncalves received her Ph.D. degree from Universidad Simón Bolívar, Venezuela. She is currently a Full Professor of Department of Computer Science & Information Technology at Universidad Simón Bolívar, Venezuela. Her research interests include database modeling, preference based queries and query processing. She has published over 53 papers in international journals, conferences and books in these areas since 2001.

E. Pınar Uça Güneş works at Open Education Faculty in Anadolu University. She received her B.A degree as an industrial engineer, then M.S. degree in the fields of Informatics and Operations Research and Ph.D. in Distance Education field in 2014. She is interested in Distance Education Management, Distance Education Programs, Social Network Approaches, e-learning, Adult Learning, Lifelong Learning.

Shona Leitch has worked in the field of academia for 14 years in various roles. She is currently the Director, Undergraduate Programs in the College of Business, RMIT University and previously was Bachelor of Commerce/Bachelor of Management Course Director in the Faculty of Business and Law, Deakin. She has previously developed and worked as the coordinator of numerous degrees at both undergraduate and postgraduate levels.Her passion lies in the areas of curriculum development and management with a focus on elearning and innovative teaching and learning initiatives as demonstrated by her research. She has received as part of a team two OLT grants on ePorftolios in Business Education and eExams. As well as research into education practices, she also continues her discipline research into privacy and ethics issues. Shona has authored over 40 book chapters, journal, conference and technical papers and she is a member of the Australian Computer Society, HERDSA and the Informing Sciences Institute.

Ivette C. Martínez has a PhD in Computer Science (2015). Main research interest are Machine Learning, genetic classifier systems, complex Systems, agent based modeling, complex networks, and the evolution of cooperation.

Giacomo Morabito is a PhD student in Economics at University of Messina (Italy).

Roberto Musotto is a PhD Student in Economics at Messina University. Corporate and Civil Suit Lawyer in Palermo (Italy).

Duygu Mutlu-Bayraktar received her PhD in multimedia learning and human-computer interaction from the Marmara University. Her research interests include multimedia learning, instructional design and technology, eye tracking and human computer interaction. She is currently working on the eye tracking about multimedia learning environment.

Eric Poitras is an Assistant Professor for Instructional Design and Educational Technology in the Department of Educational Psychology at the University of Utah. He graduated from McGill University, where he earned a graduate degree in the Learning Sciences and worked as a postdoctoral researcher at the Learning Environments Across Disciplines research partnership. His research aim to improve the adaptive capabilities of instructional systems and technologies designed as cognitive and metacognitive tools as a means to foster self-regulated learning. In particular, the capabilities of intelligent tutoring systems and augmented reality applications to capture and analyze learner behaviors in order to deliver the most suitable instructional content in domain areas such as medical diagnostic reasoning, historical thinking, and teacher professional development.

Graeme Pye received his PhD in information systems security analysis and modelling in 2009 and has been a Lecturer with the School of Information and Business Analytics, Deakin University, Victoria, Australia since 2004. His research is widely published and focuses primarily on security analysis and modelling of systems and is continuing to investigate the security and risk aspects of Australian critical infrastructure systems, their resilience and the human and social networking relationships associated with emergency management and disaster recovery. Graeme is also interested in Information Warfare, Human and Social Communication Networks and Computer Ethics, Privacy and Governance of information Systems. Dr. Graeme Pye has taught a variety of information systems subjects including systems analysis and design, advanced database, information security and risk management, business information systems, business intelligence and information systems management. Currently he is also pursuing research in aspects of student engagement for both Online and Located student learning.

Patrick Rengifo is a Computer Engineer from Simón Bolívar University (USB), Caracas, Venezuela, 2015. His interest areas are Software Engineering, and Mobile and Augmented Reality software development. He was Assistant Professor on the algorithms laboratory courses in Simón Bolívar University (2013-2015). Currently he is working at Solsteace Canada, doing Android and iOS software development.

Daniela Rodríguez holds a bachelor's degree in Computer Engineering from Universidad Simón Bolívar (Caracas, Venezuela, 2015). Her main research interest areas are Databases and Big Data. Currently, she's employed by Solsteace Canada, working on iOS software development.

Vindaya Senadheera holds a PhD in Information Systems from the Deakin University, Australia where he is presently engaged as a sessional academic and a researcher with the Deakin Business School. Vindaya's PhD is on the topic of 'social media adoption by Australian banks to communicate with the public'. As a result of his 18+ year industry experience Vindaya has developed diverse research interests in Social Media Adoption, Cloud computing, Big Data and Digital Data Streams. Graduated as a computer systems engineer, Vindaya also holds Master of information systems management degree. Prior to his involvement in research and teaching, Vindaya worked as an information systems/technology professional in customer-facing IT/IS service delivery and support leadership roles. With his extensive knowledge and experience in the business-IS/IT space, he continues to advise businesses in areas of streamlining web presence, cloud computing, and information system implementation and governance. Vindaya is also a certified Scrum Master.

Alba Utrera-Serrano is graduate in Marketing Research from the University of Almeria and former student in the Master's in Management and Business Economics at the University of Almeria (Spain). Her major research interests are in the areas of online marketing and data extraction from Internet resources.

Walter Vesperi is a Ph.D student, in Economics, Management and Statistics at the University of Messina. Research focuses on the management of knowledge flows and intellectual capital in knowledge Management. He is a member of important scientific associations (RetMES and ASSIOA).

Matthew Warren is a Professor of Information Systems at Deakin University, Australia. Professor Warren is a researcher in the areas of Information Security, Computer Ethics and Cyber Security. He has authored and co-authored over 300 books, book chapters, journal papers and conference papers. He has received numerous grants and awards from national and international funding bodies, such as: Australian Research Council (ARC); Engineering Physical Sciences Research Council (EPSRC) in the United Kingdom; National Research Foundation (NRF) in South Africa and the European Union. Professor Warren gained his PhD in Information Security Risk Analysis from the University of Plymouth, United Kingdom and he has taught in Australia, Finland, Hong Kong and the United Kingdom.

Index

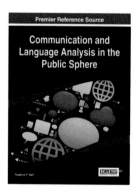